Law and New Governance in the EU and the US

Edited by

Gráinne de Búrca and Joanne Scott

HART PUBLISHING
OXFORD AND PORTLAND, OREGON
2006

Published in North America (US and Canada) by
Hart Publishing
c/o International Specialized Book Services
5804 NE Hassalo Street
Portland, Oregon
97213-3644
USA
Tel: +1 503 287 3093 or toll-free: (1) 800 944 6190
Fax: +1 503 280 8832
E-mail: orders@isbs.com
Web Site: www.isbs.com

Hart Publishing, Salters Boatyard, Folly Bridge, Abingdon Rd, Oxford, OX1 4LB
Telephone: +44 (0)1865 245533 Fax: +44 (0) 1865 794882
email: mail@hartpub.co.uk
WEBSITE: http//:www.hartpub.co.uk

British Library Cataloguing in Publication Data
Data Available

ISBN 10: 1-84113-543-7 (paperback)
ISBN 13: 978-1-84113-543-4 (paperback)

Typeset by Compuscript Ltd, Shannon
Printed and bound in Great Britain by
TJ International, Padstow, Cornwall

Preface

This volume is the result of a workshop held in Cambridge(UK) in July 2004. We are grateful to all those who attended and participated. We would like the acknowledge the financial support of Jean Monnet Professor Catherine Barnard (Cambridge University), The Center for World Affairs and the Global Economy (WAGE) and the Wisconsin Project on Governance and Regulation (WISGAR) at the University of Wisconsin-Madison. Special thanks are due to Professor David M. Trubek who has assisted in every way with the project at all stages. We are grateful to him for a very fruitful collaboration.

The Cambridge workshop formed part of an on-going collaborative research initiative in law and new governance which is taking shape within the context of an integrated project funded by the EU Framework 6 programme. This project is concerned with the emergence and spread of new modes of governance within the EU and further details can be found http://www.eu-newgov.org/.

Contents

Preface v
List of Contributors ix

Introduction: New Governance, Law and Constitutionalism
Gráinne de Búrca and Joanne Scott 1

PART I: NEW GOVERNANCE, LAW AND CONSTITUTIONALISM

1. EU Constitutionalism and New Governance
Neil Walker 15
2. Toyota Jurisprudence: Legal Theory and Rolling Rule Regimes
William H Simon 37
3. 'Soft Law', 'Hard Law', and EU Integration
David M Trubek, Patrick Cottrell and Mark Nance 65

PART II: CASE STUDIES: EUROPE

4. EU Race Discrimination Law: A Hybrid Model?
Gráinne de Búrca 97
5. New EU Employment Governance and Constitutionalism
Claire Kilpatrick 121
6. Solidarity and New Governance in Social Policy
Catherine Barnard 153
7. The European Union and the Governance of Health Care
Tamara K Hervey 179
8. Law and New Environmental Governance in the European Union
Joanne Scott and Jane Holder 211

PART III: CASE STUDIES: UNITED STATES

9. New Governance Practices in US Health Care
Louise G Trubek 245
10. Governing Occupational Safety in the United States
Orly Lobel 269
11. Information-forcing Regulation and Environmental Governance
Bradley C Karkkainen 293

12. Gender Equity Regimes and the Architecture of Learning
Susan Sturm 323

PART IV: COMPARATIVE STUDIES

13. EU Constitutionalism and the 'American Experience'
Paul Magnette and Justine Lacroix 363
14. Governance and American Political Development
Mark Tushnet 381
Epilogue: Accountability Without Sovereignity
Charles F Sabel and William H Simon 395

Index 413

List of Contributors

Catherine Barnard is Reader in Law, and Jean Monnet Chair of European Law at the University of Cambridge. She is a Fellow of Trinity College, Cambridge.

Gráinne de Búrca is Professor of Law at the European University Institute and a member of the Global Law Faculty, New York University.

Patrick Cottrell is a Lecturer in the Department of Political Science at the University of Wisconsin-Madison.

Tamara K Hervey is Professor of Law at the University of Nottingham.

Bradley C Karkkainen is Professor and Henry J Fletcher Chair at the University of Minnesota Law School.

Claire Kilpatrick is University Lecturer at the University of Cambridge, and Fellow of Emmanuel College, Cambridge.

Justine Lacroix is Professor of Political Sciences at the Université libre de Bruxelles.

Orly Lobel is Assistant Professor of Law at University of San Diego School of Law.

Paul Magnette is Professor of Political Sciences and Director of the Institute for European Studies at the Université libre de Bruxelles.

Mark Nance is a PhD candidate in the Department of Political Science, University of Wisconsin-Madison.

Charles F Sabel is Maurice T Moore Professor of Law at Columbia Law School.

Joanne Scott is Professor of European Law at University College London, and currently a Visiting Professor at Harvard Law School.

William H Simon is Arthur Levitt Professor of Law at Columbia Law School.

Susan Sturm is George M Jaffin Professor of Law at Columbia Law School.

David M Trubek is Voss-Bascom Professor of Law, and Senior Fellow, Center for World Affairs and the Global Economy (WAGE) University of Wisconsin Law School.

Louise G Trubek is Clinical Professor of Law at the University of Wisconsin Law School.

Mark Tushnet is Carmack Waterhouse Professor of Law at the Georgetown University Law Center.

Neil Walker is Professor of Law at the European University Institute.

Introduction: New Governance, Law and Constitutionalism

GRÁINNE DE BÚRCA AND JOANNE SCOTT

INTRODUCTION

THIS VOLUME EXPLORES the emergence of new approaches to governance ('new governance') in the European Union (EU) and in the United States (US). The essays represent the initial results of a research project which brings together a group of European and American scholars to examine the emergence of the new governance phenomenon in different political, geographical and policy contexts.

Three distinct but related lines of inquiry inform the collection of essays. The first line of inquiry is a practical and empirical one, entailing an examination of the actual operation of new regulatory forms in a number of specific policy fields or issue areas. By bringing together scholars working on subjects ranging from employment to health to environment and anti-discrimination, we hope to shed some light on the actual nature and characteristics of various new governance forms and their effectiveness, as well as the possible reasons for their emergence. The second line of inquiry aims to interrogate the relationship between law and new governance, both through these concrete case studies as well as through more abstract and conceptual reflections on how law and legal processes are implicated in the operation of new regulatory approaches. The third line of inquiry addresses the relationship between new governance and constitutionalism. This inquiry can be seen in a number of the essays in the volume, whether attempting to situate new governance in relation to a traditional constitutional framework, or seeking a 'theorization of the ideology' which underlies the emergent practices of governance, or, more broadly, interrogating the various possible ways of conceiving the relationship between new governance and the notion of collective self-government which is inherent in the idea of constitutionalism.

The project has not been designed as a deliberately comparative one, in the sense that we have not necessarily sought to draw specific lessons from a comparison of the US experience with that of EU. Rather, we saw a value in examining similar or even parallel developments in these two major federal-type systems, partly with a view to reflecting on whether and how the apparent trend towards 'post-regulatory' and non-traditional forms of governance transcends the particularities of a given political or geographic context. Further, while there are evident similarities between the emergence of alternatives to command-and-control regulation, and of more 'experimental' forms of governance in Europe and the United States, it can fairly be said that this development has occurred in a more self-conscious and more closely scrutinised fashion in the European Union. This is not least because of the role of the EU institutions—and in particular the Commission—in funding and advancing research on the subject, as well as in actively testing and promoting the use of new governance forms at EU level. There seems to be no similar institutional investment in conceptualising and analysing such regulatory changes in the United States. In that sense, it might be said that the trend towards new governance (or democratic experimentalism[1]) has largely emerged bottom-up in the US, with non-traditional problem-solving approaches being practised and tried out in different regulatory fields at the prompting of different sets of actors, while there have been significant top-down incentives in the European Union, in the shape of the promotion of new governance approaches in specific fields by the European Council (the EU heads of state and government) and the Commission.

WHAT DO WE MEAN BY NEW GOVERNANCE?

The concept of new governance is by no means a settled one. It is a construct which has been developed to explain a range of processes and practices that have a normative dimension but do not operate primarily or at all through the formal mechanism of traditional command-and-control-type legal institutions. The language of governance rather than government in itself signals a shift away from the monopoly of traditional politico-legal institutions, and implies either the involvement of actors other than classically governmental actors, or indeed the absence of any traditional framework of government, as is the case in the European Union and in any transnational context. In a practical sense, the concept of new governance results from a sharing of experience by practitioners and scholars across a wide variety of policy domains which are quite diverse and disparate in institutional and political terms, and in terms of the concrete problem to be addressed. Yet in each case, the common features which have been identified involve a shift in emphasis away from command-and-control in favour of 'regulatory' approaches which are less rigid, less prescriptive, less committed to uniform outcomes, and less hierarchical in nature. What can be seen already in this preliminary description is that new governance—as is suggested by the name—tends to be identified primarily by comparison with what it is not, and by contrast with some conception of traditional or 'old' regulatory approaches. Newness is not intended to signify being recent

[1] See M Dorf and C Sabel, 'A Constitution of Democratic Experimentalism' (1998) 98 *Columbia Law Review* 267.

in time, but rather something which is distinctive from what has gone before. Of course this binary or oppositional approach to defining the object of analysis has its limitations, in that it overstates the disjuncture between supposedly traditional regulatory methods and more experimental approaches and conceals the continuities between them. More importantly, it has implications for the idea of 'hybrid governance' which we will develop further below, and which forms an important theme in the various analyses and studies of new governance forms presented in this volume.

Alongside the process of definition-by-contrast, new governance forms can be depicted descriptively in terms of some of the key characteristics which they can be said to exhibit. For example, the idea of new or experimental governance approaches places considerable emphasis upon the accommodation and promotion of diversity, on the importance of provisionality and revisability—in terms of both problem definition and anticipated solutions—and on the goal of policy learning. New governance processes generally encourage or involve the participation of affected actors (stakeholders) rather than merely representative actors, and emphasise transparency (openness as a means to information-sharing and learning), as well as ongoing evaluation and review. Rather than operating through a hierarchical structure of governmental authority, the 'centre' (of a network, a regime, or other governance arrangement) may be charged with facilitating the emergence of the governance infrastructure, and with ensuring coordination or exchange as between constituent parts. A further characteristic often present in new governance processes is the voluntary or non-binding nature of the norms. While this feature is sometimes described in terms of 'soft law', the ambiguity of the notion of soft law is highlighted in several of the chapters in this volume.[2] In the EU, the much-discussed 'Open Method of Coordination' (OMC) is often presented as the archetypal, though by no means the original, example of new governance.[3] Aspects of the 'new approach to standardization' promoted by the EC Commission in the 1980s also provide an earlier example.[4] In the United States, it is more difficult to capture the idea of new governance in a single institutional form, but Hazard Analysis and Critical Control Point (HAACP) food safety plans could be cited as a canonical example.[5]

Apart from the basic exercise of depicting the operation of new governance forms in various policy fields, the primary focus of the volume is on the relationship between new governance, law and constitutionalism. It is notable that, although the new governance phenomenon has attracted

[2] See in particular Ch 3 below.

[3] See the 'OMC Research Forum' for a collection of the copious literature on this subject: http://eucenter.wisc.edu/OMC.

[4] See http://europa.eu.int/comm/enterprise/newapproach/index.htm.

[5] US Dept of Agriculture, Food Safety and Inspection Serve, 'Pathogen Reduction: Hazard Analysis and Critical Control Point (HACCP) Systems' 61 Fed Reg 38805 38816 (25 July 1996).

significant scholarly attention in recent years in the EU in particular,[6] the legal dimension remains under-explored.[7] Yet as the chapters which follow demonstrate, new governance presents significant practical and conceptual challenges for law and for lawyers, as well as for notions of democracy, self-government and constitutionalism. Many different dimensions of the possible relationship between new governance and constitutionalism are explicitly charted and explored in Neil Walker's chapter 'EU Constitutionalism and New Governance', which serves to frame discussion for several of the chapters which follow. In terms of the more specific relationship between new governance and law, below we sketch out three tentative theses. Elements of each of the three—a 'gap thesis', a 'hybridity thesis', and a 'transformation thesis'—and in some cases elements of more than one, can be seen reflected in various of the essays in this volume. These theses have a descriptive as well as a normative dimension. They offer a framework for thinking not only about the actual nature and role of law in new governance, but also about its potential nature and role.

HOW DO WE CONCEIVE OF THE RELATIONSHIP BETWEEN LAW AND NEW GOVERNANCE?

The gap thesis

In its descriptive form, the gap thesis attests to the imperviousness of law in the face of new governance, and to the existence of a gap between formal law and the practice of governance. According to this thesis, formal law, including constitutional law, is largely blind to new governance. A reading of legal texts, including constitutional texts, conceals rather than reveals or illuminates the presence and prevalence of new governance forms. Moving from descriptive to explanatory mode, law either has not 'caught up with' developments in governance, or it ignores developments which do not conform to its presuppositions, structures and requirements.

Moving from the explanatory to the more explicitly normative dimension of the gap thesis, at least two distinct if related strands can be identified. The first argues that law resists the new governance phenomenon, and the second argues that law is confronted with a reduction in its capacity. The resistance argument presents law as an actual impediment or obstacle to

[6] See now the major EU-funded research consortium which builds on existing European projects dealing with new governance: http://www.eu-newgov.org.

[7] See however the special issue of the *European Law Journal* (Volume 8, 2002) on 'law and new approaches to EU governance', upon which this current project builds. See also G de Búrca, 'The Constitutional Challenge of New Governance' (2003) 28 ELR 814. In the US setting, apart from the influential essay by Dorf and Sabel, n 1 above; see also SP Sturm, 'Second Generation Employment Discrimination: A Structural Approach' 101 *Columbia Law Review* (2001); J Liebman and C Sabel, 'A Public Laboratory Dewey Barely Imagined: The Emerging Model of School Governance and Legal Reform' (2003) 28 *New York University Review of Law and Social Change* 183 and C Sabel and W Simon, 'Destabilisation Rights: How Public Law Litigation Succeeds' (2004) 117 *Harvard Law Review* 1015.

new governance. The premises of law are not aligned with the premises of new governance. Not only does law, traditionally conceived, ignore the existence of experimental forms of governance, but through its blindness and non-recognition it may even operate to curtail and inhibit such experimentation. The reduced capacity argument, by comparison, is preoccupied not with what law does in the face of new governance, but with what it can no longer do. According to this argument, the capacity of law to steer, to inform the normative direction of policy, and to secure accountability in governance is put in peril, by virtue of the mis-match between the fundamental premises of law and the premises of new governance.

To take a high-profile example of the apparent blindness of law to the emergence of new governance in Europe, an analysis of the (unratified) EU Constitution suggests that it failed to capture and accurately depict the prevalence of new governance forms. Instead, the constitutional document downplayed the extent of the cooperative efforts between Member States which these approaches entail.[8] Tamara Hervey's chapter on health care indeed argues that there is a significant gap between formal constitutional articulation and emerging practice in this field. According to the former, health care is a matter for the Member States, but according to the latter, this policy domain is increasingly characterised by EU influence through a whole variety of governance modes. In a different setting and context, Joanne Scott and Jane Holder also point to the existence of such a gap, whereby elaborate and settled governance arrangements are nowhere visible through the prism of a traditional understanding of law, or through conventional legal documents.

In terms of resistance, whether deliberate or inadvertent, many examples of law which appear to impede the emergence and functioning of new governance can be cited. Louise Trubek and Orly Lobel both offer compelling examples of this kind in their chapters on US health care and occupational health and safety regulation respectively. Claire Kilpatrick in her chapter on EU employment policy also points to the possibility that the new (unratified) EU Constitution could have served to impede rather than to foster the emergence of transnational civil society actors in that field, whereas such broadened stakeholder participation is one of the normative presuppositions of new governance approaches. Susan Sturm argues that formal law may be discouraging organisations from undertaking positive and experimental initiatives in the field of race and gender.

From the 'reduced capacity' perspective, several contributions point to the concern that new governance may evade traditional legal mechanisms for securing accountability, or that it may circumvent important political

[8] Indeed, but for the eleventh-hour lobbying of members of the Convention which produced the first draft of the constitutional treaty, even the minimal references to 'coordination' which did ultimately appear would apparently not have been in the text: See Arts III–213, III–250(2), III–278(2) and 279(2), and the brief explanation for the adoption of these last-minute amendments (which at that time were numbered Arts III–107, III–148, III–179 and III–180) in Convention working documents CONV 849/03 and CONV 848/03.

and constitutional constraints and commitments. New governance practices may well not be subject to binding administrative procedures, and even where they are, effective review may be hard to secure.

The hybridity thesis

The 'hybridity thesis' approaches the relationship between law and new governance in a more optimistic and constructive manner. It acknowledges the co-existence and engagement of law and new governance, and explores different ways of securing their fruitful interaction. Law and new governance are posited as mutually interdependent and mutually sustaining. They potentially play off one another's strengths and mitigate one other's weaknesses. The hybridity thesis once again has a descriptive and a normative dimension, and can be presented both as fact and as desideratum.

On one account of this thesis, the hybridity of law and new governance is an interim phenomenon, a transition from a regime of formal legal ordering to a whole-hearted embrace of new governance. On another, it is both factually inevitable and normatively desirable that hybridity is a long-term phenomenon and not simply a passing stage.

The concept of hybridity is articulated in several of the chapters in this volume, most notably in the contributions by Claire Kilpatrick, by Dave Trubek, Patrick Cottrell and Mark Nance, and by Gráinne de Búrca. In Kilpatrick's, and in Trubek, Cottrell and Nance's contributions, hybridity is conceived primarily in terms of the interacton of hard and soft law, both substantively and procedurally. In the fields of employment and fiscal policy coordination, these authors argue that hybridity—in the sense of simultaneous and mutually interdependent recourse to hard and soft law—is a prominent feature of EU governance. While some clearly view soft law as a second-best and less effective alternative to hard law, Trubek and his colleagues argue that soft law may receive a more favourable evaluation in circumstances where there is a shift in the underlying theoretical framework from a rationalist/realist account, to a constructivist account. On a constructivist analysis, soft law is presented and understood less as a tool for directly constraining behaviour than as a transformative tool capable of changing behaviour. In de Búrca's chapter, hybridity is depicted in the context of an opposition between two other models of normative ordering: a traditional human rights model on the one hand, and a new governance model on the other. However, we can see even from these different depictions in several chapters that the concept of hybridity potentially refers to the interaction of many different kinds and characteristics of governance: at its most general, it refers to the combination of elements of a stylised 'new governance model' and those of a stylised 'traditional regulatory model'.

For analytical purposes, below we identify and distinguish three versions of the hybridity argument which emerge from several of the chapters which follow: 'baseline or fundamental normative hybridity', 'functional/developmental hybridity' and 'default hybridity (or 'governance in the shadow of law').[9] These different varieties of hybridity may be viewed as closely related or even overlapping, but we consider that there is nonetheless a heuristic value in distinguishing them. This is not least because the different versions of hybridity reflected in several of the chapters in this volume seemed to us to point towards the existence of a range of different understandings arguably held by different authors of both the character and the value of new governance.

Fundamental/Baseline hybridity

Of the three variants of hybridity, baseline hybridity is arguably the most restrained or even cautious in its insistence on a robust role for a traditional legally grounded framework. This form of hybridity eschews, both descriptively and normatively, the idea of pure, unadulterated new governance, or 'new governance all the way down'. On this analysis, new governance is conceived as complementary to rather than a replacement for more traditional forms of law and regulation. Fundamental or baseline hybridity insists on a continuing role for constitutional commitments and established rights, which remain binding and justiciable. This notion of a baseline of rights represents a regulatory bottom-line below which experiments in new governance may not be permitted to take us. Thus, for example, even William Simon's innovative Toyota regime analogy is said to be 'nested in larger structures that contain norms that are more approximate the themes of mainstream jurisprudence'. These include norms which aim to be responsive to concerns about individual fairness and equity. According to some models, this baseline may remain untouched by innovation in governance, operating on parallel tracks rather than interacting; a conception which Chuck Sabel and William Simon eschew in their epilogue to this volume.

In instrumental terms, fundamental or baseline hybridity may provide a partial response to those who are concerned that new governance amounts in fact to unconstrained governance, to politics without principle, or to governance by the powerful at the expense of the weak. The rise of experimental governance and new problem-solving approaches have generated profound scepticism and unbridled enthusiasm alike, and an insistence on the co-existence of the familiar (traditional, legally and constitutionally grounded regulation) with the new (experimental governance) sets a limit to the risks posed by an excessive faith in new governance. Mark Tushnet's

[9] In a recent paper ('The Coexistence of New Governance and Legal Regulation: Complementarity or Rivalry?' on file with the authors). They posit an additional version of hybridity which they call 'functional complementarity', whereby different instruments or governance techniques are required to address different aspects of a complex social problem. They draw here upon Claire Kilpatrick's example in this volume of female labour market participation in relation to which both old (non-discrimination norms), and new (European Employment Strategy) governance have been deployed, as has the provision of fiscal transfers by way of the European Social Fund.

contribution to this volume offers an example of this in a US constitutional setting. Discussing the dilemmas posed by changes in constitutional politics for those on the left (Democrats and liberals), he contrasts what are conceived as 'core' rights with 'new' rights. He argues that the former remain subject to traditional modes of justification, even as the latter enjoy innovative modes of enforcement and justification, despite the difficulties inherent in finding a principled distinction between these two categories.

A more positive version of fundamental or baseline hybridity claims not merely a continuing parallel role for traditional law and regulation, but also that new governance mechanisms may even serve to enhance the effectiveness of law's traditional role. Kilpatrick's and de Búrca's chapters offer possible examples of this in relation to the enforcement of race and gender equality rights.

Instrumental/developmental hybridity

Shifting somewhat from the dualism of fundamental/baseline hybridity, but in keeping with the more constructive aspect of the latter, the concept of development hybridity posits recourse to new governance techniques as an instrumental means of developing or applying existing and traditional legal norms. Unlike the baseline variant, developmental hybridity necessarily connotes interaction between old and new, with the new providing an institutional framework for the elaboration (and continuous transformation) of the old. The clearest and perhaps the most prominent example of instrumental/developmental hybridity in the EU context combines legally binding framework directives (laws which are binding as to their aim but leave discretion as to the manner of implementation) with new governance regimes for their implementation. Scott and Holder point to the example of the water framework directive, and to its associated multi-level, multi-actor, collaborative, common implementation strategy. The concept of 'good water quality' is elaborated within a governance frame which closely resembles the Open Method of Coordination. De Búrca, Sturm and Hervey's respective chapters also offer examples of developmental hybridity, in that they present new governance mechanisms as a means of applying, elaborating and ensuring respect for established legal or constitutional rights. Their argument applies not only in respect of 'new' rights, such as social welfare rights, the justiciability of which is contested, and which lend themselves more obviously to new governance techniques, as has long been evident in the international context in relation to the kinds of monitoring and supervisory mechanisms which operate under the International Labour Organization and the International Covenant on Economic, Social and Cultural Rights. It is also applicable in respect of what Mark Tushnet labels 'core' constitutional rights, such as equality and anti-discrimination rights. According to Sturm's analysis, the formal legal system does not displace the 'non-legalistic system', but interacts with and is deeply interwoven with it. Louise Trubek's contribution on health care policy in the US likewise accepts that recourse to medical malpractice litigation can be a means of pushing new governance (quality compliance techniques for example) in health care.

Default hybridity (governance in the shadow of law)

The concept of default hybridity rests upon the idea that legal rules—often rigid and hyper-demanding—may represent a default regime, to be complied with in the absence of participation in new governance. According to this account, law represents a 'default penalty', applicable only in the case of failure to conform to new governance demands. The default position is set precisely for the purpose of inducing people to contract out of it—and presumably into a governance regime which is considered to represent their interests better. As such it is likely to be a more specifically tailored and severe default regime than the general legal-constitutional framework presupposed by fundamental/baseline hybridity. Penalty defaults are presented as 'action-forcing', which in practice often means 'information forcing', within a new governance regime. This concept of penalty defaults emerges most clearly in the chapters by Bradley Karkkainen and Orly Lobel. Drawing on the work of Ian Ayres and Rob Gertner in contract theory, Karkkainen offers numerous examples in the sphere of US environmental governance. His clean air example also encompasses a federalism–localism dimension, whereby the threat of federal intervention serves to mobilise states in their elaboration of clean air implementation plans. Lobel in her contribution points out that contemporary penalty defaults in US occupational health and safety regulation are, however, voluntary rather than mandatory in nature. An earlier attempt to use penalty defaults to induce compliance in under-regulated areas encountered legal difficulties (reflecting the obstructive dimension of the gap thesis outline above), and was struck down by the federal courts.

The transformation thesis

The transformation thesis argues that new governance has demanded, and will increasingly demand, a re-conceptualisation of our understanding of law and of the role of lawyers. According to this thesis, the entire preceding discussion including the 'gap' and the 'hybridity' theses alike, are predicated upon an unduly formalistic and positivistic account of law. Instead, the discussion ought to focus less upon the relationship between two ostensibly independent, but interacting (or mutually blind or antagonistic) social phenomena, than on the mutually constitutive nature of these phenomena. Law, as a social phenomenon, is necessarily shaped and informed by the practices and characteristics of new governance, and new governance both generates and operates within the context of a normative order of law.

The transformation thesis can be presented at a systemic level, as is most clearly exemplified in the contribution of William Simon. Drawing inspiration from the unlikely model of an industrial system of automobile production—the Toyota Production System—used as a heuristic tool, Simon contrasts the premises of mainstream jurisprudence with the premises of an alternative jurisprudence born of new governance. This far-reaching approach suggests that the basic premises and normative presuppositions of law, legal form and legal function need to be rethought in the light of changing social practices in general, and more specific changes within public law in particular.

Other chapters reflect dimensions of the transformation thesis in a less thorough-going and more gradual or piecemeal fashion, focusing on the way in which the substantive content of certain legal norms or concepts is transformed by a given governance process. Louise Trubek, for example, argues that new governance practices in the field of US health care are leading to the rethinking of three specific legal concepts: that of participation (in relation to social inclusion), recalibrated federalism, and the role of government. Catherine Barnard in her chapter on solidarity in the EU argues that the practice of new governance could reshape and give renewed meaning to the concept of solidarity.

A central theme of many depictions of new or experimental practices of governance is the procedural role of law. On these accounts, law may play a crucial role in shaping the institutional environment in which decisions are reached, but it does not specify the need to achieve specific, preconceived goals. And even the procedures established by law may themselves be seen as self-consciously provisional and imbued with the logic of reflexive adaptation. Even if proceduralisation is understood to operate against a backdrop of existing principles and standards, these are not necessarily conceived of as fixed or rigid standards, but rather are themselves open to interpretative evolution. Thus the transformative nature of law is built into its design.

WHAT IS THE RELATIONSHIP OF NEW GOVERNANCE TO CONSTITUTIONALISM?

No less than the concept of new governance, the idea of constitutionalism is highly elusive and much contested. Nevertheless, systems of law and governance alike derive crucial legitimacy from the constitutional framework within which they operate. In the context of public policy making, constitutionalism can at a minimum be said to imply the notion of collective self-government. The third major theme of this volume seeks to inquire how novel and experimental governance forms relate, if at all, to constitutional values, norms, processes and structures. Do new governance practices elude and remain outside any constitutional framework? Do they require the articulation of a new constitutional theory tailored to their particular characteristics? Or are they in fact self-constitutionalising—new governance as constitutionalism?

In relation to the first of these three questions, it would certainly be difficult—as we argued above—even to detect the existence of the many European new governance initiatives from a reading of the EU constitutional texts, whether the unratified constitutional treaty or the existing EU treaties. The formal constitutional framework of the EU (such as it is) unlike the policy documents of the Commission and European Council, seems largely blind to the spreading practices of new governance. Far from providing a legitimating framework for the development of experimental governance forms, the EU's current constitutional framework appears to exclude the latter, which seem instead to operate free of its constraints and normative underpinnings. In relation to the second question, Mark Tushnet argues that a new constitutional theory—which to date has not convincingly been developed by those on the left in the US—is required if institutional innovations and new social practices are to be explained and justified.[10] Magnette and Lacroix, in their comparative analysis of EU and American constitutionalism, note in passing that John Dewey's idea of epistemic democracy—which has much in common with the premises of new governance—was advanced as a deliberate departure from what were then perceived as ideological and grandiose European conceptions of democracy and constitutionalism. However, they conclude their analysis by arguing that the EU today should eschew any thick version of constitutionalism based on common values and should instead adhere to a cold and abstract constitutional discipline which is more suited to its diversity of norms, identities and values. It might be said that neither the EU nor the US at present, on the analysis of these two chapters, has come up with a constitutional theory appropriate to the realities of experimental governance.

Neil Walker's chapter adopts a more comprehensive analytical approach by exploring the notion of constitutionalism, and the potential relationship between new governance and constitutionalism, from a range of different thematic perspectives. New governance might simply be subsumed into an expansive definition of constitutionalism; the defenders of new governance forms might seek to make instrumental use of constitutional norms and processes; new governance might remain entirely untouched by the 'higher practice' of constitutionalism; or the two might be structurally antagonistic to one another. Ultimately, and in forward-looking mode, he proposes a constructive notion of constitutionalism as epistemic transformation. He calls for constitutionalism to be reconceived as a 'responsible discourse of transformation' which both recalls the general aspiration of collective self-government and political responsibility, but which also provides a set of ideas and norms which can be applied to the new and more differentiated world of reflexive and experimental regulation.

[10] See also his earlier work M Tushnet, *The New Constitutional Order* (Princeton, NJ, 2003) at 172, where he considers the possibility that the idea of democratic experimentalism expounded by Dorf and Sabel, n 1 above, might provide such a theory.

CONCLUSION

The contributors to this volume began their research with a common inquiry and a clear set of questions before them. Few clear answers have emerged, but many new questions and many tentative theses have been advanced. We make no pretence at articulating or asserting a shared understanding of the nature, role and significance of new governance practices, nor of the implications of the emergence and spread of experimental governance forms for our conceptions of law and constitutionalism. To do so would belie the diversity of approaches and assumptions which clearly underpin the various contributions. What the chapters in this collection have in common, despite the differences in subject matter, analytical approach and normative outlook, is a deep interest in the phenomenon of new governance, and a related interest in the way in which this phenomenon seems to call for a rethinking of legal and constitutional categories. Collectively and separately, the chapters highlight the nature and contours of the challenge new governance presents for law and for our thinking about constitutional values and structures. This book represents the early stages of an intellectual inquiry and a research project which we hope will continue in different forms and different fora over the coming years.

Part I

New Governance, Law and Constitutionalism

1

EU Constitutionalism and New Governance

NEIL WALKER

1. INTRODUCTION

THERE ARE MANY and contested ways of defining both constitutionalism and new governance in the context of the European Union, and even more and more variously contested ways of defining the relationship between these two notions. Part of my purpose in this essay will be to map what I see as five key candidate relationships between constitutionalism and new governance—or, if you like, the key dimensions of *the* relationship between constitutionalism and new governance, and to explain why each of them tells us something of importance about the peculiar regulatory dynamic of the European Union. The sketch, then, is a cumulative one rather than a series of alternative visions, for even if some of the possible relationships set out are in mutual tension, each addresses a connection (or a disconnection) which speaks plausibly to one aspect of the EU's situation. My purpose, however, is not merely cartographical. I also want to suggest that the first four possible relationships discussed—namely subsumption, instrumentalisation, non-correspondence and structural antagonism—are all finally limiting relationships. Each plays on a different dimension of the weakness or myopia of the constitutional paradigm in the European Union, and its failure to grasp new governance fully, as well as upon a certain overemphasis on 'definition-by-contrast'[1] and a consequent fuzziness over the content and significance of the 'new' within the notion of new governance itself. The fifth possible relationship, which flows from the insight that constitutionalism's historic connection to the idea of responsible self-government requires to be rethought for the post-national domain, holds out the possibility that constitutionalism need not be viewed in these limiting terms and, accordingly, that new governance's horizons of innovation need neither be limited by these limiting terms nor depend on the wholesale rejection of constitutional discourse. It inquires instead into

[1] G de Búrca and J Scott, 'New Governance, Law and Constitutionalism' (Introduction, above).

the more profound transformative possibilities for both constitutionalism and new governance of a deeper level of mutual engagement.

2. CONSTITUTIONALISM AND NEW GOVERNANCE: MOVEABLE OBJECTS IN A LIMITING FRAME

First, though, as a prelude to examining the various candidate relationship between constitutionalism and new governance, we must address a more basic puzzle. If, as already suggested, both constitutionalism and new governance are objects whose definition is vague and highly diverse, in what sense can the normal range of conceptions of the relationship between them nevertheless be seen as limiting? To answer this question requires some investigation of the way in which the discourses both of constitutionalism and of new governance have developed in the EU context.

European constitutionalism

Let us first consider constitutionalism. Four themes in the historical development of European constitutionalism are worth emphasising for present purposes. These are in turn: nominalism, textualism, hierarchy and self-containment.

By *nominalism* we mean, simply, the tendency for constitutionalism to become anything or everything anyone claims it to be. Even at the state level, constitutionalism is a highly open-ended discourse, and this is due to a combination of its ideological potency and its wide range of options and inherent contentiousness as a form of social technology or praxis. Its ideological potency consists in the added symbolic value to be derived from claiming for one's political preferences the weight of constitutional authority.[2] The special gravitas of constitutional authority rests upon its capacity to speak, often simultaneously, to one or both of two powerfully affirmative if apparently divergent legitimating traditions in the making and sustaining of modern political community.[3] Constitutionalism invokes, first, a tradition of universalism, or at least of universalisability—the idea that constitutional claims are good claims because since the birth of modern constitutionalism and the preambles of the first constitutional charters in nineteenth-century America and France they have often purported to speak to norms or principle of good government and social organisation that hold or should hold everywhere and for everyone, with any specific claim also an instantiation of the universal. Yet constitutionalism invokes, secondly, just as weighty a tradition of particularism, here responding to an equally

[2] See, eg, N Walker, 'The Idea of Constitutional Pluralism' (2002) 65 MLR 317–59 at 331–33.

[3] P Kahn, *The Reign of Law* (New Haven: Yale University Press, 1997).

powerful emphasis in the origins of modern statehood on the specificity of each *societas*[4] and its sovereign, and on the peculiarity and special moral status of the claims that members of the same polity can make inter se. Here the strength of the constitutional claim lies in its being exclusively or especially well suited to, and indeed often already firmly embedded within and corroborated by the law or mores of a particular polity.

Constitutionalism's inherent contentiousness as a form of social technology concerns the understandable degree of divergence about what counts as and what may be manipulated as 'constitutive' within a polity, regardless of whether we take a universalistic or particularistic view of that polity. At the basic social-technological level constitutionalism produces a three-level puzzle—normative, epistemic and motivational.[5] Normatively, this has to do with the basic aims of the constitution, the version or versions of the good society it wants to effect or endorse. Epistemically, it has to do with an understanding of the key generative mechanisms—or self-understanding—of the political society in question. Motivationally, it has to do with the capacity of the Constitution to encourage human agents to activate these generative mechanisms and to provide them with institutions which enable them to do so in a way that is consistent with the Constitution's normative aspirations. If we see a Constitution as a 'model'[6] of political community, this interweaving of the normative, the epistemic and the motivational becomes clearer. A Constitution is a model in the double sense of referring back to and representing in miniature what is the supposed basis of affinity of that community, whether ethnicity, common culture, common values or shared predicament (epistemic question), and projecting forwards by supplying the means towards (motivational question) the realisation of the substantive aspirations of the polity as conceived in ideal terms (normative question). With such a range of controversial questions in play, even in the most well-established state constitutional order the scope for genuine contention, and for ideological struggle over the symbolically precious resource of constitutionalism as to what lies at its constitutive core, becomes apparent.

In the context of a post-state polity such as the EU, the mix of high ideological stakes and contentiousness at the level of social technology invites an even more rampant nominalism. As the debate over the EU's first documentary Constitution[7] has underlined, the very idea that the EU is the type of entity that ought to be conceived in constitutional terms is itself a matter of ideological controversy. It is bound up, on the one hand, with the traditional link between constitutionalism and statehood, and with the sceptical

[4] R Jackson, 'Sovereignty in World Politics: A Glance at the Conceptual and Historical Landscape' (1999) 67 *Political Studies* 431–56 at 441–44.

[5] For a study of the interaction of the epistemic and motivational dimensions in EU constitutionalism, with particular reference to the debate over the Constitutional Treaty, see N Walker, 'Europe's Constitutional Momentum and the Idea of Polity Legitimacy' (2005) 3 *International Journal of Constitutional Law* 211–38.

[6] N Walker, 'The EU as a Constitutional Project' Federal Trust Online Papers 19/04.

[7] [2004] OJ C 310 of 16 December 2004 (hereinafter 'CT').

fear that the adoption of a Constitution might imply or prefigure a partial, incipient or aspiring statehood for the EU, and on the other hand, with the efforts of the more integration-minded to bootstrap the authority of a relatively new, original and politically vulnerable polity.[8] As the failure of the French and Dutch ratification referendums in the early summer of 2005 and the subsequent decision by the June European Council to put the Constitution into deep-freeze[9] indicates, that threshold controversy over whether European constitutionalism dare speak its name is by no means resolved. It is also the case, however, that the sheer momentum of the constitutional debate has encouraged many across the spectrum of enthusiasm for integration—including those most avowedly concerned to combat creeping European statehood and so more interested in constitutionalism's authority-restraining rather than its authority-enabling properties[10]—to endorse a constitutional discourse as the most appropriate and persuasive in which to register their particular conception of the sources, mechanism, purposes and limits of EU governance (and, indeed, to do so regardless even of whether such a conception involves the reduction of the Constitution to a canonical written text.).[11] That is to say, notwithstanding the current standoff over the Constitutional Treaty, the symbolic allure of the constitutional prize has tended to cause the fabric of constitutional argument to stretch rather than tear. And this is reinforced by the sheer novelty of the EU constitutional debate, the openness of the constitutional field to diverse claims encouraged by the lack of any prior self-proclaimed constitutional text for the EU, and the absence of the discipline associated with the obligation to ground claims in the interpretation or critique of any such 'living' text.

To this ideological and practical mix we should add the genuine normative, epistemic and motivational difficulty of modelling a Constitution on the basis of any relevant 'constitutional universal' for a non-state polity. Where neither the prior cultural or political supports associated with the state (as the normal instantiation of that 'constitutional universal'), nor, relatedly, the mobilising power which law may tap by reference to these forms of prior or incipient affinity, nor even the comprehensiveness of political vision associated with the state, are available, or at least not on the same terms or to the same degree,[12] then the extent to which European

[8] See, eg, Walker n 5 above.

[9] By providing for a period of a year in which Member States might reflect on the progress of ratification, and by extending the ratification deadline from Autumn 2006 to Summer 2007.

[10] As in the famous conversion of the traditionally Eurosceptic *Economist* magazine to the idea of a European Constitution—a conversion entirely contingent upon the endorsement of a power-constraining version of the Charter of Rights See *The Economist* (4 November 2000).

[11] Of many examples, see the works of Richard Bellamy asserting a broader framework of 'political constitutionalism' against a text-centred constitutional politics; eg, 'The Constitution of Europe: Rights or Democracy?' in R Bellamy, V Bufacchi and D Castiglione (eds) *Democracy and Constitutional Culture in the Union of Europe* (London: Lothian Foundation, 1995) 153–75.

[12] Walker, n 5 above, at 216–222.

constitutionalism remains uncharted territory becomes clearer, as does the potential for promiscuous constitutional 'naming and claiming.' European constitutionalism, in short, has become a protean discourse whose ideological currency is as inflated as its social-technological foundations are unstable, and for that reason is susceptible to highly strategic and opportunistic forms of nominalism.

The second salient feature of contemporary constitutional discourse in the EU is its *textualism*. Here the solipsism of nominalism is replaced—or more often complemented—by the superficiality of text-dependence. In the case of the current constitutional treaty, textualism is in fact a product of formalism. Just because we finally may have a text in the appropriate form—one which (in the increasingly unlikely event of its unanimous ratification and implementation) is self-understood and self-authorised *as* a Constitution, or at least as a hybrid *Constitutional* Treaty—the question of what is or is not constitutional becomes resolved in the document itself. Alternatively, and perhaps more pertinently given the likely failure of the Constitutional Treaty, in the claim that the prior and extant treaty structure already constitutes a Constitution of sorts, textualism is underpinned by a kind of materialism—an emphasis upon the matter rather than the spirit of the Constitution.[13] On this view, the fact that the Treaty texts already contain some of the familiar materials of a written Constitution, in particular a detailed organogram of governmental power and of its checks and balances, is enough to validate their constitutional quality and pedigree regardless of whether their underlying motivation and telos is in any sense similar to that commonly found in the case of other written (state) Constitutions.

Yet underlying both formalist and materialist variants there is of course a preoccupation with political power. Constitutionalism seen through a textualist lens finally amounts to no more and no less than what succeeds in making it into the documentary Constitution or quasi-Constitution. As with nominalism, so too with textualism, therefore the novelty of the idea of a Constitution beyond or without a state favours an open-ended discourse, even if it is not the mere wish but rather the (putative) textual command that is crucial in the latter case. Moreover, again as with nominalism, the emphasis is on the emergence of the (formally authoritative) word rather than its implementation. A textualist approach begs the question of the impact of the text, and since, as we have seen, the difficulties of developing a relevant social technology for understanding the nature and limits of the generative power of constitutionalism are even more formidable for the post-state than for the state polity, this is a very large question to beg.

If the first two themes of European constitutionalism involve a manifest but rather shallow, and so permissive, borrowing from the state constitutional

[13] As in Weiler's idea of a 'constitution without constitutionalism'; see JHH Weiler, *The Constitution of Europe* (Cambridge: CUP, 1999) ch 1.

tradition, the statist legacy of the third and fourth themes is less apparent and often less consciously realised, but, ultimately more profound and constraining. *Hierarchy* and *self-containment* are the more venerable and more strongly established and officially endorsed themes of constitutionalism in the EU context. For the jurisprudence of supremacy, direct effect, implied powers etc, developed by the European Court of Justice (ECJ) from the 1960s onwards, and the notion of incipient constitutionalisation which grew alongside this[14] is first and foremost concerned with the assertion of the authority and integrity of the new legal order *qua* legal order.

The operative logic underpinning that process of self-assertion is at root of a traditional Kelsenian variety. It is about the positing of authoritative foundations and differentiating other norms in accordance with the pedigree provided by these foundations The legal order of the EU unfolds from the self-assuming 'judicial *kompetenz-kompetenz*'[15] of the Court in an elaborate chain of validity which encompasses different levels of norms within the Treaty-based European order as well as the supremacy or priority of EU norms over national norms. The conception of legal hierarchy contained in this model in fact contains two distinct implications. The first is that higher-order norms trump lower-order ones in cases of conflict. The second is that the higher order norms generate the lower-order norms. This formal property of the legal system, moreover, has an important institutional complement, in that the legal-normative hierarchy has also generated and is in practice articulated through and reinforced by an institutional hierarchy, one in which the key law-making institutions (Commission, Parliament and Council) and methods are situated towards the apex of the pyramid, and indeed other institutional features of the legal order—adjudication, administration and monitoring also tend to follow a 'top-down' command-and-control logic.

If hierarchy provides the operative logic of the new legal order, then self-containment is its basic premise and self-prophesising conclusion. The idea that the Constitution 'contains' its legal order[16] has closely related internal and external dimensions. Internally, it implies that the higher 'constitutional' norms of the legal system are the exclusive source of ultimate authority for the legal system. In turn, exclusiveness of source implies exhaustiveness of reach. If the constitutional norms are the only basis of authority for the legal system, then there is no part of the legal order which these norms cannot reach, no 'lower' normative arrangements which cannot finally be traced back to the authority of the highest norms. That this idea of comprehensive regulatory control is an important aspect of the constitutional self-understanding of the EU legal order is underscored by the facts of the first

[14] See, eg, P Craig, 'Constitutions, Constitutionalism and the European Union,' (2001) 7 *European Law Journal* 125–50 at 128–35.

[15] Weiler, n 13 above, at 298.

[16] See, eg, E Christodoulidis, *Law and Reflexive Politics* (Kluwer: Dordrecht, 1998) esp chs 6, 8 and 11–14.

two cases in which the ECJ, following its earlier assembly of the building blocks of hierarchy in the direct effect and supremacy line of cases, resorted to a more explicit language in describing the Treaties as the 'basic constitutional Charter' of the Community. Tellingly, these dealt, respectively, with the exhaustive reach of the 'rule of law' within the European legal order[17] and the exclusive jurisdiction of the ECJ as the Europolity's court of final authority to determine matters of European law bearing upon the key question of the respective competences of Community institutions and the Member States.[18]

And where from an internal perspective self-containment or integrity implies comprehensive scope and control, from an external perspective it implies that the EU is a separate legal order. Indeed, it is precisely its formal internal 'completeness' that vindicates its autonomy from other legal orders Within the self-containment perspective, in sum, the Constitution has a symbiotic relationship with its 'own'[19] legal order, supplying it with identity (internally) and distinctiveness (externally).

Looking at these four themes of European constitutionalism in the round, in all cases we can see the drag of the state tradition. In the case of nominalism and textualism, this operates in a loose ideological manner, in the very attempt to invest in the symbolic currency of the rhetorical language or the documentary form of a state-centred tradition. In the case of hierarchy and self-containment, the connection is deeper and more implicit. Here constitutionalism is a metaphor for the emergence and consolidation of the very idea of a legal order at the supranational level, one that draws closely on the idea of legal order relevant to statehood and the Westphalian system of states. The combination of epistemic and motivational assumptions involved—that we are dealing with a discrete political order which best regulates itself in accordance with a unitary framework of authority—may be so general and taken-for–granted as often to escape attention, but this is precisely because they are so deeply familiar from the social technology of state constitutionalism.

New governance

Turning to new governance, again we confront a concept whose exploration in one sense is highly diverse and open-ended, but in another displays a common limitation. For while the specification of what is 'new' in new governance may be more or less concrete or abstract, it invariably turns on a *categorical* distinction from the 'old.' One common starting point at the more concrete or institutional end of the spectrum is to define new governance in the EU in terms of a departure from the Classic Community

[17] Case 294/83, *Parti ecologiste 'Les Verts' v Parliament* [1986] ECR 1339.
[18] Opinion 1/91 *Re Draft Agreement on a European Economic Area* [1991] ECR 6102.
[19] Case 6/64, *Costa v ENEL* ECR 585.

Method of norm generation and of governance more generally, centring around the Commission right of initiative and the legislative and budgetary powers of the Council of Ministers and European Parliament.[20] An even more general variant of the institutionally-centred approach finds the defining feature of new governance simply in its non-legislative or only marginally legislative character, with the very idea of legislation here operating as a proxy for hierarchy.[21]. Such a view, indeed, comes very close to defining new governance as the antithesis of *legal* ordering as commonly conceived, and so, by inference, of *constitutional* ordering as the most fundamental level of legal discourse.

Other more abstract models are less quick to draw substantive inferences from institutional form. They concentrate instead on general properties of new governance, such as participation and power-sharing, multi-level integration, diversity and decentralisation, deliberation, flexibility and revisability of norms, and experimentation and knowledge–creation.[22] From this perspective, various particular regulatory forms can be assessed for their new governance credentials. These include not only the Open Method of Co-ordination (OMC)—the novel decision-making structure based on iterative benchmarking, voluntary national compliance and mutual learning that is widely perceived to be the most developed and most rapidly spreading form of new governance—but also older and more familiar devices such as partnership arrangements, comitology and even framework directives. The basic premise however, remains oppositional. The 'new' properties explicitly or implicitly acquire definition from their contrast with a model of 'old' government based on representation, singular authority, centralised command and control, rigidity and stability of norms, and the uniform application of a received regulatory formula.

Clearly, there are dangers in any binary model of regulatory forms or characteristics. Such a stylised contrast may mask the fact that many 'actually existing' old forms of government tended to incorporate some new elements, while the new forms continue to incorporate aspects of the old. In normative terms too, a binary model may encourage us to religiously favour one side in a series of nested oppositions between new and old, progressive and conservative, and so to discount the resilient worth of some of the old 'rule of law' values. Yet defenders of the conceptual currency of new governance might reasonably respond that their thinking is alert to the dangers of an unduly dichotomous approach, and that it already seeks to counter the inference of mutual exclusivity and to register that the world is invariably a

[20] See, eg, J Scott and D Trubek, 'Mind the Gap: Law and New Approaches to Governance in the European Union' (2002) 8 *European Law Journal* 1–18 at 1.

[21] See, eg, A Heritier, 'New Modes of Governance in Europe: Policy-making without Legislating?' in A Heritier (ed) *Common Goods: Reinventing European and International Governance* (Boston: Rowman and Littlefield, 2002) 185–206.

[22] See, eg, Scott and Trubek, n 20 above, at 5–6.

more complex place than any strictly binary model allows. In particular, the development of a 'theory of hybrids'[23] can help us both with the explanatory question of how old and new—hard and soft—combine and interact in practice, and with the normative question of the optimal reconciliation of the virtues associated with each.

Interesting work on hybridity is indeed emerging, and some of it can be found in the present volume.[24] For present purposes, however, we should bear in mind the obvious but not unimportant point that those for whom new governance constitutes an analytical point of departure continue to display a structural predisposition towards the new. In general terms, this has to do with the basic methodology of theory building. New governance analysis proceeds by reference to the Weberian notion of an ideal (or pure) type, in which the relations that constitute the ideal types of new (or, indeed, old) governance are the main focus of inquiry and evaluation, and provide the basic default account of the world. Indeed, the very idea of a hybrid or mixed type corroborates this founding assumption, as it suggests the primacy of the different ideal types—or basic species—from which the hybrid is formed.

In more specific terms, bias towards the new is bound up with the awkwardness of developing hybrid forms of normative as opposed to explanatory theory. Many of the more interesting insights of hybrid theorising, as suggested by de Búrca and Scott's distinction between baseline, developmental and default hybridity,[25] have to do with the causal interface between old and new, where each is conceived in general or holistic terms. Under what circumstances and to what extent, they ask, does the old underpin (baseline) or provide a catalyst (developmental) for the new, or, indeed, its disciplining counterfactual (default)? And while the answers to these questions are not normatively insignificant, in the sense that they show that the basic viability of the new tends to remain dependent upon the old, and also demonstrate how some of the normative dividends of the old and new may broadly co-exist, more detailed assessments of the optimal regulatory mix of old and new conceived of as a set of disaggregated norm-characteristics are harder to come by. This is because, if we dig down to the level of constituent variables, elements of the 'new' and the 'old tend to take the form of *logical* opposites (for example, centralisation versus decentralisation, singular versus multi-level authority, command versus deliberation, rigid and stable versus flexible and revisable norms), thereby allowing very little analytical leverage for hybrid forms to develop. Just because of the dominance and categorical quality of the initial opposition, hybridity in a normative register, then, would seem to push us either towards a crude and unlikely

[23] D Trubek and L Trubek, 'Hard and Soft Law in the Construction of Social Europe: The Role of the Open Method of Co-ordination' (2005) 11 *European Law Journal* 343–64 at 364.
[24] As previewed by de Búrca and Scott n 1 above.
[25] *Ibid*.

mix of polarised variables drawn from the opposite camps of new and old (for example, deliberatively produced *but* rigidly and stably articulated and applied norms) or, if we seek to hybridise each individual variable, towards the descriptively bereft balancing point (for example, relatively (de)centralised, or relatively (in)flexible), or, in some cases, logically incoherent 'excluded middle' (for example, relatively singular?) between these polarised variables.

The instant point is not, however, to question the long- term potential of hybridity as a way of moderating the analysis of new governance, or perhaps as a promissory note to rethink the whole explanatory .and normative paradigm of supranational regulatory innovation.[26] Rather, it is simply to confirm that the basic analytical frame through which we construct the idea of new governance creates a propensity towards oppositional thinking, and since the adoption of that frame tends in any case to be linked with an interest in and openness towards the affirmative possibilities of the new, this may result in the integrity and virtue of the new relative to the old being exaggerated.

In a nutshell, then, we may observe that the problems associated with constitutionalism at the supranational level seem to find their negative image in the case of new governance. For if, despite its diversity and internal divisions, constitutional discourse remains constrained by the legacy of an old paradigm, new governance analysis, by contrast, and again notwithstanding its significant internal differences, risks being in excessive thrall to the new. Let us now seek to examine the implications of this disjuncture between old-fashioned and new-fashioned in terms of the various candidate relationships between constitutionalism and new governance.

3. SOME CANDIDATE RELATIONSHIPS

If we recall the four major themes of European constitutionalism, we can now suggest how each of these provides the basis for one possible relationship between constitutionalism and new governance In each case, however, as intimated earlier, the connection is in some significant sense limited or compromised.

To begin again from a nominalist perspective, here we can conceive of the relationship between constitutionalism and new governance in terms of the subsumption of the latter under the former. If constitutionalism is such an open-ended discourse at the supranational level, lacking even the minimal constraints set by institutional and textual path-dependence at the state level and a certain set of social-technological assumptions about what is

[26] For thoughtful discussion, see Trubek and Trubek n 23 above. For reasons set out in the text above and further developed in section 4(a) below, however, the 'hybridity' concept may be more useful in alerting us to some of the outstanding problems with the new governance approach than in resolving these problems.

available as constitutional resources, plausible as constitutional technique and appropriate as constitutional purpose, then what is to stop us just calling new governance 'constitutional'? By a simple strategy of naming—of updating the constitutional catalogue in the light of fresh developments—do we not thereby resolve any tensions between constitutionalism and new governance?

There are two cumulative objections to such an approach. The first is that if constitutional discourse is so ubiquitous, so stretched by ideological whim and strategy, then its invocation may come to lack any significance other than as a rhetorical device. If constitutionalism is everywhere, then nowhere, the realm of new governance included, can it claim a special authority, or lend its object some special appropriateness to or core significance within supranational governance relations. Secondly, the dilution of constitutional *discourse* to the point that a claim made in the name of the Constitution carries no special authority within or special relevance to governance does not, however, imply that in *practice* there is a constitutional 'flatland'; for, as we shall see, a higher priority or greater authority may continue to be accorded to certain types of arrangements over others within the positive law and institutional workings of the supranational system. Indeed, the development of a more 'democratic' constitutional rhetoric may actually reinforce this to the extent that its permissive message distracts attention from the resilience of underlying authority structures.

For its part, the textualist strain within supranational constitutional thinking fits with an instrumentalist conception of the relationship between the Constitution and new governance. Most immediately, the new Constitutional Treaty can be viewed as an instrument through which new governance in general, and the OMC in particular find articulation in the higher echelons of the EU's regulatory system. The story of OMC's fate in the Constitutional Treaty has been told in detail elsewhere,[27] and here is not the place to repeat it. However, a number of features deserve mention insofar as they demonstrate the strengths and drawbacks of the textualist approach, and indeed point us towards other potential limitations of the constitutional vision.

First, to repeat a point, as with all constitutional texts at their point of emergence, how the Constitutional Treaty addresses the matter of new governance is in significant part a function of power politics. Yet far more so than at the level of the state, where—for better or for worse—even at transformative constitutional moments the basic structural principle of the polity, namely that of an entity with formally unlimited capacity to act, is regarded as relatively settled, such power politics at the EU level tend to respond to

[27] See, eg, G de Búrca, 'The Constitutional Challenge of New Governance in the European Union' (2003) 28 ELR 814–39 at 830f; J Zeitlin, 'Social Europe and Experimentalist Governance' in G de Búrca (ed) *EU Law and the Welfare State: In Search of Solidarity* (Oxford: OUP, 2005) 213–41.

a *double* agenda, one of both 'blueprint' and 'generative' politics.[28] The treatment of the OMC, accordingly, reflects a complex compromise over two cross-cutting macro-political questions. One involves the traditional right/left question of the emphasis to be placed on 'Social Europe'—the focus of key OMCs in economic policy, employment strategy, social inclusion, pensions etc—as a countervailing force to the single market, and the other involving the underlying structural question of the proper extent of the EU's (as opposed to Member States') competences. As with many multi-level, intersecting compromises, because of the high number of veto strategies in play, its articulation has been largely negative—more about soothing diverse anxieties than pursuing divisive aspirations. On the one hand, therefore, we find that social policy aims central to so many OMCs, and so indirectly the OMC itself, are boosted in the general statement of values and objectives in the opening provisions of the Constitutional Treaty,[29] in the 'second generation' Equality and Solidarity chapters of the Charter on Fundamental Rights[30] and in a new horizontal clause committing the Union to take account of various social polices and objectives in defining and implementing specific polices and actions.[31] Yet, on the other hand, for all that the coordination of economic and employment policies is treated as a distinctive mode of competence in the CT,[32] nowhere in the text is the OMC granted explicit constitutional status. This silence, it has been argued, resulted from a deadlock or compromise within the Praesidium of the Convention which produced the draft Constitutional Treaty between those from a state-centred perspective who were concerned at the OMC's potential for 'soft' erosion of national policy prerogatives and those of a more *communautaire* disposition who were concerned at its possible undermining of classic 'hard' supranational competences. [33] Trapped between these two opposing fears, it ultimately proved impossible for OMC to find its own distinctive constitutional voice.

In the second place, the debate on the place of the OMC in the constitutional text rather underlines the poverty of attempts to think through the idea of post-national constitutionalism in social-technological terms. No constitutional text is self-implementing, least of all one which lacks the epistemic frame of the statist model, yet remarkably little attention seems to have been paid to this fact. Commenting on the possible impact of the relevant sections of the approved constitutional text, and indeed of the alternative option of a generic OMC clause dedicated to asserting high standards

[28] D Miliband, 'Introduction' in D Miliband (ed) *Reinventing the Left* (Cambridge: Polity, 1994) 1–17 at 5.

[29] CT Art I–3.

[30] CT Part II.

[31] CT Art III–117.

[32] CT Art 1–15.

[33] Zeitlin, n 27 above, at 230.

of procedural 'due process',[34] one observer has remarked that while it appears to be common ground that 'constitutional provisions ... matter in the EU' in particular through conferring 'added legitimacy' there is nevertheless 'no clear answer'[35] *to what extent* they matter, or *how* their impact percolates through and resonates within the system. This neatly captures the widespread and complacent assumption within the Constitutional Treaty debate that putting things on a constitutional footing would somehow in and of itself be consequential rather than simply marking another consequence—the point at which political compromise had been reached.

Two questions are begged by the assumption of consequentiality. First, and more generally, what basic difference does juridification of new governance, or indeed any new form of normative ordering make? If and to the extent that the constitutional text were to impose precise or unavoidable new obligations or confer wide-ranging new powers on key organs of government or other agencies, then there might seem to be a relatively simple answer to this at the level of normative authorisation. But none of the new provisions, dealing as they do with the designation of vague objectives and general rights and the affirmation of broad jurisdictions, actually possesses that kind of semantic sting. It is difficult to see, in other words, how these provisions could be decisive in persuading or compelling key governance institutions to do what they were not otherwise minded to do, or in empowering anyone do what they were not already capable of doing.

And even if this were not so, a second set of questions of the added value of calling the text constitutional, rather than merely legal, remains unanswered. Inasmuch as the general legal code makes a difference, does the invocation of the special constitutional code make a further difference? Alternatively, even if the conferral of simple legal status makes little or no difference, might the conferral of constitutional status not still do so?

One possible answer suggested by the other two themes of EU constitutionalism—hierarchy and self-containment, is that any difference constitutionalisation makes to the promotion of new governance is more likely to be negative than positive. If we take first the theme of hierarchy, the danger is that this simply fails to correspond to or recognise the operating logic of new governance. On this view, much of what goes on in the 'underworld'[36] of new governance is hardly touched upon by a constitutional model which is fixated with pedigree norms and the commanding institutional heights of the Community method.[37] At best, then, constitutionalism and new governance

[34] For its elaboration and discussion, see G de Búrca and J Zeitlin, 'Constitutionalizing the Open Method of Co-ordination: What Should the Convention Propose?' (2003) *CEPS Policy Brief* 31.

[35] Zeitlin, n 27 above, at 240.

[36] To adapt Weiler's description of the profile of the Comitology system in, '"Comitology" as Revolution—Infranationalism, Constitutionalism and Democracy' in C Joerges and E Vos (eds) *EU Committees: Social Regulation, Law and Politics* (Oxford: Hart, 1999) 339–50.

[37] On the 'processualist' critique of documentary constitutionalism more generally, see N Walker, 'The Legacy of the Constitutional Moment' (2004) 11 *Constellations* 368–92.

are merely ships in the night, navigating their very different routes with scarcely a passing glance. And indeed, any attempt at greater familiarity, involving the examination of new governance thorough a constitutional lens, merely underlines the difficulties involved in trying to reconcile two such diverse operating logics. Thus, to return to the debates on the Constitutional Treaty, one objection to the naming and constitutional anchoring of OMC was that it would, at least implicitly, involve locating OMC in a strict hierarchy of forms of Community governance, either trumping and displacing or being trumped and displaced by certain pre-existing hard competences.[38] Yet the emergence and implementation of many new governance measures are not well understood in terms of their place in a pecking order of regulatory modalities, but rather as a set of mechanisms that through *content-dependent* persuasion and good practice can variously complement, supplement, challenge, modify, anticipate or consolidate *content-independent* forms of vertically-ordered authority. The danger, then, in trying to reduce OMC mechanisms to a logic which is commensurable with, and so competitive within, a hierarchy of forms, is of forcing square pegs into round constitutional holes.

If we move to the related idea of self-containment, the mismatch between the social technology of traditional constitutionalism and that of new governance is even more pronounced, and indeed allows us to contemplate the possibility of a structural antagonism between the two. Constitutional self-containment, as noted earlier, has both internal and external dimensions, and each threatens a key dimension of new governance. Internally, the idea that constitutional authority is exclusive and exhaustive—a preordained unitary order externally imposed upon its objects—does not fit easily with the idea of OMC as a shifting series of experimental and open-ended frameworks of voluntary compliance and emergent self-authorisation. This tension we can see, for example, in the reluctance of some to contemplate *any* form of freeze-frame constitutionalisation of the OMC in the Constitutional Treaty for fear that it might undermine its trademark flexibility and interrupt its dynamic path of development.[39]

Externally, if anything the tension is even more profound. Self-containment, as we have seen, is intimately linked to the idea of the EU as a distinct and separate legal-constitutional order. Yet so much of what is key to the social technology of EU constitutionalism clearly has a relational dimension.[40] In simple terms, the EU shares both territory and people with its Member States, and we cannot conceive of the guiding norms of the EU, the nature of its societal steering mechanisms or the motivations of its citizens

[38] See Zeitlin, n 27 above, at 230.
[39] *Ibid* 229.
[40] See, eg, N Walker, 'Postnational Constitutionalism and the Problem of Translation' in JHH Weiler and M Wind (eds) *European Constitutionalism beyond the State* (Cambridge: CUP, 2003) 27–54.

in isolation from these state structures. This relational feature is never more pronounced than in the context of new governance in general and OMC in particular, where it is precisely the failure to agree a definitive and authoritative division of competence and the recognition of the artificiality of such partitions as are in place which has provided much of the impetus for reform, and for thinking about the connection between legal orders in more fluid terms.[41]

4. THE MUTUAL (RE)ENGAGEMENT OF CONSTITUTIONALISM AND NEW GOVERNANCE

New governance reconsidered

It would seem, then, that constitutionalism may offer either too little or too much to new governance. Too little, if wearing its nominalist clothes, constitutionalism becomes a bland affair—an everyday mantra with no analytical bite; or, if wearing its textualist clothes, it is instead fated to be the casualty of complex multi-level political gridlock. Too much, if the resilient constitutional codes of hierarchy and self-containment—inherited from the state but strongly reasserted in the foundational stages of the EU—colonise and subvert attempts made in the name of new governance to rethink regulation for a post-Westphalian age. Perhaps, then, new governance has nothing to gain from constitutionalism, other than the instrumental benefits which may accrue to new governance's supporters through the strategic assertion of a symbolically powerful language in which to couch their claims. Even here, however, any victory threatens to be a Pyrrhic one if the price of adoption of the constitutional register is deference to a social technology which is ultimately at odds with that which animates new governance.

Before any such dismissive conclusion were drawn, however, new governance would have to meet its own high standards of justification and demonstrate that it was not in need of any external forms of normative support. Yet in its fixation with 'the new', new governance, as we have already noted, reveals significant weak points and blind spots. And insofar as these point to important deficiencies and limitations, might not 'old' constitutionalism offer as yet unconsidered means of assisting in overcoming these?

Earlier we identified new governance's preoccupation with a binary logic as leaving it with little sense of the value, if any, *of anything other than* new governance. Certainly in its more rigid formulations, the binary mode of identifying new governance as an important empirical and/or normative force either suggests that 'old' governance' is increasingly insignificant and/or bereft of value, or, even if it stops short of any such categorical dismissal, it nevertheless offers us no clear way of understanding or assessing

[41] See, eg, Scott and Trubek n 20 above; de Búrca n 27 above.

just how such older forms, with their opposite or countervailing regulatory logic, are supposed to complement new governance. The turn to hybridity, as we saw, signals some recognition of these problems and some attempt to move beyond them, but the legacy of the original approach is hard to shake off. Either we end up dealing in causal relationships between the old and the new conceived of as very broad generalities, or, if we take a disaggregative approach, we struggle for an effective conceptual language in which to think through the recombination of old and new.

If we try to locate what lies at the root of these difficulties, we may find it in the intensity of focus of the new governance approach upon matters of institutional design. Such a narrow preoccupation entails that questions such as the deep philosophy of governance and of political organisation which should animate that design or the wider social and political context in which the relevant institutions are embedded, tend to be ignored or relegated to secondary consideration. This is most obvious in the more concrete formulations of the new governance approach, where we see a kind of institutional fetishism in which different institutional configurations are treated as surrogates for the pursuit of some values rather than others. Yet even in the more abstract formulations of new governance, we find only a more elaborate route to the same kind of decontextualised institutional conclusion. In emphasising the context-independent value of matters such as participation, multi-level integration, diversity, deliberation, flexibility and experimental learning, new governance analysis seems intent on supplying the key ingredients necessary for *any* institutional concoction to pass the 'good governance' test.

Indeed, much of the appeal of the new governance approach seems to lie precisely in the priority it accords to the 'practical' business of supplying a checklist of widely affirmed regulatory desiderata. This is stressed far more than the inevitably more divisive question of an overall conception of governance which would relate and prioritise these various desiderata both inter se and with regard to other governance values, and which would seek to ground the whole in its overall social and political context of emergence and ramification. Yet the very concentration on a broadly palatable institutional recipe which is the source of much of its attraction may also be the most serious shortcoming of new governance analysis to the extent that it leads to avoidance or downgrading of these domains of inquiry where new governance analysis is most vulnerable.

We may demonstrate this, paradoxically, by considering one of the contributions to new governance analysis that *has* taken these questions of governance philosophy and wider socio-political context seriously, namely the work of the influential democratic experimentalist or pragmatist school.[42]

[42] See, eg, C Sabel and M Dorf, 'A Constitution of Democratic Experimentalism.' (1998) 98 *Columbia Law Review* 267; O Gerstenberg and CF Sabel, 'Directly-Deliberative Polyarchy: An Institutional Ideal for Europe?' in C Joerges and R Dehousse (eds) *Good Governance in Europe's Integrated Market* (Oxford: OUP, 2002); J Cohen and CF Sabel, 'Sovereignty and Solidarity: EU and US' in J Zeitlin and D Trubek (eds) *Governing Work and Welfare in a New Economy* (Cambridge: Cambridge University Press, 2002).

According to the experimentalists, the promise of new governance in general and OMC in particular lies in their method of addressing the tension between two aspirations of democratic authority. For democratic government is only acceptable if it both produces well-informed decisions that provide practical solutions to collective action problems, and allows participation and voice to those affected by such decisions. Whereas many theories of governance struggle to reconcile these two aspirations, and tend either to subordinate knowledge to voice or voice to knowledge, the experimentalist approach seeks to discover and exploit contexts of action in which the two can be optimally combined. For the experimentalists, a 'bottom-up' perspective, one whose point of departure is self-constituting practical problem-solving units or constituencies (who tend to be groups at the receiving end of classic command and control public sector performance) provides the best way of proceeding. It allows the 'demos' to find its own highly localised level, one where voice is most effective, knowledge and experience most relevant, and motivation most palpable. On this view, the attraction of OMC and the like is that they are sensitive to the primacy of localised understanding and praxis while offering a template in terms of which local solutions can be pooled, exchanged and developed and activity coordinated beyond the level of the basic problem-solving unit.

In developing a fully fledged and socially grounded regulatory philosophy along these lines, the experimentalist approach dramatises two particular types of problem for new governance. In the first place, there is the problem of the guarantee of the basic regulatory frame or structure of any institutional design, and, in the second place, there is the problem of the specification of the appropriate boundaries of governance.

The problem of the guarantee of the basic regulatory frame has in fact two dimensions, each of which is implicit in all forms of new governance and becomes explicit in the face of the clear normative priorities of experimentalism. The first addresses the relationship between new and old, and asks, how, in the sacrifice or subservience of 'old' values such as stability and predictability of norms to the demands of experimental learning we can continue to ensure or even presume against the erosion of these norms that we may argue are universal, or at least of resilient relevance across time and space.[43] The second concerns the danger of institutional entropy. How, given the experimentalist and 'bottom-up' basic thrust, can we find an institutional form which has the basic coherence and integrity even to guarantee its own self-reproduction? Is there not a danger either that new governance in its emphasis upon relentless revisability contains the seeds of its own destruction, or, alternatively, that it opens itself to the charge of performative

[43] For the posing of these questions in the context of the relationship between OMC and human rights protection, see de Búrca, n 27 above, at 833–35.

contradiction by placing certain anchoring premises beyond the possibility of experimental rejection?[44]

As regards the specification of the appropriate boundaries of governance and of democratic self-constitution, again the explicitness of the experimentalist approach places the problem of new governance in sharp relief. Whereas the emphasis upon a certain bundle of regulatory desiderata regardless of context means that it is often left unclear in new governance analysis at what level of government and to what extent these values should be articulated, experimentalism puts its cards firmly on the table in its identification of the coal-face, problem-solving entity as the primary unit of analysis. Yet considerations of justice, coordination and existing political culture mean that this cannot be the only key boundary for the experimentalists. As regards justice, since different problem-solving sectors are not hermetically sealed off from one another, but take decisions that involve significant externalities and indirectly affect a wide range of interests, there has to be a wider context in which these external effects can be addressed and balanced. As regards coordination, the very idea of mutual learning and adjustment within and across different OMCs and other experimental regulatory contexts presupposes a delimited zone, whether of functional activity or territory, within which such coordination takes place.

Both of these factors suggest the state, and, more importantly for present purposes, the supranational level—given the significant extant ordering and coordinating power of each—as other sites and 'outer boundaries' of political organisation beyond the basic problem-solving units. Finally, the special suitability of new governance in general and OMC in particular to the wider European supranational context is explicitly argued for by advocates of experimentalism on grounds of an existing framework of political understandings and the growing perception within that framework of the need for a revision and a renewal of the Community method.[45] On this view, against a background of growing collective anxiety as to the incapacitating inflexibility of classic Community command-and-control decision-making procedures, the new more permissive regulatory capacities of new governance are required to enhance deliberative opportunities and secure the levels of collective trust necessary to persuade Member States to relax their de facto or de jure veto powers sufficiently to save the overall EU system from

[44] One possible answer to the second objection lies in the suggestion that the basic OMC template itself be reviewed and improved by the reflexive application to this higher order level of the key aspects used in the lower order application of OMC in substantive policy sectors—benchmarking, peer review, monitoring, iterative redesign etc. See Zeitlin n 27 above. Yet, however useful an institutional design suggestion, the problem of self-reference remains. However self-critically deployed, the basic OMC methodology remains axiomatic, its original authority unchallenged.

[45] See, eg, C Sabel and J Zeitlin, 'Active Welfare, Experimental Governance, Pragmatic Constitutionalism: The New Transformation of Europe' Unpublished Paper, 2003. See also Zeitlin n 27 above.

gridlock. Here, then, the European level is presupposed not just as an objective source of authority, but appealed to as a subjective source of an ongoing commitment—as indispensable as it is elusive—to put things in common.

Reflexive constitutionalism

Taken together, the problem of anchoring the basic regulatory structure and the necessity of providing a framework of political community other and wider than that of the various problem-solving constituencies do indeed provide a significant challenge to new governance. However, it is a challenge that may be met provided that we look again at the resources of authoritative ordering that may be available through the perspective of constitutionalism.

In one sense, this may seem only too obvious a conclusion. As we have already seen, an important part of the constitutional tradition, including the oldest vector of EU constitutionalism, is concerned with the provision of a basic legal framework of political community which both trumps and is generative of other norms. Equally, that part of the tradition of constitutionalism which focuses not on the universality of norms of good governance but on the particularity of the polity has always been concerned with the bonds of affinity within even very large communities and with how these may be mobilised within a coherent social technology. Yet while these 'constitutional resources' seem to address the problems of regulatory anchorage and the construction of a wider framework of political community respectively, they threaten to do so by reasserting just these features of constitutionalism which are in most obvious tension with new governance. What price the constitutionalisation of new governance if it brings back into the picture the rigid normative and institutional hierarchy and comprehensive self-containment that new governance seeks to overcome? And what price the constitutionalisation of new governance if it falls victim to a kind of false essentialism—a 'personification'[46] of abstract community, which masks very particular interests in the name of an illusionary notion of the settled common interest, and which, indeed, provides the dubious ideological ballast to support the hierarchical operating logic and comprehensive pretensions of old-fashioned constitutionalism ?

In the most general terms, the prospect of EU constitutionalism offering a solution to the deficiencies of new governance without undermining its basic purpose depends upon EU constitutionalism nurturing a quality which it actually shares in common with the experimentalist version of new governance, namely an intense reflexivity. To be 'reflexive' means that something is capable of bending or turning back on itself. This amounts to

[46] Gerstenberg and Sabel n 42 above.

more than a providing a 'reflection'—an inert mirror or faithful model of a prior essence. Rather, it is about the possession of the quality of ipseity—of the capacity for *self*-reflection and the possibility of *self*-transformation inherent in that capacity. [47]

How does it help to reconceive of constitutionalism in reflexive terms? It does so by allowing us to think of constitutionalism as the carrier of a generic idea of responsible self-government.[48] The idea of responsible self-government is inherently reflexive in that it involves a self-assertion and a taking of responsibility as two sides of a single coin. By conceiving of itself in constitutional terms the EU is indeed, as many of the sceptics fear, making a claim to autonomy, of being a political community in its own right rather than merely a delegated and subordinate form of political authority, albeit a political community which co-exists with and does not in turn seek to subordinate other and overlapping political communities at state and sub-state level. And in making that claim to autonomy, the EU also must perforce accept full responsibility for its own affairs before both internal and external audiences. Constitutionalism, then, is the language in which both the assertion is made and the responsibility taken.

Constitutionalism is thus revealed as the indispensable 'discourse of conceptualisation and imagination'[49] whereby *any* polity conceives and thus constitutes itself as such. On this view the 'old' state tradition of constitutionalism need not be viewed in either of the negative ways portrayed earlier—neither as a paralysing legacy handed down from a quite different political context nor as a source of indiscriminate borrowing and purely opportunistic rhetoric. Rather, the state is but one species of the genus of responsible self-government, the supranational entity known as the EU another, and the generic idea itself the only basis on which we can meaningfully translate between the two contexts.

But, what, in more detail, should the generic idea of responsible self-government imply at the EU level? It was suggested above that for reflexive constitutionalism to complement and augment new governance in the EU such reflexivity should be intensely pursued. That is to say, it is not enough simply for the EU merely to style itself as a reflexive entity. Indeed, to do things merely *in the name of* responsible self-government can lead to precisely the type of 'personification' of a regulatory configuration—its reification as something possessing its own interests—that many proponents of new governance fear.[50] Rather, intense reflexivity implies close and persistent attention to the conditions in which and purposes for which the very idea of the responsible self-government of a collectivity may be justified.

[47] See, eg, B Van Roermund, 'Sovereignty: Popular and Unpopular' and H Lindahl, 'Sovereignty and Representation in the European Union? in N Walker (ed) *Sovereignty in Transition* (Oxford: Hart, 2003) 33–54 and 87–114.

[48] Walker, n 2 above, at 343–35.

[49] Weiler, n 13 above, at 223.

[50] See Gerstenberg and Sabel, n 42 above.

These conditions and purposes concern the basis on which the collective 'self' may be identified and the collective ends it seeks vindicated. Crucially, in this regard, one of the apparent constitutional weaknesses of the EU may turn out be a strength. It will be recalled that a key element in the social technology of state constitutionalism is its epistemic dimension—its understanding of the key generative mechanisms of the political society in question. Typically in the state context this involves some notion of a prior bonding element or source of affinity, and the danger is that the Constitution merely 'reflects' this rather than undertake a 'reflexive' engagement' with it. In the context of the EU no such hostages to collective fortune exist. There are no credible candidates to invest collective selfhood with a fixed prior meaning, and thus every opportunity exists for the sense of self-understanding to be constructed or transformed in the process of collective engagement itself. Or to put it another way, while the staple puzzle of state constitutionalism as a form of social technology has been to harness understanding of the epistemic foundations of the political society to the task of ongoing mobilisation of collective action, the staple puzzle of EU constitutionalism as a form of social technology is instead to establish a more basic or threshold motivation to put things in common sufficient to construct such a shared epistemic frame. The only justification of the constitutional process, then, including but by no means limited to the initial formal process of Constitution-making, lies not in the vindication of some existing essence or realisation of inherent potential, but in the productive potential of the process itself in creating and redeeming a sense of collective 'selfhood' or political community out of the emergent awareness of common interests it stimulates.

It is quite possible to imagine such a de-reified conception of constitutional order responding to the wider concerns of new governance. A reflexive constitutionalism should be one with the collective awareness and imaginative resources necessary to secure a conceptual anchor which specifies the default generative structure and normative priorities of the whole without reverting to the statist notion of a rigid and inflexible institutional hierarchy that would confront new governance with various false choices, (for example, both normative and institutional hierarchy *or* neither; rigid textual specification *or* constitutional silence, external authorisation *or* self-authorisation,) or, indeed—to recall another feature of the statist legacy—which is able to conceive of the relational or trans-polity dimension of new governance networks. Indeed, the major impediments to such a process of constitutional re-imagining are practical and ideological rather than cognitive.[51] On the one hand, as we have seen, the practical context of constitution-making invariably pits different blueprint and generative conceptions of politics against one another, and may result in uneasy and epistemically inarticulate compromises. On the other hand, the very idea of a conceptual anchorage, however light, contingent and flexible, retains

[51] See, eg, the proposal developed and discussed in de Búrca and Zeitlin n 34 above.

an idea of content-independent authoritative foundations about which partisans of new governance remain highly ambivalent.[52]

Yet a reflexive constitutionalism should also be able to overcome these practical obstacles and address these ideological concerns. For it should be capable of persuasively disseminating the idea that what binds the wider political community is no more and no less than the shared pragmatic desire to identify and secure whatever may be in the collective interest, including the conditions under which other and more intimate levels of political community or common action identified by new governance analysis as key political sites can thrive and interact in a just and well-coordinated manner. Such a pragmatic sense of constitutionalism both responds to the sceptical fear that constitution-making is simply (supranational) state-building by another name through the modesty and self-discipline of its ambitions, and answers the anti-foundationalist concern of the supporter of new governance through asserting that the only content-independent 'foundation' involved is that minimally required and presupposed in order to justify and enable the search for content-dependent solutions to collective action problems.

Of course, to end on a sober note, whether any such de-reified and thoroughly reflexive conception of constitutionalism is likely to 'catch on' at the EU level is quite another question. Many of the sceptics who have opposed the present documentary process with such success have done so precisely because they will not be convinced that the state/supranational relationship need not be negative-sum, and so wish to reject or neuter the idea of a new transnational collective political entity to stand alongside the states. Others have done so because, while perhaps less sceptical in principle, they are unhappy about the embryonic political personality or unsure about the likely mature political personality of the new collective self, and not prepared to take any chances.[53] If we take the idea of a reflexive constitutionalism in the uncharted post-national conditions of European supranationalism seriously, the latter objection should be no more valid than the former, since the personality of the collective should remain within the exclusive gift of the individuals who construct and comprise that collective. It is perhaps the deepest and most disabling paradox of European constitutionalism, however, that this can only ever be demonstrated in the doing, and that the discovery of the collective commitment to become and remain engaged with an ongoing constitutional experiment can never await the proof that such collective commitment is indeed worthwhile.

[52] See most recently, J Cohen and C Sabel, 'Extra Rempublicam, Nulla Justita?' *Philosophy and Public Affairs* (2006) (forthcoming).

[53] See, eg, N Walker, 'Europe's Constitutional Engagement' (2005) 18 *Ratio Juris* 385.

2

Toyota Jurisprudence: Legal Theory and Rolling Rule Regimes

WILLIAM H SIMON*

CONTEMPORARY ENGINEERING HAS produced distinctive ideas about organisation. These ideas have focused most on economic production, especially manufacturing, but they have broader relevance. I propose to show in this essay that a specific cluster of these ideas known as the Toyota Production System (TPS), or more generally, as 'lean production', contradicts basic premises of mainstream legal theory and implies a quite different jurisprudence.

I discuss TPS as if it were a legal system, but I am not interested in defending this characterisation on any but heuristic grounds. The jurisprudential implications of TPS are interesting because these ideas seem to underlie, in more fragmented and amorphous form, some important recent public law developments, especially in health-and-safety regulation and the delivery of public services. The engineering perspective thus has the potential both to clarify the basis of these developments and to suggest how they may evolve.[1]

The mainstream perspective to which I contrast Toyota jurisprudence is a set of premises common to the rights-and-principles and law-and-economics schools of legal theory, which together embrace most of the range of current American theory. As I use the term, however, mainstream jurisprudence does not include the tendencies some legal scholars call 'experimentalist'. 'reflexive' or 'responsive' law; still others call 'new governance', and had the term not been lately abused, might usefully be called pragmatist.[2] The Toyota

* Arthur Levitt Professor of Law, Columbia University. Thanks for help and encouragement to Paul Adler, Barbara Fried, the Hewlett Foundation, Chuck Sabel, Joanne Scott, Neil Walker, and participants in discussions at Cambridge University, Columbia Law School and the State University of New York at Buffalo Law School.

[1] The idea that TPS and related engineering ideas have important implications for public institutions comes from Charles F Sabel, 'Learning by Monitoring: The Institutions of Economic Development' in Neil Smelser and Richard Swedberg (eds) *Handbook of Economic Sociology* (Princeton, NJ: Princeton University Press, 1994).

[2] See eg, Michael C Dorf and Charles F Sabel, 'A Constitution of Democratic Experimentalism' (1998) 98 *Columbia Law Review* 267; John Braithwaite, *Restorative Justice and Responsive Regulation* (Oxford: Oxford University Press, 2002); Joanne Scott and David M Trubek, 'Mind the Gap: Law and New Approaches to Governance in the European Union' (2002) 8 *European Law Journal*. 1. The case for the term pragmatism rests on the convergence

perspective resonates with these latter tendencies. It has in some cases influenced work with these tendencies, and it may prove useful in elaborating them.

In contrast to mainstream legal thought, the Toyota system (1) emphasises the goals of learning and innovation (rather than of dispute resolution and the vindication of accepted norms); (2) combines the normative explicitness associated with formal rules with the continuous adjustment to particularity associated with informal norms (no dialectic of rules and standards); (3) treats normative decision making in hard cases as presumptively collective and interdisciplinary (rather than the heroic labour of a solitary professional); (4) fosters a style of reasoning that is intentionally destabilising of settled practices (rather than harmonising or optimising); and (5) attempts to bracket or sublimate issues of individual and retrospective fairness or blame.

Section 1 of this chapter is a stylised account of a cluster of basic themes in mainstream jurisprudence. Section 2 describes the contrasting themes of Toyota jurisprudence. Section 3 shows that the Toyota themes are visible in recent American public law developments, especially in health and safety regulation and school reform. It also discusses proposed reforms of death penalty administration in order to rebut the intuition that the Toyota perspective would be out of place in areas that are strongly charged morally. Section 4 speculates briefly about the general direction that legal theory would take if it absorbed the insights of the Toyota perspective.

1. MAINSTREAM JURISPRUDENCE

Most legal thought is committed to the following five propositions:

A. The basic functions of the legal system are dispute resolution and the vindication or optimisation of accepted social values.

In the rights-and-principles perspective, the legal system is, in HLA Hart's formulation, a 'union of primary and secondary' norms.[3] The primary norms prescribe rights, duties and powers for citizens in civil society. The efficacy and legitimacy of these primary norms depends on their convergence with informal social norms. Secondary norms allocate authority among officials to resolve disagreement and conflict about what the primary norms should be and how they should be applied and enforced. No matter how perfect the convergence between primary rules and informal social norms, disputes will arise because of bad faith or the incompleteness of social morality, and secondary norms are needed to resolve such disputes. The secondary norms may themselves express social values such as due process or democracy, or they may rest simply on the social interest in the

of some of the initiatives discussed here with John Dewey's conception of democratic government as a process of participatory learning. See John Dewey, *The Public and Its Problems* (Athens, OH: Swallow Press, 1954 [1927]).

[3] HLA Hart, *The Concept of Law* (Oxford: Clarendon Press, 1961) 77, 92–93.

resolution of conflict. Lawyers who see a broad and rich social consensus, or who cannot imagine a legitimate legal order without one, tend to see primary norms as fundamental. Those who focus on the fact of conflict and disagreement about primary norms tend to emphasise secondary norms.[4]

In the law-and-economics perspective, the distinction between primary and secondary norms is less central, and norms tend to merge with a broader array of preferences, but the picture is similar. The legal system is supposed to maximise welfare, understood in terms of current preferences. The system is an instrument for satisfying these preferences. So the task is to trade off the benefits of increased preference satisfaction through law making and enforcement against the costs of these activities so as to attain the greatest net benefit. Conflict and disagreement are treated as either costs of enforcement or as pre-existing social harms, in either case as something to be minimised.[5]

B. The dialectic of rules and standards: The legal system chooses formal rules in order to limit discretion but at the price of reducing sensitivity to factual particularity; it chooses informal norms (standards) to make decisions sensitive to context but at the cost of reduced control of discretion. Formal norms constrain decision more than informal ones. They limit the range of factors that the decision maker can consider. Legal theory attributes several potential advantages to formality, but the advantage most emphasised in general legal discourse is that formality inhibits the decision maker's ability to make decisions on the basis of illegitimate considerations—her personal or political values and goals. The narrower and more explicit the rule, the less room it allows for influence by personal values and goals, and the more readily a reviewing authority can determine whether the decision conforms to the rule.[6]

But of course, the more the rule constrains discretion, the more it also inhibits consideration of how its purposes will apply in the full context of the decision and the more often it will produce decisions at variance with these purposes. The gap between the norm's underlying goals and the decisions it produces is directly proportional to the norm's formality.

Lawyers generally tend to favor discretion-constraining rules for groups they distrust and discretion-conferring standards for groups they trust, though they do not always agree on the identity of the groups. During the Warren Court era, liberal lawyers favoured rules for the street-level public workforce—for example, *Miranda* rules for the police—and standards like 'just cause' for judges. More recently, conservatives who distrust the judiciary in criminal matters have sought to restrict their discretion through the

[4] Compare Hart previous n (emphasising secondary norms) with Ronald Dworkin, *Law's Empire* (Cambridge, MA.: Harvard, 1986) 176–275 (emphasising primary norms).

[5] Eg, Richard Posner, *Economic Analysis of Law*, 6th edn (New York: Aspen, 2003) 215–27, 563–65, 595–98.

[6] See generally, Frederick Shauer, *Playing by the Rules: A Philosophical Examination of Rule-based Decision-making in Law and Life* (Oxford: Oxford University Press, 1991) 149–55; Posner, previous n, at 556–57.

rules of the Federal Sentencing Guidelines, with the tacit but predictable effect of increasing the discretion of prosecutors, a group they trust, whose charging decisions are regulated by standards.

All these lawyers, however, tend to view the choice between rules and standards as primarily a trade-off between the costs and benefits of limiting discretion on the one hand and of decisional contextualisation on the other.

C. Legal reasoning in hard cases is interstitial.

It is a matter of pride in our legal tradition that the courts exercise their law-making power 'one case at a time'.[7] They tailor their decisions to the facts of the dispute before them. The decisions are conclusive only with respect to those facts. Their precedential effect for other cases takes the form of 'gravitational force' proportional to the proximity of their facts to the ones in the decided case.[8]

Hard cases are those for which no statute or past case plainly dictates an answer. We resolve hard cases by deriving results that harmonise with surrounding authority. We accept as presumptively valid the clear answers the authority gives for other cases and try to derive principles from them that are consistent with each and indicate how the case at hand should be resolved. A good answer is one that fits with the surrounding authority.

Ronald Dworkin's rights-and-principles account portrays 'fit' or 'integrity' as a virtue in itself. However, there are two other rationales for interstitial decision making that are widely accepted within both the rights-and-principles and law-and-economics perspective. The first emphasises the limited capacities and democratic legitimacy of courts. We need courts to resolve disputes, but their ability and authority to promulgate rules that go beyond the specifics of these cases is controversial. The second emphasises the importance of predictability. Both fairness and efficiency are served when citizens can predict when the state will intervene in private affairs. Such predictability allows successful planning of individual activity and successful coordination of joint activity. In this view, the law strives to eliminate the friction of individual interaction. This goal is served when courts respect settled precedent and innovate only when necessary (either because the law 'runs out' or because social change has rendered settled precedent intolerable).[9]

D. The core form of legal decision making is strongly differentiated from other roles and activities.

Legal theory has been most preoccupied with explaining a single phenomenon—how the judge pulls the rabbit of determinate resolution out of the hat of ambiguous authority. It treats other types of legal work as peripheral,

[7] Eg, Cass Sunstein, *Once Case at a Time: Judicial Minimalism on the Supreme Court* (Cambridge, MA: Harvard, 2001).

[8] Ronald Dworkin, *Taking Rights Seriously* (Cambridge, MA: Harvard, 1978) 111; see also Dworkin, n 4 above, at 250–54 (on the principle of 'local priority' in the assessment of precedent).

[9] Posner, n 5 above, at 560–61.

and it treats the judge's work as distinct from and independent of that of other actors even within the court system.

The rights-and-principles tradition argues that judicial decision making is strongly differentiated methodologically from other forms of public decision making. To a unique extent, judges must reason prescriptively from authority, rather than instrumentally with reference to goals. And the judge's isolation from other officials and her relative lack of accountability for the practical effects of her decisions are sometimes praised as a key elements of the judicial 'independence' that is a key feature of the rule of law.

For other theorists, the tendency to treat the judge's role in institutional isolation is more a tacit, or even regretted, habit than a matter of principle, but the habit is pervasive and longstanding. Legal theory takes little account, even within the legal system, of anyone but judges, even though we know that the practical effects of judicial intervention depend on clerks, probation officers, special masters, bailiffs, sheriffs, marshals, trustees, executors and receivers. The theorists' interest in the practices of courts typically stops at the point of judicial decision. Whether and how the decision is enforced or its broader practical impact is a matter of secondary, if any, concern. Judicial decisions are often appraised in terms of their internal plausibility, rather than in terms of their practical contribution to realising their goals.[10]

It is often pointed out that this focus on the judicial decision is parochial and anachronistic. Even within the court system, judicial activity is increasingly described as 'managerial', especially in connection with two kinds of cases. First, there are institutional reform cases in which the courts undertake to reform the administrative structures and practices of public institutions like schools and prisons that have failed to discharge their duties. Second, there are cases like those involving small drug crimes or child welfare—small cases that occur in large numbers with common patterns in which the court is expected to intervene in a fairly complex long-term manner in the hope of improving the welfare of some of the parties. Although these developments are widely recognised, they have not much affected the preoccupations of legal theory.[11]

E. Legal decision making is paradigmatically retrospective and individualist. Fairness is a central preoccupation of American common law decision making. Fairness means basically corrective justice. It is centrally concerned with

[10] There is, of course, a substantial empirical and instrumental literature on the effects of legal rules and judicial decisions. Much of this literature is theoretical and might well be called 'legal theory'. However, I exclude it from the definition of 'mainstream legal theory' because it is more peripheral to the legal culture than the judge-focused rights-and-principles and law-and-economics literature and has had limited influence on them.

[11] See Judith Resnik, 'Managerial Judges' (1982) 96 *Harvard Law Review* 374; Michael C Dorf and Charles F Sabel, 'Drug Courts and Emergent Experimentalist Government' (2000) 53 *Vanderbilt Law Review* 831.

the allocation of benefits and burdens among individuals, and with linking present treatment to past conduct. The American legal system stands ready to commit vast resources to the determination and evaluation of past conduct in order to calibrate present reward or punishment to it. The concern with fairness is longstanding, but it has recently intensified because of the increased punitiveness of the legal system in both its civil and criminal spheres. Punishment is usually predicated at least in part on retrospective fairness values, and it triggers demands for more elaborate efforts to make the relevant determinations.

Fairness is the fundamental normative commitment of the rights-and-principles school. These theorists are prone to defend fairness values as more fundamental than others or to suggest that they are more strongly suited to vindication by judges.[12] Law-and-economics is different on this point. It rejects fairness in favour of welfare as a normative touchstone. Yet, despite this distinction, law-and-economics also focuses on crafting legal rules that apportion current reward and sanctions to past individual conduct.[13] Sometimes fairness values re-enter in the form of preferences, which then become part of the welfare function to be optimised. Sometimes the results dictated by corrective justice norms turn out to be the best means of regulating behaviour in ways desirable on welfare grounds. Even when its prescriptions depart from the rights-and-principles view, law-and-economics most often proceeds from an individualist and retrospective approach. It seeks to craft incentives that induce individual, presumptively rational, actors to behave efficiently. And it accepts the common law premise that future behaviour is effectively regulated through the design of sanctions to fit past conduct in current cases.

Two problems in contemporary legal systems challenge the idea of retrospective individual liability in either the direct fairness or efficiency perspectives. The first is that much conflict arises as a by-product of conduct that is generally socially valuable. The paradigmatic traditional cases of individual retrospective liability involve intentional instances of generally noxious behaviour, say, battery or theft. But a very large class of contemporary cases—including unintentional torts and many violations of business regulation—involve conduct that is in general beneficial but that has been carried too far or conducted with insufficient precautions, often inadvertently. Legal theory has wrestled with the question of when such conduct should be regarded as blameworthy or inefficient. A key touchstone has been the idea of negligence or reasonableness. The meaning of the reasonableness norm is contested. One ambiguity refers to the relation between customary practice on the one hand and optimal practice on the other. Sometimes

[12] Dworkin, n 8 above.

[13] Louis Kaplow and Steven Shavell, *Fairness versus Efficiency* (Cambridge, MA: Harvard, 2002) 134–48.

reasonableness means the dominant practice among similar actors. Sometimes it means something more. But in either case, the inquiry in mainstream legal thought remains retrospective and individual. It is the prevalent or optimal practice at the time of the episode that counts, and whatever standard we come up with must have been within the capacity of the defendant at the time.[14]

Yet, it is often debatable whether either fairness or efficiency warrants liability based on such a retrospective inquiry. To many, fairness values do not warrant sanctions for a broad range of harms arising from unforeseen consequences of generally beneficial conduct that are nevertheless swept into our liability system. Others suggest that imposing liability may be inefficient because material compensation does not effectively redress symbolic or emotional injuries, or because the liability process does not directly induce improvements in the systemic practices that produce harm, and, to the extent that it causes actors to hide information, may inhibit improvement.[15]

A second problem arises from the fact that the defendants in a large fraction of legal controversies are organisations. It is often not clear how either fairness or efficiency dictates the imposition of liability on organisations. One strategy is to ignore or pierce the organisation and impose liability on its individual constituents when their conduct would independently warrant it. Another is to treat the organisation as if it were an individual when the elements of liability can be established on the basis of the aggregate conduct of multiple constituents acting for the organisation. Neither strategy is entirely satisfactory. With the first, decision making remains plausibly individualistic but at the cost of ignoring the distinctive dangers and problems of collective activities. With the second, the individualism seems strained. For example, while the criminal punishment of corporations does not strike most people as per se unjust, it is very hard to explain in terms of individualist fairness notions when, for example, the main effect falls on current employees and shareholders who neither encouraged nor benefited from the wrongdoing.

Moreover, while law-and-economics scholarship often treats the incentive effects of liability on organisations as tantamount to the effects on individuals, this is usually a matter of faith more than logic or evidence. Economics presupposes individual decision makers, and corporations are complex aggregations of individuals. Nevertheless, the practice of either ignoring organisations or pretending that they are individuals has long been favoured by the legal culture as a way of reconciling its individualistic doctrines with the reality of a world of organisations.

[14] Henry M Hart, Jr, and Albert M Sacks, *The Legal Process: Basic Problems in the Making and Application of Law* (William N Eskridge, Jr, and Philip P Frickey (eds)) (Mineola, NY: Foundation Press, 1994) 403–49.

[15] See, eg, Braithwaite, n 2 above.

2. THE TOYOTA PRODUCTION SYSTEM AS A JURISPRUDENTIAL PHENOMENON

TPS arises from dissatisfaction with a traditional mass manufacturing model that combines central planning with ad hoc shop floor adjustment.[16] In the traditional model, a central corps of managers and engineers promulgates rules that dictate practice to a workforce that is narrowly skilled and divided among functional departments (for example, milling, painting, cutting, polishing, assembly). Central management forecasts sales and then prescribes production targets for specific products, orders materials, and schedules each phase of the production process. Typically, the plan calls for the parts of a product to be processed separately in different departments in large batches with specialised machinery.

Invariably, adjustments are required as events depart from the plan. The pattern of orders is different from the forecast. Supplies fail to arrive on time, or they are defective. In the plant, machines break down, or parts are improperly machined. The plan contemplates a series of adjustment mechanisms for such contingencies. 'Expediters' may travel between the sales department and the factory floor to advance orders ahead in the production queue in accordance with the needs and clout of the customer. The plant can maintain a central parts inventory, or each worker can have a 'buffer' stock of spare parts at her station in case new parts fail to arrive on time or in proper condition. A specialised inspectorate or Quality Control department can review finished product and send non-conforming items back or to a special department for re-work.

TPS proponents complain that such a system is slow in responding to unanticipated changes in the volume of customer demand or in its capacity to modify or change products. It takes a long time for centralised management to absorb information indicating that changes are needed, and a long time for it to develop and implement needed changes. The traditional system tends to be quite wasteful of labour and materials, in part, because it is slow to discover defects and, when they are discovered, slow to remedy them. In addition, the system does not effectively capitalise on the knowledge and potential creative effort of most its workers. And by encouraging tolerance for errors and the expectation that they will be remedied downstream, the system fails to cultivate in workers a sense of responsibility or 'ownership'.

TPS tries to reduce reliance on forecasting, first, by configuring its sales efforts to smooth out orders, and second, by making the manufacturing process more flexible and quick. Production cues are transmitted

[16] For general accounts, see Taiichi Ohno, *Toyota Production System: Beyond Large Scale Production* (Portland, OR: Productivity Press, 1988); Shigeo Shingo, *Study of Toyota Production System from an Industrial Engineering Point of View* (Portland, OR: Productivity Press, 1981); James P Womack, Daniel T Jones, and Daniel Roos, *The Machine that Changed the World: The Story of Lean Production* (New York: Macmillan, 1990).

less hierarchically through central planners and more laterally through the shop floor. This is accomplished in part by the *kanban* system in which downstream stations signal their need for parts by returning cards upstream. Parts and products tend to be produced in smaller lots in a more continuous process with more broadly skilled workers and less specialised machinery.

The traditional model strongly differentiates between conception, which is the responsibility of central management, and execution on the shop floor. TPS attenuates this distinction. The phrase *kaizen*, or continuous improvement, connotes that process be revised in the course of its execution. TPS diffuses responsibility for the organisation of production broadly. Shop floor teams write and revise the descriptions for their jobs, schedule their members, and arrange for maintenance and repair of their equipment. Some workers meet regularly in 'quality circles' to consider problems and propose solutions. All workers are encouraged to make suggestions for improvements in the process, and such suggestions often result in changes. Inspection and quality control cease to be the exclusive preoccupation of an elite corps and become the responsibility of the entire workforce. While the old system tolerated a significant number of defects and expected many items to be re-worked, TPS espouses 'zero tolerance' for defects and has no re-work department.

The *kaizen* idea and the 'zero tolerance' norm dictate a distinctive response to production problems. A problem occurs when a defective part appears, or when a worker is unable to perform a prescribed action (say, because there is insufficient time), or when performing the prescribed action would be inconsistent with quality norms (for example, painting over dirt). The system discourages ad hoc adjustments to such problems. It does not permit workers to pass defective parts down the line, and it does not provide buffer inventory to substitute for defective parts. Instead, such problems are treated as symptoms of structural flaws to be remedied immediately. If necessary, this means stopping the line entirely until the problem is fixed. Shop floor workers have the power and duty to pull the '*andon* cord' that brings production to a halt and illuminates an electronic display that signals to the entire plant that a problem has occurred. In principle, production resumes only when the process has been revised sufficiently to eliminate the danger of recurrence. The procedure through which the solution is devised is one of consensual deliberation by representatives of any group likely to have relevant knowledge or whose cooperation is likely to be necessary to implementing the solution.

If we consider TPS as a legal system, the following points emerge:

A. Learning and innovation are key purposes of the system.

The purposes of TPS are not adequately accounted for by the preoccupations of mainstream legal theory. TPS has primary norms that reflect a pre-existing consensus about legitimate behaviour—rules that prohibit assault and theft, for example. It also has secondary norms that constitute hierarchical procedures of coercive dispute resolution. Neither kind of rule, however, plays a salient role in a successful plant, and neither is directly associated with what the participants consider the most important and distinctive functions of TPS.

From the participants' point of view, the key norms are those that constitute the problem-solving process. This process is not concerned with dispute resolution. It starts out with a shared sense among the participants that something is wrong and a shared sense of common goals. What requires discussion is not disagreement, but uncertainty. Moreover, neither the composition nor the operation of the problem-solving groups is determined by norms about authority.[17] Composition is determined by the principle that 'anyone with relevant knowledge of a problem is included, regardless of rank'.[18] Process is a matter of consensus, not a search for a pre-existing consensus, but an effort to forge a new one.

The problem-solving discussions do take place against a background of general values of 'quality'. But it would be misleading to see the discussions as efforts to vindicate or maximise these values. The values are indeterminate. The discussions are as much efforts to define them as to implement them.

For example, although early TPS proponents sometimes equated 'quality' with cost minimisation, the more recent literature speaks with contempt of 'cost-based strategies'.[19] The change apparently reflects the experience that American managers applying cost minimisation rigorously have tended to reject Toyota-style practices. They found that the Toyota approach tended to raise the costs that can most readily be measured—short-term direct labour costs—and to create benefits that are speculative (savings from future innovation) or hard to measure in advance (enhanced customer satisfaction and market share).

Similarly, 'quality' strategies like TPS are considered antithetical to managerial strategies preoccupied with stock price maximisation. Whether or not stock price maximisation is plausible goal, the strategy suffers from indeterminacy; the goal does not translate clearly into more concrete directives. In practice, it is associated with a focus on financial indicators, but

[17]

> While lower levels [in TPS] did not have much authority to make decisions without prior consultation with superiors, this apparent centralization usually took the form of 'fact-based' dialogue based on expertise rather than command-and-control domination based on positional authority....Japanese organizations had more *de jure* centralization but also more *de facto* participation than comparable American organizations.

Paul Adler, 'Flexibility versus Efficiency: A Case Study of Model Changeovers in the Toyota Production System' (1999) 10 *Organization Science* 43 at 54.

[18] John Paul MacDuffie, 'The Road to Root Cause: Problem-Solving at Three Auto-Assembly Plants' (1997) 43 *Management Science* 479 at 495. My description of TPS is based largely on the espoused principles of its proponents. Studies such as MacDuffie's and Adler's, previous n, indicate that some plants conform extensively to these principles but also that there is a good deal of variation in practice among plants that purport to have absorbed them.

[19] Cf. Ohno, n 16 above, at 8–9, 52–56 (discussing cost minimisation as fundamental goal of the system) with Rajan Suri, *Quick Response Manufacturing* (Portland, OR: Productivity Press, 1998) 54–56, 76–78 (disparaging 'cost-based organization').

the stock price performance of the firms that have taken this tack has not been superior. Paradoxically, it appears that the managers most devoted to pleasing the stock market are not the ones who end up doing so, at least in the long run.[20]

A more popular definition of quality associates it with customer satisfaction. But what products and product features customers value and how customers trade off performance and price are matters that are not fully known in advance. They are discovered in the process itself.

The quality norm is thus not a consensus to be vindicated or a value to be maximised. It is both a bet and a cultural commitment: a bet that short-term process investments will lead to discoveries that will shift cost curves; a cultural commitment that unifies and motivates the disparate groups in the production process by giving creativity and social dignity to their work.

The dimension of TPS omitted in mainstream jurisprudence is the focus on learning and innovation. TPS is, most distinctively, an effort to discover new ways of producing. The diffusion of responsibility and the stressing of the system to induce constant collaborative revision force pooling of knowledge in ways intended to generate new understanding.

B. TPS combines a strong commitment to formalisation of norms with continuous adjustment to unanticipated particularity.

TPS norms are always as articulated as possible, but they are not applied consciously in a way that would frustrate their purposes. Instead, the rules get re-considered and re-written when they come in tension with unanticipated contingency. The workers' power/duty to pull the *andon* cord and stop production represents the authority to trigger a legislative deliberation on the amendment of the rule.

The purpose of formality in TPS is quite different from its primary purpose in mainstream legal thought. Toyota formality is not designed to restrict discretion. TPS is a high-trust system with broadly educated workers who have a strong general stake in their jobs and are subject to constant peer pressure to perform well. Rather, the purpose of formal norms is to facilitate learning, or as Michel Greif puts it, 'to inspire improvements'.[21]

'Say what you do, and do what you say' is a basic premise of Toyota-style engineering.[22] As it rejects the command-and-control model of Fordist bureaucracy, TPS rejects the traditional artisanal vision in which work is

[20] James Belohlav, 'Quality, Strategy, and Competitiveness' (1993) 32 *California Management Review* 55 at 56–61. See also Masaahi Imai, *Kaizen: The Key to Japan's Competitive Success* (New York, McGraw-Hill, 1986) 49–50:

> Japanese managers have found that seeking improvement for improvement's sake is the surest way to strengthen the company's overall competitiveness. If you take care of quality, the profits will take care of themselves.

[21] Michel Greif, *The Visual Factory: Building Participation Through Shared Information* 74 (Portland, OR: Productivity Press, 1991).

[22] Joseph Casio, (ed) *The ISO 14000 Handbook* (Milwaukee, Wisconsin: American Society for Quality, 1996) 196.

regulated by tacit norms that can be grasped only by prolonged socialisation into guild and local workplace cultures. The duty to articulate forces the actors to reflect on what they are proposing to do and to communicate it as precisely as possible to their peers. Codifying the practice means that it can be more readily learned by people who did not participate in its formulation, or who do not share background experiences with the authors. The more explicitly defined the job, the broader the range of workers who can perform it. Thus it becomes easier to redeploy workers in accordance with their availability. It also increases the range of perspectives that can be brought to bear on the norm's revision. An articulated norm is more readily criticised and debated both because and it is more easily grasped and because criticism is less likely to risk personal offence when the norm is divorced from particular people.[23]

Formalisation is thus strongly associated with revisability. In TPS, a rule is simultaneously 'a point to adhere to and a point of departure'.[24]

C. Decision making is fundamentally collaborative and interdisciplinary. TPS, as we have seen, precludes the individual discretionary decision making involved in ad hoc adjustment to unanticipated particularity. On the other hand, it depends heavily on a different kind of judgment to revise continuously its rules and practices. This judgment is typically collective and interdisciplinary.

In traditional manufacturing, the process is often organised functionally, with each group or department focused on a particular activity, such as painting or machining or assembly. In TPS, production is organised more in terms of types of products, with each group performing a series of functions, and perhaps producing entire products, with a range of skills. Work is conducted by teams whose members are broadly trained and who make decisions collectively about job design, scheduling, and materials requirements. In traditional manufacturing, major unexpected problems are often handled exclusively by corps of specialists trained in a particular discipline, such as electricians or machinists. In TPS, when major problems arise, they are addressed by groups broadly representative of affected constituencies throughout the plant. These may include various shop floor teams, supervisors, suppliers, marketing people and designers.

Collaborative decision making responds to two constraints. First, the dispersal of information throughout the production process. No individual

[23] See Imai, n 20 above, at 74–78; Greif, n 21 above, at 74–76.

[24] *Ibid* at 75. See also, Paul Adler, 'Time and Motion Regained' (1993) *Harvard Business Review* 97 at 104,

> [W]orkers create a consensual standard that they teach to the system by writing job descriptions. The system then teaches these standards back to workers, who, then, by further analysis, consultation, and consensus, make additional improvements. Continual reiteration of this disciplined process of analysis, standardization, re-analysis, refinement, and restandardization creates an intensely structured system of continuous improvement.

knows enough to make key problem-solving decisions and no fixed management group could be relied on to know enough to solve all problems. Second, the need for multiple perspectives. Many problems call for multiple kinds of technical knowledge or for kinds of technical knowledge that cannot be identified at the outset. Dirt on a component might be a machining issue (if it can be eliminated in the course of machining) or a painting issue (if it can be painted over so as to make it unnoticeable) or a marketing issue (if the customer will not care about it). Team decision making increases the range of both information and technical perspectives that are considered in making the decision.

D. Decision making in TPS is intentionally destabilising.

John Womack and Daniel Jones contrast TPS with 'steady state' management.[25] In the latter, the goal is to minimise disruption and, when disruption is unavoidable, restore equilibrium as quickly as possible. By contrast, TPS involves deliberate destabilisation.[26] It induces problems with highly specified rules, unforgiving quality standards, minute synchronisation, and minimisation of inventory.

Two practices associated with TPS are relevant here. The first is benchmarking—self-assessment in terms of the performances of industry leaders. Benchmarking subjects every practice and product to comparison with the firm's most successful competitors. This approach represents a shift from the traditional practice of comparing performance to industry averages—the in-house analogue to the common law reasonableness norm. Reasonableness connotes that typical performance should be maintained in steady state. But benchmarking connotes that only superior performance is adequate. Anything less requires efforts to improve, and in a competitive market, even superior performance is unlikely to be maintained without efforts to improve. Thus, the lean production literature is full of statements disparaging adherence to custom or reasonableness. For example, Womack and Jones write:

> [T]he high achievers set specific timetables to accomplish seemingly impossible tasks and then routinely meet or exceed them. The low achievers, by contrast, ask what would be reasonable for their current organization ... to accomplish, and generally defeat themselves before they set out.[27]

[25] James P Womack and Daniel T Jones, *Lean Thinking: Banish Waste and Create Wealth in Your Corporation*, rev edn (New York: Free Press, 2003).

[26] This is not to say that TPS plants are less stable, merely that an important degree of instability is deliberate. Disruption is typically experienced as frequent when TPS methods are inaugurated but declines when they are successful:

> Today, in Toyota plants, where every worker can stop the line, yields approach 100 percent. That is, the line practically never stops! (In mass-production plants by contrast, where no one but the line manager can stop the line, the line stops constantly ... to deal with material supply and coordination problems.) Womack, Jones and Roos, n16 above, at 57.

[27] Womack and Jones, n 25 above, at 95.

As a descriptive matter, such rhetoric needs to be discounted for hyperbole. However, the rejection of the goal of equilibrium and the commitment to continuous destabilisation it implies is a critical characteristic of the TPS strategy.

The other practice associated with destabilisation is 'root cause analysis'. Problems are supposed to be traced backward through the production process. The rule-of-thumb prescribes tracing back five stages—the 'Five Whys'.[28] This means that both inquiry and solution potentially ramify beyond the point at which the problem arose. For example:

> Why is machine A broken? Because no preventive maintenance was performed.
> Why was the maintenance crew derelict? Because it is always repairing machine B.
> Why is machine B always broken? Because the part it machines always jams.
> Why does the jam recur? Because the part is warped by heat stress.
> Why does the part overheat? A design flaw.[29]

The point is that the solution to the problem may require unsettling practice at a point remote from the one at which it was identified. In the short term, this approach is often more disruptive and costly than narrower responses. John Paul MacDuffie illustrates this in a comparative study of American auto plants. He treats as evidence of scant progress in implementing lean production at a General Motors plant that a quality auditor's response to a paint defect was limited to 'charg[ing] the costs' of the defect to an earlier inspection team that should have discovered it.[30] This limited response violates the spirit of TPS. It does not inquire into the remote cause of the problem, or even of the inspectors' failure. It relies on indirect inducements to improve performance—penalties to inspectors—that, if they have any effect at all, are likely to cause low-visibility ad hoc adjustments, rather than explicit systemic revision.

The problem-solving process associated with root cause analysis is incremental in the sense that it begins with dissatisfaction with only a small part of the process and ends with a revision of only a small part. But it is not interstitial in the common law sense of 'one case at a time'. With root case analysis, the initial definition of the problem does not control its analysis or disposition. Every problem potentially implicates any of the parts of the system.

[28] Ohno, n 16 above, at 17–18.

[29] The phrase 'root cause analysis' is a little misleading to the extent that it implies that we are interested in a historical or scientific account of how the error happened. The search is, not so much for a retrospective description, as for opportunities for improvement. The 'five', of course, is a crude rule of thumb. Its blatant arbitrariness is an acknowledgment that the search for cause is potentially infinite.

[30] MacDuffie, n 18 above, at 486.

This insistence that intelligent implementation of the parts of the system requires an understanding of how each part fits into the whole is reflected in the broad training workers receive and in plant design for transparency. Plants are laid out simply and logically. Clutter and visual obstructions are minimised. Elaborate displays visible from all points in the plant summarise what is happening at each station. When a problem that requires suspension of production occurs, its nature and location are communicated immediately to the entire plant. The premise is that, at the outset, we cannot say which people in the plant will have the knowledge and skills necessary to the solution.[31]

The Toyota perspective thus resonates with a point Dworkin makes against Cass Sunstein's defense of the 'one case at a time' approach to adjudication.[32] Sunstein argues that judges do better to resolve cases in terms of relatively narrow, low-level principles. Relatively high-level principles should be disfavoured because they have implications that extend broadly across the legal system, and thus require more complex decision making, have greater potential to produce disagreement, and are more likely to upset settled expectations. Dworkin replies that we expect judges to justify their decisions in terms of principle, and there is no reason to think that the principles that provide the best justifications for decisions will be consistently of limited generality. What Dworkin calls 'justificatory ascent' means that particular claims of right potentially implicate broader structures in a way analogous to the ramifying tendency of Toyota production problems.

[31] The Toyota perspective challenges divisions, not only between work roles and groups within the firm, but also the boundaries between firms. The challenge of continuous improvement is applied to the entire process of producing a given product or product family. Just-in-time delivery of components requires close coordination with suppliers. The upstream 'root cause' of a problem may often lie beyond the boundaries of the firm. The current inter-firm divisions are provisional, and since firm boundaries tend to obscure information, suspect. Thus, the Toyota approach prescribes close collaboration and free information-sharing between firms at different stages of the production process. It urges process designers to envision and perfect the entire 'value stream' without regard to how it is currently partitioned:

> For example, when Pratt & Whitney, the world's largest manufacturer of aircraft jet engines, recently started to map its value streams for its families of jet engines, it discovered that activities undertaken by its raw materials suppliers to produce ultrapure metals were duplicated at great cost by the next firms down stream, the forgers who converted metal ingots into near-net shapes suitable for machining. At the same time, the initial ingot of material—for example, titanium or nickel—was ten times the weight of the machined parts eventually fashioned from it. Ninety percent of the very expensive metals were being scrapped because the initial ingot was poured in such a massive size—the melters were certain that this was efficient—without much attention to the shape of the finished parts. And finally, the melters were preparing several different ingots—at great cost—in order to meet Pratt's precise technical requirements for each engine, which varied marginally from those of other engine families and from the needs of competitors. Many of these activities could be eliminated almost immediately with dramatic cost savings. (Womack and Jones, n 25 above, at 20).

[32] Ronald Dworkin, 'In Praise of Theory' (1997) 29 *Arizona State Law Journal* 353 at 368–75.

But the analogy ends when Dworkin describes the goal of decision making as establishing harmony within an existing body of norms. In TPS, legitimacy does not depend on connecting decisions to established authority. (To be sure, there will usually be some such connection, but not because legitimacy requires it; rather because, as Stanley Fish emphasises, the decision makers cannot escape the influence and constraints of their cultural and practical circumstances.)[33] In TPS, legitimacy arises from the provisional consensus of the stakeholders and their commitment to re-assess readily in accordance with agreed-on criteria.

Another destabilising aspect of Toyota-style decision making arises from the interaction of its prescriptive and instrumental aspects. Rights-and-principles reasoning is prescriptive; it is concerned with elaborating goals—values with intrinsic worth. From its perspective, implementation is secondary. Law-and-economics reasoning is instrumental; it focuses on means and implementation. It usually treats the goals it seeks to further as given and fixed. In contrast, reasoning in the Toyota system encourages the re-assessment of ends in the process of implementing them. Discussion starts out as instrumental to, inter alia, defined goals of product quality, but these goals can be reconsidered in the course of problem-solving. In traditional plants that have experimented with shop floor teams and quality circles, discussion stops when it reaches 'design issues'[34] But in plants that have gone farther, design engineers may be dispatched from headquarters and assigned to work with teams in the plants. Thus, the difference between production (means) and design (goals) is eroded. Decision making in manufacturing is potentially destabilising, not only of spatially remote features of the production process, but of settled expectations about the goals of the process.

The interaction of prescriptive and instrumental thought is also salient when new products are being designed. The traditional process is a sequential and departmentalised one in which the marketing people specify customer preferences; design engineers devise specifications; process engineers translate the specification into manufacturing plans; plant engineers configure machinery and work practices to the manufacturing plans; and once production starts, line workers execute the plant engineers' instructions. By

[33] Stanley Fish, 'Still Wrong After All These Years' in *Doing What Comes Naturally* (Baltimore, MD: Johns Hopkins University Press, 1990) 356–71. As Holmes put it, 'historic continuity with the past is not a duty, it is only a necessity'. Oliver Wendell Holmes, 'Learning and Science' in *Collected Papers* (New York: Harcourt Brace, 1920) 13839.

[34]

> For example, the plant has had a persistent problem with a bracket on the brake pedal sub-assembly to which the cables for both the cruise control and power brakes are attached. The bracket often moves when the cruise control is used, resulting in misadjustment of the breaks. [T]he problem was a poor design—that the cruise control and brake cables shouldn't be attached to the same bracket, and that the bracket was in a bad location. [But to add or reposition a bracket would require] a long struggle with Detroit. (MacDuffie, n 18 above, at 484).

contrast, the Toyota style is concurrent. Teams with members drawn from all these fields work together to consider simultaneously customer needs, cost, technical performance and manufacturability. As the time for manufacture approaches, 'pilot teams' are recruited from the shop floor to work on the specification of jobs for manufacture of the new models, and they sometimes make suggestions that result in design revision. Pilot versions of the new models are sometimes built on assembly lines that are concurrently building the old models in order to facilitate a quick transition.[35]

In all these ways, TPS blurs the distinction between the prescriptive and the instrumental, or the elaboration of goals and the specification of means.

E. Individualistic and retrospective concerns are sublimated or bracketed. TPS is intensely preoccupied with mistakes, but its orientation toward them is prospective and collective. The issue is how the group will fix the problem. In his study of three auto plants, MacDuffie found the two American-owned ones preoccupied with determining who should be held responsible for mistakes. By contrast, at the Honda plant which had more fully embraced TPS, '[t]he accounting system is deliberately designed to minimise the time spent figuring out who's to blame'.[36]

In the TPS perspective, problems are more likely to result from defects in system design than from blameworthy deviance on the part of particular workers. Assigning responsibility consumes unproductive time and effort and encourages recrimination that undermines solidarity and willingness to volunteer information about mistakes. TPS thus presumes that 'a problem with our product is a problem for the whole company, not an individual or department'.[37]

The difference between 'root cause analysis' and typical common law liability analysis is revealing. The latter stops when it finds blameworthiness, and it usually measures blameworthiness by departure from established norms. On the other hand, root cause analysis is primarily concerned with how the norms could be improved. Moreover, when root cause analysis discovers violations of established norms, it does not stop. It goes on to consider whether the violations are symptomatic of some background condition that might be improved. Operator negligence, for example, might be a symptom of deficient training, or workplace distractions, or excessively long shifts. (A common law court might go on the consider these systemic factors if the plaintiff could make a case that they departed from established norms, but whether it did so would depend on the plaintiff's individual concerns, such as whether institutional liability would be necessary in order for a judgment to be collectable, rather than the potential benefits to the system.)

[35] Womack, Jones, and Roos, n 16 above, at 138–68; Adler, 'Flexibility vs. Efficiency' n 17 above.

[36] *Ibid* at 493.

[37] *Ibid.*

The TPS system emphasises intangible incentives, such as peer respect, over material ones, and group incentives over individual ones. Contingent compensation is often on a company, plant, or group basis, and rarely on an individual one.

Nevertheless, we've seen that TPS is nested in larger structures that contain norms that more approximate the themes of mainstream jurisprudence. I noted above that there are background clusters of secondary norms that allocate dispute resolution authority. There are also background clusters that are responsive to concerns about individual fairness and incentives. Three are especially notable.[38]

First, in Japanese firms, TPS is typically accompanied by a parallel personnel system that operates in critical respects more hierarchically and informally than the production system. This system provides for the ranking of employees, mostly by seniority but also on the basis of informal supervisorial assessments of performance. This ranking has a small influence on compensation and a larger one on promotions. Supervisorial judgment is checked both by administrative review and by the possibility of challenge through a union grievance process. In some companies, employees dissatisfied with their supervisors can easily transfer to a different unit.

Second, adoption of TPS typically correlates with a relatively high degree of employment security, and TPS proponents often insist that the latter is a condition of the former. Workers are likely to be more cooperative when productivity increases do not threaten their jobs and when their pay and security do not depend on their particular position in the company. Job security encourages long-term identification with the company, which in turns encourages voluntary effort.

Third, worker and employer in the Toyota-style firm typically bind themselves to each other through reciprocal investments. The firm invests in the worker by providing the more extensive training in general-purpose skills that TPS requires relative to traditional manufacturing. The worker invests in the firm by accepting back-loaded, seniority-based compensation. Each has an incentive to satisfy the other and preserve the relation.

Thus, individual fairness and incentive issues have not been ignored in TPS. However, their salience has been reduced through bracketing, muting and deferral. Fairness issues are bracketed simply by removing them from the shop floor to a separate department with separate personnel. They are muted by the bonding practices that mean that the stakes in any individual claim arising from conduct in the production process will often be dwarfed by the shared interest in preserving the relationship. And they are deferred by a system that provides rewards for success. To be sure, fairness issues can potentially arise over the division of the fruits of success. But it is a common experience that collaborators find it easier to allocate the benefits of

[38] See generally Masahiko Aoki, *Information, Incentives, and Bargaining in the Japanese Economy* (Cambridge: Cambridge University Press, 1988) 49–98.

success than the burdens of failure. By promising contingent group compensation, the system may reduce individual fairness claims by deferring some of the potential for them to a future point where, if success has occurred, the pressure to press them will have relaxed.

The bracketing, muting and deferral of individual incentive and fairness issues make Toyota Jurisprudence better able than its mainstream counterpart to address organisational actors. The basic units of Toyota Jurisprudence are groups rather than individuals. The groups, however, have fluid identities that are reconstituted continuously in the problem-solving process. Problem-solving groups may cross departmental divisions and even legal boundaries between firms. The participants are motivated by collective incentives, both material and immaterial ones, such as solidarity and craft pride. A system of rewards and sanctions calibrated to individual performance would generate centrifugal pressures that would fragment groups. Even a retrospective system preoccupied with past group performance would be disruptive because it could not take account of the fluid re-composition of groups; the groups currently being rewarded or sanctioned might not have the same composition as they did at the time of the relevant past conduct. On the other hand, the focus on collective goals and incentives makes it possible for Toyota Jurisprudence to treat groups as central.

3. TOYOTA JURISPRUDENCE AND PUBLIC LAW INNOVATION

The Toyota perspective resonates with some important recent trends in American public law that my Columbia colleagues call 'experimentalist' and that Carey Coglianese and David Lazar call 'management-based regulation'.[39] The trends are evident in several areas of health and safety regulation. They are also prominent in the approach to school reform partially codified in the No Child Left Behind Act.

Health-and-safety programmes that exemplify these tendencies include the Hazard Analysis and Critical Control Point (HAACP) food safety programme of the Department of Agriculture, the Process Safety Management Program for hazardous substances of the Occupational Safety and Health Administration (OSHA), the safety regime for nuclear power plants overseen by the Nuclear Regulatory Commission and the Institute of Nuclear Plant Operations (INPO), and the Massachusetts Toxics Use Reduction Act (TURA).[40]

[39] Dorf and Sabel, n 2 above; Cary Coglianese and David Lazer, 'Management-Based Regulation: Prescribing Private Management to Achieve Public Goals' (2003) 37 *Law and Society Review* 601.

[40] See Coglianese and Lazer, previous n, at 696–700 (HAACP and Process Safety); Bradley C Karkkainen, 'Information as Environmental Regulation: TRI and Performance Benchmarking, Precursor to a New Paradigm?' (2001) 89 *Georgetown Law Journal* 257, 354–56 (TURA); Joseph Rees, *Hostages to Each Other: The Transformation of Nuclear Safety Since Three Mile Island* (Princeton, NJ: Princeton University Press, 2003) (NRC and INPO).

These regimes proceed by requiring regulated actors to identify hazards of particular kinds and to formulate their own plans for dealing with them. The plans must be based on research (not necessarily the actor's own) showing the efficacy of the measures prescribed. The plans must be periodically reviewed and revised in the light of experience. They must specify tolerances and indicators to define satisfactory performance and corrective measures when the performance is unsatisfactory. Actors are audited for the adequacy of their plans and for compliance with them. The regimes (or related programmes) specify mandatory practice or performance standards, but the actor will also be held to the standards its own plans provide, which are expected to be higher than the mandatory ones in many respects.

Some firms will be motivated to exceed minimum standards because such performance coincides with other firm goals, such as minimising cost or smoothing product flow, or because they are subject to distinctive pressures for better performance from workers, customers or neighbouring residents. As these firms improve measurably, they demonstrate possibilities for similar firms, and give the stakeholders in these other firms and the regulators a basis for demanding more of them.

Some compliance judgments may be binary (turning on whether the actor has met a fixed threshold), but others will rank the actor on a scale that permits comparison both with its own past performance with the performances of peers. Minimum standards may ratchet up as leading performers raise expectations. Or standards may require a minimum quantum of improvement over past scores. The regulator or an industry trade association collects and disseminates information about 'best practices' associated with the highest performances. The remedial aspects of the programme tend to be less punitive than those associated with command-and-control regulation. Lagging actors are asked to diagnose themselves and formulate improvement plans, perhaps with technical assistance from the regulator. They are subjected to increased monitoring. Publication of their performance ratings may generate shaming pressures within the industry or more tangible responses from customers or investors. Continued severe performance failure may result in more punitive intervention, but the typical pattern of intervention is less one of gradually increasing harshness, and more one of prolonged cooperative intervention followed, in the most intractable cases, by complete exclusion of the actor or forced restructuring.

'New accountability' school governance programmes as pioneered in Texas, Kentucky and North Carolina, and partly mandated by the federal No Child Left Behind Act have a similar structure.[41] The federal statute does not prescribe substantive standards or practices. Instead, it requires states to set their own goals for their schools and then to develop measures

[41] See James Liebman and Charles Sabel, 'A Public Laboratory Dewey Barely Imagined: The Emerging Model of School Governance and Legal Reform' (2003) 28 *New York University Journal of Law and Social Change* 183.

to make schools accountable for efforts to fulfil the goals. State systems must develop standardised tests to measure attainment of their own goals, and must also test their students on a uniform national test. They must report the performance of each school overall and with respect to ethnic minorities, economically disadvantaged, and disabled sub-groups. All schools are expected to annually review their performances and plan for improvement.

Local education agencies must publish annual 'report cards' comparing the performance of each school with schools across the state with socio-economically comparable student populations. The agencies must provide reward to high performers and technical assistance to laggards in drafting and implementing improvement plans. Where low performing schools fail to improve, students acquire rights to transfer to other schools or to use their share of federal support for the school to purchase educational services of their choice. Persistent poor performance ultimately requires that the schools be reconstituted with new management.

The main contours of these programmes strongly resemble key features of TPS.

A. Purposes

Important features of these regimes seem designed neither to resolve disputes nor to vindicate accepted values, but to induce learning and innovation. These include the features that oblige the actors to define and justify their own standards and practices, to make them public in a way that permits others to observe their experience, and to continuously revise them in the light of shared experience. The regimes are designed to induce performance by some actors at a higher level than anything the norms currently specify.

In addition to continuous revision, the rules require special responses to problems—indicators of failure or potential for improvement in the system. There are three types of such indicators: First, relative performance scores on measures used in periodic audits, for example, the number of unplanned shutdowns at a power plant or student scores on a standardised test. Second, observations or test results indicating failure to comply with applicable practice norms, including both agency mandatory rules and the firm's plans. And third, abnormal events, near misses and breakdowns—for example, the accidental discharge of a hazardous substance in the workplace.

Poor performance on any of these indicators may lead to sanctions and dispute-resolution procedures. But the most prominent and characteristic response the systems prescribe involves neither. The firm, often in collaboration with the regulator, must investigate and develop changes designed to improve its performance. The demand is for improvement, not necessarily for vindication of a pre-existing norm. Minimum standards have to be met, but the demand for improvement may require considerably more. The ethos of these regimes is hostile to the 'compliance orientation' that takes meeting fixed standards as adequate. Moreover, the decision-making procedure contemplated for investigation and reform is consensus both within and between the regulatory agency and the firm.

Of course, these systems are nested in larger structures that include rules with mandatory standards requiring performance in accordance with current norms and procedures for non-consensual dispute resolution. A system in which these mandatory standards and non-consensual procedures played a dominant role, however, would be regarded by its designers as a failure. Nevertheless, a theorist might want to reserve the terms 'law' or 'legal system' for these more traditional norms and insist that the Toyota-style norms represented a non-legal form of social order. There would be significant costs to doing so, however. At an abstract level, the Toyota norms have significant kinship with the more traditional ones. They are both public systems of deliberate social order based on rules and related norms. Moreover, the Toyota-style systems are typically regarded by their designers and participants as alternatives to the more traditional systems.

B. Rules and standards

In all these systems, we find an emphasis on specified norms coupled with a duty to revise them continuously. Plans and performance measures should be as specific as possible. Hazard Analysis and Critical Control Points food safety plans, for example, must specify safety practices in detail, precise tolerances for problem indicators such as salmonella, and precise corrective actions when tolerances are exceeded. Yet, corrective action is a matter of re-assessment as much as enforcement. The norms should be re-written when experience indicates they can be improved.[42]

As in TPS, the systems sometimes give rank-and-file workers the duty to provoke reconsideration of a practice norm whenever its application would defeat its purposes. Institute of Nuclear Power Operation standards provide:

> If the individual actually performing the activity cannot or believes he should not follow the procedure governing that activity as written, he shall place the system/component into a stable and safe condition and inform the responsible supervisor. Situations such as this could occur if the procedure is found to be inadequate for the intended task, if unexpected results occur, or if two more procedures governing the activity conflict. The supervisor shall resolve the discrepancy in the procedure by either [determining that the procedure is in fact adequate

[42] US Dept. of Agriculture, Food Safety and Inspection Service, 'Pathogen Reduction; Hazard Analysis and Critical Control Point (HAACP) Systems' 61 Fed Reg 38805 38816 (25 July 1996) ('[In the course of corrective action, t]he HAACP plan itself might require modification, perhaps in the form of a new critical limit, or of an additional [Critical Control Point].')

or] submitting a procedure change... (no further procedural steps shall be accomplished until the procedure change is approved).[43]

In new accountability school reform, performance is measured precisely on standardised tests, but the tests are continuously revised as understanding of goals changes or as knowledge of how to measure goals improves. Administrators and teachers make and revise detailed plans for improvement at the district, school, and classroom levels.[44]

C. Interdisciplinary teams

The regulatory regimes contemplate problem-solving by interdisciplinary teams. For example, OSHA recommends for the required investigation of an unplanned release of hazardous chemicals:

> A multi-disciplinary team is better able to gather the facts of the event and to analyze them and develop plausible scenarios as to what happened, and why. Team members should be selected on the basis of their training, knowledge and ability to contribute to a team effort to fully investigate the incident. Employees in the process area where the incident occurred should be consulted, interviewed or made a member of the team. Their knowledge of the events form a significant set of facts about the incident which occurred.[45]

The Texas education statute requires site-based management teams with representatives of administrators, teachers, campus staff, parents and community members. Reformers emphasise collaboration among teachers both within and across departments and between teachers and administrators. The new system generates two distinctive pressures for collaboration. First,

[43] Institute of Nuclear Power Plant Operation, *Good Practice, Conduct of Operations* (July 1984) 18–19 (quoted in Rees, n 40 above, at 82). The rule continues:

> In cases of emergency when procedures are inadequate for the situation, plant operations personnel are directed to take such action as necessary to minimize personnel injury and damage to the plant, to return the plant to a stable, safe condition, the to protect the health and safety of the general public and the personnel on site. These actions shall be documented and, if appropriate, incorporated into a revision of the affected procedure.

[44] Liebman and Sabel, n 41 above, at 249–50.

[45] 29 CFR 1910.119, Appendix C, para 12. An earlier version of the rule specifically recommended that each team include:

> —A third-line or higher supervisor from the section where the incident occurred;
> —Personnel from an area not involved in the incident;
> —An engineering and/or maintenance supervisor;
> —The safety supervisor;
> —A first-line supervisor from the affected area;
> —Occupational health/environmental personnel;
> —Appropriate wage personnel (i.e., operators, mechanics, technicians); and
> —Research and/or technical personnel.
> (US Dept of Labor, Occupational Health and Safety Administration, Proposed Rule, 55 Fed Reg 29, 150, 29172)

performance assessment with standardised tests requires each school to teach a standard set of skills and knowledge, and this means that within the school, teachers must coordinate their teaching to ensure the proper coverage. Second, the aspiration to respond quickly to information gleaned in the course of the school year requires various forms of collaboration. Students or teachers may need to be re-assigned; new teacher training may need to be arranged; curriculum may need to be adjusted to increase emphasis on some skills and reduce emphasis on others.[46]

D. Destabilisation

These systems incorporate benchmarking and root cause analysis practices.

The Institute of Nuclear Power Operation disseminates rankings of nuclear plants based on performance indicators. Plants are distributed across five categories ranging from 'Excellent' to 'Marginal'.[47] The Texas Educational Accountability System publishes a similar set of rankings of Texas schools grouped in socio-economically homogeneous peer groups.[48] The practices of the most successful performers are often publicised. Observers of both regimes find that these activities have a powerful influence both in motivating performance through honour and shame and in diffusing knowledge about 'best practices'.

Corrective action plans are based on root cause analysis. They are most elaborate in nuclear safety, where 'significant operating event' investigations often lead to changes in operations, maintenance, training and administration.[49]

A recent controversy involved in the implementation of the HAACP system by the Food Safety and Inspection Service parallels issues MacDuffie identified in auto plant TPS implementation and illustrates the stakes in root cause. Meat tainted by e-coli H 057 was found at Gallison Wholesale Meat Company in Montana in 2002. The Food Safety and Inspection Service inspectors encouraged a recall and demanded corrective action from Gallison. However, the inspectors failed to make efforts to trace the meat back to Gallison's suppliers to see if the taint had originated with them. Operating on traditional assumptions, the inspectors assumed that it was

[46] See Charles A Dana Center, *Driven to Succeed: High Performing, High Poverty, Turnaround Middle Schools* (Austin, TX: Charles A Dana Center, 2002), available at <http:www.utdanacenter.org/downloads/products/driven/ms_vol1.pdf>

Judges are not central participants in the regimes considered here. Thus, the regimes do not alter the judicial role. An example of a reform in the spirit of TPS in which courts are central and judges become members of interdisciplinary teams—highly controversial in part for this reason—is the drug court. See Dorf and Sabel, n 11 above.

[47] Rees, n 40 above, at 98–10.

[48] Liebman and Sabel, n 41 above, at 241.

[49] See Rees, n 40 above, at 126–50.

the wholesaler's responsibility to guarantee the safety of the meat, whether the taint originated from its own processes or those of its suppliers. After a critical report from the Department of Agriculture's Inspector General insisted that HAACP required tracing back, FSIS revised its regulations to require it in such circumstances. Now problems such as this potentially implicate the entire supply chain.[50]

E. Prospectivity and remediation

These regimes are oriented toward problem solving, as opposed to blaming or punishment. The search for causes is more a search for improvement opportunities than an effort to assign blame. One finds a combination of soft incentives—shaming and honour—with extremely hard ones for persistently poor performers. When improvement seems unlikely, the regimes prescribe management change, facility shutdown or license revocation.

But purely punitive sanctions are typically not a direct part of the regime. They stand in the background, threatening intervention in cases of deliberate malfeasance, especially withholding and falsification of data. The system designers tend to bracket or sublimate such concerns. Punitive interventions are relegated to separate sub-systems of norms, not typically referred to in the regimes' self-descriptions, and often assigned to different personnel. This de-emphasis reflects assumptions that non-compliance is more often the result of incapacity than malfeasance and that the prospect of punishment deters the cooperation on which the regimes depend.[51]

F. Death penalty administration

Regulatory approaches that resonate with TPS may not be promising for all spheres, but their range has yet to be mapped. There's a tendency to think they are not well suited to issues that are highly charged morally. While there is something to this contention, consideration of Jim Liebman's proposals for reform of death penalty administration suggests that it is overstated.[52]

Liebman's proposals emerged from his extensive empirical study showing that, in about two-thirds of all cases imposing the death penalty, reviewing courts find errors sufficient to warrant post-conviction relief. This relief

[50] US Dept. of Agriculture, Office of Inspector General, Great Plains Region, 'Audit Report: Food Safety and Inspection Service Oversight of Production Process and Recall at Conagra Plan (Establishment 969)' (Sept. 2003) at 43–48.

[51] See, eg, 29 CFR 1910 119, App C, para 12:

> The cooperation of employees is essential to an effective [workplace hazardous substance] incident investigation. The focus of the investigation should be to obtain facts, and not to place blame.

[52] James Liebman, 'The Overproduction of Death' (2000) 100 *Columbia Law Review* 2030.

comes in a procedure that typically takes many years, often decades, and includes multiple rounds of review in each of the state and federal court systems.

Liebman showed how the current system is structured to 'overproduce' death sentences: Prosecutors get political capital (a reputation for toughness on crime) and procedural advantages (the opportunity to death-qualify the jury) from seeking the death penalty. Elected state court judges face a political price for checking their excesses. Neither prosecutors nor judges face much reputational cost when wrongful convictions for which they are responsible are identified because the system makes no effort to connect the mistakes with those who are responsible for them and because mistakes are discovered so long after they are made that the responsible actors are likely to have moved on. Prosecutors, judges, and juries take their responsibilities toward the accused casually because they believe (with some plausibility) that any errors they make against the accused will be remedied post-conviction. Publicly provided defence resources at trial are inadequate. Although there is a talented private bar specialising in death penalty cases, it is forced by its small size and limited resources to focus on post-conviction challenges, and hence does nothing to check the tendency of the system to overproduction at the charging and trial stages.

Liebman's reform proposal involves a curtailment of the present elaborate post-conviction review procedures in return for strengthening protections for the accused at the stages of the trial and the initial state appellate review. It includes many specific reforms long advocated by defenders, including enhanced funding and heightened qualifications for defence lawyers, open access by the defence to the prosecution's files, a requirement that confession evidence be videotaped and a prohibition on death-qualifying juries in the guilt phrase. Two aspects of the package, however, are more distinctive.

First, prosecutors must explicitly justify their charging decisions, and state judges must review sentences for consistency with both the prosecutor's rationales and decisions in other cases. The prosecutorial justification comes in a statement filed at least 120 days before announcing a decision to seek the death penalty. Comparative proportionality review is to be undertaken post-conviction by the state appellate courts.

Second, data with respect to mistakes by courts, prosecutors and defence attorneys must be compiled in a form that permits comparison across personnel and jurisdictions and be disseminated.

These proposals resonate with the Toyota perspective.

First, their goals are partly to induce learning. To be sure, the criminal justice system as a whole is necessarily strongly focused on dispute resolution and the vindication of accepted values. As long as the defendant denies allegations of the indictment, dispute resolution is critical. And just punishment is punishment that conforms to accepted values.

Nevertheless, it appears that, even among people who accept the justice of the death penalty in the abstract, there is no consensus as to when it should be imposed. The pattern of charging and sentencing in capital cases strikes most observers as erratic and as an affront to widely accepted values of equal treatment. Liebman's proposed requirements with respect to the explanation of charges by prosecutors and proportionality review by first-stage appellate courts are designed to induce reflection and to generate information that makes more consistent and thoughtful judgments possible. The proposals are not an effort to vindicate a consensus, but to make it possible for one to emerge through the public deliberative efforts of different courts, each taking account of the others decisions and reasoning.

Second, the proposals are consistent with a Toyota-style response to the dialectic of rules and standards that has played out in an especially troubling way in this area. Sentencing decisions under discretionary standards tend to be erratic or discriminatory. When reformers respond with rule-like sentencing grids in the style of the Federal Sentencing Guidelines, they often compel arbitrary results in cases they fail to anticipate or provide for. (For years, the Supreme Court could not make up its mind whether due process in death sentencing was more offended by the looseness of discretion or the rigidity of rules.) The Toyota approach suggests the possibility of continuously revisable grids. The grids would have only presumptive force. Departures would be permitted if the decision maker could give reasons for them, and each departure would be an occasion for consideration (perhaps by a sentencing commission) of whether the grids could be improved.

Third, although the element of collective decision making is not salient in the reforms, there is a tendency of the requirements of justification to encourage more engagement within prosecutorial offices and between trial judges. The need to publicly justify charging decision and the appellate review of them for consistency will encourage prosecutorial staffs to develop their practices in a more open and coordinated fashion. While trial judges will not directly deliberate with each other, they will have more reason and opportunity to take account of each other's decisions in sentencing in order to achieve consistency.

Fourth, Liebman's proposal to generate and publish comparative error data with respect to prosecutors and courts is an attempt to generate the destabilising pressures of benchmarking and root cause analysis. The hope is that rankings will encourage emulation of the most successful performers and stigmatise the laggards in ways that create pressures to reform. The attribution of the errors requires a kind of root cause analysis. The overall tendency of the proposals, which limit post-conviction review in return for more safeguards in the earlier process, is to reduce reliance on ad hoc end-of-process adjustment ('rework') in order induce improvements in early-stage routine performance.

Fifth, by shifting attention from procedures for the case-by-case rectification of past errors to systemic reforms for reducing errors, the proposals have a less retrospective and individualist orientation than conventional discourse. Capital punishment will always be fundamentally a matter of corrective justice. But doing corrective justice requires institutional capacities that cannot be developed only case by case.

4. A JURISPRUDENCE OF PROBLEM-SOLVING

The jurisprudence suggested by TPS is a jurisprudence of problem-solving. Such a jurisprudence might overlap substantially with rights-and-principles and law-and-economics legal theory. It could make ample use of the structures of moral discourse elaborated by the rights-and-principles theorists and of both the empirical and analytical techniques of the economists. It would be considerably less troubled than either of these groups tends to be about the tensions of its precepts with those of the other, since it wouldn't take either as a contender for a comprehensive theory.

However, rights-and-principles theory is primarily preoccupied with *interpretation*. A jurisprudence of problem-solving, by contrast, would be focused more on *deliberation*. Law-and-economics is primarily a theory of *optimisation* of known preferences in known circumstances. A jurisprudence of problem-solving, by contrast, would be focused more on *discovery*—on the ways in which people can deepen their understanding of both their goals and the possibilities of realising them.

John Dewey's style of pragmatism offers a philosophical basis for theories of problem-solving, but it tends to be disappointingly vague about practical application.[53] The engineering ideas and practices associated with TPS and reflected in recent public law developments might usefully complement the pragmatist approach and contribute to a problem-solving jurisprudence.

The potential benefits of a jurisprudence of problem-solving extend beyond the capacity to come to terms with recent developments and regulation and public service delivery. For, as I suggested above, a substantial range of longstanding concerns of the American legal system do not fit well with the preoccupations of mainstream legal theory. One set of these concerns is substantive; it is typified by unintentional torts and traditional health and safety regulation—laws that regulate the unintended consequences of generally beneficial conduct. A major fraction of the conduct prohibited by these regimes is not plausibly moralised and cannot be described or identified precisely for deterrence purposes. The other set of concerns involves organisational liability. Mainstream legal theory has been developed largely with reference to individuals; it has very few resources for dealing with the distinctive aspects of organisational liability. Toyota jurisprudence, which brackets moralism, acknowledges uncertainty, and takes collective action as paradigmatic, has potentially important contributions to make in both areas.

[53] See Dewey, n 2 above.

3

'Soft Law', 'Hard Law' and EU Integration

DAVID M TRUBEK, PATRICK COTTRELL AND MARK NANCE

INTRODUCTION

IN THE DISCUSSION of new governance in the European Union (EU), the concept of 'soft law' is often used to describe governance arrangements that operate in place of, or along with, the 'hard law' that arises from treaties, regulations, and the Community Method. These new governance methods may bear some similarity to hard law. But because they lack features such as obligation, uniformity, justiciability, sanctions and/or an enforcement staff, they are classified as 'soft law' and contrasted, sometimes positively, sometimes negatively, with hard law as instruments for European integration. This chapter explores the concepts of hard and soft law in order to illuminate this important aspect of the new governance phenomenon.

Of course, there is nothing new about 'soft law': it has always played a role in European integration. 'Soft law' is a very general term, and has been used to refer to a variety of processes. The only common thread among these processes is that while all have normative content they are not formally binding. Francis Snyder provided the classic treatment of soft law in the EU in 1994.[1] In his definition, Snyder describes soft law as 'rules of conduct which in principle have no legally binding force but which nevertheless may have practical effects'. In recent years there has been an increase in interest in soft law in the EU. Several studies have appeared recently.[2] Several major books that deal with soft law are coming out.[3]

[1] Other early studies include F Snyder, 'The Effectiveness of EC Law' in T Daintith (ed) *Implementing EC Law in the UK* (1995) and KC Wellens and GM Borchart, 'Soft Law in EC Law' (1989) 14 ELR 267–321.

[2] D Trubek and L Trubek, 'Hard and Soft Law in the Construction of Social Europe: The Role of the Open Method of Coordination' (2005) 11 *European Law Journal*; K Jacobsson, 'Between Deliberation and Discipline: Soft Governance in EU Employment Policy' in U Mörth (ed) *Soft Law and Governance and Regulation: An Interdisciplinary Analysis* (Cheltenham: Edward Elgar, 2004); C Joerges and F Rödl, '"Social Market Economy" as Europe's Social Model?' (2004) EUI Working Paper LAW 2004/8; D Chalmers and M Lodge, 'The OMC and the European Welfare State' (2003) Economic and Social Research Council, LSE, Discussion

While soft law has drawn increasing attention, it has not received uniform support. Thus in recent years there have been significant attacks on the use of soft law in various settings. Objections to the use of soft law in the EU include:

—It lacks the clarity and precision needed to provide predictability and a reliable framework for action;
—The EU treaties include hard provisions that enshrine market principles and these can only be offset if equally hard provisions are added to promote social objectives;
—Soft law cannot forestall races to the bottom in social policy within the EU;
—Soft law cannot really have any effect but it is a covert tactic to enlarge the Union's legislative hard law competence;
—Soft law is a device that is used to have an effect but it by-passes normal systems of accountability;
—Soft law undermines EU legitimacy because it creates expectations but cannot bring about change.[4]

Note that most of these critiques are based, explicitly or implicitly, on the view that hard law is required to achieve whatever EU objectives are in question. The authors of these critiques believe that integration requires clear guidance, uniform treatment, sanctions to deter non-compliance, and justiciability and thus can only come about through treaties, regulations or directives.

Just as hard law proponents have questioned the efficacy of soft law, so those who see merit in new governance and thus soft law have raised questions about the utility of traditional forms of hard law in the context of many of the issues confronting the EU today. Among the critiques of hard law one finds the following observations:

Paper No 11; H Cosma and R Whish, 'Soft Law in the Field of EU Competition Policy' (2003) 14 *European Business Law Review*; J Scott and D Trubek, 'Mind the Gap: Law and New Approaches to Governance in the European Union' (2002) 8 *European Law Journal* 1–18; J Klabbers, 'The Undesirability of Soft Law'(1998) 36 *Nordic Journal of International Law* 381–91; A Héretier, 'New Modes of Governance in Europe: Policy Making Without Legislating?' in Héretier (ed) *Common Goods: Reinventing European and International Governance* (Lanham, MD: Rowman & Littlefield, 2001); M Cini, 'The Soft Law Approach: Commission Rule-Making in the EU's State Aid Regime' (2001) 8 *Journal of European Public Policy* 192–207; K Sisson and P Marginson, 'Soft Regulation—Travesty of the Real Think or New Dimension?' (2001) ESRC Working Paper 32/01; J Kenner, 'The EC Employment Title and the 'Third Way': Making Soft Law Work' (1999) 15 *International Journal of Comparative Labor Law and Industrial Relations* 33–60; H Hillgenberg, 'A Fresh Look at Soft Law' (1999) 10 *European Journal of International Law*: 499–515; etc.

[3] See, eg, Mörth, previous n.

[4] For these and other critiques, see, eg, Klabbers, n 2 above; Joerges and Rödl, n 2 above; Chalmers and Lodge, n 2 above; and S Smismans, 'EU Employment Policy: Decentralisation or Centralisation through the Open Method of Coordination?' (2004) EUI Working Paper LAW No 204/01.

—Hard law tends toward uniformity of treatment while many current issues demand tolerance for significant diversity among Member States.
—Hard law presupposes a fixed condition based on prior knowledge while situations of uncertainty may demand constant experimentation and adjustment.
—Hard law is very difficult to change yet in many cases frequent change of norms may be essential to achieve optimal results.
—If actors do not internalise the norms of hard law, enforcement may be difficult; if they do, it may be unnecessary.

As we can see, arguments about hard and soft law are based largely on pragmatic and functional questions: how do these processes work; which one works best? Because the issue is pragmatic, the debate about hard and soft law cannot be resolved in the abstract or in a general way. Different domains have different needs, and 'hard' and 'soft' legal processes come in many different shapes and forms. Therefore, the discussion must be carried out in the context of particular policy domains and in light of the actual or potential operational capacities of the respective instruments in that domain.

Further, by casting the issue as a pragmatic one, we immediately recognise that the question is not necessarily one of hard *versus* soft law: there is also the issue of the possible interaction between these two approaches to governance and thus of 'hybrid' constellations in which both hard and soft processes operate in the same domain and affect the same actors. For that reason, this chapter looks at issues concerning the relationship between hard and soft law in two specific domains and explores both their relative effectiveness and their actual and potential interaction.[5]

Employment policy

The first policy domain we shall investigate is EU employment policy. The EU only has competence to regulate in only a few of the areas that affect employment. But the employment issue in Europe is so serious, and so related to basic goals of the Union, that the Union has decided it must coordinate Member State efforts to reduce unemployment and increase the percentage of the population in the workforce even though this necessarily includes activity in areas of exclusive Member State competence. To that end, the EU has created the European Employment Strategy (EES), a set of non-binding guidelines designed to govern the reform of national laws, policies and institutions in order to make them more employment-friendly. The EES includes a complex system of periodic reporting, indicators and multilateral surveillance, as well as mechanisms for benchmarking, peer review and exchange of best practices. A classic form of new governance, the EES has been a model for similar systems which now are all denominated the 'Open Method of Coordination' or OMC.

The EES itself is soft law, in that the guidelines are general, they are not binding, and there is no way to mount a court challenge to any failure to follow the guidelines. The EES, however, overlaps with EU 'hard law' in some areas, thus creating the possibility for interaction and hybridity. Among these is the field of employment discrimination, a topic that is both regulated through a hard law directive and covered by an EES guideline. Thus in this domain there exists the possibility for a 'hybrid' constellation.[6]

Fiscal policy coordination

The second domain to be explored is fiscal policy coordination. In this domain, we not only see both soft and hard law measures that deal with the same objective; we also see what appears to be a conscious effort to deploy them together to achieve maximum effectiveness. The goal of fiscal coordination in the EU is to ensure that states in the eurozone pursue and maintain the sound fiscal policies necessary for the sustainability of the euro. To that end, eurozone states are expected to keep their budgets in balance over the medium term and avoid excessive deficits in the short term.

Two very different mechanisms are deployed to achieve these goals. The first is a 'soft law' system of Broad Economic Policy Guidelines (BEPGs) that establishes non-binding standards for fiscal prudence and includes a system of multilateral surveillance designed to encourage adherence to the standards. In theory, the BEPGs and multilateral surveillance should by themselves lead to fiscal policies that would prevent excessive deficits. But the fiscal coordination system also includes a set of fixed rules that define what constitutes an excessive deficit and provides sanctions for non-compliance with these rules. Thus it includes both soft and hard elements.

Ideally, the two systems of fiscal coordination should work together. The general and non-binding BEPGs allow substantial flexibility in methods to reach sustainability thus permitting states to find paths to fiscal prudence that fit with their national needs and traditions. At the same time the fixed

[6] This chapter was completed before the issuance of Commission Recommendations for Integrated Guidelines for Growth and Jobs (2005–8) COM (2005) 141 Final. These guidelines bring together the Broad Economic Policy Guidelines and the Employment Guidelines into one structure. They put more emphasis on the integration of macro-economic, micro-economic and employment polices at the Member State level. While the Guidelines are now put together, because it does not appear that major policy changes have occurred and separate processes for fiscal coordination and employment promotion still exist, it is premature to say what effect these new developments would have on the issues analysed here should the Commission's recommendations be adopted.

and binding excessive deficit rules and the sanctions for the breach of these rules would serve as deterrents. The threat of sanctions should increase the pressure on Member States to obey both the guidelines and any specific recommendations that might emerge from the multilateral surveillance system. If the deterrent worked, it would be unnecessary to impose the sanctions.

In this chapter, we develop a conceptual framework for the analysis of hard and soft law that is drawn in part from recent work in the field of international relations (IR). We look at the literature on the role of soft law, noting that scholars have approached this phenomenon in very different ways. We explore the relative roles of hard and soft law in the two domains under study, and examine questions of hybridity.

The framework developed in this chapter is based on a synthesis of two different conceptual approaches to European integration and the application of that synthesis to the study of law. We seek to unite insights from constructivist and rationalist theories of integration and apply them to the understanding of the role law and other normative orders and governance processes may play in integration. We deploy this synthesis to analyse the two case studies, exploring the roles that law plays and paying special attention to the operation of hybrid constellations where hard and soft operate in the same policy domain.

THE DISCOVERY OF SOFT LAW IN INTERNATIONAL RELATIONS THEORY

In the literature in international relations (IR) and international law (IL) we see increasing attention being paid to the role of soft law in multilateral governance. However, there is no genuine agreement as to what soft law means, largely due to debates over whether soft law is actually 'law' and the difficulties in defining the parameters of 'hard' and 'soft' law. These concepts appear to be relatively clear, but are in fact much more complicated.[7]

In the international relations literature, the conventional conceptual definition of hard and soft law is laid out in a special issue of *International Organization* entitled 'Legalization and World Politics', which delineates three dimensions of legalisation: obligation, precision and delegation.[8] In this context, obligation means that states are legally bound by the regime and therefore subject to scrutiny under the rules and procedure of international law. Precision means that the regime's 'rules unambiguously define the conduct they authorise, require, or proscribe'.[9] Delegation means that

[7] For this reason, a prominent treatment of soft law in the legal realm brackets the deeper conceptual debate and settles for a binding (hard) versus non-binding (soft) distinction. See D Shelton (ed) *Commitment and Compliance: The Role of Non-Binding Norms in the International Legal System* (Oxford: Oxford University Press, 2000).

[8] K Abbott, R Keohane, AM Slaughter and D Snidal, 'The Concept of Legalization' (2000) 54 *International Organization*.

[9] *Ibid* at 401.

third parties have been granted authority to implement, interpret and apply the rules such that a dispute resolution mechanism and an amendment process exist. Abbott and Snidal use hard law to refer to 'legally binding obligations that are precise and that delegate authority for interpreting and implementing the law' while soft law 'begins once legal arrangements are weakened along one or more of the dimensions'.[10] While these definitions might not offer a sharp distinction between hard and soft law, this does not seem to be a high priority of the authors, as they caveat their definition by stating explicitly that 'soft law comes in many varieties: the choice between hard and soft law is not a binary one'.[11]

The treatment of hard and soft law put forth in the special issue has come under fire for ignoring crucial constitutive aspects of law. For example, Finnemore and Toope offer a compelling constructivist critique, arguing that the authors fail to account for the role of customary international law, provide no discussion of how 'obligation' is generated[12] and disregard 'the processes by which law is created and applied—adherence to legal process values, the ability of actors to participate and feel their influence, and use the legal forms of reasoning'.[13] This constructivist perspective emphasises law as 'a broad social phenomenon deeply embedded in the practices, beliefs, and traditions of societies, and shaped by interaction among societies'.[14] Despite these differences, however, both sides of the debate argue that soft law can be important.

The tension between the treatment of law as a tool for *constraining* behaviour of actors with fixed preferences versus law as a *transformative* tool capable of changing behaviour of actors by altering their identity is derivative of a broader paradigmatic divide between rationalism and constructivism in IR. Given the theoretical relevance of this divide and its potential application to soft law outside of the IR sphere, a brief digression seems appropriate in order to unpack the theoretical premises of these approaches, which will facilitate the analysis of how each conceptualises soft law and whether they are indeed complementary.

Rationalism and constructivism compared

Rationalist approaches[15] are unified by their emphasis on material factors, states as the central units of analysis, exogenous and fixed preferences of actors, rational utility maximisation and the constraining effects of an anarchic international environment. Or as Ruggie puts it, rationalist approaches

[10] K Abbott and D Snidal, 'Hard and Soft Law in International Governance' (2000) 54 *International Organization* at 421–22.

[11] Abbott *et al* n 8 above.

[12] On this point, see also C Reus-Smit, 'The Politics of Legal Obligation' (2003) 9 *European Journal of International Relations*.

[13] M Finnemore and S Toope, 'Alternatives to "Legalization:" Richer Views of Law and Politics' (2001) 55 *International Organization* 746–50.

[14] *Ibid*, at 743.

[15] Broadly conceived, rationalist approaches include classical- and neo-realism, neoliberal institutionalism, and other economics-based theories.

comprise a 'neo-utilitarian' worldview in which the world is comprised of self-regarding units with fixed identities and material interests. These approaches follow a 'logic of consequences' in which agents try to realise their preferences through strategic behaviour.[16] Outcomes are therefore typically explained in terms of individual goal-seeking under constraints.[17]

Abbott and Snidal's conceptualisation of hard and soft law is rooted in the predominant strand of rationalism, so-called 'rational functionalism' (or neoliberal institutionalism), which assumes that international institutions and legal arrangements are established for states to advance their mutual interests by solving collective action problems. Rules and institutions function to stabilise expectations, reduce transaction costs, raise the price of defection by lengthening the shadow of the future and providing a basis for issue linkage, increase transparency, provide or facilitate monitoring, settle disputes, increase audience costs of commitments, provide focal points, and increase reputational costs and benefits related to conformity of behaviour with rules.[18] Institutions can be designed to help solve a specific collective action problem, such as problems of collaboration (ie, reducing actors' incentives to defect) and coordination (ie, helping actors' choose among multiple equilibria or possible solutions).[19]

For rationalists, hard law plays a particularly important role in securing cooperation because it hedges against the mistrust that characterises the anarchic international environment. Legally binding rules deter potential violations because actors are more likely to factor in such disincentives as reputation costs, issue linkage, reciprocity and the shadow of the future into their calculus of whether or not to remain in compliance. In addition, hard law often forces actors to consider the threat of sanctions.

Although rationalists often treat states as unitary actors, there is a growing interest in exploring the relationship between international institutions and domestic politics.[20] These scholars propose accounts of international

[16] For further discussion, see J March and J Olsen, *Rediscovering Institutions* (New York: Free Press, 1989); and T Risse, 'Constructivism and International Institutions: Toward Conversations across Paradigms' in I Katznelson and H Milner (eds) *Political Science: The State of the Discipline* (New York: Norton, 2002).

[17] D Snidal, 'Rational Choice and International Relations Theory' in W Carlsnaes, T Risse and B Simmons (eds) *Handbook of International Relations* (London: Sage Publications, 2002) 74.

[18] B Kingsbury, 'The Concept of Compliance as a Function of Competing Conceptions of International Law' (1998) 19 *Michigan Journal of International Law* 345.

[19] L Martin and B Simmons 'International Organizations and Institutions' in W Carlsnaes, T Risse, and B Simmons (eds) *Handbook of International Relations* (London: Sage Publications, 2002) 196. For a rational functionalist account of regime design, see B Koremenos, C Lipson and D Snidal, 'The Rational Design of International Institutions' (2001) 55 *International Organization*.

[20] See L Martin and B Simmons, 'Theories and Empirical Studies of International Institutions' (1998) 52 *International Organization*. Eg, Martin and Simmons suggest that IR scholars have neglected domestic politics and they need to put this on the research agenda. They pose three central questions: First, under what conditions might domestic actors be willing to substitute international for domestic institutions? Second, are particular domestic actors regularly advantaged by the ability to transfer policymaking authority to the international level? Third, to what extent can international institutional decisions and rules be enforced by domestic institutions, and what are the implications for compliance?

cooperation and compliance that show how domestic institutions respond to individuals and groups in different ways and aggregate preferences, which in turn affects state behaviour.[21] Writing about Europe, Andrew Moravcsik addresses a central puzzle in the study of European integration: why have sovereign governments 'chosen repeatedly to coordinate their core economic policies and surrender sovereign prerogatives within an international institution?'[22] The conventional wisdom, Moravcsik argues, has given far too much weight to geopolitics and supranational actors. He instead suggests that the EC emerged as the result of rational decisions made by member governments in pursuit of core economic interests. Over the course of 40 years, choices for Europe crystallised not because of supranational influence, but from the relative bargaining power of the largest Member States.

Unlike rationalist approaches, which draw heavily on economic theory, constructivism is more influenced by sociology and emphasises social context, ideational factors, the role of collectively held understandings of subjects and social life, and a 'logic of appropriateness' whereby actors try to figure out the appropriate rule for a given situation. Constructivism depicts the social world as intersubjectively and collectively meaningful structures and processes.[23] Thus, social actors do not exist independently from their social environment and its collectively shared systems of meanings.[24] The social environment in which we interact defines (constitutes) who we are, our identities as social beings. Concurrently, 'human agency creates, reproduces, and changes culture through our daily practices'.[25] In this broad social sense, constructivism can be distinguished from other approaches to politics and law in its emphasis on the role of ideas and knowledge.

> Unlike positivism and materialism, which take the world as it is, constructivism sees the world as a project under construction, as becoming rather than being.[26] At bottom, constructivism concerns the issue of human consciousness: the role it plays in international relations, and the implications for the logic and methods of social inquiry of taking it seriously. Constructivists hold the view that the building blocks of international reality are ideational as well as material; that ideational factors have normative as well as instrumental dimensions; that they express not only

[21] See, eg, A Moravcsik 'The Origins of Human Rights Regimes: Democratic Delegation in Postwar Europe' (2000) 54 *International Organization* 217–52.

[22] A Moravcsik, *The Choice for Europe: Social Purpose and State Power from Messina to Maastricht* (Ithaca, NY: Cornell University Press, 1998) 1.

[23] E Adler, 'Constructivism and International Relations Theory' in W Carlsnaes, T Risse and B Simmons (eds) *Handbook of International Relations* (London: Sage Publications, 2002).

[24] Risse, 'Social Constructivism and European Integration' in A Wiener and T Dietz (eds) *European Integration Theory* (Oxford: Oxford University Press, 2004) 160.

[25] *Ibid* at 161.

[26] Adler, n 23 above, at 95

individual but also collective intentionality; and that the meaning and significance of ideational factors are not independent of time and place.[27]

From an epistemological standpoint, the constructivist approach is not interested in how things *are*, but in how they *became* what they are.[28] Thus, whereas rationalist approaches treat identity and interests of actors as exogenously given or inferred from a given material structure, constructivists ask how actors come to acquire their current identity and interests, and seek to demonstrate how interests are not objectively derived but rather are 'socially constructed and dependent on historically bounded social roles occupied by knowledgeable actors'.[29] A constructivist perspective therefore leads scholars to ask questions about the role of law in promoting processes of norm diffusion, socialisation and learning.

The alternative analytical lenses of rationalism and constructivism provide a useful starting point for thinking about the different facets of law: its meanings, its functions and its applications. When employed to analyse the relative merits of soft law, these lenses illuminate the different dimensions of soft legal instruments and offer distinct and compelling arguments in their favour. However, despite their distinctiveness, rationalist and constructivist approaches to soft law do not appear to be mutually exclusive and may, in fact, be complementary.

B. Rationalist and Constructivist Accounts of Soft Law

The IR/IL literature offers a variety of general explanations for why soft law might be preferable to hard law in some circumstances, largely from a rationalist standpoint. At least seven general (and related) explanatory themes can be drawn from the broader literature.[30]

1. *Lower 'contracting' costs.* The creation of almost any agreement entails negotiation or 'contracting' costs—coming together, learning about the issue, bargaining and so forth. When these costs are high (for example, when the issue is complex or contentious), soft law might be more appropriate

[27] J Ruggie, 'What Makes The World Hang Together' (1998) 52 *International Organization* 855–86, quoted in T Christiansen, KE Jorgensen and A Wiener, 'The Social Construction of Europe' (1999) 6 *Journal of European Public Policy* 530.

[28] Adler, n 23 above, at 100–1.

[29] J Ruggie and F Kratochwil, 'International Organization: A State of the Art on an Art of the State' (1986) 40 *International Organization*.

[30] See especially Abbott and Snidal n 10 above; C Lipson, 'Why Are Some International Agreements Informal?' (1991) 45 *InternationalOrganization*; W Reinicke and JM Witte, 'Interdependence, Globalization, and Sovereignty: The Role of Non-Binding Legal Accords' in D Shelton (ed) *Commitment and Compliance: The Role of Non-Binding Norms in the International Legal System* (Oxford: Oxford University Press, 2000); C Chinkin, 'Normative Development in the International Legal System' in *ibid*; and H Hillgenberg, 'A Fresh Look at Soft Law' (1999) 10 *European Journal of International Law* 499–515.

because non-binding norms lower the stakes for the parties involved in negotiations.[31]

2. *Lower sovereignty costs.* Legally binding agreements involve costs to Member States such as differences in outcomes on particular issues, the loss of authority of decision making in an issue area, and the diminution of sovereignty. Soft law is better equipped to promote cooperation while preserving sovereignty.

3. *Coping with diversity.* Soft law allows states to adapt their commitments to their particular situations rather than trying to accommodate divergent national circumstances within a single text. It can be used to break a deadlock in negotiations where disparities in wealth, power and interests make binding agreements impossible. Different cultural and economic structures and interests can be accommodated through the subjective application of 'soft' language such as 'appropriate measures', 'best efforts', 'as far as possible', or 'with a view toward achieving progressively'.[32]

4. *Flexibility.* The greater flexibility of non-binding legal instruments allows for renegotiation or modification of agreements as circumstances change; can accommodate diverse legal systems; and can cope better with uncertainty (for example, when the underlying problems might not be well understood, so states cannot anticipate all of the possible consequences of a legalised arrangement). Flexibility is particularly important in the fast changing and technology driven environment that is characteristic of globalisation.[33]

5. *Simplicity and speed.*[34] Soft law might be motivated by the desire to avoid formal and visible pledges by states, to avoid ratification or other cumbersome domestic procedures (in case of amendments, etc.), or to induce even the least committed states to participate.[35] It is also useful if there is potential need to reach agreements quickly (for example, on a contingency basis).

6. *Participation.* In principle, soft law permits the integration of all interested parties in the process of transnational law making.[36] Increased openness allows for more active participation of non-state actors, promotes transparency, enhances agenda setting, and facilitates the diffusion of knowledge.

7. *Incrementalism.* Soft law can also represent a first step on the path to legally binding agreements or hard law.[37]

[31] Abbott and Snidal, n 10 above, at 434.
[32] Chinkin , n 30 above, at 41.
[33] Reinicke and Witte, n 30 above, at 94–95.
[34] See Lipson, n 30 above.
[35] This aspect of soft law raises 'race to the bottom' concerns.
[36] Reinicke and Witte, n 30 above, at 94–95.
[37] *Ibid* at 95.

From the rationalist perspective, soft law promotes material and normative goals by reducing the costs of cooperation and facilitating the bargaining process upon creation of the agreement and over time. Although perhaps not as robust as hard law in its ability to constrain behaviour through credible threats of enforcement, soft law reduces barriers to cooperation and might be a precursor to harder forms of law.

Unlike rationalist approaches, constructivists have done surprisingly little to engage directly debates over the relative merits of soft law and the conditions in which soft can be effective.[38] Nevertheless, constructivism has much to offer in this regard. A growing body of constructivist research looks at how international institutions and legal norms can have an independent, constitutive effect on actors, focusing on 'the social content of the organization, its culture, its legitimacy concerns, dominant norms that govern behaviour and shape interests, and the relationship of these to a larger normative and cultural environment'.[39] Like many proponents of the OMC (as will be discussed below), constructivist scholars look at how institutions facilitate constitutive processes such as persuasion, learning, argumentation and socialisation.[40] With sustained interaction over the course of time in an institutional environment these processes influence actors' behaviour and eventually result in the creation of intersubjective knowledge and a 'norms cascade' where a critical mass of states subscribe to new norms and rules.[41]

Changes in state behaviour can also come through processes of socialisation within groups that incorporate new members through the expansion of norms, ideas and principles.[42] Constructivist scholars also underscore the importance of transnational actors in the institutional and policy processes, and are particularly mindful of the role of epistemic communities and transnational networks of policy professionals who share common values and causal understandings, which often facilitate the development and dissemination of ideas embedded in given institution.[43] From this perspective, soft law may be better equipped to promote transformative processes of

[38] It is worth noting that for constructivists, soft law, like customary law, is not always viewed as being 'chosen' in a meaningful strategic sense intended to be effective, but can evolve over time based on general practice and principle. See Finnemore and Toope (2001), fn 23.

[39] M Barnett and M Finnemore, 'The Politics, Power and Pathologies of International Organizations' (1999) 53 *International Organization* 707–8.

[40] See, eg, I Johnston, 'Treating International Institutions as Social Environments' (2001) 45 *International Studies Quarterly* 487–515 and M Finnemore, *National Interests in International Society* (Ithaca, NY: Cornell University Press, 1996).

[41] See M Finnemore and K Sikkink, 'International Norm Dynamics and Political Change' (1998) 52 *International Organization*. Note that states need not follow the same paths toward implementation of policies consistent with these norms and rules.

[42] See Johnston, n 40 above.

[43] See, eg, T Risse, S Ropp and KSikkink (eds) *The Power of Human Rights: International Norms and Domestic Change* (NewYork: Cambridge University Press, 1999) and ME Keck and K Sikkink, *Activists Beyond Borders: Advocacy Networks in International Politics* (Ithaca, NY: Cornell University Press, 1998).

norm diffusion, persuasion and learning that have a positive impact on policy outcomes by allowing a wider spectrum for deliberation in the governing process.

While rationalist and constructivist approaches in IR each offer a framework from which to construct theories and make inferences about the relative value of soft law, little work has been done to explore the possible relationship between the two. Each perspective sees value in soft law, but looks at it through very different analytical prisms. Moreover, there has as yet been effort to develop a synthetic approach that would allow scholars to deploy rationalist and constructivist insights simultaneously to deal with situations that call both for change and stability, flexibility and uniformity, change and constraint, and thus hard and soft law.

DIFFERENT SCHOLARLY APPROACHES TO SOFT LAW IN THE EUROPEAN UNION

As argued above, soft law means something different to constructivists and rationalists; perceptions of soft law are dependent on theoretical orientation. To some extent, these differences are reflected in academic discussion concerning two cases we examine in some detail in this paper. We look at arguments that support the use of the OMC in social policy and at the efforts to explain and justify the use of soft law in the effort to avoid excessive Member State budget deficits. While the case for soft law in the OMC context reflects a relatively constructivist orientation, the analysis of soft law in the context of the fiscal policy coordination reflects a more rationalist perspective.

Employment policy, the OMC and constructivism

The European Employment Strategy and the Open Method of Co-ordination of which it is the exemplar, are part of a broader movement toward 'new governance' and democratic experimentalism in the United States and European legal communities.[44] For advocates of the OMC and other 'new governance' approaches, traditional forms of command and control governance are viewed as exclusive, incapable of addressing societal complexity, static and unable to adapt well to changing circumstances, and limited in their production of the knowledge needed to solve problems. They cite the need to move from centralised command and control regulation consisting of rigid and uniform rules and hard law, toward a system of governance that promotes flexibility and learning through the uses of soft law.

The OMC can be seen as 'soft law' in contrast to the 'hard' approach of the Classic Community Method (CCM). The OMC employs general

[44] See J Zeitlin and D Trubek (eds) *Governing Work and Welfare in a New Economy: European and American Experiments* (Oxford: Oxford University Press, 2003), especially ch 1.

objectives and guidelines for Member State behaviour that are non-binding and non-justiciable while the CCM provides more or less uniform rules that are binding on Member States, are justiciable and include sanctions for non-compliance.[45]

While the CCM has worked well in many areas, it has proven less desirable in areas like employment and social policy. Given the diversity of national welfare states, which differ not only in levels of economic development, but also in their normative aspirations and institutional structures[46], and the complexity and uncertainty shrouding the social problems states must cope with at the national and local levels, top-down regulation from the EU is often not a viable way to solve social problems efficiently or effectively. In this sense, the demand for good governance in social Europe exceeds the supply provided by the traditional CCM model. In order to address broad common concerns while respecting national diversity, Europe has begun to employ different governance strategies, the most notable of which is the OMC.

How does it work?

The OMC is based upon at least six general principles: participation and power sharing, multi-level integration, diversity and decentralisation, deliberation, flexibility and revisability, and experimentation and knowledge creation.[47] It provides a soft framework that accommodates diversity, facilitates mutual learning, spreads good practices and fosters convergence toward EU goals.[48] Sabel and Zeitlin summarise the essential elements of the OMC as follows:

(1) Joint definition by the member states of initial objectives (general and specific), indicators, and in some cases guidelines;
(2) National reports or action plans which assess performance in light of the objectives and metrics, and propose reforms accordingly;
(3) Peer review of these plans, including mutual criticism and exchange of good practices, backed up by recommendations in some cases;
(4) Re-elaboration of the individual plans and, at less frequent intervals, of the broader objectives and metrics in light of the experience gained in their implementation.[49]

[45] Scott and Trubek, n 2 above, at 1; Trubek and Trubek, n 2 above.
[46] F Scharpf, 'The European Social Model: Coping with the Challenges of Diversity' (2002) 40 *Journal of Common Market Studies*.
[47] Scott and Trubek, n 2 above, at 5–6.
[48] K Jacobsson and H Schmid, 'The European Employment Strategy at the Crossroads: Contribution to the Evaluation' in D Foden and L Magnusson (eds) *Five Years Experience of the Luxembourg Employment Strategy* (Brussels: ETUI, 2003).
[49] C Sabel and J Zeitlin, 'Active Welfare, Experimental Governance, and Pragmatic Constitutionalism: The New Transformation of Europe' unpublished paper prepared for the 2003 International Conference of the Hellenic Presidency of the European Union, 'The Modernisation of the European Social Model and EU Policies and Instruments' Ioannina, Greece, 21–22 May 2003, p 24.

Because it systematically and continuously obliges Member States to pool information, compare themselves to one another and reassess current policies in light of their relative performance, scholars have contended that the OMC is a promising mechanism for improving governance in Europe.[50] The OMC first achieved prominence in the European Employment Strategy,[51] and has since spread into a number of areas of EU policy making, including social inclusion, pensions, health care, education and training, and immigration and asylum.[52]

Proponents have noted three major reasons why the OMC should be accepted as an appropriate tool for EU governance. First, many social issues confronting Europe are complex, politically sensitive, and involve a high degree of uncertainty as to which solution will achieve the desired results. OMC scholars argue that soft law allows a range of possibilities for interpretation and trial and error without the constraints of uniform rules or threat of sanction. This enables diverse Member States to develop tailored solutions to their specific problems and provides feedback mechanisms to share and build knowledge. Second, soft law processes are appropriate when the gap between the aspired norm and existing reality is so large that hard regulatory provisions will be meaningless. Softer mechanisms allow minimum levels of adherence to be established and formalise progressive advancement toward higher standards. Finally, softer forms of governance such as the OMC increase the social basis of legitimacy of the EU by allowing stakeholders to participate in the policy process and thereby facilitating knowledge diffusion and engendering a feeling of enfranchisement and investment in the system.

How can soft law make a difference?

Given these broad characteristics of the OMC, what specific mechanisms facilitate policy change and help to solve problems? A number of scholars have contributed to the effort construct an account of how the soft OMC mechanisms might operate. A major contribution to this literature can be found in the work of the Swedish sociologist Kerstin Jacobsson whose work has many affinities with constructivist scholarship.[53] Drawing on the work of Jacobsson and others, all with theoretical roots in constructivism, Trubek and Trubek[54] outline six ways that the OMC might affect change and channel behaviour:

[50] Zeitlin and Trubek, n 44 above, at 5.

[51] See D Trubek and J Mosher, 'New Governance, Employment Policy, and the European Social Model' in J Zeitlin and D Trubek (eds) *Governing Work and Welfare in a New Economy: European and American Experiments* (Oxford: Oxford University Press, 2003).

[52] Zeitlin and Trubek, n 44 above, ch 1.

[53] Jacobsson, n 2 above.

[54] Trubek and Trubek, n 2 above.

1. *Shaming.* Member states will seek to comply with guidelines in order to avoid negative criticism in peer review and Council recommendations.

2. *Diffusion through mimesis.* The guidelines and information provided by the Commission and peer states put before national policy makers a coherent policy model they are encouraged to copy; the iterative nature of the OMC, benchmarking and peer review reinforce this process.

3. *Diffusion through discourse.* The OMC process might result in the construction of a new cognitive framework or a 'new perspective from which reality can be described, phenomena classified, positions taken, and actions justified'. Broadly conceived, discursive transformation may also include the development of a common vocabulary, use of symbols (for example, indicators), and changes in ordering assumptions and views on causality.[55]

4. *Networking.* The creation of new policy networks through the OMC within national governments (through correspondence in the formulation of National Action Plans, for example) and outside of government (soliciting input from civil society and social partners) will capitalise on a more robust and diverse body of knowledge, and facilitate social processes of deliberation and learning.

5. *Deliberation.* The process of deliberation among this diverse set of actors fosters exchange of policy knowledge and experience, allows actors to get to know each other's governing systems and ways of thinking, and promotes a common identity through continued interaction, socialisation and persuasion.[56]

6. *Learning.* Hemerijck and Visser define learning operationally as 'a change of ideas and beliefs (cognitive and/or normative orientations), skills, or competencies as a result of the observation and interpretation of experience'.[57] Trubek and Mosher observe that the OMC facilitates policy learning by a series of mechanisms:

> [T]hat destabilize existing understandings; bring together people with diverse viewpoints in settings that require sustained deliberation about problem-solving; facilitate erosion of boundaries between both policy domains and stakeholders; reconfigure policy networks; encourage decentralized experimentation; produce

[55] For a detailed discussion, see Jacobsson, n 2 above.
[56] Note that Zeitlin (in unpublished comments on Jacobsson and Vifell) argues that alternative theoretical frameworks such as Cohen and Sabel's conception of directly deliberative polyarchy, in which ends and means are continuously refined in relation to one another though discursive yet disciplined comparisons of different approaches to practical problem-solving, might be better suited to capturing the interpenetration of these elements within the OMC.
[57] A Hemerijck and J Visser, 'Policy Learning in European Welfare States' (2003) Unpublished manuscript, Universities of Leyden and Amsterdam, p 5.

information on innovation; require sharing of good practice and experimental results; encourage actors to compare results with those of the best performers in any area; and oblige actors collectively to redefine objectives and policies.[58]

Evidence of effectiveness

However plausible these mechanisms may be, measuring the OMC's impact and verifying its success or failure is more difficult and has fuelled debate over the efficacy of soft law. How do we know if these soft legal instruments actually work? If they do work, how and why, and do they necessarily lead to changes in the direction of the guidelines? A number of critics have argued that because it lacks 'hard' elements, the OMC is powerless to effect real change.

There has been some effort to assess the efficacy of the OMC. Zeitlin offers a valuable heuristic by dividing the impact of the OMC into four areas: (1) substantive policy change (including broad shifts in policy thinking); (2) procedural shifts in governance and policy making (including administrative reorganisation and institutional capacity building); (3) participation and transparency; and (4) mutual learning.[59] In each of these areas, there is some evidence that OMC processes are having impact but the extent of the impact varies among the areas. One can see some shifts in policy thinking of Member States (for example, wide adoption of EU concepts and categories)[60] and in forms of administrative reorganisation (eg, better horizontal integration of interdependent policy fields, increased decentralisation of policy services within Member States and greater attention to vertical coordination between levels of governance).[61] Further, there is some evidence that OMC processes are increasing levels of participation and

[58] Trubek and Mosher, n 51 above, at 46–47.

[59] J Zeitlin, 'Conclusion: The Open Method of Coordination in Action: Theoretical Promise, Empirical Realities, Reform Strategy' in J Zeitlin and P Pochet (eds) *The Open Method of Coordination in Action: The European Employment and Social Inclusion Strategies* (Brussels: PIE-Peter Lang, 2005).

[60] See, eg, JC Barbier, 'The European Employment Strategy: A Channel for Activating Social Protection?' J Zeitlin and P Pochet (eds) *The Open Method of Coordination in Action: The European Employment and Social Inclusion Strategies* (Brussels: PIE-Peter Lang, 2005); C Ehrel, L Mandin and B Palier, 'The Leverage Effect: The Open Method of Coordination in France' in *ibid*; K Jacobsson, *Soft Regulation and the Subtle Transformation of States: The Case of EU Employment Policy* 2002/4, SCORE (Stockholm: Stockholm Center for Organizational Research, 2002); K Jacobsson and A Vifell, 'New Governance Structures in Employment Policy-making? Taking Stock of the European Employment Strategy' in I Linsenmanns, C Meyer and W Wessels (eds) *Economic Governance in the EU* (London: Palgrave Macmillan, 2005).

[61] See, eg, M Lopez-Santana, 'How "Soft" Pressure from Above Affects the Bottom: Europeanization, Employment Policy and Policy (Re)Formulation (The Spanish Case)' (2004) unpublished paper; Ehrel *et al*, previous n; and R O'Donnell and B Moss, 'Ireland: The Very Idea of an Open Method of Coordination' in J Zeitlin and P Pochet (eds) *The Open Method of Coordination in Action: The European Employment and Social Inclusion Strategies* (Brussels: PIE-Peter Lang, 2005).

transparency (eg, increased involvement of non-state and sub-national actors)[62] and promoting mutual learning among Member States.[63]

While recent empirical findings suggest that the OMC and other new modes of governance in Europe exert some positive influence through the mechanisms described above, it is difficult to establish a causal relationship between new governance processes and policy outcomes.[64] For example, changes in Member States' policy orientations might precede the launch of OMC processes, Member States themselves helped to define OMC guidelines (ie, endogeneity problems), and improvements in OMC indicators might be caused by many other factors (eg, macroeconomic changes). These empirical difficulties pose considerable problems for OMC proponents because there simply is not a wealth of concrete evidence to substantiate claims that soft law mechanisms employed by the OMC have a positive and independent effect on outcomes, which may lead some to fall back on traditional arguments in favour of hard law.

Finally, few would argue that the OMC has fully realised its promise as a change-inducing process. For those who look at the OMC through a constructivist prism, this is no surprise. For constructivists, policy changes result from transformative processes such norm diffusion, social learning and persuasion, which are all time dependent and gradual. In this sense, it is understandable that the effects of soft forms of governance are not discernable in the short or even medium term because it takes a considerable amount of time for constitutive effects or a 'norms cascade' to take place. However, viewing the OMC from a constructivist perspective does not discount the possibility that softer forms of governance may usefully be integrated with harder forms. In fact, in employment policy, arguments can be made that hybrid forms of governance already exist.

Hybridity—the EES, hard law, and the structural funds

Most discussions of the OMC tend to present the OMC as a separate governance tool that is used instead of other possible EU governance tools,

[62] See, eg, C de la Porte and P Pochet, 'Participation in the Open Method of Coordination: The Cases of Employment and Social Inclusion' in J Zeitlin and P Pochet (eds) *The Open Method of Coordination in Action: The European Employment and Social Inclusion Strategies* (Brussels: PIE-Peter Lang, 2005); D Foden, 'The Role of the Social Partners in the European Employment Strategy' (1999) 4 *Transfer*; J Goetschy, 'The European Employment Strategy, Multi-level Governance, and Policy Coordination' in J Zeitlin and DM Trubek (eds) *Governing Work and Welfare in a New Economy: European and American Experiments* (Oxford: Oxford University Press, 2003); and Jacobsson and Vifell, n 60 above.

[63] Trubek and Mosher, n 51 above, documented the presence of learning-inducing mechanisms in the EES and have shown that policies have changed over time in line with the guidelines. See also M Ferrera and S Sacchi, 'The Open Method of Coordination and National Institutional Capabilities: The Italian Case' in J Zeitlin and P Pochet (eds) *The Open Method of Coordination in Action: The European Employment and Social Inclusion Strategies* (Brussels: PIE-Peter Lang, 2005); M Ferrera, M Matsaganis and S Sacchi, 'Open Coordination Against Poverty: The New EU "Social Inclusion Process"' (2002) 12 *Journal of European Social Policy*; and Jacobsson and Vifell, n 60 above.

[64] Zeitlin, 'Conclusion', n 59 above.

namely the hard law of EU employment legislation. The perception of the OMC as an alternative to harder forms of governance is so pervasive that the European Commission argued in its White Paper on Governance that the OMC 'should not be used when legislative action under the Community method is possible'.[65] Claire Kilpatrick argues that this perception of the OMC ignores

> the most significant characteristic of the new EU employment governance: it is already a self-consciously integrated regime where the OMC, ESF, and employment law measures each play distinctive and overlapping roles in realising social justice and competitiveness objectives. From this perspective, one of the most central achievements of the EES is that it builds bridges between employment legislation...and the European Social Fund.[66]

Kilpatrick develops her ideas about hybridity in employment governance by analysing both the separate contributions of the OMC, the structural funds and various forms of hard law. In this complex model, the OMC can promote actions that complement the effect of enforcing hard law as well as providing benchmarks and indicators that measure success in meeting goals that are shared by the OMC and various directives. And the structural funds not only provide resources to help effectuate their goals; they also have a procedural dimension that complements the procedural requirements of the OMC.

Kilpatrick views the most prominent characteristic of EU employment governance to be integration. Each component—the EES, employment legislation and the structural funds—plays an important role in the single domain of employment policy; failure by one part of the whole can skew the objectives and balance of the overall hybrid regime. The trick, as Kilpatrick points out, will be choosing the appropriate policy mix to deliver an employment objective, particularly when it is unclear whether one or all of the governance tools is not, or is perceived not to be, working.

Fiscal policy coordination: Broad Guidelines, the Stability and Growth Pact, and rationalism

The EU has created a complex system of fiscal policy coordination that was designed to ensure that all EU countries maintain fiscal discipline and balance their budgets over the medium term and avoid excessive deficits. The system covers all Member States but has special provisions governing the countries in the eurozone. Member States must report on their budgetary situations and provides for multi-lateral surveillance of budgetary performance.

[65] European Commission (2001), quoted in C Kilpatrick, 'New EU Employment Governance and Constitutionalism', this volume (ch 5 below).

[66] Kilpatrick, previous n.

While the system seeks to forestall excessive deficits, it also includes provisions to deal with them if they occur. Thus it includes mechanisms, procedures, and specific rules concerning what constitutes an 'excessive' budget deficit and specifies processes to be followed if deficits become excessive. These mechanisms include monetary sanctions as a last resort.

Coordination of national fiscal policies is achieved using three basic tools: Broad Economic Policy Guidelines, multilateral surveillance, and the Excessive Deficit Procedure (EDP). Taken together, these are sometimes referred to as the Stability and Growth Pact (SGP) [67]. This system includes both soft and hard elements. It employs 'soft' methods similar to the OMC: these include the BEPGs and multilateral surveillance. But, unlike the OMC, it also includes 'hard' measures that create binding obligations and expose non-complying states to potential sanctions and litigation in the ECJ. These are set out in the EDP and SGP.

Broad Economic Policy Guidelines (BEPG)

Recognising that national fiscal policy is a common concern, the treaty requires that eurozone states maintain the budget deficit limits set out in the criteria originally set for entry into the euro.[68] The BEPGs are designed to help. Founded on Article 99,[69] these guidelines form the center of coordination efforts at the Community level.[70] They are designed to provide a broad orientation for economic policies. The Guidelines begin as a Commission draft, which then forms the basis of a report by the Council of Economic and Finance Ministers (ECOFIN) to the European Council. The Council adopts a recommendation setting out the BEPGs for Member States and the Union.[71]

The BEPGs are soft law designed to encourage cognitive and, therefore, policy convergence around a set of fiscal policies that the EU-level actors deem helpful for remaining in compliance with the initial convergence criteria. Hodson and Maher argue that the guidelines are broad and general because 'the issue is one of coordination rather than compliance with an emphasis on orientation of policy rather than defined outcomes'.[72] The

[67] The term SGP is often used to refer to all of these tools and the process in which they are designed to play a part. This is technically incorrect. While this may seem insignificant, the tools have varying legal bases that will be important to the later discussion of forms of law. The SGP consists of two Council regulations and a Council Resolution designed to enhance the operation of other tools. The BEPGs, multilateral surveillance, and the EDP were created in the Maastricht Treaty

[68] Art 99(1) (ex 103(1)).

[69] K Dyson, *The Politics of the Euro-Zone: Stability or Breakdown?* (Oxford: Oxford University Press, 2000) 36.

[70] J von Hagen and S Mundschenk, 'The Functioning of the Economic Policy Coordination' in M Buti and André Sapir (eds) *EMU and Economic Policy in Europe: The Challenge of the Early Years* (Northampton, MA: Edward Elgar, 2002) 90.

[71] Art 99(2).

[72] D Hodson and I Maher, 'European Monetary Union: Balancing Credibility and Legitimacy in an Asymmetric Policy Mix' (2002) 9 *Journal of European Public Policy*.391–407.

BEPGs themselves have been the target of reform over the years, as they were first changed in 1997 to become more specific and to include country-specific recommendations[73], and then again recently in the name of 'streamlining' so that they will now be produced tri-annually.[74] Perhaps their most important function comes in combination with the mechanism for multilateral surveillance where they form the basis for analysis and critique of national performance.

Multilateral surveillance

Multilateral surveillance is the soft law half of a hybrid tool of coordination. Article 99 EC puts in place what is often known as the 'Early Warning System'. Multilateral surveillance gives the Council, on the recommendation of the Commission, the chance to make public or confidential assessments of the policies of the Member States and to give public or confidential recommendations as a result. This assessment is based on *Stability and Convergence Programmes*, which are updated annually by the Member States and submitted to the Commission and Council. The Council of Ministers then evaluates the programmes.[75] A primary goal is to ensure that the medium-term budgetary plans are conservative enough to avoid an excessive deficit. If the Council finds that this is not the case, it may make recommendations to the Member State to correct the problem.

Council Regulation 1466/97 of 7 July 1997 implements Article 99. It focuses on 'the strengthening of surveillance of budgetary positions and the surveillance and co-ordination of economic policies' and is often portrayed as the preventative measure. António Cabral, former Director of DG Economic and Financial Affairs of the Commission, notes six different elements to the 'backbone' of 1466.[76] States must submit programmes that focus on public finances and must include 'medium-term objective of a budgetary position close to balance or in surplus and the adjustment path towards this objective'.[77] The Council provides a non-binding assessment of that programme, making recommendations for changes where it sees fit. The Council then monitors the implementation of fiscal policy to ensure that sufficient 'wiggle room' is created so as to allow the automatic stabilisers to

[73] Dyson, n 69 above, at 36.

[74] Slight modifications can be made annually. See I Begg, D Hodson and I Maher, 'Economic Policy Coordination in the European Union' (2003) 183 *National Institute Economic Review* 67–77 at 75.

[75] 'Glossary' in A Brunila, M Bui and D Franco (eds) *The Stability and Growth Pact: The Architecture of Fiscal Policy in EMU* (New York: Palgrave, 2000): 418.

[76] J Cabral, 'Main Aspects of the Working of the SGP' in A Brunila, M Bui and D Franco (eds) *The Stability and Growth Pact: The Architecture of Fiscal Policy in EMU* (New York: Palgrave, 2000) 140–1.

[77] Reg 1466/97.

work when necessary without breaching the 3 per cent deficit limit. Those outside the eurozone must include statements on the effects of their policy on exchange rate stability. Finally, while the system targets individual states, the Council also assesses each programme based on whether its contents 'facilitate the closer coordination of policies and whether the economic policies of the Member State concerned are consistent with the broad economic policy guidelines'. Regulation 1466 is soft law designed to establish an 'early warning system' to help Member States avoid an excessive deficit and the processes of Regulation 1467.

Excessive Deficit Procedure (EDP)

The Excessive Deficit Procedure (EDP) is set forth in Article 104. Should an 'excessive' deficit exist, the EDP details a procedure designed to escalate through a number of sanctions, primarily informal at the beginning (naming and shaming, peer pressure), but moving on to formal sanction in case of non-compliance. It is the hard law part of the system. The EDP is implemented through Council Regulation 1467/97 of 7 July 1997. Should the early warning system of 1466 fail to prevent a deficit beyond the 3 per cent limit; Regulation 1467 on 'speeding up and clarifying the implementation of the excessive deficit procedure' is designed to act as a corrective, or 'dissuasive',[78] measure.

Regulation 1467 entered into effect on 1 January 1999. From the beginning, however, there have been important ambiguities in its operation. To begin, Art. 104 sets out that a deficit above 3 per cent is not excessive if 'the excess over the excess over 3% is only exceptional and temporary and the (government deficit) ratio remains close to the reference value'.[79] There is considerable manoeuvrability within those limits. [80] Should a deficit qualify for this exceptional status, however, the Procedure is still initiated—the opinion of the Commission is sent to the Economic and Financial Committee for comment and returned afterwards to the Commission for final revision before being sent on to the Council. It simply requires that those facts be taken into consideration. The Member State in question may defend the deficit to the Council 'as regards the abruptness of the downturn

[78] *Ibid* at 141.

[79] Art 104 EC.

[80] Reg 1467 moves toward clarifying the multiple qualifiers in the original treaty. An excess over 3% can be considered exceptional if: '(a) it results from an unusual event outside the control of the Member State or (b) it results from a severe economic downturn', where a severe economic downturn is defined as 'an annual fall of real GDP of at least 2 per cent'. The deficit is considered temporary if budgetary forecasts as provided by the Commission indicate that the deficit will fall below the reference value following the end of the unusual event or the severe economic downturn. The Regulation fails, however, to define the ambiguous term 'close to the reference value' upon which the entire set of exceptions rests. Considering that such a qualification automatically stops the Procedure, it is imperative that such qualifiers be clear.

or the accumulated loss of output relative to past trends'.[81] This is an option only if the annual fall of real GDP was less than 2 per cent, which implies that anything above that limit would be automatically justified.[82] In the Council Resolution, however, the Member States have committed themselves to defend deficits only if the annual fall in real GDP is at least 0.75 per cent.

Once this process has been triggered,[83] the process could in theory move quickly, imposing fines as early as 10 months from the start date. It is highly unlikely, however, that the procedure could ever work so quickly due to the nature of the data required to make such decision. The clock on the process begins once an excessive deficit is 'identified', not once an excessive deficit has occurred. Cabral notes that it could take three years from the beginning of the excessive deficit before sanctions are applied.[84]

Once the Procedure moves into sanctions, the progression is relatively straightforward. The first sanction is a non-interest bearing deposit, calculated so as to make the size of the deposit dependent upon the size of the excessive deficit.[85] The continued constitution of the deposit is subject to the following criteria:

—if, after two years since it was made the excessive deficit has not been corrected, the deposit is turned into a fine;

—if, before the 2 years have elapsed the Council considers that the excessive deficit has been corrected and abrogates its previous decision on the existence of an excessive deficit, then the deposit can be returned to the Member State.

In the latter case, the cost of such a sanction is then only the interest lost on the money deposited. Once a deposit has been made, the Council assesses every year whether the excessive deficit has been resolved. For each year the excessive deficit is not resolved, the Council requires an additional non-interest bearing deposit which is turned into a fine two years after its constitution. The result is that there is always one fine that may be changed

[81] Council Regulation 1467/97, Art 2.1.

[82] *Ibid* Art. 2(3).

[83] Where 'triggered' is defined as the Commission having made the recommendation that an excessive deficit exists and once the supporting data having been having made public by either March 1 or September 1 of any year.

[84] Cabral, n 76 above, at 147. In an ambivalent judgment in 2004 case C–27/04, the ECJ effectively suspended the EDP and, in Maher's words, 'fudged the legal significance of the deadlines that are meant to be followed under the procedure and thus allowed for the Council to put the procedure in de facto abeyance'. For a detailed discussion, see I Maher, 'Economic Policy Coordination and the European Court: Excessive Deficits and ECOFIN Discretion' (2004) 29 ELR 6.

[85] The amount of the first deposit is calculated using the following formula: *deposit in per cent of GDP = 0.2 + 0.1*(deficit - 3% of GDP).*

from a non-interest bearing deposit to a fine.[86] Should a second deposit be required, the amount of the deposit as a percentage of GDP increases.[87] No single deposit may be more than 0.5 per cent of GDP.[88]

A hybrid structure

The result of this complex set of legal provision is a two-track structure. Amtenbrink and de Haan summarise the structure as follows:

> The multilateral surveillance and excessive deficit procedure employ distinct modes of co-ordination. Whereas the latter can be described as a form of closed co-ordination, the former can be regarded as an application of the so-called open method of co-ordination. The open method relies on self-commitment by the Member States, peer review and benchmarking, placing emphasis on policy learning and consensus building, while the closed method tends to have top-down policy formulation and provides for binding rules and severe sanctions. Also in terms of the distinction between hard and soft law, where hard law lies at one end of a continuum and soft law at the other, the multilateral surveillance and the excessive deficit procedures are different, the latter being 'harder'.[89]

Similarly, Imelda Maher describes the SGP as 'a combination of soft law (multilateral surveillance) and hard law (the excessive deficit procedure) with the Pact having a preference for soft law measures'.[90]

Because of the importance of the 'soft' elements in the overall system of fiscal coordination, scholars have sought to account for the use of soft law in this area. Strikingly, unlike those who have studied the 'soft law' of the OMC, these scholars have relied primarily on rationalist perspectives, often explicitly citing the work of Abbott and Snidal.[91] Using a rationalist

[86] Cabral, above n 76, at 149.

[87] Deposits beyond the first are calculated using the following formula: *deposit in % of GDP = 0.1*(deficit - 3% of GDP).*

[88] Two final points bear noting regarding the sanctions system of the EDP. First, and oddly, monetary deposits and fines can only be calculated when non-compliance stems from an excessive deficit. No regulations exist laying out the system for calculating fines should a Member State be in violation with the limit on public debt. Should a case arise in which a Member State is in compliance with the limits on excessive deficits but is well beyond the limit of 60% on public debt as a percentage of GDP, no sanctions could be levied. Cabral notes that the likelihood is small, but possible. Finally, the money gathered from sanctions is dispersed among Member States who have adopted the euro and who do not have an excessive deficit. The money is handed out according to the qualifying Member States based on their percentage of total GDP.

[89] F Amtenbrink and J de Haan, 'Economic Governance in the EU: Fiscal Policy Discipline versus Flexibility' (2001) 40 CML Rev.1075–1106

[90] I Maher, 'Law and the OMC: Towards a New Flexibility in European Policy-Making?' (2004) 2 *Journal for Comparative Government and European Policy* 2.

[91] Most notably D Hodson and I Maher, 'Soft Law and Sanctions: Economic Policy Coordination and Reform of the Stability and Growth Pact' (2004) 11 *Journal of European Public Policy* 798–813; Maher, 'Law and the OMC, previous n; and Amtenbrink and de Haan, n 89 above.

approach, these authors suggest at least eight broad (and related) reasons why soft law is employed for fiscal coordination in the EU:

1. *Reduces negotiation costs.* Soft law reduces the levels of obligation, delegation, and/or precision, and therefore makes cooperative agreements possible. In the context of fiscal coordination, very name of the central instrument that protects against excessive deficits suggests that Member States had different ideas on what should take priority: stability or growth. They realised that once they signed the Treaty it would be hard to make changes, as that would require unanimity. So, to get agreement, they kept certain provision vague and/or non-binding. Hodson and Maher observe, 'by building in considerable discretion in the Pact, scope for reform without resort to formal legal changes is possible and more likely than if formal legal instruments—including the Treaty—had to be reformed'.[92] And, Amtenbrink and de Haaan argue that by choosing a 'rather vague and legally non-binding objective for the medium term' the Member States were able to reach an agreement that otherwise might not have been available.[93]

2. *Reduces sovereignty costs.* States can limit sovereignty costs through non-binding or imprecise arrangements that do not delegate extensive powers. With respect to the Pact, soft law 'provides a ready means for member states to express concern for budgetary discipline, without actually ceding control over fiscal policy', as Member States were unwilling to delegate a significant amount of authority to the Community level.[94]

3. *Deals well with uncertainty.* Soft law is well equipped to cope with uncertainty by providing the flexibility necessary to allow for the possibility of renegotiation and/or reform that may be required as circumstances evolve over time. Building considerable discretion in the Pact makes reform possible without having to resort to formal legal changes. Soft law also is appropriate when it is impossible to specify a precise standard. This is the case for the medium term balance standard that involves complex and contestable econometric projections. Hodson and Maher contend that it was for this reason that it this standard was left in the realm of soft law.[95]

4. *Facilitates compromise.* Soft law can take divergent national circumstances into account through flexible implementation, which in turn helps states deal with the domestic political and economic consequences of an agreement. Because soft law commits states to specific forms of discourse and procedure, it makes it easier for them to understand one another and thus achieve compromise over time. For example, recent Commission proposals for reform were, to large extent, based on prior experience with the Pact.[96]

[92] Hodson and Maher, previous n, at 802.
[93] Amtenbrink and de Haan, n 89 above, at 1085.
[94] Hodson and Maher, n 91above, at 810; Amtenbrink and de Haan, n 89 above, at 1085.
[95] Hodson and Maher, n 91 above, at 803–4, 806.
[96] Amtenbrink and de Haan, n 89 above, at 1085.

5. *Improves information flows and facilitates learning.* Soft legal instruments such as benchmarking, monitoring, and review develop a common discourse that helps states learn from one another. For example, the Pact's reporting mechanisms improve transparency and reduce information asymmetry between national economies.[97]

6. *Encourages consistency and disseminates information.* Soft law can improve transparency 'by providing a code of practice for states when preparing their stability or convergence programmes for the Council and Commission and a timeline for medium term adjustment'. These measures encourage consistency in bureaucratic decision-making and inform the wider public of official attitudes.[98]

7. *Deals well with imprecision of standards and goals.* Under the Pact, some of the agreed targets (eg, medium term target of close to balance or in surplus or the general government debt level of below 60 per cent of GDP or falling) are 'unavoidably imprecise and cannot give rise to binding legal obligations or legally enforceable sanctions.[99]'

8. *Structures competition and cooperation.* Soft law may work by creating competition among Member States that ramps up reputation costs as they relate to poor performance. In addition, soft law might provide a cooperation incentive whereby poor performance by participating Member States weakens the performance and attractiveness of the eurozone as a whole vis-à-vis the rest of the world. In both of these cases, soft law can increase the peer pressure on member states to perform well. [100]

9. *Sets the stage for hard law.* Soft law may be seen as a precursor to hard law, developing shared ideas, building trust, and establishing non-binding standards that can eventually harden into binding rules once uncertainties are reduced and a higher degree of consensus ensues.[101]

We can see that scholars discussing the possible role of 'soft law' in the SGP have drawn heavily on rationalist perspectives. They have framed the issues in terms of the self-interest of states and draw heavily on the work of Abbott and Snidal. Many are primarily interested in explaining why soft law exists and deploy soft law theory merely to account for the SPG's non-binding or soft track. Unlike those who have deployed 'constructivist' approaches to put forward a theory of why soft law measures may be *preferable* to hard law in the social policy field, some analysts of the SGP may believe that the choice of soft law is a second best solution and that it

[97] Hodson and Maher, n 91 above, at 803.
[98] *Ibid.* at 803, citing P Crowley, 'Stupid or Sensible? The Future of the Stability and Growth Pact' (2003) *EUSA Review* 9–11.
[99] *Ibid*; see also Amtenbrink and de Haan, n 89 above, at 1088.
[100] Amtenbrink and de Haan, n 89 above, at 1086.
[101] Maher, n 84 above.

would have been better to set up the system exclusively in the domain of hard law.[102]

The failure of the EDP and future of fiscal coordination

However, the whole issue of hard and soft law in the area of fiscal coordination has now been reopened as a result of recent experiences with the EDP and subsequent litigation in the ECJ. In recent years, the soft law system has failed to stop number of major countries from breaching the 3 per cent budget deficit limit set out in the EDP. As a result, the Commission has tried to set in motion the hard law sanctioning system but these efforts have been blocked by several of the larger Member States that have broken the 3 per cent ceiling. The result is that all parties are now calling for changes in the SGP, although there is no agreement on what changes should be made.[103] However, several scholars have called for a recalibration of the relationship between the hard and soft elements of the system, thus bringing into direct view the elements of hybridity on which it was based.[104] This is likely to spur further inquiries into the operation of both the hard and soft elements, as well as the possibilities for interaction between them.

In the context of the SGP, some of these inquiries will focus on the inability of hard law (the EDP) to deter non-compliance and analyse why the governance structure proved incapable of effective implementation of its enforcement provisions. However, the problems faced by the SGP are not just endemic to fiscal coordination in Europe; many regulatory institutions have trouble effectively imposing sanctions, particularly in the face of violations by powerful actors. Given the difficulties of implementing hard legal sanctions, the analysis with the most fruitful application might lie within a more intensive examination of the role of soft legal instruments. Specifically, a better understanding of the soft law components of the SPG (the BEPG and multilateral surveillance), which may be cultivated by looking more closely at OMC processes and drawing more from a constructivist perspective, could produce findings that are better capable of achieving policy goals without ever having to activate of the EDP in the first place. Hodson and Maher seem to recognise this already, as their analysis is lined with indirect references to processes such as learning and diffusion that are stressed in constructivist analyses.[105]

[102] This seems to be the conclusion of Amtenbrink and de Haan, n 89 above, who rely on Abbott and Snidal to explain why soft law was deployed in the Pact, but then argue that hard law is the preferable approach to ensuring that budget deficits do not occur.

[103] Reforms to the SGP advanced by the Council were agreed to in March 2005, further vitiating the EDP by offering countries easier excuses for breaching the 3% limit.

[104] See, eg, the related symposium in (2004) 42 *Journal of Common Market Studies*.

[105] See discussion above, in section on Hybrid structure in fiscal policy.

TOWARDS A THEORY OF HARD AND SOFT LAW: THE NEED FOR SYNTHESIS AND THE ISSUE OF HYBRIDITY

The survey of the literature on employment policy and fiscal coordination reveals two major lacunae in our knowledge. The first is the failure to create an integrated approach to soft law. As we have seen, scholars attempting to explain two rather similar soft law systems (OMC and BEPG) draw on different traditions; stress different reasons for the adoption of these approaches and suggest different functional roles for soft law. At the most general level, the rationalist account suggests that soft law is a way to allow Member States to avoid hard decisions and defer making choices that, it is alleged, hard law would require. On the other hand, the constructivist story indicates that use of soft law measures like the OMC may be a better way to bring about those very decisions and facilitate the hard choices rationalists that think are being deferred. Since reality probably reflects a mix of these two motives and effects, it seems clear that we need a synthetic approach to soft law that would integrate elements of these two perspectives.

There is, however, a second lacuna that becomes apparent as we explore these cases further. Note that in both cases we see the simultaneous presence of hard and soft legal processes. This is part of the explicit design of the fiscal coordination system, but it is also present in employment policy. In that area, although the three governance pillars operate independently, they increasingly refer to each other and are evolving towards a more integrated system. A synthetic approach to the use of soft law would help us understand better the use of soft measures in areas like fiscal coordination and employment policy. But it also would serve as the first step in the development of a theory of the relationship between hard and soft law, or what we have called *hybridity,* in cases like this.

A synthetic approach to soft law

The foregoing suggests that there are virtues to both constructivist and rationalist approaches to soft law. We have seen that rationalist approaches are very useful when we want to develop an understanding of how soft law regimes have emerged. But they seem less than adequate to offer an explanation of how these mechanisms may work to bring about change. For such an explanation, it seems necessary or at least desirable to draw on constructivist approaches such as those that have developed in the effort to explain the operation of the OMC.

This suggests that insights from these two separate approaches might best be merged in some form of synthesis. Thus, the analysis of the origins of the OMC might benefit from some of the rationalist insights that have helped scholars understand the emergence of the soft track in the SGP. At the same time, if constructivist approaches were employed more fully in the study of the operation of multilateral surveillance, we might be able to frame more cogent arguments about the relative effectiveness of hard and soft law in the budgetary area. This could make it easier to see how and when soft law might be a desirable alternative rather than simply a second best solution or a way station towards hard law.

This points to the desirability of an approach that draws on both these strands of thought. Such a synthesis could build on developments within IR theory and the theory of European integration. Recently, a large number of prominent IR scholars have asserted that the so-called rationalist–constructivist divide has been overstated and that the two approaches are in fact more compatible than not.[106] Fearon and Wendt claim that there are substantial areas of agreement, and where genuine differences exist they are as often complementarities as contradictions.[107] At the same time, there have been calls to bring constructivism into studies of European integration to complement the primarily rationalist approaches used by the mainstream approaches of liberal intergovernmentalism, neofunctionalism, and multilevel governance.[108] Thus Risse argues that there are at least three ways in which constructivism enriches the understanding of the European Union:

> First, accepting the mutual constitutiveness of agency and structure allows for a much deeper understanding of Europeanization including its impact on statehood in Europe. Second and related, emphasizing the constitutive effects of European law, rules, and policies enables us to study how European integration shapes social identities and interests of actors. Third, focusing on communicative practices permits us to examine more closely how Europe and the EU are constructed discursively and how actors try to come to grips with the meaning of European integration.

Jeff Checkel's study of 'why agents comply with the norms embedded in regimes and international institutions' is an effort to develop a synthetic approach. Checkel's study shows the interrelationship of rationalist and constructivist accounts by demonstrating that certain institutional contexts are more likely to facilitate argumentative persuasion and social learning. This, in turn, can lead to the reconstitution of interests thus changing rational calculations and fostering compliance.[109]

[106] See G Hellman, 'Forum: Are Dialogue and Synthesis Possible in International Relations?' (2003) 5 *International Studies Review* 123–53 and Risse, n 24 above, for discussions of theoretical synthesis.

[107] J Fearon and A Wendt, 'Rationalism v Constructivism: A Skeptical View' in W Carlsnaes, T Risse and B Simmons (eds) *Handbook of International Relations* (London: Sage Publications, 2002) 53.

[108] Risse, n 24 above, at 159–60; see also Christiansen, n 27 above.

[109] J Checkel, 'Why Comply? Social Learning and European Identity Change' (2001) 55 *International Organization* 553–88. T Risse, 'Constructivism and International Institutions: Toward Conversations across Paradigms' in I Katznelson and H Milner (eds) *Political Science: The State of the Discipline* (New York: Norton, 2002).also suggests that rationalist and constructivist approaches could usefully be integrated to build an understanding of international negotiations that incorporate both arguing and bargaining that could provide tools to break deadlock situations.

It seems clear that a similar effort at synthesis could be developed to provide a richer account of the role of soft law in the EU. Speaking in the context of the debate over the OMC, Kerstin Jacobsson highlights the need for such a synthesis:

> A theory of the OMC and its role for domestic policy change would have to take into account both the roles of ideas, interests, and power relations in explaining policy change. It would also have to take into account the interplay of interests and ideas. Ideational change may affect how actors perceive their interests, that is, interests may change as a consequence of learning and socialization ... A theory of the OMC would, moreover, have to be a multi-level and multi-actor, able to take into account the interplay of actors, and thus interests as well as power relations, at various levels of governance: supranationally, nationally, and subnationally.[110]

Dealing with hybridity

Hybridity is emerging as an important issue in EU law as more and more scholars discover the simultaneous presence of 'hard' and 'soft' measures in the same policy domains. This is certainly true in the two domains that we have explored. Hybridity, in this sense, may be the result of conscious design or it may come about because the same objective is being pursued through two routes, one of which leads to hard measures and the other to soft ones.

The fiscal coordination system is the classic example of conscious hybridity. The system relies primarily on the BEPGs and multilateral surveillance to reach its goals. But it also includes a set of binding rules that define excessive deficits in very specific terms, create a formal process that must be followed when an excessive deficit occurs, and includes sanctions for Member States that continue running such deficits. The BEPGs both respect national diversity and are designed to encourage reform while the excessive deficit procedure and its sanctions are supposed to deter states that might be tempted to free ride by running excessive deficits that might do harm to the common currency. The hybridity that Kilpatrick has shown to exist in employment policy may not have been part of an original design but the system is evolving towards a similar pattern in which hard and soft elements are deployed in the same arena and for similar objectives.

These cases suggest that hybridity may emerge when the EU is faced with a set of difficult and potentially contradictory imperatives. Take for example the fiscal coordination system. In this case, the EU must deal with the budgets of 25 different countries. Each has its own way of doing business and each may seek a different path towards the common goal of fiscal sustainability. The coordination system must operate in a multi-level system

[110] Jacobsson, n 2 above, at 100.

where much of the competence affecting economic policy rests at the Member State level yet common interests and interdependencies mean that each state has an interest in the behaviour of the others. It must at the same time encourage and promote reforms in fiscal practice while deterring purely self-interested behaviour and free riding. Given these varied and possibly conflicting goals, it is no surprise that the Union has sought to draw on both hard and soft methods and processes and to marry them in a single system.

It is true that this system has failed to work as originally hoped. In the current economic conjuncture several states, including some of the larger ones, have breached the excessive deficit limits for some time. The soft law system could not prevent this development and the Union's inability to deploy the hard law sanctions has forced the EU to reconsider the original design. The result has been a vigorous debate about the respective roles of hard and soft law in a new system, as well as an effort to pay closer attention to ways that would make the soft law system more effective. Hopefully, this debate will contribute to the development of a clearer understanding of the respective roles of hard and soft law in this and other domains and contribute to a more robust theory of hard and soft law and hybridity.

Part II

Case Studies: Europe

4

EU Race Discrimination Law: A Hybrid Model?

GRÁINNE DE BÚRCA*

INTRODUCTION

TAKING THE EXAMPLE of the European Union (EU) Race Discrimination Directive, this chapter takes the basic intuition of the experimental governance literature, that in seeking to achieve public interest objectives and to provide for public welfare 'instead of issuing detailed regulations, or specifying how services are to be provided, the state would set general goals, monitoring the efforts of appropriate actors to achieve those goals by means of their own devising',[1] and contrasts this with what will be called a human rights perspective. From a human rights perspective, the experimental governance approach raises the concern that, once characterised primarily in terms of flexible goals, important commitments may become empty of content and, if not expressed in more substantive and specific terms, their delivery will not be susceptible to any meaningful accountability. Starting out from this point of contrast between the human rights approach and the new governance approach, the chapter uses the example of EU anti-discrimination law in the field of race to outline a hybrid approach which jettisons neither the commitments of the rights approach nor the experimentalism of the new governance approach, but which seeks to combine the essential strengths of each.[2]

RIGHTS *VS* GOVERNANCE?

The tension depicted above between the rights model and the governance model overlaps with, although it is not the same as, the contrast which has

* Thanks to Nina Boeger for excellent research assistance.

[1] C Sabel, 'Beyond Principal–Agent Governance: Experimentalist Organizations, Learning and Accountability' <http://www2.law.columbia.edu/sabel/papers/Sabel.definitief.doc>

[2] New and experimentalist governance approaches have emerged on both sides of the Atlantic, and indeed elsewhere, in part as a function of the search for better and more effective ways of tacking social and economic problems under conditions of complexity. However, the flexibility and adaptability characteristics of new governance modes also serve the related but distinct goal of coping with strong diversity within a federalised system.

been drawn between a traditional law-making approach and a 'new governance' approach in the EU.[3] To take the most important features of the former: first, a human rights model is suspicious of voluntarism and of self-regulation and is premised on some element of hierarchy in terms of answerability for the pursuit of overarching norms, while an experimentalist governance approach is premised on a more heterarchical set of arrangements with an emphasis on peer or reputational accountability. Secondly, a human rights model places importance on a degree of definition and clarity in the content of the commitment in question, while an experimentalist governance approach prioritises revisability and open-endedness in the specification of goals, with an emphasis on the role of ongoing processes to give content to those goals in changing circumstances. Thirdly, while the human rights model places importance on the role of bottom-up-actors (civil society) in monitoring, enforcing and developing the regime, it sees these crucially as relying on the existence of a set of vertical or formal norms and institutions with which to interact for both strategic (enforcement) and legitimacy-enhancing purposes. The experimentalist governance model on the other hand is more radically bottom-up in seeing social actors/stakeholders as generative of norms, and responsible for the spread and dispersal of these through their ongoing practices and activities. Fourthly, the human rights model posits a significant role for courts in ultimately enforcing the content of the legal commitment, while in the experimentalist model the role of courts is at best a residual one to monitor the adequacy of the processes established and to allow for their disruption where they are malfunctioning.

The contrast between a commitment to securing well-defined, judicially enforceable individual rights and a belief in the virtues of open-ended and flexible policy-making with an absence of hierarchical monitoring, appears fairly stark. It seems highly unlikely that someone committed to the human rights paradigm as a means towards improving the personal and social conditions of disadvantaged persons would embrace the assumptions and prescriptions of the experimentalist governance approach. However, by focusing on what is quintessentially a human rights issue—that of race discrimination—I argue in this chapter that the development and operation of EU legislation in this field provides the elements for an approach combining positive features of both models, and which does not lose the essential strengths of either. Of course it must be acknowledged that there is a risk of doing exactly the opposite, in the sense that by seeking to develop a form of hybrid model, the strengths of each of the two approaches would be lost. On the one hand it could shackle the openness and experimentalism of the governance approach to the perceived rigidity of the human rights approach; and conversely it could sacrifice the commitment to content and harder-line

[3] J Scott and D Trubek, 'Mind the Gap: Law and New Approaches to Governance in the EU' (2002) 8 *European Law Journal* 1.

enforcement of agreed values under the latter, to a more elusive and less tangible pursuit of vague goals. Nevertheless, this chapter argues to the contrary, that the model of an EU framework directive with broadly defined objectives, premised on the need for the involvement of intermediate institutions, backed up by a network of relevant institutions and stakeholders, and supported by a set of programmes intended to mobilise and resource civil society actors and to generate a body of cross-national data and research, successfully combines significant elements of the experimental governance approach while retaining some of the incentive structure, and compliance back-up of the rights model with its legal framework, judicial interpretative role and formal sanctions.

THE RACE DIRECTIVE

The EU Council and Parliament in 2000, following many years of campaigning by non-governmental organisations (NGOs) and other interests, introduced a directive 'implementing the principle of equal treatment between persons irrespective of racial or ethnic origin' in a wide range of social and economic settings.[4] This directive was adopted as one of the three parts of an overall EU anti-discrimination package, the second being a framework employment directive which followed shortly afterwards, aiming to promote equal treatment in employment on grounds of age, disability, sexual orientation and religious belief, and the third part an action programme against discrimination. The two anti-discrimination directives were seen by some as the first steps towards a new kind of European social law, based on Article 13 of the European Community (EC) Treaty which had come into force in 1999 and which enabled the Council of Ministers to take action to prohibit discrimination on a number of specified grounds. The Race Directive in particular seemed to signal a move away from the previously omnipresent requirement to show a labour-market or internal-market justification for adopting legislation in the social realm, and contained several innovative features.

This directive has certainly not been free from criticism, and several weaknesses have been identified.[5] These include the lack of positive obligations created under the directive, and its focus on individual rather than on group discrimination, since although the concept of indirect discrimination helps to identify and address collective disadvantage,[6] the kinds of remedies

[4] Council Directive 2000/43/EC of 29 June 2000. See A Tyson, 'The Negotiation of the EC Directive on Race Discrimination' (2001) 3 *European Journal of Migration and Law* 199; Mark Bell, *Anti-Discrimination Law and the European Union* (OUP, 2002).

[5] See, eg, Bob Hepple, 'Race and Law in Fortress Europe' (2004) 67 MLR 1.

[6] Statistical evidence can be used to show that a particular practice 'would' (rather than does) disadvantage members of a particular ethnic group See, however, the critique by Damian Chalmers of the way in which the indirect discrimination criterion is used to challenge structural disadvantage, and his proposal for a dialogic ('intercultural evaluation') response: 'The Mistakes of the Good European' in Sandra Fredman (ed) *Discrimination and Human Rights: The Case of Racism* (OUP, 2001).

and response mechanisms called for by the directive are primarily individually focused.[7] Other criticisms concern the very category of 'race' on which the measure is premised, and the fact that although non-EU nationals are covered by the legislation, discriminatory treatment which is based on the person's nationality rather than race—assuming that this distinction is actually workable—is not covered.[8] However, the point of using the example of the directive here is not to appraise its various weaknesses and strengths but rather simply to use it deductively in sketching a possible approach which positively combines elements of the human rights and experimental governance paradigms in addressing complex social problems.

While all EC directives can in formal terms be described as framework laws, (since they are described in the EC Treaty as binding only 'as to the result to be achieved' but leaving 'to the national authorities the choice of form and methods'), the EU's use of directives did over time tend to become more detailed and less distinguishable in nature from the formally more prescriptive EC Regulations. This development gave rise to criticism and to proposals such as those which eventually appeared in the Protocol to the EC on the Application of the Principles of Subsidiarity and Proportionality, to adopt directives in less detailed form.[9] The Race Directive, however seems to be more genuinely framework in nature, in so far as it contains a general prescription—in this case the elimination of direct and indirect discrimination on the ground of racial or ethnic origin—to which States must commit themselves, but without prescribing in detail how this is to be achieved. It is the procedural and enforcement provisions of the directive, rather than its substantive policy prescriptions, which are laid down in greater detail.

The first article of the directive states that:

> The purpose of this Directive is to lay down a framework for combating discrimination on the grounds of racial or ethnic origin, with a view to putting into effect in the Member States the principle of equal treatment.

A broad definition of direct and indirect discrimination, which is derived in part from European Court of Justice (ECJ) case law on sex equality, and which includes harassment, is given. Action to protect against the victimisation of complainants is provided for, and the burden of proof on individual complainants is required to be lessened. States are not required but are permitted to pursue a degree of affirmative action in achieving the goals of the legislation. Further, the directive contains a qualified non-regression

[7] See Mark Bell, 'Walking in the Same Direction?: The Contribution of the European Social Charter and the European Union to Combating Discrimination' in G de Búrca, B de Witte and L Ogertschnig (eds) *Social Rights in Europe* (OUP, 2005).

[8] Mark Bell, *Anti-Discrimination Law and the European Union* (OUP, 2002) ch 7.

[9] This protocol was added to the EC Treaty by the Amsterdam Treaty in 1997, and is available electronically at <http://europa.eu.int/eur-lex/en/treaties/selected/livre345.html>

clause[10] and an indication that it sets only a minimum standard, which can be seen as articulating a weak encouragement to states to ratchet their standards upwards.[11] In addition to requiring the prohibition of direct and indirect racial discrimination across a range of social fields including access to housing, health, education, social assistance, employment, in both public and private spheres, the legislation requires that states disseminate information about the aims and content of the legislation to all persons concerned, and that they establish or designate equality bodies in each state to promote the principle of race equality, including by conducting studies, publishing research, and supporting complainants. The directive states that adequate administrative or judicial remedies, including conciliation procedures where considered appropriate, should be available to those seeking redress for discrimination, and sanctions, although not stipulated in more specific terms, are required to be 'effective, proportionate and dissuasive'.

Apart from the deliberately framework or outline nature of the directive, some of its individual provisions are themselves resonant of a 'new governance' approach, to use the title of this volume. States are asked in article 11 to

> promote the social dialogue between the two sides of industry with a view to fostering equal treatment, including through the monitoring of workplace practices, collective agreements, codes of conduct, research or exchange of experiences and good practices.

They are also obliged to encourage dialogue with relevant NGOs, and they must report every five years to the Commission on how they have implemented the various obligations contained in the directive. Finally, there is an express provision concerning the possible revision of the legislation in the light of the feedback received from the states. In proposing such a revision, the Commission must take into account the views of the EU's own anti-racism agency (EUMC)[12],of NGOs and of labour and industry (the social partners).

[10] It is qualified in the sense that it does not prohibit states from reducing their current standard of race equality provision, but it is a non-regression clause in the sense that it specifies that the directive itself cannot be used as justification for a reduction in their existing standards.

[11] Art 6(1) of the directive reads: 'Member States may introduce or maintain provisions which are more favourable to the protection of the principle of equal treatment than those laid down in this Directive'.

[12] This is the Vienna Monitoring Centre on Racism and Xenophobia, which will be discussed further below. The Centre has not been altogether a success since its establishment. Having taken two years from the time of its establishment to actually begin operating, it has not had a high profile in Europe even amongst anti-racism NGOs, being outshone in this respect by the Council of Europe's smaller but more active and focused European Commission on Racism and Equality. In 2002 the EU's Vienna Monitoring Centre was subject to a critical external evaluation, and subsequently became the object of international media attention when its decision to suppress a controversial report on anti-semitism in Europe was leaked. Its future is at present uncertain since the decision of the heads of government in December 2003 to propose merging its functions into those of a broader EU human rights (later called 'fundamental rights') agency. The Commission's proposal to establish such an agency was published following a consultation process: <http://europa.eu.int/comm/justice_home/news/consulting_public/fundamental_rights_agency/report_public_hearing_en.pdf>, see now COM(2005)280.

Aside from its framework nature and from these particular provisions, on the other hand, the directive also reflects aspects of a more classical human rights instrument[13]: in particular with its focus on the individual right to complain, the unequivocal prohibition of discrimination, the emphasis on the need for enforcement of rights, as well as the emphasis on the burden of proof and adequacy of sanctions, and finally the extensive invocation of international human rights instruments in the recitals.[14] The Commission in its recent Green Paper on equality and non-discrimination also described the directive as having introduced 'a rights-based approach to discrimination'.[15]

In addition to the mixture of rights-oriented and new-governance-style provisions, however, a number of aspects of the directive's interaction with other schemes and institutional arrangements have arguably helped to shape it into an interesting hybrid instrument. In the first place, the interaction of the legislation with the EU Action Programme against discrimination is significant.[16] Secondly, the operation of the legislation takes place against the background of the establishment of a number of specific networks (in

[13] See s 2.9 of the Commissions Green Paper on Equality and Nondiscrimination COM(2004)379, drawing attention to the international human rights context of the directive. Similarly, according to a report on *Strategic Litigation of Race Discrimination in Europe: From Principles to Practice* (2004):

> It should be remembered that while the Race Directive was a European creation, the human rights violations that it seeks to address are very international in character. The strong definitions and principles adopted in the Race Directive should be adopted and promoted in other fora. The Race Directive is particularly important in strengthening the largely weak discrimination jurisprudence of the European Court of Human Rights and the decisions of the UN Treaty bodies.

The latter report was published by the Migration Policy Group, Interrights and the European Roma Rights Centre as part of a three-year project (funded by the Open Society Institute and others) on 'Implementing European Anti-Discrimination Law'.

[14]

> (2) In accordance with Article 6 of the Treaty on European Union, the European Union is founded on the principles of liberty, democracy, respect for human rights and fundamental freedoms, and the rule of law, principles which are common to the Member States, and should respect fundamental rights as guaranteed by the European Convention for the protection of Human Rights and Fundamental Freedoms and as they result from the constitutional traditions common to the Member States, as general principles of Community Law.
> (3) The right to equality before the law and protection against discrimination for all persons constitutes a universal right recognised by the Universal Declaration of Human Rights, the United Nations Convention on the Elimination of all forms of Discrimination Against Women, the International Convention on the Elimination of all forms of Racial Discrimination and the United Nations Covenants on Civil and Political Rights and on Economic, Social and Cultural Rights and by the European Convention for the Protection of Human Rights and Fundamental Freedoms, to which all Member States are signatories.

[15] COM(2004)379.

[16] The programme follows the EU's practice of supporting social legislation with a policy programme, for example the Gender Equality Programme (2001–5), the Community Action Programme to Encourage Cooperation between the Member States to Combat Social Exclusion (2002–6), and Community Incentive Measures in the Field of Employment (2002–5). Action programmes in other 'social' fields such as education and environmental policy have also been adopted.

particular the RAXEN and ENAR networks, on which see more below) to promote anti-racism law and practice and to exchange information, knowledge and experience, and in the context of the existence of an EU agency dealing with racism and xenophobia.[17] A third feature is the move towards mainstreaming anti-racism norms and concerns within other EU policies,[18] including integrating them into the so-called Lisbon agenda (ie, the triangle of economic policy, employment policy and social policy coordination).[19]

Each of these aspects—the role of the action programme, the interaction with related networks, and the move towards 'mainstreaming'—will be discussed further below. It will be clear that some of these developments are more advanced than others, that some operate more effectively than others, and that there are various inadequately functioning features. But the argument of this chapter is not so much an empirical claim that the way in which the Race Directive is operating in the context of these other strategies, institutions and instruments forms a perfect hybrid of experimental governance and a human-rights approach, but rather that the combination of the different features described provides the framework for a hybrid model which potentially combines the strengths of both approaches.

THE INSTITUTIONAL CONTEXT OF THE LEGISLATION:

The evolving role of the action programme

Due in part to force of circumstance rather than design, and in particular on account of a changing political climate which is increasingly unenthusiastic about further attempts to regulate discrimination by legislating, the EC Commission has been concentrating its energies on the Race Directive and the framework employment directive rather than on proposing new legislation[20] as had previously been contemplated, or seeking to broaden or amend the existing measures. While the Race Directive itself was negotiated

[17] This will probably soon be transformed into a broader human rights agency: see n 12 above, and further below.

[18] See COM(1998)183 An Action Plan against Racism. Also Article 8 of the Decision Establishing a Community Action Programme to Combat Discrimination 2000/750/EC and para 11 of the Preamble thereto; more recently, one of the 'chapeau' Arts of part III of the ill-fated EU Constitutional Treaty, which was the part governing all of the EU's substantive policies, Art III–3 provided: 'In defining and implementing the policies and activities referred to in this Part, the Union shall aim to combat discrimination based on sex, racial or ethnic origin, religion or belief, disability, age or sexual orientation.'

[19] See the Commission's Green paper on Equality, n 13 above. More generally, see Mark Bell, 'Combating Racial Discrimination through the Employment Strategy' (2003–4) 6 *Cambridge Yearbook of European Law*, forthcoming.

[20] An exception is the recently adopted directive on gender equality in access to goods and services, Directive 2004/113, [1994] OJ L 373/37, which had a difficult journey through the legislative process, apparently on account of the lobbying power of the insurance and advertising industries which objected to the proposal to prohibit the use of sex-based actuarial factors.

and adopted in record time, apparently because of Member States' wish that year to appear to take rapid action in response to Jorg Haider's rise to power in Austria, the high political momentum rapidly ebbed away. This was particularly evident given the growing emphasis on anti-terrorism after September 11, and many EU states delayed in implementing the directive properly or at all.[21] Any new initiatives in the anti-discrimination field seem likely to take the form of 'incentive measures' (which require only a qualified majority rather than unanimity amongst the 25 states in the Council) rather than legislation.[22] The political will which led to the adoption of a measure as broad in scope as the Race Directive, which unlike all EU other anti-discrimination laws is not confined to employment-related discrimination, seems unlikely to revive for quite some time; and while this has disappointed those campaigning for similar legislation in relation to the other grounds (such as disability, sexual orientation, age etc), it has arguably had the unanticipated effect of channelling much of the Commission's energy and focus into rendering more effective and operative, in interesting ways, the existing legislation.

In using the EU 'action programme to combat discrimination' to support the implementation and development of the Race Directive, together with the framework employment directive, the Commission has promoted the involvement of civil society actors, it has openly acknowledged the inadequacy of its understanding of the set of problems which the directive seeks to regulate, it has commissioned and funded the gathering of a broad set of data from all states, and has encouraged the establishment of transnational networks of NGOs to participate in monitoring and making operational the legislation. While the action programme was not initially conceived specifically as a support for the directives, but rather as the third and distinct part of a European anti-discrimination package alongside the two directives, it has increasingly been used to support and develop the legislation, so that the strategies under each can be seen as complementary and mutually reinforcing.

The objectives of the action programme[23]—which correspond broadly to the three strands of action funded under it[24]—are firstly analysis and evaluation (conducting research, gathering data), secondly developing the

[21] The Commission brought infringement proceedings against nine Member States (Austria, Germany, Greece, NL, UK, Ireland, Belgium, LUX, Finland), following their failure to notify implementation of the Directive on time, and recently the ECJ ruled against several of these states for failing to adopt the Directive: see C–329/04, *Commission v Germany*, judgment of 28 April 2005, C–335/04, *Commission v Austria*, judgment of 4 May 2005, C–320/04, *Commission v Luxembourg*, judgment of 24 February 2005, C–327/04, Commission v Finland, judgment of 24 February 2005.

[22] Equality Green Paper, n 13 above, at 15. A European Action Plan on Disabilities was also adopted in October 2003, COM(2003)650 final, setting out a number of initiatives to promote access of people with disabilities to employment, lifelong learning, development of new technologies and accessibility to the built environment.

[23] See Art 2 of the Council Decision 2000/750 EC establishing a Community Action Programme to Combat Discrimination (2001–6) [2000] OJ L 303/23.

[24] *Ibid*. Art 3.

capacity to combat and prevent discrimination (funding the activities of NGOs, spreading best practices), and thirdly 'promoting the values underlying the fight against discrimination' (promoting awareness through publicity, seminars, providing information). Amongst the activities which it is to support are the development and dissemination of quantitative indicators and benchmarks, and the promotion of networking and transnational cooperation. The Commission is required to cooperate regularly with NGOs and the social partners in the context of the action programme, to promote dialogue between all parties, and to encourage 'an integrated and coordinated approach' to combating discrimination. Access to the programme is open to all bodies, public and private, who are 'involved in the fight against discrimination'.

There are only passing references to legislation in the decision setting up the action programme and its priorities, one being in the first strand of action (analysis/evaluation) which mentions the evaluation of legislation in the field, and the other in the third strand (promoting values/awareness-raising) which mentions 'the organisation of seminars in support of the implementation of Community law in the field of non-discrimination'. Despite this initial failure to conceive of a structured relationship between the directives and the programme, however, there has been an evolution of the action programme in practice towards a more sustained support for the operation of the legislation, and a more organised interaction between the two instruments. At least one impetus in this direction has probably come from an initial external evaluation of the action programme in 2003 which reached the conclusion that a more integrated anti-discrimination strategy was needed, and specifically that a better interaction between the directives and the programme (or in the terms of the report, between the legislative and the programmatic aspects of the strategy) should be developed.[25] On the other hand, the evaluation report also noted that despite the lack of clarity and planning, that there had in fact been a degree of interaction in practice between the directives and the programme, at least in the area of awareness-raising. And in a follow-up evaluation report in 2004, it was said that 'the link between the programme and the strategy, and in particular between the programme and the legal approach, has been reasserted' and that 'the programme now appears to be more in line with the life cycle of the legal approach'.[26]

Under its three strands of analysis/evaluation, capacity-building, and awareness-raising, the principal ways in which the action programme has

[25] The report concluded that 'the programme must have a clearly defined role in relation to the two directives, the link between the programme-planning tool (concrete actions) and the legislative tools (directives) must be clear, and both approaches should be mutually supportive'. The evaluation report was prepared in 2003 by Deloitte & Touch, and published by the Commission's Government Services in April 2004.

[26] See the report, available online at: <http://europa.eu.int/comm/employment_social/fundamental_rights/pdf/eval/grepexsum_en.pdf>

interacted with the legislation have been through the funding of transnational networks of or umbrella NGOs active in the field of anti-discrimination, to develop their capacity and expertise further,[27] the funding of research and data collection[28] and the publicising of the EU legislation and its potential.

Strand one: analysis/evaluation

Under the action programme's first strand, the Commission provided funding for the establishment of a network of equality bodies which the Member States were required under the directive to establish or designate in order to provide support to victims of discrimination, and to issue reports and recommendations. The network was intended to promote exchanges of experience and good practice between these equality bodies. The funding was put towards a project entitled *Towards a Uniform and Dynamic Implementation of EU Anti-Discrimination Legislation: The Role of Specialised Bodies*,[29] coordinated by the Migration Policy Group NGO and led by the Dutch Equal Treatment Commission. It is a network of approximately 20 national monitoring bodies covering some or all of the grounds of discrimination listed in Article 13 EC, established with the aims of

> promoting the uniform interpretation and application of the anti-discrimination legislation, and stimulating the dynamic development of legal equal treatment in Member States, as permitted by Art 6(1) of the Race Equality Directive.[30]

This combination of a commitment to 'uniformity' and 'dynamism' will be discussed further below, but for present purposes a significant factor is the encouragement via the action programme of actors other than courts to become involved in both the interpretation and the development of the legislative standards. The participants in the network are not only the staff of national equality bodies but also invited experts and others who can usefully advise on their work. Finally, the action programme also

[27] See, for a more critical evaluation by the external evaluators of the initial tranche of funding of this second strand, <http://europa.eu.int/comm/employment_social/fundamental_rights/pdf/eval/casestudta_en.pdf>

[28] The funding available under the Programme is however limited when compared, eg, to the EQUAL initiative on employment-related equal opportunities which is backed by the European Social Fund €98.4 million over five years, as compared with. €3,000 million for EQUAL for 6six years (2000–6) <http://europa.eu.int/comm/employment_social/equal/index_en.html>

[29] *Towards the Uniform and Dynamic Implementation of EU Anti-discrimination Legislation: the Role of Specialised Bodies* <http://www.migpolgroup.com/programmes/default.asp> ('specialised bodies'), also available on the the Social Affairs Directorate General of Commission's website on the Europa server, <http://www.europa.eu.int/comm/employment_social/ >'action programme at a glance'.

[30] Meetings of the network have so far been held or scheduled within this project on the following topics: proving discrimination (monitoring, statistics, situation testing); how to meet the requirements of protection against discrimination and gender equality; equal pay; enforcement and remedies against discrimination in working life; goods and services; strategic enforcement.

funded an assessment of the equality bodies established, which was provided in a 2000 report.[31]

As far as the funding of research and data collection is concerned, the Commission has used the programme to underpin the directives by setting up groups of legal and other experts to provide it with data, including comparative information on the situation in the different Member States, as well as information about the problems encountered by each state with regard to data collection itself. Whilst the Commission is the coordinator of the action programme, the work is carried out primarily at national and at local level. The Commission seems clearly conscious of the limits of its information and the importance of continuous sources of reliable information in order to address the problems in practice. It seems indeed sceptical about its own capacity and that of national authorities to 'assess the real extent of the challenges that exist and to measure the effectiveness of legislation and policies to tackle discrimination,'[32] due to the lack of adequate mechanisms to collect data and to monitor trends and progress in Member States. One of the problems is that much of the data on discrimination, and in particular on race discrimination, is difficult to access. Other difficulties are created by privacy and data protection laws.[33] The Commission however is advocating,

[31] Promoting Diversity: 21 bodies promoting diversity and combating discrimination in the European Union: <http://www.europa.eu.int/comm/employment_social/fundamental_rights/pdf/legisln/mslegln/equalitybodies_exec_en.pdf>

The report assesses of the 21 bodies chosen on the basis of:

(1) their structure, mandate and legal basis, their independence and budget.
(2) their competences in providing services directly to victims, i.e. whether they are restricted to an advisory role or have formal powers to investigate reported cases of discrimination (UK and Ireland), whether they have standing to bring court cases (Belgium) or can act as formal quasi-judicial decision making bodies (eg, Ireland (legally biding rulings) or Holland (advisory rulings)).
(3) Their role in the political process and how far that role is formalised.
(4) Their role in information spreading, research and awareness raising.

The report concludes that whilst a small number of Member States (eg, UK, Ireland) were 'willing to go beyond the minimum standards set out in Community law' by setting up bodies with competences for all grounds of discrimination within Art. 13 EC Treaty, in most states there are shortfalls.

[32] Equality Green Paper, n 13 above, at 15.

[33] The Commission sent out questionnaires to all Member States in 2001 to find out what Member States did to collect data on discrimination, and what particular difficulties they encountered. These were followed up in 2003 in discussions with the Directors of Social Statistics in Member States. The Commission highlighted the following difficulties:

(1) Data on discrimination is generally measured by proxy indicators (eg, employment and unemployment rate) indicating the impact of discrimination rather than directly.
(2) Specific data will only be made available if there is a clear legal mandate on the part of the recipient to have it disclosed.
(3) Data on some groups will be scarce for cultural reasons and to avoid risk of stigmatisation, e.g. information on sexual orientation or the collection of data desegregated in respect of racial or ethnic origin
(4) Data, even though it may be useful, will be collected in a piecemeal manner (e.g. number complaints filed may give an indication but depends on how many people actually file them).
(5) The issue of data protection is reinforced by EU Directives on the subject.

See the discussion paper on the collection of data to measure the extent and the impact of discrimination, <http://europa.eu.int/comm/employment_social/fundamental_rights/pdf/glance/discuspap_en.pdf>

despite these sensitivities, 'a dialogue with national authorities and other stakeholders on possible ways to improve data collection in this area'.[34]

With a view to the development of indicators and benchmarks, which was one of the specific projects identified in the action programme, the Commission established a Working Group on data collection in 2003, led by the Finnish government and working in conjunction with the European Monitoring Centre on Racism and Xenophobia (EUMC),[35] in order to develop indicators to measure the existence and causes of discrimination. Two reports were commissioned and published in 2004, one a comparative study of data collection on discrimination in the US, Canada, Australia, UK and the Netherlands,[36] and the other a study on data collection to measure the impact and extent of discrimination in Europe.[37]

The other major part of the analysis/evaluation strand of the action programme which is relevant to the interaction with the Race Directive concerns the funding of 'independent experts' to assist in monitoring the transposition of the directives. The programme has funded three working groups of independent experts, coordinated by the Migration Policy Group (on racial and religious discrimination), the University of Leiden (on sexual orientation discrimination) and University of Galway (on disability) respectively, to examine the transposition of the directives into national legislation in all 25 Member States. The initial 'country reports' which were produced on racial and religious discrimination were fairly factual, concentrating on describing the situation under national law and the extent to which it corresponds with the terms of the directives.[38]

Within the Commission at the same time, a 'legal working group' of civil servants representing the Member States was also working on transposition, but it seems that these state representatives were not particularly active in promoting and developing the legislation. The aim was for them to (1) develop good practice and (2) exchange experiences over the legislation, but according to a key Commission official working in the relevant unit, many states showed little interest in their neighbour's legislation and no real benefits came out of three years of the legal working group's operation: in her view it had therefore 'outlived its life'.[39] The external evaluation

[34] Equality Green Paper, n 13 above, at 16.

[35] See n 12 above, and n 57 below.

[36] See <http://europa.eu.int/comm/employment_social/fundamental_rights/pdf/pubst/compstud04_en.pdf>

[37] <http://europa.eu.int/comm/employment_social/fundamental_rights/pdf/pubst/compstud04fin.pdf>

[38] Available at <http://www.europa.eu.int/comm/employment_social/fundamental_rights/legis/msleglnracequal_en.htm> These reports overlap to some extent with earlier reports produced outside the programme, as part of *Implementing European Anti-Discrimination Legislation*, a joint initiative by MPG, ERRC and Interrights, which does not receive Commission funding. See link at <http://www.migpolgroup.com/programmes/default>. From the individual EUMC reports, a *Comparative Analysis of National and EuropeanLlaw* was drawn up 2002 by MPG, ERRC and Interrights.

[39] Barbara Nolan, Comment at Prague Anti-Discrimination Conference, July 2004.

report on the programme indeed had already drawn attention to and criticised the 'limited exchanges between groups of experts and between the latter and the legal working group.'[40] As a consequence, the separate expert groups were merged in 2004[41] so that there would henceforth be one set of 25 experts, with one person each responsible for all the different grounds of discrimination within a given member state. The information which has emerged from this process of monitoring the legislative implementation so far gives a mixed picture, according to the Commission.[42] While the deadline for transposition of the directives passed on 19 July 2003,[43] many states had not used the three preceding years following the adoption of the directive to introduce the necessary provisions, and representatives of civil society have been critical of the lack of consultation in several states during the process of implementation. Indeed, this links with one of the interesting findings of the 2003 evaluation report of the action programme, which was that the Member States had not been active participants under the 'awareness-raising' strand of the programme either—only 9 out of 25 having sought funding which was available for this purpose. These results so far suggest on a range of fronts that the non-state actors—the NGOs, 'experts' and other civil society actors—are the more dynamic and committed interlocutors in the promotion of EU anti-discrimination legislation, thus supporting one of the assumptions on which the new governance approach is premised.

Strand two: capacity-building

The largest proportion of the action programme budget is spent on activities under this second strand, which essentially concern the funding of NGOs, public authorities, social partners, universities and other intermediate institutions of various kinds. The largest proportion of the strand two budget in turn is spent on some 27 'transnational partnerships' for the exchange of information and good practice in fighting discrimination.[44] To

[40] See n 25 above.

[41] <http://europa.eu.int/comm/employment_social/fundamental_rights/pdf/prog/budgetwork2003_en.pdf>, p 2.

[42] In some countries in 2004, draft legislation was still under discussion or had not yet even been formally tabled, or the legislation did not yet cover all of the territory of the Member State or all of the relevant levels of government. In countries where national legislation had been adopted, there was often evidence that this did not fully transpose all of the provision of the directives. Particular problems seemed to include the new definitions of direct and indirect discrimination, the notion of harassment, the introduction of novel legal concepts, and the requirement to ban racial discrimination in areas outside employment. See the Commission's Equality Green Paper, n 13 above, at 14.

[43] The deadline for the Race Directive was 19 July 2003, for the Employment Directive 2 December 2003 although some Member States have opted to avail of the right to request an addition of up to three years to implement the provisions relating to age and disability.

[44] To give an idea of the scope of the funding, among the 27 projects selected for funding, their focus included: (i) combating discrimination in public administration including health and social care, policing, trade unions, education and local authorities; (ii) equal access to goods and services; (iii) discrimination in the media; (iv) improvement of training for lawyers; (v) discrimination specifically on grounds of disability and mental health or against specific religious beliefs; (vi) multiple discrimination situations; (vii) racism in football.

qualify, there must be a range of actors from at least three states, and the activities must involve the transfer of information, lessons learned and good practices developed, and they must include a comparison of the effectiveness of processes, methods and tools related to the chosen themes, as well as exchanges of personnel, the joint development of processes , strategies and methodology, and the adaptation to different contexts of the methods, tools and processes which have been identified as good practices.[45]

Despite rising levels of interest and participation in this part of the programme,[46] the Commission was critical of the quality of the projects, although it seems likely that at least two of the reasons for this lack of quality may have lain in the criteria of eligibility for funding. On the one hand, the 'broad approach' (ie, targeting all grounds of discrimination and not only one such as race), and on the other hand, the strictly cross-border approach made it difficult for good organisations used to working with particular target groups to qualify for project funding.[47]. Dissatisfaction with the effectiveness of the first set of transnational partnerships was also expressed in a critical interim report by external evaluators.[48] In the second batch of projects selected for funding in 2004, the focus was on three key sets of activities: (1) the training of legal practitioners and NGO representatives, (2) the development of monitoring and data collection tools, and (3) networking amongst equality bodies, researchers, public authorities or civil society actors. In addition to the funding of these transnational projects, the capacity-building strand of the action programme also provides core funding to a group of four European umbrella NGOs: the European Disability Forum (EDF), the European Network Against Racism (ENAR), the European Older Persons Platform and ILGA-Europe (International Lesbian and Gay Association). Funds are used to 'allow these organisations to tackle discrimination, promote equality and involve their members in a range of activities'.[49] One example where an umbrella organisation does not exist and where the Commission declared an interest in funding one, on the basis that 'existing needs are not being met by current organizations' is that of a transnational Roma rights organisation. Finally, in a separate initiative carried out by the Migration Policy Group, one of the major NGOs which works with the Commission on anti-racism and which has been funded to

[45] This is a description of the compendium of transnational actions funded in 2001: <http://europa.eu.int/comm/employment_social/fundamental_rights/pdf/prog/compendium2001_en.pdf>, p 3.

[46] See newsletter 'Equal Rights in Practice', available from the Commission at <http://www.stop-discrimination.info>, spring 2004 (the 'newsletter'), noting a 22 % increase in applications to the Commission's call for tender in 2003, compared with the first call in 2001.

[47] Equality Green Paper, n 13 above, at 16.

[48] See n 27 above.

[49] Equality Green Paper, n 13 above, at 17; (see Action Plan Report, 2000, where the aim was to 'mainstream' the fight against racism by integrating it into many other Community policies and programmes.

carry out various projects under the action programme, a report on strategic litigation of the Race Directive which was not funded under the action programme but which clearly engages with many of the same themes and problems was undertaken.[50]

It seems in general that the capacity-building funds have greatly helped the NGOs to build up independent lobbying power at national level. Umbrella NGOs are also more likely to bring test case litigation before national courts to have them referred to the ECJ in order test the interpretation of the directives.

Strand three: awareness-raising/promoting values

In addition to a 'Europe-wide information campaign' there are three areas of activity under this final strand of the action programme: conferences, seminars for judges and practitioners, and 'special events' at national level through funding provided to ministries, NGOs and other intermediate organisations. Also in 2003 the Commission began a five-year publicity campaign under the slogan 'For Diversity—against Discrimination', with a view to heightening sensitivity towards discrimination and the benefits of diversity, and to draw attention to the existence of new legal rights against discrimination. The campaign has its own website < http://www.stop-discrimination.info> and a newsletter, and national working groups consisting of national authorities, social partners and NGOs are brought together at various times to develop awareness-raising activities.

In general, there seems to be some disappointment so far with this particular strand of activities: both in terms of a lack of adequate response to some of the tenders for funding, and also because of the failure (due to the conditions for eligibility set by the Commission) to target specific groups and messages in a more focused way. As noted above, too, the states themselves have not availed of the opportunities to apply for funding to promote awareness of race-discrimination issues and of the legislation. The potential for use of this kind of funding, however, is evident.

Complementary institutions: the agency and the networks

In addition to the support provided—albeit in an originally unplanned way—by the action programme to the functioning of the directives, the second relevant feature of the anti-discrimination regime is the operation of other institutional supports, in particular the EU agency dealing with

[50] *Strategic Litigation of Race Discrimination in Europe: From Principles to Practice*, 2004, report prepared by the MPG, Interrights and the European Roma Rights Centre as part of a three-year programme on 'Implementing European Anti-Discrimination Law' (2001–4); see link on <http://www.migpolgroup.com/programmes/default.asp>

racism and xenophobia and the various networks which have been established to tackle the same subject. While some of these have existed for a number of years—the EUMC and the RAXEN network, for example—others, including some of the networks funded by the action programme have only recently been established, and yet others—such as the European Fundamental Rights Agency—are still in the pipeline.

The rise of agencies—and more particularly their rapid proliferation in recent years—has been identified as one of the manifestations of a transformation in European governance.[51] Of course, this phenomenon has not necessarily been greeted as a positive or even neutral development by all. For some, the accountability of agencies raises significant questions,[52] and the suspicion has been expressed that the creation of new agencies and the delegation of tasks to them could be a way for the main political institutions to evade political responsibility.[53] Yet agencies in the EU context, by comparison with the US where they tend to be autonomous and powerful decision-making bodies ('the fourth branch of government') have until recently tended to be institutions whose powers were primarily information-based.[54] More recently, however, the Commission has proposed the establishment of 'regulatory agencies' in the sense of agencies which would have power either to take binding decisions or to carry out or implement policies which have been adopted by others.[55] A number of EU agencies with particular powers of this kind already exist, for example the Office for Harmonisation in the Internal Market, the Community Plant Variety Office, and the European Agency for the Evaluation of Medicinal Products. Apart from these, most of the previously established agencies at EU level—including the Vienna EUMC—are charged with gathering, analysing and disseminating information on the policy area with which they were concerned, and they have also been mandated to liaise with or to coordinate networks of actors in the relevant policy field, and they have sometimes been required to conduct research and to make proposals. Without necessarily having binding decision-making powers, EU agencies can feed into policy making in more or less influential ways by the data they gather, the expertise they marshal, the actors they mobilise and the advice they provide. A great many scholarly categorisations and taxonomies of EU agencies have been proposed,[56] analysing 'three waves of agencification' which are said to

[51] R. Dehousse, 'Misfits: EU Law and the Transformation of European Governance' Jean Monnet Working Paper 2/2002 <http://www.jeanmonnetprogram.org/papers/02/020201.html>

[52] D. Curtin, 'Mind the Gap: The Accountability of the EU Executive', 2003 Walter Van Gerven Lecture, (Groningen: Europa Law Publishing, 2004).

[53] C Harlow, *Accountability in the European Union* (OUP, 2002) 75–78.

[54] G. Majone 'The New European Agencies: Regulation by Information' (1997) 4 *Journal of European Public Policy* 262–75.

[55] See COM(2002)718,'The Operating Framework for European Regulatory Agencies' and the subsequent report of the European Parliament A5 0471/2003 of December 2003, and the Conclusions of the Council of 29 June 2004.

have occurred so far. Yet whichever taxonomy is preferred, it is undeniable that the establishment of agencies is a rapidly proliferating phenomenon in the EU context. For all their variety and range, their spread can be seen as one manifestation or dimension of the new governance trend in so far as they are transnational, information-based, largely non-hierarchical, network-coordinating organs, operating in a multi-level context and feeding into the policy-making process in different ways.

The existing anti-discrimination agency: EUMC

The European Union Monitoring Centre on Racism and Xenophobia—one of the 17 EU agencies at present—was established in 1997 by an act of the Council of Ministers,[57] even before Article 13 of the EC Treaty was in existence and at a time when the EC's legal competence to act in the field of anti-racism and indeed to set up such a centre was called into question.

The main task it was given was to provide the Community and its Member States with 'objective, reliable and comparable information and data on racism, xenophobia and anti-Semitic phenomena at the European level in order to establish measures or actions against racism and xenophobia'. On the basis of the data collected, the EUMC was expected to study the extent and development of the phenomena, to analyse their causes, consequences and effects, to work out strategies to combat racism and xenophobia and to highlight and disseminate examples of good practice regarding the integration of migrants and minority groups. One of its core activities has been to coordinate the European Information Network on Racism and Xenophobia (RAXEN), a network designed to collect data and information at national as well as at the European level, and to disseminate it in cooperation with the EUMC.

The EUMC has been dogged by various difficulties since it began its activities in 1998. It did not have fixed premises from which to operate until 1999 and was not fully staffed until 2000, and it has not had a high profile in the field of European anti-racism activities. The smaller Council of Europe body, the European Commission on Racism and Intolerance (ECRI)—with which the EUMC is called on in its founding regulation to cooperate closely—is generally acknowledged to have been more successful in carrying

[56] Some examples are E Vos, 'Reforming the European Commission: What Role to Play for EU Agencies?' (2000) 37 CML Rev 1113; M Everson, 'Independent Agencies: Hierarchy Beaters?' (1995) 1 *European Law Journal* 180; A Kreher, 'Agencies in the European Community: A Step towards Administrative Integration in Europe' (1997) 4 *Journal of European Public Policy* 225; M Shapiro, 'The Problems of Independent Agencies in the United States and the European Union' (1997) 4 *Journal of European Public Policy* 276; M Flinders, 'Distributed Public Governance in the European Union' (2004) 11 *Journal of European Public Policy* 520; D Geradin and N Petit, 'The Development of Agencies at EU and National Levels: Conceptual Analysis and Proposals for Reform', Jean Monnet Working Paper 1/2004.

[57] Regulation (EC) No 1035/97 of 2 June 1997 (OJ L 151, 10 June 1997).

out very similar tasks in the 'wider Europe', despite having fewer resources. According to the external evaluation report of the EUMC which was carried out in 2002, despite the fact that almost six years had passed since the adoption of the Regulation establishing the agency, it remained impossible to measure the effect or impact of its output, so that it could not demonstrate 'value for money' for the budget which it had committed.

The Commission subsequently acknowledged most of the criticisms made by the external evaluators, and proposed some changes to the regulation which established the EUMC agency. In the first place the Commission accepted that with regard to the agency's data collection function, the objective of comparability had not yet been achieved to any substantial degree, nor had any assessment of the effectiveness of the anti-racist policies of individual Member States been possible on the basis of its work.[58] Part of the reason for this was delay—both in the establishment of the agency itself and in the coming into operation of the RAXEN network, so that very little had yet been done in terms of overcoming the problem of the very different definitions across Member States in relation to racism and xenophobia. Another of the difficulties faced by the agency was the variability of Member State responses to the agency's attempt to hold regular round tables, to bring together national civil society actors, researchers, governments etc. The lack of a communications strategy for disseminating information and data was also criticised. Significantly, one of the proposals made by the Commission in response to the evaluation was for the agency's reports to be increasingly focused on and better linked to the EU's priorities in the fields of employment, social inclusion and anti-discrimination. Also, the Commission proposed that the agency's mandate—which was established before Article 13 EC or the anti-discrimination directives were adopted—should be amended to reflect the new legal competences.

A final criticism made by the evaluators concerned the structure and membership of the management board, which the evaluators felt was insufficiently skilled for the tasks faced by the board. Consequently, they recommended that the board should consist of member state representatives. The EUMC board itself resisted this recommendation strongly, on the grounds of the need for independence, and the Commission eventually proposed a compromise solution (mirrored in its recent proposal for the establishment of an EU Fundamental Rights Agency) whereby the membership of the management board could draw on the expertise of the existing heads of national specialised bodies (whether equality agencies, ombudspersons etc) which were required to be set up under the Race Directive. Following the findings of the external evaluation, the Commission initially published a proposal to amend the regulation establishing the

[58] Commission Communication on the European Monitoring Centre on Racism and Xenophobia, COM(2003)483.

EUMC agency to reflect the various changes proposed.[59] In particular the proposal for involvement in the management board of key personnel from the national equality bodies required under the Race Directive, and the requirement of a closer link between the activities of the agency and the priorities of the EU in anti-discrimination, social exclusion and employment, were aimed at strengthening the interaction between the Race Directive and the activities of the EUMC.

However, the proposal to amend the EUMC's framework and functioning was abruptly overtaken by more recent events. In late 2003, the European Council quite suddenly decided that EUMC's mandate should be extended to become a general European human rights agency.[60] This came as a surprise to many, since although there had been external pressure for some years on the EU to establish a fully-fledged human rights agency, the Commission had consistently rejected this proposal, including in its response to the external evaluation of the EUMC in 2002. However, following the European Council's decision to extend the agency's mandate, the Commission published a consultation document on the subject, followed by a consultation process, and ultimately by the publication of a proposal for the establishment of a new fundamental rights agency.[61] Several commentators warned of the risk that the broadening of the agency's competences would make it less likely to be capable of acting effectively against racism given the dilution in focus, but the Commission in the explanatory memorandum to its proposal for a general human rights agency refers expressly to these fears and emphasises a continuing commitment to anti-discrimination policy. In general, it appears that—despite the EUMC's own concerns—reaction to the proposal to expand the anti-racism agency to cover human rights more generally has been favourable, provided the Agency is properly resourced, well-managed and that its remit is strong enough to allow it to play a robust supporting role to the legislative and other strategies for protecting and promoting human rights.

The networks

In addition to the network of equality bodies funded by the Commission under the action programme (Equinet),[62] there are at least two other relevant anti-racism networks, as well as a general human rights network, which support the race discrimination legislation and policy of the EU. The first is the RAXEN network mentioned above, the coordination of which has been one of the core tasks of the EUMC. The second is the more recently

[59] Proposal for a Council Regulation on a European Monitoring Centre on Racism and Xenophobia (Recast version) COM(2003)483.

[60] European Council decision of 13 December 2003.

[61] See n 12 above.

[62] See <http://www.migpolgroup.com/programmes/default.asp?action=displayprog&ProgID=15>; and nn 29–31 above.

established transnational network of anti-racism NGOs, known as ENAR, which is one of the five umbrella NGOs funded under the second strand of the action programme. The third is the EU Network of Independent Experts on Fundamental Rights, which was set up by the Commission at the request of the European Parliament in 2002.

RAXEN has been one of the central tools for the EUMC in carrying out its role of providing the European Union and the Member States with objective, reliable and comparable data including examples of and models for 'good practices' at the European level on the phenomena of racism, xenophobia and anti-Semitism. The RAXEN network is composed of 25 national focal points (NFPs), one in each state, which are the entrance points of the EUMC at national level regarding the data and information collection. The NFPs are the main players in the network for collecting information, data and statistics. Within the national context, they are required to set up a national information network, which includes cooperation with the main actors in the fields of racism, xenophobia and anti-Semitism—ie, mainly governmental organs, NGOs, research bodies, specialised bodies or social partners. Three coordinating meetings of the RAXEN network are held each year.

The second major anti-racism network is ENAR, the network of European NGOs working against racism in all the EU Member States, which was established in 1998. ENAR's activities cover information exchange on EU policy developments and its anti-racism legislation, exchange of experiences and know-how, developing common strategies, inputting into the reporting done by the Vienna EUMC, the UN Commission on the Elimination of All Forms of Racial Discrimination, and the Council of Europe. Many of its activities are focused on the EU Race Directive, on developing positive action, and on ensuring that the EU 'mainstreams' anti-race discrimination norms into its other policies. The ENAR specifically seeks to cooperate with the EUMC and with other existing European and international networks and organisations.

The third relevant network, which was created in 2002 to monitor the situation of fundamental rights in the EU Member States, and has become increasingly active and prominent, is the Network of Independent Experts on Fundamental Rights.[63] Although it is not restricted to anti-discrimination law, this group of experts selected from across the Member States on the basis of their expertise in human rights issues, has every year reported on discrimination problems arising in various states, as well as making a number of specialised reports which include aspects of racism, such as in its Thematic Report on the Protection of Minorities in the European Union in 2005.[64] While the exact relationship of this network with the soon-to-be-established Fundamental Rights Agency remains unclear, it is expected that

[63] See <http://europa.eu.int/comm/justice_home/cfr_cdf/index_en.htm>

[64] <http://europa.eu.int/comm/justice_home/cfr_cdf/doc/thematic_comments_2005_en.pdf>

the network will continue to play an important monitoring and informational role.

As in any field of human rights policy, the role of NGOs and other civil society actors is crucial in providing information, spreading awareness, facilitating dialogue and debate, and lobbying for change. The specifically transnational dimension of the European anti-discrimination NGO networks is designed to enable such actors to share their experiences and pool relevant resources so that a Europe-wide anti-discrimination policy can be effectively pursued. The relationship between the various networks and the new and existing agencies and institutions is obviously also crucial to the success of attempts to identify, collect and publicise comparative data on the existence of discrimination as well as the means used to tackle it in different states and regions. Thus far, the working of the various European anti-racism networks is in its early stages, but it is clear from the mandates of the networks themselves,[65] from the way in which they have been connected through action programme funding with the legislative strategy, and from the fact that the directives themselves expressly envisage a role for NGOs in their promotion, appraisal and advice on revision, that they are key players in the operation of the EU's anti-discrimination regime.

Mainstreaming anti-racism norms

A third, although as yet less well-developed, feature of the anti-discrimination regime which is a central dimension of a new governance approach is that of mainstreaming.[66] Sometimes referred to as 'policy integration', the idea of mainstreaming is that a policy issue or area should not be treated as a compartmentalised problem or set of problems to which a solution should be found, but rather that it is to be dealt with as part of all other relevant policies, and its goals and methods should be built into those other policies. The strategy of mainstreaming seeks not only to counter the compartmentalisation of policy design and implementation, but also to take a more proactive and preventative rather than ex-post-facto problem-solving approach. The idea of mainstreaming has been most actively pursued and developed in the EU in the field of gender, where for some years the 'mainstreaming of gender' has been pursued as a strategy by the EU institutions, supported now by an explicit treaty mandate in Article 3(2) EC and by successive action programmes and 'framework strategies'.[67] Another area of

[65] See <http://www.enar-eu.org/en/about/mission.shtml> for further information on the functioning of ENAR, including its recent work programs, which and for RAXEN <http://www.antiracisme.be/raxen/raxen.htm>

[66] See, eg, Bell, n 19 above; and his'Mainstreaming Equality Norms into the E.U. Asylum Law' (2001) 26 ELR 20.

[67] See, eg, Mark Pollack, Emilie Hafner-Burton, 'Mainstreaming Gender in the European Union' Jean Monnet Paper 2/00, <http://www.jeanmonnetprogram.org>, and the special issue (vol 3, no 10, 2002) of the journal *Feminist Legal Studies* on gender mainstreaming in European public policy.

EU policy in which a mainstreaming approach has been pursued for some years is that of the environment. Again, this approach is supported by a legal mandate in Article 6 of the EC Treaty which specifies that 'environmental protection requirements must be integrated into the definition and implementation of the Community policies and activities'. There are also indications of a mainstreaming or integration approach being introduced in various other fields such as disability discrimination, social inclusion and development policy.

In the field of race discrimination, this approach is still in its infancy,[68] and does not rest the explicit legal support given to areas such as environmental or gender mainstreaming. No reference is made either in the Treaty or in any of the anti-discrimination legislation to the objective of integrating anti-racism concerns into other related policies, although the (for now) abandoned EU Constitutional Treaty, had it been successfully ratified, would have introduced such a clause.[69] However, from the time of the 1998 Action Plan against Racism, the Commission committed itself to a mainstreaming approach in seeking to challenge and address race discrimination in all of the activities and policies of the EU. Thus far, specific steps to do so can be seen in the context of the European Employment Strategy,[70] and in the area of the Structural Funds, with further initiatives promised in the field of immigration and asylum.[71] However, even if this is an approach whose potential has yet to be realised in the context of anti-discrimination, the philosophy and practice of mainstreaming is one which is increasingly taking hold across various areas of EU policy including race discrimination and human rights, and which not only has broad political support but also resonates clearly in many respects with the premises of a new governance approach.

A HYBRID MODEL

The above analysis of the EU race discrimination regime—which examined the functioning of the Directive in its institutional context, including the support and resources of the action programme on the one hand, the

[68] According to the European Network against Racism (ENAR, see n 65 above)) in its July 2004 newsletter, despite the rhetoric of the Action Plan against Racism and other EU documents, 'there has been little solid action in practice to integrate anti-racism work in a coherent and strategic manner throughout all EU policy areas. Steps have often been small and isolated.'

[69] Arts 115–122 of part III of the treaty establishing a Constitution for Europe in fact introduced a whole series of mainstreaming-type clauses, with Art III–118 focusing specifically on various forms of discrimination, including on the grounds of ethnicity or race: 'In defining and implementing the policies and activities referred to in this Part, the Union shall aim to combat discrimination based on sex, racial or ethnic origin, religion or belief, disability, age or sexual orientation.'

[70] See Bell, n 66 above.

[71] See the Commission's Green Paper on Equality, n 13 above.

European agency and various national and transnational networks on the other hand, together with the gradual moves towards a mainstreaming approach, suggests that the tension between the rights model and the governance model outlined at the start of the chapter does not necessarily preclude a successful combination of these approaches. While it is too early to appraise the concrete success or otherwise of the EU's race discrimination regime in terms of addressing the social reality of racism, it is clear that the regime has evolved into one which combines reliance on a conventional legal rights-based instrument at its core with a broader framework which embodies many of the features and premises of a new governance approach. The legislation lays down a basic legal right, but in broad and open-ended terms. Recourse to a judicial remedy is provided for—and funding has been provided for information on litigation strategies—but at the same time a whole array of other actors is drawn into the process of elaboration and enforcement of the directive both by the terms of the legislation itself as well as by the gradual evolution of the action programme and its funding priorities. While the directive contains an uncompromising legal prohibition directed to public and private actors alike, the preferred approach of the Commission is to adopt a 'dynamic' approach to its implementation,[72] and the importance of reliable comparable information, and in particular from well-informed grass-roots actors on the actual phenomenon of racism and the current methods for tackling it in each state, is treated throughout the anti-discrimination regime more generally as crucial to both the diagnosis and the treatment of this particular social problem. A mainstreaming approach, which treats race discrimination not as a self-contained social problem but as an issue integrally related to a whole range of other policies and concerns, such as immigration, employment and anti-poverty, has begun to appear. The overall 'hybrid regime' of EU anti-discrimination is thus not a twin-track approach, with a new governance strategy providing an alternative option should the legal approach fail to achieve its desired results, but rather the different approaches are yoked together in a single and increasingly integrated framework. Whether the two approaches prove to be incompatible—for example, if test-case litigation leads to judicial rulings which subsequently prove to freeze rather than to strengthen the more grassroots-generated and diversity-tolerant dimensions of the strategy—remains to be seen at a point when the regime has become more operational and the legal norms can be said to be more embedded at a social and practical level. For

[72] Professor Christopher McCrudden, speaking at a conference organised in the context of the action programme in Prague in July 2004,
(see <http://europa.eu.int/comm/employment_social/fundamental_rights/events/prag04_en.htm>) argued against an emphasis on uniformity and homogeneity in interpreting and implementing the directives, stressing that they should be seen as 'incomplete agreements' and that a diversity of approaches should be accepted, provided that all are bona fide and within the wording of the legislation.

now, however, the argument can be made that the EU anti-discrimination regime in the field of race provides a potentially promising example of a hybrid regime which constructively seeks to combine elements of a rights model and a new governance model which might otherwise be thought of as fundamentally incompatible in their methods and their aims.

5

New EU Employment Governance and Constitutionalism

CLAIRE KILPATRICK*

THIS CHAPTER'S POINT of departure is that it is important to distinguish between different ways in which European Union (EU) employment regulation can be presented as 'new'. This part of the analysis, carried out in the first section of the chapter, concludes that identifying the important *but limited and specific* ways in which EU employment regulation is new provides the necessary foundations for considering both the governance and constitutionalism implications of those changes which have occurred.

In terms of governance, recognition of this 'limited newness' substantially adjusts some of the central claims made about the changes to EU employment regulation. In particular, it is misleading and incorrect straightforwardly to assert or assume that we are witnessing a shift from hard law (the Classic Community Method) to soft law (the Open Method of Co-ordination) in the arena of EU employment regulation. Instead, I identify the key characteristics of new EU employment governance as being:

(1) a dramatic expansion of the EU governance tool-kit;
(2) hybridisation of the objectives and internal structures of those EU governance tools;
(3) a shift from responsibility for certain employment governance tasks primarily resting with public institutions (executives, legislatures, courts, public administrations) to the design of more participatory governance spaces for the elaboration of EU employment norms.

Each of these characteristics is explored in more detail in the second section of this chapter.

The last part of the chapter considers the different ways in which EU constitutionalism can be or has been connected to new EU employment governance, and what this tells us both about EU constitutionalism and new EU employment governance.

* I am particularly grateful to Joanne Scott for detailed comments and suggestions on earlier drafts of this chapter. I also wish to thank Damian Chalmers, Hugh Collins and Karl Klare for very helpful discussions and comments on earlier drafts of this chapter.

EXPLORING WHAT'S NEW ABOUT EU EMPLOYMENT REGULATION

What is new at EU level?

Over the past decade employment governance has been radically transformed at EU level. This is easily demonstrated by considering what was not present at EU level just over a decade ago. Before the end of 1993 there was:

—no general set of legal bases in the EC Treaty for creating EU employment law;
—no possibility for the social partners to make EU employment law;[1]
—no European Employment Strategy (EES), no Lisbon strategy and no Open Method of Co-ordination (OMC);
—no set of constitutional social rights destined to have a hard law status as now found in the EU Charter of Fundamental Rights (now Part II of the Constitutional Treaty).

From this perspective, therefore, *everything is new* in the sense that none of these governance tools existed before at EU level. It is worth dwelling a little further on the first of these: the absence of a general set of legal bases in the EC Treaty for creating EU employment directives. What is most interesting about this lack of competence is that it actually corresponds with extremely little utilisation of the Classic Community Method (CCM) in the employment law field.[2] Outside the area of health and safety, only six employment law directives were created before the new powers introduced at Maastricht took effect.[3] Often it is accurate to present EU law as undergoing a shift from use of the CCM to greater use of 'new old governance'

[1] The expanded roles of the social partners in EU-level employment governance are not explored in detail in this chapter. However, the chapter does address the roles social partners play in employing enterprises and in national contexts in relation to EU norms.

[2] This can be contrasted with the situation in the field of environmental law where lack of a custom-made competence did not impede the production of almost 200 directives, regulations and decisions before the SEA: for discussion see, eg, G Majone, 'The Rise of the Regulatory State in Europe' in R Baldwin, C Scott and C Hood (eds) *A Reader on Regulation* (OUP, 1998) 192 at 200.

[3] Before entry into force of the SEA, employment law measures were based on Art 94 EC (the 'common market' creation competence) or Art 308 EC (the residual common market competence). The SEA added the possibility of adopting measures at EU level relating to the health and safety of workers. The six directives were: two on gender equality at work (one on equal pay (Directive 75/117/EEC), one on equal treatment), three on business restructuring (collective dismissals, transfers of undertakings, insolvency) and one on providing employees with information about their terms and conditions of employment (Directive 91/533/EEC). All but two of these have been extensively revised in the more active post-Maastricht period. See now on equal treatment between men and women, Directive 76/207/EEC as amended by Directive 2002/73/EC; on business restructuring: Directive 98/59/EC (collective dismissals), Directive 2001/23/EC (transfers of undertakings), Directive 80/987/EEC as amended by Directive 2002/74/EC on insolvency.

tools such as framework directives as well as other new governance tools.[4] However, it can be seen that such a description works less well in the employment arena where very little EU employment law had been created prior to Maastricht, partly as a result of competence constraints.

Moreover, even entry into force of that Treaty on 1 November 1993 did not permit straightforward use of the CCM in the employment field. The opt-out by the UK's Conservative Government from the employment law legal bases introduced at Maastricht meant that they did not fully become part of EC law until 1997 when Prime Minister Blair removed UK opposition to these new employment law legal bases being used on a Community-wide basis, and led to the extension of all the directives adopted between 1994 and 1997 to the UK. Furthermore, the general Treaty competence to create anti-discrimination directives on a wide range of protected grounds was not introduced until the Amsterdam Treaty came into force in May 1999. Therefore, in many significant senses, secure production of EU employment law has been a very recent phenomenon.

Two caveats must be placed on this 'all-new' presentation of EU employment regulation. First, much was done by the courts with the little employment law in existence prior to Maastricht. The European Court of Justice and the national courts developed a flourishing judicial dialogue on some of the 1970s employment law directives.[5] Second, another important source of EU employment regulation has existed with a proper Treaty base since 1957, although it has frequently been neglected in legal scholarship. This is the European Social Fund (ESF). Unlike the government by *imperium* (attaining policy objectives through legal commands backed by sanctions) which is the traditional focus of legal scholarship, the ESF utilises the technique of government by *dominium* whereby the wealth of government is used to attain policy objectives.[6] While it is important to include the ESF in our analysis because it constitutes a different kind of source to traditional legal sources, its significance is tied to and limited by the smallness of the EU budget.[7]

Caveats notwithstanding, the sheer magnitude of the changes to EU employment regulation makes it plausible to assert that almost all of the tools for EU employment governance were created in the course of the last decade and that the thickness of EU employment governance increased dramatically as the decade progressed. In other words, 'old governance' tools (such as the legal bases to create directives) and 'new governance' tools (such as the OMC) were in fact all created within the same short time-span at EU level in

[4] J Scott and D M Trubek, 'Mind the Gap: Law and New Approaches to Governance in the European Union', 8 *European Law Journal* (2002) 1.

[5] Especially gender equality and transfers of undertakings: see S. Sciarra (ed) *Labour Law in the Courts* (Oxford, Hart Publishing, 2001), chs 2 and 3.

[6] See, on this useful distinction, T Daintith, 'The Techniques of Government' in J Jowell and D Oliver (eds) *The Changing Constitution*, 3rd edn (OUP, 1994) 209.

[7] The EU budget has never been more, and currently is less, than 1.3% EU GDP. EU Member States spend around 45% GDP; the US around 34% GDP.

the field of employment. In this sense, almost all EU employment governance is new. And that significant part which is not new—the ESF—has not only altered its own internal governance structure but has also taken on a very different aspect in its new EU governance setting, as we shall see.

What is not new in the EU and its Member States

It is important to recognise that the kind of governance tools and structures created at EU level over the past decade have existed before. Turning first to employment policy, this becomes obvious if we look at the governance of employment policy in non-EU governance sites. States have always had employment (or labour market) policies aimed at activities such as vocational training and retraining, job-matching and income replacement in periods of unemployment, underemployment, incapacity or old age. The point being made here is that employment policies have never typically been associated with a hard law 'command and control' model. Instead, the governance tasks employment policies perform generally require, on the one hand, the spending of money and, on the other, the creation of guidelines, targets, indicators and plans in attempts to steer labour markets in directions considered desirable. Both these tasks tended to be carried out in public administrative bureaucratic or tri-partite decision-making processes. Therefore, it should come as no surprise that employment policies at EU level similarly predominantly involve the same set of tools. Hence, the European Social Fund involves spending EU money 'in order to improve employment opportunities for workers in the internal market' (Article 146 EC Treaty); and OMC in the employment field (the European Employment Strategy) involves creating guidelines, indicators, targets, National Action Plans and recommendations to enable the Member States and the Community to 'work towards developing a coordinated strategy for employment and particularly for promoting a skilled, trained and adaptable workforce and labour markets responsive to economic change' (Article 125 EC Treaty).

Accordingly the novelty of the European Employment Strategy lies precisely in its creation at *EU* level. In saying this I do not wish to underplay its newness as a governance tool. First, although Member States already had employment policies as we have discussed, Gerstenberg and Sabel are right to emphasise that few if any systematically compared their employment policies with those of other Member States.[8] Second, because the EES is structured as an iterative process, providing rich information that is subject to peer review, it aims to promote cross-national deliberation and

[8] O Gerstenberg and CF Sabel, 'Directly-Deliberative Polyarchy: An Institutional Ideal for Europe?' in C Joerges and R Dehousse (eds) *Good Governance in Europe's Integrated Market* (OUP, 2002) 289 at 333.

experimental learning. Whilst the Member States deploy similar employment governance tools, they use them in highly distinctive ways and with widely differing emphases. As a result, the *potential* impact of systematic cross-national comparison and learning between Member States through the OMC is high.

Turning to social rights, the 'not really new' thesis is even truer of the inclusion of fundamental EU social rights in the EU Charter of Fundamental Rights, created in 2000 and, in revised form, now Part II of the EU Constitutional Treaty. Although it is of great interest, as we shall see, that the Charter contains a range of EU fundamental social rights, it is not all that surprising that this is the case. For a start, the constititionalisation of social rights is one of the most notable features of modern constitutions: the more recent a list of constitutional fundamental rights, the more likely it is to contain an increasing number of social rights. The most striking example of this is the South African Constitution.[9] Just as importantly, the EU was *particularly* likely to choose to include social rights in any fundamental rights catalogue. However, and distinguishing the EU Charter of Fundamental Rights from the social rights provisions in other bills of rights, the EU's historical development made it likely that *workers' rights* would be more prominent in its set of social rights than is normally the case. Fundamental social rights typically refer to rights to food, health, education, housing and a minimum income rather than to workers' rights.[10] Yet the EU's historical trajectory has placed workers' rights in a more central position than is typically the case.

Once the market-making mission of the European Community got under way, its constant companion, decade after decade at Community level, has been the need to legitimise the social dislocation created by market integration by having 'a social dimension'. Hence, at the Paris Summit of 1972, which led to the Social Action Programme of 1974 and almost all of the employment directives created before Maastricht, the Heads of State and Government urged the Community institutions to make generous and inventive use of the competences they possessed. As Michael Shanks, Director-General for Social Affairs in the Commission in this period, commented on what lay behind the legislation emerging from the 1974 Social Action Programme:

> The Community had to be seen as more than a device to enable capitalists to exploit the common market; otherwise it might not be possible to persuade the peoples of the Community to accept the common market. [11]

[9] See C Fabre, *Social Rights Under the Constitution: Government and the Decent Life* (OUP, 1999).

[10] The EU Charter does also contain some of these more typical fundamental social rights: see for example Art II–74 (right to education), Art II–94 (recognition and respect of entitlement to social security and social assistance), Art II–95 (health care).

[11] M. Shanks, 'Introductory Article: The Social Policy of the European Communities' 14 CML Rev (1977) 375 at 378.

This strongly felt need to have a social rights agenda has been accompanied, as is well known, by great difficulties, of both a jurisdictional (the difficulty of justifying supranational action) and political (the difficulty of agreeing what Community regulation should do) nature, in delivering on social rights. However, this should not blind us to the ongoing attempts to match in some way market-making initiatives with workers' rights. Indeed, before the creation of the EU Charter of Fundamental Rights, the only Charter of Fundamental Rights the Community had previously succeeded in creating, in 1989, was aimed specifically at workers. Creation of the 1989 Community Charter of the Fundamental Social Rights of Workers was closely linked to the intensification of market integration signalled by the Single European Act as successive European Councils, 'considered that, in the context of the establishment of the single European market, the same importance must be attached to the social aspects as to the economic aspects'.[12] It is true that the Workers' Charter was only a solemn declaration, and that only 11 of the then 12 Member States were prepared to sign up to it (not the Thatcher administration). The Workers' Charter has primarily been used as a justificatory resource for Community employment legislative activity and as an interpretative resource by the European Court of Justice. Nonetheless, it was seen as a step 'towards a "social constitution" for Europe' by contemporary commentators.[13] Given this background, it would have been unlikely not to see social rights, and in particular workers' rights, included in the EU Charter of Fundamental Rights.

Analysing more carefully the distinctive nature of different kinds of employment law and policy substantially adjusts common analyses of current EU employment governance developments. Such analyses view current developments as signalling a shift from hard law (the CCM) to soft law (the OMC), or as the price that had to be paid for an expansion of EU competence in the employment field.[14] Instead, it becomes evident that there are different kinds of soft and hard employment law in the EU.

Some kinds of soft law instrument, particularly those containing workers' rights such as the 1989 Community Charter of the Fundamental Social Rights of Workers and the 2000 EU Charter of Fundamental Rights, are

[12] Second Recital of the 1989 Charter's Preamble.

[13] B Hepple, 'The Implementation of the Community Charter of Fundamental Social Rights', (1990) 53 MLR 643 at 653 adding, 'It is difficult not to see the Community Charter as a step towards the creation of a European "social State"'.

[14] J Mosher and DM Trubek, 'Alternative Approaches to Governance in the EU: EU Social Policy and the European Employment Strategy' (2003) 41 *Journal of Common Market Studies* 63 at 64, 71: 'It could be said that the EES gives up the legal force of traditional regulations in order to allow the EU to deal with some core areas of social policy that were hitherto solely reserved for the Member States.' In subsequent work, D Trubek and L Trubek develop their analysis to consider different jobs performed by hard and soft law: 'The Open Method of Coordination and the Debate over "Hard" and "Soft" Law' in J Zeitlin and P Pochet with L Magnusson (eds) *The Open Method of Co-ordination in Action: The European Employment and Social Inclusion Strategies* (Brussels: PIE–Peter Lang, 2005).

hard law of a constitutional nature in the making. They are often crafted so that they could be judicially enforceable in some way or another, but are denied hard law status on a permanent or temporary basis for political reasons. Indeed the ultimate fate of the EU Charter of Fundamental Rights, and especially the social rights in it, demonstrates that what counts as 'hard' enforceability in a polycentric constitutional setting is a complex and highly contested issue.[15]

But other kinds of soft law, of which employment policy measures have always been a central example, derive their regulatory strength from government powers or capacities that do not require hard, in the sense of judicially sanctionable, legal powers. This strength may derive from providing money on the fulfilment of certain conditions laid down by the administration, or from setting up guided reporting structures to encourage the pursuit of defined policy goals, and to facilitate knowledge transfer and policy learning. Neither the ESF nor the OMC constitutes a hard law opportunity *manqué*. In these instances, soft law is shorthand for 'different from law (in its classical conception)', not 'less than law'.

What is new in both the Member States and the EU

One of the most profoundly interesting developments in employment governance is the increasingly deep and explicit integration of macro- and micro- competitiveness and social justice (with a new focus on its social inclusion variant) objectives in both traditional 'social policy' measures and traditional 'employment policy' measures. The greater integration of those objectives changes significantly the structure of the traditional instruments used to deliver social and employment policy. Employment governance can be seen as pursuing four objectives: worker protection; increasing the employment rate and lowering unemployment; including excluded groups in the labour market; increasing the competitive efficiency of employing enterprises.[16] Traditionally, worker protection was associated primarily with hard law (employment law or 'social policy' in EU parlance), whilst job creation and combating unemployment was associated primarily with soft law (employment policy). Hence, these two objectives were divided between different tools of governance and the other objectives—competitiveness, social inclusion, increasing the employment rate—were much less visible in the employment field. Although the competitiveness of firms did inform employment law it did so in rather different and less explicit ways

[15] See below, section on Constitutionalism and New EU Employment Governance.

[16] For a different classification, on which mine draws, see P Davies and M Freedland, 'The Role of EU Employment Law and Policy in the De-marginalisation of Part-time Work: A Study in the Interaction between EU Regulation and Member State Regulation' in S Sciarra, P Davies and M Freedland (eds) *Employment Policy and the Regulation of Part-time Work in the EU: A Comparative Analysis* (CUP, 2004) 63.

than it does today.[17] The same can be said of the relationship between worker protection and employment policy. Similarly, social justice within employment governance is increasingly not simply defined as worker protection: both employment law and employment policy today place greater stress on removing obstacles to labour market participation for socially excluded groups such as single parents and the disabled, even if those groups might not officially count as 'unemployed' when not economically active. Concomitantly, there is a greater emphasis on increasing the employment rate rather than on simply lowering unemployment. In sum, there has been a noticeable reorientation of the objectives of employment governance which has led to a refashioning of the tools of employment governance.

But, in developing its employment governance tools—the OMC, employment legislation, the ESF—to deliver these reoriented competitiveness and social justice objectives, did the EU lead, follow or travel alongside its Member States? The former is very often the impression given in analyses of the OMC. However, this may give a misleading impression of the development of employment policy in the EU by underplaying the central role of state and other governance sites in employment policy innovation.

In their analysis of the regulation of part-time work, Davies and Freedland suggest a reading based firmly on state employment regulation innovation.[18] They argue that the change in EU employment law and policy occurred because of a diversification, *which happened first in the Member States*, of employment regulation objectives which in turn produced the need for a different set of regulatory techniques at national and, *subsequently*, EU level. Hard and soft law was refashioned at national and EU level to meet these new objectives.

Their argument—focused on the regulation of part-time work—is worth outlining a little more fully. Drawing on national case studies, they plot a shift in several Member States[19] over the last few decades. At the beginning of this period, and conforming to a traditional regulatory pattern, Member States generally pursued the objective of worker protection by using the technique of hard law to discourage part-time work. Subsequently, there has been a common tendency in all the Member States to place a new or increased emphasis on the objectives of employment stimulation and employer flexibility, a change in approach towards moderating and encouraging part-time work and a use of the techniques of both hard and soft law to pursue these new objectives and approaches. Obviously, each Member State pursued this course in its own specific way. However, this course had

[17] On competitiveness as a new task for employment law see H Collins, 'Regulating the Employment Relation for Competitiveness' (2001) 30 ILJ 17 and C Kilpatrick, 'Has New Labour Reconfigured Employment Legislation?' (2003) 32 ILJ 135.

[18] Above n 16.

[19] The Member States analysed in the book are France, Germany, Italy, The Netherlands, Spain, Sweden and the United Kingdom.

been firmly set by domestic policy generally well before and, in any event, largely autonomously from EU employment governance developments.

Their conclusions have been reiterated in the context of a broader discussion of the recalibration of welfare regimes in Europe by Ferrera and Hemerijck who note that 'the successes achieved through domestic policy innovation in turn shaped the employment and social policy agenda of the European Union'.[20] This does nothing to diminish the interest of that developing EU employment and social policy agenda: indeed it is a primary example of policy learning in action albeit with its focus on the *EU learning* from its Member States how to develop an appropriate employment policy regime.

Conclusions

In this first section we have rejected the often-made assertion that recent developments in EU employment governance can be characterised as a shift from hard to soft law. Instead, we have noted other much more interesting developments in EU governance. There has been a dramatic expansion of the EU governance tool-kit. This expansion, and particularly the creation of the EES and the EU Charter of Fundamental Rights, has pushed a former EU Cinderella into the limelight in studies of new governance and the EU's evolving constitutional order. This expansion of the EU employment governance tool-kit took place in the context of a general reconfiguration of employment policy and employment legislation around a new more integrated and expanded competitiveness–social justice paradigm. Both these developments are fundamental to understanding the construction of the new EU employment governance regime and its two other principal characteristics, both of which were noted in the introduction: hybridity and the creation of peopled governance spaces for EU norm elaboration and revision.

THE NEW EU EMPLOYMENT GOVERNANCE REGIME

Over the last decade or so the EU has been redefined. It definitively stepped away from being an internal market with a social dimension and towards being a macro-economic area in its own right, largely because of the introduction of Economic and Monetary Union (EMU). This new Euro-economy required an EU-level employment policy, not least because, as an economic area, it was coming out badly in comparison with the US on

[20] 'Recalibrating Europe's Welfare Regimes' in J Zeitlin and DM Trubek (eds) *Governing Work and Welfare in a New Economy: European and American Experiments* (OUP, 2003) 88 at 125. Of particular relevance to the subject-matter of this paper is their discussion of the decentralisation and broadening of the participation base in formulating and delivering active labour market policy in Denmark (at 99).

growth, employment and unemployment rates. In part this is because the design of welfare systems in some Member States appears to price low-skilled workers out of jobs and to heavily discourage female labour-market participation. Compliance with the convergence criteria for EMU has also been identified as a significant factor in the EU's worsening growth and employment performance relative to the US during the 1990s.[21]

Its Member States also faced two other issues requiring an overhaul of welfare states, tax systems and labour market regulation. First, the European demographic situation is very troubling. Increasing numbers of older people and decreasing numbers of younger people lead to a new search for workers, such as women, the disabled and older workers. This requires rethinking child and elder-care provision as well as the development of flexible working models for parents, carers, the disabled and older workers. It also entails reconsideration of early retirement policies and the age at which pension rights should accrue. Second, the EU needs to find a niche in a world economy where new modes of production and consumption mean that the EU can only compete on quality and innovation. This creates needs to address low-skills, skills enhancement, educational attainment, and the maintenance of the value of human capital through life-long learning and training.

Self-identification as an 'EU-economy' in need of a labour market policy required, however, a distinct response to that pursued in state sites. The EU has very limited resources to pursue major *dominium*-led labour market reshaping; most of this money is in the hands of the Member States.[22] Nor would it be feasible, effective or legitimate to manage labour markets from Brussels. The 'innovative hybridization'[23] of employment governance in the Member States would have to find its own EU-specific translation.

Hybridisation of the objectives of EU employment governance

In the 'old governance' EU, there was little integration of policy objectives across governance tools. Instead disparate interventions occurred in the areas of social policy (primarily through legislation, plans for legislation and social rights documents) and employment policy (primarily through the European Social Fund).

Most of the literature on new employment governance in the EU has focused on the OMC (the European Employment Strategy). However, this OMC emphasis has tended to present the OMC as a separate governance tool which will therefore be used instead of other possible EU governance

[21] P De Grauwe, *The Economics of Monetary Union*, 2nd edn (OUP, 2000) 136–39.

[22] See n 7 above, and the discussion in the section on Constitutionalism and the New EU Employment Governance below.

[23] J Zeitlin, 'Introduction: Governing Work and Welfare in a New Economy: European and American Experiments' in Zeitlin and Trubek (eds) (2003), n 20 above, at 14.

tools, most particularly, the hard law of EU employment legislation. This perception—of OMC as an alternative to law—has been so strong that many influential voices have argued that it should not be allowed to happen. The European Commission therefore argued in its White Paper on Governance that the OMC 'should not be used when legislative action under the Community method is possible'.[24] Scharpf has argued that the way ahead for the European Social Model is to combine a new kind of 'softer' hard law—differentiated framework directives—with the Open Method of Coordination. This would, he argues, diminish the problems which might be associated with a shift to 'softer' forms of hard law regulation:

> since progress towards their realization would be directed by Council guidelines, while Member States would have to present action plans or reports on their effects would be periodically assessed by peer review. If evaluation should reveal general problems, the framework legislation could be amended and tightened.[25]

These proposals ignore what in my view is the most significant characteristic of the new EU employment governance: that it is already a self-consciously *integrated regime* where the OMC, ESF and employment law measures each play distinctive and overlapping roles in realising social justice and competitiveness objectives. From this perspective, one of the most central achievements of the EES is that it builds bridges between employment legislation (*imperium* measures) and the European Social Fund (*dominium* measures). The Commission's observation on OMC appears to miss the point that in a hybridised governance regime, particularly a polycentred one, all governance tools are aimed at the effective and legitimate delivery of the same broadly defined set of goals. Scharpf is therefore correct to point out that the OMC can be complementary to employment legislation. However, Scharpf overlooks the extent to which integration of governance tools constitutes already, in a very significant number of employment areas, actual practice. Moreover, he is wrong to assume that only 'soft' hard law, or what Scott and Trubek term 'new old governance', such as framework directives, couples itself with the OMC.

The first clear instances of the explicit coupling between employment directives and OMC—the directives on part-time work and fixed-term work—do indeed follow the pattern identified by Scharpf, that is, that OMC fits best with 'softer' hard law. But this may also be explained by two

[24] *European Governance – A White Paper* COM(2001)428 final 22.

[25] F Scharpf, 'The European Social Model: Coping with the Challenges of Diversity', 40 *JCMS* (2002) 645 at 664. See also J Goetschy, 'The European Employment Strategy: Multilevel Governance and Policy Co-ordination: Past, Present and Future' in Zeitlin and Trubek (eds) (2003) above n.20, 59 at 80: 'The best way to address these concerns [of a shift from hard law to soft law] is to link the OMC closely to other instruments of Community action. It would be helpful if the EES were to be associated with the other methods rather than operating in isolation'.

facts specific to these two directives. The atypical work directives, as is well known, were the products of social partner agreements under (now) Articles 138 and 139 EC. These actors may have been particularly keen to explicitly link the newly strengthened and institutionalised EES with their agreements. In addition, it is also important to bear in mind the subject matter of regulatory intervention. The purpose of the part-time work directive was not simply to protect part-time workers. It was also designed to give employers the opportunity to make use of part-time work and to give workers the option of moving between full and part-time work in accordance with their needs. These broadened objectives meant that a departure from the regulatory structure found in traditional employment law instruments was required. As Davies and Freedland remark, there is an 'integral continuity' between the Part-time Work Directive and the elements in the EES which concern part-time work.[26]

However, EU discrimination regulation demonstrates, in contrast to Scharpf's analysis, that it is not always the case that only 'softer' hard law is suitable for coupling with OMC in the employment field. A strong coupling between the OMC and employment law to achieve other objectives may require very different hard law models. For instance, the strong, and long-standing, set of EU 'hard law' commitments to gender equality is matched by an extensive focus in the EES on equal opportunities for men and women.[27] And the 2000 directives prohibiting (inter alia) age, disability and race discrimination explicitly extract the immediately preceding European Council's Conclusions on the Employment Guidelines.[28]

Moreover, it is not just recently created EU hard law or equality rights that have been connected to the EES. Links have also been made between 'old' EU hard law in other areas and the EES as it develops. The best example concerns the Community's substantial body of law on health and safety at work. In 2002, when indicators of job quality were introduced into the EES for the first time, one of these involved measuring accidents at work,

[26] Above n 16. Part-time work has played three roles in the EES: to keep older workers in the workforce, to make enterprises more adaptable and competitive and to permit effective reconciliation of work and family life.

[27] See Priority Action 6 on Gender Equality of the Employment Guidelines in effect from 2003–5.

[28] In the Race Directive (Directive 2000/43/EC) the European Council stressed 'the need to foster conditions for a socially inclusive labour market by formulating a coherent set of policies aimed at combating discrimination against groups such as ethnic minorities'. While, in the framework directive (Directive 2000/78/EC), the European Council stressed

> the need to foster a labour market favourable to social integration by formulating a coherent set of policies aimed at combating discrimination against groups such as persons with disability...and to pay particular attention to supporting older workers, in order to increase their participation in the labour market.

In the EES see Priority Action 7, 'Promote the Integration of and Combat the Discrimination Against People at a Disadvantage in the Labour Market' and Priority Action 5, 'Increase Labour Supply and Promote Active Ageing'.

and the provisions on adaptability in the EES have also been remodelled to include health and safety. Similarly, while the social partners did not explicitly link the Parental Leave Agreement and Directive with that part of the EES dealing with equal opportunities between men and women, such a link can be and has been made in the Employment Guidelines and the National Action Plans.

Finally, it is not just OMC and Community legislation which have been mutually remodelled. The objectives of the European Social Fund have also explicitly been recast to match those of the EES and employment legislation. Moreover, this remodelling has become more focused and precise over time. The Regulation on the ESF for the current programming period 2000–6 noted the introduction of the EES in 1997 and stated that it was therefore 'necessary to redefine the scope of the Fund ... to support the European employment strategy and the national action plans for employment linked to it'.[29] However, the proposed Regulation on the ESF for the next programming period (2007–13) adopts a much more tailored approach to use of the ESF to achieve EES objectives.[30] The Member States are required, under Article 4 of the proposed Regulation, to ensure that actions supported using the ESF 'promote the objectives, priorities and targets of the Strategy in each Member State and concentrate support in particular on the implementation of the employment recommendations made under Article 128(4) of the Treaty as well as of the relevant objectives of the Community in the field of social inclusion'.

The potential of the overall strength of this hybrid employment regime is formidable. Hard law—EU workers' rights—has already played an historically important role not only in liberating workers from uncongenial national employment practices but also in creating or strengthening alliances of national and transnational groups of workers and their intermediaries, often through litigation strategies.[31] Moreover, in its new hybrid environment, EU legislation can act as a seed or an anchor for a wider range of linked policy initiatives, rather than being viewed as the only game in town for EU intervention.

OMC's tools—unlike those of hard law—are ideally suited to find out whether law, or other State or public/private intervention, really works. Unlike hard law, it *can* focus on an agenda to create crèches and decent jobs. Member States have a large degree of freedom in choosing how to narrow the gender pay gap, provide genuine opportunities to reconcile work and family life and give people with disabilities the chance to participate

[29] Regulation (EC) No 1784/1999 of the European Parliament and of the Council of 12 July 1999 on the European Social Fund (OJ L 213/5), Recitals (4) and (5) of the Preamble.

[30] Proposal for a Regulation of the European Parliament and of the Council on the European Social Fund, COM(2004)493 final, Brussels (14 July 2004).

[31] C Kilpatrick, 'Emancipation through Law or the Emasculation of Law? The Nation State, the EU and Gender Equality at Work' in J Conaghan, K Klare and M Fischl (eds) *Labour Law in an Era of Globalisation* (OUP, 2002).

meaningfully in the labour market, but, ultimately, OMC can be used to ask whether they can show that their methods have worked. The enriching of the EES' governance tools—in particular, the combined use of quality indicators and recommendations—increase its suitability for these tasks. OMC provides a way of testing whether hard law or budget expenditure really works and, more broadly, of holding Member States to account on ways of achieving common policy objectives. Unlike the structural funds, OMC can measure macro-level changes instead of largely micro-level improvements.

Finally, the structural funds' governance processes and outcomes are attractive on many grounds. Unlike OMC, they provide concrete incentives for Member States to develop structured participation by a range of interested actors and institutions to work together to create progressive change on a local basis.[32]

In sum, in policy design terms, the most central characteristic of new EU employment governance is its integration. This integration gives it a regulatory strength and potential it did not previously possess. I have set out a strong version of the policy integration thesis here, because it differs so much from most analyses of new EU employment governance. However, to counterbalance this, it must be stressed that it is much easier to design joined-up EU government on paper than it is to realise it in practice. This is particularly the case in a hybrid, polycentred employment governance regime. Failure by one part of the whole to play its allotted role skews the objectives and balance of the overall hybrid regime. Hence, choosing the appropriate policy mix to deliver an employment objective will be very different in a scenario where each governance tool is expected to do its job, and in a scenario where one or all of the governance tools is not, or is perceived not to be, working. Therefore, when the UK Government presses for OMC to be privileged as a mode of policy intervention over EU employment legislation, suspicions are appropriately aroused that this is because it perceives the OMC to be less effective in practice than other EU governance tools.[33] In part, it may be fears and concerns of this kind that motivated the Commission in its White Paper on Governance to argue against the OMC ousting legislative action.[34]

Peopled governance spaces for norm-elaboration and revision

The last fundamental change in the EU employment regime we wish to highlight and to analyse is a shift away from conceiving of legal standards, expenditure activities, or labour market management as being definitively

[32] J. Scott, 'Law, Legitimacy and EC Governance: Prospects for "Partnership"'(1998) 36 *JCMS* 175.

[33] See C Kilpatrick and M Freedland, 'How is EU Governance Transformative? Part-time Work in the UK' in Sciarra, Davies and Freedland (eds), n 16 above, at 299 especially 343ff.

[34] See n 24 above and accompanying text.

in the hands of public institutions which create and interpret norms relating to these activities. A new characteristic can be discerned across EU instruments in the employment field: legislation, expenditure and labour market management. This characteristic is explicitly requiring *both public and private actors* to be involved in EU normative instructions through activities such as elaboration, implementation, adjustment, review and comparison. Moreover the range of both public and private actors involved in EU employment governance has expanded. The public actors include the executive, the legislature, Parliaments, public administrations at all levels, agencies and courts. The private actors include unions, employers, groups of workers or their elected representatives and other civil society associations.

Employment legislation

The four principal areas of EU employment legislation over the last 'long' decade concern equality legislation,[35] atypical work[36], working time[37] and worker representation.[38] In each of these areas, new linked roles have been given to public and private actors. Before examining these linkages in more detail it is worth underlining that none of these roles existed at EU level in pre-Maastricht EU employment legislation. Moreover, while similar public–private links to those recently introduced at EU level had been made before in the legislation of some Member States, the model used in the worker representation directives is new at both EU level and in the Member States.

One set of linkages emerges from the new discrimination directives. The effectiveness of the judicially enforceable rights created by the race and gender equality directives is to be given greater weight by creating a new public enforcement agency in each Member State.[39] Moreover, these agencies, along with voluntary associations engaged in combating discrimination, are given new rights to support or act on behalf of individuals in judicial and administrative proceedings.[40] It is in the nature of many central anti-discrimination concepts that they require, and have received in the EU judicial

[35] The Burden of Proof Directive (97/80/EC), the revised Equal Treatment Directive (both on gender equality), the Parental Leave Directive (96/34/EC); the Race Equality Directive (2000/43/EC); the Framework Directive on Age, Disability, Religion/Belief, Sexual Orientation (2000/78/EC).

[36] The Part-time Directive (97/81/EC); the Fixed-term Directive (99/70/EC); the telework agreement (2002).

[37] The Working-time Directive of 2003 (2003/88/EC) which consolidates the original 1993 Directive and subsequent amending directives; the Young People at Work Directive (94/33/EC).

[38] The European Works' Councils Directive (94/45/EC); the Information and Consultation Directive (2002/14/EC); Directives Requiring Worker Involvement in the new European Company (2001/86) and European Co-operative (2003/72/EC, OJ L 207/25)).

[39] Art 13 Directive 2000/43/EC; Art 8a ETD.

[40] Art 7(2) Directive 2000/43/EC; Art 6(3) ETD.

context, extensive and revisable elaboration. However, this elaboration was patchy in the past, often because of the absence of an adequate nexus of informed local actors to organise litigation strategies. A further linkage between Member States and private actors is created by providing that the Member States should encourage and promote the social partners and non-governmental organisations to engage in dialogue on combating race and gender discrimination and promoting equality.[41]

A very different linkage between public and private actors is created in the directives on atypical work, parental leave and working-time. In these directives, the most distinctive new feature is that bargained agreements between, depending on the directive, 'management and labour', 'the social partners' or 'the two sides of industry' can set or derogate from a wide range of legislative standards. These legislative standards are either laid out in detail in the directive (working-time) or sketched out in the directive (atypical work, parental leave) and left to the Member States to flesh out, either legislatively, through bargained standard-setting, or through a mixture of legislation and bargained statutory adjustment. The most far-reaching use of the bargained statutory adjustment technique is in the Working-time Directive. The directive lays down a series of detailed basic entitlements to inter alia a maximum working week of 48 hours, rest-breaks, daily rest and weekly rest as well as additional protection for night-workers. However, it then provides that all of these standards can be adjusted by bargained agreement either at industry level or in individual enterprises and workplaces.[42] In other words, the legislative standard functions primarily as a starting-point for the working-time standards which will ultimately be applied to workers in the EU as a result of bargained agreements.

This technique is taken one step further in the worker representation directives of the post-Maastricht period. These directives all aim to ensure that employing enterprises inform and consult their workers on important decisions in the life of the enterprise. Each directive deals with a different kind of employing enterprise: Community-scale undertakings, European Companies and, most recently, all enterprises with more than 50 employees. Each directive contains a legislative information and consultation model. However, this legislative model is explicitly set up as a default setting, to operate only where no information and consultation arrangement bargained between employers and their workforces has been created. Moreover, the directives provide additional regulatory incentives for the creation of rapid bargained agreements on information and consultation.

We can illustrate this more clearly by looking at the European Works Council Directive of 1994. Community-scale undertakings can comply with

[41] Arts 11 and 12 Directive 2000/43/EC; Arts 8b and 8c ETD.

[42] In relation to the 48-hour limit, bargained agreements can only adjust the length of the reference period over which the 48 hour maximum will be averaged, up to a maximum of 12 months (the basic reference period is set at 17 weeks).

the directive's goal that they should inform and consult their workforces in one of three ways: through statutory compliance, bargained compliance or rapid bargained compliance. Incentives for bargained compliance are created by the possibility of avoiding the detailed arrangements on information and consultation in the statutory default model. For instance, under a bargained agreement there is no requirement (as there is under the default model) to hold an information and consultation meeting with worker representatives covering

> the economic and financial situation, the probable development of the business and of production and sales, the situation and probable trend of employment, investments, and substantial changes concerning organisation, introduction of new working methods or production processes, transfers of production, mergers, cut-backs or closures of undertakings, establishments or important parts thereof, and collective redundancies. [43]

However, standard bargained compliance remains subject to certain legislative constraints as to who can make the agreement and what it should cover.[44] These constraints are removed in the case of rapid bargained compliance, that is, compliance with the directive before its date of transposition. Here the only requirements are that the Community-scale undertaking has an agreement, with any employee-side signatory, providing for the transnational information and consultation of the entire workforce.[45] The role played by the legislative standard in this setting, where the legislative design incentivises intra-firm compliance with a broadly defined legislative goal, is very different from the traditional obligation–sanction role played by legislative standards. The workings of the European Works Council Directive in practice clearly demonstrate this. At present, almost three-quarters of the Community-scale undertakings in which the information and consultation obligations have been triggered[46] have taken the rapid bargained compliance route and almost all of the remainder have taken the bargained compliance route.[47] The statutory default model has played two main roles: to act as an incentive to reach agreement and to provide a flexible template for those bargained agreements.

The structural funds: the ESF

The structural funds demonstrate even more clearly than employment legislation the need to bring together a relevant set of public and private actors

[43] Annex EWC Directive, para 2.
[44] Art 6 EWC Directive.
[45] Art 13 EWC Directive.
[46] The directive must be triggered either by management or workers, and this has happened in just under one-third of the two thousand or so enterprises covered by the Directive.
[47] See P Lorber, 'Reviewing the European Works Council Directive: European Progress and UK Perspective' (2004) 33 ILJ 191.

in order to obtain the means to carry out broadly defined EU employment objectives.

The critical staging post here is the significant reforms of the structural funds in 1988. These introduced the principle of partnership, a principle that has been retained in the 1993 and 1999 rounds of reforms. The Regulation laying down general provisions governing the structural funds states that Community actions under the funds shall be drawn up in a partnership between the Commission, the Member States and a 'representative partnership' designated by the Member State. In designating this partnership at national, regional, local or other level Member States are required to 'create a wide and effective association of all the relevant bodies, taking account of the need to promote equality between men and women'. The partnership covers the preparation, financing, monitoring and evaluation of assistance.[48]

Aside from this general regime, the 1988 reforms also created a new instrument: the Community Initiatives. These are programmes with an earmarked budget (between 5–10 per cent of the Structural Funds budget depending on the programming period) to be spent on specified themes. In the current period (2000-6) one Community Initiative is ESF-funded. This is the EQUAL initiative.[49] EQUAL is a transnational programme which promotes new means of combating all forms of discrimination and inequality in the labour market, as well as focusing on the position of asylum seekers and refugees. According to the Commission, EQUAL differs from the ESF mainstream programmes in its function as a laboratory (principle of innovation) and in its emphasis on active cooperation between Member States.[50] Its themes mirror the EES. It is implemented by strategic partnerships called EQUAL Development Partnerships (EDPs), which may operate at a local, regional or national level. An EDP can be funded to pursue one of the specified themes. To obtain funding it must state the rationale for its project, the EDP's objectives, what is innovative about the project, who will benefit, explain how it will empower the partners and its beneficiaries and enter into transnational cooperation agreements with EDPs in other Member States pursuing the same theme.

To show the potential of the ESF, I briefly outline one of these Equal Development Partnerships (EDPs) in the UK: *Building London: Creating Futures*. Altogether, there have been 195 EDPs in the UK, 82 in the first round in 2002 and 113 in the second round in 2005. The *Building London: Creating Futures* EDP pursues the adaptability theme. It aims to formulate a sub-regional coordinated programme to ensure that disadvantaged people

[48] Art 8 of Regulation 1260/1999 of 21 June 1999 laying down general provisions of the Structural Funds (OJ L 161/1).

[49] See <http://europa.eu.int/comm/employment_social/equal/index_en.html>.

[50] However, in the 2007–13 programming period it is proposed to move EQUAL back into the mainstream ESF programmes: Inforegio, *Factsheet 2004*, 1.

have equal opportunities to access, retain and progress in present and future Central London construction jobs. For example, the EDP notes that of 145,000 Construction Skills Certification Scheme Cards issued only 404 of them went to women because of disempowerment and childcare responsibilities. The EDP also deals with barriers faced by ethnic minorities and older workers in accessing Central London construction jobs. The EDP has 14 partners comprising training providers, employers, local authorities, community groups and unions. The lead partner is the London Borough of Southwark. Other partners include the Construction Industry Training Board, the Union of Construction and Allied Trades and Technicians (UCATT), the Lambeth Women's Workshop and Women's Education in Building. Beneficiaries are to be identified through outreach and referral measures, trained and supported in training and at work, and given help with dependant care, travel and equipment costs. One of the aims is to ensure that trained individuals retain a job for six consecutive months. The trade union, UCATT, for instance, will train and develop individuals as 'learning representatives' in the workplace. The London EDP has transnational cooperation agreements with EDPs in France and Germany. It was approved to spend between 2 and 5 million euros.

Good governance and partnership is even more thoroughly integrated into the proposed operation of the structural funds for the next programming period which runs from 2007-13.

We have seen that the 1999 'parent' Regulation for the structural funds 2000–6 contains the principle of partnership.[51] However, its accompanying 'daughter' Regulation on the ESF is silent on issues of governance and partnership.[52] This is not true of the 'daughter' Regulation on the ESF proposed for the 2007-13 period, Article 5 of which is dedicated to 'Good Governance and Partnership'.[53] Three aspects are worth mentioning. First, stress is placed on the territorial—local and regional—dimension of the ESF. Second, in programming, implementing and monitoring the ESF, Member States should ensure that the social partners are 'involved' and that non-governmental stakeholders are 'adequately consulted'. Third, and most interestingly, those managing the Member State's programme must encourage 'adequate participation and access' to funded activities by the social partners and NGOs. For NGOs this is particularly to be the case in the domain of social inclusion and gender equality. For the social partners, 'adequate participation and access' are further underwritten by fencing off a percentage of the ESF solely for activities jointly undertaken by the social partners, in particular to promote adaptability of workers and enterprises.

[51] Above, n 48.
[52] Above, n 29.
[53] Above, n 30.

The European Employment Strategy

The Employment Guidelines 2003–5 devote a special section to 'Good Governance and Partnership in the Implementation of the European Guidelines' calling on the involvement of parliamentary bodies, social partners and other relevant actors in the implementation of the EES.[54] The Commission has been keen to stress that 'from the very beginning the EES was an open process'.[55] However, one of the EES' major problems has been that it has been seen, and has generally proved in practice, to be an activity carried out, with varying degrees of commitment, solely by government officials.[56] The disjunction between theory (involvement by a wide range of public and private actors) and practice creates three serious problems for the EES as a governance tool. The first is an effectiveness problem: without public and private actors 'buying into' the EES it simply will not function particularly as it lacks the more obvious sticks and carrots generally available under legislation and the ESF. The second is a legitimacy problem: without enough relevant public and private actors being involved, the EES risks having very little legitimacy. The third is a visibility problem: until the EES is owned and deployed by a wide range of relevant public and private actors it will be largely ignored by the media and the general public.

These problems, and the costs of the non-EES,[57] have had two perceptible effects on its development. First, it has pushed the issue of who participates in the EES higher up the political agenda. Second, a change has occurred in which public and private actors are seen as relevant and how they should be included in the EES. While the 2003-5 Employment Guidelines state that good governance and partnership is important, in practical terms this amounts to little more than exhorting the *relevant actors* 'in accordance with national tradition and practices' to *implement* the EES. In 2004, both the Spring European Council[58] and the Council's

[54] Council Decision of 22 July 2003 on Guidelines for the Employment Policies of the Member States (OJ L 197/13). However, see G de Búrca who points out that the stronger commitment to wider participation in the Commission's proposed Guidelines was watered down by the Council: 'The constitutional challenge of new governance in the European Union', 28 ELR (2003) 814 at fn 99.

[55] Para 1.4, Communication from the Commission to the Council, the European Parliament, the Economic and Social Committee and the Committee of the Regions: *The Future of the European Employment Strategy (EES) "A Strategy for Full employment and Better Jobs for All"* COM(2003)6 final, Brussels (14 January 2003).

[56] For an excellent detailed assessment see J Zeitlin, 'Conclusion: The Open Method of Coordination in Action: Theoretical Promise, Empirical Realities, Reform Strategy' in Zeitlin and Pochet with Magnusson (eds) n 14 above.

[57] See, in particular, the two reports of groups led by Mr Wim Kok. The first, requested by the Spring European Council of 2003, reported in November 2003: *Jobs, Jobs, Jobs. Creating More Employment in Europe*. The second, a broader report on how to revitalise the Lisbon Strategy, was set up by the Spring European Council of 2004, and reported in November 2004, *Facing the Challenge. The Lisbon Strategy for Growth and Employment*.

[58] Presidency Conclusions, Brussels, 25/26 March 2004, paras 43 and 44.

Recommendations to the Member States under the 2003-5 Employment Guidelines,[59] took a different tack. In order to ensure that support and advocacy for change reaches beyond Governments, the Member States were called upon to build *Reform Partnerships* involving *the social partners, civil society and the public authorities*. We can see here that a richer set of public and private actors is enumerated as having a role to play. Moreover, that role is not simply to 'implement' the Employment Guidelines; instead their envisaged role is to be involved in a more structured and far-reaching partnership with the Government of each Member State.

Even more far-reaching changes are in prospect as a result of the Kok Group's Mid-term Review of the Lisbon Strategy[60] and the decision of the new Commission President, Mr Barroso, to prioritise the revitalising of Lisbon. The 'new start' for Lisbon proposed by the Barroso Commission rotates around three central concepts, one of which is mobilising support for change.[61] In the Commission's view,

> establishing broad and effective ownership of the Lisbon goal is the best way to ensure words are turned into results. Everyone with a stake in Lisbon's success and at every level must be involved in delivering these reforms. They must become part of national political debate.[62]

Three significant changes are proposed to make this happen. First, there will be a shift away from *implementation* of EU Employment Guidelines towards *elaboration* at Member State level, after *broad discussion*, of the action needed to create more and better jobs and the commitments and targets that should be made in that specific Member State to achieve that goal. Second, these new integrated programmes for growth and jobs (national Lisbon programmes) should be given a higher public profile by being looked after by a 'Mr' or 'Ms Lisbon' in each Member State. Third, greater legitimacy and visibility should be given to the national Lisbon Programmes by discussions with the social partners and by their being adopted by Government following a debate in the national Parliament.[63]

[59] Council Recommendation 2004/741/EC of 14 October 2004 on the implementation of Member States' employment policies (OJ L 326/49).

[60] Above, n 57.

[61] The other two are more focus (ie, just two overriding priorities: growth and jobs) and simplifying and streamlining Lisbon.

[62] Communication to the Spring European Council, 'Working Together for Growth and Jobs: A New Start for the Lisbon Stategy' COM(2005)24.

[63] The Spring European Council of 23/24 March 2005 endorsed a weaker version of these proposals: see para 38(c) of the Presidency Conclusions:

> Member States will draw up, on their own responsibility, "national reform programmes" geared to their own needs and specific situation. Consultations on these programmes will be held with all stakeholders at regional and national level, including parliamentary bodies in accordance with each Member State's specific procedures. The programmes will make allowance for national policy cycles and may be revised in the event of changes in the situation. Member States will enhance their internal coordination, where appropriate by appointing a Lisbon national coordinator.

Conclusions

I have set out in some detail the linkages drawn between public and private actors in EU employment instruments in order to demonstrate what an important and transversal characteristic of EU employment governance it now is. To be sure, legislation, the ESF and the OMC link public and private actors in distinctive ways. Nonetheless, a general feature of EU employment governance is that more heavily populated governance spaces have been designed to deliver employment objectives that combine in new ways competitiveness and social justice.

CONSTITUTIONALISM AND NEW EU EMPLOYMENT GOVERNANCE

What has new EU employment governance got to do with EU constitutionalism and the documentary constitutional activity that has recently taken place in the EU, resulting in the EU Charter of Fundamental Rights and the (unratified) Constitutional Treaty which now contains that Charter?

This raises a preliminary question: why has constitutionalism been connected to EU employment governance at all? It is not immediately obvious why any positions have or need to be taken on the relevance of constitutionalism to EU employment governance. The connection rests, it seems to me, on what Neil Walker has termed 'the sheer open-ended inclusiveness of what may be signified under the constitutional sign'.[64] While questions about what the EU does in the employment field, and its relationship with its States and its citizens in that arena, 'can be in fact be framed in a variety of different discourses, [they] are also capable of being brought together, or condensed, under the wide umbrella of a constitutional register'.[65] That is to say, in recent years choices have been made—by politicians and scholars in particular—to bring the language of constitutionalism to bear on the EU[66] in order to explain and enhance its legitimacy.[67] The place given to employment governance in those analyses of constitutionalism depends on how one explains the EU and what is accordingly prescribed to enhance its legitimacy.

[64] N Walker, 'Europe's Constitutional Momentum and the Search for Polity Legitimacy' in JHH Weiler and CL Eisgruber (eds) *Altneuland: The EU Constitution in a Contextual Perspective*, Jean Monnet Working Paper 05/04, 22.

[65] *Ibid.*

[66] M Poiares Maduro notes that 'The currency of constitutionalism has become the dominant currency of the debates on European integration': 'How Constitutional Can the European Union Be? The Tension Between Intergovernmentalism and Constitutionalism in the European Union' in JHH Weiler and CL Eisgruber (eds) n 64 above at 1.

[67] This is not to deny the importance presence of constitutional denial in relation to the EU: see N Walker, n 64 above, at 26–27 discussing inter alia D Grimm, 'Does Europe Need a Constitution?' (1995) 1 *European Law Journal* 282. As Walker notes (27) the very invocation of a constitutional frame in relation to the EU is not innocent of social meaning as it 'conveys the message that the EU is the kind of entity which is suitable for constitutional treatment'.

What strikes me as most interesting is that it is entirely possible to construct a range of respectable arguments on the relationship between EU governance and constitutionalism. In this section I explore these different positions on EU employment governance and constitutionalism. Before doing so, it is worth thinking about the reasons lying behind the existence of such a wide range of positions. Part of the explanation for this range of positions lies in the focus from which EU employment governance is approached in discussions on constitutionalism. First, is the focus on EU employment governance as it is and how it actually operates, as it is and could operate or as it should be? Second, is attention directed to the *substantive focus* of EU employment governance or on how various actors are involved in EU employment governance? Approaches most interested in the substantive focus of EU employment governance will think about issues such as the policy areas on which EU employment governance has focused, whether 'hybridity' constitutes a threat to social justice and so on. Those whose primary concern is the identification of the *appropriate actors* of EU employment governance will be interested in issues such as the roles given to those actors, how the actors are selected, and how those actors interact over time. Third, what is the constitutional position focused upon? Is it the extant formal constitutional framework, the 'living' constitution and practices of governance, the position in the Constitutional Treaty, or some other possible constitutional settlement containing a different set of EU employment governance instruments which reflect a different set of EU aspirations and goals in the employment field?

My limited purpose is to demonstrate the possibility of cogent, though differing, constitutional positions on the EU and illustrate the place and treatment which EU employment governance receives within those positions. I group these positions into two broad categories: transformative EU constitutionalism and intergovernmental EU constitutionalism.

Transformative EU constitutionalism and new EU employment governance

I use the term transformative EU constitutionalism to embrace a range of positions which see the EU as 'becoming' constitutionalised and which take an expansive approach to constitutionalism. For transformative constitutionalists, the debate provoked by the current (unratified) Constitutional Treaty is not in any sense an end-point of EU constitutional discussions. Moreover, that debate and its outcomes are not exhaustive of EU constitutionalism; instead, they imperfectly reflect some of the concerns of that broader and ongoing debate. Two quite different variants of transformative constitutionalism are identified: 'state of nation-states' constitutionalism and processual constitutionalism.[68]

[68] I borrow 'processual constitutionalism' from Neil Walker, n 64 above, at 29.

'State of nation-states' constitutionalism

One variant of transformative EU constitutionalism urges the EU to be more 'state-like' in providing an adequate set of employment and social welfare guarantees: what Habermas calls a 'state of nation-states'.[69] It focuses both on the need to improve the substantive content of the EU component of the 'European social model' and on the need to stimulate a genuinely transnational civil and political society. Perhaps the most distinctive substantive proposal of this brand of EU constitutionalism is its bolder social spending plans for the EU. Hence Philippe Schmitter has proposed that the monies currently allocated to agricultural subsidies and structural and regional funds should be redirected to giving a Euro-stipendium to any citizen of the EU whose income is less than one-third of the average EU income.[70]

It is clear that this vision departs radically from the current EU position and the position in the Constitutional Treaty, in particular by allocating a large role to the EU in visible citizen-directed social spending. It views it as important for social and employment rights and other instruments to be provided by the EU, and not to rely primarily on alternative sources such as the Council of Europe or national sources. Two main reasons seem to underpin this strand of constitutionalism's prescription of EU-provision of a much more extensive set of social rights. One is the need to build a stronger feeling of 'we' amongst the citizens of the EU, to make them more of a 'people' than the 'peoples' of Europe. The second is the need for the EU to provide for the citizens of Europe what its States increasingly cannot or will not be able to provide because of global economic integration. The EU is seen as both a cause and a product of this global economic integration. The EU's role becomes one then of *conserving* the *distinctive* European social model that has been developed by its Member States.[71]

Although the Constitutional Treaty most certainly does not fulfil these aspirations, it can be examined to see whether it takes any steps towards fulfilling such state-supportive aspirations. The main new source pointing in this direction is the set of social rights contained in the EU Charter of Fundamental Rights.[72] This contains rights supporting transnational civil society as well as substantive social rights. So far as substantive rights are concerned, the Charter contains a significant number of employment rights including rights to equality on a wide range of grounds, rights to fair and

[69] J Habermas, 'Why Europe Needs A Constitution', (2001) 11 *New Left Review* 5 at 8.

[70] PC Schmitter, *How to Democratize the European Union ... and Why Bother?* (Lanham: Rowman and Littlefield, 2000) 44ff. See also Habermas n 69 above at 17, who notes that in his new EU 'full budgetary powers would not be necessary in the beginning'.

[71] See, eg, Habermas, n 69 above, at 6.

[72] Though see also Art I–47 on 'The principle of participatory democracy', in particular, its citizens' right of legislative initiative and Art I–48 on 'The Social Partners and autonomous social dialogue'.

just working conditions and to reconcile family and professional life. In relation to transnational civil society, the Charter contains rights to collective bargaining, collective action and to freedom of association.

However, this strand of constitutionalism would wish the Charter to contain a strong set of justiciable EU social rights binding on both the EU itself and its Member States in a wide range of circumstances. Its proponents would therefore be particularly concerned about the potentially large hurdles placed in the way of the EU Charter fulfilling the role they would like to see it play in the Member States by the horizontal clauses of the Charter. In particular, Article II–111 states that the provisions of the Charter are addressed to the Member States 'only when they are implementing Union law' and states that the Charter 'does not extend the field of application of Union law beyond the powers of the Union or establish any new power or task for the Union, or modify powers and tasks defined in other parts of the Constitution'.

Moreover, the Constitutional Treaty places additional obstacles on the fostering of transnational civil society. While freedom of association is protected in the EU Charter of Fundamental Rights,[73] since Maastricht the EU has explicitly excluded its competence to act in this area.[74] Moreover, one of the main last-minute changes to the Constitutional Treaty, at the insistence of the UK Government, was to require courts using the EU Charter of Fundamental Rights to have due regard to the explanations drawn up by the Conventions involved in the drafting of the Charter and subsequently the Constitutional Treaty.[75] This change was primarily intended to ensure that courts would not extensively interpret the rights to freedom of association and to strike embodied in the Charter in a way that would allow national limits on collective action by unions to be challenged, in particular in relation to *transnational* collective action.[76] These limitations on transnational

[73] See Art II–72 EU Constitutional Treaty:

> Everyone has the right to freedom of peaceful assembly and to freedom of association at all levels, in particular, in political, trade union and civic matters, which implies the right of everyone to form and join trade unions for the protection of their interests.

[74] Art 137(6) EC Treaty; retained as Art III–210(6) EU Constitutional Treaty: 'This Article shall not apply to pay, the right of association, the right to strike or the right to impose lockout'.

[75] See new Art II–112(7): 'The explanations drawn up as a way of providing guidance in the interpretation of the Charter of Fundamental Rights shall be given due regard by the courts of the Union and of the Member States' and the Declaration on the Charter annexed to the Constitutional Treaty which contains the Explanations.

[76] See, eg, that the Explanations tie the meaning of freedom of association to the more restricted meaning in Art 11 ECHR rather than the meaning given to it by the ILO's Committee of Experts on Freedom of association. Note also in relation the Charter's guarantee of collective action (Art II–88 EU Constitutional Treaty) that the Explanations provide that:

> The modalities and limits for the exercise of collective action, including strike action, come under national laws and practices, *including the question of whether it may be carried out in parallel in several Member States*.

activities by unions are significant in themselves. However, these restrictions clearly have broader implications for all of the voluntary associations making up a nascent transnational civil society.

Processual constitutionalism

The 'state of nation-states' variant of transformative constitutionalism can be contrasted with processual constitutionalism.[77] Processual constitutionalists are not simply making the point that 'constitutional' practices should be more expansively defined so as to go all the way down from formal constitutional documents to micro-processes of governance. Their point is that constitutional practices are in fact *primarily located and produced* in these micro-processes of governance rather than in formal constitutional texts.

In both its substantive and procedural focus, processual constitutionalism can be contrasted with state-building transformative constitutionalism. It is less exercised about pinning down precise social 'positive integration' gains. It also focuses more on the identification of *already instituted* governance sites as 'constitutional' than on the stimulation of transnational civil society stressed, inter alia, in the 'state of nation states' literature. From this point of view, the new peopled governance spaces we have identified as a key characteristic of new EU employment governance are central constitutional practices in the EU. So far as employment is concerned, the focus so far by processual constitutionalists has rested almost exclusively on the OMC.[78] Nonetheless the constitutional prescriptions of processual constitutionalism in relation to the OMC may be useful in relation to the ESF and EU employment legislation too. Although this view of constitutionalism sees the real constitutional action as going on below the surface of formal constitutional documents, and argues that such practices should be included in the concerns of mainstream constitutional law scholarship, it also views it as important to afford appropriate recognition and support to these constitutional practices in formal constitutional texts.[79] Gráinne de Búrca charts how the Convention failed to introduce into the Constitutional Treaty general requirements of transparency and participation across all the OMC processes. Indeed, the OMC receives no explicit mention in the Constitutional Treaty at all.[80] Although its *tools*—guidelines and so on—are recognised in the Constitutional Treaty's provisions on the Broad Economic Policy Guidelines,[81] the Employment provisions[82] and in the new

[77] I borrow this term from Neil Walker, n 64 above.

[78] Gerstenberg and Sabel, n 8 above; de Búrca, n 54 above.

[79] See, eg, J Holder and J Scott's chapter on environmental governance in this volume where they discuss 'embedded constitutionalism' in which 'the practice of governance has spawned a process of constitutionalisation from within'. Yet these new governance processes 'have failed even to ripple the constitutional surface of the EU'.

[80] Above n 54.

[81] Art I–15(1) and Art III–179.

[82] Art I–15(2) and Art III–206.

wording of the clauses on social policy,[83] no constitutional *values* underpinning these OMC processes were enshrined in Part III of the Constitutional Treaty. Nor are the types of constitutional values sought by processual constitutionalism found in Part II of the Constitutional Treaty: the EU Charter of Fundamental Rights. Rights protecting freedom of association are actually of limited use in deciding who should be allowed to participate, to deliberate or to act as representatives in a particularly constituted governance space. Who, for instance, should be allowed to bargain away the statutory limits on night work contained in the Working-time Directive on behalf of the workers who will otherwise be protected by those limits?[84]

Intergovernmental constitutionalism and EU employment governance

In intergovernmental constitutionalism the focus is placed more on analysing the constitutional framework as traditionally defined (not the expansive definition of 'constitutional' used by processual constitutionalists) and on the EU as it is (not as it should be as in 'state of nation-states' constitutionalism). In sum, the focus is on the existing Treaty framework, on the changes wrought to that framework by the Constitutional Treaty and on the relationship set up by those sources between the EU and its Member States.

Distinctive strands of intergovernmental constitutionalism emerge for two important reasons. First, there is descriptive disagreement over *how intergovernmental* the EU currently is: this affects how employment governance is viewed and what kind of constitutionalism the EU needs. Second, different positions can and are taken on the desirability of social and employment protection and governance in a market economy.

Maduro argues that, looking back, we can now see that the EU obtained legitimacy in the past from a strong version of intergovernmental constitutionalism. In that set-up, the policies of the EU were both enforced and constrained by a limited form of constitutionalism, providing regime legitimacy to the EU. However, what those EU policies were to be was largely decided under the logic of intergovernmentalism, in bargains between democratically legitimate states that represented their publics, and provided polity legitimacy to the EU.[85]

Now there can be no doubt that intergovernmentalism has not gone away. No-one is arguing that there has been a shift to a position in which the EU is a *pouvoir constituant* that no longer needs the agreement of the

[83] Art I–15(3) and Art III–213.

[84] On the very difficult issues raised by such questions in specific national contexts, see, eg, P Davies and C Kilpatrick, 'UK Worker Representation after Single Channel' (2004) 33 *ILJ* 121.

[85] Above n 66.

Member States to change its formal operating framework and acts on behalf of its 'people'.

The concerns highlighted by an intergovernmental legitimacy set-up, in which EU constitutionalism plays the role of policing the effective and appropriate exercise of functionally limited, delegated, EU powers have been and will continue to be important in assessments of the EU's actions in the field of employment. From this perspective, it is no easy task to see how provision of employment rights by the EU can be justified given the division of labour between the EU and the Member States set out both in the current constitutional framework and clarified and strengthened by the Constitutional Treaty. This is reflected in arguments noting that the justifications for introduction of many pieces of EU employment legislation in the past were 'in truth rather weak'.[86] Even when, post-Maastricht, it has become easier to find an appropriate legal base for employment legislation, resolving the competence problem, it is difficult to fulfil the requirements of the subsidiarity principle, according to which the EU should act 'only if and insofar as the objectives of the proposed action cannot be sufficiently achieved by the Member States'.[87] Some variants of intergovernmental constitutionalism are also conservative in political terms. This leads to worries that the EU could confer rights on citizens, workers and unions additional to those currently provided at national level, and that this is an unwarranted and unacceptable intrusion of EU law into sensitive political choices properly left to the Member States.[88] Such concerns have left an extremely heavy imprint on the EU Charter of Fundamental Rights and explain in particular the additional restrictions placed on the rights to freely associate and to engage in collective action.[89]

The question therefore is not whether intergovernmentalism is present or absent in the EU constitutional framework. The question is whether the EU can continue to be legitimised *solely* by reliance on this 'intergovernmentalism & functional EU constitutionalism' model. EU employment governance has become part of a descriptive disagreement over the extent to which the EU can continue to be solely legitimised in this way. Those who argue that this is still largely the way the EU works tend to argue that there is not very much EU employment governance and nor is there likely to be.

[86] P Davies commenting on the distortion of competition argument used to introduce the collective dismissals directive in 1975, 'The Emergence of European Labour Law' in W McCarthy (ed) *Legal Interventions in Industrial Relations: Gains and Losses* (Oxford, Blackwell, 1992) 330.

[87] Art 5(2) EC Treaty. See the expanded definition in Art I–11(3) of the Constitutional Treaty.

[88] At their most extreme, such Euro-sceptic stances, exemplified by parts of the UK Conservative party, become transformative in their advocacy of the abolition of substantial parts of the EU employment governance structure and, more broadly, their desire to turn the EU into a much looser free trade association.

[89] See above nn 73–76.

Moravscik provides an argument at the strong intergovernmental end of this spectrum.[90] In his view, the development of the EU over the last five decades has given us the EU its Member States want—no more, no less. The old legitimacy set-up is therefore still the appropriate legitimacy set-up. The Constitutional Treaty's role is to clarify and synthesise this stable and *constitutionally mature* framework in which the States provide polity legitimacy and EU constitutionalism provides regime legitimacy by ensuring the proper exercise of those EU powers. Moreover, the EU system is also stable because those powers are unlikely to expand anytime in the near future. In his view, developments in social and employment policy do not belie that assessment. Hence, the substantive results of employment and social policy by coordination have 'been extremely modest, if present at all'.[91] EU employment and social expenditure is limited and looks very unlikely to increase: there will be no European minimum citizens' income or welfare state.[92] Why? There is simply no functional pressure for the Member States to give the EU greater powers in this field.[93]

However, Maduro argues that the current EU constitutionalism debate has arisen precisely because the EU can no longer simply rely on its previous legitimacy set-up. This is because that legitimacy set-up relied upon the EU's actions being clearly traceable to a set of limited functions. However, because of the significant expansion in EU competences (express and implied), increased recourse to majoritarian decision making at EU level, and the spillover effect of the rules on market integration:

> The borders of Union action are no longer defined by the express competences that the States have attributed to it and are, instead, the flexible product of the political action of a broad range of social actors that attempt to promote their interests in a new level of decision-making whose political authority is such as to allow for the pursuit of a broad and highly undetermined set of public goals.[94]

Such an approach, transposed to the employment context, envisages a more expansive role for the EU in employment governance from that emerging from stronger versions of intergovernmentalism. The result, for

[90] A Moravscik, 'The European Constitutional Compromise and the Legacy of Neo-functionalism' (2005) 12 *Journal of European Public Policy* 1.

[91] *Ibid* at 18.

[92] Accordingly he comments (p 28) on Schmitter's EU minimum income proposal (n 70 above):

> Such schemes would surely succeed in "democratising" the EU, but only at the expense of its further existence. The impracticality of such schemes demonstrates the lack of a realistic alternative to current, indirect forms of democratic accountability.

[93] See also, G Majone, 'Europe's "Democratic Deficit": The Question of Standards' (1998) 4 *European Law Journal* 5 at 10:

> The attempt to legitimate the Community by developing European standards of social justice is bound to fail under present circumstances because it goes against the clearly expressed preferences of the governments and the citisens of the Member States.

[94] Above, n 66 at 10.

the foreseeable future, will be the pragmatic, and potentially uneasy, co-existence of intergovernmentalism with the broader pursuit of EU polity-building actions. This is the kind of assessment made of EU employment law by Hugh Collins. He argues that we should not be surprised that the Member States are reluctant to cede competence over central areas of historical industrial compromise as reflected in national strike laws. Accordingly the solution proposed in the Constitutional Treaty—to continue to exclude competence over freedom of association, strikes and lockouts, while providing fundamental rights oversight by the EU in these areas—is a sensible recognition for the foreseeable future of both the rights at stake and the diversity of the States' positions.[95] However, outside these sensitive areas, 'the remainder of employment law, particularly those parts that are perceived to constitute essential ingredients in the themes of social inclusion, competitiveness and citizenship, seem destined to become subject to processes and dialogue at a European level with a view to the creation of common minimum standards'. [96] While the EU can appropriately set out broadly defined employment governance principles, it will often best be left to the social partners and the Member States to flesh out the details of that framework.[97] This also indicates that the peopled governance spaces which are so central to processual constitutionalism and are a key feature of EU employment governance may receive less attention in even socially progressive versions of intergovernmental constitutionalism. This is not only because this kind of constitutionalism tends to be less focused on identifying governance practices of this kind as 'constitutional'. It is also because intergovernmental constitutionalism is more likely to identify the State as the place where these practices are to be carried out and where *better choices* about who should participate, deliberate or represent the relevant 'people' will be made: where workplace agreements adjusting statutory standards will be made, where Employment Guidelines will be implemented, and where European Social Fund partnerships will be constructed.

CONCLUSIONS

This chapter has sought to demonstrate that the transformation of employment regulation at EU level since Maastricht is fertile ground for studies of both 'new governance' and of EU constitutionalism. One of the most difficult, but also stimulating, problems I faced when writing this chapter was

[95] H Collins, *Employment Law*, Clarendon Law Series (OUP, 2003) 251–52.
[96] *Ibid*.
[97] *Ibid*:

> Although the European Community has a vital role to play in articulating the broad reach of these principles [of competitiveness, social inclusion and citizenship], their detailed implementation can be achieved through a variety of methods and levels of governance.

that, in considering the relationship between new governance and constitutionalism, the 'new governance' path can seem to lead down one constitutionalism path only: that of processual constitutionalism. Although this is a deeply interesting path, it did not seem fully to capture the range of ways in which employment governance was important to debates on EU constitutionalism. This is because EU employment governance is 'new' in the other ways outlined in this chapter as well: there is much more of it than there was pre-Maastricht, its objectives are different, and a much wider range of tools exists to pursue those new objectives in an integrated manner at EU level. My core argument has been that to understand EU governance properly and to assess the wide range of constitutional positions in which employment governance plays a role, it is vital to consider the full range of EU employment governance tools and the objectives they are called upon to pursue. The four tools focused on in this chapter are legislation, expenditure, the OMC and fundamental social rights. Consideration of all of these governance tools provides, in turn, the constitutional tools for an important debate on how these activities should best be carried out in the EU in order to ensure, in the words of the Constitutional Treaty, 'unity in diversity' in a 'social market economy'.

6

Solidarity and New Governance in Social Policy

CATHERINE BARNARD

INTRODUCTION

SOLIDARITY IS ONE of the defining values of the European Union. The Laeken declaration describes Europe as:

> [T]he continent of liberty, solidarity and above all diversity, meaning respect for others' languages, cultures and traditions. The European Union's one boundary is democracy and human rights.[1]

The importance of solidarity to the European Union is recognised by the European Coal and Steel Community (ECSC), European Community (EC) and European Union (EU) Treaties and, more strikingly, the Treaty establishing a Constitution for Europe (Constitutional Treaty). The aim of this chapter is to examine how solidarity, a concept which originated in the welfare systems of nation states, has been borrowed and developed at European Union level. In particular, it considers what contribution solidarity can make to the debate about new governance in the field of social policy.

The chapter begins by briefly examining the various ways in which the Treaties have recognised solidarity before considering its use by various actors, in particular the Community institutions and the Community courts. It then considers whether solidarity can or should be a tool of new governance, and what new governance mechanisms can bring to the EU's understanding of solidarity.

SOLIDARITY AS A VALUE, AN OBJECTIVE AND A PRINCIPLE

Solidarity is a concept which originated in the social welfare systems of the Member States, particularly those of France, Belgium and Germany.

[1] European Council Meeting in Laeken, Presidency Conclusions (14 December 2001) 00300/1/01, p 21.

Advocate General Fennelly defined solidarity in his opinion in *Sodemare*[2] as the 'inherently uncommercial act of involuntary subsidization of one social group by another'.[3] In the national system it has meant that national taxpayers pay their taxes to help look after their fellow nationals who need assistance. This sense of solidarity is derived in part from a shared nationality, and in part from a shared sense of identity. As Cremona puts it, solidarity carries a sense of 'mutual dependence in addition to unity of purpose and common interest'.[4] Together these abstract ideas work to create a sense of responsibility for the weaker members of the group: thus *national* citizenship leads to the evolution of a sense of national solidarity.

Given solidarity's well-established provenance in the founding Member States, it is perhaps not surprising that solidarity was expressly recognised in the first of the foundation Treaties, the ECSC Treaty of 1951. Its Preamble provided that:

> Recognising that Europe can be built only through real practical achievements which will first of all create *real solidarity*, and through the establishment of common bases for economic development.

Reference to the principle of solidarity was also made in the Preamble to the EEC Treaty of 1957. This provided:

> INTENDING to confirm the *solidarity* which binds Europe and the overseas countries and desiring to ensure the development of their prosperity, in accordance with the principles of the United Nations,

However, 'solidarity' was not mentioned in the text of the Treaty itself until 1992 when it was included in Article 2 EC under the heading of Community tasks.[5] At the same time it was also included in the Preamble to the Treaty on European Union (TEU) which provides:

> DESIRING to deepen the *solidarity* between their peoples while respecting their history, culture and their traditions,

Solidarity also appears in Article 1 TEU as a task of the Union 'to organise, in a manner demonstrating consistency and *solidarity*, relations between the Member States and between their peoples'.

The word solidarity has made a number of appearances in the Constitutional Treaty: it appears in the Preamble of both the Constitutional

[2] Case C–70/95 *Sodemare SA, Anni Azzurri Holding SpA and Anni Azzurri Rezzato Srl v Regione Lombardia* [1997] ECR I–3395.

[3] Para 29. The meaning of solidarity in the EU context is considered further in C Barnard, 'EU Citizenship and the Principle of Solidarity' in M Dougan and E Spaventa (eds) *Social Welfare and EU Law* (Oxford: Hart, 2005).

[4] See also M Cremona, 'EU Enlargement: Solidarity and Conditionality' (2005) 30 ELR 3, 3.

[5] 'The Community shall have as its task ... the raising of the standard of living and quality of life, and economic and social cohesion and solidarity among Member States'.

Treaty[6] and the Charter of Fundamental Rights[7] and again in the statement of the Union's values.[8] Solidarity also appears in the list of the Union's objectives where the term solidarity is used in three different ways: first, it talks of 'solidarity between generations'[9]; secondly, it talks of 'solidarity among Member States',[10] an idea which is given more concrete expression in Article I–43 which requires the Union and its Member States to 'act jointly in a spirit of solidarity' if a Member State is the victim of terrorist attack or natural or man-made disaster;[11] and thirdly, it refers to 'solidarity and mutual respect among peoples' in respect of the Union's relations with the outside world.[12]

This review shows that the Treaty drafters view solidarity as both a value and an objective of the Union.[13] The Court of Justice has also recognised solidarity as a principle.[14] For example, in the 1978 case of *Benzine en*

[6] The Preamble provides:

> Believing that Europe, reunited after bitter experiences, intends to continue along the path of civilisation, progress and prosperity, for the good of all its inhabitants, including the weakest and most deprived; that it wishes to remain a continent open to culture, learning, and social progress; and that it wishes to deepen the democratic and transparent nature of its public life, and to strive for peace, justice and solidarity throughout the world.

[7] 'Conscious of its spiritual and moral heritage, the Union is founded on the indivisible, universal values of human dignity, freedom, equality and solidarity;'

[8] Art I–2:

> The Union is founded on the values of respect for human dignity, liberty, democracy, equality, the rule of law and respect for human rights, including the rights of persons belonging to minorities. These values are common to the Member States in a society in which pluralism, non-discrimination, tolerance, justice, solidarity and equality between men and women prevail.

[9] Art I–3 para 3 provides:

> It shall combat social exclusion and discrimination, and shall promote social justice and protection, equality between women and men, solidarity between generations and protection of the rights of the child.

This usage was earlier recognised by the Court of Justice in Case C–50/99 *Podestà v CRICA* [2000] ECR I–4039 para 21 in respect of those in employment and those in retirement.

[10] Art I–3 para 3 continues: 'It shall promote economic, social and territorial cohesion, and solidarity among Member States.'

[11] See also Council Regulation 2012/2002 establishing the European Union Solidarity Fund, [2002] OJ L311/3) which has been used in cases of the storm and flooding in Malta in Sept 2003, the forest fire in Spain in the summer of 2003 and the flooding in Southern France in Dec 2003: see EP and Council Dec 2004/323/EC, [2004] OJ L104/112.

[12] Art I–3 para 4 says:

> In its relations with the wider world, the Union shall uphold and promote its values and interests. It shall contribute to peace, security, the sustainable development of the Earth, solidarity and mutual respect among peoples, free and fair trade, eradication of poverty and protection of human rights and in particular the rights of the child, as well as to strict observance and to development of international law, including respect for the principles of the United Nations Charter.

[13] For a detailed discussion of this theme, see M Cremona, 'Values in the EU Constitution: the External Dimension' in Susan Millns and Monica Aziz (eds) *Values in the Constitution of Europe* (Ashgate Press, forthcoming).

[14] Solidarity has not been recognised as such by the Treaty drafters (Art 6 TEU lists only 'liberty, democracy, respect for fundamental right and fundamental freedoms, and the rule of law' as 'principles' of the EU).

Petroleum[15] the Court talked of the '*principle* of Community solidarity which is one of the foundations of the Community'(emphasis added), [16] a view now shared by the Member States which also have recognised solidarity as a general principle of Community law.[17]

The different uses of solidarity—as a value, as an objective and as a principle—highlights the flexible nature of the concept, suggesting that it can serve a variety of functions. On the one hand, it can serve as a rhetorical device enabling decision makers to invoke the concept as a *value or an objective*, to guide policy development. On the other hand, solidarity as a *principle* might serve a more substantive role justifying legislative decisions; and in this context the use of the solidarity principle might be reviewable by the Courts. This very flexibility makes solidarity a potential tool of new governance and worthy of further investigation. In the next section I consider the use of solidarity by the various institutional actors, in particular the legislative institutions—the Commission and the Council. I then consider how the Community Courts have responded to this usage. Given the origin of the term in the national welfare systems, my examination will focus on the field of social policy as broadly construed.

THE USES OF 'SOLIDARITY' BY THE VARIOUS INSTITUTIONAL ACTORS

Solidarity as used by the legislative institutions

Introduction

In this section I consider two uses of solidarity that, for the sake of exposition, I have distinguished as 'hard' and 'soft'. By 'hard' uses I mean situations where the institutions use solidarity as a guiding 'principle' for legislation; by 'soft' uses I mean situations where solidarity serves as an 'objective' or 'value' guiding the shape of other policies and/or Community expenditure.

'Hard' uses of solidarity

'Solidarity' has been used as a guiding principle in EC legislation to justify what are, in essence, 'sacrifices'[18] by certain undertakings/companies to assist others in their sector. This usage of solidarity was first seen in the

[15] Case 77/77 *Benzine en Petroleum Handelsmaatschappij BV v Commission* [1978] ECR 3079 para 15.

[16] For a more recent example, see Case C–84/96 *Netherlands v Commission* [1999] ECR I–6547 para 47.

[17] See, eg, the arguments raised by the governments in Case C–308/95 *Netherlands v Commission* [1999] ECR I–6513 para 20 and Case C–445/00 *Austria v Council* [2003] ECR I–000 para 78.

[18] Joined cases 26 and 86/79 *Forges de Thy-Marcinelle et Monceau SA v Commission (concrete reinforcement bars)* [1980] ECR 4155 para 10.

1970s in respect of the anti-crisis policy in the iron and steel sector where the reference to solidarity in the Preamble to the ECSC Treaty provided the basis for the Commission to justify a variety of interventionist measures. For example, in *Valsabbia*[19] the Court noted that

> [t]he anti-crisis policy in the iron and steel sector is based on the fundamental principle of solidarity between different undertakings, proclaimed in the preamble to the ECSC Treaty and given practical expression in numerous articles, such as Article 3 (priority accorded to the common interest, which presupposes the duty of solidarity), Article 49 et seq. (a system of financing the Community based on levies).

The case concerned overproduction in the steel sector, particularly of concrete reinforcement bars. As the Court noted, in pursuance of the principle of solidarity the Commission began by taking non-compulsory measures designed to bring the supply of iron and steel products more into line with demand.[20] When this did not work, the Commission introduced a compulsory system of prices, by General Decision 962/77,[21] and the method used to fix the level of the prices was a 'discretionary and technical matter governed by the principle of solidarity'.[22] The Court found that the General Decision was compatible with the ECSC Treaty. The legality of the General Decision was again challenged in *Forges de Thy-Marcinelle*[23] and once again the Court upheld the validity of the measure, noting that 'even if the measure in dispute did require sacrifices of certain undertakings for the sake of Community solidarity, it did not cause them undue hardship'.[24]

In another move to address over production in the steel sector, the Commission issued Decision 2794/80[25] laying down steel production quotas, and providing the power to fine undertakings which exceeded their quotas. This Decision was based on Article 58 ECSC which permitted a quota system to be adopted only if there was a 'manifest crisis' in the sector which was so serious as to jeopardise all the undertakings in the Community. The quota system was intended to deal with the crisis by imposing a general reduction in supply intended to bring supply and demand back into equilibrium and to check the fall in prices. In *Ferriera Padana SpA*[26] the Court dismissed arguments that the quota system adopted (which applied to all

[19] Joined cases 154, 205, 206, 226 to 228, 263 and 264/78, 39, 31, 83 and 85/79 *SpA Ferriera Valsabbia and others v Commission* [1980] ECR 4046 para 59.

[20] Para 59.

[21] Decision 962/77/ECSC, [1977] OJ L114/1.

[22] Para 71.

[23] Joined cases 26 and 86/79 *Forges de Thy-Marcinelle et Monceau SA v Commission (concrete reinforcement bars)* [1980] ECR 4155.

[24] Para 10. In Case 276/80 *Ferriera Padana SpA v Commission* [1982] ECR 517 the Court dismissed arguments that the quota system adopted led to the 'irregular application of the principle of solidarity'.

[25] [1980] OJ L291/1.

[26] Case 276/80 *Ferriera Padana SpA v Commission* [1982] ECR 517.

undertakings and not just to large and inefficient undertakings) led to the 'irregular application of the principle of solidarity'. In *Klochner-Werke*[27] the Court was more expansive. It noted that Article 58 ECSC was based on solidarity between all Community steel undertakings in the face of a crisis and sought an equitable distribution of the sacrifices between all steel undertakings.[28] The Court continued that 'those undertakings must strive together in a display of Community solidarity so as to enable the industry as a whole to overcome the crisis and survive'.[29] For that reason, the Court said, no single undertaking, by pleading special financial difficulties, could seek to exempt itself and exceed the production quotas.[30]

Even though there is no equivalent of Article 58 ECSC in the European Community Treaty, the idea of solidarity between producers in a specific sector has been extended beyond coal and steel to a number of areas covered by the EC Treaty, notably agriculture, fisheries and transport. In respect of agriculture, the Court recognised in *Eridania Zuccherifici*[31] that in dividing quotas between individual undertakings on the basis of their actual production under the system established by Regulation 1785/81[32] the Council was acting in accordance with the principles of regional specialisation and solidarity. The solidarity principle was expressly recognised in the Preamble to Regulation 934/86,[33] amending Regulation 1785/81, which provided that 'a demonstration of solidarity should be asked of all producers concerned so that the deficit recorded following the period of 1981/82 to 1985/86, amounting in budgetary terms to some 400 million ECU, may be eliminated'. This resulted in an elimination levy (referred to as a solidarity levy[34]) being charged to manufacturers of sugar during the following 5 years in respect of the production of certain types of sugar. This levy was upheld by the European Court of Justice in *Société sucrière agricole de maizy*.[35]

[27] Case 263/82 *Klockner-Werke v Commission* [1983] ECR 5075.

[28] Para 17, wording reiterated by AG Biancerelli in Case T–120/89 *Stahlwerke Peine-Salzgitter AG v Commission* [1991] ECR II–279. See also Case 81/83 *Acciaierie e Ferriere Busseni SpA v Commission* [1984] ECR 2951 para 18. In respect of a later Decision fixing quotas, see Case 64/84 *Queenborough Rolling Mill Company Ltd v Commission* [1985] ECR 1829. See also Case 92/88 R *Assider v Commission* [1988] ECR 2425 where the Court found that the Commission measure 'did not exceed the level of sacrifices which the Commission may validly impose on steel undertakings for the sake of solidarity'; and AG Mischo's Opinion in Joined Cases 167 and 212/88 *Assider and Italy v Commission* [1987] ECR 1701.

[29] Para 19.

[30] Similarly, in Case 64/84 *Queenborough Rolling Mill Company Ltd v Commission* [1985] ECR 1829 para 11 the Court said that the 'principle of solidarity does not allow the applicant to rely on fixed delivery contracts in order to justify the fact that it exceeded its quotas'. See also Joined Cases 63 and 147/84 *Finsider v Commission* [1985] ECR 2857 paras 29–32.

[31] Case 250/84 *Eridania zuccherifici nazionali SpA and others v Cassa conguaglio zucchero and the Italian Ministry of Finance and the Treasury* [1986] ECR 5804 para 20.

[32] [1981] OJ L177/4.

[33] [1986] OJ L87/1.

[34] AG Lenz's Opinion in Joined Cases C–143/88 and C–92/89 *Zuckerfabrik Suderdithmarschen AG v Hauptzollamt Itzehoe* [1991] ECR I–415 para 147.

[35] Case C–172/95 *Société sucrière agricole Maizy and Société sucrière de Berneuil-sur-Aisne v Directeur régional des impots* [1996] ECR I–5581.

Sugar is not the only agricultural sector in difficulty; the dairy sector has also suffered from major structural surpluses. This led the Council to adopt two Regulations (856/84[36] and 857/84[37]) introducing a levy on quantities of milk delivered beyond a predetermined reference quantity. Regulation 857/84 allowed Member States to vary the percentage applied to the reference quantities in order to allocate additional reference quantities to producers who had adopted milk production development plans. As Advocate General Van Gerven noted in *Cornée*,[38]

> [t]his provision therefore enables a system of solidarity to be established in which abatements are imposed on all producers in order to grant supplementary reference quantities to certain producers who find themselves in a situation which justifies specific aid.

When, in *Spain v Council*[39] the Spanish government argued that Spain should not form part of the Community regime because it had played no part in creating the Community surpluses, since there was a milk production deficit in its industry,[40] the Council and Commission rejected such arguments. They reasoned that the fact that even though Spain had not contributed to the creation of Community surpluses, not including Spain in the new Community regime was 'contrary to the principle of solidarity'.[41] The Court seemed to agree, ruling that the Council had not committed a manifest error in finding that the situation in the Spanish milk industry was sufficiently different to justify differential treatment.[42]

[36] [1984] OJ L90/10.

[37] [1984] OJ L90/13.

[38] Joined Cases 196/88, 197/88 and 198/88 *Cornée and others v Cooperative agricole laitière de Loudeac (Copall)and Laiterie cooperative du Trieux* [1989] ECR I–2309 para 5.

[39] Case 203/86 *Spain v Council* [1988] ECR 4563.

[40] Para 22.

[41] Para 24.

[42] Para 26. In a similar vein, but this time in the context of the wine industry, see Case C–375/96 *Zaninotto v Ispettorato Centrale Repressione Frodi* [1998] ECR I–6629 paras 45–48 where the Commission argued that the burden of the surplus was not placed on Italian producers alone but was redistributed among all Community producers in accordance with the principle of solidarity (a word not mentioned in the relevant regulation), an approach consistent with 'the prohibition of discrimination as interpreted by the Court'. The Court seemed to agree, noting the Commission's wide discretion in pursuing the objective of improving conditions on the wine market and that

> all Community producers, regardless of the Member State in which they are based, must together, in an egalitarian manner, bear the consequences of the decisions which the Community institutions are led to adopt in the exercise of their powers in order to respond to the risk of an imbalance which may arise in the market between production and market outlets

The Court repeated these sentiments in Case C–56/99 *Gascogne Limousin Viandes SA v Office National Interprofessionnel des Viandes de l'Élevage et de l'Aviculture (Ofival)* [2000] ECR I–3079 para 40 in the context of the early-marketing premium for calves which had been introduced to help improve and restore balance to the market for beef and veal which had been seriously disturbed by consumer fears concerning BSE.

The express language of solidarity has also been used to address specific problems in the fisheries sector. For example, in 1998 the Council introduced a 'solidarity mechanism' in its Regulation on the total allowable catches for certain stocks of highly migratory fish[43] under which a certain tonnage of bluefin tuna was deducted from the quota allocated to three Member States for re-allocation to two other states on which the quota reduction had the greatest impact. Once again, in *Italy v Council*[44] the Court upheld the Council's measure.

The other area where major structural changes have been necessary is in transport, particularly inland waterway. Council Regulation 1101/89[45] helped to achieve a substantial reduction in overcapacity in the inland waterways sector (particularly in the Benelux countries and France and Germany) by introducing a scrapping scheme coordinated at Community level but financed by the industry itself. Each Member State whose waterways were linked to those of another Member State had to set up a Scrapping Fund; all owners of a vessel had to contribute to one of those funds. When a vessel owner scrapped a vessel he was entitled to a scrapping premium. In *Schiffart*[46] the Council justified its Regulation as a 'solidarity measure that was appropriate and beneficial for the whole sector', an argument that the Court of Justice accepted.

'Softer' uses of solidarity

So far we have seen how the solidarity principle has been used to justify Community legislation which shares the burden of restructuring. This is what I have termed the 'harder' use of the solidarity principle. The cases demonstrate that it is for the *Community* legislature to apply the solidarity principle to the sector;[47] *individual undertakings* cannot voluntarily apply the solidarity principle themselves for fear of breaching Article 81 on anti-competitive behaviour.[48]

However, I now wish to consider 'softer' use of the solidarity principle, where solidarity serves as an 'objective' or 'value' guiding the shape of other policies and/or Community expenditure. Social cohesion provides a good example. Article 2 EC lays down the Community objective of promoting 'economic and social cohesion and solidarity among the Member States'. This is given concrete expression in the cohesion policies set out in

[43] Council Reg 49/1999, [1999] OJ L13/64.

[44] Case C–120/99 *Italy v Council* [2001] ECR I–7997.

[45] [1989] L116/25.

[46] Joined Cases C–248/95 and C–249/95 *SAM Schiffart GmbH, Heinz Stapf v Germany* [1997] ECR I–4475 para 74. See also Case C–414/93 *Teirlinck v Minister van Verkeer en Waterstaat* [1995] ECR I–1339 where the headnote (but not the judgment) talks of the 'financial solidarity between the scrapping funds'.

[47] Case T–14/89 *Montedipe SpA v Commission* [1992] ECR II–1155para 286. This argument is developed further in the text attached to nn 71ff below.

[48] *Ibid.*

Title XVII (on economic and social cohesion and the structural funds) and subsequently fleshed out by detailed regulations. The Commission describes the Structural funds (ERDF, EAGGF, ESF and FIFG),[49] the Cohesion Fund, the funds aimed at preparing the CEECs for accession and the Solidarity Fund collectively as 'instruments of solidarity'.[50] The European Council also recognised the value of the solidarity principle to the 'success story' of the European Union. In its Laeken Declaration it said:

> As a result of mutual solidarity and fair distribution of the benefits of economic development, moreover, the standard of living in the Union's weaker regions has increased enormously and they have made good much of the disadvantage they were at.[51]

Solidarity is also seen as a key component of the European social model, a model characterised by systems offering a high level of social protection, the social dialogue and services of general interest.[52] As the Commission put it in its Communication of 2000 on the European Social Policy Agenda:[53]

> In the future, modernising the European social model and investing in people will be crucial to retain the European social values of solidarity and justice while improving economic performance.

Solidarity is thus seen as a vital part of the 'virtuous circle of economic and social progress' based on a mix of social policy (social quality/social cohesion), economic policy (competitiveness and dynamism) and employment policy (full employment/quality of work).[54] The European Council, in its own European Social Agenda agreed at Nice, also emphasised the importance of the solidarity principle as a feature that distinguishes the European social model. Under the heading 'Modernising and improving the European social model', it says that:

> To prepare for the future, the Union must rely on its achievements. It must continue to promote its inherent values of solidarity and justice as enshrined in the Charter of Fundamental Rights.[55]

[49] European Regional Development Fund, European Agricultural Guidance and Guarantee Fund, European Social Fund, Financial Instrument for Fisheries Guidance

[50] Jacques Delors characterised economic and social cohesion in terms of 'competition that stimulates, cooperation that reinforces, and solidarity that unites'. He called the solidarity that stems from the EU's structural policies the 'basic cement of Europe': Cremona, 'EU Enlargement', n 4 above.

[51] European Council Meeting in Laeken, n 1 above, at p20.

[52] Nice European Council, para 11.

[53] COM(2000)379, 6. See also COM(2001)104, 3 and 8.

[54] *Ibid.*

[55] Para 11. Similarly, under the heading 'Modernising Social Protection' it notes that the modernisation of social protection systems must meet the requirements of solidarity: that is what is at stake in the action we have to take on retirement and health and to achieve an active welfare state that strongly encourages participation in the employment market.

The Charter of Fundamental Rights itself contains a specific Title headed 'Solidarity' which embraces a range of social rights (eg, workers' rights to information and consultation, collective bargaining and action, protection in the event of unjustified dismissal, fair and just working conditions, prohibition of child labour and protection of young people at work, social security and social assistance, health care, environmental and consumer protection).

It may well be that this softer use of solidarity serves little more than a rhetorical function. However, solidarity is an important statement of the values underpinning the allocation of resources in the Union and provides a standard against which subsequent policy can be assessed. This raises the question as to the meaning of solidarity and how that meaning is determined. This question will be reconsidered after we examine how the Community Courts have responded to solidarity.

How the Community courts have responded to solidarity

Introduction

For many years, the Court of Justice has used the term solidarity as a synonym for the duty of cooperation laid down in Article 10 EC,[56] both between the Community institutions and the Member States[57] and between the Member States and the Community institutions. [58] The Court has also

[56] Joined cases 6 and 11/69 *Commission v France* [1969] ECR 1175 para 16. These sentiments were reiterated by AG Slynn in Case 57/86 *Greece v Commission* [1988] ECR 2855. In his opinion in Case 187/87 *Land de Sarre and others v Ministre de l'Industrie, des P et T et du Tourisme* [1988] ECR 5013 AG Slynn highlighted the links between the principles of 'effet utile' and of 'Community solidarity', a theme also developed by the Court of Justice in Joined Cases C–63/90 and C–67/90 *Portugal and Spain v Council* [1992] ECR I–5073 paras 51–53.

[57] Eg, Case T–139/99 *Alsace International Car Services (AICS) v European Parliament* [2000] ECR II–2849 para 41 concerned the duties owed by the Community institutions to the Member States. The Court of First Instance said:

> in accordance with the principles of sound administration and solidarity as between the Community institutions and the Member States, the institutions are required to ensure that the conditions laid down in an invitation to tender do not induce potential tenderers to infringe the national legislation which is applicable to their business.

[58] This use of the solidarity principle has spilled over into the field of the CFSP. Art 11(2) TEU provides:

> The Member States shall support the Union's external and security policy actively and unreservedly in a spirit of loyalty and mutual solidarity.
> The Member States shall work together to enhance and develop their mutual political solidarity. They shall refrain from any action which is contrary to the interests of the Union or likely to impair its effectiveness as a cohesive force in international relations.

See also the revised wording in Art I–15 of the Constitution:

> Member States shall actively and unreservedly support the Union's common foreign and security policy in a spirit of loyalty and mutual solidarity and shall comply with the Union's action in this area. They shall refrain from action contrary to the Union's interests or likely to impair its effectiveness.

used solidarity as an explanation for why the duty of cooperation exists,[59] and as a buttress to support the duty of cooperation.[60] However, it is only in more recent years that the Court has actually engaged with the principle of solidarity, first in response to its use by the Community legislature and secondly in respect of its use by private parties. Most recently the Court has used solidarity in a more pro-active way to impose obligations on the Member States in the context of its case law on citizenship. We shall consider these different attempts by the Court to engage with the principle of solidarity.

The courts' response to the use of solidarity by the legislative institutions

The very fact that the Court has identified solidarity as a general principle of law suggests that Community policies can be reviewed to see whether they comply with the principle of solidarity. As we have seen in the cases involving the 'harder' use of the solidarity principle (those involving restructuring in the steel, transport and agricultural sectors), the Court has recognised and largely supported the legislature's use of the solidarity principle to justify burden sharing. However, as we have also seen the review has been with the lightest of touch.[61] In this respect the Court's attitude to solidarity has much in common with its approach to subsidiarity.[62] Therefore, in cases such as *Ferriera Padana SpA*[63] and *Klochner-Werke*[64] the Court did not scrutinise the substance of the solidarity arguments put forward by the legislature, nor did it consider their application to the facts

[59] See, eg, Case C–278/98 *Netherlands v Commission* [2000] ECR I–1501, where, in AG Alber's Opinion at para 84, he reports that according to the Dutch government, the correction procedure under Art 5(2)(c) of Reg. 729/70 'merely specifies that in the procedure to determine the clearance of accounts the duty of cooperation in good faith which always exists between the Commission and the Member States on the basis of Community solidarity must apply'.

[60] See, eg, AG Darmon's Opinion in Case C–9/89 *Spain v UK* [1990] ECR I-1383 para 45:

> Furthermore, what we have here is merely the application to the particular case of the common fisheries policy of the principle of Community solidarity, which the Court has already recognised as one of the foundations of the Community, as well as the obligation on Member States to cooperate in achieving the objectives of the Treaty as laid down in Art [10] of the EEC Treaty.

In a similar vein, see the tone of the questions asked in Case C–112/00 *Eugen Schmidberger, Internationale Transporte und Planzüge v Republik Österreich* [2003] ECR I–5659.

[61] Case C–233/94 *Germany v Parliament and Council (Deposit Guarantee Schemes)* [1997] ECR I–2405; Case C–84/94 *UK v Council* [1996] ECR I–5755; Case C–377/98 *Netherlands v Parliament and Council* [2001] ECR I–000.

[62] See generally, A Toth, 'A Legal Analysis of Subsidiarity' in D O'Keeffe and P Twomey (eds) *Legal Issues of the Maastricht Treaty* (Chichester: Chancery, 1994). See also the essays by Steiner and Emiliou in the same volume as well as N Emiliou, 'Subsidiarity: An Effective Barrier Against "the Enterprises of Ambition"' (1992) 17 ELR 383; A Toth, 'The Principle of Subsidiarity in the Maastricht Treaty' (1992) 29 CML Rev 1079.

[63] Case 276/80 *Ferriera Padana SpA v Commission* [1982] ECR 517.

[64] Case 263/82 *Klockner-Werke v Commission* [1983] ECR 5075.

of a particular case, contenting itself instead with an endorsement of the general need for solidarity in the sector. Indeed, in the process of upholding solidarity in a particular sector, the Court has also been willing to enforce arrangements based on solidarity. Therefore, in *Germany v Commission (sheepmeat)*[65] the Court noted that Community aid paid to sheepmeat producers was 'based on the notion of solidarity'.[66] For this reason, it upheld the Community's powers to impose penalties on traders who had 'committed irregularities when making an application for financial aid'.

On the other hand, the Court has shown itself willing to ensure that the criteria laid down in the Treaty are satisfied and so will not be blinded by solidarity arguments to allow any legislative proposal to stand. Therefore, in *Fabrique de fer de Charleroi SA*[67] the Court found that the Commission had misused its powers in granting an additional quota to an undertaking which was the sole steel producer in the state (this rule benefited a particular Danish company) since this was not envisaged by Article 58 ECSC. The Court rejected the Danish government's contention that the principle of solidarity between Community undertakings justified a further effort on the part of some of those undertakings to ensure the survival of undertakings in a special situation.[68]

The Court of First Instance has also suggested that it might scrutinise the solidarity principle more closely in the context of state aid. In *AIUFFASS*[69] the CFI explained that Articles 87(3)(a) and (c) introduce two derogations from free competition 'based on the aim of Community solidarity, a fundamental objective of the Treaty'. Article 87(3)(a) gives the Commission discretion to authorise aid to promote the economic development of areas where the standard of living is abnormally low or where there is serious unemployment, while Article 87(3)(c) gives the Commission discretion to allow state aid to facilitate the development of certain economic activities or of certain economic areas, where such aid does not adversely affect trading conditions to an extent contrary to the general interest. In exercising its discretion whether to approve such aid under Article 87(3), the CFI said that the Commission had to ensure that 'the aims of free competition and Community solidarity are reconciled, whilst complying with the principle of solidarity'. It continued that '[t]he influence of Community solidarity may vary depending on the circumstances; it has more of an influence to the detriment of competition in the crisis situations described in paragraph 3(a) than in the cases provided for in paragraph 3(c)'.

[65] Case C–240/90 *Germany v Commission* [1992] ECR I–5383.

[66] Para 26.

[67] Joined Cases 351 and 360/85 *Fabrique de Fer de Charleroi SA and Dillinger Huttenwerke AG v Commission* [1987] ECR 3639.

[68] Para 21.

[69] Case T–380/94 *Association Internationale des utilisateurs de fils de filaments artificiels et synthétiques et de soie naturelle (AIUFFASS) and Apparel, Knitting & Textiles Alliance (AKT) v Commission* [1996] ECR II–2169 para 54.

The courts' response to the use of solidarity raised by individuals and undertakings

Increasingly, individuals—and more usually companies—have invoked the principle of solidarity to justify agreements which provide important welfare provision in the Member States. It is in this area that the Court has found it most difficult to respond to the use of solidarity. The problem lies in the fact that while, on the one hand, the idea of workers working together themselves or with their employers in a spirit of solidarity is something to be admired, [70] on the other hand, the uncontrolled joint activity of such groups risks coming close to an agreement between undertakings which might fall foul of competition law. The Court has therefore scrutinised most carefully arrangements between individuals and undertakings or between undertakings which they themselves have justified in the name of solidarity. For example, in *Montedipe*[71] the Court of First Instance rejected the argument put forward by the polypropylene producers that a reciprocal assistance contract in the case of necessity did not breach Article 81. The Commission had argued that 'solidarity and competition are mutually antagonistic' and that 'only the authorities could occasionally take action to reconcile them'. The Court agreed, noting that the 'principle of burden-sharing among undertakings by common agreement is contrary to the concept of competition which Article [81] ... is intended to uphold'.[72]

On the other hand, a rigorous application of Community competition law to pension or sickness schemes organised by employers could have a destructive effect on key pillars of a national welfare provision. Therefore,

[70] Case C–201/01 *Maria Walcher v Bundesamt für Soziales und Behindertenwesen Steiermark* [2002] ECR I–8827 para 49 AG Mischo:

> Indeed, one would be more inclined to salute the solidarity which, in certain circumstances, employees can, as here, demonstrate towards their employer and to criticise the opposite conduct, which is to pursue immediately all available legal remedies to obtain full payment of salary when due, even at the risk of accelerating the collapse of the undertaking.

See also AG Cosmas' Opinion in Joined Cases C–157/94, C–158/94, C–159/94 and C–160/94 *Commission v Netherlands* [1997] ECR I–5699 para 97:

> An economic activity the results of which by definition affect every individual (particularly in the case of the supply of electricity) or, at least, wide sectors of the population, must be carried out with particular regard to, inter alia, the need to contain the cost and to ensure certain basic forms of solidarity between those who do or may benefit from that activity.

[71] Case T–14/89 *Montedipe SpA v Commission* [1992] ECR II–1155.

[72] Para 286. See also Case T–61/89 *Dansk Pelsdyravlerforening v Commission* [1992] ECR II–1931 where the Court said that Art 81(1) still applied to a cooperative association of fur breeders based on solidarity and fairness; Case T–136/94 *Eurofer ASBL v Commission* [1999] ECR II–263 para 73:

> The circulation of such information, which is normally regarded as a trade secret, made it possible for each company to determine its competitors' past or present conduct on each market and established between them a system of solidarity and mutual influence that led to the coordination of their economic activities. This exchange of information thereby resulted in the normal risks of competition being replaced by practical cooperation and in conditions of competition different from those obtaining in a normal market. Such conduct is incompatible with Art 65(5) of the ECSC Treaty.

in some cases the Court has used the principle of solidarity[73] to justify arguing that where the activity is based on national solidarity, it is not an economic activity and therefore the body concerned cannot be classed as an undertaking to which Community competition rules apply.

This approach was first adopted in the case of *Poucet and Pistre*[74] where the Court held that certain French bodies administering the sickness and maternity insurance scheme for certain self-employed persons and the basic pension scheme for skilled trades, were not to be classified as undertakings for the purpose of competition law. The schemes, to which affiliation was compulsory, provided a basic pension,[75] regardless of the financial status and state of health of the individual at the time of affiliation. The schemes were also non-funded which meant that they operated on a redistributive basis, with active members' contributions being directly used to finance the pensions of retired members. This, the Court said, was the embodiment of the principle of solidarity.[76]

Solidarity was also reflected in the grant both of pension rights to those who had made no contributions and of pension rights that were not proportional to the contributions paid. There was also solidarity between the various social security schemes, with those in surplus contributing to the financing of those with structural difficulties. The Court therefore concluded that:

> It follows that the social security schemes, as described, are based on a system of compulsory contribution, which is indispensable for the application of the principle of solidarity and the financial equilibrium of those schemes.
>
> ... [O]rganisations involved in the management of the public social security system fulfil an exclusively social function. That activity is based on the principle of national solidarity and is entirely non-profit-making. The benefits paid are statutory benefits bearing no relation to the amount of the contribution.

The Court concluded: 'Accordingly, that activity is not an economic activity ...' and so EC competition law did not apply.

[73] T Hervey, 'Social Solidarity: A Buttress against Internal Market Law?' in J Shaw (ed) *Social Law and Policy in an Evolving European Union* (Oxford: Hart, 2000). In a different context, and outside the scope of this paper, but in a similar vein, is the view expressed in *La Cinq SA v Commission* [1992] ECR II–1 para 58 that:

> If commercial broadcasting undertakings were admitted as active members of the European Broadcasting Union alongside public–service broadcasting organisations, the Europevisions programme-exchange system itself could not remain what it is: a system of solidarity between organisations of the same nature indirectly supporting the weakest members.

[74] Joined Cases C–159/91 and C–160/91 *Poucet and Pistre v AGF and Cancava* [1993] ECR I–637.

[75] The features of these schemes are helpfully summarised by AG Jacobs in his Opinion in Case C–67/96 *Albany International BV v Stichting Bedrijfspensioenfonds Textielindustrie* [1999] ECR I–5751 para 317.

[76] See also AG Cosmas' views in Case C–160/96 *Molenaar v Allgemeine Ortskrankenkasse Baden-Württemberg* [1998] ECR I–843 paras 80 and 82; AG Tesauro's views in Case C–120/95 *Decker v Caisse de Maladie des employés privés* and Case C–158/96 *Kohll v Union des caisses de maladie* [1998] ECR I–1831 paras 20–23.

Poucet and Pistre can, however, be contrasted with *FFSA*[77] where the Court found there was insufficient solidarity in the scheme to justify taking it outside the scope of European Community law. The case concerned a French supplementary retirement scheme for self-employed farmers.[78] Membership of the scheme was optional and, unlike *Poucet*, the scheme operated on a capitalisation (rather than a redistributive) basis which meant that the benefits depended solely on the amount of contributions paid by the recipients and the financial results of the investments made by the managing organisation. On these facts the Court concluded that the managing body carried out an economic activity in competition with life assurance companies and so the Community competition rules, in particular Article 81, applied. Neither the social objective pursued (it was created by the government to protect those whose income was lower and whose average age was higher than those of other socio-economic categories and whose basic old-age insurance was not sufficient), nor the fact that it was non-profit-making, nor the requirements of solidarity (for example, contributions were not linked to the risks incurred and there was no prior questionnaire or medical examination and no selection took place) altered the fact that the managing organisation was carrying out an economic activity.

In the light of *FFSA* it is not surprising that in *Albany*[79] the Court found that a pension fund charged with the management of a supplementary pension scheme set up by a collective agreement concluded between organisations representing employers and workers in a given sector, to which affiliation had been made compulsory by the public authorities for all workers in that sector, was an undertaking within the meaning of Articles 81, 82 and 86. of the Treaty. The Court noted that, like *FFSA*, the scheme operated in accordance with the principle of capitalisation, in respect of which it was subject, like an insurance company, to supervision by the Insurance Board; and, the Court added, as with *FFSA*, this conclusion was not affected by the facts that the fund was non-profit making, that it pursued a social objective, and that it demonstrated elements of solidarity.[80] However, the Court

[77] Case C–244/94 *Fédération française des Sociétés d'Assurances* [1995] ECR I–4013 discussed by Laigre, 'L'intrusion du droit communautaire de la concurrence dans le champ de la protection sociale' [1996] *Droit social* 82.

[78] Case C–67/96 *Albany* [1999] ECR I–5751 para 325.

[79] Case C–67/96 [1999] ECR I–5751 para 87. see also Joined Cases C–180/98 to C–184/98 *Pavlov and Others* [2000] ECR I–6451.

[80] The solidarity was reflected by the obligation to accept all workers without a prior medical examination, the continuing accrual of pension rights despite exemption from contributions in the event of incapacity for work, the discharge by the fund of arrears of contributions due from an employer in the event of the latter's insolvency and by the indexing of the amount of the pensions in order to maintain their value. The principle of solidarity was also apparent from the absence of any equivalence, for individuals, between the contribution paid, which is an average contribution not linked to risks, and pension rights, which are determined by reference to an average salary. Such solidarity makes compulsory affiliation to the supplementary pension scheme essential. Otherwise, if 'good' risks left the scheme, the ensuing downward spiral would jeopardise its financial equilibrium (para 75). This would increase the cost of pensions for workers, particularly those in small and medium-sized undertakings with older employees engaged in dangerous activities, to which the fund could no longer offer pensions at an acceptable cost (para 108).

did recognise that the solidarity elements justified the exclusive right of the fund to manage the supplementary scheme under Article 86(2) and so there was no breach of Articles 82 and 86.

Although the Court's initial enthusiasm for the principle of solidarity seemed rather to have cooled after *FFSA*, the principle was again successfully invoked in *Sodemare*.[81] The Court ruled that Articles 43 and 48 on freedom of establishment did not preclude a Member State from allowing only non-profit-making private operators to participate in the running of its social welfare system by concluding contracts which entitled them to be reimbursed by the public authorities for the costs of providing certain social welfare services. Having noted that Community law did not detract from the powers of the Member States to organise their social security systems[82] the Court added:

> It is clear from the documents before the Court that that system of social welfare, whose implementation is in principle entrusted to the public authorities, is based on the principle of solidarity, as reflected by the fact that it is designed as a matter of priority to assist those who are in a state of need owing to insufficient family income, total or partial lack of independence or the risk of being marginalised, and only then, within the limits imposed by the capacity of the establishments and resources available, to assist other persons who are, however, required to bear the costs thereof, to an extent commensurate with their financial means, in accordance with scales determined by reference to family income.[83]

The Court accepted the Italian government's reasoning that since non-profit making private operators, by their very nature were not influenced by their need to derive profit from the provision of services, they could pursue social aims as a matter of priority. Thus, in *Sodemare* the Court used the principle of solidarity to reinforce its view that Community law was not just about unrestricted access for all economic operators to the market in other Member States and so found there was no breach of Community law and Articles 43, 48 and 49 in particular.

Since *Sodemare* the Court has carefully examined the facts of individual cases to consider whether there is a sufficient degree of solidarity to justify a finding that the activity is not economic and so falling outside the scope of Community law (*Poucet and Pistre)*, or insufficient solidarity and so Community law applies (*FFSA*). For example, in *AOK*[84] the Court found

[81] Case C–70/95 *Sodemare v Regione Lombardia* [1997] ECR I–3395.

[82] Para 27.

[83] Para 29.

[84] Joined Cases C–264/01, C–306/01, C–354/01 and C–355/01 *AOK Bundesverband, Bundesverband der Betriebskrankenkassen (BKK), Bundesverband der Innungskrankenkassen, Bundesverband der landwirtschaftlichen Krankenkassen, Verband der Angestelltenkrankenkassen eV, Verband der Arbeiter-Ersatzkassen, Bundesknappschaft and See-Krankenkasse v Ichthyol-Gesellschaft Cordes, Hermani & Co.* (C–264/01), *Mundipharma GmbH* (C–306/01), *Gödecke GmbH* (C–354/01) *and Intersan, Institut für pharmazeutische und klinische Forschung GmbH* (C–355/01) [2004] ECR I–000. See also Case C–218/00 *Cisal di Battistello Venanzio & C.Sas v Istituto nazionale per l'assicurazione contro gli infortuni sul lavoro* [2002] ECR I–691 concerning compulsory insurance against accidents at work and

that the sickness funds in the German statutory health insurance scheme were involved in the management of the social security system where they fulfilled 'an exclusively social function which is founded on the principle of national solidarity and is entirely non-profit-making'.[85] Since the funds were obliged by law to offer their members essentially identical benefits, irrespective of contributions, and they were bound together in a type of community founded on the basis of solidarity which enabled an equalisation of costs and risks between them and they did not compete with one another or private institutions,[86] they fell on the *Poucet and Pistre* side of the line and so their activity could not be regarded as economic in nature. On the other hand, in *Wouters*[87] the Court said that because a professional regulatory body such as the Bar of the Netherlands was neither fulfilling a social function based on the principle of solidarity nor exercising powers which were typically those of a public authority, it did engage in an economic activity and so was subject to Community law.

This brief review shows that the Court has used the solidarity principle to ensure that Community law does not have the effect of eroding some of the EU's broader social policy objectives ,[88] which of course include solidarity. In this way the principle of solidarity has reinforced the principle of subsidiarity—the local provision of services and facilities has largely been preserved from the reach of European Community law—in the name of solidarity.

Making pro-active use of solidarity

While the defensive use of the solidarity principle is now reasonably well established, it is in the field of EU citizenship that the Court has introduced

occupational diseases; Case C–355/00 *Freskot AE v Elliniko Dimosio* [2003] ECR I–5263 the term undertaking within the meaning of Art 87 of the Treaty did not cover a body such as ELGA (Greek organisation for agricultural insurance) in respect of its activities under the compulsory insurance scheme against natural risks; Case T–319/99 *FENIN v Commission* [2003] ECR II–357 concerning the bodies which run the Spanish national health system; Joined Cases C–266/04 to 270/04, C–276/04 and C–321/04 to C–325/04 *Nazairdis SAS v Organic* [2005] ELR I–000 concerning a basic social security scheme founded on a solidarity mechanism.

[85] Para 51.

[86] Paras 51–53.

[87] Case C–309/99 *Wouters, Savelbergh, Price Waterhouse Belastingadviseurs BV v Algemene Raad van de Nederlandse Orde van Advocaten* [2002] ECR I–1577 para 58. See also Case C–55/96 *Job Centre Coop Arl* [1997] ECR I–7119.

[88] See, eg, Case C–67/96 *Albany International BV v Stichting Bedrijfspensioenfonds Textielindustrie* [1999] ECR I–5751 para 59:

> It is beyond question that certain restrictions of competition are inherent in collective agreements between organisations representing employers and workers. However, the social policy objectives pursued by such agreements would be seriously undermined if management and labour were subject to Art [81(1)] of the Treaty when seeking jointly to adopt measures to improve conditions of work and employment

Joined Cases C–270/97 and C–271/97 *Deutsche Post v Sievers* [2000] ECR I–929 para 57 on Art 141 on equal pay where the Court said that:

> [T]he economic aim pursued by Art [141] of the Treaty, namely the elimination of distortions of competition between undertakings established in different Member States, is secondary to the social aim pursued by the same provision, which constitutes the expression of a fundamental human right.

a more ambitious and positive use of the concept: to impose financial obligations on the host state to provide certain benefits to the migrant citizen.[89] This was first seen in *Grzelczyk*.[90] Grzelczyk, a French national studying at a Belgian university, supported himself financially for the first three years of his studies but then applied for the minimex (the Belgium minimum income guarantee) at the start of his fourth and final year. While Belgian students could receive the benefit, migrant students could not.[91] As a result, Grzelczyk suffered (direct) discrimination contrary to Article 12.[92] The Court said that Grzelczyk, a citizen of the Union, could rely on Article 12 in respect of those situations which fell within the material scope of the Treaty[93] which included those situations involving 'the exercise of the fundamental freedoms guaranteed by the Treaty and those involving the exercise of the right to move and reside freely in another Member State, as conferred by Article [18(1)] of the Treaty'.[94]

The Court then considered the limits laid down in the residence directives, in particular the limits imposed by Article 1 of the Students' Directive 93/96 which requires migrant students to have sufficient resources when exercising the rights of free movement. The Court said that while a Member State could decide that a student having recourse to social assistance no longer fulfilled the conditions of his right of residence and so could withdraw his residence permit or decide not to renew it,[95] such actions could not be the automatic consequence of a migrant student having recourse to the host State's social assistance system.[96] The Court continued that beneficiaries of the right of residence could not become an 'unreasonable' burden on the public finances of the host State.[97] Therefore, the Belgian authorities had to provide some temporary support (the minimex) to the migrant citizen, as they would to nationals, given that there existed 'a certain degree of financial solidarity' between nationals of a host Member State and nationals of other Member States.[98] In other words, due to this 'certain degree of financial solidarity' between the Belgian taxpayer and the French migrant student, derived from their common (EU) citizenship, the student could enjoy the social benefit but only for so long as the student did not become

[89] While I shall focus on the position of migrant EU citizens, there is also solidarity between EU nationals and nationals benefitting form association agreements, although the details of this are less clear: Case C–257/99 *R v Secretary of State for the Home Department, ex p Barkoci and Malik* [2001] ECR I–000 para 78 'with a view to respecting human dignity and demonstrating solidarity'.

[90] Case C–184/99 [2001] ECR I–6193.

[91] Para 29.

[92] Para 30.

[93] Para 32.

[94] Para 33, citing Case C–274/96 *Bickel and Franz* [1998] ECR I–7637.

[95] Para 42.

[96] Para 43.

[97] Para 44.

[98] *Ibid.*

an unreasonable burden on public finances. In *Bidar*[99] the Court built on the ruling in *Grzelczyk* to justify finding that the UK was obliged to treat legally resident migrants equally with nationals in respect of access to maintenance grants and loans. However, the Court said that the UK would be justified in imposing a three residence requirement before the individual could claim maintenance grants and loans.

The solidarity principle also helps to explain *Baumbast*.[100] Baumbast was a German national who had been working in the UK and continued residing there with his family once his work in the EU had ceased. While he had sufficient resources for himself and his family, his German medical insurance did not cover emergency treatment in the UK, as required by Directive 90/364 on persons of independent means.[101] For this reason the British authorities refused to renew his residence permit. The Court said that he could rely on his directly effective right to reside under Article 18(1) but this right had to be read subject to the limitations laid down in the residence directives.[102] It then qualified this remark by adding that the limitations and conditions referred in Article 18(1) had to be applied 'in compliance with the limits imposed by Community law and in accordance with the general principles of that law, in particular the principle of proportionality'.[103] It concluded that, given neither Baumbast nor his family had become a financial burden on the state, it would amount to a disproportionate interference with the exercise of the right of residence if he were denied residence on the ground that his sickness insurance did not cover the emergency treatment given in the host Member State.[104] When viewed through the lens of solidarity, it could be argued that there was a sufficient degree of solidarity between Baumbast and the British taxpayer to justify him (and his family) receiving emergency medical treatment on the NHS.

The reliance on the solidarity principle to justify imposing additional financial obligations on the host state in respect of EU migrants is a remarkable development. It raises the question of whether solidarity can be invoked by all EU migrants, including those who have recently arrived in

[99] Case C–209/03 *R (on the application of Danny Bidar) v London Borough of Ealing, Secretary of State for Education and Skills*, judgment of 15 March 2005, not yet reported.

[100] Case C–413/99 *Baumbast and R v Secretary of State for the Home Department* [2002] ECR I–7091. See also the reference in Para 44 of *Grzelczyk* to Dirs 90/364 and 90/365 which, like Dir 93/96, 'accepts a certain degree of financial solidarity'. See also AG Geelhoed's comments in *Bidar* para 31:

> The notion of 'unreasonable burden' is apparently flexible and, according to the Court, implies that Directive 93/96 accepts a degree of financial solidarity between the Member States in assisting each other's nationals residing lawfully in their territory. As the same principle is at the basis of the conditions imposed by Directive 90/354, there is no reason to presume that this same financial solidarity does not apply in that context too.

[101] Para 88. See also Case T–66/75 *Hedwig Kuchlenz-Winter v Commission* [1997] ECR II–637 paras 46–7.

[102] Para 90.

[103] Para 91.

[104] Para 93.

the host state, especially those seeking education.[105] *Bidar* suggests that the answer is no: that only those who enjoy a certain degree of integration in the host state can expect equal treatment in respect of certain benefits like maintenance grants and loans. In paragraph 56 the Court referred to the need for Member States to show 'a certain degree of financial solidarity with nationals of other Member States' in the organisation and application of their social assistance systems. It then continued in paragraph 57 that:

> In the case of assistance covering the maintenance costs of students, it is thus legitimate for a Member State to grant such assistance only to students who have demonstrated a *certain degree of integration* into the society of that State. (emphasis added)

The Court then makes clear that length of residence is a key indicator of integration:[106]

> [T]he existence of a certain degree of integration may be regarded as established by a finding that the student in question has resided in the host state for a certain length of time.

Thus, *Bidar* emphasises a 'quantitative' approach:[107] the longer migrants reside in the Member State, the more integrated they are in that state and the greater the number of benefits they receive on equal terms with nationals. The corollary of this is that in respect of newly arrived migrants there is insufficient solidarity between them and the host state taxpayer to justify requiring full equal treatment in respect of social welfare benefits. This was the view taken by Advocate General Ruiz-Jarabo Colomer in *Collins*.[108] Collins, who was Irish, arrived in the United Kingdom and promptly applied for a job-seeker's allowance (JSA) which was refused on the grounds that he was not habitually resident in the UK. The Advocate General distinguished the facts of *Grzelczyk*[109] (and the Court's reference

[105] See AG Geelhoed's opinion in Case C–413/01 *Franca Ninni-Orasche v Bundesminister für Wissenschaft, Verkehr und Kunst* [2003] ECR I–13187 where he referred to the need for a minimum degree of financial solidarity towards those residents who are students but holding the nationality of another Member State and concluded that a resident like Mrs Ninni-Orasche with a 'demonstrable and structural link to Austrian society' could not be treated in Austria 'as any other national of a third country' (para 96). This is particularly so in the field of education where, as AG Geelhoed noted in Case C–224/98 *D'Hoop* [2002] ECR I–6191 para 41 European integration has created an environment conducive to transnational education. Interstate education is, moreover, viewed as an important instrument in promoting mutual solidarity and tolerance as well as the dissemination of culture throughout the European Union.

[106] Para 59. See also AG Geelhoed's remarks in Case C–413/01 *Ninni-Orasche v Bundesminister für Wissenschaft* [2003] ECR I–13187 paras 90–91. For an emphasis on the contextual approach which takes account of length of residence and degree of integration, see AG Ruiz-Jarabo Colomer's opinion, in Case C–138/02 *Brian Francis Collins v Secretary of State for Work and Pensions* [2004] ECR I–000 paras 65–67.

[107] This idea is developed further in Barnard, *Bidar* (2005) 42 CML Rev 1465.

[108] Case C–138/02 *Brian Francis Collins v Secretary of State for Work and Pensions* [2004] ECR I–000.

[109] Para 66.

to solidarity) and concluded that Community law did not require the benefit to be provided to a citizen of the Union who entered the territory of a Member State with the purpose of seeking employment while lacking any connection with the state or link with the domestic employment market.[110] The Court decided the case on a different basis but reached the same conclusion.

Even in cases where the Court does not make express reference to the solidarity principle, as in *Trojani*,[111] solidarity resonates in the background. Trojani, a French national, was a short-term resident in Belgium. He had been living in a Salvation Army hostel where, in return for board and lodging and some pocket money, he did various jobs for about 30 hours a week as part of a 'personal socio-occupational reintegration programme'.[112] As with Grzelczyk, Trojani was denied the minimex on the grounds that he was neither Belgian, nor a worker under Regulation 1612/68. While the Court of Justice left it up to the national court to decide whether Trojani was in fact a worker, it did consider the rights he might enjoy from being a citizen. The Court said that while he did not derive the right to reside in Belgium from Article 18, due to his lack of resources,[113] since he was lawfully resident in Belgium he could benefit from the fundamental principle of equal treatment laid down in Article 12.

This raises the question as to the basis for assuming that the host state (and in particular the host state taxpayer) should pay benefits to the migrant indigent citizen. The answer would seem to lie in some, albeit attenuated and unarticulated, notion of solidarity between those who are citizens of the Union. If this is the case then solidarity assumes considerable political, financial and legal significance. But where and how is its meaning being discussed? It is in this context that a consideration of solidarity as a tool of new governance becomes particularly pertinent.

SOLIDARITY AS A TOOL OF NEW GOVERNANCE?

As the previous sections have shown, the most striking feature of the use of solidarity is its very flexibility: it is capable of being used by a variety of actors (the EU institutions, the Member States and private parties) in a variety of ways (positively, to impose obligations on states, individuals and undertakings, and negatively to protect the erosion of individual rights). It is also multi-level: it is used vertically and horizontally. Its vertical use can be seen in the way it facilitates relations between the EU institutions and the Member States (the Article 10 usage), between EU institutions and subnational actors (especially in the context of regional aid), between the state

[110] Para 76.
[111] Case C–456/02 *Trojani v Centre public d'aide sociale de Bruxelles* [2004] ECR I–000.
[112] Para 9.
[113] Para 36.

and its own nationals (*Poucet and Pistre*), and between the state and migrant nationals *(Grzelczyk* and beyond). Its horizontal use can be seen in the way it facilitates relations between states (again this can be seen in the context of Article 10 usage), and relations between private parties in the national context (between workers in pension schemes) and in the transnational context (between producers in the steel, agriculture, fisheries and transport sectors). And these usages and levels are themselves interdependent, not least because they are all conducted with the framework of European Community law.

The flexible, multi-level context in which solidarity operates suggests that solidarity has much in common with the more familiar new governance tool, subsidiarity. Yet, the two principles are different: while subsidarity is about power sharing, solidarity concerns burden sharing and burden sharing has direct financial implications. This means that there should be debate and deliberation about the meaning of solidarity. To what extent is this happening? In those areas where we have identified a 'softer' use of the solidarity principle and the EU institutions, especially the Commission, have precipitated discussion, then the process does have a structured deliberative quality. For example, in its Communication on the Social Policy Agenda[114] the Commission identified the need to make 'social dialogue at all levels' contribute to the challenges of promoting 'competitiveness and solidarity and the balance between flexibility and security'. It then outlined action to be taken:

—Consulting the social partners at European level with a view to identifying areas of common interest including those offering the best possibilities for collective bargaining;
—Closely monitoring and continuously updating the study on representativeness of social partners at European level;
—Launching a reflection group on the future of industrial relations;
—Promoting interaction between social dialogue at European and national level through national round tables on issues of common interest (work organisation, future of work, new forms of work);
—Reviewing with the social partners the functioning of the social dialogue structures (at both cross-industry and sectoral levels) and, if necessary, propose adaptations;
—Invite social partners to develop their own initiatives in areas of their responsibility to adapt to change.

A similar desire for discussion and engagement can also be detected in the Union's Cohesion Policy for 2006 and beyond. According to its Regional Policy website,[115] the Commission welcomed discussion on the new Policy.

[114] COM(2000)379, 23.
[115] <http://europa.eu.int/comm/regional_policy/debate/forum_en.htm>

It said that following the publication of the Second Cohesion report in 2001 which contained a list of 10 questions for debate,[116] there followed a 'lively debate' among Member States, regional authorities, economic and social actors and European citizens, the contributions to which were all published on the website. In the light of this debate, the Commission adopted its third Cohesion Report followed by a proposal for new legal instruments.

It is difficult to assess just how influential the public debate has been on shaping the Commission's final proposals but at least there has been some attempt to engage with the relevant actors to give concrete meaning to solidarity in the regional context. However, where the Court draws on the principle of solidarity, the same wide-ranging debate is simply not available. Decisions such as those in *Grzelczyk* may precipitate knee-jerk, often hostile reaction from the press,[117] but this can scarcely count as deliberation. On the other hand, when scrutinised from a deliberative perspective, the Court's judgments do create space for Member States at least to articulate their views on solidarity and proportionality. The decision in *Collins*,[118]

[116] The questions are:

(1) How is it possible to further economic convergence and preserve the European model of society?
(2) How should Community policies be made more coherent? How should the contribution of other Community policies to the pursuit of cohesion be improved?
(3) How should cohesion policy be modified in preparation for an unprecedented expansion of the Union? Should cohesion policy also address territorial cohesion in order to take better account of the major spatial imbalances in the Union?
(4) How can cohesion policy be focussed on measures which have a high Community added value ?
(5) What should be the priorities to bring about balanced and sustainable territorial development in the Union?
(6) How should the economic convergence of lagging regions of the Union be encouraged?
(7) What kind of Community intervention is required for other regions?
(8) What methods should be used to determine the division of funds between Member States and between regions?
(9) What principles should govern the implementation of Community intervention?
(10) What should be the response to increased needs with regard to the economic, social and territorial dimensions of cohesion?

[117] See, eg, the recent concerns reported in the British press about the 'influx of students from the accession countries'. A report form the Higher Education Policy Institute <http://www.hepi.ac.uk/> articles predicted that 30,000 students will arrive from the accession countries and that this is 'likely to increase competition for places ... If the government does not provide the extra places, some of these will be displacing UK students'. Recent reports in the British press suggested that it would cost £900 million a year to educate EU students in British universities, a figure expressly rejected by Alan Johnson, the Minister for Higher Education who suggested a figure of around £30 million: Letter to *The Times* (4 Feb. 2004) p 19. For a flavour of the debate, see L Clark, 'Britain faces huge bill for upkeep of students from EU' *Daily Mail* (22 Mar 2004) p 2.

[118] Case C–138/02 *Brian Francis Collins v Secretary of State for Work and Pensions* [2003] ECR I–000. See also AG Geelhoed's Opinion in Case C–413/01 *Franca Ninni-Orashe v Bundesminister für Wissenschaft, Verkhr und Kunst* [2003] ECR I–13187 para 86 where he highlighted the 'specific circumstances' of *Grzelczyk* in comparison with the newly arrived Mrs Ninni-Orasche.

concerning the Irish work seeker, illustrates how this might occur. It will be recalled that Collins was refused job-seeker's allowance on the grounds that he was not habitually resident in the UK.

The Court said that, as a work seeker and a Union citizen he was entitled to benefits of a 'financial nature intended to facilitate access to employment in the labour market of a Member State'. It then subjected the 'habitual residence' requirement to a conventional discrimination analysis. It noted that because the rule disadvantaged those who had exercised their rights of free movement it would be lawful only if the UK could justify it based on objective considerations unrelated to nationality and proportionate to the aim of the national provisions. Following *D'Hoop*,[119] the Court accepted that it was legitimate for a national legislature to wish to ensure that there was a genuine link between the person applying for the benefit and the employment market of that state, and that the link could be determined by establishing that the claimant has 'for a reasonable period, in fact genuinely sought work' in the UK. Thus, the Court accepted the UK's arguments that there were limits to a state's obligation to pay benefits to all migrants but required the state to articulate the conditions for access to the benefit. It said that while the residence requirement was appropriate to attain the objective it was only proportionate if it rested on clear criteria known in advance, judicial redress was available and the period of residence was not excessive.

Thus, the consequence of decisions such as *Collins* and *Grzelczyk* is that they place the onus on the host Member State to explain the reason for limiting the availability of the benefit to the migrant, to articulate what is meant by 'unreasonable burden' and to explain why steps taken by the state are proportionate. In this way, it could be argued that the Court is imposing an obligation on Member States to give reasons for its decisions and in so doing, proceduralises the approach to solidarity.

CONCLUSIONS

Solidarity can be viewed as a tool of new governance, helping to shape policies in other areas and as a linchpin to justify legislative decisions on burden sharing. However, as we have also seen, its presence in the ECSC Treaty suggests that it is not all that 'new', albeit its recent use by the Court, at a time when governance is under the spotlight, makes it a subject worthy of study. Solidarity can also be seen as benefiting from new governance mechanisms—in particular deliberation—to give it substance, shape and meaning. In respect of decisions which impact on national welfare states, this is of particular importance. If national populations perceive that decisions are

[119] Case C–224/98 [2002] ECR I–6191.

taken in the name of solidarity between Union citizens by officials in Luxembourg or Brussels but without any involvement from national or sub-national actors this could undermine the already diffuse sense of solidarity between those citizens. On the more positive side, if the EU is to have a genuine social face to complement the single market, a Union informed by the values of solidarity, whose meaning is developed through a constant dialogue with the various actors is surely better than one which is not.

7

The European Union and the Governance of Health Care

TAMARA K HERVEY

INTRODUCTION

WITHIN THE EUROPEAN Union (EU), the organisation and delivery of health care services is the responsibility of the Member States. So affirm both the EU's Constitutional Treaty[1] and its 'constitutional court', the European Court of Justice.[2] Yet the case study described in this chapter paints quite a different picture, in which the European Union is becoming increasingly involved in the governance of health care. Here, 'governance' means the use of legal and political authority, wealth and information, to exercise control in the management of relationships and resources in the pursuit of social and economic ends.[3] Through the health care case study, the chapter explores the changing roles of law in EU governance processes and the EU's constitutional construct, and highlights some uncertainties or problems with our understandings of 'new' governance in the EU.

Health care makes a good case study for three main reasons. First, health care is a field of governance in which (any significant) EU activity and involvement is relatively new. This allows isolation and analysis of particular 'moments of governance' or catalysts for emerging processes, at least to some extent free from the 'background interference' of several years of EU

[1] Art III–278(7) CT.

[2] See, for instance, Case 238/82 *Duphar* [1984] ECR 523, para 16; Cases 159 & 160/91 *Poucet and Pistre* [1993] ECR I–637, para 6; Case C–70/95 *Sodemare* [1997] ECR I–3395, para 27; Case C–120/95 *Decker* [1998] ECR I–1831, para 21; Case C–158/96 *Kohll* [1998] ECR I–1931, para 17; Case C–157/99 *Geraets-Smits and Peerbooms* [2001] ECR I–5473, para 44.

[3] In the EU context, the term 'governance', as opposed to 'government', is useful as it avoids the implication that the EU is, or is becoming, or should become, a (federal) state. More importantly, it also allows us to capture the rich insights of political science literature, such as that on policy-networks, and multi-level governance, and to move away from an exclusive focus on the 'classic Community method' of governance, as outlined in the Commission's *European Governance: A White Paper* COM(2001)428. See J Scott and DM Trubek, 'Mind the Gap: Law and New Approaches to Governance in the European Union' (2002) 8 *European Law Journal* 1; C Scott, 'The Governance of the European Union: The Potential for Multi-Level Control' (2002) 8 *European Law Journal* 59.

governance activity. Second, health care is a field which presents complex problems, especially in the context of the various challenges to the 'European social model' that currently occupy national social welfare systems in European states. Considering the EU's involvement here may illuminate the potential of different types of governance mechanisms, and mixes of such modes of governance, in tackling such social problems.[4] Third, many of the various EU 'modes of governance'[5] are present in the field. In the EU, health care is also a policy area in which governance can be said to be strongly 'multi-level', in the sense of involving interactions between sub-national, national, EU, and transnational institutions and actors. The case study shows the operation of various different modes and levels of governance within the lens of one policy area of activity.

Following this brief introduction, the main body of the chapter is a narrative exploration of the explosion in EU involvement in the governance of health care. The starting point for the narrative is a relatively recent development in EU internal market litigation (the *Kohll* litigation). After explaining the significance of this litigation, as a catalyst for the inception of various other governance processes, the narrative traces each, by reference to the documentary records. The modes of governance at issue include harmonising regulation; explicit constitutional reform (the Constitutional Treaty); a proposed 'open method of coordination'; 'persuasive convergence' through EU-coordinated cooperation; and funding, information collection and dissemination. The chapter then considers the different and changing roles for (constitutional) law within these various modes of governance, noting in particular that 'traditional' conceptualisations of EU 'constitutional law' capture only part of the story about governance processes applicable to health care in the EU. Finally, the chapter touches on a number of hermeneutical and normative problems that arise for EU legal scholars from the specifics of the case study. Many of these have echoes in the other contributions to this collection.

THE EUROPEAN UNION AND THE GOVERNANCE OF HEALTH CARE

The starting point for this chapter's story of EU health care governance is a relatively recent development in EU internal market litigation, concerning the freedom to receive and provide cross-border services within the EU (the *Kohll* litigation).[6] In adopting this as the starting point for the narrative, the

[4] Many of the chapters in this volume deal with the question of 'hybridity' between old and new governance forms. See the Introduction for an overview.

[5] See also T Hervey and J McHale, *Health Law and the European Union*, (Cambridge: CUP, 2004) ch 2.

[6] There are other related litigation developments, in fields such as the free movement of goods (Case 215/87 *Schumacher* [1989] ECR 617; Case C–120/95 *Decker* [1998] ECR I–1831); free movement of health care services themselves across borders (Case C–322/01 *Deutcher Apothekerverband* v *0800 DocMorris and Waterval* 11 [2003] ECR I–14887; and, potentially, EU competition law (but see Cases C–264/01, C–306/01, C–354/01 and C–355/01 *AOK Bundesverband and others* [2004] ECR I–2493.

case study foregrounds certain processes of 'hard' law, in particular that of adjudication, rather than other explanatory factors, for instance those focused more on 'softer' legal mechanisms, or indeed political power. The reference to internal market litigation situates the analysis, at least at its inception, within the assumptions of 'traditional' EU constitutionalism, and the 'classic Community method' of governance.[7] Here, the EU's constitution operates in a 'top-down' mode, with distinct spheres of competence between EU institutions and those of the Member States and regional or even local actors. Indeed, much of the negative response to the (actual or potential) substantive outcomes of the *Kohll* litigation[8] can only be understood within this traditional framework.

However, in this study, the *Kohll* litigation is not read as the end point or outcome, but rather as a key catalyst for the inception of various other ('new' and also less new) governance processes, which, if carried through, will alter the conceptual map within which we situate the EU's involvement in the governance of health care. Most of these other governance processes do not fit easily within a traditional construct of EU constitutionalism. Their elaboration will inform the contours of a framework for analysis of what various modes of 'new governance' might mean for the roles of (constitutional) law, in relation to EU health care governance.

[7] See further Neil Walker, Ch 1 of this volume. Some of the 'classics' here include S Weatherill, *Law and Integration in the European Union*, (Oxford: Clarendon, 1995); M Poiares Maduro, *We The Court: The European Court of Justice and the European Economic Constitution* (Oxford: Hart, 1998); JHH Weiler, *The Constitution of Europe* (Cambridge: CUP, 1999); F Scharpf, *Governing in Europe: Effective and Democratic?* (Oxford: OUP, 1999); and A Stone Sweet, *Governing with Judges: Constitutional Politics in Europe* (Oxford: OUP, 2000).

[8] V Hatzopoulos,'Health Law and Policy: The Impact of the EU', forthcoming in *Selected Courses of the Academy of European Law 2003* (unpublished paper); Y Jorens, 'The Right to Health Care Across Borders' in R Baeten, M McKee and E Mossialos (eds) *The Impact of EU Law on Health Care Systems* (Brussels: PIE Peter Lang, 2003); E Steyger, 'National Health Care Systems Under Fire (but not too heavily)' (2002) 29 *Legal Issues of Economic Integration* 97; AP Van der Mei, 'Cross-Border Access to Health Care within the European Union: Some Reflections on *Geraets-Smits and Peerbooms* and *Vanbraekel*' (2002) 9 *Maastricht Journal of European and Comparative Law* 1; V Hatzopoulos, 'Killing National Health and Insurance Systems but Healing Patients?' (2002) 39 CML Rev 683; R Baeten, 'European Integration and National Healthcare Systems: A Challenge for Social Policy' (2001) 8 *infose* 1; J Nickless, 'Were the European Court of Justice Decisions in *Kohll* and *Decker* Right?' (2001) 7(1) *eurohealth* 16; T Van der Grinten and M de Lint, 'The Impact of Europe on Healthcare: The Dutch Case' (2001) 7(1) *eurohealth* 19; W Palm, J Nickless, H Lewalle and A Coheur, *Implications of Recent Jurisprudence on the Coordination of Health Care Protection Systems* Summary Report produced for DG Employment and Social Affairs (Brussels: AIM, 2000); K Sieveking, 'The Significance of the Transborder Utilisation of Health Care Benefits for Migrants' (2000) 2 *European Journal of Migration and Law* 143; C Garcia de Cortazar, '*Kohll* and *Decker*, or That is Somebody Else's Problem' (1999) 6 *European Journal of Health Law* 397; A Cabrai, 'Cross-border Medical Care in the European Union-Bringing Down a First Wall' (1999) 24 ELR 387; 'EU Patients Entitled to Treatment Abroad' *Irish Times* (13 July 2001); 'Ruling Frees NHS Patients to Seek Treatment Abroad' and 'A Healthy Opportunity' *Sunday Times* (15 July 2001); 'NHS May Pay for EU Care' *Independent on Sunday* (15 July 2001).

The *Kohll* litigation

Article 49 EC provides that 'restrictions' on the freedom to provide services within the EU 'shall be prohibited'. Originally, it was tacitly assumed that the material scope of Article 49 EC did not extend to 'public services', such as health care services, because the essential characteristic of a 'service'—that it be provided for 'remuneration'—was not present.[9] However, in a series of rulings beginning in 1998, the European Court of Justice (ECJ) has found that, in some circumstances, health care reimbursed under a national social security scheme may fall within Article 49 EC.[10] So, for instance, the ECJ has found that a system requiring prior authorisation where treatment is sought from a health care provider with whom the insurance fund has not entered into an agreement (which would in practice include health care providers in other states) constitutes prima facie a 'restriction' in the sense of Article 49 EC.[11] According to the doctrine of direct effect,[12] a litigant may enforce her rights in primary EU law (here, Article 49 EC) before national courts. The significance of this interpretation of the Treaty is that, prima facie, individual patients may enforce a right to have health care, given in another Member State, reimbursed by the national health (insurance) system of their home Member State.

However, the potentially disruptive effects of the extension of Article 49 EC to national health care systems[13] are mitigated by a number of factors.

[9] The essential characteristic of remuneration is that it constitutes consideration for the service in question; Case 263/85 *Belgian State* v *Humbel* [1988] ECR 5365, para 17. However, remuneration need not come directly from the recipient of the services; Case 352/85 *Bond van Adverteerders* [1988] ECR 2124.

[10] Case C–158/96 *Kohll* v *Union des Caisses de Maladie* [1998] ECR I–1931, para 29, applying to *extramural* health care (taking place outside a hospital); the principle applies also where *intramural* health care (within a hospital) is reimbursed by a national sickness insurance fund, even where such reimbursement is on the basis of regulated pre-set scales of fees; Case C–157/99 *Geraets-Smits and Peerbooms* [2001] ECR I–5473 paras 55–58; Case C–368/86 *Vanbraekel* [2001] ECR I–5363, para 42; see also Case C–385/99 *Müller-Fauré and van Riet* [2003] ECR I–4509; Case C–8/02 *Leichtle* 18 [2004] ECR I–2641. The ECJ has not yet ruled on the application of the Treaty to the provision of health care services under a national health system financed largely by public taxation. The English High Court has ruled that the principles developed by the ECJ in *Geraets-Smits* and *Müller-Fauré* do apply in the context of the UK NHS, funded largely through public taxation; see *R (on the application of Yvonne Watts)* v *Bedford Primary Care Trust and Secretary of State for Health* [2003] EWHC 2228 (Admin), 1 October 2003. This case has now been referred to the ECJ under the preliminary rulings procedure, Art 234 EC, see Opinion of the Advocate General in Case C–372/04, 15 December 2005.

[11] Case C–385/99 *Müller-Fauré*, n 10 above, paras 37–45, para 103.

[12] A central, Court-developed part of the process of 'constitutionalisation' of EU law, in the traditional constitutional mode. See, eg, B de Witte, 'Direct Effect, Supremacy and the Nature of the Legal Order', in P Craig and G de Búrca (eds) *The Evolution of EU Law* (Oxford: OUP, 1999).

[13] These concern the impact of the rulings on the stability and internal balance of national health (insurance) systems, and the viability of their social goals. Certain Member States, for instance, those Member States that provide higher standards of service, better value for money, a greater choice for patients, or whose medical profession enjoys a high reputation, might

The first is the structure of Article 49 EC itself, and the other internal market provisions of the Treaty, as interpreted by the ECJ. Potentially, Article 49 EC may be read as an essentially deregulatory mechanism of governance. Indeed, deregulation based on litigation may be seen as the quintessential mode of 'old governance' in the EU—the 'grandmother of old governance'. However, the Member States of the EU do not have a tradition of neo-liberal economics with which classical market deregulation is associated. Rather, the Member States of the EU have tended to reflect a 'social market' tradition, in which public intervention in the free operation of markets is accepted and indeed expected, either as required to prevent various 'market failures' (social values as 'market perfecting or correcting'), or as to promote values of social justice as ends in themselves.[14] The ECJ has taken account of the 'social market' tradition, by constructing the internal market as more than a simple deregulatory space. One element of this jurisprudence is the development of the principle that restrictions on

experience an unpredictable influx of patients. This may have an impact on standards of national health care provision for nationals, for instance longer waiting lists. The rulings may have a detrimental effect on health care planning and capacity maintenance. States calculate their health care needs by reference to their populations. Too much movement of patients might result in overburdening of some hospitals, and corresponding under use of others, possibly leading to closures. This could jeopardise the social principle of effective health care accessible to all, which underpins the national health (insurance) systems of all Member States. The ability of patients to access (and be reimbursed for) innovative treatments that might not be recognised as reimbursable within their home state may imply a loss of control over the reimbursement of such new and 'unproven' treatments. Thus, decisions about cost-effectiveness in terms of determining which treatments are to be reimbursed within a particular national health (insurance) system may no longer be kept within the 'closed' national system, with its own 'home-grown' experts, but must be subject to exogenous assessment. Ultimately, the decision to reimburse certain types of treatment, and not others, in the context of limited overall resources for health care, constitutes a choice to allocate resources to meet the health care needs of one part of the population rather than another. The same reasoning applies to the use of EU law by litigants seeking to avoid waiting times for health care services under their national health (insurance) systems. States use hospital waiting lists in effect as a tool to constrain spending. Waiting lists also arise as a logical consequence of policy decisions about resource allocation. The ability of certain (litigious) patients to utilise EU law in these circumstances may be regarded as an inappropriate judicial interference with political processes. There are also concerns about the assumption of the Court in *Kohll* that a similar standard of health care applies across the EU. It is not clear whether different quality standards with respect to treatment in hospitals could be used to justify a refusal to reimburse, on the grounds that Member States may justify additional national regulatory measures if these are essential for protection of public health. In general, then, these kinds of pressures may jeopardise the overall structure of national health (insurance) systems, their financial and administrative arrangements, and questions of access to and quality of treatment.

[14] On deregulation, the internal market and the EU's socio-economic constitution, see for instance Poiares Maduro, n 7 above; F. Scharpf, *Governing in Europe*, n 7 above; on social law in particular, see S. Deakin, 'Labour Law as Market Regulation' in P. Davies *et al* (eds) *European Community Labour Law: Principles and Perspectives* (Oxford: Clarendon Press, 1996); G Majone, 'Which social policy for Europe?' in Y Mény, P Muller and J-L Quermonne (eds) *Adjusting to Europe: The Impact of the European Union on National Institutions and Policies* (London: Routledge, 1996); W Streek, 'Neovoluntarism: A New European Social Policy Regime?' (1995) 1 *European Law Journal* 31.

the freedom to provide and receive services may be *justified* in various circumstances.[15]

Second, the disruptive potential of the *Kohll* litigation is significantly mitigated by the juridical structure within which such litigation takes place. The principles of internal market law, including its scope (here, application to health care systems), have been developed in the context of the ECJ's power to give authoritative interpretations of EU law under Article 234 EC. Article 234 EC involves a reference from a national court to the ECJ for a 'preliminary ruling' in a case concerning a question of EU law, before final resolution of the case at the national level. Thus the principles enunciated by the ECJ are given effect in national legal orders by national courts. The Article 234 EC procedure cuts both ways.[16] On the one hand, it requires national courts to apply EU law within their own legal orders—embodying the idea that 'every national court is an EU court'. This means that the detailed working out of the processes of integration (here, the application of Article 49 EC to health care systems) is removed from the highly visible political arena, where differences in approach may be extremely difficult to reconcile, to the judicial arena, where solutions are reached by an 'impartial' body, relatively shielded from public scrutiny. Here, respect for the rule of law and the authority of courts help to ensure compliance with EU-level norms. This is particularly so where *national* courts actually apply EU law, which is the case with directly effective provisions such as Article 49 EC. On the other hand, under Article 234 EC, national courts retain an important 'gatekeeping' control, in that they are the ultimate arbiters of any litigation, and indeed of whether to refer to the ECJ at all.[17] The crucial part of any litigation involving the free movement of patients based on rights in Article 49 EC, that is, the question of justification, is, technically at least, a question of fact for the national court.[18]

Granted therefore, the potentially disruptive effects of the extension of Article 49 EC to national health care systems are significantly mitigated. However, even so, the *Kohll* litigation, within the construct of directly

[15] Relevant objective public interest justifications include the social protection provided by national social security systems (Case C–272/94 *Guiot and Climatec* [1996] ECR I–1905); the financial viability of such social security systems (Case C–120/95 *Decker* [1998] ECR I–1831; Case C–158/96 *Kohll* [1998] ECR I–1931; Case C–157/99 *Geraets-Smits and Peerbooms* [2001] ECR I–5473; Case C–368/86 *Vanbraekel* [2001] ECR I–5363; Case C–8/02 *Leichtle* [2004] ECR I–2641; and consumer protection (Case 205/84 *Commission* v *Germany* [1986] ECR 3755, para 30; Case C–288/89 *Gouda* [1991] ECR I–4007, para 27; Case C–76/90 *Säger* [1991] ECR I–4221, para 15; Case C–275/92 *Schindler* [1994] ECR I–1039, para 58).

[16] See, in general, T Tridimas, 'Fragmentation, Efficiency and Defiance in the Preliminary Reference Procedure' (2003) 40 CML Rev 9–50.

[17] But see Case C–224/01 *Köbler* [2003] ECR I–10239, in which the Court held, for the first time, that a national supreme court (the Supreme Court of Austria) should have referred a case under Art 234 EC (or rather, should not have withdrawn a reference).

[18] See G Davies, 'Health and Efficiency: Community Law and National Health Systems in the Light of *Müller-Fauré*' (2004) 67 MLR 94.

effective EU internal market law, significantly raises the levels of uncertainty for governments of Member States, and other relevant actors (such as health care providers, insurance funds), in terms of the application of EU law to their norms and practices in health care provision and its reimbursement. Both rational actor-oriented, policy-network and institutionalist accounts of EU governance processes would tell us to expect a response to such uncertainty, be that explained by reducing the (transaction) costs associated with uncertainty; or by network or institutional opportunism. Drawing on the discourses of these different explanatory accounts for EU governance processes,[19] the *Kohll* litigation may be read as a catalyst for the bringing into play of a number of modes of governance with which the EU is now engaging in the governance of health care.

A 'High Level Reflection Process' and Commissioner Byrne's reflection process

The initial most visible institutional and governmental response at EU level to the *Kohll* litigation came in the Health Council[20] of 26 June 2002. The Council invited health ministers and representatives of civil society to take part in a 'high-level process of reflection' on patient mobility and health care developments in the EU. This 'High Level Reflection Process' (HLRP) took place during 2003, and played an important agenda-setting role, with the final Report[21] containing some 19 recommendations, which are now being carried forward in a number of ways. The HLRP Report focuses on five themes, the fourth of which—'reconciling national health policy with

[19] Over time, the explanatory discourse on EU 'integration' has been overlaid by a discourse about the EU as a system of governance. See, eg, K Armstrong, 'Legal Integration: Theorizing the Legal Dimension of European Integration' (1998) 36 *Journal of Common Market Studies* 155; K Armstrong, 'The New Institutionalism' in P Craig and C Harlow (eds) *Lawmaking in the European Union* (Deventer: Kluwer, 1998); K Armstrong and S Bulmer, *The Governance of the Single European Market* (Manchester: MUP, 1998); Scharpf, n 7 above; G Majone, *Regulating Europe* (London: Routledge, 1996); G Majone, 'A European regulatory state?' in J Richardson (ed) *European Union: Power and Policy-making* (London: Routledge, 1996); G Marks, L Hooghe and K Blank, 'European Integration from the 1980s: State-Centric v. Multi-Level Governance' (1996) 34 *Journal of Common Market Studies* 3; G Marks *et al*, *Governance in the European Union* (London: Sage, 1996); J Richardson, 'Policy-making in the EU: Interests, Ideas and Garbage Cans of Primeval Soup' in J Richardson (ed) *European Union: Power and Policy-making* (London: Routledge, 1996); S Hix, 'The Study of the European Community: The Challenge to Comparative Politics' (1994) 17 *West European Politics* 1; M Jachtenfuchs, 'Theoretical Perspectives on European Governance' (1995) 1 *European Law* Journal 115; J Peterson, 'Decision-Making in the European Union: Towards a Framework for Analysis' (1995) 2 *Journal of European Public Policy* 1; Scott and Trubek (eds) special issue vol. 8 no 1 of (2002) *European Law Journal*; Commission, *European Governance: A White Paper* COM(2001)428 final.

[20] In spite of the lack of formal competence in the field, the Health Ministers of the Member States of the European Union have been meeting regularly at least since the mid-1980s.

[21] High Level Reflection Group, *High Level Reflection Process on Patient Mobility and Healthcare Developments in the European Union* HLPR/2003/16, 9 December 2003.

European obligations'—explicitly concerns the need to respond to the *Kohll* litigation. The Report highlights the legal uncertainty concerning the application of EU rules to health care systems, and various possible responses are mooted. These include: Treaty reform; secondary legislation; Commission communications; Member State initiatives and bilateral cooperation; and a permanent cooperation mechanism at EU level.

The Commission formally responded to the HLRP Report in April 2004, in COM(2004)301 final,[22] which suggests 12 areas where the EU could take matters forward. Interestingly, the press release on COM(2004)301[23] highlights only three elements of the 'package'—better provision of information to patients; establishing an Open Method of Co-ordination (OMC) on the reform of health care; and an 'action plan' on '*e-health*'—none of which involves 'old' or regulatory modes of governance. Perhaps this is related to the contentious nature of EU involvement in health care governance, a matter which was being played out in the negotiations for the Constitutional Treaty (see below), at the same time as COM(2004)301 was being drawn up. In fact, a number of other modes of governance are also covered, including proposed EU-level legislation on the mutual recognition of professional qualifications, enforcement of existing EU-level harmonisation legislation on data protection in the health care field, re-routing of EU public health funding for research on the motivations for cross-border patient mobility, and re-routing of EU structural funding towards health care infrastructure and skills development, especially in the new Member States. COM(2004)301 also covers the use of Commission communications (soft law measures) to clarify the legal position in response to the uncertainties raised by *Kohll*. In fact, this part of COM(2004)301 does not appear to fully encapsulate all the elements of the relevant ECJ rulings.[24]

Furthermore, Commissioner David Byrne[25] launched his own electronic Reflection Process in July 2004. The Byrne Reflection Process (BRP) was guided by a strategy paper, ostensibly seeking the views of governments and civil society, but also strongly articulating the Commissioner's vision for 'a new EU Health Strategy'.[26] Byrne's strategy paper has a strong emphasis on mainstreaming health into all EU policies, on multi-level participation, and, in a significant departure from the HLRP, a strong and explicit linkage of

[22] *Communication from the Commission Follow-up to the High Level Reflection Process on Patient Mobility and Healthcare Developments in the European Union* COM(2004)301 final.

[23] IP/04/508, 21 April 2004.

[24] The Commission states that 'Any hospital care to which you are entitled in you own Member States, you may also seek in any other Member State', see, COM(2004)301 final, p 7. In fact, at least one of the relevant cases, *Geraets-Smits and Peerbooms*, concerns the receipt of hospital care to which the patient *would not have been entitled* in his home state.

[25] Commissioner for DG SANCO until 22 November 2004, when Commissioner Markos Kyrianou took over under the Barroso Commission.

[26] D Byrne, 'Enabling Good Health for all: A Reflection Process for a New EU Health Strategy' 15 July 2004, <http://europa.eu.int/comm/health/ph_overview/strategy/health_strategy_en.htm>.

health and economic growth,[27] bringing health into the Lisbon agenda, and related processes. Both COM(2004)301 and especially the BRP suggest an independence of action on the part of the Commission that needs to be taken into account in assessing the implications of the follow-up to the HLRP (see 3 below).

'If it moves, harmonise it'[28]: regulatory 'old governance' responses

The HLRP Report and COM(2004)301 both propose certain elements of 'old governance' as a response to the *Kohll* litigation. Also, alongside the HLRP, the EU legislature was quietly agreeing a consolidation of the principal legislative measure governing the implications of the free movement of persons for national social security systems, which of course include health care systems, Regulation 1408/71/EEC.[29] The Commission identified three further areas where 'old governance' could apply: a proposed new directive on the free movement of services,[30] one on the free movement of medical professionals, and the enforcement of the Data Protection Directive in the field of health care.

In terms of the latter, data protection is covered by Directive 95/46/EC.[31] This is binding EU secondary legislation, which sets harmonised standards of data protection within the Member States—in other words, it is a classic piece of 'field occupation' by EU law.[32] The Commission observed in COM(2004)301 that the implementation of the provisions of the directive in the health care sector in Member States may need some work. To this effect, the Commission offers to 'work with the Member States ... to raise awareness of these provisions'.[33] This is somewhat different from the classical modes of implementation and enforcement of EU legislation by the Commission envisaged by the Treaty, and indeed by the directive itself,[34]

[27] 'Europe [sic] needs a paradigm shift from seeing health expenditure as a cost to seeing effective health policies as an investment. Europe should look at what health puts in to the economy and what illness takes out', Byrne strategy paper, previous n, at 6.

[28] See C Barnard, *The Substantive Law of the EU* (Oxford: OUP, 2004) 535.

[29] Regulation 883/2004/EC, [2004] OJ L166/1.

[30] COM(2004)2 final.

[31] [1995] OJ L281/31.

[32] The directive aims to ensure that the level of protection of the rights and freedoms of individuals with regard to data protection is equivalent in all Member States; preamble, recital 8. As noted in recital 10, EU-level harmonisation in this area must not result in any lessening of the protection afforded by national laws concerning the right to privacy. See Case C–101/01 *Lindqvist* [2003] ECR I–2971, para 96. However, Member States do retain a certain 'margin for manoeuvre' in implementing the directive; preamble, recital 9. Although the directive sets out basic principles and standards with respect to the lawfulness of data processing, it is left to the Member States to set the precise conditions within which such processing is lawful; Art 5.

[33] COM(2004)301 final, p 13.

[34] Arts 22–24. However, Art 27 provides that Member States and the European Commission are required to promote both national and EU-level codes of conduct in relation to specific sectors. This approach fits well with the turn to 'new' modes of governance in the EU.

and presumably would sit alongside the possibility of enforcement through Article 226 EC or the direct effect of the directive's provisions.[35]

In COM(2004)301, the Commission took the opportunity to promote an existing proposal for legislation to amend the Directives on the Mutual Recognition of Professional Qualifications.[36] The proposal is regarded as highly problematic, both in general and specifically in the health care sector.[37] Problems with the proposal in this sector centre around questions of notification of professional malpractice procedures and confidential exchange of information relevant to the free movement of professionals. Perhaps to soften the ground, the Commission refers to an EU-funded Belgian project ('Sysex'), which has done some preparatory work here. This highlights linkages between the classic Community method of governance, and other methods of governance, including through use of EU funding.

'Money, money, money': convergence through EU funding, data collection and dissemination

The HLRP Report, COM(2004)301 and the BRP Report all envisage the use of EU funding, including to collect and disseminate relevant data, as a mechanism for responding to the *Kohll* litigation. The HLRP Report called for a refocusing of the EU's structural funds, towards health infrastructure development and health status improvement, and some skills development, especially in the new Member States. The Commission responded that the EU already supports investment in health, and that this will be continued. Investment in skills development is presented as essential, as, if insufficient human capacity is built over the forthcoming years, the freedom of movement (of medical professionals, patients or both) implied by internal market

[35] See Cases C–465/00, C–138/01 and C–139/01 *Österreichischer Rundfunk* [2003] ECR I–4989, para 101. For an application of the directive in the context of 'health care information', see Case C–101/01 *Lindqvist* [2003] ECR I–2971.

[36] COM(2002) 119 (amended by COM(2004) 317) on mutual recognition of professional qualifications. Council reached political agreement on a common position on 18–19 May 2004, with the German and Greek delegations voting against; the common position was adopted on 21 December 2004; Directive 2005/36/EC was adopted in September 2005, OJ 2005 L 255/22.

[37] In the UK, for example, health and social care regulators have argued that the new proposals may result in harm to patient safety, noting for example, the element of the proposal that health professionals be allowed to practice in another Member State for a period of up to 4 months per year without having been registered with the host Member State's regulating authority. See R Watson, 'GMC Opposes EU Proposal to Allow Greater Freedom of Movement for Doctors' (2002) 325 *British Medical Journal* 795. In Ireland, the health regulatory bodies—the Medical Council, Dental Council, Opticians Board and the Pharmaceutical Society of Ireland—all called upon the Tanaiste to stop the proposed directive which would enable health practitioners to practice in Ireland without any registration there. They were concerned that a health professional who had been struck off in another Member State could practice in Ireland without having registered. See <http://www.nursingboard.ie/ABANews/Directive19NOV02.html>. The European Parliament supported these concerns: see 'EU Work Plan Puts Patients at Risk' 18 July 2002 <http://www.bbc.co.uk/1/hi/health>; 'EU Rejects Foreign Doctors Plan' 27 November 2003 <http://www.bbc.co.uk/1/hi/health>.

law may mean skills shortages in the poorest Member States. This is also presented as a justification for EU-level information sharing about capacity planning, and subsequent coordination of policy.[38]

Second, COM(2004)301 identified 'health technology' as the largest contributor to escalating costs of European health care systems. Evidence-based analysis of new health care technologies (in comparison with existing (cheaper) therapies) is carried out at national level, in a fragmented way. The only EU-level work here is that of the 'Transparency Committee' under Directive 89/105/EEC.[39] The Commission suggests a coordination of 'collaboration and projects already assisted under the public health programmes' through a 'coordinating mechanism', implying a blend of funding and 'new governance' through coordination. However, in the first instance, only a study on such a mechanism will be commissioned. The language in this part of COM(2004)301 suggests a sense that this response to *Kohll* is, in the view of the Commission at least, unlikely to attract sufficient support to be taken forward. This reflects the long-standing lack of a true 'single market' in pharmaceuticals across the EU.[40]

Third, one of the key opportunities arising from the *Kohll* litigation is the possibility of developing 'European centres of reference', offering highly-specialised treatments for patients with rare diseases, and offering a focal point for research and information dissemination. These would be appealing for individual Member States lacking the financial or human capacity to provide such specialised treatment. A clear 'EU value added' can be seen here, consistent with the principle of subsidiarity. Similarly, the *Kohll* litigation offers opportunities for cross-border health care provision to be developed in border regions,[41] and in fact, this is happening to some extent already, in the EU-supported 'Euregios'. Funding from the public health programme is to be directed to evaluation of the Euregio health projects, to assess the most successful in terms of cooperation on health care.[42] The

[38] Information sharing allows for planning. Current trends show critical shortages in health care professionals in the near future.

> 'If the overall numbers and specialisations of health professionals are not adequate, this still represents a serious risk for health systems across the Union, with the impact being felt hardest in the poorest Member States.'

In this context, it will be difficult for any one country to invest in training health professionals without knowing other countries will do likewise.

Therefore the Commission invites the Member States to consider a 'concerted strategy'.

[39] Directive 89/105/EEC on the transparency of measures regulating the pricing of medicinal products for human use and their inclusion in the scope of national health insurance schemes [1989] OJ L40/8. On the limited practical effect of the directive, see Hervey and McHale, n 5 above, at 323–27; L Hancher, 'Creating the Internal Market for Pharmaceutical Medicines: An Echternach Jumping Process?' (1991) 28 CML Rev 821.

[40] See Hervey and McHale, n 5 above, at ch 8.

[41] See A Coheur, 'Integrating Care in the Border Regions' (2001) 7(4) *eurohealth* (2001) 10; R Busse 'Border-crossing Patients in the EU' (2002) 8(4) *eurohealth* 19.

[42] COM(2004)301 final, p 9 'The Commission plans to support a project under the public health programme to evaluate Euregio health projects and to assess the most successful regions in terms of cooperation on health care'.

implication is that convergence of national approaches, based on these models of best practice, would follow. The public health programme is also to support research on the motivations for cross-border health care. This will presumably be used to inform decisions in the context of other governance processes, including the 'old' regulation and 'new' methods, such as the OMC.

COM(2004)301 notes that the lack of interoperability of health care information systems across Europe represents a significant barrier to reaping the benefits of cross-border health care. The public health programme is to be used to begin the process of developing an EU-wide 'Health Information and Knowledge System'. However, the Commission's enthusiasm in this context needs to be seen in the light of the significant systemic inertia that would have to be overcome to attain such a system. The Commission is also using its '*e-Europe 2005*' action plan in this area.[43] One strand of *e-Europe 2005* is the '*e-health* action plan',[44] which will provide EU funding for a number of developments. For instance, an EU 'electronic health card' is to be developed, involving a common approach to patient identifiers and electronic health record architecture.[45]

COM(2004)301 proposes a 'health systems information strategy', which will be taken forward through the public health programme, and the *e-health* action plan. The Commission is to contribute to developing health information systems ranging from local networks through to 'Europe-wide systems for spotting emerging health threats'. In order for such a Europe-wide system to function, compatibility of national and local data systems feeding into it will be essential. The Commission is to work with the European Medicines Evaluation Authority (EMEA) towards a pharmaceuticals information strategy, which will include developing a database containing a harmonised set of information on all licensed medicines in the EU.[46] The process of developing such a database may prompt convergence in national practice in terms of data collection and presentation. In general, the Commission also plans to collect and disseminate data from within primary health care and hospital sectors. Where funding is also used for information gathering at EU level, this provides the Commission with a significant lever, in terms of its own information, rather than being reliant on national sources of information, either slow to arrive or non-existent, or potentially filtered through national administrative institutions.

[43] Commission, *eEurope 2005: An Information Society for All An Action Plan to be Presented in view of the Sevilla European Council, 21/22 June 2002*, COM(2002)263 final.

[44] Commission, *e-Health—Making Healthcare Better for European Citizens: An Action Plan for a European e-Health Area*, COM(2004)356.

[45] According to the Commission, this card is to be rolled out in 2008.

[46] COM(2004)301 final, p 12.

'C'mon, c'mon, let's get together': 'persuasive convergence'

Although the HLPR Report is at pains to stress that 'the organisation and financing of healthcare and social protection systems' are the responsibility of Member States,[47] nevertheless, it concludes that 'exchanges of best practice would be valuable for all Member States'.[48] To this end, the HLPR Report suggests a permanent cooperation mechanism at EU level. This is echoed by COM(2004)301[49] and the BRP Report.[50] The motivation for this is partly expressed by reference to the *Kohll* litigation,[51] but also by reference to common challenges to national health care systems from technological development, ageing populations and rising public expectations.

Under Article 152(2) EC, the Commission has now decided to establish a 'High Level Group on Health Services and Medical Care' (HLG on HS&MC), of senior officials from Member States, chaired by the Director General of DG SANCO, in order to drive this process of cooperation and coordination. It will call on external experts, as necessary. Other stakeholders are to be involved only indirectly, not as full members.[52] In many of its work areas,[53] EU funding will also be used to support policy developments, and some may also (or instead) be taken forward by the OMC.

[47] It devotes several paragraphs to this assertion, setting out a long list of national responsibilities. The *Kohll* rulings are read as recognising 'the need for Member States to be able to plan health services to ensure access ... avoid undermining the financial balance of the social security system, and control costs ...'.

[48] COM(2004)301 final, p 10.

[49] '[a] consensus has ... developed that a framework at European level to facilitate cooperation and to shape developments is needed, but is lacking', COM(2004)301 final, p 4.

[50] 'There is overwhelming support for the Commission's role in steering exchange of best practice', BRP Report, p 5.

[51] Community law gives patients mobility entitlements, but their exercise is difficult in practice, so cooperation of Member States would help; the consequences of the litigation for national health care systems are unclear, this can also be alleviated by cooperation.

[52] 'Civil society stakeholders from the health sector should also be involved on a regular basis, in particular through the European Union Health Forum. Representatives of regional and local authorities with responsibility for health care should also be able to contribute, as in most Member States the responsibility for providing health services is at regional or local level.' COM(2004) 310, p 16.

[53] COM(2004)301 envisages a number of areas of activity, including exchange of best practice on 'provision of information to patients on how to get treatment in other Member States, and get your NHS to pay for it'; exchange of information on networks of health experts and centres of excellence across the EU; cooperation to 'ensure that where Europe does have an impact on health or health systems, it does so in a positive way'; identifying common elements in national statements on the rights and duties of patients; exchange of information and cooperation on capacity-sharing, by a pooling at EU level of experience gained by existing local initiatives in cross-border health care; drawing up a contractual framework for healthcare purchasing; data sharing between Member States on health care professionals, their specialisms, distribution and mobility (in collaboration with the Commission and 'relevant international organisations'); and coordinating assessment of new health technologies.

A health care Open Method of Coordination

The HLRP Report mooted the possibility of a 'health care OMC' as a response to the uncertainty arising from the *Kohll* litigation. At the same time as COM(2004)301, the Commission issued COM(2004)304 final[54] proposing such an OMC, covering both health and social care. The focus of COM(2004)304 differs from that of COM(2004)301. The opening paragraph sets the tone, situating European social and health protection systems as 'an important part of the European social model'. COM(2004)304 also recalls the EU's pedigree in promoting convergence of social protection objectives and policies,[55] rather than stressing the need for a response to a new situation.

Recalling that the Barcelona European Council, March 2002, set three principles for reform of social protection systems, including health care, COM(2004)304 sets objectives based on these principles. The principles are: ensuring access to care, on the basis of universal access, fairness and solidarity; promoting high quality care; and ensuring the financial sustainability of health care and social protection systems. These are high-sounding principles, to which all interested actors can easily sign up. The Employment, Social Policy, Health and Consumer Affairs Council endorsed the OMC's principles in October 2004. However, the detail of how such social entitlements are delivered currently varies widely between Member States, and an OMC process in the field of health care will face significant challenges.[56]

OMC processes in other areas place significant reliance on the identification of 'hard' quantitative objectives and indicators, in particular as a basis for the evaluation and benchmarking stage of the process. However, it is extremely difficult to compare national health systems of the Member States, given their independent historical, cultural and institutional contexts, and the multidimensional aspects of health care. If a health OMC is to be effective, extreme caution will be needed in the formulation of indicators and the interpretation of results. Of the three principles on which the objectives of the health OMC are based, only the financial sustainability of national health (insurance) systems is readily susceptible to quantification. What cannot be so easily quantified is 'best practice', in terms of

[54] *Modernising Social Protection for the Development of High-Quality, Accessible and Sustainable Health Care and Long-term Care: Support for the National Strategies using the 'Open Method of Coordination'*. See also Commission communication, *The Future of Health Care and Care for the Elderly: Guaranteeing Accessibility, Quality, and Financial Viability* COM(2001)723 final; Joint report by the Commission and the Council, *Supporting National Strategies for the Future of Health Care and Care for the Elderly* Council Doc 7166/03, 10 March 2003.

[55] In particular, by reference to 1992 Council Recommendation 92/442/EEC on the convergence of social protection objectives and policies.

[56] See R Busse, 'The 'OMC' in European Health Systems' <http://www.tu-berlin.de/fak8/ifg/mig/files/2002/lectures/pdf/Lisbon3105-RB.pdf>.

not simply more efficient health care provision, but a more 'patient-centred' approach to health care provision.

Moreover, the health OMC faces opposition in Council and national parliaments,[57] to the effect that the case for an OMC process has not been persuasively made by the Commission. Council's October 2004 conclusions make clear that the OMC is to have a 'light touch', and should not impose excessive administrative burdens. National health ministries must be directly involved. Overlaps between existing EU institutions and processes[58] must be avoided.

Indicators, on which the OMC will be based, are to be developed from 2004, by reference to work done originally under the action programme on health monitoring[59] and subsequently the public health programme.[60] All Member States are to submit, by March 2005, 'preliminary reports' on the challenges facing their systems. The Commission will analyse these and propose 'development and reform strategies' for 2006–9. The first 'Joint Report' will be adopted in 2007.

'Reflecting the will of the citizens and States of Europe':[61] The constitutional reform

At the same time as the HLRP was carried out, the governments of the Member States were considering the latest version[62] of the EU's evolving 'constitutional document', the Constitutional Treaty (CT).[63] The CT has now been agreed, but of course it will not enter into force unless it is ratified by national constitutional process in each Member State before it enters into force.[64] One of the aims of the CT is to clarify the division of competences between the EU institutions and those of the Member States.[65] The division

[57] See, eg, UK Parliament House of Commons Select Committee on European Scrutiny, Thirty-Second Report (28 October 2004).

[58] The Social Protection Committee; Employment Committee, Economic Policy Committee and HLG on HS&MC.

[59] Decision 1400/97/EC [1997] OJ L193/1.

[60] Decision 1786/2002/EC [2002] OJ L271/1. See the European Community Health Indicators Projects 1 and 2, 1998–2001, and 2001–4; PGN Kramers, 'The ECHI Project' (2003) 13 *European Journal of Public Health* 1.

[61] Art I–1 CT.

[62] On the EU Constitution as process, see J Shaw, 'Postnational Constitutionalism in the European Union' (1999) 6 *Journal of European Public Policy* 579; B de Witte, 'The Closest Thing to a Constitutional Conversation in Europe: The Semi-Permanent Treaty Revision Process' in P Beaumont, C Lyons and N Walker (eds) *Convergence and Divergence in European Public Law* (Oxford: Hart, 2002).

[63] For details on the novel 'constitutional convention' method, see G de Búrca, 'The Drafting of the European Union Charter of Fundamental Rights' (2001) 26 ELR 126; K Lenaerts and M Desomer, 'New Models of Constitution-Making in Europe: The Quest for Legitimacy' (2002) 39 CML Rev 1217.

[64] Art IV–447 CT.

[65] The necessity of such a clarification is particularly associated with German legal and political commentators, see J Schwarze, 'Constitutional Perspectives of the European Union with Regard to the Next Intergovernmental Conference' (2002) 8 *European Public Law* 241. See also U di Fabio, 'Some Remarks on the Allocation of Competences between the European Union and its Member States' (2002) 39 CML Rev 1289.

of competences within the EU is a highly politicised area of EU constitutional law, reflecting concerns about 'creeping competence', the extension of EU competence into ever wider areas.[66] The context here is the uncertain legitimacy of the EU as a '*demos*-less' polity, exercising powers once exclusively held by the democratically legitimated sovereign entities of its Member States.[67]

The general concerns about the division of competences in the EU are reflected in microcosm in the context of the EU's involvement in health care, and, more generally, health policy. In the CT, 'common safety concerns in public health matters' are explicitly deemed to be a matter of 'shared competence'.[68] This was probably seen as desirable,[69] in the light of the ECJ's apparent constraining of Article 95 EC as a basis for Community public health competence, in the *Tobacco Advertising* ruling.[70] By contrast, the 'protection and improvement of human health' is stated to be an area where the EU may take only 'supporting, co-ordinating or complementary action'.[71] In such areas, national laws may not be harmonised.[72] It is likely that most elements of governance of health care systems would not fall within the terms 'common safety concerns in public health matters', as 'public health' enjoys a specific meaning in this context.[73] However, health

[66] Legally speaking, this happens because the precise extent of Community competence is not always easy to determine, for a number of reasons. Community competence includes *implied competence*, where the Treaty does not grant an explicit power, but requires the achievement of an objective (Cases 281, 283–5, 287/86 *Germany* v *Commission* [1987] ECR 3203). Competence in a particular field is rarely exclusively allocated to the EU institutions, but is most often *shared* with national institutions, leading to boundary disputes about the proper limits of Community competence, expressed in legal terms by reference to the principles of subsidiarity and proportionality (Art 5(2) and (3) EC). Some legal basis provisions may be expressed in very *general* terms, leaving doubt as to their precise scope in a particular context (See particular, Art 308 EC). Along with Art 95 EC, this is explicitly mentioned in the Laeken Declaration as a possible site for adjustment by the Constitutional Convention; see G de Búrca and B deWitte, 'The Delimitation of Powers between the EU and Its Member States' in A Arnull and D Wincott (eds) *Accountability and Legitimacy in the European Union* (Oxford: OUP, 2002) 204. The European Court of Justice has not developed a complete doctrine of the allocation of powers between Member States and EU institutions. De Búrca and de Witte contrast the position with respect to other elements of European constitutional law, where the Court has developed quite comprehensive jurisprudence.

[67] For a starting point on the (copious) literature on the subject, see P Craig and G de Búrca, *EU Law: Text, Cases and Materials* (Oxford: OUP, 2002) ch 4; P Craig, 'The Nature of the Community: Integration, Democracy and Legitimacy' in P Craig and G de Búrca (eds) *The Evolution of EU Law* (Oxford: OUP, 1999) 23–50; A Arnull and D Wincott (eds) *Accountability and Legitimacy in the European Union* (Oxford: OUP, 2002); Scharpf, n 7 above; Weiler, n 7 above; JHH Weiler and M Wind (eds) *European Constitutionalism beyond the State* (Cambridge: CUP, 2003), especially M Poiares Maduro, 'Europe and the Constitution: What if This is as Good as it Gets?' therein; N Walker (ed) *Sovereignty in Transition* (Oxford: Hart, 2003).

[68] Art I–14 CT.

[69] See M Giannakou, member of the Constitutional Convention, 'Thoughts on the EC Treaty Provisions Regarding Public Health' CONTRIB 229 CONV 536/03 (4 February 2003).

[70] Case C–376/98 *Germany* v *Parliament and Council (Tobacco Advertising)* [2000] ECR I–8419.

[71] Art I–17 CT.

[72] Art I–12(5) CT.

[73] See, generally, Hervey and McHale, n 5 above, at ch 3.

care governance probably does fall within 'the protection and improvement of human health'. Thus, the Treaty implies a basis for mechanisms of 'new governance' in health care, for instance, the HLG on HC&MT or the health OMC. It also strongly implies the exclusion of EU 'old governance' mechanisms from the health care field.

Probably more importantly, the 'internal market' is also an area of shared competence. As we have seen, the catalyst for the EU's recent increased involvement in health care is internal market litigation, and the Commission seeks to respond utilising internal market legal bases where it proposes 'old governance' measures, such as a new directive on services. Therefore, to a large extent, these provisions, although presented as intending to constrain 'creeping EU competence' in the health field, appear to simply consolidate the existing position.

However, on its face, the CT attempts to constrain 'creeping competence' in the health field, by explicitly stating that responsibility for health care systems is a matter of national competence. This clause originated as a proposed addition to Article III–122, which refers to 'services of general interest', and is in Title I of Part III CT on 'provisions of general application'. The proposal gained initial support from over 10 Member States. This would have read:

> 1. The Constitution shall in no way prejudice the responsibilities of the Member States for the determination of their policies, organisation and delivery of health services and medical care provided within the framework of a social security scheme.
> 2. The responsibilities of the Member States referred to in paragraph 1 shall include in particular the management of health services and medical care and allocation of resources to them, and standards applied.

However, in the Irish draft, the clause was moved to Article III–278(7). It now reads:

> Union action shall respect the responsibilities of the Member States for the definition of their health policy and for the organisation and delivery of health services and medical care. The responsibilities of the Member States shall include the management of health services and medical care and the allocation of the resources assigned to them.

A number of observations may be made. Legally speaking, the location of a provision in a legal text may make a difference to its interpretation. So, here, the earlier version, under Title I, would have had a stronger effect than a provision later in the Treaty. The final version limits 'Union action', whereas the earlier version limits 'the Constitution'. While it is not entirely clear what the legal significance of this distinction might be, one possible interpretation is that 'Union action' predominantly relates to action of the legislative and administrative institutions of the EU; that is, its main focus is secondary legislation. 'The Constitution' seems to be wider, including within its focus the primary text of the CT itself. The (perceived) challenge to the organisation of national health systems comes inter alia from the application by the ECJ and national courts of the Treaty provisions on freedom to provide and receive services. These remain essentially unchanged in the CT.[74] While the final text might limit the ability of the Commission, for instance, in the development of a health OMC, the earlier text seems to at least attempt to go further towards encouraging the ECJ to develop a different approach to the scope of the directly effective Treaty provisions on the internal market.

Nevertheless, the overall thrust of the CT is that health care is a matter for Member States. 'Organisation and delivery of health services and medical care' is to be the responsibility of the Member States, and the CT explicitly states that the 'Union shall respect' such responsibilities. This is reflected in the list in Article I–17, of 'areas of supporting, co-ordinating or complementary action', which, as we have seen, strongly implies the exclusion of EU 'old governance' mechanisms from the health care field. However, unlike the earlier text proposed for Article III–122, the current provision does nothing to curtail the application to health care systems of the 'grandmother of old governance'—that is, deregulatory internal market litigation.

GOVERNANCE, LAW AND EU CONSTITUTIONALISM

What does the health care case study reveal about the changing roles of law in the context of the EU's new governance processes? What do these mean for the EU's constitutional arrangements? What hermeneutical or normative uncertainties or problems do 'new governance' mechanisms bring? The final section of this chapter brings together some preliminary observations on these interrelated questions from the health care case study, and draws some parallels with other contributions to this collection.

Roles of (EU) law: beyond harmonisation

EU lawyers have tended to downplay the significance of EU Treaty law that requires cooperation on the part of Member States, focusing only on the negative aspects of policy areas where regulatory harmonisation is explicitly excluded. The implication is that policies where the EU plays a 'supporting, co-ordinating or complementary' role are not very important. A focus on new governance methods challenges that assumption. Also, EU lawyers have only recently begun to consider the significance of soft EU law.[75] The

[74] Arts III–144–50 CT.

[75] See L Senden, *Soft Law in European Community Law* (Oxford: Hart, 2004). For early exceptions, see F Snyder, 'Soft Law and institutional practice in the European Community' EUI Working Paper LAW No 93/5; K C Wellens and G M Borchardt, 'Soft law in European Community Law' (1989) 14 ELR 267.

health care case study shows how the legal obligations of Member States to cooperate or participate in new and persuasive convergence governance structures (OMC); funding, information collection and dissemination) and the use of soft interpretative norms may underpin future significant Europeanisation effects, through indirect or voluntary policy convergence, and may affect the articulation and dissemination of legal norms and values within the EU's constitutional order.

First, the roles of law in OMC include the imposing of procedural obligations to report within certain timeframes, and provide information within certain parameters. Soft law generated under OMC persuades rather than coerces national actors to conform to European standards; although national or sub-national actors may adopt hard law in response to OMC processes. In the health care context, OMC faces particular difficulties in translating indicators with respect to the *quality* of care into the process. It is here that relationships between an OMC process on health care, and a *right* to access quality health care may come into play.[76] Relations between the OMC process and (fundamental) rights in EU law have been elaborated in a number of contributions to the literature.[77] Bernard has argued that the OMC process may provide an opportunity for the EU to pursue a social rights agenda, by reference to the fundamental social rights contained in the Charter of Fundamental Rights of the European Union (EUCFR).[78] Such social rights would include a 'right to health care' (Article 35 EUCFR). OMC may then provide an alternative framework to litigation, within which the contested relationships between the internal market and the 'European social model' may be resolved.

Obviously it is too soon to assess the policy content outcomes of the proposed health OMC. To the extent that the OMC process is successful in tackling the similarly complex social problems of unemployment and social exclusion, and to the extent that health care can be likened to those policy areas, a health OMC may be a fruitful mechanism of governance in the EU. For instance, OMC may provide the framework for resolving uncertainties about relationships between economic indicators (such as health as a driver of economic growth) and human-rights-based values (such as health as a human right),[79] through comparison of the relative success of locally or

[76] See J Zeitlin, 'Opening the Open Method of Coordination' Committee of the Regions Conference, 30 September–1 October 2002, <http://www.cor.eu.int/pdf/omc/zeitlin.pdf>.

[77] See, in particular, N Bernard, 'A "New Governance" Approach to Economic, Social and Cultural Rights in the EU' in T Hervey and J Kenner, *Economic and Social Rights under the EU Charter of Fundamental Rights: A Legal Perspective* (Oxford: Hart, 2003); K Armstrong, 'Tackling Social Exclusion through OMC: Reshaping the Boundaries of EU Governance' in T Börzel and R Cichowski (eds) *State of the Union: Law, Politics and Society* (Vol 6) (Oxford: OUP, 2003) 170; F Scharpf, 'The European Social Model: Coping with the Challenges of Diversity' (2002) 40 *Journal of Common Market Studies* 645.

[78] Bernard, previous n.

[79] The BRP Report highlights problems with the interpretation of health as a driver of economic growth, observing that values such as health as a human right may be underemphasised as a consequence. BRP Final Report, p 3.

regionally developed health policy blends of the values of the internal market and the 'European social model'.

Second, one of the key Treaty obligations of the Commission, often underplayed by 'old governance' and traditional constitutional accounts of the EU, is to foster cooperation between the Member States in various policy areas.[80] When describing these policies, legal commentators often focus on the 'negative' aspects of their legal bases, in particular the fact that harmonisation of national policies through binding EU-level norms, such as directives, is explicitly precluded by the Treaty. However, these legal bases also include *positive* obligations on the Member States, to liaise with the Commission and to coordinate policies and programmes accordingly. Thus, national policy in the relevant field may not lawfully develop in a vacuum, but multi-level coordination and cooperation is required by EU 'constitutional' law.

Further, such legal bases formally grant the Commission a general power of initiative to propose measures which will promote cooperation between the Member States in those areas, potentially leading to convergence of national policies. In the health field, Article 152(2) EC is an example of such a legal basis provision. It provides that 'Member States shall, in liaison with the Commission, coordinate among themselves their policies and programmes' in the areas of 'improving public health, preventing human illness and diseases, and obviating sources of danger to human health',[81] and gives the Commission competence to 'take any useful initiative to promote such coordination'. The extent to which those areas include governance of health care systems is highly contentious in the EU context. Nevertheless, the Commission has taken several initiatives to promote policy coordination in the governance of health care systems, including the establishment of the HLG on HS&MC, the Byrne Reflection Process and the health OMC.

Third, EU law plays a crucial role in legitimating the disbursement of EU funding, which can also promote Europeanisation through voluntary convergence. Although the EU's budget is modest,[82] the EU institutions have traditionally used the provision of financial incentives to promote the integration process. This mode of governance, largely neglected by legal scholarship, involves the use of the wealth of governing institutions to achieve

[80] See, eg, Art 99 EC on economic policy; Art 127 EC on employment; Art 137 (2)(a) and 140 EC on social policy; Art 149 EC on education; Art 151 EC on culture.

[81] Art 152(1) EC.

[82] It is important to be clear about the size of the EU's budget. The idea, at times perpetuated by the British media, of swathes of 'Brussels bureaucrats' is a gross exaggeration. In fact, the European Commission employs fewer people than a large county council in England; see A Hayes, 'The EU and Public Health beyond the Year 2000' (1998) 4 *eurohealth* 2. The EU budget represents only a fraction of levels of public spending in the Member States. It is obvious from this that the EU, as currently constituted, cannot possibly replace health spending in the Member States. The EU's redistributive interventions in the health field are small-scale, in the totality of health spending across the EU as a whole.

policy aims.[83] Where funding is used to generate and share information, there are close links with technocratic modes of governance. Although a long-standing technique of governance in the EU context, the use of funding to promote particular policies, or steer developments, including the adoption of hard law, at national level, now deserves greater attention from EU legal scholars,[84] in the context of 'new governance' discussions.

The EU, through its research and technology policy, has funded medical research since the mid 1980s.[85] The public health programme[86] also provides funding for medical research, and other matters concerned with health care delivery. A key element of these programmes is the sharing of best practice across borders and the forging of networks in particular fields, in order to provide a forum for shared knowledge and expertise. Over time, it may be that the experiences of collaboration may feed into national policy processes, thus prompting gradual convergence or 'Europeanisation' of national policies, or, ultimately, laws. From this convergence of approaches, EU-level financial support may also lead to the adoption of principles or values that eventually feed through to EU-level legislation,[87] or other modes of governance, such as OMC. For instance, the public health programme has been used to develop health indicators that are likely to form the basis of the health OMC.

Judicial review of Commission action disbursing EU funds is a failsafe legal mechanism of last resort to ensure disbursement consistent with agreed goals and parameters,[88] although strict *locus standi* rules make this an impractical route for challenge to or participation in the formation of those goals for any other than the 'privileged' applicants of EU institutions and Member States.[89] Further, in policy areas where governance is shared

[83] The technique of government by *dominium*; see T Daintith, 'The Techniques of Government' in J Jowell and D Oliver (eds) *The Changing Constitution* (Oxford: OUP, 1994); see further, T Daintith and A Page, *The Executive in the Constitution: Structure, Autonomy and Internal Control* (Oxford: OUP, 1999); see also Claire Kilpatrick, Ch 5 in this volume. What the EU does not fund is also relevant; see for instance the Commission's refusal to fund stem cell research under the Framework Six Programme; for further information see T Hervey and H Black, The European Union and the Governance of Stem Cell Research' (2005) 12 *Maastricht Journal* 3.

[84] For exceptions to the trend of neglect, see, eg, J Scott, *Development Dilemmas in the European Community* (Buckingham: Open University Press, 1995); J Scott, *EC Environmental Law* (London: Longman, 1998); J Kenner, 'Economic and Social Cohesion: The Rocky Road Ahead' (1994) *Legal Issues of European Integration* 1.

[85] See Council Resolution on the First Framework Programme of Research [1983] OJ C208/1; Decision 85/195/EEC Establishing a Multiannual Research Action Plan in the Field of Biotechnology, [1985] OJ L83/1, which included the use of biotechnology in health care.

[86] Decision 1786/2002/EC of the European Parliament and of the Council of 23 September 2002 Adopting a Programme of Community Action in the Field of Public Health (2003–2008) OJ L271/1.

[87] See, for instance, the case of 'orphan medicines' (for treating disorders affecting not more than five in 10, 000 persons), discussed in Hervey and McHale, n 5 above, at 244–45.

[88] Case C–106/96 *UK* v *Commission (Poverty IV)* [1998] ECR I–2729.

[89] Art 230 EC; Case 25/62 *Plaumann* [1963] ECR 95; Case C–50/00P *Unión de Pequeños Agricultores (UPA) v Council* [2002] ECR I–6677.

between EU and (sub)-national levels, the legal structure of Article 230 EC may preclude the use of litigation as a 'good governance' check.[90] Non-litigation routes to promote mechanisms of good governance, including principles of good administration, or value-for-money standards, may have a more significant role.

A governance mechanism closely related to the use of funding is the collection and dissemination of data at EU level, either by the Commission, or by specialist EU agencies, such as the EMEA. In certain circumstances, the Commission is obliged in EU law to collect and disseminate data across the EU.[91] Member States, under the 'duty of sincere cooperation',[92] are obliged to cooperate in this process. Where data collection is mandated at EU level, the need to produce standardised and comparable data sets in order to fulfil obligations in EU law may give a significant push towards convergence of national practices towards a 'Europeanised' standard. For instance, if the Commission and EMEA develop standardised health systems information data sets, to prepare for and respond to emergent health threats, as is being proposed, then national, regional or local administrations will be obliged to provide data in the 'Europeanised' form.

Changes in data collection or dissemination practices may reveal information that affects the policy-making process at national levels. Further, the enhanced ability of individual citizens, or NGOs, to compare data across Member States may increase opportunities not only for political pressure, but also for litigation strategies, at national or sub-national levels. For instance, several Member States have recently adopted statements of 'patients' rights'. The Commission proposes the EU-level collection of information on the rights of patients,[93] in order to promote cross-border health care—both to increase patient confidence in health care in other Member States and to assist in the formation of contractual relationships between health care funds in one Member State with health care providers in another. Comparisons of rights enjoyed by patients in other Member States may throw light on (perceived) deficiencies in particular Member States, increasing political pressure for reform. It may also provide alternative interpretations of patients' rights, bringing opportunities to challenge existing national interpretations of provisions common to several Member States, by reference to interpretations in legal systems of other Member States. This is particularly so within the context of common membership of

[90] For instance, Art 230 EC implies the identification of 'an act of the EU institutions'. So where, for instance, the Court finds that there is no such act (see, eg, Case T–461/93 *An Taisce* [1994] ECR II–733) then judicial review will not be available. In a new governance setting, where responsibilities of public and private actors at different levels may be imprecisely defined, these types of problems are exacerbated.

[91] Eg, in employment (Art 128 EC); social policy (measures based on Art 137(2)(a) EC); education (Art 149(2) EC).

[92] Art 10 EC.

[93] Either through the High Level Group on Health Services and Medical Care or by the OMC.

the Council of Europe, with the European Convention on Human Rights and European Social Charter, both of which include rights relevant to health care, and indeed the provisions of the EUCFR, now part of the CT.[94] The Commission's collection and dissemination of information, for instance on patients' rights may, in time, lead to comparisons between national systems within the EU, and cross-fertilisation of standards development and interpretation of the content of various elements of a 'right to health care' recognised in the CT.

Finally, the Commission uses interpretative communications (soft law) in dialogue with the ECJ and national courts, in order to determine the contours of EU 'hard law'. Although the Commission has no formal constitutional authority to determine the scope or content of EU law (that being for the ECJ or national courts), such communications may have significant persuasive effects.[95] Communications may structure social or economic behaviour as if they were binding legal norms, in that individuals may rely on them in arranging their affairs. This may be seen with the Commission's communication COM(2004)301 final on the *Kohll* ruling. It remains to be seen whether the Court will be persuaded to develop its jurisprudence consistently with this communication, so as to remove the application of *Kohll* in situations where the patient would not have been entitled to the particular hospital care at issue in her home state. In a classical constitutional framework, this type of use of soft law might offend the doctrine of separation of powers,[96] to the extent that the Commission (an administrative/legislative institution), acting in a quasi-judicial role, may be 'usurping' the judicial function. However, the EU has always accommodated this role of soft law,[97] and the increased prominence of new governance simply brings into the spotlight an existing governance mechanism, reminding lawyers of the relevance of non-binding legal norms in exercising control in the management of relationships and resources in the pursuit of social and economic ends.

[94] For further discussion, see T Hervey, 'The Right to Health in EU law' in T Hervey and J Kenner (eds) *Economic and Social Rights under the EU Charter of Fundamental Rights* (Oxford: Hart, 2003) 193–222; T Hervey, 'We Don't See a Connection: the 'Right to Health' in the EU Charter and European Social Charter' in B De Witte and G de Búrca (eds) *The Protection of Social Rights in Europe: Changes and Challenges*, (unpublished paper) 305–385.

[95] The Commission has used such soft law measures in internal market law; see Commission Comunication concerning the Consequences of the Judgment Given by the Court of Justice on 20 February 1979, in Case 120/78 *Cassis de Dijon* [1980] OJ C256/2; and in the field of competition law, for instance, see M Cini, 'The Soft Law Approach: Commission Rule-making in the EU's State Aid Regime' (2001) 8 *Journal of European Public Policy* 192; Senden, n 75 above, at 143–48.

[96] On the problems of applying a traditional 'separation of powers' approach to EU governance, see C Joerges, 'The Law's Problems with the Governance of the European Market' in C Joerges and R Dehousse, *Good Governance in Europe's Integrated Market* (Oxford: OUP, 2002) especially 19–22.

[97] See Senden, n 75 above.

Constitutionalism

The health care case study reveals strongly that the CT's formal articulation of the constitutional norm to the effect that the governance of health care is a matter for Member States is at odds with the emerging practice that suggests various sites at which the governance of health care is becoming, or at least may become, 'Europeanised'. It is difficult to read the CT as a 'brake' on the emerging health care governance practices discussed above, as there is little evidence that the CT seeks to deal directly with the interrelationship between the internal market and health care, which is what would be required to end 'competence creep' in this policy area. Starting with the obvious and simple observation that written constitutional texts do not necessarily capture operative constitutional norms and practices, what does this mean for EU constitutionalism?

At least in the health care context, the 'creeping competence' discourse represents genuine concerns about the legitimacy of governance, in terms of both process and outcome. These reflect not only generic constitutional concepts, such as accountability or protection of individual rights, but also sector-specific interests or values, such as the equal access of citizens to public health care provision, the solidarity of health care systems, and effective use of public resources for health care delivery. In the European context, these can be characterised as 'constitutional values', in that they form a relatively stable and agreed foundation, within which politically contentious and non-stable policy decisions about health care are made.[98]

The health care case study suggests that a reliance on a traditional, allocation of powers, constitutional model for the EU may prove profoundly problematic in ensuring constitutional protections, at least in a policy area such as health care governance. Such a model implies, inter alia, an EU Member State hierarchy, within which it is essential to 'get right' the formal allocation of competences; (at least symbolic) lines of accountability of separate 'executive' institutions to elected representative institutions;[99] delegation of authority from legislative to executive actors; a regulatory structure where individually enforceable legal norms are the ones that matter; control of regulatory activity and acts of relevant institutions through judicial review. If our constitutional model assumes that health care governance is a matter for Member States, there is a danger that questions about the protection of constitutional values in the new governance arrangements operating in the EU escape constitutional scrutiny. If the EU's constitution tells us that health care is a matter for Member States, then we can safely leave

[98] See M Tushnet, *The New Constitutional Order* (Princeton, Princeton University Press, 2003).

[99] See eg P Lindseth, 'Delegation is Dead, Long Live Delegation: Managing the Democratic Disconnect in the European Market-Polity' in C Joerges and R Dehousse (eds) *Good Governance in Europe's Integrated Market* (Oxford: OUP, 2002).

scrutiny to national constitutions. The very involvement of the EU in the governance of health care suggests that this particular model of EU constitutional law simply does not capture the processes at play: the practice of governance has been decoupled from the nation state, and cannot be readily re-coupled.

Rather, the health care case study implies that we need a constitutional model which accomodates heterarchy of legal authority;[100] within which competence is shared and competences are exercised within multi-level governance mechanisms; within which various actors participate in governance, rather than acting as agents for a delegating authority; where non-enforceable legal norms matter;[101] and where control mechanisms take into account all of the above, and, therefore, must go beyond judicial review. The relationships between governance institutions within that multi-level system need to be understood not simply within a binary EU-national government framework. For instance, the Commission is proposing further cooperation between health care providers on capacity sharing, observing that a number of cross-border capacity sharing arrangements already exist, and that the bodies involved have worked out how to tackle problems of cross-border cooperation. These projects have grown up out of local initiatives. The Commission is now suggesting a cooperation mechanism that goes directly from local to EU level (either through HLG on HS&MC, or through OMC) cooperation, and that bypasses both Council, and national executives and parliaments altogether. The challenge for EU constitutional law is to encapsulate such interactions within its framework of analysis, so as to ensure that constitutional norms are protected therein. The details of such a framework are not developed here,[102] but the health care case study suggests its contours include institutional balance, legitimacy and participation.

Institutional balance

One possible narrative from the health care case study, drawing on institutionalist/rational actor accounts, would present the Commission's 'purposive opportunism'[103] arising from the application of new governance mechanisms in health care governance. According to this narrative, new governance does not significantly destabilise the independent agency, or even

[100] See, for instance, N MacCormick, *Questioning Sovereignty* (Oxford: OUP, 1999); N Walker, 'Late Sovereignty in the European Union' and M Poiares Maduro, 'Contrapunctual Law: Europe's Constitutional Pluralism in Action' in N Walker (ed) *Sovereignty in Transition* (Oxford: Hart, 2003); N Walker, 'The Idea of Constitutional Pluralism' (2002) 65 MLR 317–59.

[101] See Senden, n 75 above.

[102] See, in particular, the chapters in the first part of this volume.

[103] This is well-represented in existing literature—see, for instance, Armstrong and Bulmer, n 19 above.

hegemony, of the Commission as the linch pin of Community law and policy making. For instance, the change of emphasis from the HLRP Report in COM(2004)301 and even more so the BRP (which adds the Commission-led linkage of health with the Lisbon agenda) may be read as Commission 'recapturing' the policy initiative from the Member States or Council, and indeed from the civil society participants in the HLRP. The Commission's long-standing use of the wealth of government, and technocratic governance techniques, blending judicious use of EU funding and information coordination, coupled with OMC, situates the Commission as a central driver and clearing house for generation and dissemination of policy ideas, allowing the Commission control over these governance processes. This narrative would raise classical concerns about the Commission's vulnerability to 'capture'. Not new, these are even made explicit in the BRP Report, which suggests that the health agenda may be susceptible to capture by powerful interests in the food, tobacco or pharmaceutical industry.[104]

However, the health care case study also supports a more subtle narrative, in which Council, national governments and even parliaments (although perhaps not civil society) seek to reassert control, with some success. This arises, for instance, in the institutionalisation of coordination and cooperation, through comitology, such as the HLG on HS&MC. This classical form of executive governance in the EU's constitutional order allows for flexibility, but without national administrations ceding to the Commission all control of governance processes. Its critique is well known in EU legal literature.[105] Another example is the health OMC. National parliaments and Council are sceptical about the need for an OMC in this field at all. The difficulty of quantifying elements of health care makes OMC processes difficult to apply. The upshot is that Council has rewritten this OMC to leave a large margin of discretion to Member States, possibly to the extent that operating an OMC process at all may not be an efficient use of administrative resources, and it may in the end be quietly dropped, or allowed to wither through de facto lack of real participation.

[104] BRP Report, p 4.

[105] See C Harlow, *Accountability in the European Union* (Oxford: OUP, 2002) especially ch 3; M Andenas and G Türk (eds) *Delegated Legislation and the Role of Committees in the EC* (The Hague: Kluwer, 2000), especially G Schäfer, 'Linking Member State and European Administrations: The Role of Committees and Comitology', and AE Toeller and HCH Hofmann, 'Democracy and the Reform of Comitology' therein; C Joerges and E Vos (eds) *EU Committees: Social Regulation, Law and Politics* (Oxford: Hart, 1999), especially G Ciavarini Azzi, 'Comitology and the European Commission' therein; E Vos, 'The Rise of Committees' (1997) 3 *European Law Journal* 210; K St Clair Bradley, 'The European Parliament and Comitology: On the Road to Nowhere' (1997) 3 *European Law Journal* 230; R Pedler and G Schäfer (eds) *Shaping European Law and Policy: The Role of Committees in the Political Process* (Maastricht: European Institute of Public Administration, 1996); K St Clair Bradley, 'Comitology and the Law: Through a Glass, Darkly' (1992) 29 CML Rev 691.

The health care case study suggests that the EU's constitutional concept of institutional balance[106] may provide a framework within which the relative powers of at least EU-level institutional actors may be held in fruitful tension. One potential response to the problems of comitology in EU constitutional law has been through the concept of 'institutional balance'.[107] However, new governance raises questions about the application of institutional balance in a context of multi-level activity, where local, regional and national institutions also share competence and shape policy development. What kind of entitlement to 'institutional balance' could form a platform for empowerment of (excluded) civil society groups, where new governance structures imply their participation? Could an entitlement to 'institutional balance' prevent the quiet dropping of a health OMC?

Legitimacy

A number of the US participants in the conference that preceded the publication of this collection observed that the use of new mechanisms of governance to solve complex social problems in any other than neoliberal ways appears to require the application of these new mechanisms of governance 'under the radar', that is, relatively isolated from high profile media or other public scrutiny. While a fixation with neoliberalism is not so entrenched in European political life, elements of this 'under the radar' phenomenon appear also in the EU health care case study, for instance, in the use of Article 234 EC as a site for deregulatory litigation, and consequent governance responses to instability thereby created; or in the press release on COM(2004)301, which highlighted only the 'soft' and cooperative, and not the normative, governance responses proposed by the Commission.

Whilst the 'under the radar' phenomenon may be desirable in terms of policy outcomes, it raises questions about traditional constitutional understandings of legitimate governance, through representation of informed citizens by law makers, accountability of executives to elected legislatures, and so on. Questions arise as to whether the participatory elements of new governance offer sufficient legitimacy to compensate for the lack of informed debate among a wider citizenry. There is also a concern about the generation and application of fundamental constitutional values (see below).

[106] See K Lenaerts and A Verhoeven, 'Institutional Balance as a Guarantee for Democracy in EU Governance' in C Joeges and R Dehousse, *Good Governance in Europe's Integrated Market* (Oxford: OUP, 2002).
[107] Although in fact the ECJ has declined to find the comitology system 'unconstitutional', see Case 25/70 *Koster* [1970] ECR 1161 and Case 302/87 *European Parliament v Council (Comitology)* [1988] ECR 5615.

Participation

One feature of 'new governance' is said to be a move from representation towards participation. As in the US case,[108] the EU involvement in health care governance reveals the emergence of novel institutional structures that may enhance participation in governance processes. In particular, a health OMC will presumably draw on a wide range of 'partners', for instance, in developing its benchmarks and indicators, and feeding back instances of good practice into the policy loop. If the health OMC moves ahead, various relevant actors, such as health care funds, hospitals, health care professionals and patients, are likely to be included in the various stages of the OMC process.

Participation applies at all policy stages, including policy initiation. The application of new methods to health care governance suggests a focus on representation of a wider range of interested actors, even at the policy initiation stage, as participators in agenda-setting. The membership of the agenda-setting High Level Reflection Group included not only health ministers and the European Parliament, but also other key stakeholders, that is, representatives of patients, professionals, providers and purchasers of health care. Rather than bringing in a wider range of stakeholders later in the policy cycle, in particular, in the implementation of EU law phase under the 'traditional' construction of EU law, stakeholders were involved from the very beginning. The use of new governance methods here may help to avoid, for instance, 'agency capture' of the Commission by entrenched interests, for instance, those of the pharmaceutical industry, reflecting a generalised concern framed in terms of the representativity of the EU's agenda-setting institutions and processes.

On the other hand, the HLRP only met for a year. The real work of taking the detail of the policy forward will be done by the HLG on HS&MC, which excludes civil society as full members, even though they were included at the High Level Reflection stage. It also also excludes parliaments (European and national) except in the most indirect ways. This seems to be a return to an older mode of governance for the EU.[109] This is also exemplified in the health OMC. OMC is said to offer significant changes to sites for participation, and in particular to link sub-national with EU levels. However, for the health OMC, Council has explicitly written in the direct participation of national health ministries, thus removing the possibility of bypassing that national site of governance and control.

The health care example raises questions about who the 'representatives of civil society' are, especially where they interact 'at EU level'. For instance, the 'civil society' members of the High Level Reflection Group were

[108] See L Trubek, 'New Governance Practices in US Health Care' in this collection.

[109] The legal basis of the HLG on HS&MC is also interesting—unlike the Social Protection Committee, which has a Treaty basis in Art 144 EC, it is set up by Commission Decision.

International Mutual Association (AIM); Standing Committee of the Hospitals of the EU (HOPE); European Health Management Association (EHMA); European Patients Forum (EPF); European Social Insurance Partners (ESIP); Standing Committee of European Doctors (CPME). All are EU-wide networks of national representatives of civil society, so by definition operate at a distance from individual patients, health care professionals and health care funders and purchasers within the Member States, although all can claim representativity indirectly through national organisations which form their membership. It is unclear how the members of the High Level Reflection Group were selected. However, they are all groups which had already worked closely with the Commission, which could suggest a 'semi-closed' network, again reverting to potential problems of 'capture'. In the case of one group, the 'European Patients' Forum', the group itself owes its existence to a request from the Commission that such a group be created.[110] One potential role for the law here is to allow challenge to the processes by which 'civil society' groups become 'insiders' in EU governance processes,[111] and a counterbalance to the power of the EU institutions, especially the Commission—in effect to require civil society to structure and present itself in a way which is appealing to the EU institutions, rather than self-chosen.[112]

Backstop or kickstart? Constitutional values

Several of the contributors to this collection observe that 'new governance' often emerges within a pre-existing framework of hard law, suggesting that such a framework may be one of the drivers of new governance phenomena.[113] Hard law provides the framework, or backstop, within which experimentation and problem-solving among relevant stakeholders may flourish, and lead to desired or efficient policy outcomes. Hard law, including litigation, can also be used to destabilise entrenched institutional arrangements that are failing to achieve their objectives,[114] thereby 'kickstarting' new governance arrangements. The roles of such legal 'backstopping' rules

[110] 'The European Patients' Forum should be seen as a response to recent calls by the European Commission and other EU institutions to have one pan-European patient body to address and be consulted on issues concerning the interests of patients in the European healthcare debate.' <http://www.europeanpatientsforum.org>.

[111] The inclusion of other EU-wide networks excluded from EU-level processes has already arisen in the context of Case T–135/96 *UEAPME* 1998 ECR II–2335.

[112] See generally, G De Búrca and N Walker, 'Law and Transnational Civil Society: Upsetting the Agenda?' (2003) 9 *European Law Journal* 387.

[113] See, in particular, Bradley Krakkainen; Ch 11 and Susan Sturm, Ch 12 of this volume.

[114] See CF Sabel and WH Simon, 'Destabilization Rights: How Public Law Litigation Succeeds' (2004) 117 *Harvard Law Review* 1015.

include promoting accountability and ensuring adherence, in the context of experimental devolved governance, to centrally-agreed broad policy goals.

The EU health care case study is consistent with the observation that various new governance mechanisms follow from particular types of hard law rules, and in particular with the observation that litigation may play a destabilising role, such that existing entrenched actors and institutions are enticed or forced into new ways of interacting and using new problem-solving mechanisms. One interesting element of the responses to the *Kohll* litigation is the extent to which policy discussions that were not strictly indicated by the uncertainties raised are now included in EU health care governance. The *Kohll* litigation seems to have 'kickstarted' various broader policy discussions, in particular based on solving of shared problems in the provision of health care within the 'European social model' in the twenty-first century.

Much of the legal commentary criticising the *Kohll* litigation has been on the basis that the application of the law of the internal market to health care provision in the Member States of the EU destabilises the financial arrangements for national health care provision. This is presented as undesirable. In contrast, a 'new governance' reading of such destabilisation suggests that it should rather be embraced, as opening up opportunities for the application of governance mechanisms that will generate more efficient policy outcomes.

However, new governance mechanisms in themselves provide only the *processes* within which policies are generated, and, potentially, new soft and hard regulatory norms are adopted.[115] In the context of complex social problems, such as how to continue to provide universal access to quality health care, in the current European context, unless new governance moves towards agreed objectives, in terms of normative standards, then applying internal market law to public services that have hitherto been considered to be outside of 'the market' may turn out to be more destabilising than is desirable. Whether the European Court of Justice, or indeed national courts, are able to provide the contours of such normative standards in the context of health care provision, remains to be seen, although certain values, for instance, solidarity, appear to be consistently appearing in the jurisprudence.[116] Under 'old governance', although we may not agree with the precise contours of these backstopping values, at least we know which institutions and mechanisms (largely, courts and litigation, with the possibility of legislation where Community competence allows) are responsible

[115] See, eg, O Gerstenberg and CF Sabel, 'Directly-Deliberative Polyarchy: An Institutional Ideal for Europe?' in C Joeges and R Dehousse, *Good Governance in Europe's Integrated Market* (Oxford: OUP, 2002).

[116] T Hervey, 'Social Solidarity: A Buttress against Internal Market Law' in J Shaw (ed) *Social Law and Policy in an Evolving European Union* (Oxford: Hart, 2000) 31.

for generating them.[117] Under 'new governance' arrangements, it is less clear whence these values emanate. In the context of health care, Community competence is highly contested, and there is no equivalent of the framework directive(s) present in the race equality or environmental spheres. In this case, new governance can offer opportunities, but it also presents risks that core values, against which new governance mechanisms are framed, are developed and perpetuated by institutions and other actors that escape (to some extent) *both* classical *and* 'new' modes of accountability and representativity or participation.

CONCLUSION

What emerges clearly from the health care case study is that the 'traditional' conceptualisations of EU (constitutional) law, and its relationships with national legal regimes, do not capture the wide variety of governance processes brought to bear in the EU context, certainly in the case of governance of health care. 'Europeanisation' is so much more than deregulatory litigation with a bit of top-down harmonisation, implemented by national administrations, wherever formal competence provisions allow. Our accounts of the roles of law in the governance of Europe need to take account of law's roles in containing 'soft convergence' processes, such as persuasive coordination, provision of funding, and collection and dissemination of information, as well as in the more visible 'new governance' processes, especially the OMC.

What is also clear is that 'old governance' still plays an important role. This chapter's narrative is of a governance space opening up for the EU in the wake of the archetypal 'old governance' mechanism—internal market litigation. Far from abandoning 'old governance' legislative responses, the EU institutions, especially the Commission, are keen to pursue them, *alongside* the array of new governance mechanisms now also available. The extent to which the Commission can exploit all such possible sites for governance is subject to constitutional principles of institutional balance, as well as the practicalities of the Commission's limited resources.[118]

The health care case study shows that litigation remains a core site for the contestation of core ideological ('constitutional') values (such as equality and solidarity of citizens) within the EU's juridical construct. This finding merely confirms in the context of services much of the existing 'EU

[117] See Grainne de Búrca, Ch 4 in this volume.

[118] For instance, given the lack of a single market in pharmaceuticals, evidence-based analysis of new health care technologies is a possible site for Europeanisation, but the Commission is decidedly lukewarm on this.

constitutional literature', citing litigation on free movement of goods.[119] The possibility of individual legal challenge to national welfare settlements, even at the fringes, affects the balance of powers between EU and national or even sub-national institutions in the health care field. This constitutional rebalancing, along with the various governance responses to the resultant instability, deserves the attention of EU (constitutional) lawyers, in terms of both its processes and its substantive policy outcomes.

[119] See Poiares Maduro, n 7 above; Weatherill, n 7 above; JHH Weiler, 'The Community System: The Dual Character of Nationalism' (1982) 1 *Yearbook of European Law* 257.

8

Law and New Environmental Governance in the European Union

JOANNE SCOTT AND JANE HOLDER*

INTRODUCTION

THIS BOOK DEMONSTRATES that 'new governance' approaches pervade an increasingly wide array of policy spheres. This chapter, as well as that by Karkkainen, suggests that environmental governance provides unusually rich material for the study of new governance in both the European Union (EU) and the United States (US). The profligacy of the available examples,[1] the diversity and novelty of the processes and the relative longevity of their life-span all attest to its significance. The insights gleaned are of value beyond the environmental sphere, and in thinking more generally, about the relationship between (constitutional) law and governance. This chapter offers two European examples of new governance in environmental policy. Though these examples form just a small part of the elaborate world of new governance in this area, they offer important insights into this world and into some of the questions which it poses for law.

The first case study is concerned with environmental assessment, and specifically with the manner in which this concept has evolved. Twenty years after the inception of environmental assessment in the EU, the legislative framework has undergone considerable revision, and its scope of application has been much extended. This incremental process of change rests upon governance processes which bear testimony to the pragmatist ideal of federalism as experimentalism, constituting diverse laboratories for innovation, and linking structures for learning.[2] Contrary to many of the processes

* Many thanks to Bill Simon, Dave Trubek, Sharon Turner, and the other participants in the Cambridge workshop for their very useful comments. Thanks too to the various officials who agreed to be interviewed in the course of writing this paper. Many thanks to Despina Chatzimanoli for her excellent editing.

[1] See generally, H Heinelt, H Malek and AE Toller (eds) *European Union Environmental Policy and New Forms of Governance* (Ashgate, 2001).

[2] This idea has a long history in the United States. See, eg, *New State Ice Co. v Liebman*, 285 US 262, 311 (1932) (Brandeis, J, dissenting): 'It is one of the happy incidents of the federal system that a single courageous State may, if its citizens choose, serve as a laboratory'.

under discussion in this book, environmental assessment has a history in the EU.[3] In terms of its evolution, a number of iterations have occurred, leading to repeated instances of revision and review. Consequently, and exceptionally, we are in a position to evaluate 'whether in practice the back-and-forth between central agencies and local ones' has been effective.[4]

The second case study is concerned with the implementation of the EU Water Framework Directive (WFD). In the face of intense political disagreement, the obligations laid down in this more recent instrument are characterised by extreme flexibility. The core requirements are ill-defined, and the exceptions open-ended. According to the surface language of law, Member States enjoy considerable autonomy in implementation. Yet beneath this surface language, there has emerged, spontaneously, a forum for multi-level collaborative governance. Once again, this is seen to be deeply experimentalist. Contrary to the previous example, we lack here a history such as would permit an evaluation of outcomes and impact. But, even now, this case study is interesting from the perspective of law. Not only has there emerged—at a descriptive level—a gap between law and the practice of governance, but the premises which underpin the two seem starkly different, even antithetical, in their orientation.

The core claim in this chapter is an empirical one. It is suggested that there is emerging in the EU a unique approach to federalism which can readily be called experimentalist. So central is this approach that it is seen to emerge even where it is not explicitly mandated. In environmental assessment it emerged *ab initio* on the basis of the legislative text. In the water domain it has been concealed by a legislative framework which rests on different, and increasingly misleading, premises.

The emergence of experimentalist federalism in the EU stands in contrast to the classic community method. Whereas the former is collaborative and multi-level, laying considerable emphasis upon soft law, the latter is based upon clear divisions of competence and recourse to binding legislation. Yet it has been against the backdrop of this classic community method that (constitutional) law has emerged and evolved in the EU. Consequently, experimental federalism poses stark and difficult questions for law and for lawyers. It is not enough to report the existence of a 'gap' between law and the practice of governance, telling though this may be in thinking about the relationship between law and politics. The challenge lies also in contemplating the role of,

[3] Of course, it has an even longer history in the United States. A form of environmental assessment was first introduced by the National Environmental Policy Act 1969 (NEPA), s 102(a) 42 USC 4321–4361. For a review of the effects of this aspect of the legislation, see S Taylor, *Making Bureaucracies Think: The Environmental Impact Statement Strategy of Administrative Reform* (Stanford University Press, 1984). For a broader review of NEPA, including its environmental impact assessment strategy, see LK Caldwell, 'The National Environmental Policy Act: Retrospect and Prospect' (1976) 6 *Environmental Law Reporter* 50.

[4] M Tushnet, *The New Constitutional Order* (Princeton University Press, 2003), p 169.

and implications for, law in the face of shifting patterns in the practice of governance. The final section of this chapter offers some preliminary observations on this relationship in the context of the two environmental examples under discussion here.

ENVIRONMENTAL ASSESSMENT: FEDERALISM AS EXPERIMENTALISM

Environmental assessment[5] describes a process of predicting the likely effects of a proposed project, plan or policy on the environment prior to a decision being made about whether these should proceed. The significance of the procedure lies in the fact that it forces developers, administrators, and policy makers to think through the consequences for the environment of their decisions. Whilst clearly providing a procedural framework for decision making, environmental assessment does not regulate the substance of the decision—the outcome. Instead, all that is required is that the decision maker is availed of the information derived from the assessment procedure, and that this is taken into account when the decision is being made. This means, for example, that it is quite possible for a harmful (in environmental terms) project to be granted development consent. Importantly though, aspects of the environmental assessment procedure suggest that in practice it is capable of making a difference in favour of environmental protection. One such element having particular relevance for a discussion about new forms of governance and their constitutional importance stems from the opportunity that environmental assessment provides for a broad constituency of people and groups to become informed and to some extent engage in the decision-making process. This means that environmental assessment allows for the generation of a broad range of information and its exchange between government, industry, environmentalists and the public. Such rights of participation may also bring responsibilities for the provision and assessment of environmental information, particularly on behalf of the proponent of the project or policy. In the EU's form of environmental assessment,[6] this opportunity for participation has recently been enhanced with the result that in environmental assessment there are now many sites and scales of interaction between governmental and non-governmental bodies and some blurring of the traditional divisions between the public regulation of environmental problems, and the role of private actors.

A further important element is the requirement that the decision maker evaluate various options or alternatives to the proposed project or policy.

[5] Environmental assessment is a collective term, for the environmental impact assessment of projects, and strategic environmental assessment of plans, policies and programmes.

[6] Directive 85/337/EEC [1985] OJ L175/40. This was amended in 1997 (Directive 97/11/EC [1997] OJ L73/5) and 2003 (Directive 2003/35/EC [2003] OJ L156/17 on participation). See generally, J Holder, *Environmental Assessment: The Regulation of Decision-Making* (OUP, 2004), ch 1.

This provides a degree of anticipatory control because environmental harm may be prevented or reduced by identifying possible alternative sites, designs or technology at an early stage in the consent process. There is some evidence that this requirement has proved to be a forceful one, at least in the context of environmental assessment procedures invoked in cases of nature conservation.[7] In general, though, the regulatory nature of environmental assessment (that it does not mandate a particular outcome or standard) means that evaluating the *difference* that the procedure has made in terms of environmental protection is notoriously difficult. As Bartlett notes:

> the theorist or analyst who looks only for dramatic impacts or only for obvious direct effects is likely to be unimpressed ... Comprehending the significance and potential of EIA requires appreciation of the complexity of ways that choices are shaped, channelled, learned, reasoned and structured before they are officially made.[8]

There are, however, some recent signs that environmental assessment is capable of swaying decision making away from certain development projects. In the United Kingdom, for example, the central reason for the Secretary of State's refusal of development consent for a 'global port'[9] was the planning inspector's consideration of the likely effects of the development on designated conservation sites which had been identified in the course of the environmental assessment process. (Interestingly, the inspector had criticised the 'functional' assessment of these effects and plans for 'compensation' advanced in the developer's environmental statement, submitted as part of the process).

Turning to the form of regulation exercised by environmental assessment, though originally out of synch with the European Union's command-and-control approach to regulation, today the procedure looks increasingly typical of the Union's favoured approach. The original instrument, dating originally from 1985, is characterised by broad flexibility and rich proceduralisation. Member States retain considerable flexibility in implementation. Framework rules, combined with derogations, opt-outs, and textual ambiguity combine to concede considerable room for Member State manoeuvre. Against this backdrop of flexibility, procedural instruments—transparency, participation requirements and the like—are deployed to enhance accountability in implementation.

The effectiveness of Environmental Impact Assessment (EIA) as an instrument of environmental regulation has been much discussed. Views differ

[7] See case study on the European Commission's assessment of alternative routes for the purposes of the Habitats Directive (Directive 92/43/EEC [1992] OJ L206/7 in Holder, previous n, pp 158–62.

[8] RV Bartlett, 'Ecological Reason in Administration: Environmental Impact Assessment and Administrative Theory', in R Paehlke and D Torgerson (eds) *Managing Leviathon: Environmental Politics and the Administrative State* (Behaven, 1990), 82.

[9] At Dibden Bay, discussed as a case study in Holder, n 6 above, ch 6.

starkly, not least between those who regard environmental assessment, instrumentally, as a means of informing decision makers of the possible environmental consequences of a proposed project or action,[10] and those who propose, more fundamentally, that environmental assessment inculcates environmental protection values amongst those taking decisions.[11] The latter consider that environmental assessment contributes to changing the culture in which decisions are made, leading to a type of 'social learning'. Here, we are concerned less with its effectiveness in absolute terms, and more with relative effectiveness, temporally conceived. The EIA Directive has been repeatedly reviewed and revised. Review and revision takes shape within the framework of processes constituted by the directive itself. The directive provides the tools for iterative evaluation and adaptation. It is with these processes and tools that this case study is concerned.

Central in this regard is the concept of information exchange.[12] According to this, the Member States and the Commission shall exchange information on the experience gained in applying the directive. In particular, the Member States shall inform the Commission of the criteria and/or thresholds adopted for selecting projects to be assessed.[13] Concerns about the quality of the information submitted by Member States led, in the Strategic Environmental Assessment Directive (SEA),[14] to a demand that Member States 'ensure that environmental reports are of sufficient quality to meet the demands' of the directive.[15]

Information exchange is supplemented by a Commission reporting requirement. On the basis of the information received, the Commission is charged with issuing five-yearly implementation reports, examining the application and the effectiveness of the directive. The Commission is responsible, on the basis of these, for submitting such additional proposals as are necessary for the amendment of the directive, with a view to ensuring that it is applied in

[10] Eg, as discussed by LK Caldwell, *Between Two Worlds: Science, the Environmental Movement and Policy Choice* (CUP, 1992).

[11] This is the view of Taylor, *Making Bureaucracies Think*, n 3 above, and, more recently, H Wilkins, 'The Need for Subjectivity in Environmental Impact Assessment'(2003) 23 *Environmental Impact Assessment Review* 401.

[12] Directive 85/337/EEC, n 6 above, Art 11.

[13] The Directive rests upon a distinction between Annex 1 and Annex II projects. Whereas the former are by definition to be subject to assessment, the latter are to be subject to assessment where they are likely to have significant effects on the environment.

[14] Directive 2001/42/EC on the Assessment of the Effects of Certain Plans and Programmes on the Environment [2001] OJ L197/30.

[15] *Ibid*, Art 12(2). This goes on to provide that Member States shall communicate to the Commission any measures they take concerning the quality of these reports. The Strategic Environmental Assessment Directive was to be implemented from the middle of 2004, and the first Commission report is not due until the middle of 2006, and at seven yearly intervals thereafter. Thus, to date, the impact and justiciability of this quality requirement is not yet clear. On the important issue of the quality of environmental reports, see the Institute of European Environmental Policy <http://www.ieep.org.uk>. A more recent study does not seem to be available.

a 'sufficiently coordinated manner'.[16] To date the Commission has issued three such implementation reports.[17]

Innocuous though these informational requirements may appear, it is suggested that they underpin an approach to governance which is peculiarly well-suited to conditions of complexity and diversity. This approach makes a virtue out of necessity, harnessing disagreement and diversity as resources for innovation and learning. These tools exemplify, in many important respects, the distinctive character of European federalism, which rests increasingly upon coordination not harmonisation, and upon supervised decentralisation.

The approach to review and revision which underpins the EIA Directive readily lends itself to analysis according to a democratic experimentalist frame. According to this:[18]

> (i) lower level actors are granted autonomy to experiment with solutions of their own devising within broadly defined areas of public policy:[19]

As noted above, Member States are permitted considerable flexibility in the implementation of the EIA Directive. This extends not only to the range of projects to be assessed[20] and to the nature of the information to be gathered,[21] but also to the manner in which the assessment findings are to be taken into account in the development planning process.[22] The directive has

[16] Directive 85/337, n 6 above, Art 11(4).

[17] The first report was published in 1993 and covered the period up to the beginning of July 1991 (with some additional information from July 1991 to March 1992). See COM(93)28 final—vol 12. An update of this report was issued in 1997 and covered the period from 1990 until the end of 1996. A third five-year report was published in 2003 (*Report from the Commission to the European Parliament and the Council on the Application and Effectiveness of the EIA Directive: How Successful are the Member States in implementing the EIA Directive?*

[18] This characterisation of democratic experimentalism draws *directly* upon Sabel and Gerstenberg's characterisation of it in 'Directly Deliberative Polyarchy: An Institutional Ideal for Europe' in C Joerges and R Dehousse (eds) *Good Governance in Europe's Integrated Market* (OUP, 2002), pp 291–92.

[19] As Bill Simon noted in his comments on an earlier version of this chapter, this has a strange ring in the EU setting. Here, it is not so much that lower level actors are granted autonomy. Rather, it is the case that higher level actors (the EU) choose not to impede the autonomy of the Member States through the adoption of constitutionally permitted legislation setting out detailed and prescriptive substantive values. In the end the result is the same.

[20] Projects of the kind listed in Annex I must be subject to assessment. Those listed in Annex II (a much longer list) shall be made subject to assessment only where Member States consider that their characteristics so require. This requirement has been read by the European Court alongside Art 2, as requiring assessment wherever projects are likely to have significant effects on the environment.

[21] This is specified in Art 5, and includes today a description of the main alternatives studied by the developer and an indication of the main reasons for his choice. Assessment of the information to be supplied is made on the basis of relevance and reasonableness, the latter having regard, inter alia, to current knowledge and methods of assessment.

[22] Art 8 provides that the results of the consultations and information gathered must be 'taken into consideration' in the development consent procedure. The directive does not institute any substantive 'bottom-line' whereby egregiously negative effects will necessitate a refusal of development consent.

no substantive core, and even damaging projects may proceed. This flexibility has been somewhat curtailed by the European Court. The Court has held repeatedly that Member States may not exempt in advance entire categories of project, except in so far as this category as a whole is not likely to have significant effects on the environment.[23] Similarly, in 'screening' projects for assessment, Member States are obliged to consider not merely their scale, but also their nature and location.[24] Likewise, the environmental effects of the project cannot be determined by reference to the characteristics of that single project. On the contrary, Member States must have regard to their cumulative effects, in order that the objective of the directive not be circumvented by 'the splitting of projects'.[25] All this notwithstanding, heightened flexibility continues to reign.

> (ii) in return, these lower level actors are required to furnish higher-level units with rich information regarding their goals as well as the progress they are making towards achieving them:

As noted previously, Member States and the Commission are to exchange information on the experience gained in applying the directive, and the Commission is charged with issuing periodic implementation reports. In practice, the provision of information by Member States is by way of response to a Commission questionnaire. In addition, however—in even the most meagre of the Commission's three reports (the 1997 update)—the Commission also makes recourse to additional sources of information. To illustrate, the latest (2003) report was prepared by the Impact Assessment Unit of the School of Planning of Oxford Brookes University, in conjunction with a steering committee of staff from DG Environment, and a representative from the Member States. This team sought further (post-questionnaire) clarification from most Member States on key aspects of their implementation processes. This included the circulation of a further set of questions to the Member States, following an initial review of responses received. Secondary literature and databases (including the Enimpas database on EIA in transboundary context) were also examined by the team for further evidence of EIA practices within the Member States.[26] It is in the light of this that the Commission is able to claim that the report is 'structured around the transposition and implementation of Directive 97/11/EC and the operation of the EIA Directive as a whole, rather than on the basis of the individual questions posed by DG Environment's questionnaire', and to conclude

[23] See, eg, Case 72/95 *Kraaijeveld* [1996] ECR I–5403, para 50. This is a very difficult burden to discharge, and it remains uncertain how this might be achieved in practice.

[24] Case C–392/96 *Commission v Ireland,* para 65.

[25] *Ibid*, paras 73–83.

[26] Above, n 17 (third report), 'Methodology' at p 12, and Appendix One for the full text of the relevant questionnaires. See pp 52, 65, 90 and 96 for instances where secondary literature were used to inform the Commission's observations.

that 'this facilitated a more comprehensive overview of progress on transposition and implementation and highlighted key issues that warrant further attention'.[27]

Much emphasis is placed by the Commission in the reports upon the difficulties encountered as a result of information deficits which result from a lack of, or inadequate, Member State monitoring of EIA practice.[28] Such gaps are repeatedly highlighted in the reports, in a bid to encourage the collation of more reliable and comprehensive data, and better monitoring and research on the operation of EIA.

> (iii) the lower level actors agree to respect in their actions framework rights of democratic procedure and substance, as these are elaborated in the course of experimentation itself:

The basic claim for participation in environmental assessment is that it contributes to the correctness or validity of decisions, by allowing assertions to be checked against the views of those who have local knowledge of an area, or are interested parties. More fundamental claims for participation now rest upon a deliberative ideal that better outcomes may be arrived at and, furthermore, that the process of deliberation is capable of inculcating environmental values which may encourage an ongoing sense of environmental responsibility for those involved in decision making (both participants and authorities). A view of environmental assessment as an expression of 'local democracy'[29] means that the procedure has become increasingly identified with this deliberative ideal.

The EIA Directive grants individual rights to participate in the assessment process. Article 6 establishes rules for the participation of the public, while also granting Member States discretion to establish the 'detailed arrangements' for the provision of information and consultation. The directive requires that Member States must ensure that any application for development consent and the accompanying environmental statement (compiled by the developer according to guidance in Article 5 and Annex IV) 'are made available to the public'.

[27] Above, n 17 (third report), pp 12–13.

[28] See, eg, in the 2003 Report (n 17 above), pp 50, 64, 36, 95–96.

[29] See, in the UK, the most notable example, the decision of the House of Lords in *Berkeley v Secretary of State for the Environment and Fulham Football Club (Berkeley No. I)* [2000] WLR 420, [2001] AC 603, (2001) 13 JEL 89, as per Lord Hofmann at 430:

> the directly enforceable right of the citizen which is accorded by the [EC EIA] Directive...requires the inclusive and democratic procedure prescribed by the Directive in which the public however misguided or wrong headed its views may be, is given the opportunity to express its opinion on the environmental issues.

For an evaluation of the shift from environmental assessment as technical procedure to mechanism for local democracy, see R McCracken, 'Environmental Assessment: From Technocratic Paternalism to Participatory Democracy?' paper given at the Enforcement of EC Environmental Law Seminar, King's College London, June 2003.

The framework for public participation has been subject to evolution over time, with significant amendments introduced in 1997 and 2003. The former seem attributable largely to the review and revision process under discussion here, and are indicative of the democratic experimentalist idea that process, as well as outcomes, is to be regarded as provisional, and as subject to continuous improvement on the basis of information pooling on comparative performance and best practice. These include the introduction of obligatory reason giving requirements,[30] greater clarity about timing in terms of information provision and the expression of public opinion,[31] and a strengthening of public participation opportunities in the transboundary assessment of projects.[32] The latter (2003 amendments) reflect, predominantly, developments at the international level, with the entry into force of the Aarhus Convention.[33] These include a broadening of the categories of information to be made available to the public,[34] a requirement that the public likely to be affected by the proposed development, be notified of the arrangements for public participation,[35] and a requirement that the public be given 'early and effective' opportunities to participate in decision-making procedures.[36] It also revises existing procedures by entitling the public 'to express comments and opinions when all options are open to the competent authority or authorities before the decision on the request for development consent is taken'.[37] This potentially engages the public in the consideration of alternatives, before options have become fixed. Also significant is the requirement that the main reasons and considerations on which the decision is based must include information about the public participation process, and be articulated 'having examined the concerns and opinions expressed by the public'.[38] This requirement potentially requires the decision maker to internalise the participatory elements of environmental assessment.

The formal framework for participation has then been strengthened in a number of important respects. Today,[39] the provisions aim at a more inclusive,

[30] Directive 97/11/EC, n 6 above, Art 9(1).
[31] *Ibid.* Art 6(2).
[32] *Ibid.* Art 6(3).
[33] *Convention on Access to Information, Public Participation in Decision-Making, and Access to Justice in Environmental Matters* at: <http://www.unece.org/env/pp/>.
[34] Directive 2003/35/EC Art 3(4) amending Art 6(2) and (3). In addition to the information gathered by the developer in the form of an environmental statement, and the main reports and advice issued to the competent authority or authorities at the time the public is informed of the request for development consent, information which comes to light after this initial notification and which is considered relevant to the final decision must also be conveyed to the public. This suggests that the framers of the directive conceive of environmental assessment as a process, with participation a feature of several stages of this.
[35] Directive 2003/35/EC Art 6.
[36] *Ibid.* Art 3(4) amending Art 6.
[37] *Ibid.* Art 3 amending Art 6(4).
[38] Art 3(6) amending Art 9.
[39] In fact, the 2003 reforms are not due to take effect until 25 June 2005, but analysis here presupposes these changes.

less technicist environmental assessment procedure, with public involvement in decision making expressed in the manner of an entitlement to participate, and to access to the courts to enforce its provisions. This is an advance on the more restricted information disclosure and consultation provisions of current forms of assessment. However, deficiencies still remain. There are no legal requirements for public participation at the initial screening stage,[40] or in respect of the 'scoping' of the assessment to be conducted. Consultation at these stages is merely encouraged by way of the Commission's guidance notes.[41] Nonetheless, the previously weak provisions have been significantly strengthened to encourage active public participation.

> (iv) the periodic pooling of information is intended to reveal the defects of parochial solutions, and allows for the elaboration of standards for comparing local achievements. It exposes poor performers to criticism from within and without, making good ones (temporary) models for emulation:

The implementation reports are stated to be part of a process for identifying the strengths, weaknesses, costs and benefits of EIA and implementation practices, and for identifying where improvements could be made and/or where the provisions of the directive or its implementation could be clarified or strengthened.[42] It is telling in this respect that in the United Kingdom there have been disagreements between central government and the devolved authorities as to the scope of the information to be submitted. This is said to reflect fears on the part of the relevant central government department that to highlight differences in implementation would serve also to highlight weaknesses in its preferred approach: precisely the point of information pooling and peer review.

The reports seek to do more than identify shortcomings and weaknesses in Member State implementation, and also to highlight examples of good practice. The Commission observes in its most recent report.

This review has produced a great deal of information on the operation of EIA in the Member States of the EU. It has reviewed 'best practice' and practice that is less than good. A Member State may have arrangements in place that are at the 'cutting edge' of best practice in one respect and in others display only a weak commitment to the EIS processes as a whole.[43]

[40] Above, n 17 (third report), p 49 where the Commission observes that only three Member States currently consult the public before arriving at a screening decision on Annex II projects. The Commission finds in its latest implementation report that consultation in respect of scoping takes place in around half of the Member States, it being legally required in only some cases (p 53).

[41] See DG Environment website: <http://europa.eu.int/comm/environment/eia/home.htm>. See, eg, the scoping guidance which provides a consultations 'checklist' (p 23) and emphasises that '[c]onsultations will help to ensure that all the impacts, issues, concerns, alternatives and mitigation which interested parties believe should be considered in the EIA are addressed' (p 11). Further guidance is given on how and who to consult.

[42] Above, n 17 (third report), p 15.

[43] Above, n 17 (third report), p 96.

Self-evidently the reports examine the legal framework for implementation. But they do more. They include also analysis of implementation practices within the Member States, including those which may be considered supererogatory having regard to the legal requirements of the directive. Thus, 'best practice' includes practice which is better than that which is legally required, and the reports engage with implementation practices and not merely with legal norms. So, for example, to take up the theme discussed above, the latest report examines mechanisms and measures for facilitating and promoting public participation in EIA, including those which go beyond those legally required.[44]

Moving on, there can, more generally, be no doubt that these experimentalist processes of review have generated far-reaching revision and strengthening of assessment obligations. Three of the most important amendments introduced in 1997 have their origins in the Commission's implementation reports.[45] The evolution of the public participation requirement has already been discussed. Also, additional instruments have been deployed in an attempt to steer Member State implementation. Included among these are frequent recommendations for Member States to make more use of existing Commission guidance. A range of detailed guidance notes have been produced on the basis of the findings included in the five-year reports. In the latest report, for example, the Commission notes that

> it envisages preparing *interpretative and practical oriented guidance* with the involvement of experts from the Member States as well as other stake holders like NGOs, local and regional authorities and industry

as well as considering what further amendments should be introduced.[46]

Before moving on, three more points merit observation:

First, there is an increasing awareness that one function of these experimentalist processes is to consider the scope of environmental assessment. Thus, in the SEA Directive, the Commission is explicitly invited to consider the

[44] Above, n 17 (third report), p 78.

[45] See the table at pp 27–28 of the 2003 report (n 17 above) which summarises the amendments introduced and locates their origin. This shows that the other main sources for amendments include the case law of the European Court, international conventions, and the introduction of new, related, Community legislation. The three amendments in mind here concern a.) the requirement that all projects subject to EIA require development consent (Art 2(1); b.) the introduction of screening selection criteria in Annex III (See also Art 4(3) requiring that these be taken into account). Screening is defined in the relevant Commission guidance document as that part of the EIA process which determines whether an EIA is required for a particular project; and c.) the introduction of a formalised 'scoping' procedure (Art 5(2)). Scoping is defined in the relevant Commission guidance document as: 'the process of determining the content and extent of the matters which should be covered in the environmental information to be submitted to the competent authority for projects which are subject to EIA'.

[46] Above 14, p 8. For the text of the various guidance documents, see the DG Environment website at: http://europa.eu.int/comm/environment/eia/eia-support.htm

possibility of extending the scope of the directive to other areas/sectors and to other types of plans and programmes.[47]

Second, it is striking that the insights gleaned in the course of review of this instrument have been applied also in articulating new obligations, in new instruments. There has been spill-over from instrument to instrument. This is particularly apparent in the case of the SEA Directive which applies to plans and programmes, rather than to individual projects.[48] This instrument is powerfully imbued with the lessons learned in the course of repeated review of the earlier EIA Directive. To give just one example:[49] Analysis of alternatives is considered a key element of environmental assessment, perhaps even the most important,[50] because it encapsulates a preventive approach. In the original EIA Directive, consideration of alternatives formed no more than an adjunct to the central but basic body of information to be provided by the developer.[51] 'The failure on the part of the developers to take account of alternatives where this would be justified'[52] was recognised by the European Commission as a major deficiency in the quality of environmental statement during the first implementation phase. The amending directive was drafted in the light of these concerns, and elevated the status of this category of information to a mandatory requirement.[53] The information to be provided shall include 'an outline of the main alternatives studied by the developer and an indication of the main reasons for his choice, taking into account the environmental effects'.[54] Still, however, the onus of considering alternatives remains on the developer, with no requirement on the part of the authorities to show that alternatives have been considered, and to make this available to the public, such as exists in the case of the consideration of mitigating measures.[55]

[47] Above, n 14, Art 12(3). This is placed in the context of efforts to further integrate environmental protection requirements in accordance with Art 6 EC. See also, Art 5 of Directive 2003/35/EC on public participation. This provides, again, that the Commission will consider the possibility of extending its scope to cover other (than those currently listed in Annex I) plans and programmes relating to the environment.

[48] Above, n 14.

[49] One could also draw here upon the example of public participation, where the 1997 EIA amendments were mirrored almost exactly, except for an additional reference to the public being given an early and effective opportunity to give their opinion on the draft plan or programme (which in turn spilt-over to the 2003 amending directive).

[50] M Hertz, 'Parallel Universes: NEPA Lessons for the New Property' (1993) 93 *Columbia Law Review*. 1668 at 1679, considers analysis of alternatives to be at 'the heart of the environmental impact statement'.

[51] This fell in to the subsidiary category of 'additional information' to be provided only when the Member State considered it relevant, and only where the developer might reasonably be required to compile the information. See Art 5(1) in conjunction with Annex III, para 2 of Directive 85/337/EC, n 6 above.

[52] Report from the Commission on Implementation of Directive 85/337/EEC COM(93)28, p 43.

[53] Above, n 14, Art 5(3).

[54] Above, n 14, Art 5(3)

[55] Above, n 14, Art 9(1).

In theory, in itself, the development of strategic environmental assessment considerably extends the alternatives which may be considered in a decision-making process by allowing a broad range of criteria to be incorporated by the assessment of different options at an earlier stage.[56] Certainly a notable feature of the SEA Directive is the potential for enhanced attention to be given to the consideration of alternatives. The Commission was keenly aware—by dint of its reporting activities—of the continuing deficiencies underlying the EIA Directive in this regard. Insights from EIA spilled over to SEA, with the result that where an environmental assessment is required, the environmental report must identify, describe and evaluate the likely significant effects on the environment of implementing the plan or programme, and 'reasonable alternatives' to it, taking into account he objectives and the geographical scope of the plan or programme.[57] There is also a requirement to describe the 'zero-option' or the do-nothing alternative.[58] When a plan or programme is adopted, the authority must provide a statement of how the assessment was conducted and the reasons for not adopting the alternatives considered.[59] This suggests that the authority must more fully internalise the 'alternatives' requirement, rather than paying lip service to it.

Third, there is some evidence of cross-level experimentation. Within the European Commission, environmental assessment is being expanded, so that a form of policy appraisal now operates to review the internal formulation of European-level legislative and policy proposals, taking into account social, economic and environmental factors.[60] This builds upon the idea of environmental assessment, but extends it to encompass a broader sustainability assessment. This involves the amalgamation of existing sectoral assessment procedures into a single, standardised, procedure. Crucially, for the purposes of this chapter, the emergence of European-level sustainability (or impact) assessment offers an example of a feedback loop in law and policy making. The Commission's current development of this assessment regime for its *internal* procedures is viewed as providing a testing ground for the future application of a similar system in the Member States. The Commission has recognised that it would not be tenable to expect Member States to endorse an expanded conception of assessment, except in so far as this already applies to its own procedures. In particular, DG Environment foresees that the experience of applying a broad-ranging

[56] M Partidario, 'Strategic Environmental Assessment—Principles and Potential' in J Petts (ed.), *Handbook of Environmental Impact Assessment: Vol. 1 Processes, Methods and Potential* (Blackwell, 1999), p 67.

[57] Art 5(1) to be read in conjunction with Annex I of the SEA Directive, n 12 above.

[58] Annex I(b) states that information shall be provided by the developer on, inter alia, 'the relevant aspects of the current state of the environment and the likely evolution thereof without implementation of the plan or programme'.

[59] Above, n 14, Art 9.

[60] See COM(2002)272 final.

impact assessment procedure to its internal activities means that 'we will have the practical experience of operating the Commission's own integrated assessment procedures and will thus also have the moral high ground' when it comes to promulgating a similar model for Member States.[61] Thus, we see the Commission embracing and building upon the concept of environmental assessment as originally applied to the Member States. In turn, we see it preparing for a fundamental re-drawing of the concept as it currently applies to the Member States; on the basis of experience gained in the conceptualisation and application of the concept at the European level.

IMPLEMENTING THE WATER FRAMEWORK DIRECTIVE: LOOKING BENEATH THE SURFACE

The second case study has something in common with the first. It too may be conceived in experimentalist vein. Here again we have a directive (the Water Framework Directive—WFD) which leaves considerable autonomy to the Member States. [62] Like the EIA Directive, this contains a plethora of information pooling and reporting requirements. But there is more. Though not self-evident on the basis of the text of the directive, there has emerged a WFD governance forum, which is committed to the pooling of information and experience, and to the elaboration of standards for comparing local achievements. It represents a radical and, in some ways surprising, instance of experimentalism in the EU.

The WFD provides a legislative framework for the protection and improvement of water quality in the EU, and for sustainable water use. It applies to all kinds of water resources such as rivers, lakes, ground water, estuaries and coastal waters. The legislative framework is complex, providing for a range of procedural and substantive obligations, and a wide array of exceptions. The details need not detain us here. Suffice it to say, for the purpose of this chapter, that the directive aims at the integrated river basin management of waters, with the ultimate goal that Member States achieve 'good' surface water and groundwater status by the end of 2015.[63] For groundwater, 'good' is defined in terms of its quantitative and chemical status. For surface water, chemical status combines with ecological status. The concept of 'good' remains open-ended. This is notably the case for groundwater, and as regards the ecological status of surface water.

[61] See Holder, n 6 above, at 166.

[62] Directive 2000/60/EC Establishing a Framework for Community Action in the Field of Water Policy [2000] OJ L327/1. This was adopted in 2000 after many years of embattled negotiation.

[63] *Ibid*, Art 4(1)(1) for surface water, and Art 4(1)(b) for groundwater. The obligation is somewhat qualified in the case of artificial or heavily modified bodies of surface water (See Art 4(1)(a)(iii)).

It has been said that the 'incorporation of ecological considerations into the meaning of good status is, perhaps, the most progressive aspect of the strategy'.[64] Yet the concept of good ecological status is barely defined. Annex V identifies the quality elements which will make up an assessment.[65] It also provides, at a very general level, a normative definition of ecological status in each of the status classes (for example, good and moderate). These are supplemented by definitions of the conditions of the specific quality elements in each status class, for each water category. Implementation will require the establishment of methods and tools for ecological assessment, the establishment of parameters (metrics) for assessment, and of values (and value ranges within a given class). As William Howarth puts it:

> The exercise of applying Annex V of the Directive in practice is of considerable technical complexity, given the range of water categories that are involved and the diverse range of parameters that need to be taken into account in determining the status of any particular water. This is clearly an undertaking demanding a high level of relevant scientific expertise and common understanding across the Member States.[66]

It is immediately apparent in the light of the above that the implementation phase is all important. The directive constructs a number of implementation 'routes': legislative (requiring the adoption of European-level 'daughter directives');[67] executive (implying the empowerment of the European Commission within the framework of 'comitology' structures);[68] and Member State (conceding Member State autonomy in implementation).[69]

[64] W Howarth, 'Environmental Quality Standards and Ecological Quality Standards' (forthcoming Journal of Environmental Law).

[65] These fall into three groups of elements: biological, hydromorphological, and chemical and physico supporting elements.

[66] Above, n 64, p 20.

[67] See, eg, n 62 above, Art 16 which provides for the adoption of legislation concerning pollutants which present a significant risk, and Art 17 which provides for the adoption of legislation to prevent and control groundwater. See Decision 2055/2001 establishing the list of priority substances in the field of water policy [2001] OJ L331/1.

[68] See above, n 62, Art 20 which provides for the technical adaptation of the directive, and empowers the Commission to adopt guidelines on the implementation of Annexes II and V. The comitology system allows the Commission to exercise delegated powers, except in so far as its proposed actions do not accord with the opinion of a European-level committee, comprising representatives of the Member States. Where the committee view is out of synch with that of the Commission, the matter under consideration will pass from the Commission to the Council; that is to say from the executive back to (one part of) the legislative branch (the European Parliament being the other part, which is all but excluded). See Council Decision 1999/468/EC, and on the controversy over the European Parliament's (lack of) involvement see:

[69] This is the default position. The Member States are bound to implement the WFD into national law by 22 December 2001, and to achieve the objectives within the timeframes specified.

According to surface appearance, these three routes are emphatically different, both in terms of their decision-making mechanics, and their underlying constitutional premises. Put crudely, by way of illustration, the legislative route would appear to be premised upon centralisation, and the Member State route upon barely mitigated decentralisation. In the former, it is for the Community institutions to act, in accordance with the classic community method. In the latter, it is for the Member States to act, in accordance with the precepts of their domestic political and legal order.

Yet, it is the argument of this chapter that, in the case of the WFD, surface appearance is misleading in the extreme. In particular, the concept of Member State autonomy in implementation does little to capture the practice of governance in this sphere. The formal picture of Member State autonomy belies a complex reality which is characterised by multi-level, experimentalist, governance. This rests upon informal structures and recourse to soft law. As will be seen below, it is the argument also that there is greater convergence, and fluidity, as between the different implementation routes than the text of the directive might imply. Critical to these arguments is an understanding of the practical framework for Member State implementation.

In practice, Member State implementation takes shape against the backdrop of the so-called Common Implementation Strategy (CIS).[70] Nowhere mentioned in the directive, this provides an informal forum for Member State cooperation in implementation.[71] The CIS provides for 'open co-operation' between the Member States, and between the Commission and

[70] 'Common Implementation Strategy for the Water Framework Directive: Strategic Document' (Strategy Document). See also the follow-up document: 'Common Implementation Strategy for the Water Framework Directive: Carrying Forward the Common Implementation Strategy for the Water Framework Directive—Progress and Work Programmes for 2003 and 2004' (1st review) and the more recent: 'Moving to the Next State in Common Implementation Strategy: Progress and Work Programme for 2005 and 2006' (as agreed by the Water Directors on 2–3 December 2004) (2nd review). For these and other related information go to: <http://europa.eu.int/comm/environment/water/water-framework/implementation.html> or to the CIRCA site: <http://forum.europa.eu.int/Public/irc/env/wfd/library?l=/framework_directive&vm=detailed&sb=Title>. See the very useful 'resource document' issued by the European Environmental Bureau (EEB) in 2004 ('"Tips and Tricks" for Water Framework Directive Implementation' (2004) at: <http://www.eeb.org/activities/water/200403_EEB_WWF_Tips&Tricks.pdf>;A second useful report: 'EU Water Policy: Making the Water Framework Directive Work' (2005) may be found at: <http://www.eeb.org/activities/water/making-WFD-work-February05.pdf>.

[71] The WFD Common Implementation Strategy represents just one example of informal Member State cooperation in implementation in the environmental sphere. A similar pattern emerges as a result of the wide-ranging activities of IMPEL—the European Union Network for the Implementation of Environmental Law. See: <http://europa.eu.int/comm/environment/impel/>.This is an informal network of European regulators concerned with the implementation and enforcement of environmental legislation. Note also that the CIS structures are being used even in respect of areas falling outside of the WFD Thus, an initiative on flood prediction and prevention has been launched under its auspices, headed by the Netherlands and France, and charged with preparing 'best practice' documents, drawing on experiences in the Member States.

the Member States, in the implementation of the WFD. It reflects a 'new partnership working method', involving scientific as well as political actors, creating networks of specialists from different Member States and different levels of governance.[72] Against the backdrop of a dauntingly ambitious and complex framework directive, CIS provides for collaboration in implementation and in environmental problem solving.

With CIS, we find a dramatic and unexpected expression of new governance, nestling beneath the surface of Member State autonomy or sovereignty in implementation. The collaborative governance which this spawns is strongly imbued with the characteristics of experimentalism and resembles, in many important respects, the archetypal experimentalist tool, the Open Method of Coordination.[73] Like the OMC, it is committed to information sharing and the benchmarking of best practice. The Commission also deploys a 'scoreboard' approach, charting progress on implementation in respect of the WFD.[74]

The CIS was agreed by the Commission and the Member States (and Norway) in May 2001. It was reviewed and adjusted in 2003, and again in 2005.[75] This CIS was conceived by the EU Water Directors in appreciation of the substantial and shared challenges confronting Member States in the implementation of the WFD. The Water Directors are Member State representatives, with overall responsibility for water policy. In most cases, a Water Director will be the head of a Member State's water division, situated within the ministry for environment. Informal meetings of the Water Directors and the Commission are a regular, biannual, event, and are hosted by the Member State holding the Presidency of the European Council. They are co-chaired by the Commission and the Council President.

CIS proceeds on the basis of three working levels. Working Groups are charged with the preparation of technical, non-binding, guidance documents, and with ensuring necessary consultation at a technical level. The Strategic Coordination Group is chaired by the Commission and comprises

[72] Strategy Document, above n 70, at p 2. It remains to be seen to what extent this new partnership approach will spill over to the area of compliance, with the Commission coming to adopt a more deliberative, consensual, approach to enforcement. Further research is needed on this key issue of compliance in this setting.

[73] For an up-to-date account of the vast literature on this subject see the OMC forum at: <http://eucenter.wisc.edu/OMC/>. See, in particular, the recent contributions by Jonathan Zeitlin for an excellent overview (in particular 'Introduction: The Open Method of Coordination in Question' and 'The Open Method of Coordination in Action: Theoretical Promise, Empirical Realities, Reform Strategy' in Jonathan Zeitlin and Philippe Pochet, with Lars Magnusson (eds) *The Open Method of Coordination in Action: The European Employment and Social Inclusion Strategies* (Brussels: PIE-Peter Lang, 2005)). Like certain of the OMCs, WFD also uses a 'scoreboard' to assess and publicise Member State progress on transposition and reporting. See: <http://europa.eu.int/comm/environment/water/water-framework/transposition.html>.

[74] See: <http://europa.eu.int/comm/environment/water/water-framework/scoreboard.html>.

[75] Strategy Document and 1st and 2nd reviews, n 70 above.

participants from each Member State. It is charged with discussing the activities of the working groups, and with seeking to ensure coordination as between their different activities. It also prepares the necessary documentation for the Water Directors. The Water Directors steer and drive the process.

There is some vagueness on questions of participation.[76] Emphasis is laid upon the importance of 'active involvement' on the part of 'stakeholders, NGOs and civil society'; it is stated that the strategy should 'be based on the principles of openness and transparency encouraging creative participation of interested parties'.[77] The European Environmental Bureau (EEB) and WWF 'welcome the commitment of the European Commission, the Member States and Norway to transparency and public participation shown by the introduction of the Common Implementation Strategy for the Water Framework Directive' and note that their participation 'has been positive and very informative'.[78] 'For the first time stakeholders' and environmental NGOs' opinions and positions were sought to gather a broad range of views and ideas on implementing EU water laws.'[79] Involvement is to be decided on a case by case basis, depending on the scope and topic of the relevant process or working group.

> By identifying the kind of involvement needed for each situation..., the Commission and the Member States intend to ensure both the effective participation of and contribution from the interested parties and to enhance their understanding of the different elements related to the process. The basic idea is to promote an open and clear exchange of views and concerns between all the parties directly responsible for the implementation of the Water Framework Directive and those who will be interested in, or affected by, it.[80]

As regards the strategic coordination group, it provided that alongside the Commission Chair, and Member State participants, 'NGO's and stakeholders may be invited as observers and/or consulted'.[81] As regards the working

[76] See the CIS, 'Public Participation in Relation to the Water Framework Directive', Guidance Document no 8. Again, all relevant documents may be accessed at CIRCA: <http://forum.europa.eu.int/Public/irc/env/wfd/library?l=/framework_directive&vm=detailed &sb=Title>.

See also the criticisms of the EEB regarding the insufficiency of involvement of environmental NGOs in the Pilot River Basin integrated testing exercise ('Tricks and Treats', n 70 above, pp 59–60). In the United Kingdom, participation also raises the question of the involvement of representatives from the devolved authorities. Sharon Turner, in her comments on a draft, observes that 'Scotland has been very proactive in insisting it has appropriate representation and Northern Ireland is becoming more assertive'.

[77] Strategy Document, above n 70, at p 14.

[78] EEB, 'Tricks and Treats', n 70 above.

[79] EEB, 'Tricks and Treats', n 70 above, p 64.

[80] Strategy Document, n 70 above, at pp 14–15.

[81] Strategy Document, n 70 above, at, p 12.

groups, '[p]articipants from stakeholders and NGO's should be invited when they can contribute to the work with a specific expertise'.[82] As regards the working groups, all Member States (and other participating countries), stakeholders and NGOs may nominate experts to the groups.

To give just one example, the working group on ecological status comprises more than 70 participants (compared to an average size of 30–40). The vast majority are drawn from relevant Member State ministries and agencies.[83] This includes some 'regional' representation.[84] A small number of additional participants are drawn from a variety of European[85] and international organisations,[86] industry,[87] and civil society.[88]

CIS comprises four key activities or modules: information sharing; the development of guidance on technical issues; information and data management; and application, testing and validation.

CIS leads to the production of guidance documents.[89] These documents are to be 'developed in a pragmatic way based on existing practices in Member States'. They are based on best available knowledge at the time, but conceived as 'living documents', to be subject to ongoing review and updating.[90] They shall be 'practical, operational and policy and implementation oriented' and 'practical testing [in pilot river basins] should be part of the development of the guidance document'.[91] To take just one, singularly

[82] Strategy Document, n 70 above, at p 13.

[83] Working Group 2A, 'Overall Approach to the Classification of Ecological Status and Ecological Potential'. The final version was agreed by the Water Directors on 24/25 November 2003, Annex II.

[84] For example, the Scottish Environmental Protection Agency (SEPA) fields two representatives, and the Agence de l'Eau Rhône-Mediterraneé-Corse a single representative. The term 'regional' is used as a convenient shorthand for the sub-state level, and does not imply any judgment on the credibility of any people's claim to nationhood.

[85] EEA (European Environmental Agency), CEN (the European Centre for Harmonisation), JRC (the Joint Research Council).

[86] ICPDR (International Commission for the Protection of the Danube River), ETC/WTR (the European Topic Centre on Water, an international consortium brought together to assist the EEA in providing environmental information to the Member States, and to develop an environmental information network (EIONET: European Environmental Information and Observation Network)).

[87] ECPA (European Crop Protection Industry), EUREAU (Union of Water Supply Associations).

[88] The European Environmental Bureau fields two participants, and the STAR project (a transnational research project under the auspices of the 5th framework programme) fields one.

[89] For details of the guidance documents adopted see the CIRCA Information Exchange Platform at: <http://europa.eu.int/comm/environment/water/water-framework/information.html>. See also the EEB report 'Tricks and Treats', n 70 above, where the EEB offers advice to environmental NGOs as to how they should use the CIS guidance documents. They 'must challenge well-trodden paths and suggest alternatives'; 'improve the guidance documents by critically participating in the Pilot River Basin testing exercise' and '[h]ighlight issues that have been overlooked...'; and 'request that there is public participation as early as possible in the WFD implementation process' (p 12).

[90] Strategy Document, n 70 above, at p 14

[91] Strategy Document, n 70 above, at p 5.

important example, the WG on Ecological Status (Ecostat) has issued guidance which elaborates indicators and values for measuring water status, and for defining the nebulous concept of 'good' water status.[92] This confirms:

> Much of the guidance document is based on Member States' existing national experiences of assessing and classifying surface waters or on the interim outcomes of some of the development work currently underway. As implementation progresses and Member States begin to monitor and assess the ecological status of water bodies, the richness of Member States' practical experiences with ecological classification in relation to surface water categories will increase. New ways of dealing with some of the technical challenges, such as controlling the risk of misclassification, may be identified. The sharing of this growing body of experience among Member States will benefit all and should be encouraged.[93]

This working group is also responsible for coordinating an intercalibration exercise[94] and for reporting the results. This is intended to ensure that the class boundaries (for good ecological status) are consistent with the normative definitions laid down in the directive, and are comparable across the Member States.[95]

The EEB observes that 'CIS guidance documents can be effective in helping to achieve the WFD objectives', but that '[n]evertheless, in a few cases the guidance documents deviate from "best practices" and potentially undermine WFD requirements'.[96] This is attributed to the consensual nature of CIS decision making, and to the danger that this generates a lowest common denominator type approach. For this reason the EEB urges environmental NGOs and other stakeholders to engage critically but constructively in the formulation and re-formulation of guidance documents.

CIS is an informal process, leading to results which are non-binding on the Member States. Nonetheless, it operates within a framework intended to enhance Member State accountability in implementation. Pivotal in this respect is the elaborate reporting regime which the WFD constructs. Member States are required, on a regular basis, to submit a variety of far-reaching reports to the Commission.[97] These are to include copies of river

[92] Above, n 83.

[93] *Ibid*, Foreword.

[94] Intercalibration is one of the most politically sensitive aspects of the WFD/CIS process. The CIS dimension is seen as paving the way for a formal Commission decision pursuant to Art 21 comitology procedures. Intercalibration is concerned with ensuring the comparability of Member State assessments as regards the boundaries between ecological quality classes. As the EEB puts it: the 18 month intercalibration exercise is intended to 'establish a common understanding on status quality assessment and harmonised class boundaries that is consistent with the WFD normative definitions.' (EEB, 'Tricks and Treats', above, n 70, at p 51).

[95] See especially: 'Towards a Guidance on the Establishment of the Intercalibration Network and the Process on the Intercalibration Exercise, Guidance Document no 6, available at CIRCA, n 70 above.

[96] EEB, 'Tricks and Treats', n 70 above, at p 64.

[97] See generally n 62 above, Art 15.

basin management plans, together with updates, and interim progress reports with respect to measures planned. Member States are to include also summary reports of their programmes for the monitoring of water status,[98] thereby enabling the Commission to monitor Member State arrangements for monitoring. The Commission, in turn, is required to follow-up with the publication of its own reports. These are intended to review progress in implementation. In the case of the Commission's regular implementation report, it shall also review the status of surface water and ground water in the EU, and a survey of Member State river basin management plans, including suggestions for the improvement of future plans.[99]

Given the informal nature of the CIS, it is unsurprising that there is nothing in the WFD which makes it imperative for Member States to organise their reporting activities in the light of CIS guidance. There is nothing which makes it obligatory for Member States to measure and report performance according to CIS indicators and values. In practice, however, two features of the reporting regime create space for reporting, and review of performance, to proceed on the basis of CIS derived benchmarks. First, in practice, Member State implementation reports of this kind are issued by way of response to a Commission questionnaire. Thus, the Commission is free to draft its questions in such a way to elicit information framed in these terms. Second, as noted, it is incumbent upon the Commission to evaluate progress in implementation, and to incorporate its assessment, together with proposals for future improvements, in a report to be submitted to the European Parliament and the Council. Here again, there is ample scope for the Commission to measure performance relative to CIS benchmarks. As in the OMC, review by reference to shared targets and indicators, will operate to enhance transparency by facilitating cross-comparison of performance, and comparison relative to evolving best practice.

It is notable that CIS institutional arrangements are themselves regarded as provisional, and as subject to revision in the light of experience. The implementation strategy proceeds in phases. The first phase came to an end in 2002 and was followed by a review of progress and the elaboration of a work programme for the next phase. This review led to a major re-drawing of the organisational frame for implementation. One central concern in the re-organisation was the need to induce better integration as between the different implementation activities. This led to a revised institutional structure, designed to streamline the work, and to address cross-cutting issues more effectively.[100] A second review was conducted in December 2004, setting

[98] See generally n 62 above, Art 8 and Annex V.

[99] See generally n 62 above, Art 18. The first implementation report is to be submitted by the Commission in 2012 and subsequent reports on a six year cycle thereafter.

[100] Whereas previously there existed eight working groups and three Expert Advisory Fora, the activities of two of the three advisory fora have been shifted to working groups, and the number of working groups reduced from eight to four. From eleven groups in total, there are now five. The integration theme was also concerned with inter-linkages between the WFD and other areas of EU environmental policy.

out a work programme for the years 2005–6.[101] This includes a detailed overview and analysis of the make-up and activities of the CIS working groups. In looking back at earlier reforms, it concludes:

> [T]he results of the CIS WP 2003/2004 are impressive and useful. In addition, the planning and management of the activities under the work programme improved considerably. Building on these positive experiences, the CIS process should continue to further ameliorate its operation in order to continue to deliver results of high quality and value for the WFD implementation during the work period 2005/2006.[102]

Significant also from a re-organisation perspective, is the emphasis placed upon learning from experience. CIS has taken shape not only on the basis of prior planning, but also in the light of the pragmatic demands of problem solving. Thus, for example,

> [c]ertain pragmatic working experiences and procedures have been established in 2001/2002 which were necessary so that the Guidance Documents could be prepared. The former working groups have thereby established a number of additional groups such as steering groups, drafting groups and expert groups.

These organic working procedures have received formal endorsement in the course of review, and will be continued as best practice during the second phase. However, the endorsement is not uncritical. There is recognition of a danger that, with the new concentrated structure, these additional groups will emerge as de facto working groups, leading once more to an increase in the number of such groups, and to related coordination problems. Efforts are therefore made to clarify the nature, function and working methods of 'additional groups', and to specify more closely the relationship between these and the formal working groups.[103] The strategic coordination group is charged with monitoring the establishment of such groups, and with ensuring that a balance between the need to create small efficient units, and the risk of creating a fourth working level, is maintained.[104]

There is then evidence of an interesting dialectic as between 'bottom' and 'top' in the evolution of the strategy. Unanticipated solutions have emerged to meet practical need, and have received formal endorsement at a later

[101] Above, n 70 (2nd review).
[102] *Ibid*, p 6.
[103] See in particular, n 70 above (1st review), Annex A. This provides for the following ad hoc structures: steering teams (the team of WG leaders is sometimes joined by other members who would like to be more actively involved in the preparation of the meetings and the steering of the work); drafting teams (a number of active members a WG invited to prepare a specific document for a meeting, in order to assist the team of WG leaders); expert networks or expert workshops (external experts gathered on an ad hoc basis if and when the necessary in-depth knowledge on a specific subject is not available in the WG. The WG defines the task for the experts and the members of the WG are invited to nominate the appropriate expert).
[104] Above, n70 (1st review), p 9.

stage. At the same time, with formalisation have come critical engagement and a concerted attempt to anticipate and offset the kinds of difficulties to which these practical solutions might give rise.

This reflexivity as regards institutional form has generated a high degree of self-consciousness as regards the division of authority as between the three working levels (the working groups, the strategic coordination group, and the meeting of the water directors). The process of review of working methods led not only to a consolidation of existing lines of authority, but also to attempts to re-enforce the accountability of lower level actors to those at a higher level, and of the technical branch to the political branch.

Thus, the new working groups are to report regularly on their progress to the strategic coordination group.[105] Whereas the strategic coordination group is to be empowered—within the framework of ongoing review of the work programme—'to decide upon refinements and changes in the mandates, timetables and priorities', any such changes must 'recognise the overall agreed priorities in the work programme'. 'New working areas, substantial changes to the work programme and the establishment of new working groups will need to be decided by the Water Directors'.[106]

This self-consciousness as regards questions of accountability is reflected also in the new criteria for the establishment of supporting groups.[107] These groups are to operate on the basis of a precise mandate or terms of reference drawn up by the umbrella working group. [108] They are to work with the highest possible level of transparency, in order to enable the working group to follow and to contribute to their activities. Considerations of effectiveness and accountability underpin the design and reform of CIS.

LAW AND NEW APPROACHES TO GOVERNANCE

We have presented here two cases studies in 'new' environmental governance. It is suggested that these studies attest to the emergence of a unique form of federalism in the EU. This federalism, by contrast to the classic community method, is experimentalist and multi-level, and is seen to emerge regardless of whether it is contemplated by the legislative frame. These two examples, like the other examples discussed in this volume, raise profound and difficult questions for law and for constitutionalism. This chapter will conclude with some tentative comments on the legal dimension of the new environmental governance discussed above.

[105] Where relevant, the chairs of the working groups participate in the meetings of the strategic coordination group.

[106] See generally n 70 above (1st review), pp 11-12.

[107] Above, n 70 (1st review), Annex 1.

[108] See also n 70 above (2nd review), pp 17, setting out criteria for ad hoc supporting structures.

In many respects environmental assessment offers a classic illustration of the changing nature and function of law in new governance. As Supiot puts it, '...the law is relinquishing the job of establishing substantive rules, but is instead concentrating on affirming principles and laying down procedures'.[109] Environmental assessment relies upon procedural techniques to bring about a change in behaviour, such that the underlying principles (especially that of sustainable development) may be better respected. However, in the European example, this does not exhaust the role of law. Additionally, law provides a framework for the evaluation and evolution of the procedures and principles which underpin environmental assessment. Law provides a framework for the scrutiny of existing practices, and for their continuous improvement.

We have presented the story of the evolution of environmental assessment as an experimentalist one. Revision and spread of environmental assessment are seen to rest upon an iterative process of information pooling and comparison of best practice. There has emerged a sustained and organised system for ongoing law reform which is embedded in experience, and positively harnesses the pluralism of the EU in the name of learning on the basis of diverse experience. Here, the multiplicity of sites and levels of European governance emerge as opportunity not threat. The processes and mechanisms for revision imply the construction of a relationship between state and federal level which is collaborative, not hierarchical, and which is premised upon the positive value of diversity, experimentation and learning. The institutional arrangements in question depend upon, rather than resist, political fragmentation. Member States (or sub-state units) are not passive recipients of federal ordinances, but active co-equal participants in the iterative process of reform.

The core mechanisms under consideration in this example—namely, the information pooling and reporting requirements—provide a framework for experimentalist revision. This framework is constituted by law. It is set out in ordinary legislation. In the environmental sphere, the framework has been consolidated through the enactment of legislation 'standardizing' and 'rationalizing' the information pooling and reporting requirements.[110] Pervasive in environmental law, these processes are also evident in many other policy spheres.[111] It is not an exaggeration to state that the underlying approach to governance has emerged as a key characteristic—or

[109] A Supiot, 'Governing Work and Welfare in the Global Economy' in J Zeitlin and DM Trubek (eds) *Governing Work and Welfare in the New Economy*, p 388.

[110] Council Directive 91/692/EEC [1991] OJ L377/48. The Commission questionnaires are drawn up on the basis of an established committee procedure, and are published in the form of Commission decision. For two recent examples see, Commission Decision 2004/461/EC laying down a questionnaire to be used for annual reporting on ambient air quality assessment under Council Directive 96/62/EC.

[111] By way of example, one can find equivalent processes in the areas of sex discrimination, and consumer protection.

hallmark—of European law making and of a distinctively European approach to federalism. Still, the processes have failed even to ripple the constitutional surface of the EU. Embedded in, and regulated by, 'ordinary' legislation, these processes are nowhere acknowledged as constitutionally salient. They do not feature in the EC treaties, nor in the Pailed European Constitution. They merit not a mention in treatises examining the constitutional law of the EU, remaining the little noticed preserve of the specialist substantive lawyer.

In explaining this lack of constitutional visibility, it may be that the concept of 'hybridity' will help. In this example, as in many of the others discussed throughout this volume, new governance comes together with old. The new supplements but does not supplant the old. Thus, these novel processes for experimentalist revision take shape in a framework which is all too familiar. This familiar framework rests upon recourse to conventional, binding, instruments (directives[112]) and conventional legislative procedures (in this case, the co-decision procedure[113]). This familiar frame both diverts attention from the novel processes under discussion, and facilitates their smooth accommodation. The processes do not provoke any formal transformation in constitutional law, but nor do they meet resistance in constitutional law terms. On the surface, little has changed. Beneath the surface, the practice of governance is much altered.

It is this kind of example which may be thought to have spawned an approach to constitutionalism in the EU which has been characterised as 'constitutional processualism' or 'constitutional materialism'.[114] According to this view,

> constitutional discourse and practice within the European Union should not been seen exclusively or even mainly as a matter of Treaties and self-styled constitutional documents.

On the contrary, these grand constitutional moments are just a part of a broader constitutional canvas which includes governance processes which are not acknowledged or regulated by the treaties, but which

> are viewed by dint of the pervasiveness of their practice and/or their transformative effect upon the general structural and cultural template of European regulation, as vital constitutional processes which are in danger of being obscured by the focus on surface activity.[115]

[112] As suggested in an earlier piece, 'new' and 'old' in terms of governance are situated on a spectrum. Framework directives exhibit features of both old and new and have been previously characterised as 'new, old, governance'.

[113] See Art 251 EC for a description of this. The Commission enjoys the right of legislative initiative here, with the Council and the European Parliament being co-equal partners in the adoption of legislation.

[114] N Walker, 'After the Constitutional Moment' Federal Trust Paper 32/93 at: <http://www.fedtrust.co.uk/main.asp?pageid=267&mpageid=67&subid=277&groupid=6>.

[115] *Ibid*, p 6.

Of course the concept of the constitutional is much contested, and there is no self-evident threshold according to which constitutional import may be assessed. Ultimately, as Walker concedes, the construction of the concept implicates values and preferences, and constitutes a battle-ground for the advancement and/or denigration of new forms of governance.

With the Water Framework Directive (and CIS), the picture with regard to law is yet more complex and unsettled. Here we find elaborate collaborative processes, spanning sites and levels of governance. By contrast to the previous example, these processes appear to be neither constituted nor regulated by any recognisably *legal* act. An exhaustive reading of the treaties and of relevant legislation would give no hint of the existence or operation of CIS. Bearing in mind the formal sources of EU law, these processes seem to operate entirely beneath the legal radar, invisible to 'ordinary' as well as to constitutional law. This lack of visibility may be attributed, at least in part, to the informal and voluntary nature of multi-level collaboration in CIS, and to the 'softness' of the instruments which ensue.

To say in the water domain that new governance is invisible to law is to highlight just one aspect of the relationship between law and new governance. It is not simply that law neither constitutes nor captures the practice of governance. It is also that the premises of governance are, in many respects, at odds with the premises of law. There is a palpable tension—or a gap[116]—between law and the practice of governance. Whereas the former is based upon a settled vertical and horizontal division of competences, the latter is experimentalist, collaborative, fluid and multi-level.

According to the legal (WFD legislative) framework, implementation powers are parcelled out between distinct authorities, operating at different levels of governance. Most notably, the powers are divided between the Member States on the one hand, and the European Union institutions on the other. According to this framework, this division of power represents a zero sum game. The European institutions are deprived of those powers which the Member States enjoy. Conversely, powers are vested at the European level at the direct expense of the Member States. The legal picture is characterised by a division of clearly circumscribed blocks of implementation authority to distinct levels of governance, operating on the basis of divergent institutional configurations and decision-making procedures.

In practice, however, we find that there is considerable convergence as between the EU (legislative) and Member State implementation routes. There is also considerable fluidity between them. Surface appearances conceal a vastly more interesting, if vastly more complex, reality.

[116] The existence of such a gap has been previously noted. See J Scott and DM Trubek, 'Mind the Gap: Law and New Approaches to Governance in the EU' (2002) 8 *European Law Journal* 1, and G de Búrca, 'The Constitutional Challenge of New Governance in the EU' (2003) 28 ELR 814.

As seen, CIS exemplifies a collaborative, participatory, partnership-based approach to environmental governance. Accordingly, Member State implementation takes shape in a multi-level setting which is strongly experimentalist in tone. European-level legislative implementation appears, by contrast, to rest upon the 'classic community method', by virtue of its emphasis upon the adoption by the Community institutions of legally binding 'daughter directives'. In practice, however, the Commission is committed to developing its legislative proposals in 'a spirit of open consultation'. To this end, and in 'in parallel with the activities under the Common [Implementation] Strategy', it has established multi-stakeholder consultative fora, comprising Member State and Commission representatives, NGOs, industrial associations and outside experts. [117] These bodies—Expert Advisory Fora (EAFs)—strongly resemble CIS working groups in form, and have come to constitute the key bodies preparing the way for legislative implementation.[118] Institutionally, there are striking similarities.

Likewise, the line between the two routes is not, in practice, emphatically drawn. CIS review led to the transformation of two of the EAFs (groundwater and reporting) into CIS working groups; implying a de facto transfer from the legislative (European level) to the Member State branch.[119] One critical factor motivating this change was a recognition of the need to integrate better the activities of the Working Groups and the EAFs. This had proved difficult in practice, with the 'cross-implications between policy development [legislation] and ongoing implementation [Member State] ...only discussed in the last stages of Guidance development'.[120]

[117] Strategy Document, n 70 above, at pp 6–9.

[118] Three such bodies were established during the first phase (2001–2): EAF on Priority Substances and Pollution Control, EAF on Groundwater, and the EAF on Reporting. To take the activities of the EAF Groundwater as an example: The Commission established this to assist in the preparation of a proposal for a groundwater daughter directive pursuant to Art 17 WFD At a first meeting the EAF discussed a position paper prepared by the Commission, and provided guidance on the lines to be followed when developing a legislative proposal on groundwater. An extended issue paper was discussed at a second meeting, and the first elements of a legislative proposal presented at a third. At a fourth meeting, on 25 June 2002, the main draft outline of a proposal for a groundwater directive was presented. 'Overall, the proposal received a positive response from member States'. Thus, indisputably, preparation of this proposal proceeded on the basis of open cooperation between the Commission and the Member States, in the context of a multi-national, multi-actor, implementation network.

[119] Of course, there is nothing to prevent the Commission drawing up a formal proposal for a daughter directive, in accordance with the terms of the WFD But even in areas where further implementing legislation is not explicitly envisaged by the WFD, the Commission could anyway put a formal proposal, simply relying upon a legal basis in the EC Treaty rather than a secondary basis in WFD.

[120] Above, n 70 (1st review), p 6. There is fluidity too as between the executive (comitology) and Member State route. Thus, the recently published CIS guidance on reporting (30 November 2004) is self-consciously presented as a first step in developing a comprehensive guidance document on reporting, to be adopted in accordance with the WFD Art 21 committee procedure. This reflects the broader CIS perspective that guidance documents produced under its auspices may form the basis for guidelines adopted under the Art 21 comitology procedure (Strategy Document, n 70 above, at p 2).

The failure of law to perceive CIS would seem to cast doubt upon law's capacity to steer and constrain its operation. CIS seems to take shape in a legal black hole. Yet, it would be wrong to conclude that it operates on a basis which is normatively fickle and unconstrained. On the contrary, it operates on the basis of institutional arrangements and working procedures which are routinised. In reality, CIS spawns (provisionally) settled practices, and (provisionally) settled normative expectations. Examples cited would include the establishment and role of supporting groups, and the manner in which the respective authority of the three working levels has been defined and circumscribed.

The explicit regularisation of form and procedure, and the self-conscious settling of normative expectations around these, is justified in the language of accountable as well as effective governance. These normative expectations are not entrenched in any recognisably legal form, but they are (provisionally) entrenched in the reflexive practice of governance.

On this account, CIS represents something of an enigma in legal terms. On the one hand, formally, it is invisible to (and at odds with) law, and unconstrained by legal norms. On the other, it is notably 'law-like' in its character. It is born of agreement between the Commission and the Member States. It is encapsulated in documentary form (the strategy document), this being subject to formal amendment over time, on the basis of settled consensual procedures. This document sets out the institutional arrangements for CIS, as well as identifying its underlying values, and the means to ensure respect for them. In many ways, the constitutive and regulatory framework 'look' distinctly legal albeit, as observed, the relevant documents are not packaged in any recognisably legal form.

Thus, we find with CIS a strange constellation; in formal terms a legal vacuum, but in material terms a high degree of formalisation and regularisation. In the light of this, it is possible to think of CIS as representing an example of what we might call *embedded constitutionalism*. The practice of governance has spawned a process of constitutionalisation from within, and a settling of expectations around certain core values; transparency, participation, accountability and the like. This process of constitutionalisation in CIS rests upon an uncertain combination of continuity and change. Procedures and practices coalesce around the relevant values but, as seen, they are subject to continuous scrutiny and revision in the light of rational self-criticism and reflection. Experimentalism emerges as a key value in the immanent constitutionalisation of governance.

This concept of embedded constitutionalism is resonant of much thinking on constitutionalism in the United Kingdom, with its emphasis upon 'political' as opposed to 'legal' constitutionalism.[121] Martin Loughlin, for example, in a recent contribution to this debate, presents a conception of

[121] For a discussion and further references see A Tomkins, *Public Law* (OUP, 2003).

public law as practice.[122] According to this, 'public law is generated through usage', and not just simply laid down from above. 'Standards of conduct are internal to the practice', there being 'no ultimate standard of correctness'; 'the way that it is generally done within the practices supplies its own justification'.[123] As such, Loughlin argues, 'the subject of public law cannot be grasped without having regard to a myriad of informal practices concerning the manner in which the activity of governing is conducted'.[124] For Loughlin, public law includes, but extends beyond, positive law, and positive public law is seen as acquiring meaning through the practice of governance.

Of course, this idea of embedded constitutionalism begs many, difficult, questions. Not least, accountability questions loom large. Presented by one practitioner as a deeply unconstitutional, pragmatic response to a hopelessly over-ambitious directive, CIS is conceived as sanctioning legislation by committee.[125] First, decision making is seen to take shape within a virtual normative vacuum, the WFD failing even to specify the most essential elements of policy.[126] Second, accountability to government, and via government to parliament, may seem attenuated in CIS. Doubts may arise as to the capacity of the Water Directors—government officials representing the Member States—to exercise effective and continuing oversight in areas of immense density, technical complexity and rapid change. It is notable also that the European Environmental Bureau presents a mixed, though improving, picture of the provision of opportunities for public participation in the implementation of the WFD within the Member States.[127]

There also arises the question of the relationship between embedded and formal constitutional law. At a descriptive level we would point to the possibility for spill-over as between embedded and formal constitutionalism. One sees in the new governance prototype—comitology—a crystallisation in law of the immanent practices and values of governance. Comitology, like CIS, started life in a virtual legal vacuum; not constituted and only barely regulated by law.[128] Today, by contrast, it is embodied in, and regulated

[122] M Loughlin, *The Idea of Public Law* (OUP, 2003). See generally ch 2, especially pp 29–30 and points 8–16 of the concluding chapter.

[123] Above, n 122, pp 15–16.

[124] Above, n 122, p 30.

[125] Interview with national official in UK.

[126] The need for the legislative act to define essential elements has long been recognised by the European Court as an element of lawful delegation to the executive branch Of course, formally, this requirement would not apply here as there is no delegation as such, merely collaboration in the drawing up of non-binding guidance notes.

[127] Art 14 WFD requires that governments should encourage active involvement of interested parties in the implementation of the Directive, and obliges them to allow for public information and consultation in the development of River Basin Management Plans. The second EEB report ('EU Water Policy', n 70 above) notes examples of good as well as bad practice, and some improvements in the quality of public participation during the year 2004. Still, it concludes that 'most Member States follow a minimalist legal approach'. (p 31)

[128] For the early ECJ case-law sanctioning 'comitolgy', albeit requiring that the 'basic elements' be laid down in the delegating legislation, see Case 23/75 *Rey* Soda [1975] ECR 1279, Case 5/77 *Tedeschi* [1977] ECR 1555 and, for a later example, Case 16/88 *Commission v Council (Fisheries)* [1989] ECR 3457.

by, (constitutional) law.[129] The formal legal framework—legislative and judicial—is, however, in substance, strongly derivative of the practice of governance; be it in terms of the enforcement of internally generated, increasingly regularised, rules of procedure,[130] or in terms of its formal entrenchment of inter-institutional political settlements on comitology.[131] There is a fascinating story to be told here. Suffice it for now, however, to emphasise the existence of a powerful link between formal law and the practice of governance, and of a marked spill-over as between embedded and formal constitutionalism.

This is not to suggest that there is no role for law independent of the practice of governance, or that constitutionalism should be conceived solely as enforceable self-regulation in the constitutional domain. On the contrary, the comitology story is suggestive of an interesting constitutional hybrid. It is the role of formal constitutional law to bring to bear certain values which are constitutionally entrenched, and to protect certain rights which are constitutionally guaranteed. In comitology, the vindication of the principle of transparency (conceived in terms of access to documents) would be a good example.[132]

In developing this argument, it is useful to draw upon the work of Henry Monaghan, writing in a US constitutional setting many years ago.[133] He argues in favour of a distinction between 'true constitutional rules' and 'constitutional common law'.[134] For Monaghan only the former should be

[129] See Art EC, and Council Decision 87/373/EEC [1987] OJ L197/33, as amended by by Council Decision 1999/468/EC [1999] OJ L184/23. See also, for a discussion of the copious case law of the ECJ, C Joerges and E Vos (eds) *EU Committees: Social Regulation, Law and Politics* (Hart Publishing, 1999), and especially the chapters by Vos and St Clair Bradley therein.

[130] Case C–263/95 Germany *v Council (Construction Products)*. Also, establishing Standard Rules of Procedure Council Decision, see 1999/468 [2001] OJ C38/3.

[131] It is equally important to observe that the EU constitutional framework played an important role in shaping these political settlements. In particular, the institution of the co-decision procedure greatly enhanced the role of the European Parliament in the legislative procedure, and concomitantly empowered the parliament in its long-standing quest for a more significant role in comitology (see the chapter by St Clair Bradley, n 129 above). To appreciate the derivative nature of formal rules on comitology, compare the *modus vivendi* between the Council, European Parliament and Commission, initialled on 20 December 1994 [1996] OJ C102/1, and the European Parliament's Resolution of 18 January 1995 [1995] OJ C43/37on the one hand, with Council Decision 1999/468/EC(n 129 above) on the other. Not only is the formal framework strongly based upon the *modus vivendi*, but it is subsequently fleshed out by a similar Agreement between the European Parliament and the Commission on procedures for implementing Council Decision 1999/468/EC [1999] OJ L256/19. Practice informs the formal framework both before and after its enactment. The 1987 Decision (n 129 above) consolidated the comitology procedures which had grown up in practice, and was fleshed out by the Resolution on the modification of the procedures for the exercise of implementing powers conferred upon the Commission—'comitology' [1998] OJ C313/101. To complete the picture, see, finally, the Proposal for a Council Decision amending Decision 1999/468/EC COM(2002)719 final.

[132] Eg, T–188/97 *Rothmans v Commission*, judgment of 19 July 1999.

[133] HP Monaghan, 'Foreward: Constitutional Common Law' (1976) 89 *Harvard Law Review* 1.

[134] *Ibid*, p 33.

conceived as judicially protected constitutional exegesis, whereas the latter should be regarded as constitutional common law, and consequently as reversible by the political branch. He offers the example of the constitutionally guaranteed due process fair hearing requirement. Whereas this constitutionally compelled requirement must be shielded from political intrusion, not 'all the specific components of the right to hearing cases embody fundamental, immutable constitutional principles'.[135] On the contrary,

> a considerable portion of the details of implementation consist of minutiae below the threshold of constitutional concern ... If details may vary from one jurisdiction to another, it is because they do not materially diminish the effectiveness of the implementation which is constitutionally guaranteed.[136]

Against this backdrop, Monaghan contemplates the appropriate role for courts. Whereas the Supreme Court must protect those rights which are constitutionally compelled (the fair hearing requirement), it should exhibit greater deference in enforcing requirements which are constitutionally inspired but not constitutionally compelled (the minutiae giving effect to this requirement). As regards the latter, Monaghan suggests, the Court might perform a dual function. On the one hand, it might check that the variable procedures and practices giving effect to constitutional requirements are 'minimally adequate'. On the other, it might 'proceed on a frankly experimental basis in the hope of achieving the 'best implementing rule on a cost–benefit analysis'.[137]

Leaving aside the detail of Monaghan's rich and prescient analysis, it will be apparent that his argument is suggestive for the EU. Indeed already one could give examples of such an approach. The European Court, interpreting the EC Treaty, takes it upon itself to ensure that remedies available in the event of a breach of EU law not be such to preclude the effective vindication of rights guaranteed in EU law.[138] With some exceptions, it does not insist upon a harmonised approach to remedies, but is tolerant of diversity, subject to the variable Member State resolutions being considered minimally adequate having regard to the constitutionally guaranteed requirement of effectiveness. Similarly, the Court of First Instance (CFI) has adopted an approach to the constitutionally compelled principle of democracy which is susceptible to variation in institutional form, according to the established practice of governance.[139]

[135] *Ibid*, p 25 (footnotes excluded).
[136] *Ibid*, p 26.
[137] *Ibid*.
[138] See, for a full discussion, M Dougan, *National Remedies before the Court of Justice: Issues of Harmonisation and Differentiation* (Hart Publishing, 2004).
[139] Case T–135/96 *UEAPME v Council*, judgment of 17th June 1998. It is possible to be critical of the CFI's concept of 'representativity' as democracy in this case, while still applauding the more general notion of diversity in institutional form in the realisation of core constitutional values. Note that the principle of democracy is not explicitly laid down in the Treaty.

More generally, this distinction between constitutionally compelled requirements and mechanisms for their implementation might usefully inform the European courts' approach to new governance. It offers a means of embracing embedded constitutionalism, and the experimentalist advantages which this entails. At the same time, it offers a guarantee of minimum adequacy as regards compliance with constitutionally compelled rights and values. Significantly, and in keeping with the experimentalist spirit underpinning Monaghan's own analysis, it might additionally be appropriate for courts to check upon the adequacy of procedures for securing reflexivity in the practice of governance.

New governance poses hard questions for law. The observations here are preliminary and tentative. What at least, we hope, is clear is that the study of constitutional law in the EU necessitates also the study of the practice of governance. The pure, unadulterated, study of constitutional law is less troubled and less untidy. But, equally, it is less exhilarating. The EU represents a remarkable and innovative experiment in federalism. Beneath the surface of apparently obscure areas of policy, there lie many surprises which pose daunting conceptual and practical challenges for law and for lawyers.

Part III

Case Studies: United States

9

New Governance Practices in US Health Care

LOUISE G TRUBEK*

INTRODUCTION

EIGHTY-TWO PER CENT of Americans rank health care among their top issues.[1] People are satisfied with health care when they can get it but are afraid they will not be able to secure it. Over 45 million people were without health insurance during 2003.[2] Inadequate health care quality has been well documented. Compounding the problems is an extremely complicated health care scheme. Health care coverage is provided through a mixed public, private, and non-profit system. It delivers services through local provision with federally controlled programmes such as Medicare. This complicated framework for providing health care has thwarted the use of technology, which has been so crucial to modernising other industries. Despite the development of evidence-based information and new technology, the problems of the uninsured, cost escalation and improving quality are still threatening the viability of the health care system.

There is a sense that these problems can be resolved. This belief is related to the realisation that the old system of governance cannot solve these problems, but there are new techniques and theories that can help resolve problems. The old tools include centralised government entitlement programmes with primary authority at the Washington level, inflexible rules, self-regulation and heavy reliance on litigation.[3] However, since the 1970s, critics from the left and right of government regulation and the administrative state have called for alternatives to this vision. Out of this critique have emerged new approaches to governance that are not simply deregulation.

* University of Wisconsin Law School. Thanks to Jessica Levie and Tom O'Day for their excellent research and editing help. I would also like to thank the students in my 2002, 2003, and 2004 health law courses.

[1] Paul Krugman, 'The Health of Nations' *New York Times* (17 Feb 2004) at A23.

[2] US Census Bureau, *Income, Poverty, and Health Insurance Coverage in the United States: 2003* (August 2004) 14.

[3] For an extensive discussion of these issues see, William H Simon, 'Solving Problems v. Claiming Rights: The Pragmatist Challenge to Liberal Legalism' (2004) 46 *William and Mary Law Review*.

The inability of the old set of tools, legal theories and institutions to resolve the problems was highlighted in the failure of the Clinton health plan and the partial failure of managed care in the 1990s. These failures set the stage for a series of collaborations of people searching for new ways of resolving these ongoing problems. This new approach is called 'new governance' and consists of devolution, public-private partnerships, stakeholder collaboratives, new types of regulation, network creation, coordinated data collection, benchmarking and monitoring. This type of 'new governance' changes the way law is created and administered. It restructures relationships among markets, government and the professions and re-opens the age-old issue of how best to maintain social and environmental values in a market economy. New governance is a third way between traditional administrative law and total deregulation. It recognises that, while privatisation can bring important new tools to help solve problems (like market-based approaches), 'private markets cannot be relied on to give appropriate weight to public interests over private ones without active public involvement'.[4]

In health care, there has always been a mix of self-regulation, market forces and government regulation.[5] As one observer asked, 'How can professionalism be balanced with corporate or government oversight and measurement of the quality and costs of care provided by physicians?'[6] The problem has been understanding how to balance these, in the context of the problems that have to be resolved. The context includes gridlock in Washington, the political interest in shifting power to local levels, the potential of technology, the scepticism about professional expertise, and the desire for more individual responsibility and involvement.

As these new governance practices take hold, they become a challenge to the way in which we view government and the way law works. The New Deal/Great Society model seems out of touch and disfavoured. The new governance practices are a way of seeking new methods to resolve real social problems. Sceptics of new governance, such as Mark Tushnet, believe that the issues of transparency, fragmentation, unproven success of new tools and imbalance of power are major obstacles to the promise of new governance.[7] On the other hand, Tushnet has characterised the conservatives as having a vision and agenda that is persuasive and may be implemented and sees new governance as one of the few efforts to create a liberal counterpoint.[8] Other scholars have more confidence that new governance alliances

[4] Lester M Salamon, 'The New Governance and the Tools of Public Action: An Introduction' (2001) 28 *Fordham Urban Law Journal* 1635.

[5] Troyen A Brennan, 'The Role of Regulation in Quality Improvement' (1998) 76 *Milbank Quarterly* 709.

[6] Lawrence P Casalino, 'Physicians and Corporations: A Corporate Transformation of American Medicine?' (2004) 29 *Journal of Health Politics, Policy and Law* 869.

[7] Mark Tushnet, *The New Constitutional Order* (Princeton, 2003).

[8] *Ibid.*

and tools can win favour and move beyond the unpersuasive, New Deal bureaucratic model to achieve a more just society.[9]

This paper examines the way new governance tools are being incorporated in resolving health care problems. The first section discusses stakeholder collaborations. These collaborations are the arenas in which the leading actors are developing ways of dealing with three health care conundrums: how to embed technology, how to eliminate racial and ethnic disparities and how to achieve universal coverage. These alliances are not one format; the format will depend on the nature of the problem and the actors involved. The second section describes new governance techniques in these three problem areas. The description documents how efforts to resolve these three problem areas moves from traditional regulation to a different set of strategies. The final section takes a broad view of these new practices and shows that legal theories and concepts must be rethought in order to have the practices successfully resolve the health care conundrums.

STAKEHOLDER COLLABORATIONS

There is an underlying energy among many actors who sense an opportunity to drastically revise and improve the way health care is delivered in the United States, despite its overwhelming problems. This optimism stems from two sources: a shared understanding among the stakeholders that change is essential for the economic and personal health of the nation and a confidence that they can figure out how to do it. The stakeholders realise the limitations of the health care system must be overcome in order for the US to continue to have a strong, growing economy and provide excellent high-quality health care for all people. One physician reformer has noted that we have the most expensive health care system in the world and fail to be number one on all other worldwide indicators.[10] A new set of actors in health care have the confidence that they can solve the problems. These reformers are revising existing institutions, creating new arenas, and founding monitoring organisations. The new actors are participating in this series of collaborations and dialogues in all types of governance. Local, state and federal governments are working at the policy level with health care institutions, as well as business and consumer groups. Health care institutions are working together to make changes, such as developing standardised data collection tools that will work within and across institutions. At the patient–provider level, the interaction is changing from a hierarchical relationship to that of sharing of expertises.[11] Within these institutions and arenas,

[9] Michael C Dorf, 'After Bureaucracy' (2004) 71 *University of Chicago Law Review* 1245.

[10] Dr Jeff Grossman, Address at The Digital Healthcare Conference (23 June 2004) (presentation on file with author).

[11] Institute of Medicine, *Crossing the Quality Chasm: A New Health System for the 21st Century* (Washington DC, 2001).

the actors are able to interact, carry out and initiate the reforms necessary to improve health care. These approaches can be referred to as new governance practices.

Under traditional regulation, stakeholders did not interact with each other, either because there was no need or because of long-time adversarial positions. The realisation that collaboration between actors was necessary developed out of challenges in the late 1980s and 1990s. The first challenge was the move to managed care, developed and led by employer purchasers. These employers believed that they were paying too much money for low-quality services. Many of these leading employers were devotees of quality management in their own businesses. The move to managed care was unsuccessful partially due to resistance by consumers and physicians. The second event was the Clinton health plan debacle. This major effort at the federal level to produce universal coverage failed and was a tremendous blow to the proponents of a centralised single system to deliver health care. The final event was the potential for massive development of information technology that had been transforming other industries such as banking and securities. Despite the tremendous importance of technology to the economic welfare and individual health, the move to technology is moving slower than in other industries for two reasons. First, there has been tremendous resistance to creating the standards necessary to exchange and protect the information. Second, there is reluctance by medical providers to invest in technology because of costs, perceived loss of autonomy and the fear of a centralised data set.

These three experiences emboldened key stakeholders to overcome traditional animosities and self-interests in order to achieve health care reform. The actors are creating new arenas, which encourage the collaboration that previously had been difficult to achieve. They realise that bringing varied expertise and broad experiences to the collective governance structure is essential.[12] Active participation of health care actors—providers, consumers, government and employers—is necessary to solve the persistent conundrums. Each entity has important information that, when shared with all stakeholders, improves the understanding of and the ability to address a problem. Sometimes this process is called 'bootstrapping' where separate organisations come to a unified vision for future goals.[13] These new collaborations may decide to bring in more organisations or have local pilot projects to see what works. This exploration leads to something different and perhaps more ambitious than what they started out with.

Four sets of actors are now emerging as proponents and leaders of alternative approaches to solve the health care conundrums through these new collaborations: the pioneering physician, the concerned payor, the active

[12] Orly Lobel, 'The Renew Deal: The Fall of Regulation and the Rise of Governance in Contemporary Legal Thought' (2004) 2004 *Minnesota Law Review* 342.

[13] Wendy Netter Epstein, 'Bottoms Up: A Toast to the Success of Health Care Collaboratives: What Can We Learn?' (2004) 56 *Administrative Law Review* 3.

consumer and the facilitating government leader. These actors have the characteristics of the 'policy entrepreneur,' crucial to the implementation of these new routes.[14] These policy entrepreneurs participate together in various networks, alliances and forums in order to solve health policy problems. Each policy entrepreneur brings to the alliance a constituency that eventually must accept working with the new alliances. This requires the entrepreneur to work well with the disparate stakeholders and simultaneously assure that their constituency accepts the collaboration and sees it as a way to achieve the constituency's goals.

The role of physicians is crucial in order for new governance in health care to be successful. Historically, professionalism was a way for physicians to mediate between the tensions of a market-driven approach to health care and the alternative of government regulation. Professional values and institutions have been viewed as necessary in order for physicians to maintain an independent role between the market and regulation. This worked successfully for physicians for a period of time. However, business and consumer advocates complained that physician control was resulting in higher costs, lack of access and inconsistent quality of care. The managed care revolution in the 1980s—businesses' attempt to create a competitive market—drastically undermined these traditional professional institutions and controls and damaged the overall leadership of physicians. The recent backlash against managed care, created in part by the actions of health care providers, has emboldened them to once again assert their leadership role. The managed care backlash came about in part by an alliance between physicians and consumers to fight the intrusion of the 'outsiders' into the physician–patient relationship. Although physicians won this battle, managed care had changed the environment in which they practised through the development of large integrated hospital and clinic systems, where most physicians now practise; the creation of evidence-based medicine; and increased reliance on allied health care professionals. As one observer noted, 'physicians are weakened but not vanquished'.[15] In attempting to reassert their leadership role, physicians noted the effectiveness of business leaders in advancing quality in health care through the use of networks. They now emulate these network collaborations by working with a wide variety of stakeholders.

Although physicians are asserting a new role, the concerned employer-payor, who emerged in the 1980s to control health care costs, is still active and prominent. Employers wanted to control health care costs because they are a major factor in their profitability and sustainability, since health care coverage in the United States is largely provided through the workplace.

[14] Thomas R Oliver, 'Policy Entrepreneurship in the Social Transformation of American Medicine: The Rise of Managed Care and Managed Competition' (2004) 29 *Journal of Health Politics, Policy and Law* 701.

[15] Jill Quadagno, 'Physician Sovereignty and the Purchasers' Revolt' (2004) 29 *Journal of Health Politics, Policy and Law* 815.

Since the 1980s, employers have expanded their activities to improving quality and have even become active in solving the problem of the uninsured.[16] The leading voice of business in health care is the Leapfrog Group, a consortium of more than 100 large employers that have mobilised to use their purchasing power to affect the health care system. The Leapfrog Group, although national, has substantial influence on business actions at the state and local level. It exerts a major external force on the internal workings of health care institutions and professional groups through the production and dissemination of benchmarks on the quality and cost of health care procedures.

The rise of consumers as key players in health care is related to both the use of markets in health care as one tool of controlling costs and the rise in chronic diseases that must be controlled by the patient's own involvement. Therefore, two consumer roles are important in health care: the role of the purchaser of health care services and the patient active in their own health care. After managed care, employer purchasers now realise that more allies are needed to develop and implement any new health care system design. They view a strong consumer role as essential to any sustainable changes to the system. They also believe that giving consumers a greater voice in the purchase and delivery of health care is essential to creating a cost-effective and high-quality system.

Patients are also being called upon to take more active control over managing their personal health care and in designing their health care benefits.[17] A major model for quality improvement, for example, is planned care based on the successful disease management model. It relies on a bottom up, patient empowerment, community-linked approach.[18] The role of the consumer as a co-producer of good health, as well as a consumer choosing appropriate and quality services, is now a major theme in health care reform. Some advocate for the development of intermediary organisations to assist consumers in participating in their own care both through selection of benefit packages, taking on responsibility for following protocols, and for disputing when their care is inadequate.

Government is still a crucial actor in these new arenas. While it may no longer be the authoritative directing agency, as envisioned in the traditional command-and-control model, government actors are needed for ultimate sanctioning, as sources of funding, and accountability for fair and equitable processes. They are also major payors for health care directly for many groups and therefore, share some of the roles discussed for private employers.

[16] Milt Freudenheim, '60 Companies to Sponsor Health Care for Insured' *New York Times*, (27 Jan 2005) at C1.

[17] Christopher Querem, 'Aligning Health Care Incentives' (2003) (unpublished MS on file with author); see also, Institute of Medicine, *Health Literacy: A Prescription to End Confusion* (Washington DC, 2004).

[18] Institute for Health Improvement, *The Business Case for Planned Care* (2003).

Their participation in the collaboratives is essential to assuring that health care services, even if devolved, are fair, equitable and effective.

There are internal and external mechanisms that affect the potential success of these collaboratives.[19] The first is the internal interests of the stakeholder. For instance, physicians are not a monolithic group. Surgeons, for example, may be threatened by some quality standards in different ways that paediatricians are affected. Small businesses have different interests and power than the Fortune 500 companies. And the success of the collaborative may depend on who within the organisation is participating and their relationship to their constituency. For example, the participation of the head of a stakeholder organisation may provide certain kinds of authority, but if the head of the organisation cannot sell the collaboration to the rest of the organisation, the goals of the collaborative may be undermined.

The external mechanisms that affect the success of the collaboration are the transparency of collaborative, dampening of innovation due to fears of liability and regulations, and the absence of difficult to organise constituencies. State and federal administrative procedure acts, and open records and open meetings laws, do not apply to many of these collaboratives because they are not organised as public bodies. This makes the availability of information about their activities difficult to find and makes their work seem suspicious. In addition, fears of litigation based on malpractice may also be an obstacle to development and implementation of innovative techniques. Substantive government regulations that do not allow innovative systems, such as payment for quality, are also external checks on the effectiveness of collaborations. A third external barrier is the absence of participation by patients and consumers who have traditionally had difficulty organising due to their diverse income, race, ethnicity, gender and geography.[20]

Various models of collaboratives are negotiating how to solve three of the health care problems confronting the US health care system. The way to address each problem will depend on the nature of the problem and may involve different stakeholders and different tools. One example is the rapidly developing collaboratives that seek to reduce the uneven quality of health care services. These collaboratives are addressing the problem though developing data collection, agreeing on standard benchmarks and disseminating this information to the public. Businesses' development and use of standards and guidelines to improve quality and encourage the adoption of technology initially threatened the leadership of physicians.[21]

[19] John Braithwaite *et al*, 'The Governance of Health Safety and Quality', unpublished MS on file with author (2004), 27, fig.3.

[20] John Harley Warner, 'Grand Narrative and its Discontents: Medical History and the Social Transformation of American Medicine' (2004) 29 *Journal of Health Politics, Policy and Law* 769.

[21] Kevin Fiscella, 'Within Our Reach: Equality in Health Care Quality', paper given at the *Symposium, Racial and Ethnic Disparities in Health Care Treatment*, The Harvard Civil Rights Project (18 May 2004), unpublished MS on file with author.

Physicians and other health care institutions are now both cooperating with these business-led collaborations and leading the development of alternative collaborations. These networks can restore the weakened professional influence and leadership of physicians through these newer networks of professionals. [22] These networks, however, include not only physicians, as in the older model, but others who share values and interests, such as consumer groups, business groups and government groups. The consumers are necessary to provide and utilise the information system in order to choose the best providers and also in managing their own care. Business is essential because they pay for health care for a substantial percentage of the population and possess expertise on how to produce business quality. The government is essential to assure that all the relevant stakeholders are part of the quality system and that they themselves as payors will pay for quality. These emerging collaborations for quality are the places where practices are developed and monitored; ideally, each stakeholder returns to his or her organisation to implement the best practices and systems reforms advocated by the collaboration.

NEW GOVERNANCE PRACTICES

Converting the US health care system to an excellent producer of high-quality care for a reasonable price is a daunting task. Health care reformers are concentrating now on three specific issues: implementing technology, reducing racial and ethnic disparities, and expanding coverage. In each area, there is a new set of tools and institutions being deployed to solve these problems and solving each problem will require a tailored approach using the panoply of potential tools, such as devolution, public–private partnerships, new types of regulation, network creation, coordinated data collection, benchmarking and monitoring. The stakeholders involved will change, depending on the problem being addressed. Similarly, the levels at which the intervention occurs will depend on which is the most effective to solve the problem.

Embedding Technology: From Command-and-Control to Standards and Local Collaborations

An electronic-based system may improve health care quality by giving providers and consumers access to information necessary to make health care decisions, as well as improve communication between provider and patient and among providers.[23] Improving health care technology could cut

[22] Deborah A Savage, 'Professional Sovereignty Revisited: The Network Transformation of American Medicine?' (2004) 29 *Journal of Health Politics, Policy and Law* 661; William D. White, 'The Physician "Surplus" and the Decline of Professional Dominance' (2004) 29 Journal of Health Politics, Policy and Law 853.

[23] Simon, n 3 above, at 58–59.

administrative costs, reduce health care inefficiency, and improve health care quality by creating new high-technology medical records that provide better data. Further, an electronic system could be used to rapidly detect and respond to bioterrorism attacks, as well other population health issues, such as SARS.[24] However, there has been tremendous resistance to creating the standards necessary to exchange and protect the information and there is reluctance by medical providers to invest in technology because of high costs, perceived loss of autonomy, and fear of a centralised data set.

The first effort to encourage the health care system to move to adopt technology was the Health Insurance Portability and Accountability Act of 1996 (HIPAA). HIPAA delegates power to the Department of Health and Human Services (HHS) to promulgate rules to advance health care technology through uniform standards for electronic transactions, privacy protections and security of data. The production of the rules relied on the traditional federal Administrative Procedure Act rule-making process and took many years and many hearings to finally produce pages of pages of rules. The proponents of HIPAA relied on the command-and-control model.

However, the rules-based system seemingly proposed in HIPAA was never quite the old model. First, the concept underlying the need for a standardised system across competing providers and insurers was initiated by a series of public-private collaborations, known as HIPAA Collaboratives. State-based and local collaboratives consist of all the stakeholders including business, government, technology experts, and providers from all types of backgrounds. Prior to the creation of HIPAA, these groups were already in existence, trying to create local technology standards. In fact, their work was one of the impetuses behind the enactment of HIPAA. Since HIPAA has been enacted, these groups have been helping their members comply with HIPAA by providing information and sharing techniques.[25] While there is no formal relationship between the Collaboratives and HHS, they have a mutual dependence. HHS provides the 'stick' of the rules while the Collaboratives provide best practices and local implementation so that the vision can be achieved. These Collaboratives continue to provide information back to HHS to improve implementation. These groups also linked with each other and created websites to share information within their own regions.[26] Further, HHS, in charge of enforcement, has emphasised that they have little interest in conventional enforcement; indeed, there is no budget for enforcement.

In the last several months, there has been a major initiative to further embed technology led by a bi-partisan alliance between former Republican Speaker Newt Gingrich and Representative Patrick Kennedy.[27] This reflects the continued reports that describe how advanced technology could radically

[24] Newt Gingrich and Patrick Kennedy, 'Operating in a Vacuum' *New York Times* (3 May 2004) at A25.

[25] Epstein, n 13 above.

[26] *Ibid.*

[27] Gingrich and Kennedy, n 24 above.

transform the quality and reduce the cost of health care.[28] The Bush Administration has proposed a national health care regional infrastructure, which will be responsible for coordinating all private sector initiatives into the National Health Information Infrastructure.[29] The goal is to create a comprehensive knowledge-based network of interoperable systems capable of providing information anytime, anywhere. It is, however, not a central database of medical records. The role of the federal government is to ensure that standards are in place to allow the interoperable systems: the model is the banking information infrastructure. The proposal funds demonstration projects at the local because local governance facilitates a high level of trust and it is easier to align incentives that have local appeal. The proposal is for 'regional' systems that could be smaller or larger than states. These local health systems seem to build on the success of the HIPAA Collaboratives and move beyond the centralised, rule-based HIPAA system.

This proposal tracks new governance in that it suggests the devolution of governance from the federal government to local and state entities.[30] Devolution recognises that idea of 'subsidiary': that 'all government tasks are best carried out at the level closest to those affected by them.'[31] This reordering involves more than shifting power from the federal government to more local entities. The technology proposals recognise that the federal government may not be the best entity to completely solve social problems, but it retains a strong role for the federal government in setting standards, monitoring compliance and providing incentives through funding.[32] It allows local public and private groups to respond to local conditions and reduce fears of excessive data collection in Washington.

Devolution does not mean there is no role for coordinating institutions and systems. The local groups, each of which has its own method of addressing technology, also share their knowledge, successes and failures with other groups by way of a nation group that facilitates the exchanges. This requires some form of orchestration, either through horizontal sharing or through multi-level feedback, where a larger entity takes the information and experience and distributes it to other like programmes. Orchestration is also necessary to ensure that the quality of the services provided at the local level is adequate and to prevent the race to the bottom, which can occur with isolated and fragmented local projects.

The idea of experimentation is closely linked to devolution, since the more local an entity is, the easier experimentation becomes. Often, experimentation

[28] Institute of Medicine, n 11 above.

[29] Dr. William A. Yasnoff, Address at The Digital Healthcare Conference (23 June 2004) (presentation on file with author).

[30] Lobel, n 12 above.

[31] *Ibid.*

[32] See Louise G Trubek and Maya Das, 'Achieving Equality: Health Care Governance in Transition' (2003) 29 *American Journal of Law and Medicine* 411.

occurs outside the realm of regulation or parallel to it.[33] Experimentation can also be seen as similar to continuous quality improvement because organisations should be constantly experimenting with what works and what does not.[34]

It is also closely linked to networking, through the process of finding out from organisations in the field what already works or does not work and adapting to this. The use of networks also changes the role of government because it no longer regulates or commands organisations to achieve desired outcomes. While negotiation through networks may be difficult, rules and standards that have been negotiated by the networks may be better complied with because of the negotiation process.[35]

Traditional governance has been sceptical of collaboration between private and public. The positive relationship between the HIPAA Collaboratives, which consist of public and private groups including providers and insurers, and the national standard development has been mutually supportive. New governance embraces such networks,[36] recognising that public and private entities have different strengths that can be used in concert to solve public problems.[37] The local HIPAA Collaboratives implement the national standards in different ways, creating diverse systems of compliance while still producing an ability to communicate nationally and meet federal standards.

Eliminating racial and ethnic disparities: From anti-discrimination litigation to quality assurance tools[38]

There is revived interest in eliminating racial and ethnic disparities in health care treatment. Studies have shown that minority Americans receive less health care and what they do receive tends to be lower quality care.[39] These differences remain even when alternative explanations, for example, insurance status and income, are controlled for.[40] There are substantial new reports emerging that document the issue. These reports are implicitly critical of the old approaches to overcoming disparities.[41]

[33] Louise G. Trubek, 'Lawyering for a New Democracy: Public Interest Lawyers and New Governance: Advocating for Health Care'(2002) 2002 *Wisconsin Law Review* 594.
[34] *Ibid.* at 587.
[35] Epstein, n 13 above.
[36] Salamon, n 4 above, at 1634.
[37] *Ibid.* at 1633–34.
[38] Fiscella, n 21 above.
[39] Sidney D Watson, 'Race, Ethnicity and Quality of Care: Inequalities and Incentives' (2001) 27 *American Journal of Law and Medicine* 208–9.
[40] *Ibid.* at 208.
[41] Institute of Medicine, *Unequal Treatment* (Washington DC, 2003); See also, Healthy People 2010 at <http://www.healthypeople.gov/About/goals.htm>.

The traditional approaches to eliminating disparities in health care were based on the civil rights litigation approach dating from the 1960s and the passage of the Civil Rights Act of 1964. Title VI litigation was considered a major tool to eliminate racial and ethnic disparities. Lawsuits were brought against hospitals and communities where discriminatory practices were alleged. In addition, command-and-control enforceable rules were issued by the Department of Health, Education and Welfare and successor agencies, accompanied by an enforcement unit.[42] Since the 1960s substantial credence and energy were devoted to this approach. Federal agencies were responsible for enforcement of this law and there was also private litigation. Over the past 20 years, however, the civil rights litigation approach has been unable to eliminate health disparities due to a lack of success in the courts, a dearth of lawyers willing to take the cases to court and weak outcomes even when litigation has been successful. At the federal agency level the enforcement has been unsuccessful. Further, what action has been taken has been reactive not proactive. There were never sufficient lawyers, persuasive fact situations or effective remedies to make the federal enforcement approach work.[43]

In response to the documentation of the persistence of health disparities, there is a major initiative led by reformist health care leaders to adopt a quality-based approach to the provision of health care as an indirect route to achieving equality. A recent report called 'Within Our Reach' indicated that 'leveraging existing quality assurance systems to monitor and address disparities could substantially reduce the disparities in healthcare treatment'.[44] The confidence in the ability to reduce disparities is based in the confidence in new quality strategies. But there are two problems with implementing quality: the complex regulatory structure of health care and the existing malpractice framework.

The first problem is the complex regulatory structure in health care. Since the late 1990s, reformers from the medical sector and concerned business purchasers have promoted quality as an achievable and necessary goal for the health care system.[45] Although the US has one of the most expensive health care systems in the world, the quality of care that health care consumers receive is mixed. The Agency for Healthcare Research and Quality's *National Healthcare Quality Report* indicates that the US system currently does not do enough to prevent diseases, diagnose them early to improve treatment outcomes or provide coordinated care to patients with chronic

[42] Title VI of the Civil Rights Act of 1964, 42 United States Code § 2000d (2000).

[43] Watson, 'Race, Ethnicity and Quality of Care', n 39 above; Marianne Engelman Lado, 'Unfinished Agenda, The Need for Civil Rights Litigation to Address Racial Discrimination and Inequalities in Health Care Delivery' (2001) 6 *Texas Forum on Civil Liberties and Civil Rights* 16.

[44] Fiscella, n 21 above.

[45] See Leapfrog, <http://www.leapfroggroup.org/>.

diseases.[46] Since health care is a combination of self-regulation and professional values and institutions, the effort to embed quality involves increasing regulatory governance while including the traditional self-regulation and professional roles. This is an explanation for the complexity of merging quality improvement with a traditional government regulatory framework.[47] Any framework for implementing quality must integrate the physician voice into the mechanism.

The second problem with implementing quality is the existing malpractice framework. There is widespread agreement that the malpractice litigation system is failing in compensating injured parties and to deter future negligence. The proponents of the quality assurance system assert that it will do a better job of deterring negligent behaviour as well as preventing unnecessary errors. However, there is no consensus as to how to compensate patients who are injured through negligent or non-negligent behaviours. Many alternatives have been proffered such as no-fault, enterprise liability or new types of redress such as medical courts or arbitration.[48] One reason for the lack of action is the uncertainty as to how to tie in the compensation system with the quality assurance system. They must be in tandem; otherwise, there will be no buy in to the new quality systems and the substantial reform of the existing malpractice framework. The new compensation system must demonstrate that it will advance quality care and fairly compensate injured patients. This new quality system has to create a culture of safety within the health care system. For example, it is likely that the standards for care that are being produced by the new stakeholder quality alliance groups will be used to establish the standard for competency and health care providers will be held to that standard.[49] In order for this to be successful, physicians must accept that the new standards are fair to them and consumers must believe that the new system will fairly reward injured patients. These new systems must proceed together.

If the problems with quality can be resolved, it will open the way not only to a high-quality health care system, but also to reduce health disparities. It is by making reduction of health disparities a core value of providing quality health care that the system can deal effectively with this controversial subject. By recognising health care disparities as a quality problem, it forces the organisations that are subject to and participate in the quality initiatives to deal with racial and ethnic disparities. Once they are committed to the assessment and measuring of quality, they then must also examine these

[46] Agency for Healthcare Research and Quality, *National Healthcare Quality Report* (2003) available at <http://qualitytools.ahrq.gov/qualityreport/download_report.aspx>.

[47] Brennan, n 5 above.

[48] Paul C Weiler, 'Fixing the Tail: The Place of Malpractice in Health Care Reform' (1995) 47 *Rutgers Law Review* 1157.

[49] Michelle M Mello *et al*, 'The Leapfrog Standards: Ready to Jump from Marketplace to Courtroom' (2003) 22 *Health Affairs* 46.

issues for racial and ethnic minorities who are part of their delivery system. It puts particular pressure on public purchasers, such as Medicaid and Medicare, who provide health care for a substantial number of minority Americans. Thus, since we have seen quality initiatives that started in private, employer-based plans spread to Medicaid and Medicare, the same could happen for initiatives on racial and ethnic disparities.

There are still, however, important methodological challenges to using this quality approach to monitoring and addressing racial/ethnic disparities. The key issue is data collection. There has been substantial controversy over the collection of racial and ethnic indicators in the United States. Many believe that the information can be used for racial profiling and other discriminatory purposes. In addition, there are controversies over the definition of ethnic groups, such as what it means to be Hispanic/Latino and the confusion over multiple ethnicities. Nonetheless, there appears to be a consensus across the stakeholders that the collection of this data is essential in order to eliminate racial and ethnic disparities.

The quality approach to reducing disparities results in a different role for lawyers than the civil rights litigation approach embodied in the Title VI and HHS enforcement model. The lawyer's role would no longer be as an advocate for the individual and institutions that alleged discrimination by the health care provider or the health care system generally. It would therefore decentre the court as the main arena for redressing the harm that came from discriminatory conduct. The major emphasis would be placed on reforming internal health care systems through a combination of creating incentives for positive outcomes and evidence-based medicine. Employees and government payors would tie payment to quality outcomes that would include compliance with outcomes that have a significant affect on preventing disparities. Examples of such outcomes are good prenatal care, normal birth-weight babies, and proven chronic care management. The civil rights model, therefore, which is based on an adversarial lawyer and court complex would no longer be the dominant model. The performance of physicians and the medical institutions, combined with carefully developed guidelines and benchmarks, would be the tools for reducing disparities.

It is clear that many of the new chronic care models rely on physician leadership in implementing and controlling the system. The quality purchasers are leading in the push for aligning the incentives to encourage the use of these techniques but the physicians are participating in a clear effort to make sure that they are part of the process. For example, in a recent policy statement issued by the AMA endorsing chronic care management as a way to achieve quality, they stressed that the physician who was the primary doctor for the patient be incorporated into the patient management system and not be bypassed. [50] They want to maintain control and avoid a system like managed care that will diminish their expertise.

[50] American Medical Association, Report of the Council of Scientific Affairs (2004).

Vision of universal coverage: From a centralised single system to linked state experimentation

The lack of universal coverage has long been the most noted deficiency in US health care. The effects of uninsurance are notable in personal health, additional costs and on the economic health of the nation. The lack of insurance in the US results in poor health for those residents who are uninsured. In addition, it results in the shifting of the costs for providing care of the uninsured on to two sets of payors: the employers pay more than their share because of the shifting of uncompensated care costs by the medical establishment; and the government payors who are forced to raise taxes in order to cover their share of uncompensated care. It also affects the economy by encouraging job lock where employees cannot move to the position that matches their talents because of their fear of losing health care coverage.

The Clinton health plan was an effort to achieve a seamless universal system through an elaborate, federally controlled, all-embracing system. The Clinton health plan was defeated in part because it was viewed as an attempt to replace the existing, diverse and complex health care system with a mammoth bureaucracy. The failure is viewed as a vote against centralised, government-dominated, bureaucratically controlled governance.[51]

At the same time as the failure of the Clinton health plan, there was a concerted attack on entitlement programmes. The elimination of the entitlement status of the major welfare programme for poor people—Aid for Dependent Children (AFDC)—was a tremendous blow for the progressives, who since the New Deal, had dreamed of the adoption of the European 'social citizenship' model.[52] The maintenance of the entitlement to Medicaid is a continual battle. The battle over entitlements, coupled with the Clinton plan failure, undermined the progressive belief that an entitlement/rights approach was a likely route to universal coverage.

A new incremental approach, based on new programmes and proposals, was generated in the wake of the Clinton plan's failure.[53] States have addressed the issue of coverage by expanding eligibility for Medicaid to more low-income children and parents[54] as well as accessing the federal State Children's Health Insurance Program (SCHIP) funds.[55] SCHIP is an expansion of health care coverage targeting uninsured children. The federal

[51] Louise G Trubek, 'Health Care and Low-Wage Work in the United States: Linking Local Action for Expanded Coverage' in Jonathan Zeitlin and David M Trubek (eds) *Governing Work and Welfare in the New Economy* (Oxford, 2003).

[52] Joel F Handler, *Social Citizenship and Workfare in the United States and Western Europe: The Paradox of Inclusion* (Cambridge, 2004).

[53] Symposium, *Facing Health Care Tradeoffs: Costs, Risks and the Uninsured*, La Follette Policy Report (Robert M. La Follette School of Public Affairs, University of Wisconsin-Madison, Winter 2003–4).

[54] Trubek, 'Health Care', n 51 above.

[55] Institute of Medicine, n 11 above.

government, in enacting SCHIP, encouraged states to experiment with various approaches to insuring children and families with the additional funding. States seized on an approach of increasing health care coverage to low-income Americans state by state via government programmes. There is now a rich array of state approaches to providing coverage for the uninsured. Networks of state government officials, legislators, and governors across states spread 'best practices' and encouraged united action to support the programmes.[56] Combining public programmes with employer-based coverage is also being proposed through further expansion of Medicaid and encouraging small business to offer health care coverage through a combination of tax credits and subsidies from government programmes.[57]

There is now an acknowledged consensus that some form of universal coverage for residents is essential for the economic and personal health of the US.[58] In part the consensus is based on the incremental approach, which is state-based, public and private coverage mix. In the recent presidential election both major presidential candidates endorsed the incremental route to expanding coverage. However, the move to the state-based experiments in health care coverage can be seen as resulting in an even more fragmented, differential package benefits. The proponents of the incremental system are demonstrating that the expansion will include quality coverage and promotion of healthy life styles and cost-effective treatment. This approach emphasises the individual's participation as a consumer and a self-managing patient. It also includes methods insure that the benefits paid are guided by medical science. It deemphasises the bureaucratic, single set of universal benefits and administration. It also aims to assure that the relationship between the physician and patient is a core element.[59]

However, there are problems with a state-based system. First, the states are struggling to maintain their commitment to health care due to the current fiscal crisis at the state level. It is striking how the governors have rallied around their newly ambitious health care coverage programmes and have, to a great extent, resisted cutbacks. One observer noted:

> State officials explained why SCHIP seemed largely immune to significant cuts, citing its strong popularity among consumers, providers, and politicians; the fact that it was small and inexpensive (relative to Medicaid) and not an entitlement (making it a programme that policy makers felt they could 'control'); its high federal matching rate (making it a less attractive target for cuts); and its success at

[56] Trubek, 'Health Care', n 51 above.

[57] *Facing Health Care Tradeoffs*, n 53 above; Barbara Zabawa, 'Breaking Through the ERISA Blockade: The Ability of States to Access Employer Health Plan Information in Medicaid Expansion Initiatives' (2001) 5 *Quinnipiac Health Law Journal* 1.

[58] See, eg, Paul Fronstin, 'The "Business Case" for Investing in Employee Health: A Review of the Literature and Employer Self-Assessments' (March 2004) 267 *Employee Benefit Research Institute*.

[59] Mark Schlesinger, 'Reprivatising the Public Household? Medical Care in the Context of Public Values' (2004) 29 *Journal of Health Politics, Policy and Law* 969.

> its critical objective—insuring low-income children. But these same officials hinted that continued fiscal pressures could result in future cuts to SCHIP.[60]

This statement highlights the crucial importance of increasing federal funding and supporting states in their innovation.[61] This might include new types of flexible standards and requirements that both encourage innovation but also guarantee financial integrity and coverage for the most vulnerable and high-cost groups.[62] New technology can encourage movement between public and private plans (so-called seamless enrolment) by simplifying even complex eligibility requirements. Information technology enables people to move from public plans to private coverage and vice versa with no loss of coverage when their job and income situation requires.[63] The seamless system requires horizontal networks within the states and communities to allow public programmes and private employers to communicate and share information on eligibility.

The critics of the incremental approach assert that the abandonment of the rights/entitlement model guarantees that the universality, essential for an effective and efficient health care system, will never be achieved. They argue that the fiscal constraints of state government and the elimination of judicially reviewable entitlements will undercut coverage and low-income people will once again lose coverage.[64] However, they admit that the political will for the single-payor, rights/entitlement route is gone. In order to be persuasive, the groups promoting the incremental approach must demonstrate their ability to work together and resist retrenchment.[65]

LAW, GOVERNANCE AND HEALTH CARE

While solving the three health care problems requires different tools, all share some of the same new governance practices. In understanding how these new governance practices challenge the New Deal/Great Society administrative state, four shifts are highlighted: new types of participation, multi-level public and private networks, different roles for government and an understanding of law as 'soft'—flexible rules with informal sanctions.

[60] Ian Hill *et al*, The Urban Institute, *Squeezing SCHIP: States Use Flexibility to Respond to the Ongoing Budget Crisis, New Federalism: Issues and Options for States* (Washington DC, 2004).

[61] The Kaiser Commission on Medicaid and the Uninsured, *Medicaid's Federal-State Partnership: Alternatives for Improving Financial Integrity* (California, 2002) available at <http://www.kff.org/medicaid/4068-index.cfm>.

[62] *Ibid.*

[63] *Facing Health Care Tradeoffs*, n 53 above.

[64] David A Super, 'The Political Economy of Entitlement' (2004) 104 *Columbia Law Review* 633. See also Timothy S Jost, *Disentitlement?* (Oxford, 2003).

[65] See Steve Lohr, 'The Disparate Consensus on Health Care for All' *New York Times* (6 Dec 2004) at C16.

Each of these shifts presents serious challenges to the conventional understanding of how law and governance should work and can be effective. In order for these new practices to be viewed as significant alternatives to the traditional, command-and-control/rights-based conventional governance, a convincing case must be made that these new mechanisms can be effective in delivering large-scale, accountable and legitimate resolutions to health care problems.

New types of participation

The new governance practices in the three problem areas demonstrate a shift to new ways in which decisions are made and participation occurs in health care. Traditionally, disadvantaged groups were able to participate through public interest lawyer advocacy at the administrative agency, social movements at the legislative level, and litigation against discrimination and malpractice.[66] In recent years, the old system often did not achieve the desired result of making health care more equitable and efficient. Health care failures, like the centralised Clinton health plan and the civil rights litigation strategy[67], are examples of the inadequacy of the older model. However, in the struggle to make the older models of participation work, some techniques emerged that can be identified as part of the new system. These include state-based expansion of access, consumer–physician alliances, the patient empowerment movement and the acknowledgement of racial and gender biases in health care.

The positive insight from the Clinton health plan demise was that, after that failure, states were able to expand coverage for the uninsured through a combination of new federal funding and encouragement of flexibility in the states. The flexibility allowed at the state level resulted in a wide group of actors participating in the development of each state's own strategies. The coverage that resulted from that process has proved popular and increased the funding and influence of local providers and institutions, such as community health centres and free clinics.

The second insight was the ability of consumers and physicians to work together to challenge the negative aspects of managed care. This alliance achieved a reduction in the rigidity of managed care procedures. Consumers and physicians realised from this success that the quality indicators that business developed as part of managed care could be a tool for improving the quality of care for even disadvantaged patients. Consumers in particular are beginning to see that alliances with unlikely allies can improve their ability to obtain the type of programmes that they advocate.

[66] Trubek, 'Lawyering', n 33 above.
[67] Trubek and Das, n 32 above.

The patient empowerment movement was based initially on dissatisfaction with the quality of health care delivery. It arose from the alternative treatment movement, as well as a desire for patients to control their own treatment. This created the concept of the consumer as an independent actor in the health care arena. The activated consumer, making health care decisions based on quality and cost information, is a continuation of that movement. The interface of the longstanding patient rights vision with the newer patient empowerment movement opened the path to a more active role for patients/consumers in the level of clinical and institutional decision making.[68]

An understanding of how race, gender and ethnic aspects impact health care outcomes developed out of the discrimination/civil rights approach to reducing disparities. The civil rights critique of the existing health care system had a powerful effect on the conventional belief that the health care system was unbiased. However, the failure to reduce disparities by the civil right approach led concerned people to seek to move beyond gridlock and be open to new approaches to solving racial and ethnic disparities.

There is energy now for creating more equitable participation in health care through the stakeholder collaborations, based on these insights within the current political climate. There remain barriers to fully implementing the new practices. The first barrier is the lack of explicit measurement of the participation of disadvantaged groups in any of these new practices.[69] There needs to be an explicit focus on participation in these new practices. This requires a guideline on the importance of such participation and a method of monitoring that the guidelines are actually being met. The second barrier is that these practices are being conducted in a variety of sites with a variety of actors. They are difficult to locate and view for purposes of monitoring and evaluating effectiveness. The old entitlement programmes were much easier to track through the public availability of documents and required, though limited, methods of participation.[70] These new practices do not have procedural requirements, like the Administrative Procedure Act, and are not easily judicially reviewable. A third barrier is uncertainty about who will be the advocates for disadvantaged groups. While individual patients can be effective at the patient–physician level, representatives of the interests of the disadvantaged groups are essential at the institutional and policy level. Advocates for disadvantaged group participation can be lawyers or reformist physicians and others committed to an all-inclusive health care system. These advocates play the role of assuring that the barriers to participation are removed; for example, ensuring collection of data on the

[68] Sydney Halpern, 'Medical Authority and the Culture of Rights' (2004) 29 *Journal of Health Politics, Policy and Law* 835.

[69] Brandon L Garrett and James S Liebman, 'Experimentalist Equal Protection' (2004) 22 *Yale Law and Policy Review* 321.

[70] Super, n 64 above, at 726.

number and characteristics of the uninsured that is reliable for programme and policy development.[71] These advocates may also play an important role in diffusing the liability debate that is a barrier to implementing the new quality tools. They could advocate for monitoring institutions that assure abusive and negligent behaviour is prevented and sanctioned.[72] The traditional public interest lawyers had systems for funding and legitimacy that were developed in the 1960s and 1970s. These new advocacy roles in the new governance practices are more fluid and less subject to external requirements than the traditional, public interest advocacy of the earlier period. For example, a consumer group that wanted to participate in one of the collaboratives could be excluded and there would no administrative or judicial review required, because these collaboratives are organised as private groups.

Multi-level public and private networks

Health care in the US has always been a messy mix of private market, self-regulation and state and federal programmes. Nonetheless, there is a decided shift in the relationship between these four elements in the new governance practices. Most commentators agree the momentum has decidedly shifted to the states and public–private partnerships.[73] This was a surprise to most longstanding health care reformers who always assumed that any universal coverage and improved quality had to be based on a national, uniform programme like Medicare.

The success of state experimentation leading to positive change can be seen in both the expansion of coverage and in curbing the abuses of managed care. The demise of the Clinton health care plan, changes in federal regulations, and the passage of SCHIP allowed the states to experiment. The ability of individual states to be leaders resulted in a diffusion of good practices. A second example is the enactment of legislation in the states to protect patients, challenging the nascent managed care movement. The state enactments catalysed sweeping changes in the way health care was delivered by the managed care companies all over the country. This story delivered the message that action by individual states could be diffused through the national market without the necessity of uniform, national legislation.[74]

In President Bush's proposals for disseminating new technology in health care and in the Medicare Modernization Act, there is both a commitment

[71] Wisconsin Public Health and Health Policy Institute, *Issue Brief, No. 5* (Madison, October 2002).

[72] William M Sage, 'Unfinished Business: How Litigation Relates to Health Care Regulation' (2003) 28 *Journal of Health Politics, Policy and Law* 387.

[73] See generally John Holahan (ed) *Federalism & Health Policy* (Washington DC, 2003).

[74] Mark A Hall, 'The "Death" of Managed Care: A Regulatory Autopsy', unpublished MS, on file with author.

to regionalism, described as below the Washington level but not necessarily at the state level, and also incentives for providing the infrastructure through public–private networks.[75] This is consistent with the academic discussion about 'new regionalism' and 'new localism'.[76] Scholars note that in order to achieve the values of local autonomy, there needs to be a legal regime that encourages local participation. Limiting centralised power is not enough to create greater diversity and participation. However, regional units have been difficult to achieve. The challenge, therefore, of proposing regional structures in the US is daunting. Nonetheless, many of the hospital/health care systems, as they become large and integrated, including several million users, may be a base for public–private structures that might provide a framework for successful health care delivery at a devolved level.[77]

Different roles for government

The New Deal view of government as the controlling, commanding presence is no longer accurate. A role for government does continue, but new governance practices can result in confusion about what that role is. [78] Government remains an important stakeholder in the evolving collaborations. It assumes a coordinating role in implementation of health care services and organises activities so that each actor can do whatever it does best. With entitlements on the decline, government has a crucial role in orchestrating and justifying programmes.[79] The various ways in which government can be involved include facilitating collaboration; monitoring programmes for effectiveness; collecting data; using regulation and funding to assure quality; correcting imbalances in participation, as when low-income patients and small businesses find it difficult to participate; and through sanctioning in order to prevent privatisation failure and to assure that actors participate fairly.

The need for monitoring is particularly evident in assuring participation of all the stakeholders, transparency of the information that is generated and holding the health care system accountable for achieving its benchmarks. [80] Government can monitor through public law litigation,[81] enactment of

[75] Yasnoff, n 29 above.
[76] David J Barron, 'A Localist Critique of the New Federalism' (2001) 51 *Duke Law Journal* 377.
[77] Trubek and Das, n 32 above.
[78] Mark Schlesinger, 'On Government's Role in the Crossing of Chasms' (2004) 29 *Journal of Health Politics, Policy and Law* 1.
[79] Super, n 64 above.
[80] Sidney D Watson, 'REL Reform: Mandating Systems Reform to Reduce Racial, Ethnic and Language Disparities in Health Care', paper given at the *Symposium, Racial and Ethnic Disparities in Health Care Treatment*, The Harvard Civil Rights Project (18 May 2004), unpublished MS, on file with author.
[81] Charles F Sabel and William H Simon, 'Destabilisation Rights: How Public Law Litigation Succeeds' (2004) 117 *Harvard Law Review* 1016.

statutory requirements for information availability and dissemination[82] and requiring self-regulatory systems.[83]

One recent example shows the challenge for the state in effectively transitioning from a command-and-control, central authority to a more flexible manager. This challenge emerged from the privatisation of traditionally government-provided health care prevention and outreach services to low-income people. The state now contracts with health care organisations to provide these services. Increasingly, the contracting organisations are using small, community-based organisations to reach minority patients. These nonprofits are undertaking a substantial responsibility for raising funds and providing services for the underserved and underrepresented. This privatisation has risks for low-income people who rely on these services, as well as for the credibility of the entire health care system. In order for this approach to succeed, the state has to maintain its financial commitment, monitor the quality of the care, and share information on the quality of services. The danger is that if the state does not assume these responsibilities, the privatised system will collapse with serious consequences for patients and the system as a whole.[84]

Soft law

Guidelines, benchmarks and standards that have no formal sanctions are referred to as soft law. Soft law is an important component of new governance practices. Traditional regulation relies on uniform rules, sanctions if the rules are not followed and court challenges for noncompliance.[85] This hard law approach has proved inadequate in many cases in regulating health. First, the use of court challenges to enforce regulations has been ineffective, due to the complexity of the problems seeking to be solved, the lack of fit between the institutional structures that are causing the failures with the remedies provided by courts and the recent unwillingness of judges to undertake massive reforms through court systems. The failure of the anti-discrimination paradigm in racial and ethnic disparities is an example.[86] Secondly, there is the famed gap between law on the books and law in action. Uniform rules are not automatically enforced by the agencies, nor

[82] Vernellia R Randall, 'Eliminating Racial Discrimination in Health Care: A Call for State Health Care Anti-Discrimination Law', paper given at the *Symposium, Racial and Ethnic Disparities in Health Care Treatment*, The Harvard Civil Rights Project (18 May 2004), unpublished MS, on file with author.

[83] Garrett and Liebman, n 69 above.

[84] Rick Lyman, 'Once a Model, A Health Plan is Endangered' *New York Times* (20 Nov 2004) A1, A11.

[85] David M Trubek and Louise G Trubek, 'Hard and Soft Law in the Construction of Social Europe: The Role of the Open Method of Coordination' (forthcoming 2004) *European Law Journal*.

[86] Watson, 'REL Reform', n 80 above.

does enforcement necessarily lead to the desired outcome. [87] The perceived inability of the HIPAA rules to advance the consumer's interest in health data collection is an example of the gap between law in the books and effective achievement of the goal. Another failure of traditional regulation is the use of malpractice litigation as the major to prevent errors and improve quality. The randomness of the cases, the high costs of litigation, including lawyers' fees, and the resistance of health care institutions to utilise the information of failures in a self-regulatory way, are all problems with the hard law approach.

A choice may not be required between hard and soft law. Different modes may be required for different issues and combining them may be useful when they are complimentary. An example is found in reducing the racial and ethnic disparities in health care treatment. The move to using the 'law of quality compliance' includes soft law instruments such as benchmarking, data collection and reporting.[88] There is, however, still a role for court and legislative requirements to compel the collection and format for the data collection. 'This classic legal construct, which grounds the problem of disparities in the law of civil rights, may now be giving way to shared ownership with the law of health care quality.'[89] The discussion of the ability of the discrimination model to effectively co-exist with the quality-assurance model is just beginning.

There is also a continued role for new types of regulation, particularly those that combine hard law and soft law. The standard setting technology regulations are an example of regulation that is necessary. A second example is the use of action-forcing regulations where health care institutions must put in place quality assurance and compliance programmes in order to get continued accreditation and funding. A third example is regulations that foster discussions among patients, field-level workers, and family.[90]

CONCLUSION: PUTTING THE PIECES TOGETHER

Rand Rosenblatt[91] in a recent article posits that we are entering into a fourth age of health law. He describes the first three ages as the authority of the medical profession, modestly egalitarian social contract and market competition. This fourth age, in his opinion, is linked to a more general shift to new governance. This paper supports that view and shows that this fourth age is developing rapidly.

[87] Trubek and Trubek, n 85 above.

[88] Sara Rosenbaum and Joel Teitelbaum, 'Addressing Racial Inequality in Health Care' paper given at the *Symposium, Racial and Ethnic Disparities in Health Care Treatment*, The Harvard Civil Rights Project (18 May 2004), unpublished MS, on file with author.

[89] *Ibid.*

[90] Braithwaite *et al*, n 19 above.

[91] Rand Rosenblatt, 'The Four Ages of Health Law' (2004) 14 *Health Matrix* 155.

The larger issue is whether this evolving system can be both popular and effective. The partial failure of managed care and the Clinton health plan was due in part to the inability of the reformers to demonstrate that people would be better off and fairly treated under that governance system. In envisioning this fourth age, it will be important to maintain the positive aspects of the earlier ages, such as social contract, physician trust, and innovation that market forces bring. Hybrid solutions would be a way of reforming while reassuring everybody that, despite the changes, the essential stability of the system is in place.[92] Despite the seemingly overwhelming problems of reforming health care provided in the US, it remains one of the top concerns among residents. Health care actors sense this opportunity and are working to develop new practices. These new practices, in turn, challenge conventional institutions and processes.

[92] Clark C Havighurst, 'Starr on the Corporatizion and Commodification of Health Care: The Sequel' (2004) 29 *Journal of Health Politics, Policy and Law* 947.

10

Governing Occupational Safety in the United States

ORLY LOBEL

IN THE UNITED States, 'labour law' is a distinct and separate field from 'employment law'. While labour law involves a semi-privatised model of collective bargaining between workers and employers, employment law has developed as a command-and-control regulatory model of worker protection. Yet, at the same time as unionism is becoming increasingly rare in most American industries, the limits of a command-and-control approach to workplace policies have become more and more pronounced in the new, post-industrial economy. This chapter describes the expansion of third-way governance-based policies—complementing command-and-control and market-based strategies—with which the US Occupational Safety and Health Administration (OSHA) has been experimenting. It explores the possibilities of administrative governance through the context of occupational safety and the new energy surrounding a bureaucratic agency's efforts to rethink its traditional regulatory roles. Since the establishment of OSHA within the US Labor Department in the early 1970s, the agency and its regulatory practices have been the source of controversy and conflict. In political debates, the agency has been described as cultivating 'a culture of regulatory excess that eats away at the vitality of our economy'.[1] Often, OSHA has been described by legal scholars as the paradigmatic case of bureaucratic failure and regulatory unreasonableness. Both as a response to external critique and as part of its own learning processes, the agency has continuously struggled with its self-identity and positioning, its relationship with private industry and its institutional structure. For more than two decades it has been experimenting with a variety of governance-based strategies that would supplement its core enforcement activities. In its 2003–8 five-year strategic management plan, OSHA aims to dramatically increase its compliance assistance activities, its growing number of cooperative programmes and to generally promote 'a safety and health culture'

[1] Senator Hutchison, Testimony before Congress, 1995. For a longer in-depth inquiry of the context of occupational safety and labour regulation in the United States, see generally, Orly Lobel, 'Interlocking Regulatory and Industrial Relations: The Governance of Workplace Safety', 57 *Administrative Law Review* 1071, 2005.

through education and training, public/private alliances and structural impact. A study by the Federal General Accounting Office (GAO) that was completed in March 2004 provides initial evaluation of these new governance experiments. The current plan, however, is to move beyond the framework of peripheral fragmented experiments to a concerted effort to transform the nature of regulatory administration. To do so, the agency must overcome a variety of regulatory and political impediments, including the need to change the default questions and answers of what administrative agencies can and should do. The first section of this chapter describes the realities of OSHA, fraught with budgetary constraints, political resistance and a weak legal mandate. The second section describes inadequacies of traditional regulatory approaches to safety and health regulation in today's employment context. The next section describes several programmes which OSHA has developed in response to these limits, primarily the expanding initiatives under the agency's Office of Cooperative Programs. The final section critically assesses these governance innovations and reveals why OSHA has yet to develop a more comprehensive framework that integrates the concept of effective governance into the core of its regulatory activities. A set of legal and political impediments needs to be overcome in order to move regulatory governance beyond experimentation. In particular, questions about resources allocation, balanced coercive and cooperative options, and an adequate role for all stakeholders, including workers, are crucial for a legitimate shift to new governance approaches. The context of occupational safety illustrates the difficulties of evaluating success in a transitional administrative framework, within a confined period of time, and in relation to both the complexities of regulating the new economy and our diverse normative commitments.

THE REGULATORY MANDATE OF THE OCCUPATIONAL SAFETY AND HEALTH ADMINISTRATION

The American Occupational Safety and Health Administration (OSHA) is often used in regulatory debates as the prime example of regulatory failure and bureaucratic pathologies. Over three decades ago, following a series of fatal occupational accidents during the activist climate of the late 1960s, the federal Occupational Safety and Health Act of 1970 (OSH Act) was adopted 'to assure so far as possible every working man and woman in the Nation safe and healthful working conditions and to preserve our human

[2] On the move from a traditional regulatory model to a new governance paradigm in both theory and practice, see generally, Orly Lobel, 'The Renew Deal: The Fall of Regulation and the Rise of Governance in Contemporary Legal Thought' (2004). 89 *Minnesota Law Review* 342. For a longer in-depth inquiry of the context of occupational safety and labour regulation in the United States, see generally, Orly Lobel, 'Interlocking Regulatory and Industrial Relations: The Governance of Workplace Safety', 57 *Administrative Law Review* 1071, 2005.

resources'.[3] Since its establishment and throughout its existence, the agency has been fraught with controversy and resistance and there have been multiple political and legislative attempts to weaken the agency's authority.[4] The agency is persistently attacked by business interests for being outrageously intrusive and unreasonable and criticised by labour for being exceptionally slow and ineffective. OSHA officials themselves frequently decry the agency as dangerously under-staffed, under-funded, under-appreciated, and overly-attacked by all sides.

Ironically, businesses' attacks on the agency's regulatory intrusiveness co-exist with ongoing realities of high occupational injury and disease rates. Over a dozen workers are killed daily in the United States during on-the-job accidents and over a hundred more die every day from work-related disease.[5] The risk is burdened unequally across sectors and segments of the labour market and the most vulnerable, low-skilled, and disorganised workers bear the risks of the most serious injuries.[6] Despite the soaring costs of occupational related care, exceeding $200 billion per year, government spending on workplace safety has never reached the levels of other social issues and OSHA's budget continues to steadily decline.[7] Moreover, despite a pervasive image of omni-presence, the reality of OSHA—a low-budget, understaffed, overextended agency—translates into little enforcement. With a staff of little over 2,000 employees, today's OSHA is in charge of the safety of more than 115 million American workers at over eight million worksites.[8] Even the most at-risk industries are estimated to be inspected on average only once every 10 years.[9] Thus, although OSHA received wide authority to regulate production across all industries, the legislative mandate provides the agency few resources to enforce safety standards. The penalty under the OSH Act for wilfully endangering workers is a misdemeanour, carrying a maximum penalty of six months' imprisonment. Put in perspective, a comparison to environmental regulation is striking, since in

[3] Pub L No 91–596, 84 Stat 1590 (1970). See also, David P Mccaffrey, *OSHA and the Politics of Health Regulation* (Plenum Publishing, 1982); Thomas O McGarity and Sidney A Shapiro, *Workers at Risk: The Failed Promise of Occupational Safety and Health Administration* (Westport, CT: Praeger, 1993).

[4] Graham K Wilson, *The Politics of Safety and Health: Occupational Safety in the United States and Britain* (Oxford: Oxford University Press, 1985) 43; Sidney A Shapiro, 'Occupational Safety and Health: Policy Options and Political Reality' (1994) 31 *Houston Law Review*. 13, 25.

[5] AFL-CIO 13th Annual Report on Occupational Safety (2004) at <http://www.afl-cio.org>.

[6] Eg, in recent years, the number of fatal work injuries among foreign-born Hispanic workers has steadily been rising. *Ibid*.

[7] Amy Goldstein and Sarah Cohen, 'Bush Forces a Shift in Regulatory Thrust: OSHA Made More Business-Friendly' *Washington Post Sunday* (15 August 2004).

[8] OSHA vital statistics, available at <http:www.osha.gov>; AFL-CIO 13th Annual Report, n 5 above.

[9] David Weil, 'Assessing OSHA Performance: New Evidence from the Construction Industry (2001) 20 *Journal of Policy Analysis and Management* 651, 654–55.

almost all measures of regulatory commitment, US environmental policies have been stronger than workplace policies. For example, the maximum penalty for wilfully endangering a protected fish under the Clean Water Act is 15 years of imprisonment.[10] In practice, OSHA rarely prosecutes for violation of safety standards and the monetary fines allowed by the legislative act are equally low. Fines are routinely decreased after negotiation and citations are often downgraded from 'willful violations' to less severe citations.[11] For example, a GAO study found that OSHA cites maximum penalty in only 2.1 per cent of all violations with penalties, then after negotiation, maximum penalty is in effect imposed on less than 1 per cent of the violations.[12] Critiques have described these agency practices as creating 'a culture of reluctance' to bring meaningful regulation to the workplace.[13] The American National Safe Workplace Institute has described the low sanctions for occupational safety as an attitude of 'human expendability', where 'blue-collar blood pours too easily'.[14]

REGULATORY INNOVATION IN THE CONTEXT OF POLITICAL VULNERABILITY

OSHA practices and the limits of its reach no doubt epitomise the relative power of business interests and the political weakness of labour interests in the United States. However, they also signify more general failures of the traditional top-down command-and-control model employed by regulatory agencies, as well as the changing circumstances of the new world of work. The thinness of the traditional regulatory approach to occupational risk prevention has failed to fulfil the promise of safety to all workers.

In its early days of existence, OSHA promulgated hundreds of pages of regulation.[15] Rules were often too complex, vague, needlessly detailed or simply unsuited to fit the realities of production and work.[16] Most disturbingly, increasingly, there has been a proven disconnect between compliance with substantive rules and the safety of workers. Recent studies in industrial safety indicate that standards frequently diverge from the major

[10] Thomas O McGarity and Sidney A Shapiro, *Workers at Risk: The Failed Promise of the Occupational Safety and Health Administration* (Westport, CT: Praeger, 1993) 220.

[11] See, David Barstow, 'California Leads in Making Employer Pay for Job Deaths' *New York Times*, (23 Dec 2003).

[12] General Accounting Office, *Occupational Safety & Health: Penalties for Violations Are Well Below Maximum Allowable Penalties* (1992) available at <http://www.gao.gov.

[13] Barstow, n 11 above.

[14] Joseph A. Kinney, 'Why Did Paul Die? *Newsweek* (10 Sept 1990), 11, at 11 cited in Sidney A Shapiro, 'Occupational Safety and Health: Policy', n 4 above, at 39.

[15] SH Fleming, 'Charting a New Course Toward Workplace Safety and Health' (1996) 7 *Job Safety And Health Quarterly* 9, 10.

[16] McGarity and Shapiro, *Workers at Risk*, n 3 above, at 42.

sources of fatalities and injuries in the workplace.[17] Explicitly, regulatory standards about protective machineries, the adoption of particular technologies or a particular blueprint on production processes have been incapable of addressing the realities of safety management. For example, at many workplaces, a majority of injuries are related to ergonomics or soft tissue injuries from repetitive motions or strenuous physical work, for which OSHA has no standard. Therefore, even with perfect compliance, industrial studies predict that uniform occupational safety regulation can only prevent less than 25 per cent of occupational injury.[18] In effect, at least in certain industries, violations of OSHA standards account for only less than 20 per cent of fatal accidents.[19] At the same time, there is widespread agreement among industrial safety professionals that most accidents can in fact be prevented by better safety management.[20] Rather than a result of any particular violation of existing OSHA standard, workplace accidents are most often attributable to defects in planning, internal communication, definition of responsibilities and authority, deficiencies in training, inadequate supervision and an overarching absence of a culture of safety.[21]

OSHA's practice of adopting substantive rules and enforcing these rules invariably on all firms has perpetuated the image of an agency that is insensitive to the costs of its regulatory demands. These realities of top-down detailed regulation and zealous enforcement have led to intense resistance by industry. Since the early 1980s, industry litigated against almost every single safety and health standard that OSHA sought to promulgate. The landmark case was the US Supreme Court Benzene decision, which struck down exposure standards, holding that OSHA must first establish the existence of a 'significant risk' before it regulates preventative standards.[22] Since the Benzene case, litigation against OSHA's regulatory activities persisted, and in fact, in the atmosphere of command-and-control adversarialism, every single health standard that OSHA has ever promulgated has been challenged in court, usually by both labour and industry. The impact of judicial review, private resistance and new legislative hurdles on issuing administrative rules have all burdened and ossified administrative rule-making in

[17] See eg, John Mendeloff, 'The Role of OSHA Violations in Serious Workplace Accidents' (1984) 26 *Journal of Occupational Medicine* 353

[18] Lawrence Bacow, *Bargaining for Job Safety and Health* (1980) 40.

[19] John Mendeloff, n 17 above. Mendeloff found that violations accounted for 13–19%of 645 fatality cases that he studied.

[20] Centers for Disease Control & Prevention, Occupational Injury Panel, 'Occupational Injury Prevention' in *Injury Control in the 1990s: A National Plan for Action* (1992) 329, cited in Dean J Haas, 'Falling Down on the Job: Workers' Compensation Shifts from a No-Fault to a Worker-Fault Paradigm' (2003) 79 *North Dakota Law Review* 203.

[21] John Braithwaite, *To Punish or Persuade: Enforcement of Coal Mine Safety* (1985).

[22] *Indus. Union Dep't. v Am. Petroleum Inst*., 448 US 607 (1980); *Cotton Dust, Am. Textile Mfrs. Inst., Inc. v Donovan*, 452 US 490 (1981).

general and OSHA's standard setting activities in particular.[23] As a result, while in some areas detailed standards have produced little safety improvement, other areas, posing significant risks, have been left dangerously unregulated.[24]

Akin to the limits of regulatory standards, enforcement practices of the agency have increasingly proven to be limited in their effects. OSHA's enforcement practices are traditionally top-down random wall-to-wall inspections, seeking violations of its substantive rules in various worksites, followed by prosecution and sanctions. Pursuant to the agency's motto, 'you see it, you cite it', inspectors are generally obliged to cite every identified violation.[25] Yet a substantial number of empirical and comparative studies have pointed to the limits of this adversarial model.[26] As other authors in this volume have argued, punishment in the case of good faith efforts to comply with government regulation can produce counter-productive effects of resistance, de-moralisation, and evasion tactics.[27] Confrontational enforcement diminishes the willingness of firms to cooperate and share information with the agency, as well as with other private firms on cost reduction, innovative techniques and mutually beneficial problem solving.[28] Experienced OSHA inspectors describe firms who exemplify true intent and willingness to improve their safety, suggesting that with those firms, repeat citations for marginal violations through augmented fines risks sending the message that 'there is no pleasing OSHA'.[29]

Moreover, while a top-down enforcement pattern may have been suited for the first wave of occupational safety regulation, the introduction of new governance techniques becomes even more essential when a regulatory regime has been operating for several decades—at the stage when the government agency aims to move from broad stroke prohibition to fine-tuning and sophisticated targeting. It has long been empirically shown that repeat

[23] See, eg, Comprehensive Regulatory Reform Act of 1995, s 343, 104th Cong. See also, generally, William S Jordan, 'Ossification Revisited: Does Arbitrary and Capricious Review Significantly Interfere with Agency Ability to Achieve Regulatory Goals through Informal Rulemaking?' (2000) 94 *Northwester University Law Review* 393; Jerry L Mashaw, 'Reinventing Government and Regulatory Reform: Studies in the Neglect and Abuse of Administrative Law' (1996) 57 *University of Pittsburgh Law Review* 405.

[24] See, eg, W Kip Viscusi, *Risk by Choice* (Cambridge, MA: Harvard University Press, 1983) 78–100 (arguing that while OSHA regulates standards with little benefits, it does not regulate significant risks of carcinogenic substances.).

[25] KSG Case Program, *Regulatory Reform at OSHA* C102–97–1371.0 p 3.

[26] Eugene Bardach and Robert A. Kagan, *Going by the Book: The Problem of Regulatory Unreasonableness* (1982), p 104–16. See also, Robert Kagan, *Adversarial Legalism: The American Way of Law* (2003).

[27] See also, William Simon, 'Solving Problems versus Claiming Rights' (2004) 46 *William and Mary Law Review* 127; Susan Sturm, 'Second Generation Employment Discrimination' (2001) 101 *Columbia Law Review* 458, 460–62; Braithwaite, *To Punish or Persuade*, n 21 above.

[28] See also, GAO 2004 Report, p 26, available at <http://www.gao.gov.>.

[29] *Ibid.*

OSHA inspections on the same firms have a significantly diminishing impact.[30] Recent studies examining OSHA's performance in improving safety conditions in large construction sites with high inspection rates find that despite substantial enforcement efforts, repeat inspections have only a modest effect on compliance with OSHA standards.[31] Moreover, the agency has found that the prospect of inspection every few years fails to significantly deter employers and to induce them to alter their safety practices prior to and after an inspection has taken place. OSHA inspectors report that alterations made following an inspection are merely 'temporary fixes' rather than systemic long-term reforms.[32]

Finally, at the same time that the role of the state in regulating the market is evolving, the realities of occupational risks are posing new challenges for regulators. The new global economy has dramatically altered the nature of work and employment. In the past several decades, firms have shifted from mass industrial production to post-industrial manufacturing, digital and service markets. The typical economic enterprise of the industrial era was a large and long-term firm. Production was relatively stable, menial tasks were narrowly defined, and roles were segmented. By contrast, production today is more heterogeneous, volatile and includes complex contractual chains. This has made it more difficult for a centralised agency to promulgate and enforce universal top-down rules that will fit all firms.[33]

EXPERIMENTATION WITH COOPERATIVE GOVERNANCE

The shift from a traditional regulatory to a new governance model, based on cooperation and partnership with private industry, has been promoted by the federal administration for several decades. In the mid-1990s, during the Clinton administration, the political platform of 'reinventing government' was epitomised in Al Gore's 'New OSHA' initiative, designed to 'cut obsolete regulations', to 'reward results, not red tape', to create 'grassroots partnerships' between regulator and regulated parties, and to 'negotiate' rather than 'dictate'.[34] The 'New OSHA' emphasised that government officers should focus on reducing injuries rather than 'rack(ing) up their numbers of inspections, citations, and fines. Rather, they are supposed to focus

[30] Jean-Jacques Laffont and Jean Tirole, 'The Politics of Government Decision-Making: A Theory of Regulatory Capture' (1991) 106 *Quarterly Journal of Economics* 1089; Alison D Morantz, 'Has Regulatory Devolution Injured American Workers: A Comparison of State and Federal Enforcement of Construction Safety Regulations' Stanford Law and Economics OLIN Working Paper no 308 (June 2005) available at <http//sarn.com/abstracts=755026>.

[31] Weil, n 9 above.

[32] KSG Case Program, n 25 above.

[33] Orly Lobel, 'Orchestrated Experimentalism in the Regulation of Work' (2003) 101 *Michigan Law Review* 2146.

[34] President's Memorandum on Regulatory Reform, 31 Weekly Comp Pres Doc 363 (4 Mar 1995).

on the underlying purpose of their agency. For many, this is a radical change from the traditional regulatory mentality.'[35]

During the Bush administration, the agency continued the idea of changing the 'traditional regulatory mentality'. In 2004, an official government statement declared 'OSHA is not just a regulatory agency anymore'.[36] In a 2005 speech, acting OSHA director, Jonathan Snare, emphasised the need to further develop 'outreach, education and compliance assistance' and 'cooperative and voluntary programs' along side with 'strong enforcement'.[37] The speech reflects OSHA's stated plans to further dramatically increase its cooperative outreach activities in the near future. In its 2003–8 management plan, OSHA has recognised that the American workforce has changed in significant ways over the past several decades: increased diversity in production and heterogeneity of workforces, a shift from goods to services, and a decrease in the percentage of workers employed in stable full-time jobs[38]:

> These demographic and workplace trends complicate the implementation of occupational safety and health programs and argue for enforcement, training, and delivery systems that are different from those that have been relied upon to date.[39]

OSHA's current goal is defined as the promotion of a safety and health culture through compliance assistance, cooperative programmes and the development of strong leadership in the private sector. Interestingly, the focus on a safety *cultúre* is also the key component that the International Labor Organization (ILO) is now promoting in its new focus on injury prevention worldwide.[40]

The focus of industry safety cultures is manifested through a variety of new governance approaches. In recent years, OSHA has expanded its non-traditional activities, now devoting over 30 per cent of its entire budget to new cooperative governance approaches.[41] The programmes range from sophisticated enforcement and targeting plans, through recognition programmes of beyond compliance programmes, to support of voluntary industry wide initiatives. Under its 'Office of Cooperative Programs', OSHA is developing a range of non-adversarial programmes. The Voluntary Protection Program (VPP) certifies employers with exemplary safety records

[35] OSHA Maine 200 Application, cited in Malcom K Sparrow, *The Regulatory Craft: Controlling Risks, Solving Problems, and Managing Problems* (2000), pp 86–87.

[36] John L Henshaw, Head of OSHA in a speech (21 April 2004).

[37] Snare speech, American Bar Association OSH Law Committee Key West, Florida (2 March 2005), available at <http://www.osha.gov/pls/oshaweb/owadisp.show_document?p_table=SPEECHES&p_id=838.

[38] OSHA 2003–8 management plan, <http://www.osha.gov/StratPlanPublic/strategicmanagementplan-final.html>.

[39] *Ibid.*

[40] ILO, *World Day for Safety and Health at Work*, World of Work (June 2004), pp 26–27.

[41] GAO 2004 Report, n 28 above, at p 22.

as 'Star' firms. The primary attraction of a 'Star' certification is the exemption of participating firms from routine random inspections. To be recognised as a 'star member', a firm must have below-industry-average injury rates for several years. It also must adopt and maintain an internal safety programme, which includes an analysis of the safety hazards in their worksites and have clear procedures for prevention and control. A safety programme also commits to routine employer-conducted inspections of the workplace, investigations of 'near-miss' incidents and means by which employees can complain of unsafe practices and circumstances without fear of reprisal.[42] OSHA also requires participating firms to encourage employee involvement and provide employees with general safety training. Under the VPP, OSHA has recently developed the Special Government Employees (SGE) initiative which trains workers at participating VPP sites to serve alongside OSHA officials 'as full-fledged members of evaluation teams'.[43] The new VPP Mentoring Program matches participating firms with candidates that seek assistance in preparing for certification.[44] Participating sites host 'VPP days' and reach out to other firms within the industry to encourage them to join the programme.[45] While the VPP is mainly tailored for larger firms because of its extensive planning requirements, the Safety and Health Achievement Recognition Program (SHARP) is the equivalent programme for smaller firms in high hazard industries. Again, the recognition of exemplary safety and health management practices exempts from general inspections. Firms that apply to SHARP first receive free and largely confidential consultation through the On-site Consultation Program,[46] an OSHA-funded state-run programme.

Two other cooperative programmes at OSHA are designed to bring together various stakeholders in order to create an ongoing learning environment. The Strategic Partnership Program (SPP) consists of local partnerships with the goal of targeting specific hazards or industries, mainly in the construction industry. The programme is designed to assist firms in integrating lessons from multiple worksites by creating partnerships of groups of employers, employees, employee representatives, as well as educational institutions. Similar to VPP and SHARP, the programme offers incentives in the form of exemption from routine inspections, although OSHA withholds the right to inspect the most severe types of hazards. Finally, the Alliance Program is designed to support national or regional problem-solving forums, which include large firms, trade associations, and at times, non-profit organisations, government agencies and labour unions. Alliances are

[42] *Chamber of Commerce v Department of Labor* 174 F3d 206, 335 US App DC 370, 18 OSH. Cas (BNA) 1673, 1999 OSHD.

[43] OSHA Directives, CSP 03-01-001.

[44] <http://www.vpppa.org>. The programme is coordinated by the Voluntary Protection Programs Participants' Association.

[45] GAO 2004 Report, n 28 above, at28.

[46] The programme is also referred to at times as 'the State Consultation Program'.

designed to 'reach out to, educate, and lead the nation's employers and their employees in advancing workplace safety and health'.[47] Such goals are defined loosely and they are closely related to OSHA's general outreach activities, including training, industry voluntary guidelines and dissemination of information.

CORE AND PERIPHERY IN REGULATION AND GOVERNANCE: EVALUATING OSHA'S COOPERATIVE SHIFT

While the promotion of new governance approaches to federal occupational safety regulation has been carried under the leadership of both Democratic and Republican administrations, the fine details and underlying commitments to the goals of the agency make for significant differences in evaluating the myriad of new programmes, experiments, and initiatives at OSHA. OSHA's cooperative programmes signify the shift from command-and-control model of risk regulation to a new governance model that fosters public/private partnership, encourages industry cooperation, and allows flexibility in policy implementation.[48] These new regulatory approaches involve industry in a more dynamic and ongoing way and offer positive incentives to beyond-compliance safety initiatives. They are therefore no doubt a necessary response to the shortcomings of universal top-down standards and confrontational enforcement. The risk, however, is that cooperative initiatives can also signify a decline in the political commitment to public regulation of the new workplace. Given OSHA's limited resources, programmes must be prioritised and effectiveness must be monitored. Moreover, in order to ensure the legitimacy of the programme, workers themselves—the greatest stakeholders in the safety regulation schema—must be involved. Finally, the different models must be evaluated on an ongoing basis to ensure transparency and public accountability.

Resource allocation and effective targeting

A broader repertoire of agency tools allows better targeting and use of the ongoing availability of traditional government sanctions. An agency strapped for resources, facing a shrinking budget and extensive regulatory resistance, can in fact upgrade its traditional enforcement levels with sophisticated targeting and escalated sanctions, leveraging limited resources by the introduction of innovative comprehensive governance techniques.

However, merely relying on positive incentives and giving up the use of coercive government sanctions risks a permissive regime that fails to deter

[47] See, <http://www.OSHA.gov.>
[48] Lobel, 'The Renew Deal', n 2 above.

bad faith violators. Today, OSHA's cooperative programmes are in effect voluntary, offering an opt-out from routine inspections, penalty reductions and formal recognition of good safety practices. The question is whether the agency reaches the firms that most require targeting. In contrast to the contemporary voluntary programmes, during the Clinton administration OSHA developed a programme that was aimed to target dangerous workplaces to enter into partnership with the agency under the threat of targeted enforcement in the case of refusal. In this context, firms would face an actual choice between effective cooperation or increased sanctions. This attempt to promote balanced enforcement and governance was met with great resistance by industry interests, who demanded instead a programme that was 'true voluntary'.[49] In particular, industry contested the requirement to implement private 'comprehensive safety and health programs' (CSHP) that would require firms look 'beyond specific requirements of law to address all hazards'. Internalised private CSHPs would seek to prevent injuries and illnesses, 'whether or not compliance is at issue'.[50] In other words, the programme sought to impose 'beyond compliance' requirements for those choosing partnership, asking firms to make comprehensive changes to their safety practices even in areas in which there were no existing OSHA rules, such as ergonomics injury. Industry argued that this was an attempt to introduce ergonomics standards and other hazard rules through the backdoor, without the promulgation of formal rules.[51] The US Chamber of Commerce, in a paradigmatic adversarial move, challenged the Clinton-era cooperative compliance programme, contesting the adoption of the programme by OSHA without following notice and comment requirements under the Administrative Procedure Act (APA).[52] In 1999, the Federal Court of Appeals of the District of Columbia accepted the claim—holding that the programme was not properly adopted by OSHA—and thus invalidated the programme.[53] OSHA had developed the programme as a 'directive' rather than a 'rule', and the agency claimed that the directive was a 'general statement of policy', not subject to rule-making requirements. Because of the increased formalisation and ossification of the administrative rule-making process in recent years, OSHA and other federal administrative agencies have become increasingly accustomed to 'non-rule' initiatives, issuing decisions under such rubrics as policy statements or 'good guidance'.[54] Yet, in this case, although OSHA claimed that CCP was no more than 'a formalised inspection plan', the court described the directive as the 'practical equivalent of a rule obliging employers to comply or to suffer the

[49] *Ibid.*

[50] *Chamber of Commerce v Dept of Labor*, OSHA 174 F3d 206, 335 US App DC 370, 18 OSH Cas. (BNA) 1673, 1999 OSHD (CCH) p 31, 787.

[51] *Chamber of Commerce*, pervious n. See also Sparrow, n 35 at 252–53.

[52] 5 USC § 553; §§ 556, 557.

[53] *Chamber of Commerce*, n 50 above.

[54] Lobel, The Renew Deal, n 2 above.

consequences'.[55] The court decision demonstrates the difficulties administrative agencies encounter when they attempt to integrate new governance approaches into their core regulatory practices. While merely voluntary programmes such as the ones OSHA is currently expanding do not encounter resistance and contestation, formalising an initiative that integrates both sticks and carrots is subject according to Chamber of Commerce ruling to strict rule-making requirements. Following the Chamber of Commerce decision, OSHA could have decided to issue the CCP directive as a rule, following notice and comment procedures, a process that could have taken several years to complete. Instead, the agency abandoned the Clinton era programme, developing instead its 'purely voluntary' programmes, including VPP, SHARP, SPP, and Alliance, as industry demanded.[56] This has led commentators to critically argue that 'regulatory agencies are more likely to face legal challenge when they declare the basis for their exercise of discretion—however rational—than when they exercise their discretion in an arbitrary manner without declaring it'.[57]

A legislative proposal from the Clinton administration, the Comprehensive Occupational Safety and Health Reform Act (COSHRA), which would have reformed the OSH Act to include universal requirements on comprehensive safety programmes at all firms and active participation of workers in the governance of safety was also abandoned, following strong resistance of the business community.[58] In 1998, OSHA drafted a Safety and Health Program Rule, which would have similarly required most employers to establish a workplace safety and health programme to ensure compliance with OSHA standards.[59] Despite OSHA's continuing official position that 'effective management of worker safety and health protection is a decisive factor in reducing the extent and severity of work-related injuries and illnesses and related costs', the rule was withdrawn in 2002.

OSHA continues to regularly use discretion in all of its interactions with private parties, through decisions about targeting, investigation, inspection, citation and prosecution. The current structure that has emerged from the confrontational initiative is that of voluntary programmes which are confined to separate departments, and cooperative and sanctioned interactions that are fragmented. The newness of 'new governance' is not the availability of discretion and flexibility in the actions of government. Government agencies have always used certain degrees of discretion to accommodate variance and change. Rather, successful new governance approaches ideally

[55] See, Sparrow, n 35 above, at pp 252–53.

[56] See, Sparrow, n 35 above, at p 254 ('If the regulated community did not appreciate novel programs based on structured discretion, OSHA figured, they could have it the old way.')

[57] *Ibid.*

[58] The Comprehensive Occupational Safety and Health Reform Act; HR 1280, 103d Cong. Title II (1993).

[59] 29 CFR 1900.1, Docket no, S&H–0027.

signify the formalisation of flexible practices into integrated and coherent programmes that promote ongoing learning and can be continuously deliberated, evaluated and improved.

Stakeholder participation and regulatory beneficiaries

Although studies have repeatedly shown that worker participation improves safety, OSHA has failed to systematically institutionalise the role of workers in the governance of occupational health and safety.[60] This can explain why labour interests have characterised the recent expansion of cooperative programmes as anti-labour tactics: 'the agency apparently needed to find a way to justify its increasingly irrelevant existence in this anti-regulatory, anti-enforcement, business-controlled Republican administration'.[61] They further describe these initiatives as 'window dressing on a deadly crisis facing low-wage workers'.[62] Under the title 'Building Alliances Minus Unions', an AFL-CIO affiliate recently described OSHA's newest initiative, the 'Alliance Program' as a deliberate effort to exclude workers.[63] The 2004 AFL-CIO Report on Safety further calls to 'fight behavior-based safety programmes, incentive programmes and injury discipline programmes that discourage workers from reporting injuries and illnesses'.[64]

The fear of promoting greater partnership between government agencies and private industry while excluding the most natural stakeholders within the regulatory triangle is a valid concern. OSHA requires some employee involvement for participating in its cooperative programmes, but does not provide guidance on what such involvement may entail. While under the OSH Act workers are entitled to request an inspection, accompany inspectors during an inspection and receive relevant information about compliance; they are not entitled to receive monetary compensation for time spent pursuing workplace safety issues.[65] Unionisation increases enforcement of labour regulation, yet most firms today in the United States are not unionised.[66] Ironically, while workplace safety is a social area that readily lends itself to stakeholder participation, both labour and industry in the

[60] See e.g., David Weil, 'Are Mandated Health and Safety Committees Substitutes for or Supplements to Labor Unions?' (1999) *Industrial and Labor Relations Review* 339; Matthew W Finkin, 'Employee Representation Outside the Labor Act: Thoughts on Arbitral Participation, Group Arbitration, and Workplace Committees' (2002) 5 *University of Pennsylvania Journal of Labor and Employment Law* 75.

[61] Confined Space website (labor-based).

[62] OSHA '"Summits" With Friends While Hispanic Workers Continue to Die' <http://www.confinedspace.org>.

[63] Goldstein and Cohen, n 7 above.

[64] The AFL-CIO 13th Annual Death on the Job Report (2004).

[65] Occupational Safety and Health Act of 1979, 29 USCA §§651–678. *Leone v Mobil Oil Corp* 523 F2d 1153 (DC Cir 1975).

[66] David Weil, 'Enforcing OSHA: The Role of Labor Unions' (1991) 30 *Industrial Relations* 20.

American workplace have largely resisted legal reforms that would promote participation.[67] For employers, the promotion of partnerships involving workers is understood as an attempt to revive collective action at work. In the contemporary largely anti-union atmosphere of post-industrial production, even a hint of unionism is enough to raise industry resistance. For the American labour movement, requirements set by government about employer–employee partnerships raise the fear of management domination and a further substitute for independent unionism.[68] In part, OSHA's avoidance of institutionalising worker participation in the governance of safety is a result of the historical divisions between the fields of labour and employment law.[69] Specifically, safety employee–management committees raise the question of employee participation schemes under the National Labor Relations Act (NLRA). The NLRA prohibits employer practices that 'interfere with, restrain, or coerce' workers in the exercise of their rights to self-organisation, collective bargaining and other concerted activities.[70] In classifying the legality of employee participation, courts have relied on an adversarial understanding of labour relations to unpack different forms of workplace governance. In several recent cases, the courts ordered to disband employee safety committees, holding that the committees were unfairly dominated by the employers, who structured the committees, were involved in defining safety reform proposals, and paid the employees for their time on the committees.[71] The decisions on the legality of instituting worker safety participation programmes take two types of questions into account—substantive and procedural. Substantively, employee involvement is acceptable on subject matters that are of interest to management, that is, quality of production, investment, R&D and efficiency.[72] Issues that pertain to the 'terms and conditions of employment', which are subject to collective bargaining under the NLRA, are not allowed in the participatory schema and must be excluded from multilateral discussions. Procedurally, interactions that are set up to simply derive input from workers are distinguished

[67] Randy S Rabinowitz and Mark M. Hager, 'Designing Health and Safety: Workplace Hazard Regulation in the United States and Canada' (2000) 33 *Cornell International Law Journal* 373, 431.

[68] Teamwork for Employees and Managers Act of 1997: Hearing on s 295 Before the Senate Committee on Labor and Human Resources, 105th Cong. 49 (1997) (testimony of Jonathan P Hiatt, Gen Counsel, AFL-CIO) (calling for 'employee involvement' only in the context of 'an independent voice').

[69] See, Orly Lobel, 'Agency and Coercion in Labor and Employment Relations: Four Dimensions of Power in Shifting Patterns of Work' (2001) 4 *University of Pennsylvania Journal of Labour & Employment Law* 12.

[70] National Labor Relations Act (NLRA) 29 USC §158a(1)(1935).

[71] Electromation; *E.I. du Pont de Nemours & Co.*, 311 NLRB 893 (1993); See also, *Polaroid Corp*, 329 NLRB 424 (1999); Michael H LeRoy, *Employer Domination of Labor Organizations and the Electromation Case: An Empirical Public Policy Analysis,* (1993) 61 *George Washington Law Review* 1812.

[72] S 8, NLRA.

from those that involve conceding decision-making powers to workers. The latter type of interactions are more likely to be viewed by the courts as illegal bargaining or 'dealing with' workers outside the labour law framework, absent an independent, full-fledged union.

Despite the framework of illegality, in practice, the NLRA ban on company unions has little effect on the actual decision of management to create employee participation programmes. In practice, employee safety committees in non-unionised firms are widespread.[73] Almost all large American companies report that they have installed some form of employee participation.[74] These include employee involvement programmes, worker-management committees, teams, quality circles, work councils and employee representation on the firm's board.[75] Both empirical quantitative data and ethnographic studies show that such committees can play crucial roles in improving safety, facilitating communicating and increasing learning and problem solving capacities.[76] In the 2004 GAO study on OSHA's cooperative programmes, firms attribute much of the success their participation to employee involvement.[77] Ironically, however, because of the current legal prohibition on company initiated labour organisation, the wider the variety of workplace issues addressed by participatory committees and the greater decision-making power granted to employees, the greater risk for the employer that the participation will be found in violation of labour laws.

Despite a broad consensus that the flat prohibition on cooperative forms of worker–management organisation is outdated and does not fit today's political economy, no successful labour law reform has been legislated since the 1950s.[78] In 1996, the Teamwork for Employees and Managers Act (TEAM) was passed by both houses of Congress but vetoed by President Clinton.[79] The TEAM Act was designed to amend the NLRA to allow for more cooperative relationships between employees and the employer.[80] Unions saw the TEAM Act as not adequately prohibiting company-dominated labour organisations and demanded more assurances that employers would not use employee participation to thwart union representation efforts.[81] Although the Clinton administration supported a similar reform to amend the adversarial stance of the NLRA and to reform the OSH act to

[73] Dennis Devaney, 'Electromation and DuPont: The Next Generation', (1994) 4 *Cornell Journal of Law & Public Policy* 3, 16.

[74] See, Lobel, 'Agency and Coercion', n 59 above.

[75] *Ibid.* at 150–52.

[76] Gregory R Watchman, 'Safe and Sound: The Case for Safety and Health Committees Under OSHA and the NLRA' (1994) 4 *Cornell Journal of Law & Public Policy* 65.

[77] GAO 2004 Report 13.

[78] See also, Cynthia Estlund, 'The Ossification of Labor Law' (2002).102 *Columbia Law Review* 1527.

[79] Commission on the Future of Worker-Management Relations, US Dep't of Labor & US Dep't of Commerce, *Fact Finding Report* (1994).

[80] Lobel, 'Agency and Coercion', n 59 above.

[81] TEAM at 34.

include worker involvement, the administration opposed the TEAM Act because it failed to provide the needed assurances demanded by labour. The result was that while all parties, labour and industry, democrats and republicans, supported reform of the NLRA, no reform was achieved. The ultimate result is that employers are able to informally experiment with a wide range of worker participation forms under the shadow of informality, while government agencies like OSHA fail to monitor and creatively incorporate these private experiments into their regulatory schema.

Transitional governance: Measuring success and data transparency

The Government Accountability Office (GAO) has recently conducted a year-long study of OSHA's cooperative programmes, including interviews with participating firms, managers, employees, safety professionals, economists, lawyers and public officials. The study's findings are generally positive. The GAO report concludes that the new cooperative strategies have improved safety and health practices by allowing OSHA to play a 'collaborative, rather than a policing, role with employers'.[82] Participation in the programmes seems to reduce injury and illness rates, improve the relationships between industry and the public agency and promote productivity and work relations in participating firms. Accident rates for participating sites are significantly lower than at comparable firms, [83] and in several studies, companies report that the introduction of safety programmes cut worker compensation claims dramatically.[84] According to OSHA data on VPP, participating firms experience a lost-workday rate over 50 percent below the average for their industries, as well as a decline in accident rate compared to their own figures prior to joining the programme.[85] When the Clinton administration promoted the cooperative compliance programme, which combined cooperative incentives with the threat of traditional enforcement, OSHA found that employers self-identified a dramatically greater number of hazards than could have been cited top-down by the agency and they significantly lowered their injuries rates compared to prior years.[86]

Although the GAO study finds positive effects of the programmes, the evaluation is far from conclusive. First, the study emphasises that OSHA

[82] GAO 2004 Report, n 28 above, at 43.

[83] Jospeh Rees, *Reforming the Workplace: A Study of Self-Regulation in Occupational Safety* (Philadelphia: University of Pennsylvania Press, 1988) (Cal-OSHA data).

[84] Emily A.Spieler, 'Perpetuating Risk? Workers' Compensation and the Persistence of Occupational Injuries, (1994) 31 HOUS. L. REV. 119, 155; Rees, previous n (Cal-OSHA data).

[85] <http://ww.osha.gov/dcsp/vpp/index.html>; GAO 2004 Report, n 28 above, at 25–26.

[86] Harvey Simon and Malcolm Sparrow, *Kennedy School of Government Case Program: Regulatory Reform at OSHA*, KSG Case Study no 1371.0 (Cambridge, MA: KSG Press, 1997).

does not currently collect complete, comparable data that would enable full evaluation of the programmes. GAO similarly suggested in a different report that OSHA collect more data for the evaluation of the state consultation programme. In 2002, OSHA sponsored a study on the programme, finding positive outcomes of reduced violations, citations and decline in injury and illness rates. GAO, however, again stated that long-term evaluation would require further data collection. OSHA reacted to these appraisals by attempting to expand the OSHA Data Initiative which it originally used to collect information on its enforcement activities. However, the Office of Management and Budget (OMB) recently denied OSHA permission to extend the data collection to all employers. Consequently, it is important to acknowledge that the collection of information itself requires investment and long-term commitment. Without an emphasis on large-scale and ongoing data mining, successful initiatives will continue to be labelled as 'anecdotes' or peripheral 'experiments'. (See Appendix 1.)

Second, a basic problem that underlies the ambivalent assessment of OSHA's new governance approaches is that the agency does not systematically differentiate between its programmes and models under the rubric of OSHA's cooperative compliance office. As we saw, there are key differences between programmes that combine both cooperation and sophisticated targeting and those that merely offer positive incentives to recognise exemplary firms. The latter type of cooperative programme raises the concern of self-selection effects, where the agency simply recognises the achievements of those responsible actors who volunteer to participate. In such a context, even when safety rates are above average for participating firms, the causal link between the governance tool and success rates is provisional.

Third, as other authors in this volume demonstrate, success of new governance initiatives cannot be measured solely through one-dimensional criteria. For example, while it is important to estimate the number of hazards that members of cooperative governance abate per year, it is equally important to consider more systemic improvement to the culture of safety. For example, it is not easy to quantify the benefits of improved problem-solving capacities, employee empowerment and increased awareness and knowledge about risks prevention, all of which facilitate long-term performance. For example, the 2004 GAO study found that participation in the cooperative programmes creates trust between management and agency officials, as well as between management and employees.[87] A change in the perception of the agency from that of an opponent to a partner and a shift from an atmosphere of fear to that of mutual respect is a broader benefit to promote systematic change in private industry. In fact, a more legitimate image of the role of the agency can allow OSHA to reinforce traditional

[87] GAO Report 2004, n 28 above.

regulatory protections and allow the escalation of enforcement in appropriate contexts without as much resistance as it has traditionally encountered. A positive safety culture can also expand beyond the narrow issues of injury prevention and have greater systemic impact on industry-wide learning.

A related problem of adequate monitoring and effective evaluation of new governance approaches at OSHA has been the issue of transparency. OSHA currently publishes the names of worksites that it has identified as having the highest rates of injuries and illnesses. This is a practice that other federal agencies have similarly undertaken in recent years. For example, the Environmental Protection Agency (EPA) now annually publishes the top 10 toxic polluter facilities in each industry.[88] The goal is that through increased transparency and public data, private actors will be able to make informed choices that take into consideration responsible safety records. For example, reporters, consumers, sub-contractors, suppliers and workers can investigate on where it was riskiest to work and whether the agency is effectively pursuing recalcitrant actors. OSHA reports that many firms that participate in their cooperative programmes now require their subcontractors to also meet the elevated safety standards.[89] The hope is that subcontractors would have incentives to improve their safety practices if they would be widely published. However, public information does not come without struggle in this conflict fraught field. While OSHA willingly began publishing the names of firms with high injury rights, it would not reveal actual injury rates despite repeat requests by reporters. In 2003, OSHA cited the trade secret exception to revealing public information embedded in the Freedom of Information Act in order to deny disclosure of this data. OSHA argues that some employers are reluctant to share information on cost reduction and innovative techniques, although through the new alliance programme there has been more willingness to share.[90] OSHA's stance on the public disclosure of high injury rates was successfully appealed, when recently a federal court ordered the agency to disclose for the first time the company names and the worker injury and illness rates of the American workplaces with the worst safety records.[91] The court found that since the agency requires companies to post at worksites the number of hours employees worked, such information cannot be deemed confidential.

A final caveat for evaluating OSHA's new governance practices is that in order to successfully implement new governance strategies, issues that have been traditionally kept separate must be creatively linked. The new governance model recognises that doctrinal divides and boundaries between legal

[88] The Toxic Release Inventory (TRI) provides a national database of annual amounts released by manufacturers.

[89] GAO 2004 Report, n 28 above, at 28.

[90] *Ibid* at 26.

[91] Julia Preston, 'Judge Orders Agency to Disclose Safety Records' *New York Times* (3 Aug 2004).

fields are contingent and are often defined through negotiation and revision. It therefore encourages the questioning of these divides through openness and fluidity of policy domains. New governance approaches that promote private participation, collaboration, and experimentation have great potential to illuminate how widely dispersed issues are connected at the level of those who are most influenced by them. While under a traditional regulatory model, law is fragmented into distinct, specified sub-fields, new governance approaches can take a more holistic approach to problem solving and public design. OSHA now acknowledges that certain workplace safety issues have been overlooked and neglected due to the problematic divisions between policy fields. In 2003, the agency recognised that the most serious vocational risks include workplace violence and motor vehicle accidents, two areas that have not been traditionally addressed by the agency. Motor vehicle fatalities have generally been covered by the Department of Transportation, with OSHA's jurisdiction vastly limited. Similarly, workers' compensation programmes are governed by state laws and the OSH Act prohibits OSHA from displacing or affecting 'in any manner' any state workers' compensation law. Some private insurers already offer rate reductions to employers participating in voluntary compliance programmes, and OSHA has formed some alliances and partnerships with private insurers, but reports that others are hesitant to interact with OSHA for fear that clients will view them as 'agents of OSHA'. Some state plans coordinate between their workers' compensation programmes and their state occupational safety programme, sharing the same data for both departments. Similarly, across the ocean, the British occupational health and safety administration was merged with the worker compensation programme, leading to vast changes in the ability of the state to use information and learn, as well as use ex-post and ex-ante incentives together. In the federal OSH Act, the prohibition on OSHA to promulgate rules that can affect worker compensation regulation is inherently inefficient. The separation between policy fields, and the rigid, yet contingent, division of labour among administrative agencies (like with the division between labour/employment law) creates unnecessary overlaps and disincentives for systemic improvements in the social field of occupational safety.

CONCLUSION

Workplace safety regulation requires more than promulgating rules about hazard abatement. In our contemporary political economy, effective prevention requires employers to systematically identify hazards, self-assess compliance, evaluate effectiveness and track their own progress on hazard control. In addition, workplace risk prevention must involve those most affected by the requirements on safety—workers themselves. In order for OSHA to reinvent its regulatory tools in effective ways a myriad of legal barriers must be removed, including historical dichotomies between labour and employment laws and the divides between administrative regulatory prevention and private initiatives. The lessons of OSHA's straddle between experimentation and the evolution of its core regulatory practices are demonstrative of the difficulties of transitional public design. A key moral is that when schemes are left informal, and in some ways 'outlawed', the public ability to learn, deliberate and support best practices is fundamentally inhibited.

Appendix 1

The Information Catch in a Transitional Period

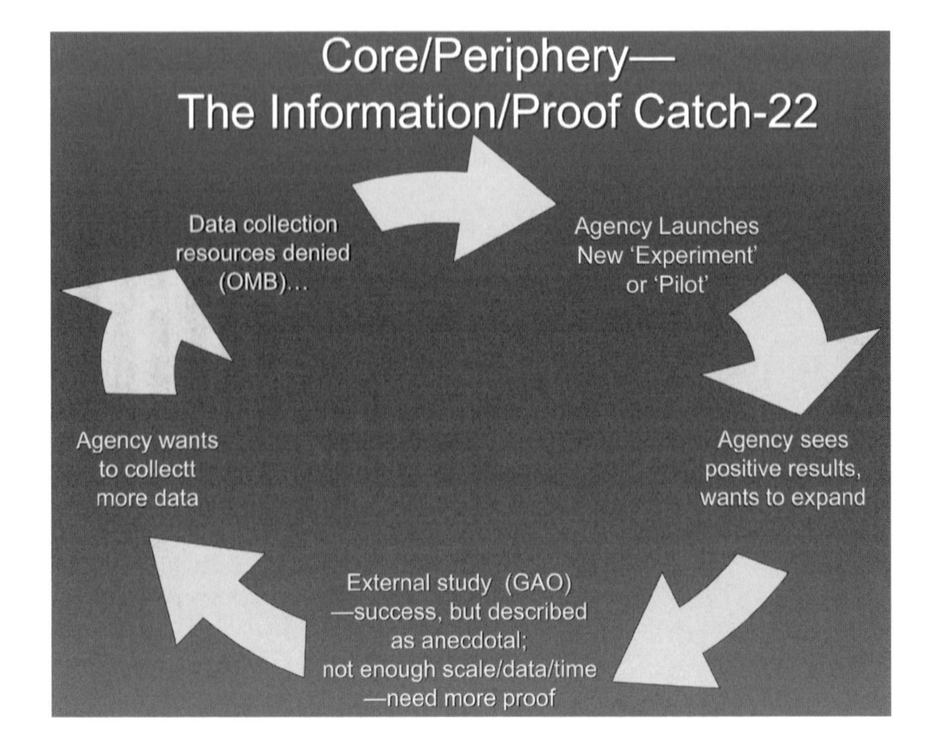

Appendix 2

Growth of OSHA Cooperative Programmes

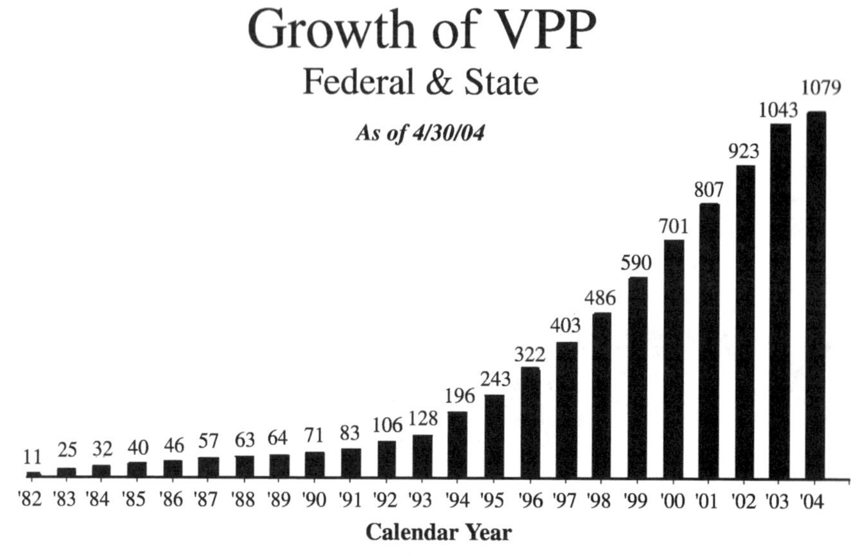

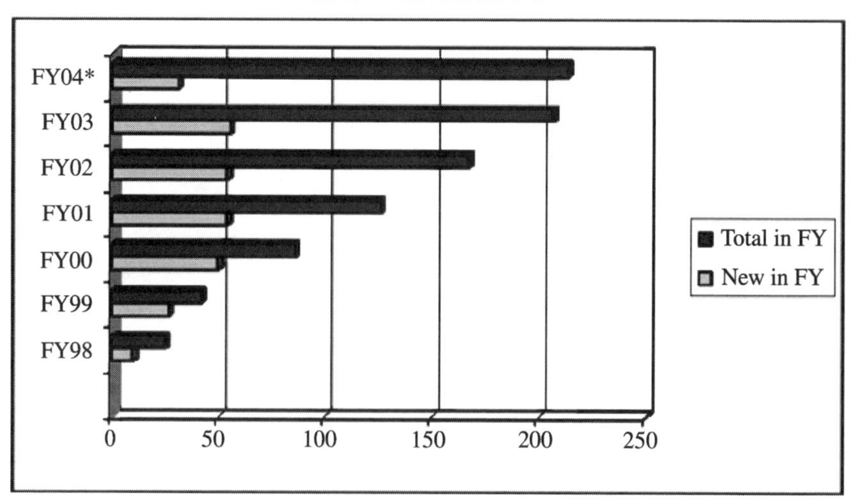

Source: OSHA Office of Partnership & Recognition

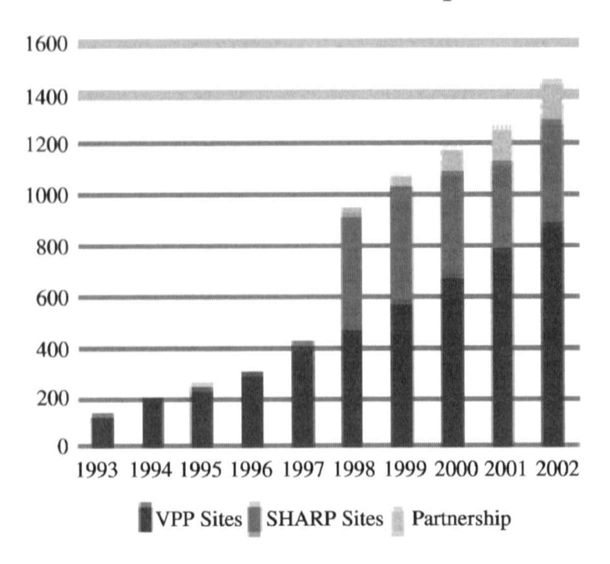

Appendix 3

Proposed FY2006 Budget (Dollars in Millions)

	FY 2005	FY 2006	Change
	$	$	$
Safety and Health Standards	16.0	16.6	0.6
Federal Enforcement	169.7	174.3	4.6
State Programs	91.0	92.0	1.0
Technical Support	20.7	21.7	1.0
Federal Compliance Assistance	70.9	73.3	2.4
State Consultation Grants	53.4	53.9	0.5
Training Grants	10.2	0	-10.2
Safety and Health Statistics	22.2	24.5	2.3
Executive Direction and Administration	10.1	10.7	0.6
Total, OSHA Budget Authority	464.2	467.0	2.8
Full Time Equivalents **(includes 8 reimbursable FTE)*	2,208	2,208	–

Selected OSHA Workload Data

	FY 2005	FY 2006	Change
Notices of Proposed Rulemaking	4	3	–1
Final Rules	4	4	–
Federal Inspections	37,700	37,700	–
State Program Inspections	58,000	58,000	–
Total VPP Federal VPP Sites	993	1,264	271
Consultation Visits	31,500	32,250	750

Source: News release <http://www.osha.gov>.

11

Information-forcing Regulation and Environmental Governance

BRADLEY C KARKKAINEN

ENVIRONMENTAL REGULATION IN the United States is shifting from reliance on direct regulatory prescription of mandatory rules of behaviour to the use of a varied basket of more flexible regulatory strategies. First-generation environmental laws empowered expert agencies to specify both environmental objectives and the permissible means to achieve them.[1] This top-down, interventionist approach, pejoratively labelled 'command-and-control regulation', has been widely criticised. Rules of this type, it is said, are often both over- and under-inclusive.[2] They tend to be costly to implement, inflexible, insensitive to local variations in the costs and benefits of environmental improvements, and they may stifle innovation.[3]

Recent reform efforts have served up an array of alternatives, including:

—market-based mechanisms, such as taxes, fees, and cap-and-trade permitting systems[4]

—environmental contracting[5] with individual facilities[6], firms,[7] or entire sectors[8]

[1] M Graham, *The Morning After Earth Day: Practical Environmental Politics* (Washington, DC: Brooking Institution Press, 1999) at 1–2.

[2] D Farber, 'Environmental Protection as a Learning Experience' (1994)27 *Loyola Los Angeles Law Review* 791 at 794–95.

[3] B Ackerman and R Stewart, 'Reforming Environmental Law' (1985) 37 *Stanford Law Review* 1333 at 1335–36.

[4] See R Hahn and R Stavins, 'Incentive-Based Environmental Regulation: A New Era for an Old Idea?' (1991) 18 *Ecology Law Quarterly* 1 at 7–12.

[5] See generally E Orts and K Deketelaere, 'Introduction: Environmental Contracts and Regulatory Innovation' in E Orts and K Deketelaere (eds) *Environmental Contracts* (London: Kluwer Law International, 2000) at 1, 15–19; ED Elliott, 'Toward Ecological Law and Policy' in M Chertow and D Esty (eds) *Thinking Ecologically: The Next Generation of Environmental Policy* (New Haven, Yale University Press, 1997); J Freeman, 'The Contracting State' 28 *Florida State University Law Review* 153 (2000).

[6] See, eg, D Dana, 'The New "Contractarian" Paradigm in Environmental Regulation' 2000 *University of Illinois Law Review* 35 at 36 (discussing 'facility-by-facility' agreements in which 'regulators contractually commit not to enforce some requirements ... in return for the regulated entities' contractual commitments to take measures not required under existing formal law'.)

[7] See N Gunningham and D Sinclair, *Leaders and Laggards: Next-Generation Environmental Regulation* (Sheffield: Greenleaf Publishing, 2002) (describing the Australian

—devolved, collaborative, 'place-based', multi-party governance in integrated watershed management[9] and ecosystem management.[10]

The common assumption underlying these initiatives is that centralised regulatory agencies have a limited capacity to gather and process relevant information, constraining their ability to specify effective and economically efficient rules.[11] The alternative approaches devolve authority to localised actors deemed better situated to make context-sensitive decisions.[12]

Among the alternative approaches, market-mimicking strategies—especially marketable permit or cap-and-trade systems—have received a disproportionate share of scholarly notice. Less widely celebrated is the emergence of a 'contractarian' paradigm[13] in which regulated entities 'contract around' otherwise applicable rules by bargaining with regulators and, in some cases, regulatory beneficiaries.[14] These bargains may take the form of conditional waivers that transform previously mandatory rules into default rules defining the background against which bargaining takes place.

Experiments in collaborative 'place-based' ecosystem management in places like the Chesapeake Bay, the Florida Everglades, and the San Francisco Bay-Delta region carry this devolutionary thrust a step further. These programmes seek to manage, in an integrated way and at ecologically-defined scales, the entire suite of causally interconnected resources and stressors that jointly comprise the ecosystem.

State of Victoria's Environmental Improvement Plan programme promoting tripartite contracting among firms, regulators, and community organisations).

[8] See R Stewart, 'A New Generation of Environmental Regulation?' (2001) 29 *Capital University Law Review* 21 at 80–86 (describing sector-specific 'environmental covenants' in Europe and Japan); D Fiorino, 'Toward a New System of Environmental Regulation: The Case for an Industry Sector Approach' (1996) 26 *Environmental Law* 457.

[9] See J Cannon, 'Choices and Institutions in Watershed Management' (2000) 25 *William and Mary Environmental Law and Policy Review* 379.

[10] See B Karkkainen, 'Collaborative Ecosystem Governance: Scale, Complexity, and Dynamism' (2002) 21 *Virginia Environmental Law Journal* 189; JB Ruhl, 'A Manifesto for the Radical Middle' (2002) 38 *Idaho Law Review* 385.

[11] See ED Elliott, 'Environmental Markets and Beyond: Three Modest Proposals for the Future of Environmental Regulation' (2001) 29 *Capital. University Law Review* 245 (describing conventional regulation as 'an inch wide and a mile deep' its reach limited by high information costs); Ackerman and Stewart, n 3 above, at 1336–37 (stating that conventional regulation places excessive information demands on regulators); B Karkkainen, 'Information as Environmental Regulation: TRI and Performance Benchmarking, Precursor to a New Paradigm?' (2001) 89 *Georgia Law Journal* 257.

[12] Cf. D Farber, 'Triangulating the Future of Reinvention: Three Emerging Models of Environmental Protection' (2000) *University of Illinois Law Review* 61 (identifying self-regulation, bilateral bargaining, and collaborative governance as leading reinvention models); Dana, n 6 above, at 37 (arguing regulators seek 'decentralized and contextualized' solutions because 'centralized, one-shoe-fits-all solutions' are 'clumsy, costly, and ... unhelpful' in resolving complex and variable problems).

[13] See Dana, n 6 above; Orts and Deketelaere, n 5 above, at 1.

[14] See J Johnston, 'The Law and Economics of Environmental Contracts' in *Environmental Contracts*, n 5 above, at 271, 286; S Hsu, 'A Game-theoretic Approach to Regulatory Negotiation and a Framework for Empirical Analysis' (2002) 26 *Harvard Environmental Law Review* 33.

Conventional natural resource and environmental programmes proceed piecemeal by isolating discrete categories of problems, abstracted from their local ecological context. Disregarding ecological interdependencies, this fragmentary approach leads to regulatory gaps, inconsistencies, redundancies, counterproductive interventions, and over- and under-regulation.

In contrast, integrated management aims to be more sensitive to local ecological context and causal interdependencies. This complex, multidimensional task demands a great deal of inter-agency, inter-governmental, and public–private coordination, collaboration, and information-pooling at ecosystem scales. Complexity also militates in favour of epistemic humility and an open-ended, experimentalist management style that both generates and responds to new learning. Participants seek continuously to improve their understanding of the system through ongoing scientific investigation, ecological modelling, and monitoring, coupled with 'adaptive management' strategies that treat management interventions as provisional and experimental, subject to re-evaluation and revision in light of new learning and dynamic changes in the system itself.

These hybrid public–private institutional collaborations represent the most significant instantiation of new governance in contemporary US environmental regulation. Like other new governance arrangements, they are '"networked" and "multilevel"', with 'decisionmaking processes that are neither hierarchical nor closed, and that permit persons of different ranks, units, and even organizations to collaborate as circumstances demand'.[15]

Critics charge that devolutionary and collaborative approaches are susceptible to rent-seeking strategic bargaining, domination by powerful and self-interested economic actors, and excessive transaction costs.[16] This chapter examines two types of legal rules that may be used to discipline and ensure accountability in these newly emerging institutional arrangements.

The first type of rule is the 'regulatory penalty default'. The term 'penalty default' was coined by Ian Ayres and Robert Gertner who observed that some default rules in contract law are non-majoritarian, imposing harsher terms than contracting parties might prefer. To avoid the penalty, parties 'bargain around' the default rule to reach explicit, less onerous contract terms.[17] This approach, Ayres and Gertner argued, is especially useful in cases of information asymmetry, where a party otherwise might withhold

[15] C Sabel and W Simon, 'Destabilization Rights: How Public Law Litigation Succeeds' (2004) 117 *Harvard Law Review* 1015, at 1019.

[16] See D Spence and L Gopalakrishnan, 'Bargaining Theory and Regulatory Reform: The Political Logic of Inefficient Regulation' (2000) 53 *Vanderbilt Law Review* 599; R Steinzor, 'Reinventing Environmental Regulation: The Dangerous Journey from Command to Self-Control' (1998) 22 *Harvard Environmental Law Review* 103, 141–43; C Coglianese, 'Is Consensus an Appropriate Basis for Regulatory Policy?' in *Environmental Contracts*, n 5 above, at 93.

[17] I Ayres and R Gertner, 'Filling Gaps in Incomplete Contracts: An Economic Theory of Default Rules' (1989) 99 *Yale Law Journal* 87, at 91–93.

information so as to shift undisclosed risks to the other party. Creating a countervailing incentive to disclose information in the course of bargaining, penalty default rules exhibit an 'information-forcing' character.

This chapter argues that some regulatory rules operate as *regulatory penalty defaults*, coupling harsh background requirements with opportunities for regulated parties to 'bargain around' the default baseline toward alternative arrangements. Like contract penalty defaults, regulatory penalty defaults are both information-forcing and action-forcing. They induce regulated parties to investigate, disclose, and undertake affirmative self-regulatory measures that achieve public objectives more effectively and presumably at less cost. Variants of the regulatory penalty default approach account for some of the most important policy successes in US environmental law.

A second type of disciplining rule is the 'destabilization right', providing a legal avenue to disentrench failing institutions. Chuck Sabel and Bill Simon coined the term in the context of public law litigation—constitutional or statutory challenges to current institutional arrangements in public education, welfare, prisons, and policing—where courts and litigants increasingly recognise the limits of 'command and control judging' that attempts to impose effective institutional reforms from the bench.[18] A better approach, Sabel and Simon argue, is to disentrench the failed institutional arrangement and set broad performance goals for its successor, shifting the burden to the defendant to initiate institutional reconstruction and opening the door to multi-party collaboration in an open-ended, experimental process of institutional redesign.

This chapter extends Sabel and Simon's work in two ways. First, it argues that an administrative (rather than judicial) destabilisation right held by a central regulatory body can provide discipline and accountability to ensure that local new governance institutions adhere to their commitments. This approach can serve as a check on regulatory capture, strategic bargaining, policy distortions resulting from asymmetric information, and other procedural ills.[19]

Second, this chapter argues that in US environmental law, an important destabilisation right already exists in the 'citizen suit' which allows interested citizens to seek judicial redress if regulated parties or agency administrators violate legal requirements.[20] Although most commonly used to compel strict enforcement of conventional regulatory standards and procedures, the citizen suit can also operate as a destabilisation right, disentrenching underperforming institutions and forcing their reconfiguration.

[18] See Sabel and Simon, n 15 above.

[19] See Coglianese, n 16 above.

[20] See B Thompson, Jr, 'The Continuing Innovation of Citizen Enforcement' (2000) *University of Illinois Law Review* 185 (labelling citizen suits 'a defining theme of the modern environmental era').

REGULATORY PENALTY DEFAULTS: THEORY AND PRACTICE

The pioneering work of Ayres and Gertner in contract theory defined a penalty default rule as a gap-filling rule that intentionally imposes a harsher outcome than the parties themselves might prefer, thereby creating an incentive to contract around the default rule toward an explicit alternative term.[21]

Ayres and Gertner argued that penalty default rules are especially valuable in contexts of information asymmetry, where they might enhance efficient contracting by eliciting privately held information that the informed party might otherwise have an incentive not to disclose.[22] Their principal example is *Hadley v Baxendale*.[23] In *Hadley*, a miller sued a shipper seeking recovery of lost profits occasioned by delayed shipment of a crankshaft necessary to run the mill. The court held that damages beyond those reasonably foreseeable by the defendant were unavailable, unless the defendant knew or had reason to know of special circumstances that might give rise to such damages. The miller and similarly situated parties might prefer a rule allowing all consequential damages, but under that rule ultra-sensitive parties could shift unusual risks to unsuspecting shippers through non-disclosure. The *Hadley* rule effectively penalises non-disclosure, and consequently creates an incentive to disclose in the course of contract bargaining. Because penalty default rules create incentives that elicit asymmetrically held information, Ayres and Gertner described them as 'information-forcing'.[24]

While contract law consists largely of interpretive or gap-filling default rules,[25] environmental regulation typically has grander designs. Environmental law assumes that strong medicine is required to change the behaviour of parties who would gladly externalise environmental costs if they were able. The regulator usually tackles the challenge head-on with mandatory rules prescribing the behaviour the regulated party must undertake, subject to coercive sanctions for non-compliance.

Sometimes, however, environmental regulations operate as default rules, offering regulated entities the opportunity to 'bargain around' the otherwise applicable rule by undertaking a self-initiated alternative deemed a satisfactory substitute. Regulatory penalty default rules are a specialised subset of

[21] Ayres and Gertner, n 17 above, at 91–93 ('Penalty defaults are designed to give at least one party to the contract an incentive to contract around the default rule and therefore to choose affirmatively the contract provision they prefer.')

[22] *Ibid*. ('[P]enalty defaults are purposefully set at what the parties would *not* want—in order to encourage the parties to reveal information to each other or to third parties').

[23] *Hadley v Baxendale*, 156 Eng Rep 145 (Exch 1854).

[24] See Ayres and Gertner, n 17 above, at 91–95.

[25] See EA Farnsworth, *Contracts*, 3rd edn (New York: Aspen Law and Business, 1999) §1.10, at 36 ('the great bulk of the general rules of contract law ... are subject to contrary provision by the parties').

default rules,[26] imposing harsh default terms and thereby creating stronger incentives for regulated parties to come forward 'voluntarily' with acceptable alternatives. Like their contract cousins, regulatory penalty default rules can be *information-forcing*, inducing disclosure of information held asymmetrically by the regulated party. They might also induce parties to produce new information, a useful feature if the regulated party is best situated to produce the desired information. Finally, regulatory penalty defaults sometimes have an *action-forcing* character, inducing the regulated party to undertake an affirmative action it is otherwise disinclined to pursue, so as to avoid the negative consequences of the default rule.

Despite the early predominance of mandatory command-and-control rules in environmental law, examples of penalty default rules can be found in 1970s regulatory enactments. Additionally, some rules initially conceived as mandatory have been revised to operate as penalty default rules. In other cases, innovative regulatory programmes have incorporated penalty default strategies.

In a recent article, I argued that the environmental impact statement (EIS) requirement of the National Environmental Policy Act (NEPA) has evolved into an inadvertent penalty default rule. Government agencies have learned that they can 'bargain around' the requirement to produce a costly and dilatory EIS by redefining projects to include mitigation measures that reduce expected environmental impacts below the EIS-triggering threshold.[27] Other examples of penalty default rules embedded within federal environmental laws include the Resource Conservation and Recovery Act's 'land ban', the Clean Air Act's federal implementation plan (FIP) provision, and the Endangered Species Act's prohibition on adverse modification of endangered species habitat, coupled with the habitat conservation plan (HCP) provision allowing a partial opt-out if specified conditions are met. The paradigmatic case of an information-forcing penalty default rule, however, is California's Proposition 65. These examples are discussed in the sections that follow.

PROPOSITION 65: THE UNCERTAIN THREAT OF CIVIL LIABILITY

In 1986 California voters adopted a ballot initiative known as Proposition 65, the Safe Drinking Water and Toxic Enforcement Act,[28] requiring businesses to

[26] Ayres and Braithwaite applied the penalty default concept to regulation, but did not develop the concept in depth. See I Ayres and J Braithwaite, *Responsive Regulation: Transcending the Deregulation Debate* (New York: Oxford University of Press, 1992), 108–9 (urging regulatory contracting around either 'majoritarian' or 'penalty' default rules). See also D Farber, 'Taking Slippage Seriously: Noncompliance and Creative Compliance in Environmental Law' (1999) 23 *Harvard Environmental Law Review* 297, at 315–16 and fn 76 (suggesting that scholarship on contract penalty defaults 'might have some lessons for environmental law').

[27] See B Karkkainen, 'Toward a Smarter NEPA: Monitoring and Managing Government's Environmental Performance' (2002) 102 *Columbia Law Review* 903.

[28] Safe Drinking Water and Toxic Enforcement Act of 1986, California Health and Safety Code §§25249.5–25249.13. For a history of Proposition 65, see M Barsa, 'California's Proposition 65 and the Limits of Information Economics' (1997) 49 *Stanford Law Review* 1223.

give 'clear and reasonable warning' to anyone they expose to listed carcinogens and reproductive toxins.[29] Failure to warn subjects the violator to stiff civil penalties enforceable by the attorney general or by citizen suit,[30] unless the exposure poses 'no significant risk'.[31] Implementing regulations define 'significant risk' for carcinogens as a 1-in-100,000 risk of cancer assuming a lifetime of exposure.[32] Proposition 65 places the burden on businesses to identify and warn those exposed or, alternatively, to reduce exposures below the actionable 'significant risk' threshold.[33]

Most commentary on Proposition 65 focuses on the ubiquitous warning labels it inspires, and whether they are an effective and responsible means of informing the public about toxic hazards.[34] The evidence suggests that Proposition 65 warning labels have caused consumers to avoid some products, leading manufacturers to alter product formulations.[35]

For environmental exposures, however, the effect of Proposition 65 warnings is murkier. Environmental exposure warnings typically consist of advertisements, community-wide mailings, or signs posted at a polluting facility. The effectiveness of these means of communication is uncertain.[36] Nonetheless, informed observers argue that Proposition 65 has contributed to significant reductions in environmental releases of listed pollutants, albeit through somewhat less direct means than warnings themselves.[37]

Because environmental exposure pathways are often difficult to trace, managers of polluting facilities are not certain who is exposed, at what level, and over what spatial scale, leaving further uncertainty as to how best to warn affected persons. Proposition 65 demands 'clear and reasonable'

[29] California Health and Safety Code §25249.6 ('No person in the course of doing business shall knowingly and intentionally expose any individual to a chemical known to cause cancer or reproductive toxicity without first giving clear and reasonable warning to such individual.') Businesses with fewer than 10 employees are exempt. See *ibid.* §25249.11(b).

[30] *Ibid.* §25249.7(b)–(d) (violation subject to civil penalty of up to $2,500 per day, with action brought by Attorney General, district attorney, city prosecutor, or 'any person in the public interest').

[31] *Ibid.* §25249.10(C).

[32] 22 California Code Regs §12703(b) (defining 'no significant risk' as a level 'calculated to result in one excess case of cancer in an exposed population of 100,000, assuming lifetime exposure at the level in question').

[33] See Barsa, above n 28, at 1224, 1240–41 (describing actions by businesses to reformulate products and reduce environmental releases as to avoid Proposition 65 warnings).

[34] See, eg, Barsa, above n 28; C Rechtschaffen, 'The Warning Game: Evaluating Warnings under California's Proposition 65' (1996) 23 *Ecology Law Quarterly* 303.

[35] See R Smith, 'California Spurs Reformulated Products', *Wall Street Journal* (1 Nov 1990) at B1 (arguing Proposition 65 had a national impact as manufacturers reformulated products to avoid warning requirements); C Rechtschaffen, 'How to Reduce Lead Exposures with One Simple Statute: The Experience of Proposition 65' (1999) 29 *Environmental Law Reporter* 10581 (stating that manufacturers removed lead from many consumer products to avoid warning requirements).

[36] See Rechtschaffen, n 34 above.

[37] See D Roe, 'Toxic Chemical Control Policy: Three Unabsorbed Facts' (2002) 32 *Environmental Law Reporter* 10232 (crediting Proposition 65 with helping to reduce air emissions of carcinogens 85% from1988 to 1997, exceeding a 50% decline nationally).

warnings, but it does not define what counts as 'clear and reasonable'. Implementing regulations authorise several methods for warning of environmental exposures, including signs 'in the affected area', advertisements 'which target the affected area', and mailings to 'occupants of the affected area'.[38] But the polluter must determine the 'affected area' and choose the 'most appropriate' method under the circumstances, and the warning must be provided 'in a conspicuous manner and under such conditions as to make it likely to be read, seen or heard by an ordinary individual in the course of normal daily activity'.[39] These indefinite standards leave ample room for second-guessing and litigation over the legal adequacy of any particular warning. Polluters relying on newspaper advertisements and mailings have faced legal challenges arguing that their warnings reached too few people or targeted the wrong communities.[40] Under California law, these are questions of fact for jury determination.[41]

In principle, toxic polluters can avoid the duty to warn by reducing pollution below the 'no significant risk' threshold.[42] But the complex risk assessments necessary to make this determination typically lie beyond the scientific and technical capacity of the ordinary polluting facility, and are themselves open to dispute and legal challenge in a proceeding in which the burden of proving 'no significant risk' lies with the defendant.[43] As Proposition 65 co-author David Roe explains, 'Scientific uncertainty results in legal uncertainty for private industry'.[44]

Just when things look bleakest from the polluter's perspective, however, Proposition 65 throws a lifeline, authorising a regulatory agency, the Office of Environmental Health Hazard Assessment (OEHHA), to establish numerical thresholds that will be deemed to meet the 'no significant risk' test.[45] By voluntarily meeting these standards, polluters can avoid the duty

[38] 22 California Code Regs §12601(d).

[39] *Ibid.*

[40] See M Freund, 'Proposition 65 Enforcement: Reducing Lead Emissions in California' (1997) 10 *Tulane Environmental Law Journal* 333 (describing successful legal challenges to adequacy of warnings by posting at plant gates, newspaper publication, and mass mailings).

[41] See *Ingredient Communication Council, Inc v Lungren*, 4 Cal Rptr 2d 216 (Cal Ct App 3d Dist 1992).

[42] See California Health and Safety Code §24249.10(c) (exempting from warning requirements any 'exposure for which the person responsible can show that the exposure poses no significant risk assuming lifetime exposure at the level in question').

[43] See *Consumer Cause, Inc v Smile Care*, 91 Cal App 4th 454 (Cal Ct App 2001) (in suit for failure to warn, defendant has the burden to prove 'no significant risk' even if plaintiff offers no affirmative evidence of health risk at expected exposure levels). In *Smile Care* plaintiffs sued dentists who failed to warn patients that fillings contain mercury, a listed carcinogen. Plaintiffs offered no evidence of medical harm, but the court held that the mere allegation of failure to warn of exposure to a listed substance shifted the burden to defendants to prove 'no significant risk'.

[44] See Roe, n 37 above.

[45] See California Health and Safety Code §25249.12 (authorising state agencies to adopt implementing regulations); 22 Cal Code Regs §§12701–12711 (authorising regulatory adoption of No Significant Risk Levels ('NSRLs') for carcinogens at numerical exposure thresholds deemed to pose no significant risk).

to warn and inoculate themselves against liability. But first, the standards must be established. This gives toxic polluters in California an unusual incentive to cooperate with regulators in setting and justifying regulatory standards, and to produce and disclose credible toxicity and exposure information to advance the regulatory process.[46] Under Proposition 65, California has established nearly 300 regulatory standards for toxic pollutants at a far faster pace and with lower administrative costs than under conventional regulatory approaches, largely due to the extraordinary levels of industry cooperation engendered by Proposition 65.[47]

Proposition 65 illustrates a creative use of the penalty default approach to advance environmental regulation. Ordinarily, the regulatory agency bears the burden of producing the information necessary to justify regulation. Polluters consequently have a perverse incentive *not* to produce or reveal crucial toxicity and exposure data.[48] Proposition 65 reverses the incentive by adopting an intentionally harsh background rule—a broad and uncertain duty to warn, coupled with stiff liability for failure to warn adequately. Proposition 65 then invites polluters to 'contract around' the penalty default by cooperating in the regulatory process, first by revealing or generating information necessary to establish regulatory standards, then by 'voluntarily' reducing emissions below the numerical standards. The Proposition 65 penalty default rule is both information-forcing and action-forcing.

Critics argue that Proposition 65 is too draconian, and contrary to initial expectations it has spawned few imitators .[49] A full assessment Proposition 65's merits is beyond the scope of this chapter, but without question Proposition 65 illustrates the powerful potential of the regulatory penalty default mechanism.

REINVENTING CONVENTIONAL RULES AS PENALTY DEFAULTS: THE ENDANGERED SPECIES ACT

Recognising that 'command-and-control' regulation can be exceedingly burdensome, agencies sometimes seek to reinterpret conventional rules as

[46] See Roe, n 37 above.

[47] See *ibid*.; J Applegate, 'The Perils of Unreasonable Risk: Information, Regulatory Policy, and Toxic Substances Control' (1991) 91 *Columbia Law Review* 261, at 309–10 and fn 263; Barsa, above n 28, at 1240 (stating that California set nearly 300 regulatory standards 'without prompting a single legal challenge' leading a review panel to conclude that 'by federal standards, Proposition 65 has resulted in 100 years of progress in the areas of hazard identification, risk assessment and exposure assessment').

[48] See M Lyndon, 'Information Economics and Chemical Toxicity: Designing Laws to Produce and Use Data' (1989) 87 *Michigan Law Review* 1795.

[49] See P Stenzel, 'Right-to-Know Provisions of California's Proposition 65: The Naivete of the Delaney Clause Revisited' (1991) 15 *Harvard Environmental Law Review* 493, at 494 and fn 8 (describing early hopes of environmentalists that Proposition 65 would spread to other states); R Lovett, 'Prop 65's Non-Toxic Legacy', *Sacramento Bee* (30 Nov 1997), at Forum 1, 6 (describing how Proposition 65's perceived inflexibility and stringency led to failure of similar measures elsewhere).

penalty defaults. Broadly speaking, these are a subset of what Dan Farber calls 'affirmative slippage', a divergence between nominal regulatory requirements and actual practice, authorised by the regulatory agency in pursuit of more effective or cost-efficient regulation.[50] In an unusually bold effort to refashion conventional rules, the Clinton-era Department of the Interior dramatically expanded the use of Habitat Conservation Plans, transforming an obscure and rarely used waiver provision, §10(a) of the Endangered Species Act (ESA), into the centrepiece of endangered species and ecosystem conservation policy.

Section 9 of the ESA prohibits the 'take' of listed species of fish and wildlife.[51] The statute defines 'take' to include 'harm',[52] and by regulation 'harm' extends to adverse habitat modification that disrupts essential behaviours.[53] The result can be a blanket prohibition on economically valuable but habitat-modifying activities, such as forestry or urban development, on lands hosting endangered species.[54]

Congress amended the ESA in 1982 to create an escape hatch for landowners gripped by this sweeping prohibition. The presence of listed species of butterflies had barred developers from building new housing on San Bruno Mountain, in the densely populated San Mateo peninsula just south of San Francisco. The developers offered to scale back their development, dedicate most of the land as a habitat reserve, and undertake affirmative habitat enhancements such as removing non-native vegetation, replanting native species, and funding a permanent management programme. This plan, they argued, offered major improvements in habitat quality in exchange for small reductions in habitat acreage, producing greater net environmental benefits than the ESA-mandated 'hands-off' approach. The US Fish and Wildlife Service accepted the logic of this proposal, but lacked legal authority to strike the deal.[55] Congress then intervened, amending the statute to add a new §10(a) authorising issuance of permits for the 'incidental take' of listed species provided it would not 'appreciably reduce' the

[50] Farber, n 26 above, at 299 (defining 'affirmative slippage' and noting that some cases of 'affirmative slippage' involve penalty default rules).

[51] 16 USC §1539(a)(1)(B) (prohibiting any person to 'take' any species of fish or wildlife listed as 'endangered'); 50 CF R §§17.31(a), 17.71 (by regulation, extending prohibition on 'take' to fish and wildlife listed as 'threatened').

[52] 16 USC §1532(19) (defining 'take' to include 'harass, harm, pursue, hunt, shoot, wound, kill, trap, capture, or collect, or to attempt to engage in any such conduct').

[53] 50 CF R §17.3 (defining 'harm' to include 'significant habitat modification or degradation where it actually kills or injures wildlife by significantly impairing essential behavioral patterns, including breeding, feeding, or sheltering'); *Babbitt v Sweet Home Chapter of Communities for a Great Oregon*, 515 US 687, 691 (1997) (upholding habitat modification rule as a reasonable agency interpretation of the statute).

[54] The Fish and Wildlife Service's limited monitoring and enforcement capabilities allow many violations to proceed undetected and undeterred. See Hsu, n 14 above, at 58–59, 61; Dana, n 6 above, at 38–39.

[55] See *Friends of Endangered Species v Jantzen*, 760 F 2d 976 (9th Cir 1985).

species' prospects for survival and recovery in the wild, and provided further that the activity fall within an agency-approved Habitat Conservation Plan designed to 'mitigate and minimize' adverse ecological impacts.[56]

In enacting §10(a), Congress anticipated that similar 'win-win' opportunities would arise elsewhere, justifying regulatory variances in exchange for enhanced species protection.[57] The §10(a) waiver provision was rarely used, however. Landowners generally found the cost of producing Habitat Conservation Plans outweighed the benefits. Indefinite and highly discretionary statutory standards made permit approval uncertain, and a history of spotty §9 enforcement undercut incentive to seek permits if activities were unlikely to trigger regulatory scrutiny in any event.[58] Yet the unpredictable threat of ESA enforcement created its own complications, especially for large developers who found it difficult to arrange financing under this legal cloud.

Interior Secretary Bruce Babbitt saw the California gnatcatcher—a small and undistinguished songbird dependent on the southern California coastal sage scrub habitat, then rapidly vanishing to urban sprawl—as an opportunity to leverage a more forward-thinking ecosystems policy. Listing the gnatcatcher threatened to curb development across a broad swathe of fast-growing San Diego, Orange, and Riverside Counties, at enormous cost to landowners, developers and local governments.[59] Babbitt calculated that listing could force southern California to devise strategies to contain sprawl and forestall threats to other coastal sage-dependent species. The gambit paid off. Landowners, developers, state and local officials, conservationists and federal agents joined forces to develop ambitious regional multi-species conservation plans, setting aside large core habitat reserves and rewriting local land use rules to restrict development on the periphery of the reserves.[60]

[56] 16 USC §1540(a).

[57] See Sen Rep No 97–418, 97th Cong, 2d Sess 10 (1982) ('In some cases, the overall effect of a project may be beneficial to a species, even though some incidental taking may occur. An example is the development of some 3000 dwelling units at San Bruno Mountain near San Francisco ... Absent the development of this project, these butterfly recovery actions may well never have happened.')

[58] See K Sheldon, 'Habitat Conservation Planning: Addressing the Achilles Heel of the Endangered Species Act' (1998) 6 *New York University Environmental Law Journal* 279. Incidental take permits are not available 'as of right' but instead are discretionary. See 16 USC §1540(a) (Secretary 'may issue' permit if applicant meets statutory requirements and 'such other conditions as the Secretary may require').

[59] See M Ebbin, 'Is the Southern California Approach to Conservation Succeeding?' (1997) 24 *Ecology Law Quarterly* 695.

[60] The Southern California plans technically arose under §4(d), which authorises the Secretary to promulgate special rules to protect 'threatened' species. By avoiding a default regulation that extends the prohibition on 'take' to 'threatened' species unless a §4(d) rule provides otherwise, the gnatcatcher rule operates as the functional equivalent of a §10(a) permit. See R Fischman and J Hall-Rivera, 'A Lesson for Conservation from Pollution Control Law: Cooperative Federalism for Recovery under the Endangered Species Act' (2002) 24 *Columbia Journal of Environmental Law* 45, at 94–109.

Following the California model, Habitat Conservation Plans became a showcase of Clinton-era regulatory reinvention. Some 360 HCPs covering 30 million acres were negotiated by September 2001,[61] transforming §9 from an inflexible, uniform mandatory rule to a penalty default rule setting the baseline for bargaining toward locally tailored solutions that reconcile habitat conservation needs with economically beneficial land uses. To secure regulatory approval, regulated parties must produce detailed information on land characteristics, species counts, habitat requirements, vegetation types, and environmental stressors, and they must develop site-specific affirmative conservation plans at a level of contextual detail unlikely ever to be achieved by top-down regulatory prescription.

The de facto penalty default rule in the HCP context was designed to operate neither as a penalty nor as a default rule. Instead, §9 was intended as an ordinary mandatory rule. The consequences of that rule turned out to be so harsh, however, that it could easily serve as a penalty default when coupled with the §10(a) partial waiver provision.

THE ACCIDENTAL PENALTY DEFAULT: NEPA AND THE BURDEN OF PROCEDURE

The National Environmental Policy Act (NEPA) is one of oldest and most venerated, yet simultaneously among the most reviled of US environmental laws. It is also one of the least well understood. Most academic debate surrounding NEPA concerns the effectiveness of the Environmental Impact Statement (EIS), the encyclopaedic compendium of expected impacts and alternatives that a federal agency must produce before undertaking any action that 'significantly affects' the environment.[62] In all but the most extreme cases, however, federal agencies can avoid NEPA's EIS requirement by redefining projects to keep the expected environmental impacts below the statutory threshold of 'significant'.[63]

This strategy is known as the 'mitigated FONSI' (Finding of No Significant Impact). A mitigated FONSI allows the agency to avoid producing an EIS by adding mitigation measures to a proposed project, and then conducting a more modest inquiry known as an Environmental Assessment (EA), leading to a formal agency finding that, as mitigated, the project will

[61] See US Fish and Wildlife Service, *Habitat Conservation Plans and the Incidental Take Permitting Process: Frequently Asked Questions* (Nov 2001).

[62] See National Environmental Policy Act, 42 USC §4332(2)(c) (requiring federal agencies to 'include in every recommendation or report on proposals for legislation and other major Federal actions significantly affecting the quality of the human environment, a detailed statement by the responsible official' on environmental impacts and alternatives to the proposed action).

[63] See Karkkainen, n 27 above, at 932–36.

have 'no significant impact' on the environment. The use of mitigated FONSI has been upheld by the courts.[64]

Mitigated FONSIs appear to represent a large fractional share of the roughly 50,000 FONSIs produced annually, indicating that agencies generally find it less costly to undertake mitigation than to undergo the lengthy and cumbersome EIS process.[65] A 1993 survey concluded that 'agencies appear to rely heavily on mitigation measures to justify ... findings of no significant impact (FONSIs)'.[66]

Many environmentalists and legal scholars regard the mitigated FONSI as a dodgy way of avoiding NEPA's information production and disclosure requirements.[67] One must assume that projects proceeding under mitigated FONSIs start out above the statutory threshold of 'significant' environmental impacts—otherwise, the agency could avoid an EIS through an ordinary unmitigated FONSI. It is precisely in that terrain that an EIS is normally required to ensure 'fully informed decision-making'. But the mitigation plan used to justify a FONSI is developed without benefit of an EIS, raising concerns that the agency has not adequately considered all the environmental impacts and mitigation alternatives.[68]

Seen from another angle, however, the mitigated FONSI is just a simplified means to achieve NEPA's core objective of improving government's

[64] As one court explained,

> [A]n EIS must be prepared only when significant environmental impacts will occur as a result of the proposed action. If, however, the proposal is modified prior to implementation by adding specific mitigation measures which completely compensate for any possible adverse environmental impacts stemming from the original proposal, the statutory threshold of significant environmental effect is not crossed and an EIS is not required. (Cabinet Mountains Wilderness v. Peterson, 685 F.2d 678, 682 (DC Cir. 1982)).

[65] See A Herson, 'Project Mitigation Revisited: Most Courts Approve Findings of No Significant Impact Justified by Mitigation' (1986) 13 *Ecology Law Quarterly* 51, at 68–69 (stating that agencies 'know the EIS process involves considerably more expense and delay' than the simpler EA/mitigated FONSI procedure); E Blaug, 'Use of the Environmental Assessment by Federal Agencies in NEPA Implementation' (1993) 15 *Environmental Professional* 57, at 58 (lower cost is a leading reason agencies choose EAs instead of EISs).

[66] See Blaug, n 6 above5, at 57. Some agencies say they rarely use mitigated FONSIs, while others use them frequently. According to Blaug, nine agencies said that up to half of their EAs led to mitigated FONSIs, one said a 'majority' one 80%, and one 95%. See *ibid*. at 59.

[67] See, eg, W Rodgers, Jr, *Environmental Law* 2nd edn (St. Paul: West Publishing, 1994) at 893–94 ('[T]here always has been something suspiciously circular about the practice of mitigated FONSIs: the agencies contend with conviction that they don't have to write EISs to consider all the bad things that might happen because they already have given careful thought to, and taken precautions against, all the bad things that might happen.'); Glitzenstein, 'Project Modification: Illegitimate Circumvention of EIS Requirement or Desirable Means to Reduce Adverse Environmental Impacts?' (1982) 10 *Ecology Law Quarterly* 253, at 271–78.

[68] See P Eglick and H Hiller, 'The Myth of Mitigation under NEPA and SEPA' (1990) 20 *Environmental Law* 773, at 776; cf. M Herz, 'Parallel Universes: NEPA Lessons for the New Property' (1993) 93 *Columbia Law Review* 1668 , at 1712–13 (noting the 'inherent circularity' in requiring an EIS only if investigation reveals that environmental impacts are 'significant' so that 'only by going through the process can the agency decide whether it is necessary to go through the process').

environmental performance.[69] On this approach, the agency need identify only the most important environmental consequences of its proposed action and mitigate the harm to a 'not significant' level. By this unexpected route, the mitigated FONSI integrates environmental considerations into an early stage of project design, and produces environmentally beneficial outcomes.

To be sure, the approach is backhanded. NEPA's authors expected the information revealed in the EIS, together with political pressure produced by public disclosure, to inform the selection of mitigation measures and drive improvements in environmental performance. Instead, the formal EIS process proved so costly and cumbersome that agencies go to great lengths to avoid it, even at the price of adopting costly mitigation measures. The EIS thus becomes not the direct vehicle for improved environmental decision-making, but a de facto penalty default that applies only if the agency fails to identify a satisfactory mitigation plan.

Additional complications mar this story of inadvertent policy success, however. The statute does not require that promised mitigation measures actually be implemented, and courts have interpreted CEQ guidance on the subject as non-binding.[70] Nor are projects typically monitored to verify the accuracy of pre-decision predictions or to adjust mitigation measures in response to unexpected results.[71] Thus a mitigation plan set forth in a mitigated FONSI might not be implemented, or if implemented may be less effective than promised.

The solution is straightforward: post-project monitoring to ensure that mitigation measures are effective, coupled with 'adaptive mitigation' strategies to adjust mitigation measures as necessary.[72] So modified, NEPA could become a model penalty default regulation, imposing a burdensome—but hardly pointless—default procedure, the comprehensive Environmental

[69] See G McDonald and L Brown, 'Going Beyond Environmental Impact Assessment: Environmental Input to Planning and Design' (1995) 15 *Environmental Impact Assessment Review* 483, at 487 (stating that 'practitioners ... have found it more expedient and logical' to integrate environmental considerations into project design and planning at an early stage 'rather than waiting until the EIS report was completed ... inconveniently late in the project to make design changes'); Herson, n 6 above5, at 68 (arguing that if mitigated FONSIs prevent environmental harms, the result is 'consistent with NEPA's underlying purpose').

[70] CEQ guidance indicates that only binding mitigation measures can support a mitigated FONSI, but the guidance itself has been held non-binding. See *Cabinet Mountain Wilderness v Peterson*, 685 F.2d 678, 682–83 (DC Cir. 1982) (dismissing CEQ guidance as 'merely an informal statement, not a regulation' and 'not ... persuasive authority'). While some courts require mitigated FONSIs to be based on specific and enforceable mitigation measures, others have found a general commitment sufficient. See Rodgers, n 67 above, at 894 ('case law on mitigated FONSIs is thoroughly divided around the proposition of how firm and binding the mitigation must be to avoid an EIS').

[71] CEQ regulations recommend but do not require monitoring to verify that mitigation measures are implemented. See 40 CF R 1505.2(c).

[72] See Karkkainen, n 27 above, at 938–46 (proposing post-project monitoring and adaptive mitigation).

Impact Statement, while inviting regulated parties to avoid the penalty default by building creative and credible mitigation strategies into the project at the early planning stages.

PENALTY DEFAULT ON A TIME FUSE: THE RCRA LAND BAN 'STATUTORY HAMMER'

Frustrated by the slow pace of EPA action to regulate hazardous waste disposal, Congress amended the Resource Conservation and Recovery Act (RCRA) in 1984 to add the Land Disposal Restriction (LDR) programme, popularly known as the 'land ban'.[73] Notwithstanding its name, the land ban did not prohibit all land disposal of hazardous waste. Instead, it called for a series of phased prohibitions, unless the wastes are processed in accordance with EPA-promulgated treatment standards.

The intent of the phased prohibition was to pressure EPA to develop treatment standards by the statutory deadlines, lest the harsher default prohibitions take effect. Despite its record of inaction over the previous decade, the agency accomplished this Herculean task on time for every category of waste subject to the land ban.[74] The land ban also created powerful incentives for the hazardous waste disposal industry to produce and disclose information EPA needed to promulgate the requisite standards, and not to interfere with the standard-setting process.[75]

The land ban is often described as a 'statutory hammer', but the underlying logic is that of a regulatory penalty default on a time fuse, one that kicks in by statutory command on a date certain in default of agency action within the prescribed period.[76] Not all 'statutory hammers' have the character of penalty defaults, however. For example, some permitting schemes deem a permit to have been issued if the permitting agency fails to act on the application by a date certain.[77] Others provide that proposed rules

[73] Codified at 42 USC §§6924(d)–(m), RCRA §§3004(d)–(m). See Stewart, n 8 above, at 58 (stating the 'land ban' was enacted under perceptions of 'gross neglect of duty by EPA').

[74] See R Hill, 'An Overview of RCRA: The 'Mind-Numbing' Provisions of the Most Complicated Statute' (1991) 21 *Environmental Law Reporter* 10254 (land ban provides 'a strong incentive for EPA to develop and promulgate the required standards on time to avoid the serious disruptions in the economy that would result from an inability to legally dispose of any hazardous wastes').

[75] See M Zinn, 'Policing Environmental Regulatory Enforcement: Cooperation, Capture, and Citizen Suits' (2002) 21 *Stanford Environmental Law Journal* 81, at 114 (land ban 'made regulatory advocates of regulated firms, which hoped to forestall the land ban by encouraging EPA to adopt more palatable rules within the 32-month deadline').

[76] See S Shapiro and R Glicksman, 'Congress, the Supreme Court, and the Quiet Revolution in Administrative Law' (1988) *Duke Law Journal* 819, at 839 ('Congress has given the EPA a certain period of time to regulate; if at the end of the specified time the agency has failed to act, the 'hammer' falls, and the regulatory result set forth in the statute automatically goes into effect.')

[77] See J O'Reilly, 'Burying Caesar: Replacement of the Veterans Appeals Process is Needed to Provide Fairness to Claimants' (2001) 53 *Administrative Law Review* 223, at 250 and fn 160 (describing 'statutory hammer' schemes in which permit issues automatically in default of agency action by a specified date).

automatically take effect if the agency fails to promulgate final rules by a date certain.[78] In such cases, the agency may be indifferent to the outcome and simply allow the permit to issue (or the rule to take effect) by default without expenditure of additional agency resources. For its part, the legislature may simply want to ensure that *some* rule is in place by the specified time, and grant the agency discretion to choose between the default and an agency-devised alternative. Plainly, however, the intent and effect of the RCRA land ban was to put in place a regulatory penalty default. All available evidence indicates that it has been a highly effective device.

FORCING 'COOPERATIVE' FEDERALISM: SIPS, FIPS AND THE CLEAN AIR ACT

The Clean Air Act is founded upon a federalist division on labour.[79] Under the statute, the federal EPA establishes health-based National Ambient Air Quality Standards (NAAQS) for ubiquitous 'criteria' pollutants.[80] It is then up to the states to develop State Implementation Plans (SIPs) specifying enforceable emission limitations, monitoring requirements and enforcement programmes.[81] States have broad discretion to choose the appropriate mix of regulatory tools and to allocate the pollution reduction burden, but their SIPs must be approved by the federal EPA, which reviews them for completeness and for substantive adequacy as means to achieve national air quality standards.[82] Backstopping this 'cooperative federalism' scheme, EPA is mandated to impose a Federal Implementation Plan (FIP) in the absence of an approved SIP.[83]

The background threat of direct federal regulation is a powerful inducement for states to develop their own Clean Air Act implementation plans. The vast majority of states now operate under EPA-approved SIPs,[84] and in most cases these have led to major reductions in air pollution[85] and

[78] M Magill, 'Congressional Control over Agency Rulemaking: The Nutrition Labeling and Education Act's Hammer Provisions' (1995) 50 *Food and Drug Law Journal* 149, at 150–51 (describing statute providing that proposed rules take effect if FDA fails to promulgate final rules within a prescribed time period).

[79] See J Dwyer, 'The Practice of Federalism under the Clean Air Act' (1995) 54 *Maryland Law Review* 1183, at 1193.

[80] 42 USC §7409. The statute requires a 'primary' standard at a level 'requisite to protect the public health' *ibid.* §7409(b)(1), and a 'secondary' standard at a level 'requisite to protect the public welfare' *ibid.* §7409(b)(2), but the secondary standard is usually pegged to the primary standard.

[81] 42 USC §7410(a).

[82] *Ibid.* §7410(c).

[83] *Ibid.* §7410(c)(1)(B).

[84] See Dwyer, n 79 above, at 1198 (noting that 'the vast majority of states' develop state implementation plans because allocation of the cost of pollution reduction is 'enormously important on the state and local level').

[85] According to EPA, ambient levels of carbon monoxide fell 65% nationally between 1983 and 2002, ground-level ozone 22%, lead 94%, NO2 21%, particulate matter (PM10) 13%, and sulphur dioxide 54%, despite significant population and GDP growth. US Environmental Protection Agency, *National Air Quality and Emissions Trends Report* (2003), at 4.

substantial benefits to human health,[86] even where compliance with federal air quality standards has been less than perfect.[87]

The Clean Air Act FIP/SIP requirements clearly exhibit the architecture of a regulatory penalty default: direct federal regulation kicks in if the state fails to produce an acceptable pollution control plan. Why such a scheme? The highly technical task of setting health-based air quality standards is most efficiently assigned to a single expert (federal) agency with superior technical, administrative and fiscal capacities, eliminating redundancy of effort. States, however, are better situated to decide how to allocate the pollution control burden among sources in a local airshed, especially insofar as these affect local land use and economic development.[88] Prior to federal intervention, however, most states failed to regulate air pollution effectively.[89] The prospect of direct federal regulation under a FIP threatens loss of local control, possibly accompanied by severe economic and political consequences. The choice for the states, then, is no longer whether to regulate, but rather who will regulate. They must either try to regulate wisely and well, or leave the job to distant federal officials who may be less sensitive to local economic and political conditions. Against that background, the incentive to undertake the politically difficult challenge of regulating air pollution becomes compelling.

The courts have held that this forced cooperative federalism scheme does not violate the anti-commandeering principle of *New York v US*,[90] because it involves mere 'inducement' and not 'outright coercion' of the states.[91] As one leading commentator notes, 'Formally, at least, states always have an exit option.'[92]

[86] EPA estimates that Clean Air Act regulations save 200,000 lives and prevent 22 million lost work days annually. US Environmental Protection Agency, *The Benefits and Costs of the Clean Air Act*, 1970–90 (Oct 1997) ('Section 812 Report'). An OMB analysis found that the health benefits of EPA's major air quality programmes outweigh costs by at least 5 to 1. US Office of Management and Budget, Office of Information and Regulatory Affairs, *Informing Regulatory Decisions: 2003 Report to Congress on the Costs and Benefits of Federal Regulations* (2003), at 9 and Table 3.

[87] In 2003, 124 air quality control regions in 33 states were in non-attainment of air quality standards for at least one criteria pollutant, exposing 126 million people to substandard air quality. US Environmental Protection Agency, *National Air Quality and Emissions Trends Report* (2003) at 170, Table A-19.

[88] See D Esty, 'Revitalizing Environmental Federalism' (1996) 95 *Michigan Law Review* 570, at 614–17 (arguing that if solutions depend on 'locality-specific factors' states or local communities should decide); Dwyer, n 79 above, at 1198 ('[B]ecause air pollution regulation has a substantial impact on local economic development, states may believe they can achieve the federal goals more efficiently and with less disruption of local economies than bureaucrats who answer to headquarters in Washington, DC.')

[89] See T Page, 'The Limits of Devolution in Environmental Law' (1997) *University of Chicago Legal Forum* 527.

[90] *New York v US* 505 US 144 (1992) (striking down federal statute compelling states to adopt nuclear waste management programmes on grounds that 'Congress may not simply commandeer the legislative processes of the States').

[91] *Virginia v Browner*, 80 F 3d 869 (4th Cir 1996), at 881.

[92] Dwyer, n 79 above, at 1198.

Some critics contend that SIPs are actually one of the weak points of the Clean Air Act. EPA lacks the administrative, financial and technical capacity to fill the regulatory void if many states decline to adopt SIPs.[93] Political pressures on EPA also militate against aggressive SIP review, rendering the FIP threat weaker in practice than on paper.[94] Finally, EPA review of SIP adequacy rests largely on information supplied by the states, and may reflect incomplete pollution source inventories, uncertain air quality modelling and inadequate monitoring. Consequently, states have both the opportunity and the motive to 'game' the SIP review process with rosy air quality forecasts that may not be borne out in practice.[95]

Notwithstanding these concerns, the Clean Air Act's SIP–FIP penalty default scheme appears to be least moderately successful. It has induced most states to take responsibility for air pollution control within their boundaries, despite obvious political and financial costs. States have committed substantial legal, technical and administrative resources to the task, in most cases making far greater commitments than they would have absent the FIP incentive. By all accounts, the air is cleaner and public health better protected than prior to the Clean Air Act.

Like the RCRA land ban, the SIP–FIP scheme operates on a short time fuse: states have a statutory grace period within which to develop, submit, and win EPA approval for their SIPs, and EPA may not impose a FIP until that period expires.[96] The presumption here, as for the land ban, is that the penalty default is needed only as backup, to take effect if the party fails to undertake the desired regulatory effort. Unlike the land ban which exploits a draconian regulatory default rule, however, the operative 'penalty' in the FIP case is not the certainty of harsh regulatory outcomes, but rather political and economic uncertainty stemming from loss of local control over regulatory matters of great local significance.

STRUCTURING NEW GOVERNANCE

The foregoing examples illustrate creative uses of penalty default mechanisms in conventional environmental regulation. What has any of this to do with new governance? Properly structured, penalty default rules might be used to induce meaningful participation in locally devolved, 'place-based',

[93] See G Smith and E Grillo, 'Let's Clear the Air Once and for All: Municipal Liability for Failing to Comply with Section 110 of the Clean Air Act' 44 (1995) *Catholic University Law Review* 1103, at 1130.

[94] See R Percival *et al*, *Environmental Regulation: Law, Science and Policy* 4th edn (New York: Aspen Law and Business, 2003), at 531–32.

[95] See R Adler, 'Integrated Approaches to Water Pollution: Lessons from the Clean Air Act' (1999) 23 *Harvard Environmental Law Review* 203, at 243–45.

[96] States have three years after a NAAQS is promulgated to submit a SIP. EPA then has 12 months to approve or disapprove, and 24 months to promulgate a FIP.

collaborative, public–private hybrid new governance institutions, aimed at integrated, adaptive, experimentalist management of watersheds and other institutions.

Consider the problem of integrated watershed management. Although nationally uniform, technology-based regulations have curbed pollution from large industrial and municipal wastewater 'point' sources, the Clean Water Act (CWA) does little to address polluted run-off from diffuse 'non-point sources' like farms and city streets, so that water quality remains a problem in many lakes and streams.[97] Moreover, notwithstanding its stated objective to 'restore and maintain the chemical, physical, and biological integrity of the Nation's waters',[98] the CWA's narrow operational focus on point-source pollution control leaves aside many crucial aspects of aquatic ecosystem management, such as the degradation of wetlands and other aquatic and riparian habitats, declining populations of aquatic species, proliferation of invasive species and related ills.[99] These problems are deeply interconnected: poor water quality damages aquatic habitats and contributes to declining species populations, while the loss of riparian buffers, filtering wetlands, and filter-feeding shellfish compounds water quality problems.

Scientists, natural resource managers and environmental policy experts have long urged that law and policy be redirected toward integrated management of this entire suite of interrelated problems at watershed scales.[100] Yet despite avowals of support from the highest governmental circles to local grassroots activists, integrated watershed management remains at the periphery of US environmental policy, taking a back seat to conventional point-source regulatory controls.

A resurgent Total Maximum Daily Load (TMDL) programme in the 1990s, reinforced by a far-reaching TMDL rule proposed the Clinton administration, brought renewed hope that states might finally be compelled to address non-point source pollution and integrated watershed

[97] See R Adler, 'Addressing Barriers to Watershed Protection' (1995) 25 *Environmental Law* 973, at 990 ('Polluted runoff is the largest source of water pollution in the United States and a major source of physical and hydrological impairment and habitat loss.')

[98] Federal Water Pollution Control Act §101(a), 33 USC §1251(a).

[99] See National Research Council, *Restoration of Aquatic Ecosystems: Science, Technology, and Public Policy* (Washington, DC: National Academy Press, 1992), at 342.

[100] See National Research Council, previous n 99, at 342 (urging 'management of all significant ecological elements in a comprehensive approach ... on a watershed or other landscape scale'); Adler, n 97 above, at 977–79 (describing watershed management as a response to 'the futility of trying to solve complex, interrelated water problems through individual decisions on thousands of discrete but connected activities'). But cf. O Houck, 'TMDLs: The Resurrection of Water Quality Standards-Based Regulation under the Clean Water Act' (1997)27 *Environmental Law Reporter* 10329 at 10331–43 (arguing that integrated watershed management is impossibly complex and compares unfavourably to technology-based regulation which despite shortcomings has improved water quality).

management.[101] Under §303(d) of the CWA, states are required to identify 'impaired' waters—those not meeting water quality standards—and to establish binding caps (TMDLs) on total pollutant loadings, translatable into individual allocations for each pollution source, in each impaired water body segment.[102] TMDLs thus threaten stricter limits on pollution discharges into impaired waters than are ordinarily required under the CWA. If a state fails to produce an adequate TMDL, §303(d) requires EPA to produce a federal TMDL.[103]

Because the statute lacks firm deadlines for submission and approval of impaired waters lists and TMDLs, however, §303(d) was largely ignored by EPA and the states for many years.[104] Beginning in the1980s, a rash of citizen suits successfully advanced the theory that persistent failure to submit the required lists amounted to 'constructive submission' of inadequate lists, obligating EPA to impose TMDLs where states had failed to do so.[105]

The litigation blitz forced EPA to re-examine §303(d). Reversing course, the Clinton administration abandoned its defensive litigation posture and pursued an aggressive policy offensive, promulgating a new rule reinterpreting §303(d) to promote integrated watershed planning and requiring states to include enforceable controls on non-point sources in their TMDLs.[106] The rule—later suspended and finally withdrawn by the Bush administration[107]—would also require states to establish continuous water quality monitoring and modelling programmes, providing the basis for subsequent adjustments to TMDLs if the initial measures did not improve water quality to acceptable levels.

The Clean Water Act's TMDL requirements incorporate a 'forced cooperative federalism' penalty default scheme closely resembling the Clean Air

[101] A top EPA official explained that TMDLs 'if done properly, can inform, empower, and energize citizens, local communities and States to improve water quality at the local, watershed level. The basic information derived from a sound TMDL could liberate the creative energies of those most likely to benefit'. Testimony of GT Meham III, Assistant Administrator for Water, before the Subcommittee on Water Resources and the Environment, Committee on Transportation and Infrastructure, US House of Representatives (15 Nov 2001).

[102] 33 USC §1313(d)(1)(A) and (C).

[103] Id. §1313(d)(2).

[104] See R Glicksman, 'The Value of Agency-Forcing Citizen Suits to Enforce Nondiscretionary Duties' (2004) 10 *Widener Law Review* 353, at 373–74 (attributing inaction to EPA's emphasis on technology-based regulations and consequent lack of EPA pressure on states).

[105] See id. at 375–79. Initial lawsuits failed due to the absence of enforceable statutory deadlines. The legal breakthrough came when courts held that 'if a state fails over a long period of time to submit proposed TMDLs, this prolonged failure may amount to the "constructive submission" by that state of no TMDLs' obligating EPA to act. *Scott v City of Hammond*, 741 F 2d 992 996–97 (7th Cir 1984).

[106] See 65 Fed Reg 43,586 (13 July 2000) (final EPA rule revising requirements for states to establish and enforce Total Maximum Daily Loads (TMDLs) of pollution from point and non-point sources into impaired waters).

[107] See 66 Fed Reg 53044 (18 Oct 2001) (postponing effective date to 30 April 2003); 68 Fed Reg 13608 (19 March 2003) (withdrawing TMDL rule).

Act's SIP/FIP scheme.[108] States can be expected to develop TMDLs because they fear the uncertain political and economic consequences if they leave the job to federal regulators. In some cases, this threat appears to be working. For example, overcoming a long history of failed efforts at interstate cooperation, New York and Connecticut jointly developed and secured EPA approval for a TMDL for dissolved oxygen in Long Island Sound, incorporating phased reductions in nitrogen loadings from various categories of point and non-point sources in both states.[109]

TMDLs also embrace a second and more interesting penalty default. Developing and implementing TMDLs is costly and technically demanding, requiring comprehensive water quality and discharge data, detailed scientific information, and sophisticated hydrological and pollutant dispersal modelling capabilities that severely test the fiscal, technical and administrative capacities of most states.[110] Some argue that the resource demands of TMDLs could divert effort from other important water quality and aquatic ecosystem management initiatives. This concern led many states to oppose the Clinton EPA's aggressive TMDL rule.[111]

But the desire to avoid the costly, straightjacketing, formal TMDL process has also triggered a new round of proactive efforts to improve water quality in impaired waters. For example, the Chesapeake Bay Program—a sophisticated, basin-wide collaborative effort by EPA, the states of Maryland, Virginia and Pennsylvania, local governments, NGOs and leading private sector actors to restore aquatic ecosystem health in the nation's largest estuary—has undertaken with EPA approval a self-directed collaborative and experimental 'parallel TMDL' process to assign pollutant loads basin-wide and on a tributary-specific basis, with the goal to improve water quality to levels that would remove Bay waters and tributaries from impaired waters lists by 2010, a year before formal TMDLs are due. The Chesapeake Bay Program acknowledges that achieving this ambitious goal will require an integrated effort, including new land use policies, agricultural nutrient management planning, restoration of wetlands and riparian forest buffers, integration of groundwater and surface water management and restoration of filter-feeding oyster populations. By pre-empting the need for formal

[108] See S Birkeland, 'EPA's TMDL Program' (2001) 28 *Ecology Law Quarterly* 297, at 318–19 ('Both programs confer substantial responsibility on states to devise and implement pollution controls according to local economic and environmental conditions, within parameters set by applicable air and water quality standards' and 'EPA may exert substitution authority where a state fails to meet its statutory and regulatory obligations').

[109] See EPA Long Island Sound Office, News Release, 'EPA Takes Action to Control Nitrogen Pollution in Long Island Sound' (5 Apr 2001).

[110] See O Houck, 'The Clean Water Act TMDL Program V: Aftershock and Prelude' (2002) 32 *Environmental Law Reporter* 10385, at 10389–96.

[111] See Letter from National Governors' Association to President Clinton, 6 July 2000 (expressing governors' concerns about fiscal impact, perceived inflexibility, and onerous procedural requirements of TMDL rule).

TMDLs through proactive watershed management, Chesapeake Bay Program partners hope to preserve flexibility for ongoing experimentation and integrated approaches to ecosystem restoration and management.[112] The TMDL penalty default threat has lent discipline and a new sense of urgency to a collaborative new governance effort in the basin that has otherwise tended to advance by fits and starts.

These creative efforts may be undercut by the Bush administration's withdrawal of the Clinton-era TMDL rule, restoring the status quo ante of an ineffective predecessor rule. EPA claims to be working on new TMDL revisions to improve upon both the status quo and the Clinton-era rule,[113] but the current administration's broad retreat from environmental protection objectives suggests little cause for optimism.

For our purposes, however, the present status of the TMDL rule is less important than the regulatory mechanism it illustrates. Let us suppose the case for collaborative, integrated, experimentalist approaches to watershed management is as strong as leading scientists and natural resource managers claim. Let us also concede the sceptics' point that good intentions alone are insufficient to induce parties to undertake the costs and burdens of environmental protection and to refrain from strategic behaviour. Against those assumptions, a penalty default rule structured along the lines of the Clinton-era TMDL rule—to trigger onerous procedural and substantive requirements if flexible experimentation fails—might be a powerful spur to action. Such an approach could focus the attention of local actors squarely on objectively measurable environmental performance targets and create a sense of urgency in devising and implementing effective, locally tailored implementation strategies, while still allowing wide latitude for local institutional and policy experimentation. A well designed penalty default approach, in short, appears capable of imposing discipline, accountability, and transparency from above on locally flavoured, bottom-up, flexible new governance experimentation from below.

ADMINISTRATIVE DESTABILISATION RIGHTS: DISENTRENCHMENT FROM ABOVE

Chuck Sabel and Bill Simon recently advanced a provocative theory of 'destabilisation rights', defined as 'claims to unsettle and open up public institutions that have chronically failed to meet their obligations and that are substantially insulated from the normal processes of political accountability'.[114] On their

[112] See Chesapeake Bay Program, *Chesapeake Bay 2000:Water Quality Protection and Restoration, An Innovative Approach*.

[113] See EPA Press Release R-068, 'Final Withdrawal of 2000 TMDL Rules Takes Effect' (13 Mar 2003).

[114] Sabel and Simon, n 15 above, at 1020.

view, much recent 'public law litigation'—typically, litigation to vindicate constitutional or statutory rights allegedly violated by important public institutions like schools, prisons, police forces or various arms of the welfare state—seeks as a remedy the destabilisation and disentrenchment of the failing institutions. The aim and effect of these suits, they argue, is to 'widen the possibilities of experimentalist collaboration'[115] in crafting far-reaching institutional restructuring, while avoiding the pitfalls of a detailed, prescriptive, judicially imposed remedy. This reorientation in public law litigation, they argue, is part of a broader trend away from 'command-and-control' solutions and toward experimentalist 'new governance'. Analyzing the cases, they conclude that a prima facie case for destabilisation consists of two elements: first, a clear and persistent violation of standards, and second, 'political blockage',[116] that is, a structural defect in the conventional mechanisms of political accountability that systematically blocks movement toward a solution to the underlying problem.

All of Sabel and Simon's examples revolve around constitutional and statutory civil rights provisions,[117] but the destabilisation rights construct also has applications beyond the civil rights context. In particular, a form of *administrative* destabilisation right may prove useful as a disciplining mechanism in the context of centrally coordinated networks of locally devolved, collaborative new governance institutions—the sort of two-tiered structure of accountability contemplated by advocates of the brand of new governance styled 'democratic experimentalism'.

In their seminal work 'A Constitution of Democratic Experimentalism',[118] Dorf and Sabel argued that more was required of an effective new governance regime than simple devolution of authority to local, multi-party collaborations. Central to their experimentalist vision is the idea that local experiments should operate in parallel, allowing tailoring to local circumstances and maximising opportunities for experimentation, comparative benchmarking and horizontal diffusion of successful innovations. A critical element in their regulatory architecture is a central coordinating and monitoring body—the 'new center', as democratic experimentalists style it. The function of the new centre is to collect and pool information from varied local experiments, to distil lessons learned, to formulate (in consultation with local units) provisional minimum performance standards, and to intervene when local experiments go awry.

In a subsequent work, *Beyond Backyard Environmentalism*, Sabel and his colleagues argued that a similar structure should form the backbone of an experimentalist environmental policy, again contending that simple

[115] *Ibid.* at 1020.
[116] *Ibid.* at 1062.
[117] *Ibid.* at 1022–28 (school equity and adequacy); *ibid.* at 1029–34 (mental health); *ibid.* at 1034–43 (prisons); *ibid.* at 1043–47 (police abuse); *ibid.* at 1047–52 (housing).
[118] M Dorf and C Sabel, 'A Constitution of Democratic Experimentalism' (1998) 98 *Columbia Law Review* 267.

devolution to local collaborative initiatives was not an adequate response to the deficiencies of conventional command-style regulation. Central coordination and monitoring, they argued, were essential to ensure accountability, transparency, diffusion of successful experimental models and achievement of minimum performance objectives. More generally, managing complex ecological problems intelligently over the long run would require mechanisms for rigorous, system-wide institutional learning, which in turn depend on effective coordination of the disparate parts of the regulatory system.[119]

Reactions to these proposals ranged from enthusiasm,[120] to quizzical interest,[121] to deafening silence, to noisy rejections,[122] to vituperative *ad hominem* attacks.[123] A common theme among the critics is doubt concerning the coordinating and disciplining role of the 'new center'. How, sceptics ask, might the new regulatory centre impose discipline and minimum standards on the locally devolved parts, without falling back on the same old rigid, hierarchical, top-down, command-style rules and straightjacketing procedural formalisation of the past? Are not democratic experimentalists trying to have it both ways, to 'have our central government and reject it too?'[124]

The answer, of course, is 'Yes'. The democratic experimentalist architecture seeks to retain an important role for the regulatory centre, but to redefine that role by replacing a highly prescriptive, rule-bound, top-down management approach with one that devolves most operational authority to decentralised units but insists on transparency and accountability for performance and retains the right to intervene in the event of palpable failure at the local level.

That architecture is not difficult to envision in other organisational settings. In the 1950s, for example, many business corporations became so centralised and bureaucratic that operating units were largely reduced to carrying out detailed commands from corporate headquarters. More recently, successful and innovative corporations have adopted decentralised structures, granting operating units substantial autonomy to set their own goals, targets, work rules, production plans and so on, but nonetheless holding local units accountable to the corporate centre for financial performance, product quality, environmental outcomes and other firm-wide

[119] C Sabel, B Karkkainen and A Fung, 'Beyond Backyard Environmentalism' in J Cohen and J Rogers (eds) *Beyond Backyard Environmentalism* (Boston: Beacon Press, 2002).

[120] See, eg, O Lobel, 'The Renew Deal: The Fall of Regulation and the Rise of Governance in Contemporary Legal Thought' (2004). 89 *Minnesota Law Review* 342.

[121] See, eg, Farber, n 12 above.

[122] See, eg, S Foster, 'Environmental Justice in an Era of Devolved Collaboration' (2002) 26 *Harvard Environmental Law Review* 459.

[123] See, eg, T Lowi, 'Frontyard Propaganda' in *Beyond Backyard Environmentalism*, n 119 above, at 71 (dismissing *Beyond Backyard Environmentalism* as 'propaganda' for 'the decadent phase of classical liberalism').

[124] *Ibid*. at 70–71.

performance objectives.[125] Persistent failure at the local level to achieve satisfactory performance along one or more of these dimensions invites an intervention from headquarters—such as reassigning key managers or re-examining goals, targets and operating assumptions. We are perhaps less accustomed to government operating in this way, but at bottom the concept of coordinated decentralisation is not so difficult to understand.

My modest ambition here is to reintroduce the Sabel–Simon notion of 'destabilization rights' and adapt it to elaborate on the redefined role of the 'new center' in experimentalist regulation. The idea is that while refraining from prescribing *ex cathedra* and in excruciating detail the procedures, standards, goals, objectives, performance targets, operating principles, institutional forms and mandatory rules by which local units must operate, the 'new center' might retain the whip hand through an administrative destabilisation right over local arrangements. That is, the centre would retain the right to intervene, destabilise and disentrench local efforts that are deemed to be failing, either because they are chronically underperforming relative to expectations, or because they evidence regulatory capture, distortions arising from strategic bargaining on the part of one or more participants, or any of the other assorted procedural defects from which devolved, collaborative deliberation is said by its critics to suffer. These two elements—chronic underperformance relative to established norms, coupled with 'political blockage'—correspond to Sabel and Simon's prima facie case for a destabilisation remedy in the public law litigation context.

The crucial difference, of course, is that the sort of destabilisation right proposed here is an administrative control mechanism, not a judicial remedy for a constitutional or statutory violation. The two are not incompatible. In principle at least, we might authorise both external checks on the entire system through the judicial process and internal checks on the performance of local units through central administrative oversight and a right of destabilising administrative intervention. In either case, the destabilisation right concept captures the sort of cure that experimentalists would think appropriate in cases of chronic underperformance and process failure: disentrenchment of the failing institutional arrangements coupled with a normative critique, creating an opening for a fresh start under new arrangements that are not prescribed in detail from above, but instead are fashioned by the participants in response to the critique. In such cases, the destabilisation remedy can have powerful and far-reaching effects, and its availability can serve as a useful disciplining influence on participants in locally devolved processes.

This conception should go some way toward clarifying the relationship between the 'new center' and the local parts in democratic experimentalist theory.

[125] See W Simon, 'Toyota Jurisprudence' in this volume.

CITIZEN SUITS: DISENTRENCHMENT FROM BELOW

Most US environmental statutes authorise private citizens to bring enforcement actions against private parties who violate regulatory requirements or government officials who fail to perform mandatory duties.[126] Most citizen suits are of the first type: for example, a citizen—or an NGO on behalf of its members—might sue a polluter for violating an effluent limitation under the Clean Water Act.[127] Typically, these suits aim to secure strict enforcement of conventional regulations in circumstances where the regulatory agency has overlooked the violation, whether inadvertently or intentionally as a matter of enforcement policy.[128]

Citizen suits to compel agencies to perform nondiscretionary duties are the more interesting category for our purposes. Many of these are so-called 'deadline suits' to compel the agency to promulgate a rule, issue a report, or take some other mandatory action by a date certain specified in the statute.[129]

While some suits to enforce nondiscretionary duties may amount to little more than procedural nitpicking,[130] others have had far-reaching effects. Citizen suits have compelled agencies to launch entire new regulatory programmes like the Prevention of Significant Deterioration (PSD) regulations under the Clean Air Act[131] or the ambitious Clinton-era Total Maximum Daily Load (TMDL) rule to address water pollution exceeding established water quality standards. Endangered Species Act lawsuits have proven especially potent, occasioning large-scale reconfigurations of federal land management policies, such as the Clinton-era Northwest Forest Plan—an ambitious ecosystem management, monitoring, and restoration plan for federally owned forests in the Pacific Northwest devised in response to a series of ESA citizen suits to protect the endangered northern spotted owl and various salmon species, and incorporating elements of collaborative, watershed-based planning and adaptive management.[132] ESA citizen suits

[126] The Clean Water Act, for example, provides that

> any citizen may commence an action on his own behalf (1) against any person .... alleged to be in violation of (A) an effluent standard or limitation under this Act, or (B) an order issued by the Administrator or a State with respect to such a standard or limitation, or (2) against the Administrator where there is alleged a failure by the Administrator to perform any act or duty under this Act which is not discretionary. (Federal Water Pollution Control Act (Clean Water Act) §505(a), 33 USC §1365(a)).

[127] See Thompson, n 20 above, at 204 (stating that 'the vast majority of citizen suits to date' have sought to enforce Clean Water Act permit requirements).

[128] See *ibid*.. at 190–92 (stating that undetected violations, deferential enforcement policies and inadequate agency staffing lead to under enforcement of environmental laws).

[129] See Glicksman, n 104 above, at 356.

[130] For example, critics charge that suits to compel the Fish and Wildlife Service (FWS) to produce legally non-binding endangered species recovery plans divert scarce agency resources from more critical tasks like additional species listings.

[131] See Glicksman, n 104 above, at 358–61 (describing the history of the PSD Program).

[132] See M Blumm, 'The Amphibious Salmon: The Evolution of Ecosystem Management in the Columbia River Basin' (1997) 24 *Ecology Law Quarterly* 653, at 663–74 (describing success of ESA citizen suits in the Pacific Northwest, prompting the Clinton administration to propose the Northwest Forest Plan as an alternative to continued legal gridlock).

were also important factors motivating the launch of the Everglades restoration project,[133] the San Francisco Bay-Delta initiative[134] and other new governance arrangements for integrated and collaborative ecosystem management.

Occasionally, citizen suits have been used to thwart novel collaborative governance regimes. For example, in *Oregon Natural Resources Council v Daley*, environmentalists successfully invoked the citizen suit provision of the Endangered Species Act to undercut the Oregon Coastal Salmon Restoration Initiative, a collaborative, adaptive ecosystem management governance effort undertaken in hopes of averting Endangered Species Act listings of several salmon species. The court held that the National Marine Fisheries Service could not rely on 'future efforts' and 'voluntary measures' in the Restoration Initiative as the basis for its listing determinations.[135] Since the parties had agreed to collaborate in large measure to avoid the straightjacketing regulatory restrictions that would accompany ESA listing—that is, to avoid the regulatory penalty default of ESA regulation—the court's ruling was a major setback that, if widely followed, may bode ill for future efforts to use the penalty default threats of ESA listing to motivate voluntary participation in new governance undertakings.

On the other hand, citizen-initiated litigation has also been used to destabilize and disentrench established institutional practices and modes of governance that are palpably failing to provide integrated, place-sensitive, and adaptive environmental and natural resource management. A leading example is Mono Lake, a saline terminal lake in California's Sierra Nevada whose freshwater tributaries had been diverted by the Los Angeles Department of Water and Power (DWP) under appropriative water rights granted by the state Water Resources Board, leading to declining lake levels and ecological harm.[136] The National Audubon Society sued to force administrative reconsideration of these water diversions. The California Supreme Court held that the state had failed to adequately consider its 'public trust' obligation to manage water resources in a manner consistent with protection of ecological, recreational, and aesthetic values.[137] Recognising that reconciling

[133] See J Fumero and K Rizzardi, 'The Everglades Ecosystem: From Engineering to Litigation to Restoration' (2001) 13 *St Thomas Law Review* 667 (describing how citizen suit and intergovernmental litigation in Florida destabilised traditional water management arrangements, leading to emergence of collaborative ecosystem restoration efforts).

[134] See E Rieke, 'The Bay-Delta Accord: A Stride toward Sustainability' (1996) 67 *University of Colorado Law Review* 341.

[135] See *Oregon Natural Resources Council v Daley*, 6 F Supp 2d 1139, 1159 (1998)

[136] See C Arnold, 'Working Out an Environmental Ethic: Anniversary Lessons from Mono Lake' (2004).4 *Wyoming Law Review* 1.

[137] *National Audubon Society v Superior Court*, 658 P 2d 709 (Cal 1983). The Mono Lake litigation was decided under the common law public trust doctrine, closely linked but not identical to statutory citizen suit provisions. See R Schiller, 'Enlarging the Administrative Polity: Administrative Law and the Changing Definition of Pluralism, 1945–1970, (2000) 53 *Vanderbilt Law Review* 1389, at 1448–49 (tracing environmental citizen suit provisions to Joe Sax's earlier work on the public trust doctrine).

Los Angeles' water supply needs with the ecological needs of Mono Lake required more than a once-off reassignment of water rights, however, the court refrained from issuing a highly prescriptive remedy, instead remanding the matter to the Water Board for reconsideration while emphasising the continuing, permanent nature of its 'public trust obligation'. What eventually emerged from follow-up litigation, administrative proceedings, and negotiations among the DWP, city officials, environmentalists, state agencies and others was a collaborative conservation effort that seeks to couple water conservation measures in Los Angeles with continuous monitoring and adaptive management of Mono Lake and its tributaries, allowing freshwater diversions at adjustable levels calibrated to the ecological needs of the lake. The resulting new governance arrangement—a multi-party, intergovernmental, interagency, public-private collaboration—is widely viewed as a model for ecologically sensitive water management throughout the arid West, where water is the critical limiting resource for environmental protection, economic development, and population growth.[138]

Similarly, citizen suits under the Endangered Species Act played an important role in disentrenching failing natural resource management institutions in the Columbia River of the Pacific Northwest, opening space for collaborative, adaptive new governance approaches.[139] In other cases, such as the San Francisco Bay Delta, mere anticipation of the consequences of potential Endangered Species Act lawsuits has operated to disentrench established institutional arrangements in favour of new governance solutions[140]—a development that blurs the boundary between available but unexercised destabilisation rights and regulatory penalty defaults.

These examples suggest the possibility that future generations of citizen suit provisions might be structured with bottom-up destabilisation, disentrenchment, and penalty default effects in mind. In this way citizen suits might be adapted to play a positive role in the emergence of new governance regimes, rather than serving as the handmaiden of conventional 'command-and-control' regulation, a role for which they are much criticised.[141]

[138] See H. Doremus, 'Water, Population Growth, and Endangered Species in the West' (2001) 72 *University of Colorado Law Review* 361 ('The link between ... water, urban population growth, and the protection of endangered species, has become impossible to ignore. Water, the essential element whose limited availability defines the West, is the fulcrum of the relationship'.).

[139] J Volkman, 'The Endangered Species Act and the Ecosystem of Columbia River Salmon' (1997) 4 *Hastings West–NorthWest Journal of Environmental Law and Policy* 51.

[140] See, eg, E Rieke, n 134 above (describing emergence of the CALFED Bay-Delta Program under threat of Endangered Species Act and Clean Water Act litigation).

[141] See, eg, C Sunstein, 'What's Standing After Lujan? Of Citizen Suits, Injuries, and Article III' (1992) 91 *Michigan Law Review* 163, at 221 (describing citizen suits as 'part and parcel of a largely unsuccessful system of command-and-control regulation').

CONCLUSION

This chapter has argued that two kinds of legal rules, regulatory penalty defaults and destabilisation rights, can play a useful and possibly central role in motivating, structuring and disciplining environmental new governance institutions in the United States. Regulatory penalty default rules—harsh backstopping rules forming the default background against which regulated parties are invited to bargain for alternative solutions—already play a significant role in conventional environmental regulation. Given their information-forcing and action-forcing character, regulatory penalty default rules appear suitable for adaptation to a new role—creating incentives for parties to enter into collaborative new governance arrangements in pursuit of environmentally beneficial outcomes, so as to avoid the harsher consequences that might follow from failure to do so.

The second category, destabilisation rights, is adapted from Chuck Sabel and Bill Simon's work on the new public law litigation. This chapter has argued for employing destabilisation rights in two new governance contexts. First, destabilisation rights might operate as a top-down administrative check on local collaborative processes, allowing a central regulatory body to intervene to disentrench local institutional arrangements that are demonstrably failing to achieve stated performance objectives and are suffering process failures. Second, destabilisation rights might operate through citizen suit provisions, allowing bottom-up, citizen-initiated disentrenching interventions to destabilize demonstrably failing institutions and thereby create space for experimental alternatives.

Regulatory penalty defaults and destabilisation rights share some deep similarities. Both are legally enforceable categories of 'hard law' rules, backed by the coercive power of the state. Both seek to impose discipline and accountability on otherwise reluctant actors. But neither relies on direct regulatory prescription of mandatory rules of behaviour, thus avoiding the pitfalls of conventional 'command-and-control' style rules. Instead, these rules operate by indirection. Regulatory penalty defaults change the baseline for negotiation and make genuine cooperation more attractive than shirking or strategic bargaining. Destabilisation rights authorise interventions that upset failing institutional arrangements, but by refraining from prescribing detailed solutions they clear the way for a 'fresh start' collaborative search for novel alternatives.

Regulatory penalty defaults and destabilisation rights thus go some distance toward answering the sceptics of new governance who question how it is possible both to have discipline, accountability, central coordination and oversight, yet to avoid the pathologies of excessively prescriptive 'command-and-control' style rules.

12

Gender Equity Regimes and the Architecture of Learning

SUSAN STURM

INTRODUCTION

SCHOLARS AND PRACTITIONERS in a variety of regulatory areas have embraced 'new governance' as a promising approach to addressing complex public problems and, in the process, revitalising democracy. Proceeding under different names and with different points of emphasis,[1] this approach shares an emphasis on regulation through centrally coordinated local problem solving. Public agencies encourage local institutions to solve problems by examining their own practices in relation to common metrics and comparing themselves to their most successful peers.[2] Problem solving operates through direct involvement of affected and responsible individuals.[3] Information about performance drives this process. Its production and disclosure enables problems to be identified, performance to be compared, pressure for change to mount and the rules themselves to be revised. Public bodies coordinate, encourage and hold accountable these participatory, data-driven problem-solving processes.[4]

As a strategic response to particular problems under particular conditions, new governance is uncontroversial. Its claim as an overarching general regulatory theory, however, has provoked questions about its feasibility and

[1] The language of 'new governance' scholars includes democratic experimentalism, empowered participatory governance, a structural approach, legal pragmatism, reflexive law, and open method of coordination. For a comprehensive overview of new governance scholarship, see Orly Lobel, 'The Renew Deal: The Fall of Regulation and the Rise of Governance in Contemporary Legal Thought' (2004) 89 *Minnesota Law Review* 342.

[2] See Michael C Dorf and Charles F Sabel, 'A Constitution of Democratic Experimentalism' (1998) 98 *Columbia Law Review* 267; William Simon, 'Solving Problems v. Claiming Rights: The Pragmatist Challenge to Legal Liberalism' (2004) 46 *William and Mary Law Review* 127; Susan Sturm, 'Second Generation Employment Discrimination: A Structural Approach' (2001) 101 *Columbia Law Review* 458.

[3] See Archon Fung, *Empowered Participation: Reinventing Urban Democracy* (Princeton: Princeton University Press, 2004).

[4] Joanne Scott and David Trubek, 'Mind the Gap: Law and New Approaches to Governance in the European Union' (2002) 8 *European Law Journal* 1.

legitimacy. What motivates genuine institution learning, institutional reflection and peer comparisons? How do these informal processes produce generalisable norms that express public values? What prevents these problem-solving processes from re-inscribing the power dynamics they are intended to redress? What about institutions which resist cooperating in (or investing the resources required to enable) effective problem solving, or that lack the grass roots mobilisation and intermediary institutions that have been present in the most successful new governance examples? What prevents the legitimation of purely symbolic, process participation with limited impact on substantive outcomes?

These questions provoke deeper engagement with the mechanisms and drivers of participatory problem-solving and cross contextual learning: the 'how' and the 'where' of new governance. New governance's traction depends upon strategically located actors engaged in ongoing and insistent questioning about the adequacy of the status quo and efforts to reform it. Sustaining this mobilisation in turn requires leadership, not only at the top but also at crucial everyday decision points. New governance theory must explicitly focus on developing the culture and political economy for sustaining institutional change. It must also account for how public norms will be advanced when circumstances do not encourage robust public problem solving. These challenges map out the agenda for the next phase of new governance theory and practice: (1) developing the architecture of learning, mobilised participation, institutionalisation and accountability necessary to motivate and legitimate participatory problem solving; and (2) working through the relationships between new governance and more traditional regulatory approaches.

This agenda brings the issue of scope to the forefront. Should new governance develop incrementally, through the accumulation of successful experiments in particular regulatory contexts? Or is new governance best pursued as an overarching regulatory theory that transcends problem area and context, and that assumes constitutional dimension. To be sure, regulatory ambitiousness has elevated the visibility, impact, and stature of new governance. But it also increases the urgency of engaging with the scepticism about its viability. If public problem solving requires a set of conditions to work, then new governance theory must grapple with how those conditions can best be fostered. It must also address head-on the consequences of requiring new governance methods where those conditions do not currently exist.

This kind of knowledge requires in depth study of new governance initiatives that have produced effective problem solving, and the role of public institutions in their success. The methodology of institutional analysis provides a focus for pushing our conceptual frameworks about law and public problem solving.[5] Theoretical and practical innovation develops through

[5] See Edward L Rubin, 'The New Legal Process, The Synthesis of Discourse, and the Microanalysis of Institutions' (1996) 109 *Harvard Law Review* 1393.

in-depth examination of particular contexts in which practitioners in different institutional locations have actually integrated learning, mobilisation, accountability and institutionalisation into their participatory problem-solving systems, which have in turn been linked across institutional and political domains. This methodology permits theorising from practices that themselves reflect a tacit or sometimes articulated theory of action. It starts with an intervention in a particular context or problem, and follows the web of relationships, processes, and structures that interact to produce or prevent a normatively desirable outcome. The process of identifying experiments that institutionalise ongoing learning and change provides a small but significant response to the most sceptical of the new governance critics. If it is happening, it can happen. It also permits a critical assessment of whether and when new governance operates as intended. Finally, close examination of an ongoing new governance initiative offers an opportunity to observe and theorise about the mechanisms that enable or discourage learning, empowerment, participation and accountability, and the forms of public intervention that foster their development.

Recent public interventions to address workplace inequality provide a particularly ripe area for institutional analysis and comparison. In the United States, the problem of employment discrimination has been the focus of traditional regulatory intervention for the past 40 years. Compliance agencies, such as the Equal Employment Opportunity Commission and the Office of Federal Contracts Compliance Programs in the Department of Labor have occupied centre stage of these public interventions.[6] Recently, a different public approach to the problem has emerged to address women's marginalisation and under-participation in universities, particularly in the sciences. The primary public protagonist in this initiative is not a traditional compliance agency, but is instead the National Science Foundation (NSF), a public agency that is deeply involved in supporting scientific advancement, NSF has used its funding role to foster institutional transformation within universities aimed at increasing the long-term participation of women in the sciences. This initiative exhibits many features central to new governance approaches: self study, participatory problem solving, experimentation, benchmarking and centralised bodies providing pooling and assessment of bottom-up innovation. At least in some contexts, practitioners seemed to be grappling quite effectively with the questions of learning, mobilisation, accountability and institutionalisation that lie at the frontiers of the new governance debate.

This case study reveals the pivotal role of linkages in making new governance work. Its regulatory design built in the development of problem-solving intermediaries, as both a new institution and a new role. Problem-solving intermediaries link issues, strategies and tools which must be connected to

[6] See John Skentny, *The Ironies of Affirmative Action* (Chicago: University of Chicago Press, 1996).

address complex problems but ordinarily operate independently. These new institutions and roles have, under certain conditions, enabled organisational learning, fostered mobilisation and produced accountability that still encourages local experimentation.

The study of gender equity initiatives also offers a comparative dimension. The United States' domain specific strategy for developing new governance methods to address inequality contrasts with the more 'constitutional' strategy, reflected in the European Employment Strategy[7] and Northern Ireland's recent equality regulation,[8] and that some have argued to be inchoate in Article III–118 of the Constitutional Treaty.[9] Although the American and European examples each utilise new governance principles, they differ in their scope and institutional design. In the United States, the gender project was developed in a particular context, at the initiation of a non-regulatory public agency acting as a problem-solving intermediary, working in conjunction with scientists, activists and universities. In Europe, the regulatory regime developed through a deliberate, political process of general policy and governmental reform. Although this chapter does not itself undertake a comparison of the US and EU gender projects, it offers a framework for critically assessing the promise of constitutionalism, as compared to domain specific experimentation, as a developmental strategy for new governance.

This chapter first extrapolates from new governance critiques to generate an analytical framework for empirical investigation and theory building. It then describes and analyses the linkage strategies used in the NSF gender-in-science initiative to meet the challenges of promoting organisational learning, sustaining mobilisation and providing accountability while facilitating problem solving. Finally, it considers the implications of this contextual analysis for the relationship of new governance and constitutionalism.

THEORY ELABORATION FROM NEW GOVERNANCE CRITIQUES

The first generation of new governance work has provoked scepticism about its legitimacy and feasibility. This section develops this scepticism as an analytical framework for empirical investigation and theory development.

How does new governance enable learning and benchmarking?

New governance depends on the capacity for ongoing learning at the individual and organisational level. It proceeds through a continual process of

[7] See David M Trubek and James S Mosher, 'New Governance, Employment Policy, and the European Social Model' in Jonathan Zeitlin and David M Trubek (eds) *Governing Work and Welfare in a New Economy* (Oxford: Oxford University Press, 2003).

[8] See Christopher McCrudden, 'Mainstreaming Equality in the Governance of Northern Ireland' (1999) 22 *Fordham International Law Journal* 1696–775.

[9] See Jo Shaw, 'Mainstreaming Equality and Diversity in European Law and Policy' (unpublished manuscript).

identifying problems, generating solutions, and monitoring practices and outcomes. Error-identification requires an organisation set up to enable those who experience everyday operations to 'identify shortcomings and opportunities and to assess alternatives and make the feasible ones work'.[10] Benchmarking involves 'an exacting survey of current and promising products and processes which identifies those products and processes superior to those the company presently uses, yet are within its capacity to emulate and eventually surpass'.[11] Each of these processes presumes the capacity, opportunity, and incentive to gather, analyse, and act upon information about shortcomings in current practice. Participants must either come to the table with these skills and resources in hand or develop them as part of the problem-solving process. Problems stemming from structural arrangements, such as how decisions are made, require the capacity to identify and question underlying organisational norms.

The scholarly literature shows that many organisational environments discourage this form of institutional learning.[12] Many organisations are not set up to prompt critical assessment of day-to-day performance. Employees operate within organisational routines, which limit their perception of problems. The triggers for detecting and acting on problems do not exist in many organisations. This may be particularly true for public and non-profit organisations, which do not participate in market competition. These organisations may also have out-dated or rudimentary data systems, and lack basic knowledge about their performance. As a result, many problems go unnoticed or unreported. This organisational blindness intensifies when the organisational culture devalues the importance of the problem. Communication channels up the organisational hierarchy further muddy and filter the information flow.[13] Often, information revealing problems is 'delinked' from decision makers in a position to institute change. This is both because those with the information about problems do not participate in decision making, and because decision makers lack regular access to those who know where the problems occur. Organisations tend to decouple day-to-day activities from goals or knowledge generated outside those routines.[14]

[10] Charles F Sabel, 'Learning by Monitoring: The Institutions of Economic Development' in Neil J Smelser and Richard Swedberg (eds) *The Handbook of Economic Sociology* (1996), 149, 154

[11] Dorf and Sabel, n 2 above at 286.

[12] Chris Argyris and Donald A Schon, *Organisational Learning: A Theory of Action Perspective* (Addison Wesley 1978); Donald C Langevoort, 'Organised Illusions: A Behavioral Theory of Why Corporations Mislead Stock Market Investors and Cause Other Social Harms' (1997) 146 *University of Pennsylvania Law Review* 101.

[13] See generally Richard H Hall, *Organizations: Structures, Processes, and Outcomes* , 9th edn (Prentiss Hall, 2004).

[14] Douglas J Orton, and Karl E Weick. 'Loosely Coupled Systems: A Reconceptualization' (1990) 15 *Academy of Management Review* 203–23; Alexandra Kalev, Frank Dobbin and Erin Kelly, 'Two to Tango: Affirmative Action, Diversity Programs and Women and African-Americans in Management' (2004) (unpublished manuscript on file with author).

These observations prompt questions about whether new governance problem-solving processes can work as envisioned. If new governance simply layers problem-solving processes on top of static organisational processes, it is unlikely to provoke meaningful organisational learning or change. If, however, it increases the capacity and incentives for learning, and 'couples' learning and action, transformation seems more plausible. The capacity for organisational learning is not itself static or given; interventions can enable and motivate learning within and across organisational domains.

Thus, an important area for future inquiry involves whether and how new governance methods can develop the infrastructure and culture needed to produce effective collaborative problem solving. What triggers problem identification and analysis, particularly if market or competitive pressures do not produce these incentives or cultures? What processes, roles and structures enable learning to take place across domains outside routine communication and incentive systems? What strategies enable knowledge generated through deliberative problem solving to influence pivotal decisions and routines? And what sustains these intentionally disruptive processes over time, particularly when they cut against the grain of routines or embedded values they are intended to revise?[15]

New institutionalist and networking scholarship offers one promising direction for this inquiry. This scholarship situates organisations within the institutional environments in which they operate and that influence their practices.[16] An organisational field could include the labour markets supplying workers, regular collaborators and competitors, professional networks, advocacy groups, funders and public regulators.[17] Much of the new institutionalism scholarship has emphasised the constraints these organisational fields impose 'by forcing units in a population to resemble other units that face similar constraints'.[18] But this scholarship also suggests that organisational fields other than markets can also prompt for organisations to question and change current practice in light of peers' successes. The

[15] Organisational theorists and sociologists refer to these patterned interactions as scripts: observable, recurrent activities and patterns of interaction characteristic of a particular setting. Stephen R. Barley and Pamela Tolbert, 'Institutionalization and Structuration: Studying the Links between Action and Institution' (1997) 18 *Organization Studies* 93, 98. See also James G March and Johan P Olsen, *Rediscovering Institutions: The Organizational Basis of Politics* (Free Press, 1989).

[16] See generally W Richard Scott, 'Unpacking Institutional Arguments' in Walter W Powell and Paul J DiMaggio (eds) *The New Institutionalism in Organizational Analysis* (Chicago: University of Chicago Press, 1991), 164.

[17] DiMaggio and Powell, in a classic article, offer three such mechanisms: coercion, mimetic processes or modelling, and normative pressures. Paul DiMaggio and Walter W Powell, 'The Iron Cage Revisited: Institutional Isomorphism and Collective Rationality in Organizational Fields' (1983) 48 *American Sociological Review* 147–60.

[18] Walter W Powell, 'Expanding the Scope of Institutional Analysis' in Powell and DiMaggio, n 16 above.

question is whether and how new governance initiatives can harness the normative potential of particular environmental fields. An important focus for the next phase of new governance inquiry is documenting the practice fields shaping organisations' normative commitments, incentive structures and practice routines, the role of various organisational fields in encouraging or discouraging public problem solving, and how regulatory approaches can be linked to bootstrap the regulatory potential in existing organisational fields.

Finally, organisational scholarship has identified the role of professionals and other norm intermediaries as key carriers of ideas across organisational fields.[19] They carry ideas as they move among organisations and through participation in professional networks: conferences, workshops etc. This emphasis on identifying mediating roles played by repeat players opens up another fruitful area of inquiry about the mechanisms for transmitting usable knowledge and encouraging benchmarking across practice domains.

How does new governance mobilise effective problem solving and change?

New governance methods involve high energy, resource intensive, and sustained attention. Effective problem solving requires the capacity to determine the impact of current practices on affected individuals, and continually to renew the commitment to addressing those problems. The resulting destabilisation unsettles order and certainty, and thus cut against the grain of organisational tendencies toward stasis. Remedying problems of public significance—such as discrimination, pollution, police abuse or educational inadequacy—usually requires reallocating priorities and power. These moves often trigger resistance or backlash. Moreover, the conditions that support destabilisation—acknowledged crisis, innovative leadership, high growth etc—may not last. New governance approaches must be able to provide the architecture to sustain its processes and substantive achievements when these triggering conditions change, or to build in a process of renewing the problem-solving motivation and capacity.

Grass roots participation and transformative leadership can play a significant role in overcoming these tendencies to maintain the status quo.[20] By involving and empowering those with an interest in change—both

[19] DiMaggio and Powell, n 17 above, Lauren B Edelman, Sally Riggs Fuller, Iona Mara-Drita, 'Diversity Rhetoric and the Managerialization of Law' (2001) 106 *American Journal of Sociology*. 1589.

[20] See, eg, James S Liebman and Charles F Sabel, 'A Public Laboratory Dewey Barely Imagined: The Emerging Model of School Governance and Legal Reform' (2003). 28 *New York University Review of Law and Social Change* 183.

reform-minded insiders with direct decision-making responsibility and outsiders who are directly affected by the problematic conditions—new governance, at least in theory, builds in the mobilisation needed to sustain ongoing change. Grass roots participation is important for several reasons. First, it provides knowledge uniquely in the hands of those directly affected by the problems under consideration. These affected actors live in the convergence of multiple governance systems and experience the output of intersecting systems. They know how systems that look good on paper break down in practice, information that is essential for the root cause inquiry that is so important to effective problem solving.

This direct connection to the relevant problems gives rise to a second significant role for countervailing power in new governance regimes: applying pressure to question the adequacy of the status quo and to take action to address identified problems. The relevant outsiders occupy a position that links their fate directly to the values at stake in the regulatory project.[21] Their identity and experience in that affected position, if mobilised, connects them to the role of asking insistent questions and pressing for change needed to address persistent problems. Outsiders also, by definition, do not occupy formal positions of power, and thus are less subject to the pressures of order maintenance and power preservation that militate against destabilising the status quo.

Finally, outsider participation can provide legitimacy to new governance regimes by giving those affected by decisions a voice in determining how those problems will be addressed. This participation value lies at the core of democratic principle and fair process. Citizen participation is particularly important in addressing complex problems because most problems are not exclusively technical; they necessarily involve prioritising and choosing among values under conditions of scarce resources. For that reason, ongoing participation by those affected is needed if they are to have influence when value choices are actually made.

Grass roots participation in new governance processes also can provide a means of building a cadre of transformative leaders. These processes place change agents at the table with those in formal leadership positions, and involve them in decision making. This ongoing access multiplies the opportunities to exercise informal leadership.[22] This process expands the pool of transformative leaders able to assume formal leadership roles.

However, sceptics have questioned the legitimacy and feasibility of grass roots participation in new governance deliberations. The legitimacy questions stem from the potential lack of representativeness and accountability of

[21] See Lani Guinier and Gerald Torres, *The Miner's Canary: Enlisting Race, Resisting Power, Transforming Democracy* (Cambridge, MA: Harvard University Press, 2003); Michael Dawson, *Behind the Mule: Race and Class in African American Politics* (Princeton: Princeton University Press, 1995).

[22] See Debra E Meyerson, *Tempered Radicals: How People Use Difference to Inspire Change at Work* (Cambridge, MA: Harvard Business School Press, 2001).

those who directly participate. Some deliberative processes operate outside formal democratic institutions, and may lack methods of accountability connecting direct participants to the concerns and views of the group they represent, or providing feedback to and from those direct participants.[23] Unless accountability concerns are built into the process of selecting and working with community members, participants may not reflect the perspectives of the larger group, and may not be perceived as legitimate proxies for the views of their 'constituents'.

The feasibility questions stem from differences in power and capacity among the deliberative community. Disempowered groups may lack the resources, skills and technical knowledge to participate effectively in problem solving.[24] They may also distrust deliberative processes that are set up and run by management, and thus or filter crucial information. Time constraints, experiences of failure in the past and concerns about the risks of coming forward often discourage people from active participation. New governance scholarship is at best vague about the processes for developing a group's capacity to engage effectively and enabling them to participate as 'equals' in the deliberative process. This literature has yet to grapple fully with the challenge of constructing effective processes that also enable meaningful participation by disempowered groups, and that do not simply privilege experts.[25] What if the capacity to participate effectively does not exist at the outset or emerge in the course of participatory problem solving? Is far-reaching social equity both a goal and a precondition for its success?[26] If so, then equality is necessary for new governance to work in the first place.[27] Can new governance processes themselves generate occasions and capacity for mobilisation necessary to shape substantive agendas and to legitimate and hold accountable the problem-solving process? How can countervailing power simultaneously be harnessed through participation in the new governance processes and yet remain sufficiently 'outside' to perform its 'countervailing' function?

How does new governance provide centralised accountability without undermining local experimentation?

A third constellation of questions involves concerns about accountability. Normatively motivated change must be internalised within a particular

[23] William E Scheuerman, 'Democratic Experimentalism or Capitalist Synchronization? Critical Reflections on Directly-Deliberative Polyarchy' (2004) 17 *Canadian Journal or Law and Jurisprudence* 101, 118.

[24] Archon Fung and Erik Olin Wright, 'Thinking About Empowered Participatory Governance' in Archon Fung and Erik Olin Wright (eds) *Deepening Democracy: Institutional Innovations in Empowered Participatory Governance* (London: Verso, 2003).

[25] See Helen Hershkoff and Bennett Kingsbury, 'Crisis, Community, and Courts in Network Governance' (2003) 28 *New York University Review of Law and Social Change* 322.

[26] Joshua Cohen and Joel Rogers, 'Power and Reason' in Fung and Wright, n 24 above, at 248–53.

system, both to take account of local circumstance and to embed changes in the routines determining practice. But without sources of external pressure, accountability and support, internally motivated change can be fleeting, fragile and simply absent in the domains most in need of reform. New governance approaches look to public bodies to provide centralised accountability by (1) inducing and supporting deliberative problem solving; (2) requiring the adoption of process norms and local experimentation; (3) devising and propagating common metrics for assessing and comparing outcomes; (4) creating incentives for these institutions to make process and performance information available and to compare their performance with peer institutions; (5) pooling information from local problem solving; and (6) monitoring performance and inducing improvement.[28] New governance theory elaborates the role of judicial and regulatory intervention in supplying the necessary architecture and incentives for institutional learning and cross-institutional comparisons in problematic private[29] and public institutions.[30] This process is designed to induce local actors to produce diagnostic standards and information about institutional practices in relation to those standards, which simultaneously enables local problem solving and central monitoring and accountability. New governance presupposes public agencies' capacity to perform this function.

But creating public agencies that can actually perform these roles is easier said than done. The process of influencing local practice does not emerge simply by creating a system that requires institutions to interact with a central body. Indeed, new institutionalism and implementation scholarship shows that local institutions can be quite effective in defusing the impact of external bodies, particularly regulatory actors, on their core practices.[31] Without a centralised norm that is creating or leveraging capacity and motivation, only the pioneers will progress. But imposing deliberative processes and performance standards in domains lacking the features necessary to relate the performance standards to learning goals can have perverse effects, produce purely symbolic compliance, and even undercut the capacity to change.[32]

[27] Scheuerman, n 23 above, at 118.

[28] See sources cited in n 2, above.

[29] Sturm, n 2 above.

[30] Charles F Sabel and William Simon, 'Destabilization Rights: How Public Law Litigation Succeeds' (2004) 117 *Harvard Law Review* 1015.

[31] *See* William Clune, 'A Political Model of Implementation and the Implications of the Model for Public Policy, Research, and the Changing Role of Lawyers' (1983) 69 *Iowa Law Review* 47; Lauren B Edelman, Howard S Erlanger and John Lande, 'Internal Dispute Resolution: The Transformation of Civil Rights in the Workplace' (1993) 27 *Law and Society Review* 497, 500 (showing how symbolic legitimation can occur through developing rituals of legality that do not in fact influence practices).

[32] See Kimberly D Krawiec, 'Cosmetic Compliance and the Failure of Negotiated Governance' (2003) 81 *Washington University Law Quarterly* 487.

Public regulatory agencies face serious challenges in obtaining necessary information, building cooperative relationships, and developing communities of practice among peer institutions. Local organisations may not produce reliable information, particularly about the cultural and institutional dynamics that prevent change. Centralised organisations may lack sufficient cultural fluency to decipher the adequacy and reliability of the information they do receive. They may also face resistance to any external oversight of local decision making. To facilitate a learning community, these institutions must be viewed as legitimate conveners of peer interaction. Public interventions justified by failure may thwart the necessary openness and engagement for collaborative problem solving to work. If external accountability standards are imposed on organizations with inadequate, systems with low internal accountability they could discourage experimentation and produce perverse incentives and symbolic compliance.[33] Will public institutions, particularly the lower courts, actually assess the adequacy of problem-solving processes, or will they defer to the decisions of the institutions they are supposed to monitor, thereby legitimating purely symbolic processes?[34] Compliance continues to play a much needed role in dislodging resistant actors who are violating basic public norms. But regulatory agencies have internalised a compliance culture, which complicates their capacity to operate effectively as facilitators of public problem solving.

Public agencies also face considerable obstacles in developing common performance metrics that will simultaneously prompt local experimentation and provide accountability.New governance's potential as a form of public normative elaboration hinges on the efficacy of these performance metrics. It is crucial that they measure what is actually valued, and give information revealing where the problems lie and why they persist. But the relationship of these metrics to desired practice and local innovation often remains ambiguous at best. One concern is that the aspects of performance most amenable to quantitative metrics may not be those most important to learning, but will nonetheless assume priority simply because they are measured.[35] Quantitative metrics often point to where problems are occurring, but not why they are occurring. In a context of mobilised public engagement and ongoing problem solving, these measures can prompt further investigation into the root causes. Without the infrastructure and activism needed to

[33] This is the central point of Richard Elmore's friendly critique of Liebman and Sabel's defence of the No Child Left Behind Act as an example of experimentalist regulation. See Richard Elmore, 'Details, Details, Details' (2003) *New York University Review of Law and Social Change* 315.

[34] This is a core concern levelled at the structural approach to second generation employment discrimination by new institutionalists. See, eg, Edelman *et al*, n 31 above; Krawiec, n 32 above.

[35] See Richard Elmore, 'Details, Details, Details' (2003) 29 *New York University Review of Law and Social Change* 315.

contextualise quantitative metrics so that they trigger self-diagnosis and remediation, however, performance standards can operate like rigid rules.[36] The localities most in need of improvement may be most vulnerable to this dynamic.

These learning, mobilisation and accountability questions highlight where further theoretical and empirical work is needed to develop new governance's potential—and to understand its limits—as a regulatory approach. They also provide concrete direction for empirical investigation by identifying the areas where careful examination and analysis will push current boundaries in our understanding. The chapter now applies this analytical framework to a case study of NSF's gender equity initiative in academic science.

THE GENDER PROBLEM IN ACADEMIC SCIENCE: ESTABLISHING THE NEED FOR A MULTI-DIMENSIONAL APPROACH

Hundreds of studies have documented the fact of women's under-participation in university faculties.[37]

> Despite advances made in the proportion of women choosing to pursue science and engineering careers, women continue to be significantly underrepresented in almost all science and engineering fields, constituting only approximately 22%of the science and engineering workforce at large, and less than 20% of science and engineering faculty in 4-year colleges and universities.[38]

Until recently, public interventions have produced reports, discrete programmes and new institutional positions but little long-lasting change or generalised impact. As a first step in assessing new initiatives, it is important to understand why gender inequality has proven so difficult to remedy through conventional administrative, judicial and political interventions.

The dynamics contributing to faculty women's under-participation are complex and multi-dimensional, for a variety of reasons. First, gender inequity in universities takes variable forms, ranging from the structural to

[36] See Gordon Whitman, 'Making Accountability Work' (2003) 29 *New York University Review of Law and Social Change* 361.

[37] See <http://www7.nationalacademies.org/cwse/gender_faculty_links.html>.

[38] NSF ADVANCE, *Increasing the Participation and Advancement of Women in Academic Science and Engineering Careers*, Program Solicitation NSF 02–121 (2002). At MIT, for example, the small number of women faculty in the School of Science (15 tenured women vs 197 tenured men in 1994) had remained unchanged for at least 10 and possibly 20 years. *Reports of the Committees on the Status of Women Faculty at MIT*, <http://web.mit.edu/faculty/reports/> (March 2002) at 3.

the cognitive to the interactive to the intentional.[39] Alongside these more subtle and structural forms of gender bias, blatant forms of exclusion or unequal treatment, of the type that typified women's experience in the late 1960's, does continue to occur in some departments and universities.[40] These differences in approach require diverse strategies to reach the relevant actors, incentives, and dynamics.

Second, the dynamics producing gender bias and under-participation operate on multiple levels. Decisions reproducing gender bias operate at the level of the organisation, but are also sustained by broader cultural and practice fields. Women are trained in and recruited from different institutions. Departmental decision makers also interact with their counterparts in other institutions, as well as in professional networks that both cooperate and compete in field development. Even within organisations, gender bias involves interactions across multiple levels of university interaction. Practices implicating women's participation are both highly decentralised and interconnected with those of other departments and the central university. [41] The decisions and practices reproducing marginalisation are a product of culture.[42] Transforming these patterns requires multi-level intervention at the level of underlying assumptions, institutional behaviours, processes and organisational fields.[43]

Third, the conduct contributing to women's under-participation is diffuse in time, place and manner. Large gaps in current status result from the accumulation of small differences.[44] These differences arise in a wide range of decisions that shape the trajectory of a faculty member's career: providing mentorship, defining the applicant pool, evaluating candidates, building research teams, constructing informal professional networks, inviting speakers, assigning teaching and committee responsibilities, negotiating salaries, allocating resources and selecting departmental and university leadership. Many people and institutions may participate in the production of these small treatment differentials. They can occur within a particular department, within the larger university or across a research field. A response

[39] For an excellent summary of the issues and the voluminous literature, see Virginia Valian, *Why So Slow: The Advancement of Women* (MIT Press, 1999).

[40] See, eg, *Jew v University of Iowa*, 749 F Supp. 946 (D Iowa, 1990); *A Study of the Status of Women Faculty in the Sciences at MIT*, <http://web.mit.edu/fnl/women/women.pdf>.

[41] Robert Birnbaum, *How Colleges Work: The Cybernetics of Academic Organization and Leadership* (San Francisco: Jossey-Bass Publishers, 1988), 14–21.

[42] Edgar H Schein, *Organizational Culture and Leadership*, 3rd edn (San Francisco: Jossey Bass, 2004).

[43] Cathy A Trower, 'Assessing and Evaluating Impact', presentation at NSF ADVANCE National Conference, April 20 2004, available at <http://www.advance.gatech.edu/2004conf/3a_trower.ppt>.

[44] See Jonathan Cole and B Singer, 'A Theory of Limited Differences: Explaining the Productivity Puzzle in Science' in H Zukerman, JR Cole and JT Bruer (eds) *The Outer Circle: Women in the Scientific Community* (New Haven, CT: Yale University Press, 1991); Valian, n 39 above.

directed only at the problem's visible manifestation will not necessarily reach the series of decision points that combine to produce persistent inequality.

Fourth, gender bias is difficult to detect at the level of the individual, except in its most egregious form. Because it is often automatic or unconscious, those involved in it do not necessarily know of their bias. Gender bias often interacts with other motivations and factors; it is only through observing patterns over time that gender's role becomes visible.[45] Those who experience bias may not themselves understand their experiences in relation to gender. Even if they do, they may see their experience as unusual or unique, or simply not worth the risk or trouble that might accompany an individual complaint. They may also resist claiming gender as a public identity or explanation for their status.[46]

Fifth, gender bias is linked with and yet distinct from other problems with governance, decision making, participation and bias. The participation of people of colour on faculties remains extremely low, for both reasons common to gender marginalisation and for reasons that are distinctive to the dynamics of racial and ethnic inequality. Faculty hiring, promotion and governance practices can be problematic and unfair in ways that may be experienced more acutely by women but that have far broader effects. Gender bias is integrated with and often results from inadequate organisational systems and conflict resolution processes. Some of the dynamics affecting women's participation also affect universities' capacity to adapt to other complex problems, such as the rigidity of disciplines and their resistance to interdisciplinarity and collaborative scholarship, and their undervaluation of teaching.

Finally, gender equity initiatives are deeply interconnected with and dependent upon other governance and regulatory systems both inside and outside the university. They depend upon the participation of university leaders who have broader responsibility for the governance of their domains, and who treat gender equity as one of a much larger set of values and concerns. Those involved in gender advocacy are not focused exclusively on questions of faculty participation, and are also involved in addressing broader constituencies both within the university environment and in the larger social environment. Their relationships with broader professional, regulatory and advocacy constituencies affect their approach to gender equity issues arising within the university context.[47]

[45] *Ibid.*; Joyce Fletcher, *Disappearing Acts: Gender, Power, and Relational Practice at Work* (Cambridge, MA: MIT Press, 2001).

[46] Massachusetts Institute of Technology, *A Study on the Status of Women Faculty in Science at MIT*, <http://web/mit/edu/fn1/women//women.html> (March 1999) 10–11 (hereinafter 'MIT 1999 Report').

[47] See Mark Suchman and Lauren Edelman, 'Legal Rational Myths: The New Instituionalism and the Law and Society Tradition' (1996) 21 *Law and Social Inquiry* 903, 905.

Gender bias is thus a multi-dimensional problem. Its remediation requires operating both deeply within particular contexts (to get at the micro-level and cumulative interactions) and broadly across contexts (to enable the reworking of the environmental conditions and incentives that shape internal practices). Multi-dimensional problems require multi-dimensional solutions. Particular programmes that work in a particular context must be sustained over time and connected with other programmes that influence the overall gender dynamics. This requires a sustained institutional change strategy that bridges the different interventions needed to change culture. The next section introduces the NSF ADVANCE initiative as a form of public problem solving doing just that.

INSTITUTIONAL INTERMEDIARIES: A NEW PUBLIC APPROACH TO GENDER EQUITY

The National Science Foundation's ADVANCE exemplifies a new approach to the goal of increasing the participation and advancement of women in academic science and engineering careers.[48] This section describes NSF's role as an institutional intermediary enabling remediation of complex problems cutting across boundaries. It also documents the development of problem-solving intermediaries within the University of Michigan's ADVANCE Program which, like many other ADVANCE institutions, mirrors NSF's bridge building strategy.

NSF as national institutional intermediary

NSF is an independent federal agency that 'promotes and advances scientific progress in the United States by competitively awarding grants and cooperative agreements for research and education in the sciences, mathematics and engineering'.[49] A major supporter of academic science, the agency resists the label of regulator, notwithstanding its considerable impact on the

[48] The National Science Foundation is an independent federal agency created by the National Science to 'promote the progress of science' and 'advance the national health, prosperity, and welfare' (Foundation Act of 1950, as amended, 42 USC §§ 1861–75). NSF funds research and education through grants and cooperative agreements with universities and colleges, school systems, business, informal science associations and other research organisations. For a description of NSF, see http://www.nsf.gov/od/lpa/news/publicat/nsf04009/intro/start.htm.

[49] ADVANCE, *Increasing the Participation and Advancement of Women in Academic Science and Engineering Careers*, Program Solicitation NSF 05–584<http://www.nsf.gov/pubs/2005/nsf05584/nsf05584.pdf>. 'With an annual budget of about $5.5 billion, we are the funding source for approximately 20 percent of all federally supported basic research conducted by America's colleges and universities. In many fields such as mathematics, computer science and the social sciences, NSF is the major source of federal backing.'<http://www.nsf.gov/about/glance.jsp>.

practices of the universities it funds. NSF operates primarily as a grant-making rather than a compliance agency, although as such it does have responsibilities for monitoring compliance with legal requirements concerning diversity.[50] The agency has significant and ongoing involvement in the core work of the organisations it seeks to influence. NSF's goal is 'to support the people, ideas and tools that together make discovery possible'.[51]

NSF's involvement with gender issues stems from its general capacity-building relationship with universities. From its inception, NSF has emphasised workforce development as integral to its goal of supporting scientific discovery and advancement. NSF uses scientific inquiry as the overarching methodology for all of its work, including its project to advance women's participation. Thus, neither gender equity nor compliance structures NSF's overall involvement with universities. NSF's gender agenda grows out of its larger commitment to advancing science through developing the workforce. Through its grant-making power, NSF uses its access, resources and legitimacy to promote environments in which women and men will succeed as scientists.

NSF's role is in part a normative one. NSF puts gender, as well as race, on the table as a legitimate value integrally connected to the larger goal of advancing science.[52] It legitimates gender as a normative enterprise through science's language and method, as well as its own reputation for rigor and merit-based decision making. NSF has achieved the status of a brand signifying merit and organisational excellence.[53] It has harnessed its reputation for rigour and scientific method to legitimating gender equity as a value.

[50] Government Accounting Office, Women's Participation in the Sciences has Increased, but Agencies Need to Do More to Assure Compliance with Title IX <http://www.gao.gov/new.items/d04639.pdf> at 11 (July 2004).

[51] *Ibid.*

[52] The argument proceeds as follows: Excellence in discovery and innovation in science and engineering derives from an ample and well-educated work force. Global competition is intensifying such that the United States may not be able to rely on the international labour market to fill unmet skill needs. Domestic talent is likely to decline unless the Nation intervenes to improve success of scientists from all demographic groups, especially those that have been underrepresented in scientific and engineering careers. That means taking steps to increase the successful participation of women and people of colour. National Science Board, *The Science and Engineering Workforce: Realizing America's Potential* (14 Aug 2003) available at <http://www.nsf.gov/nsb/documents/2003/nsb0369/nsb0369.pdf>.

[53]

> The 'NSF brand' represents merit-reviewed excellence; openness and inclusiveness; inspiring, pace-setting research at the constantly-changing frontier; and a commitment to a free marketplace of ideas that spans ethnic, social, economic and geographic boundaries. The Foundation strives to be influential and agile, serving as a creative catalyst for change. Finally, the 'NSF brand' represents accountability, building and maintaining the public trust. ('The Promotion of Excellence in Research: the Experience of the National Science Foundation', remarks of Joseph Bordogna, available at <http://www.nsf.gov/news/speeches/bordogna/05/jb050408_frenchamerica.jsp>).

High quality research establishes the need to address gender under-participation as a strategic, as well as a moral imperative. Although a history of deliberate gender exclusion certainly characterises many universities, NSF articulates forward-looking goals premised on how current conditions perpetuate under-participation and why eliminating these barriers will advance scientific priorities.

NSF's role is also distinctive because it has focused on creating institutional environments that support women's advancement, rather than focusing solely on advancing the careers of individual women. NSF developed this strategy through learning from its own failures, a methodology that it subsequently built into the ADVANCE Program. Until the late 1990's NSF encouraged women's increased participation primarily through individual support helping women with grants at pivotal stages of their careers. Prompted in part by the MIT report, NSF undertook an analysis of its gender programmes and determined that its current strategy was not making a dent in the problem.

> We noticed that people getting grants renewed and renewed. We had a cacophony of programs for women. We were not getting any critical mass. We were having a small impact. [54]

NSF concluded that it would be difficult to enable women to advance without changing the institutional environments that shaped their interests and opportunities.

This analysis led NSF to adopt ADVANCE—a foundation-wide effort to increase the participation and advancement of women in academic science and engineering careers. NSF announced that it would fund initiatives to change university culture through its 'Institutional Transformation Awards'. These awards support innovative and comprehensive programmes for institution-wide change. NSF ADVANCE does not prescribe particular programmes, strategies, or outcomes. It instead promotes a methodology for strategically connecting knowledge and action to address identified problems. NSF does this through supporting strategies, institutions and roles that enable informed problem solving to occur at the point when it can influence decision making.

The NSF builds institutional analysis and knowledge-sharing into the core of its gender initiative, based on the premise that gender under-participation must be understood if it is to be effectively addressed. ADVANCE's guidelines established clear expectations that grantees will develop programmes, priorities and policy through systematic inquiry. This approach includes inquiry (1) demographic studies about the status of women's participation at the institution, required both by base line studies at the outset of the grant term and ongoing data according to 12

[54] Interview with NSF Deputy Director, 17 March 2004.

indicators[55]; (2) self-analysis and academic research on the dynamics causing gender bias and preventing and enabling institutional change; (3) benchmarking analyses of what other institutions know, both about the scope and nature of gender bias in their own institutions and, more importantly, about programmatic and strategic responses that have worked; and (4) evaluation of the impact of different interventions, including ongoing programme evaluation and feedback.[56]

NSF's public intermediary role works through the operation of three key factors: reciprocity in its relationship with grantees, a capacity building orientation and leveraging its central location within a pre-existing university network and practice community.

Reciprocity

NSF structures its grantee relationship in terms of mutual responsibility and mutual benefit, thus creating conditions permitting the development of trust which in turn necessary to fosters the risk taking necessary to identify and address gender issues.[57] NSF's position and philosophy opens the possibility of working collaboratively with grantees specifically and universities more generally. NSF programme officers come from the university community and many will return after their term at NSF ends. From the outset, NSF invites interaction with prospective grantees as part of the grant application process. It also encourages information sharing among prospective and current grantees by articulating expectations in the grant solicitation that new grants will build on the efforts of prior grant recipients.

NSF ADVANCE operates through negotiated agreements that structure what those in the network refer to as a collaboratory—an ongoing network of experimentation and knowledge-sharing among NSF and its grantees.

[55] The following NSF guidelines for data collection shall serve as the model for annual data collection and reporting for annual reports of progress for year 2, 3, and 4 of the award:
Number and percent of women faculty in science/engineering by department
Number and percent of women in tenure-line positions by rank and department
Tenure promotion outcome by gender
Years in rank by gender
Time at institution and Attrition by gender
Number of women in S&E who are in non-tenure-track positions (teaching and research)
Number and percent of women scientists and engineers in administrative positions
Number and percent of women S&E faculty in endowed/named chairs
Number and percent of women S&E faculty on promotion and tenure committees
Salary of S&E faculty by gender (controlling for department, rank, and years in rank)
Space allocation of S&E faculty by gender (with additional controls such as dept., etc.): baseline and year 5
Start-up packages of newly hired S&E faculty by gender (with additional controls such as field/department, rank, etc.)

[56] ADVANCE, Program Solicitation NSF 05–584, n 49 above.

[57] See Charles Sabel, 'Studied Trust, 'Building New Forms of Cooperation in a Volatile Economy' (1993) 46 *Human Relations* 1133.

Collaboration agreements operate like a constitution for the interactions between NSF and its grantees, and among the grantees themselves. They define reciprocal responsibilities for both NSF and those it funds. NSF and grantees commit to shared goals and mutual responsibilities for information gathering, standard setting, evaluation and monitoring, and sharing knowledge with the field. Grantees agree to set up the institutional infrastructure needed to accomplish their proposed programmes, gather necessary data, evaluate their progress, work cooperatively with evaluators and monitors, work closely with NSF and other grantees, and disseminate their results and best practices. NSF assumes 'major responsibility for providing general oversight and monitoring to help assure effective performance and administration, as well as coordination of all the ADVANCE Institutional Transformation programmes as part of an initiative designed to achieve national science and engineering workforce goals'.[58] These responsibilities include holding ADVANCE meetings, coordinating pertinent information regularly among grantees, offering technical advice and guidance and providing feedback to awardees based on reports, periodic site visits and 'the many contacts and interchanges involved in the monitoring'.

NSF's method of developing quantitative indicators to establish the basis for data gathering and evaluation illustrates its collaborative stance. The agency views quantitative indicators as necessary to track progress, enable comparability across institutions and signal problem areas warranting greater attention. It was important from the outset that these indicators reflect the best available understanding of the types of decisions that needed to be tracked, as well as the realistic possibilities of obtaining the data. So, NSF brought the grantees together to brainstorm with NSF staff about what those measures should be. The group then had to justify to NSF programme staff the indicators thus identified. NSF and grantees continue to think about revising these indicators, and one of the grantees has undertaken a major research project, with NSF support and broad grantee participation, to refine common indicators that enable comparability across institutions and also enable tailoring to specific context.

Programme officers are also in a position to work through problems and issues that arise over the course of the grant. This enables a working relationship to develop. Many grantees communicate regularly with the NSF programme officer and staff, and rely on NSF to help them work through difficult problems or to enlist additional support. Programme staff are themselves bound by the ethic of data-based evaluation. Both NSF and grantees are subject to outside review and are accountable to NSF oversight bodies. This provides the framework to develop a working relationship within the context of accountability, which in turn provides a context permitting more formal evaluation without necessarily destroying the trust relationship needed for future problem solving

[58] Draft Collaboration Agreement.

Capacity building

Unlike the typical regulatory relationship, universities seek out contact with NSF ADVANCE. This is because NSF brings concrete benefits to the table in the form of resources, expertise and legitimacy. NSF's monitoring role is linked to capacity building: developing adequate knowledge, incentives and institutional infrastructure so that universities can tackle the difficult problem of increasing women's participation. This capacity-building emphasis differs from a compliance orientation, which focuses on evaluating whether current practices comply with affirmative action and anti-discrimination requirements. A capacity-building approach treats data gathering and monitoring as a form of learning.[59] As with any complex problem warranting NSF's attention, learning is needed to understand and address gender equity.

NSF focuses explicitly on building the capacity of universities to understand and address gender under-participation. Grantees must develop the organisational infrastructure needed to implement the grant as part of the approval process. They also commit to investing institutional resources to developing the infrastructure to sustain these projects over the long run. This requirement prompts change even within institutions that do not receive funding. Unsuccessful grantees report that participating in the application process itself jump-started a change process within the university. Grantees also agree to participate in a learning community consisting of other grantees as well as interested non-grantees who participate in meetings, web exchanges and networks. They commit to maintaining a public website as part of a 'dissemination mechanism' and participate in reverse site visits and grantee meetings.[60] NSF encourages grantees to develop partnerships with industry, government, professional societies and other not-for-profit organisations.[61]

This capacity-building orientation affects the meaning of failure, to both NSF and to its grantees. Failures and errors serve a positive role. They provide the basis for obtaining a grant in the first place, by identifying baseline conditions justifying the grant award. They produce information about where the system is failing. They also provide the necessary trigger for action and for increasing support to take that action. Disclosing problems does not increase the risk of being targeted for sanctions. It instead identifies the locations where additional knowledge, resources and attention are

[59] See Sabel, n 10 above.

[60] ADVANCE: FAQs for Institutional Transformation Proposals, NSF 02-126, 1. ADVANCE grantee websites are available at <http://www.nsf.gov/home/crssprgm/advance> (last visited 8 July 2004).

[61] ADVANCE, Program Solicitation NSF 05–584, n 49 above, at 16. With respect to the identity of 'project partners', the Program Solicitation mentioned that '[p]artnerships involving industry, government, professional societies and other not-for-profit organizations are encouraged but not required'. ADVANCE, Program Solicitation NSF 05–584, n 49 above, at 4.

needed. So, for example, NSF's third year review of the University of Michigan found considerable progress in hiring, but high attrition rates of senior faculty which undercut the impact of this progress. NSF's response was not to threaten sanctions but instead to focus attention on why people leave and how the programme needed to expand its focus to track and respond proactively to these challenges. This response prompted increased support and encouragement from NSF. The university's capacity to learn from failure was itself a sign of success. This 'failure theory of success' reduces the risk and increases the rewards associated with identifying problems. The prospect of benefiting from data gathering and monitoring increases the willingness to gather information necessary to identify problems and to share that information with NSF. This is in contrast to a compliance framework, where failure prompts increased monitoring or sanctions and thus discourages genuine self-evaluation.

The capacity building orientation also provides NSF with a richer, more varied range of incentives with which to influence conduct. NSF provides substantial resources, expertise and contacts to enable institutions to address the problem of women's under-participation. NSF's role in developing data-gathering capacity is one example:

> Principal investigators knew they'd be asking for data that would be difficult for them to get- especially given that these may be people without the standing to get the kind of information they need (faculty asking for tenure data, etc.). NSF needed to back up their requirements with some kind of ongoing relationship. The bigger, more systemic programs at NSF are all done this way.[62]

In addition, NSF provides expertise and access to the most current tools available to address gender in science, including policies, programmes, strategies, research analyses and protocols. NSF programme officers know the people in the field who know the most about particular issues, and provide grantees with access to those experts. This wide array of tools creates strong incentives for universities to interact with NSF. It also provides NSF with flexibility and variation in its use of incentives and accountability. A 4 million dollar grant certainly provides universities with considerable incentive to open up lines of communication and work closely with the agency. NSF monitors how the money is spent and whether grantees are fulfilling the commitments made at the outset of the grant relationship. Departure from the commitments in the cooperative agreement must receive written approval from the NSF programme officer. NSF also requires outside review. This monitoring role brings with it the possibility of holding back funds if these commitments are not honoured. Information gathering is thus about improving 'knowledge people, and tools' generally and gender inclusiveness particularly.

[62] Interview with NSF Program Director, 17 March 2004.

Leveraging pre-existing networks and practice communities

The question remains, does all of this capacity and relationship building with particular institutions advance the field more generally? .How does NSF affect the many institutions that unsuccessfully apply for funding or do not even apply? The answer lies with NSF's location within a thick network of pre-existing relationships among universities. Universities interact regularly with each other completely apart from NSF's role. They compete with each other for students, faculty, funding and status. They cooperate with each other to share research, knowledge and strategies. They are part of varied professional and disciplinary networks that regularly meet and share research and strategies. Universities already have incentives to pay attention to the practices and outcomes of other universities. They also meet regularly in the course of their ongoing work.

NSF piggy backs on these pre-existing competitive and cooperative relationships. Apart from its gender role, NSF is located in the middle of these communities of practice. It is 'a central clearing house for the collection, interpretation and analysis of data on scientific and technical resources in the United States'.[63] It participates in these professional networks, and supports many of their activities. Universities thus pay attention to the activities of other NSF grantees because they cannot afford not to keep up with their competitors. So, if the University of Michigan out-competes Stanford in recruiting top flight scientists who happen to be women, Stanford sits up and takes notice. Universities also pay attention because NSF stands for quality and rigour. It regularly sets and then revises standards of practice through its grant-making activities. Its ADVANCE project simply leverages that role.

By leveraging pre-existing relationships, NSF can thus have an impact far beyond the institutions it actually funds. The information disseminated about what works and what does not work has a natural audience of highly attentive consumers with independent motivation to learn from and outdo each other. NSF also has developed collaborative relationships with other institutional intermediaries that use and support ADVANCE's work.

This model of leveraging relationships is mirrored in ADVANCE's approach to grant-making. Grant applicants also are required to create an infrastructure that builds partnerships among existing institutions and individuals with expertise, resources and leadership that could be harnessed to ADVANCE's work. It encourages grantees to use inter-departmental and professional networks within particular universities to create pressure for change. Departments and fields also cooperate and compete within universities. ADVANCE encourages development of departmental incentives to take gender participation seriously and to learn from and try to improve upon the efforts of peer departments.

[63] <http://www.nsf.gov/od/lpa/news/publicat/nsf04009/intro/start.htm>.

Many other regulatory agencies require information production and disclosure in the context of monitoring compliance. But NSF ADVANCE has developed a strategy that, when implemented, overcomes the major regulatory contradictions that have limited the impact of information disclosure and monitoring. ADVANCE has been able to get inside universities to obtain information about where and why problems are occurring and what can be done about them. It has been able to bring different actors to the table to collaborate around difficult problems. It has developed considerable public knowledge about causes and potential strategic responses to gender bias. It has forged a learning community among universities, one that produces both cooperation and competition driving institutional change. It has introduced incentives that profoundly affect how institutions make decisions, and implemented a system of accountability that seems to keep universities at the table as engaged participants

The role of linkages and pivot points

NSF represents a different kind of governmental strategy for promoting gender equity than the usual regulatory agency. Two key concepts characterise ADVANCE's institutional intermediation approach: linkages and pivot points. [64] Individual and institutional bridge builders bring together issues, actors, knowledge and incentives around a common problem. These linkages are both substantive and strategic. Substantive linkages connect problems sharing common goals, causes or remedies. Bringing issues together for consideration changes the understanding of each issue and enables identification of common causes and remedies. Linkages also connect actors who operate independently in relation to the problem but whose actions are in fact interdependent. This interdependence may be knowledge based. The information needed to understand the problem and identify solutions may be dispersed among different actors who do not ordinarily share information. Institutional intermediaries create new information flows bridging these knowledge gaps. They also generate opportunities to act on available knowledge, and bringing usable information to those in a position to act. Strategic linkages leverage incentives and tools from one domain to another, thus increasing the tools for motivating change. Treating issues together enhances the knowledge, incentives or collaboration needed to address each. Either the actions of one affect the success of the other or certain steps require coordination of actors who otherwise lack opportunities or incentives for joint action.

Institutional intermediaries forge linkages through their attributes as insider-outsiders, their organisational position requiring them to interact regularly with very different types of stakeholders, and their hybrid, problem-solving strategies. These linkages occur at strategic locations or pivot

[64] For a helpful analysis of the role of linkages in the international law context, see David W Leebron, 'Linkages' (2002) 96 *American Journal of International Law* 5.

points that either perpetuate or alter prevailing assumptions and practices. Through the creation and exploitation of pivot points, intermediation institutionalises occasions for detecting problems and reshaping underlying structures and assumptions.[65] This approach is simultaneously internal and external; it is both embedded enough to overcome the information asymmetries that characterise traditional monitoring relationships and independent enough to avoid capture. NSF can also wield internal legitimacy and still remain sufficiently outside routines to destabilise the status quo. Problem-solving intermediation thus creates the conditions that have fuelled benchmarking and learning-by-monitoring in the private sector; it forges mechanisms and occasions for ongoing error detection, learning and problem solving.[66] It develops the conditions for grass-roots mobilisation and for generating new leadership committed to sustaining ongoing change. Although it does not solve the legitimacy questions, its attentiveness to the conditions for effective involvement at least creates the possibility for creating accountable participation. It is too soon to determine long-term impact, but as the next section illustrates, at least in some universities these interventions have already had concrete impact on the level of women's participation in a relatively short period of time.

University of Michigan ADVANCE: Institutional intermediation on the ground

The University of Michigan, one of nine institutions initially funded through ADVANCE, mirrors the institutional intermediary strategy adopted by NSF. Michigan received an ADVANCE grant for a programme adopting NSF's multi-level, data driven, participatory approach sketched out by NSF. It has developed a series of individual, departmental and campus-wide initiatives. These initiatives respond quite directly to the conditions and barriers to women's participation described in the previous section. Individual initiatives include faculty career advising, research funds and networks supporting women scientists and engineers. Departmental initiatives support departments aiming to improve their climates through departmental transformation grants and self studies. Campus-wide initiatives include data-based workshops for disciplines, interactive theatre interventions and a programme called Science and Technology Recruiting to Improve Diversity and Excellence (STRIDE).[67]

> This committee provides information and advice about practices that will maximize the likelihood that well-qualified female and minority candidates for faculty

[65] Cf. Claire Moore Dickerson, 'Corporations as Cities: Targeting the Nodes in Overlapping Networks' (2004) 29 Iowa Journal of Corporate Law 533.
[66] See Sturm, n 2 above, at 523; William H Simon, 'Toyota Jurisprudence' in this volume (Ch 3).
[67] <http://www.umich.edu/~advproj/about.html>.

> positions will be identified, and, if selected for offers, recruited, retained, and promoted at the University of Michigan. The committee works with departments by meeting with chairs, faculty search committees, and other departmental leaders involved with recruitment and retention.[68]

Less discussed but perhaps even more significant, Michigan's ADVANCE grant institutionalised a structure that, from the outset, placed gender equity experts at the table with high-level university administrators and gender equity advocates. The overarching institutional change strategy harnesses the knowledge and social capital of individuals and institutions with a track record for effective problem solving. Michigan ADVANCE uses its resources to support collaborations among advocates, experts and governance actors, and to locate those collaborations at crucial decision points such as faculty search processes and leadership development and selection. It provides change agents with the information, networks and resources to maximise their legitimacy and impact. The role of individual and institutional problem-solving intermediaries as catalysts for change is pivotal.

It is important to note the Michigan ADVANCE operates along side and, to a limited extent, in collaboration with compliance approaches. Claims involving serious discrimination, particularly sexual harassment, are outside the purview of ADVANCE and are addressed through compliance actors, including the General Counsel and the Office of Institutional Equity. The Affirmative Action office continues to process discrimination complaints and bears responsibility for government reporting.[69] The General Counsel reviews publications, reports and policies produced through ADVANCE for their compliance with prevailing law. The Office of Institutional Equity and Human Resources collaborate to a limited extent with ADVANCE, and have incorporated successful ADVANCE initiatives into University-wide policy and practice. To a limited extent, compliance and ADVANCE actors have worked together when their functions overlap. Thus, problem-solving intermediation does not supplant the role of compliance in addressing serious discrimination.

Although Michigan has just completed year three of a five year grant, various quantitative and qualitative measures indicate that the ADVANCE strategies have had positive effects for women scientists and for their departments. These effects are seen in the form of hiring and demographic shifts; process, policy and role changes; and increased awareness, understanding and commitment at multiple levels of the institution. ADVANCE reports 'significant progress regarding the recruitment of women scientists

[68] <http://sitemaker.umich.edu/advance/STRIDE>.
[69] Interview with Director of Office of Institutional Equity.

and engineers at the University of Michigan'.[70] Thirteen per cent of new hires in the sciences and engineering were women in 2001 and 39 per cent were women in 2004. As a proportion of all science and engineering tenure track offers, 15 per cent of offers went to women in 2001 and 41 per cent in 2004.[71] An NSF review panel of six external auditors reported an 'increased hiring of women scientists and engineers in a number of departments, with some hiring women for the first time in many years'.[72] The result is an increase in the number of departments moving from 'token' representation of women (defined as less than 18 per cent of tenure track faculty) to 'minority' representation (18–36 per cent), and the NSF review panel noted that this shift 'may be of significant impact in improving the climate for women in those departments'.[73]

The NSF site visit auditors found multi-level support, accompanied by the programmatic strategies of ADVANCE, has had 'transformative' effects:

> Throughout our interviews with programme participants we heard stories of transformation. Senior male faculty reported a complete change in their perspective or that of their male colleagues after hearing a presentation from STRIDE or seeing the CRLT players. Junior women faculty reported significant changes in the climate of their individual departments, with comments such as 'now certain things can't happen', 'certain topics can now be discussed in my department that couldn't be raised before', and 'we are more willing to speak up or call people on issues than before'. Several departments showed a major turnaround in attitudes and practices; the astronomy department was 'transformed' according to one respondent, with two new hires of women faculty following the STRIDE intervention and faculty discussion.[74]

Institutional intermediation thus represents an institutional, strategic and role innovation. It does not replace governance, mobilisation and compliance approaches. On the contrary, it leverages the potential and incentives of these approaches to identify and address problems. It does this by creating linkages connecting actors' knowledge, incentives, values and practices, and by targeting organisational pivot points that redefine cultural norms and practices. These linkages and pivot points destabilise the status quo and enable multi-dimensional and coordinated analysis and action. The next section explores the theories-in-action that orient and, we hypothesise, help understand when and why problem-solving intermediaries enable sustainable change.

[70] UM ADVANCE Program Overview <http://www.umich.edu/~advproj/overview.pdf>.
[71] *Ibid.*
[72] Site Visit: University of Michigan NSF ADVANCE Program, 1 (2004), available at <http://sitemaker.umich.edu/advance/files/sitevisit.pdf>.
[73] *Ibid.*
[74] Site Visit: University of Michigan NSF ADVANCE Program, 6 (2004), available at <http://sitemaker.umich.edu/advance/files/sitevisit.pdf>.

STRATEGIES OF INSTITUTIONAL INTERMEDIATION: LINKAGES AND PIVOT POINTS

Three related intervention theories animate the work of these institutional intermediaries: (1) functional integration of gender equity and core institutional practice, even as it maintains gender as a distinct normative and critical category; (2) development of bridge builders who play a key role in promoting necessary learning, coordination, collaborating and rethinking; and (3) building in the architecture for continually regenerating mobilisation and leadership. These theories share an emphasis on the role of linkages and pivot points in destabilising problematic routines and motivating learning necessary to reshape practice.

Functional integration: Embedded advocacy and accountable governance

Institutional change will not result simply from policy change, even if participatory and deliberative problem-solving processes produce reform in policies and priorities. Knowledge about and commitments to gender equity also have to be strategically linked, at particular moments in time, to the myriad routines and decisions that actually determine access, opportunity and participation.[75] This requires a process of institutional internationalisation. Internalisation means incorporating inclusiveness into the way department chairs, deans, search committees and other leaders do business. It also means that knowledge about problems and their solutions influences day-to-day practices, and those committed to gender and racial participation have a place at the table. It institutionalises processes and roles with responsibility for revising current practice in light of new information. Internalisation focuses on institutional stakeholders with the power, incentives and capacities to influence policy and practice over the long run. It requires active participation by insiders.

The design of ADVANCE undertakes that internalisation process through functional integration: building deliberation and problem solving about gender into values, roles and processes of an institution. Gender issues are self-consciously linked to governance routines, incentive structures, and institutional priorities. The ADVANCE initiatives employ three pivotal strategies for functional integration: problem framing, constructing roles for those with primary responsibility for the initiative and establishing the processes and occasions for doing the work.

[75] Cf. Robin Ely and Debra Meyerson, 'Theories of Gender in Organizations: A New Approach to Organizational Analysis and Change' in B Shaw and R Sutton (eds) *Research in Organizational Behavior*.

Functional integration through problem framing

The ADVANCE initiatives connect gender equity problematics and goals to core institutional concerns, and at the same time preserve gender as a distinct analytical and normative category. NSF explicitly links its gender equity goals to the broader normative frame of advancing scientific inquiry and achievement. It encourages applicants and grantees to explore how women's advancement could improve the quality and dynamism of the overall academic enterprise.[76] Local empirical analysis of gender inequality's causes and solutions also operates to connect gender to underlying institutional dysfunction preventing full, inclusive and productive faculty participation in academic science. How is women's under-participation a signal for more general and generic institutional dysfunction? The analysis that NSF grantees are required to undertake reveals that in a given context, gender equity cannot occur without changing governance structures generally, which in turn benefits the overall institution. This conceptualisation prompts those primarily concerned with gender to identify underlying causes, shared interests and institutional strategies that must be addressed to achieve gender equity. It also encourages governance actors to integrate gender analysis into ongoing decision making. At the same time, women's full participation remains a distinct and significant goal.

Functional integration helps considerably in dealing with potential backlash. By backlash, we refer to opposition or resistance to equity initiatives based on perceptions of unfairness, counter-productivity, or illegality. As one Dean put it, there are 'some that are hostile, to the point where they fight against it. They view what we're doing as set-asides, quotas'.[77] Backlash often proceeds on an assumption that diversity and merit are two opposing concepts, and that efforts to include women and people of colour are at the expense of excellence and on the backs of majority group members. Functional integration by definition connects gender equity to questions of institutional mission. This is the direction suggested by the Supreme Court's recent decision in the Michigan cases.[78] Functional integration also responds directly to the concern that diversity is at the expense of quality by explicitly showing that gender cannot be addressed without correcting underlying institutional problems, and that creating conditions more conducive to gender participation will also redound to the benefit of others affected by the same dynamics.[79]

[76] 'By supporting the groundwork necessary to transform institutional practices systemically, the institutional transformation awards seek to create positive, sustainable, and permanent change in academic climates'. ADVANCE: *Increasing the Participation and Advancement of Women in Academic Science and Engineering Careers,* Program Solicitation NSF 02–021, available at <http://www.nsf.gov/pubs/2002/nsf02121/nsf02121.htm>.

[77] Interview with Dean and co-PI, 1 June 2004.

[78] *Grutter v Bollinger*, 123 S Ct. 2325 (2003); *Gratz v Bollinger*, 123 S Ct, 2411 (2003).

[79] See Guinier and Torres, n 21 above.

Where functional integration of substantive concerns has occurred, it has helped gender equity advocates institutionalise continuing interaction and productive tension between routines and vision. This integrative framing of gender with dominant professional and institutional concerns also provided multiple entry points for those dissatisfied with the status quo.[80] Many women found it difficult or risky to place and keep gender on the agenda when the issues were framed in terms of either intentional discrimination or special privileges for women. They expressed reluctance to claim gender as an identity category unless it could be related to their professional identity and status. Some expressed unwillingness to point fingers or to claim gender bias because they did not want to adopt what they referred to as victim status or to be perceived as whiners. The dual agenda approach opened up the range of critical frameworks which would prompt and legitimate a response. It also created alliances between those concerned about gender and those concerned about dysfunctional governance patterns that affected departmental quality. As gender became legitimised as a category, in part because NSF has recognised its relationship to the scientific project, women expressed greater willingness to include gender as a distinct concern and to identify themselves as women concerned about gender equity in the workplace. Thus, substantive functional integration effectively mobilised a broader range of stakeholders.

Functional integration through role hybridity

ADVANCE also promoted functional integration through the creation of hybrid roles for those centrally involved in its work. NSF encouraged Michigan's ADVANCE to set up the grant so that the people responsible for implementation lie at the intersection of two complementary practice spaces. The first is the ADVANCE space: problem-solving work that cuts across multiple institutional and disciplinary domains linked by gender analysis. The second is core operational goals, functions and authority: the decision-making and routine practices of institutional governance. The ADVANCE players are situated so that they link and move back and forth between the two domains, both substantively and structurally.

Functional integration results in part from a strategy of accountable governance. Those with significant administrative responsibilities assume direct and public responsibility for gender equity in general and for implementation of the NSF ADVANCE grant in particular. For example, the deans of the three major colleges also became Co-Principal Investigators (Co-PIs) on the NSF ADVANCE grant. They were essentially drafted into the project, without complete appreciation of what they were signing on to do, but over

[80] See Mary Fainsod Katzenstein, 'Feminism within American Institutions: Unobtrusive Mobilization in the 1980's' (1990) 16 *Journal of Women in Culture and Society* 27.

time become invested in the success of ADVANCE. This move formalised responsibility and accountability for the success of ADVANCE. Over time, it also enhanced and solidified the Deans' commitment to gender equity as a priority.[81]

To scientists, NSF grantee responsibilities are familiar and legitimising, and they carry reputational value and consequences. The same strategy also brings those with core leadership responsibility out of their normal setting and authority structures into the ADVANCE space, where they have the opportunity to think creatively, to interact in an open-ended way with those directly affected by the problem, to brainstorm with an interdisciplinary group of faculty and experts and to problem-solve. As one ADVANCE protagonist described it, 'people with access and power [were] given a different conceptual framework for thinking about their role, which influenced the way in which they carried out their policymaking responsibilities'. Deans and chairs gained access to information they otherwise lacked. 'I can't tell you how many times there was shock and surprise at the table—learning about the way things work'.[82] Involving governance actors as direct caretakers of ADVANCE enabled the linking of normative commitments, policy change, incentives and accountability. Initiatives particular to ADVANCE were generalised beyond the scope of what ADVANCE requires.

Importantly, functional integration simultaneously works in the opposite direction through embedded advocacy: gender equity advocates and experts move in and out of leadership positions with core operational responsibilities. ADVANCE proliferates occasions for gender advocates and experts to participate in decision-making arenas. Abby Stewart, ADVANCE's Principal Investigator, assumed a high level administrative responsibility within the dean's office. She had regular contact with department chairs in her dual role as Academic Dean and ADVANCE PI.

The grant involves pre-existing organisations such as the Center for Research on Teaching and Learning, the Center for Education on Women, and the Institute for Research on Women and Gender in the planning and implementation of crucial ADVANCE functions. These organisations have some formal responsibilities for ADVANCE related work, such as conducting evaluations, running networking programmes, facilitating workshops and consulting. They regularly interact with decision makers about the work, and act as intermediaries between ADVANCE and the constituencies of their organisations. As a second example, a dean has created an advisory committee of women faculty, which meets regularly with him, as well as with department-level leaders. In addition to these governance tasks, the

[81] Site Visit, University of Michigan ADVANCE Program, 19–24 September, at 1, available at <http://sitemaker.umich.edu/advance/files/sitevisit.pdf>

[82] Interview with Dean and Co-PI, 1 June 2004.

advisory committee has monthly meetings with the larger group of women they represent, which have in some cases resulted in successful policy recommendations on the college-wide level. This partial integration of gender experts and advocates into governance routines has provided crucial source of learning, accountability and destabilisation. Because of these emergent, hybrid roles, co-PI Deans collaborate regularly with respected colleagues who are not constrained by administrative necessity and who are accountable to the constituencies most directly affected by and interested in the success of the initiative. In the words of one participant, 'we are like the little burr'.[83]

Functional integration through routine organisational processes

Finally, functional integration is occurring at the University of Michigan at the level of daily routines and practices. Regular gatherings such as chairs meetings and faculty searches have at times become mini 'constitutional moments' in which norms are elaborated, practices rethought in light of normative commitments and new knowledge, and accountability processes developed. These occasions are used to put on the table the underlying structures and values that shape daily practice. In the university context, this often involves how decisions get made about bringing new members into the community and allocating responsibilities and benefits among existing members. The collection of information revealing structural problems, coupled with regularised occasions to discuss that information, generates the urgency and collective will to change institutional routines. This can give rise to new public commitments that result when there is collective activity around documented problems.

ADVANCE has been quite self-conscious in its strategy of regularising occasions for institutional reflection about structural questions relating to gender and other related concerns. This includes integrating gender issues into already existing meetings or reviews, such as faculty meetings, chair and dean meetings, departmental and salary reviews and accreditation and other ongoing evaluations. It also has been achieved by creating new forms of regular interaction integrating gender and governance concerns. For example, ADVANCE has given rise to monthly meetings of women science chairs. Data gathering relevant to gender issues has also been integrated into operations, for example by building iterative reporting and monitoring into the process of getting resources from the central administration to run a search and hire a candidate. When individuals with multiple forms of accountability regularly move back and forth across ADVANCE and core operational spaces, meetings and other encounters have the potential to raise insistent questions, disrupt business-as-usual and produce policy informed by generalisable learning. This destabilisation of routines and reflection about practices can otherwise be a rare event in academic governance.

[83] Interview with ADVANCE participant, 28 Jan 2005.

Functional integration also enables the process to move in the other direction—from mini-constitutional moment back into organisational routine. In other words, functional integration creates new relationships and experimental spaces connecting governance, mobilisation and compliance roles, often with the intervention of bridge builders. This enables actors at University of Michigan to use the learning that comes out of the gender equity initiative in the course of routine decisions and practices, such as designing search processes, allocating work and leadership roles and distributing resources.

The role of bridge builders: Connecting domains, discourses and knowledge

Achieving change within universities is like herding cats. Power is highly dispersed. Departments often lack information about each other and about central administrative priorities and initiatives; central administrators lack reliable information about departmental decisions and practices. Departments and disciplines do not regularly interact; they value different types of knowledge and communicate using different language and styles. Yet, as we have seen, gender and racial under-participation results from accumulation of this kind of decision making, and from cultural and institutional patterns that cut across these domains but are difficult to observe or change from any one location. Often, the processes, structures and incentives to cross these synapses do not exist.

ADVANCE has introduced the role of bridge builders as a way of institutionalising this much-needed synapse-crossing. Bridge builders are individuals who are able to operate across different domains and levels of activity to understand and influence the interaction of actors, incentives, routines, and goals. The role is not unique to ADVANCE; bridge builders can be found informally in many settings. ADVANCE, however, places bridge builders at the centre of its implementation strategy and builds their role into the structure of the change ADVANCE principal investigators and STRIDE faculty are two examples of ADVANCE-inspired problem-solving intermediaries.

Bridge builders are defined by their characteristics, their institutional location, and their roles. First, their characteristics: bridge builders come to the position with a track record of effective participation in the institutional arena generally and around issues of fair treatment in particular. They have previously been involved extensively but informally in problem solving, as bridge builders, trouble shooters, and mentors. This background affords them legitimacy with different constituencies coming into the role. They also bring deep cultural knowledge of the institution—its values, informal power structures and minefields.

Second, their institutional location: bridge builders sit at the convergence of interdependent but distinct governance domains. They have cross-cutting responsibility and authority for influencing practices relevant to the participation of women faculty. This problem orientation affords them institutional authority and resources to work with individual faculty members, chairs, deans, advocacy leaders, central administrators, compliance actors—anyone affected by or in a position to affect women's participation as faculty. The Principal Investigators of ADVANCE, for example, interact at the individual level, with faculty who are experiencing difficulties in their departments or who are considering leaving the University. They meet regularly with chairs, deans and other governance actors. They work closely with advocacy and research institutions involved in studying or providing services. They convene and participate in groups and networks of faculty and administrators concerned about gender equity. They thus have access to different levels of problem articulation and intervention, and can move across levels without the usual conceptual and bureaucratic constraints. They can participate in the decision-making bodies within these different domains as they impact gender. They thus have multiple sources of accountability, from both the top and the bottom.

Third, their role: bridge builders facilitate problem solving. They integrate existing knowledge about the problem and its potential remediation. They work with individuals who bring problems to their attention by virtue of their public identification as problem solvers. They work with researchers to generate knowledge about the problem and its remediation, which they in turn share. They identify patterns revealed through both individual complaints and systematic evaluation. They locate current and potential collaborators who bring different perspectives, forms of institutional legitimacy, and forms of power. They bring the right people to the table to collaborate on problems that cut across their responsibilities and interests.

ADVANCE has provided the Michigan gender equity initiative with the opportunity and resources to identify individuals and institutions already performing a mediating role, provide them with institutional legitimacy and support, and enhance their capacity to perform these roles. ADVANCE also employs programmatic interventions that breed and enable new bridge builders and institutions.

The bridge builders in the ADVANCE projects play several crucial linking functions. First, they provide an overarching conceptual framework for the gender initiative, one that connects an understanding of the culturally and institutionally rooted dimensions of the problem to programmatic intervention, system design and institutional change.[84] This conceptual orientation prompts actors to think about their efforts in relation to each other and to larger goals and analyses. This framework informs their self-evaluation.

[84] Indeed, the most recent NSF ADVANCE solicitation requires grant applicants to articulate the conceptual framework underlying their concrete programmatic proposals. See Program Solicitation, n 38 above.

Second, bridge builders' history, skill set and position make them multilingual. Bridge builders work on the individual, group, and system level. They also move back and forth between the local institutional, multi-institutional and national level. This boundary spanning across different domains provides them with cross-cutting cultural and institutional knowledge and relationships. This form of institutional capital enables them to translate normative commitments into the language of particular communities, and in turn, to rethink general normative principles in relation to the experiences of particular contexts. This fluency also enables them to determine when they lack the necessary legitimacy, knowledge or fluency to communicate within particular domain. An understanding of the importance of communication has prompted their emphasis on recruiting and developing new bridge builders to perform a similar function in their own practice domains. The job of communicating with scientists about the nature and scope of the problem required participation of actors with legitimacy within each disciplinary realm. NSF has played a tremendous role in legitimising gender equity as a serious subject that is amenable to the rigorous techniques and methodologies that characterise NSF's approach to scientific research and development.

Third, bridge builders use small scale problem solving and trouble shooting to generate occasions for mobilisation and systems change.[85] They have the flexibility and mandate to intervene strategically when action is needed. Bridge builders construct experimental spaces to address problems that would otherwise remain on the back burner, and help redesign governance systems to address both gender equity issues and more general issues of institutional fairness and effectiveness. Dilemmas can become occasions for change, an entry point that is focused on a manageable issue but embedded in a pattern of interactions to which the mediating actor has access. Individual incidents, such as the threatened departure of a senior faculty woman or a search yielding no diverse candidates, provide opportunities for problem and pattern identification. Institutional failures thus operate as triggers for reflection and problem solving. Exposure to multiple realms over time and space enables interventions that ratchet up and down the different locations at which gender inequality functions. It also facilitates the cross-domain knowledge sharing so crucial to linking the local and the centre, both within a particular university and among a network of universities.

The architecture of accountability: Developing movers and shakers

We have been describing a process of integrating concerns about equity into the fabric of daily decision making. This process entails ongoing questioning and revising practices in light of the problems identified. Such a process

[85] One active participant in ADVANCE at Michigan referred to this role as becoming an 'articulate pain in the ass'. Cf. Meyerson, n 22 above.

is difficult to sustain over the long run, particularly when normal incentives and routines cut against devoting time and resources to these questions. Leadership often surfaces as a key factor in enabling this ongoing change—strategically located individuals who exercise power to influence choices and priorities. In the context of universities, this kind of leadership must be exercised not only by the central administration, but at the many different locations determining access and participation. This power stems both from formal authority and from mobilisation by those committed to increasing the participation of women and people of colour. Effective and committed leaders have played central roles in jumpstarting gender and racial initiatives. But change efforts cannot last if they remain dependent upon a few key change agents. Many creative reform efforts have foundered when reform-minded presidents leave office or faculty reformers move on. Moreover, the mobilisation efforts that produce leadership and accountability are quite difficult to sustain. The long-term viability of a public problem-solving approach to gender and racial inclusiveness depends upon the capacity to institutionalise the regeneration of leadership and mobilisation.

ADVANCE explicitly focuses attention and resources on replenishing existing commitments and fostering new leadership. ADVANCE self-consciously creates regular opportunities for those concerned about gender equity to interact, to develop shared understandings about the problems, to develop their capacities to shape their environments and to assume responsibility for action. Those who receive individual faculty support for their career advancement often have institutional responsibilities attached to the receipt of funds that encourage their development as leaders both in their fields and in the institution. Small grant programmes exist to provide recognition and leadership for those who want to participate. Faculty development work takes place often in group contexts which give the opportunity for similarly situated actors to develop ongoing networks for information exchange and support. The emphasis on micro-environments creates multiple and lower risk opportunities to mobilise and exercise leadership. The NSF grant legitimised forms of mobilisation consistent with professional identity. This every-day mobilisation is occurring as the same time as those with formal governance responsibilities are developing the tools to groom new leadership. The NSF and Michigan ADVANCE projects self-consciously link the development of individuals' capacity to thrive with a sense of the possibility of change at a more systemic level.

Effective mobilisation occurs when there are pivot or leverage points that attract and enable joint, normatively focused practice. In the gender context, these may be occasions for analyzing individual problems in relation to group or institutional concerns or experiences. These micro-occasions make underlying dynamics visible, so that one can identify an issue as a gender or institutional dysfunction concern that warrants action. As this understanding develops, routine decisions become occasions for exercising situational leadership. In addition to building capacity and hope, the gender equity initiatives have created a new range of occasions in which people can understand themselves as part of a larger phenomenon and act in accordance with this realisation. ADVANCE uses meetings focused on capacity building and leadership development to perform this mobilisation function. They simultaneously energise, equip and motivate individuals to act, and create the opportunities for them to put this energy into effect. These meetings focus on concretely supporting and advancing the participants' work, and connecting that personal advancement to participation in institutional change. Very busy people regularly attend! The strategy is to locate the need and the energy and then to develop a project or intervention to sustain that energy and link it to institutional practices. These pivot points often lie at the intersection of resources, an occasion to act, and a space in which issues can be raised without substantial risks to individual participants.

Multiplying the occasions for people to exercise leadership in informal but influential contexts has the potential to open up additional leadership roles as well as continually reconstruct the meaning of leadership in the context of the demands of a particular project. The Dean of the Engineering School, also an ADVANCE PI, created an Advisory Committee of female faculty to work with him on gender-related issues. He meets with them at least once a semester. Some of the members of this committee are also part of STRIDE so 'there is another flow of information that goes through the institution'. The group is interested in the broader picture as well'.[86] In addition, the committee has a monthly meeting with faculty on issues related to women; it meets with each department chair, and with every female candidate as she nears the end of the hiring process. They also wrote a report making recommendations based on these conversations. According to the Dean, the Engineering School has put some of those recommended policies into place.

Another example at the level of the National Science Foundation ADVANCE Project is the continually expanding cross-institutional leadership of people like Abby Stewart and Virginia Valian from Hunter College. Such roles are sustainable because the relationships forming across ADVANCE grantees are ongoing, through the interplay of meetings, site visits and communication over websites.

ADVANCE also used the strategy of building on pre-existing institutions that have a track record and a commitment to gender issues at the university. The University of Michigan's Center for the Education of Women (CEW) and Institute for Research on Women and Gender (IRWG) are two examples of institutional actors who bring skills, such as research, and capital, such as networks, to the collaboration. They had a considerable track record in addressing gender issues at Michigan, and brought different constituencies and skills to their work. ADVANCE involved them from the outset; they assumed roles in the ADVANCE work that built on their strategic position within the university. This avoided some of the turf battles that can

[86] Interview with Dean and Co-PI, 2 June 2004.

arise among advocacy groups, and bootstrapped the institutional capital and resources of these groups to the ADVANCE initiative.

These three strategies—promoting functional integration, bridge builders and ongoing mobilisation—permeate NSF's gender equity approach. Combined with NSF's pivotal location within a web of collaborative and competitive relationships, these strategies provide powerful responses to the 'how' questions that are so crucial to new governance's efficacy.

CONCLUSION: THE IMPLICATIONS OF THE GENDER EQUITY EXAMPLE FOR NEW GOVERNANCE AND CONSTITUTIONALISM

The NSF case study shows the powerful role that linkages, forged by problem-solving intermediaries, played in orchestrating the conditions necessary for effective and accountable problem solving. This crucial role for linkages has been emerged in other public regulatory arenas as well. In the area of international governance regimes, linkages have been key in forming trans-governance regulatory regimes that include non-state actors and regulatory networks 'exchanging information, coordinating national policies and working together to address common problems'.[87] In the area of organisational change, linkages relating local organisations to their larger social environment have been identified as a dominant factor influencing their structure and direction.[88]

The gender equity example also documents the particular circumstances contributing to problem -solving intermediaries' effectiveness in playing this linking role. NSF is an evidence-based intermediary organisation. It operates within a pre-existing community of practice among varying levels within universities. It builds on the prior mobilisation of activists concerned about gender inequality. It carries tremendous legitimacy and resources, enabling it to form vertical collaborative relationships with grantees, and to facilitative horizontal interactions among universities.

The confluence of these variables in the NSF case triggers a question about genders, networks and mobilised stakeholders needed to forge these crucial linkages. Will constitutional approaches increase the likelihood that these conditions and institutions will develop? Or, will they produce symbolic or cosmetic processes that essentially legitimate the status quo? One

[87] Anne-Marie Slaughter 'Global Government Networks, Global Information Agencies, and Disaggregated Democracy' (2003) 24 *Michigan Journal of International Law* 1041, 1043; Oran P Young, *Governance in World Affairs* (Cornell University Press, 1999), 193. This coordinated activity may take place either formally, through the mandate of international conventions, or informally, through regularised interactions of governmental and non-governmental actors at different levels. These activities may result in binding norms, shared expectations, guidelines or combinations of these forms.

[88] See W Richard Scott and John W Meyer, 'The Organization of Societal Sectors: Propositions and Early Evidence', in Powell and DiMaggio, n 16 above.

response to this risk would be to eschew constitutionalism and instead adopt a purely incremental, domain-specific strategy for introducing new governance processes: Develop new governance only in contexts with adequate infrastructure and networks. But this approach suffers from the opposite limitation. It fails to build the infrastructure to engage in the form of public problem solving necessary to address complex problems. It also assumes that this capacity is static, and that it can be managed or predetermined by those designing regulatory interventions.

Perhaps a way out of this dilemma is to use pragmatism and root cause analysis (the methodologies of new governance) to develop more nuanced strategies for scaling up new governance as a regulatory approach. We may need to rethink what we mean by constitutionalism and its relationship to problem solving. The first step of this inquiry entails figuring out the right theoretical and empirical questions: Where are the recurring breakdown points in public problem-solving efforts and why are they occurring? How could public institutions be better equipped to overcome those barriers? Are any of these barriers traceable to general patterns reachable through overarching shifts in incentives or institutional design? How could we rethink the roles of different types of public and quasi public agencies to increase the repertoire of public institutions involved in this problem-solving work? Are there particular prerequisites for public problem solving (such as improved data-gathering capacity) that could be pursued generally without necessarily legitimating normative outcomes resulting from superficial or illegitimate processes? What is the appropriate mix of overarching processes and contextualised experiments?

In many respects, scholars of new governance face many of the same challenges confronting new governance practitioners. The unanswered questions lie at the intersection of disciplines, institutions and regulatory systems. Their engagement requires fluency across these various domains, as well as the capacity to bridge the normative and the empirical. We too must learn to be bridge builders, mirroring the challenge of the problem-solving projects themselves.

Part IV

Comparative Studies

13

EU Constitutionalism and the 'American Experience'

PAUL MAGNETTE AND JUSTINE LACROIX*

THE CONSTITUTIONALISATION OF the European Union has given a new impetus to an old question: to what extent can a Constitution contribute to the emergence and consolidation of 'patriotic feelings' beyond the nation-state? The most enthusiastic supporters of the EU's Constitutional Treaty see it as a first step towards a political body founded on the recognition of a set of 'common values'. Many American scholars share this view: Bruce Ackerman echoes a widespread state of mind when he expresses his hope that 'constructive affirmations of common citizenship will instil the civic pride and hope that may propel the European Union beyond the limits reached by the dynamics of fear and humiliation' so that it will eventually bypass its present stage, which is that of a 'hollow shell that will be crushed in one or another of the crisis that make up human history'[1]

Explicitly or not, the 'American model' is one of the central references of this debate. Some refer to it to demonstrate that a highly abstract and initially contested fundamental law can become, with the passing of time, the symbol of what unites a non-ethnic polity. Sceptics retort that this hypothesis ignores the dramatic process of nationalisation which has characterised American history since its inception, and they add that it depended on such specific conditions that it cannot be replicated. In any case, it seems very difficult to reflect upon the EU's constitutional future without referring, at least implicitly, to the American experience. In this chapter, we argue that this comparison between the United States and Europe is more misleading than illuminating. The European Union has generated its own constitutional grammar, and the Europeans should not try to duplicate the American path by promoting a 'constitutional patriotism' founded on common values and opposition to an external 'other'. The adoption of a European

* We would like to thank Richard Bellamy, Dario Costiglione and Kalypso Nicolaïdis for their helpful comments on earlier drafts of this paper.

[1] B Ackerman, 'Prologue: Hope and Fear in Constitutional Law' in EO Eriksen, JE Fossum and AJ Menendez (eds) *Developing a Constitution for Europe* (London: Routledge, 2004), xvi-xvii.

Constitution should not give birth to a 'Euro-patriotism', be it purely constitutional. Instead of mimicking the 'American model', Europeans should rather value their value-free Constitution and the deliberately cold and abstract constitutional discipline.

'WE VERSUS THEM': CONSTITUTIONAL PATRIOTISM IN THE UNITED STATES

That the United States do generate strong patriotic feelings, and that the US Constitution of 1787 is the object of a public cult which is part and parcel of this patriotism, is beyond doubt. Yet, what strikes most 'foreign' observers when they examine the American debates about the nature of patriotism and the role played by the Constitution in the construction and persistence of patriotic feelings, is what divides US scholars as much as what they have in common. To put it briefly, the core of the debate is the degree of 'abstractness' of American patriotism. On the one hand, liberals argue that the fundamental law should be neutral towards the moral and religious views citizens espouse. Since Americans live in a pluralist society, the Constitution should not affirm any conception of the good life. Instead, it should provide a framework of rights that respect persons as free and independent individuals, capable of choosing their own values and ends.[2] On the other hand, some authors denounce this public philosophy as flawed. They argue that it is rather the historical construction of a 'thick' American identity which makes America what it is. To be sure, being American is not a matter of ethnic or religious affiliation; it is a genuinely 'civilian' identity. But this identity consists of a set of beliefs, tastes, references, shared understandings and aspirations built into the practice of American citizenship which give it its strength and value. Cut off from the moral world in which it finds its roots and its motivational resources, American patriotism would dissolve. In Michael Sandel's words,

> civic resources ... are still to be found in the places and stories, memories and meanings, incidents and identities, that situate us in the world and give our lives their moral particularity. Political community depends on the narratives by which people make sense of their condition and interpret the common life they share; at its best, political deliberation is not only about competing policies but also about competing interpretations of the character of a community, of its purposes and ends.[3]

The significance of this philosophical discussion should not be underestimated. It shows that, in the very country which is taken as a model of how

[2] J Rawls, *A Theory of Justice*, Cambridge, (MA: Harvard University Press 1971); R Dworkin, *Taking Rights Seriously* (Cambridge, MA: Harvard University Press, 1977); B Ackerman, *Social Justice in the Liberal State* (New Haven, CT: Yale University Press, 1980).

[3] M Sandel, *Democracy's Discontent: America in Search of a Public Philosophy* (Cambridge, MA: Harvard University Press, 1996) 349–50.

constitutional patriotism should work, its precise nature and development continues to be hotly debated.

However, the strength of the consensus which underlies this controversy is equally striking. Beyond their divergences, American scholars agree on the basic axiom of American constitutional patriotism: 'America was born of the conviction that sovereignty need not reside in a single place'.[4] The idea that American constitutionalism finds its origin and most solid foundation in the concept of 'dispersed sovereignty' has been noticed by all European commentators of American politics, from Tocqueville to Arendt and Habermas. Different ideologies give rise to different interpretations of this principle, but it is rarely contested as such. Liberals highlight its protective value: echoing Montesquieu and the Founding Fathers, they restate that a compound republic prevents the dangers of factionalism and corruption by opposing power to power[5]; within the different branches of power, as among them, rivalries ensure a fair process of deliberation.[6] On their side, communitarians stress the formative virtue of dispersed sovereignty: 'proliferating sites of civic activity and political power can serve self-government by cultivating virtue, equipping citizens for self-rule, and generating loyalties to larger political wholes'.[7] Scholars inspired by such a vision of politics—one which sees a 'thick' identity rooted in concrete contexts as an indispensable component of a stable polity—have even endeavoured to demonstrate empirically how dispersed sovereignty produces those civic resources which are the republic's blood.[8] Sitting somewhere in between these two lines of thought, 'liberal republicans' try to reconcile these views by describing the American Constitution as the source of a dualist system which organises the confrontation of citizenship and privacy so as to 'economize on virtue'.[9] Whatever the extent of their disagreement on the degree of moral agreement required to make the polity work, and despite the fact that they value it for different reasons, American scholars at least agree on this fundamental constitutional principle: sovereignty is and should remain dispersed. Discussions on the foundation of the community may thus continue unabated, since they take place within a conceptual matrix which is beyond discussion.

This is precisely what constitutional patriotism is about: it offers a conceptual basis and a shared language which helps maintain political conflicts within the margins of the constitution. This public philosophy is 'constitutional'

[4] Sandel, previous n, at 346

[5] J Shklar, 'The Liberalism of Fear' in S Hoffman (ed) *Political Thought and Political Thinkers* (Chicago University Press, 1998).

[6] C Sunstein, *Designing Democracy, What Constitutions Do* (Oxford: Oxford University Press, 2001).

[7] Sandel, n 3 above, at 348.

[8] RD Putnam, *Making Democracy Work: Civic Traditions in Modern Italy* (Princeton, NJ: Princeton Univeristy Press, 1993).

[9] B Ackerman, *We the People: Foundations* (New Haven, CT: Yale University Press, 1991).

to the extent that the supreme law is the symbol of what the adversaries have in common: the conflict does not oppose those who defend the Constitution to those who reject it, but rather two competing interpretations of the meaning of the constitution.

However, one can discern two ways for being a 'Constitutional Patriot'. The first version is patriotic in a general sense. In this strictly liberal conception, the invocation of the Constitution bears witness to the parties' loyalty to the polity and their attachment to its legal and political foundation. The second version is 'patriotic' in a more restrictive sense. In this more communitarian reading, constitutional loyalty cannot be dissociated from the defence of a pattern of thought which is deemed genuinely 'American'. This latter interpretation, which links values and norms, has actually been more much more widespread than the liberal one. From its very inception, constitutional debates in the US have indeed been shaped by a constant and widespread desire to stress the uniqueness of their public philosophy. What's more, in this deliberate strategy of distinction, American politicians and scholars have usually used 'Europe'—be it an oversimplified and sometimes caricatured Europe—as the symbol of the 'other' constitutional model, against which their own original way could be assessed and magnified. To a large extent, what unites American intellectuals, despite their disagreements, is their consensus on a fundamental constitutional axiom which is seen as typically American. Theirs is a Western culture, but it is defined by peculiar constitutional devices which are based on an American pattern of thought—as opposed to the other West: Europe.

Many historians have convincingly shown that the Founding Fathers were moved by an ambition to renovate the political science of their time, and that in their book this meant distinguishing themselves from European 'dogmas'. For the Men of Philadelphia and their followers, Europe meant Britain, and Britain in turn symbolised unfair authority, corruption, aristocratic disdain and decay. What the Founders rejected was not just the colonial state, but also a philosophy of government which was deemed inherently bad. Their revolution was not only political, it was also moral and intellectual. Britain was the homeland of 'over refined, over elaborated, dogmatic metropolitan formulas in political thoughts'[10] that had to be replaced by pragmatic and commonsensical arguments, more fitted to the Americans' own mores. Sure, the Founding fathers invented the idea of a 'compound republic' and made the notion of 'dispersed sovereignty' the core of their own constitutional thought because it corresponded to the '*de facto* constitutional order that they ... had known for generations'.[11] Yet, their intellectual revolution consisted also in replacing a 'foreign' sophisticated

[10] B Bailyn, *To Begin the World Anew: The Genius and Ambiguities of the American Founders* (New York: Vintage Books, 2004), 32.

[11] *Ibid.*

rhetoric by an 'indigenous' pragmatic pattern of thought, 'nourished in the awareness of provincial simplicity and innocence'.[12] The Revolution was seen as an antidote to moral decay. For those who fought for the Independence, the American Revolution had not only a political sense but also a deep moral signification which linked self-government with the need to cultivate public virtues.[13] As Bernard Bailyn indicates, this intellectual revolution was a source of strong patriotic pride:

> Britain was no longer the bastion of liberty it once had been. America—in the simplicity of its manners, its lack of luxury and pomp, its artlessness, homeliness, lack of affectation and cynicism—America had taken Britain's place as the moral guardian and promoter of liberty.[14]

The political and moral revolution symbolised by the Constitution had been made possible by a diffuse American patriotism which, in turn, it strengthened.

Fifty years later, Tocqueville's portrait of American democracy helped to consolidate this constitutional patriotism. The young French aristocrat not only stressed the uniqueness and the exemplarity of the American experience—with a touch of religious style echoing indigenous narratives—he also highlighted the democratic virtues of the Constitution, anticipating the critics that would denounce its elitist bias. The French magistrate, upset by Napoleonic excesses, shared the Founding Fathers' fear of despotism and factionalism. But he was primarily concerned by a third risk—which was less central to the Founders' reflections: that of civic apathy and confinement of the citizens to the private sphere, another phenomenon paving the way for an omnipotent state. That Tocqueville found the remedy to this European evil in the American Constitution only confirmed the prescience of the Founders and the value of their philosophy of government. Federalism and local independence, nourishing a rich associative life, were a functional substitute for the role the aristocracy played in the constitutional monarchy idealised by Montesquieu. Tocqueville was venerated for having confirmed—from an outsider viewpoint, which gave his judgement a certain impartiality—that America had replaced Britain as the symbol of a free society. Dispersed sovereignty was the solution the Europeans were desperately looking for. By stressing this point, Tocqueville helped the Americans take conscience of their own civic culture and of the specific nature of their political theory. He helped them understand that their Constitution echoed their history, their moral and religious universe and even their geography.

[12] *Ibid.*, at 34.

[13] G Wood, *The Creation of the American Republic, 1776–1787* (Chapel Hill: University of North Carolina Press, 1969), ch 3.

[14] Bailyn, n 10 above, at 34.

This patriotic praise of the Constitution has lasted until nowadays. Highlighting the 'unexplored promises' of the American Constitution, and using Europe as a counter-example, has remained a constant attitude in American constitutional discussions. Two examples, taken at the beginning and end of the twentieth century, may illustrate this. In the pre-New Deal period, contemplating the rise of social conflicts and contentions raised by new regulatory politics, John Dewey formed his theory of 'epistemic democracy' in large part because he feared a Europeanisation of American politics. Reified concepts, ideological perceptions, mystic theories of the state (all typically European phenomena) concealed the real nature of the issues, generated unfounded conflicts and reduced the problem-solving capacity of democracy. Understanding democracy as a learning process and the state as an experimental institution—against the 'mythical' European concept of the state—could help prevent these deviations. Again, decentralisation, local experiences, exchange of views, comparison through wider deliberation (ie, epistemic democracy) could contribute to public enlightenment. To be sure, Dewey did not idealise the American democracy of his time—nor did he caricature European societies. He saw, with much more clarity than many of his followers, the limits of the Founders' imagination, which 'did not travel far beyond what could be accomplished and understood in a congeries of self-governing communities'.[15] An he knew that the Americans had to rethink their principles because they 'have inherited, in short, local town-meeting practices and ideas' but now 'live and act and have (their) being in a continental national state'.[16] Still, it is in Tocqueville's idea of a dispersed democracy that Dewey found the source of a renewed public education reconciling small communities and the great society. And it is in the Europeanisation of the American tradition—the domination of class struggles and ideological visions—that he saw the major dangers.

This desire not to be European is, again, transparent in a recent work of reinterpretation of American constitutionalism such as Ackerman's *We the People*. The author stresses in the very first page of his book how unfortunate it is, in his eyes, that America is 'an intellectual colony, borrowing European categories to decode the meaning of its national identity'.[17] Determined to break with this tradition, he invites his readers to perceive the US Constitution as a 'genuinely distinctive pattern of constitutional thought and practice' and to approach it 'without the assistance of guides imported from another time and place'.[18] Actually, this reading of the American Constitution does not abandon European references, but it uses them as a counter-model. In Ackerman's book, as in the Founding Fathers'

[15] J Dewey, *The Public and Its Problems* (New York: H Holt, 1927; reprint Ohio University Press, 1954), 111.
[16] *Ibid.*, at 113.
[17] Ackerman, n 9 above, at 3.
[18] *Ibid.*

argument, American constitutionalism is the solution to Europe's evils. The Westminster model exhibits 'vicious pathologies': 'taxes may be designed so that the social groups supporting the Opposition are forced to pay the bulk of the revenue; benefits may be distributed so that Government supporters appropriate the lion's share'.[19] Majoritarianism is, in other words, the mother of all political evils. To those who would argue that those forms of factionalism are the price to be paid for clear-cut oppositions guaranteeing a wide mobilisation of the citizens, Ackerman first answers that this is a *faux semblant*: 'This emphatic and repeated show in Parliament contrasts oddly with the mass apathy and fractional conviction swirling about the country.'[20]. He then takes the defence of the American model, feigning to wonder, 'Which is worse: irresponsibility, opacity and indecisiveness or factional tyranny by the parliamentary majority?'[21] In a constitutional order based on the axiom of dispersed sovereignty, he concludes, these evils can be avoided: 'Every initiative must appeal to the interests and ideologies of a host of independent politician/statesmen, who themselves have gained the soft support of popular majorities' and this makes sure that a proposal 'serves the permanent interests of the community'.[22] Moreover, in Ackerman's eyes, such a system has major epistemic advantages: it 'allows a host of politicans/statesmen to play the role of policy initiator' and this may explain why 'there is more fresh thinking on more problems in the American system'. In the end, 'there are many problems that profit from a healthy eclecticism: perhaps, over time, the American system encourages lawmakers to move beyond the narrow limits of "clear" ideologies'.[23]

Such a caricature of the constitutional 'good, bad and ugly'[24] may make us smile—especially after the 2004 presidential campaign. But it is useful when it reminds us that anti-Europeanism—be it a soft anti-Europeanism, moved by a desire to understand and value one's own nature, or a hard one made of resentment—has been a constant feature of American constitutional theory. To be sure, American patriotism is a complex phenomenon, in which the philosophy encapsulated by the Constitution only plays a relative role. The social *ethos* of the 'American dream' and the universalistic ambition of American citizenship—with the memories of its betrayals—are the most powerful sources of loyalty to the nation.[25] Still, the Constitution is a crucial element of these collective feelings, not just because it sets the rules

[19] *Ibid.*, at 256.
[20] *Ibid.*, at 255.
[21] *Ibid.*, at 322.
[22] *Ibid.*, 255–56.
[23] *Ibid.*, at 256.
[24] R Bellamy and J Schonlau, 'The Good, the Bad and the Ugly: The Need for Constitutional Compromise and the Drafting of the EU Constitution' in L Dobson and A Follesdal (eds) *Political Theory and the European Constitution* (London: Routledge, 2004).
[25] J Shklar, *American Citizenship* (Cambridge, MA: Harvard University Press, 1991).

of the game, but because it symbolises a public philosophy which made the settlement of the country's major existential crises possible. The fact that the original compact gave rise to violent oppositions ending up in a Civil War, and that they could nevertheless be bypassed, has consolidated the value of the Constitution. Through its reinterpretations of the original compact, after the political *aggiornamenti* of the Reconstruction and of the New Deal, the court contributed to legitimise the Constitution,[26] so that it could symbolise the principles of a reconciled nation. Since then, the sacralisation of the Constitution by the professional body of lawyers, the continuing practice of stressing what is genuinely American (and hence not European) in it,[27] and the 'near religious veneration' of which the *Federalist Papers* have become the object, have continued to convey this constitutional culture.[28] What defines loyal citizens—by opposition to traitors, be they racist, communist or terrorist—is precisely their willingness to confine their disagreements to the places and mechanisms prescribed by the constitution, and to formulate them in constitutional terms. The presence of an indisputable common ground is what makes disagreements tolerable. Such a 'common ground' is precisely what is called for by the tenants of a 'constitutional patriotism' for the European Union. Yet, does it match a Union of states?

MIMETISM AND OPPOSITION: EUROPEAN CONSTITUTIONAL PATRIOTISM AND THE 'AMERICAN MODEL'

Despite the fact that the concept of 'constitutional patriotism' was coined with very specifically European concerns in mind, the 'American model' has been a constant reference in the debates it has given rise to. When he introduced this concept in the late 1970s, German political scientist Dolf Sternberger had a very specific aim: he sought to redeem the nature of patriotism in a country where the word itself sounded odd, the Federal Republic of Germany (FRG). In substance, his argument went as follows: since Nazism had rendered any ethnic conception of nationhood unacceptable in post-war Germany, and since the German 'people' was divided into two states, the only resource available to build a new form of civic link in the FRG were the values encapsulated in the Fundamental Law of the Bonn Republic. The rule of law, liberal democracy, federalism and 'social market economy', despite their apparent abstractness, are values which have, he argued, generated convictions and behaviours that can be likened to those which form the basis of patriotism. By repudiating the past—the centralist,

[26] Ackerman, n 9 above.
[27] GP Fletcher, *Loyalty: An Essay on the Morality of Relationships* (Oxford: Oxford University Press, 1993).
[28] Bailyn, n 10 above, at 104.

authoritarian, racist, inegalitarian features of the Reich—and by providing the German people with liberal–democratic ambitions, the Fundamental Law was the highest symbol of this 'new era' in the history of their country. Sternberger's argument was thus primarily rooted in a German context, yet the values of the FRG Fundamental Law obviously reflected those of its American godfather, and in the course of his demonstration Sternberger referred to the US as a plausible example of how a 'civil religion' can cement a nation. A few years later, when the concept was used to address other issues, the historical precedent of the United States was again taken as an example. The liberal political movements who used 'post-national' and 'constitutional' links to rethink the German law of nationality in the 1980s—arguing that if 'Germanhood' were based on political principles rather than ethnic features, it could be extended to foreigners settled in the Federal Republic, provided they share the values and objectives formalised by the Constitution—once again took America as a political model.

In the early 1990s, the phrase 'constitutional patriotism' became popular in the discussions on a third issue, the political meaning of European integration, when Jürgen Habermas borrowed this concept in his writings on European identity. Arguing that the 'communautarian' vision of nationhood doesn't match the EU's diversity—and would contradict the EU's commitment to protect diversity against centralising and standardising trends—he supported a 'post-national' conception of citizenship, inspired by the 'republican' tradition. Citizens cannot and do not need to forget their national identity to become truly European citizens. Yet, this does not prevent them from forming a political community, to the extent that they share constitutional values and are ready to assess their own national tradition in the light of these principles. In the future European Union, the same principles would have 'to be interpreted from the vantage point of different national traditions and histories. One's own national tradition will, in each case, have to be appropriated in such a manner that it is related and relativised by the vantage point of other national cultures'.[29] Habermas' conceptual references were drawn from the writings of the European Enlightenment, and primarily from the concept of a 'civic nation' associated with the French Revolution. But when he endeavoured to demonstrate the plausibility of this scenario, he shifted to the US—and Switzerland—as an historical illustration of how a political community can be built on the basis of a public philosophy formalised by the constitution.

Since then, the 'American experience' has become the paradigm of constitutional patriotism for those Europeans who think about the possibility of building a polity beyond the nation-state, and the experience of the

[29] J Habermas, 'Citizenship and National Identity. Some Reflections on the Future of Europe' (1992) 12(1) *Praxis International* 1–19 at 7.

European Convention, so often compared to the precedent of Philadelphia, has made this comparison ever more popular. To be sure, this American reference is not always explicit. Indeed, the proponents of a European wide constitutional patriotism have struggled to demonstrate that a non-statist Constitution makes sense and that the EU is a polity whose constitutional foundations may be written down in a legal text, without turning it into a Federal State such as the United States. But escaping from the statist matrix actually proves very difficult.

Habermas's recent intellectual evolution is an interesting illustration of these conceptual difficulties. Initially, in the wake of the public discussions raised by the ratification of the Maastricht Treaty in the early 1990s, he sought to demonstrate that the EU could form a distinctive constitutional patriotism, without becoming a super state. His case was, however, conceptually vague. Habermas first argued that the EU is different from a communautarian nation-state because it is based on civic, rather than ethnic foundations. So far, so good. But what, then, distinguishes Habermas's post-national polity from a multinational state? French sociologist Dominique Schnapper makes a good point when she recalls that, in the republican tradition: 'It is the effort to break from identities and memberships that are felt to be natural through the abstraction of citizenship which characterises the national project'.[30] Understood in these republican terms, Habermas's polity appears as a nation writ large—something he implicitly acknowledges when he takes Switzerland and the United States as illustrations.

Far from alleviating this conceptual weakness, Habermas has deepened it in his more recent writings about constitutional patriotism. Anxious not to be seen as a naive idealist, Habermas has taken the critique of the civic nationalists seriously. In substance, these authors claim that constitutional patriotism 'does not provide the kind of political identity that nationality provides'[31] because 'the intellectual adherence to abstract principles—human rights, respect for the state of law—cannot replace, at least in the foreseeable future, the sentimental and political mobilisation that is aroused by the internalisation of the national tradition'[32]. Habermas retorts that the first mistake of those who think that constitutional patriotism is impossible, would be forgetting 'the voluntaristic character of a civic nation, the collective identity of which exists neither independent of nor prior to the

[30] D Schnapper, *La Communauté des citoyens: Sur l'idée moderne de nation* (Paris: Gallimard, 1994), 99.

[31] D Miller, *On Nationality* (Oxford: Clarendon Press, 1995), 163.

[32] Schnapper, n 30 above, at 79. These critiques are unfair to Habermas when they feign to believe that he sees 'constitutional patriotism as a substitute for nationality of the more familiar sort' (Miller, previous n, at 163) as Habermas nowhere imagines substituting, but complementing nationality with constitutional patriotism.

democratic process from which it springs'.[33] The practice of citizenship requires symbols, representations, narrative etc, but these are not offered by race or history, they are built by the political community. Habermas draws two consequences from this beginning.

Firstly, he considers that the link between nationality and citizenship is not conceptual but historical and that nothing prevents the forming of a larger civic bond: 'why should this generation of a highly artificial kind of civic solidarity—a 'solidarity among strangers'—be doomed to come to a final halt just at the borders of our classical nation-states?'.[34] Secondly, he states that, far from being a constraint, the history of national citizenship is a resource for this larger civic bond:

> the artificial conditions in which national consciousness came into existence recall the empirical circumstances necessary for an extension of that process of identity-formation beyond national boundaries. These are: the emergence of a European civil society; the construction of a European-wide public sphere; and the shaping of a political culture that can be shared by all European citizens.[35]

Although he denies projecting 'a familiar design from the national onto the European level',[36] Habermas finally gives a very conventional version of constitutional patriotism. He argues that the adoption of a European Constitution could be the 'symbolic crystallization' of a 'political act of foundation', echoing the arguments of those republicans who acknowledge that 'the enacting of a formal Constitution can be an historic act that plays a very significant role in national history'.[37] For the German philosopher, a charter of fundamental rights would help emphasise 'the common core of a European identity' by recalling 'the character of the painful learning process it has gone through' and the 'lasting memories of nationalist excess and moral abyss'. Federal-type institutions would also help politicise the stakes and set up social policies so as to embed 'economic arguments for an ever-closer union into a much broader union'. Moreover, while preserving multilingualism as a symbol of the mutual recognition of national cultures, the European Union should use English 'as a working language at face-to-face level, wherever the parties lack another common idiom'.[38] One can wonder, then, if Habermas does not simply theorise the classic federalist vision for Europe which remains so popular in Germany. A Constitution embodying

[33] J Habermas, 'Why Europe Needs a Constitution?' (2001) 11 *New Left Review* 5–26, at 15.
[34] J Habermas, *Après l'Etat-nation: Une nouvelle constellatioj politique* (Paris: Fayard, 2000) 109.
[35] Habermas, n 33 above, at 16.
[36] Habermas, n 33 above, at 18.
[37] Miller, n 31 above, at 163.
[38] Habermas, n 33 above, at 6, 19, 9, 21.

shared political principles—and symbolising the break with a bitter past—would make political mobilisations on issues of social justice possible. These mobilisations would, in turn, strengthen the citizens' sense of trust and solidarity and ultimately their attachment to the EU's basic principles. By recalling that a civic identity should be build through the democratic experience, and by drawing the institutions and policies that could arouse a transnational political mobilisation in Europe, Habermas intends to show that 'constitutional patriotism' is not a perspective as disembodied as is often said. But he tries so hard to convince the most traditionalist republicans, that he ends up adopting their arguments and undercutting his own.

In his writings inspired by the war in Iraq, Habermas went one step further than describing the EU as an FRG writ large. He added the only element of a national scenario he had left aside so far: opposition to an 'Other'. On 31 May 2003, Habermas teamed up with the French philosopher Jacques Derrida to produce a manifesto on the new European identity which was published simultaneously in the *Frankfürter Allgemeine Zeitung* and *Libération*. In their argument, the 'rebirth of Europe' occurred on 15 February 2003, when millions marched on the streets against the American foreign policy in Iraq.[39] This European identity could be seen in their eyes as a counterweight to the United States. Not having experienced the horrors of twentieth-century warfare on their own soil, Americans lack the Europeans' peculiar capacity to understand and accept differences. The Europeans, on the contrary, cultivating the memory of their own past, are endowed with a specific 'civilizing' mission: that of acting as a counterweight to the 'callous superpower' US. The loop is looped, so to say: as the Americans had formed their constitutional pride in opposition to Europe, so Europeans could now find the moral glue of their own polity in a conscious opposition to the US. Paradoxically, America is both the model and the counter-model of this Euro-patriotism.

It is worth recalling that post-nationalism initially considered that Europe's 'Other' was Europe itself.[40] By making a decisive break with the populist nationalism of their own past, the Europeans were supposed to fight their former selves, not some Schmittian 'enemy'. Shifting from a reflexive attitude towards a more trivial polemical behaviour, Derrida and Habermas actually replicate the strategy of these American intellectuals who highlight the 'Americanness' of their identity by contrasting it to the European other. In so doing, they also resort to affective motives and abandon the original plea for a rational and critical foundation of collective identities.[41] Moreover, they

[39] J Derrida and J Habermas, 'Europe: Plaidoyer pour une politique extérieure commune' *Libération* (31 May 2003), 44–46.

[40] J Lacroix and K Nicolaïdis, 'Order and Justice Beyond the Nation-State: Europe's Competing Paradigms' in R Foot and A Hurrell (eds) *Order and Justice in International Relations* (Oxford: Oxford University Press, 2003) 125–54.

[41] JW Müller, 'Europe: Le pouvoir des sentiments: L'europatriotisme en question' (2004) *La République des idées*, at <http://www.repid.com/aticle.php3?id_article=192>.

contradict the very foundation of post-nationalism when they contemplate the emergence of a single European demos. The two thinkers indeed conclude that the Europeans will accept democratic discipline, that is the authority of the majority over the minority, when they understand themselves as being constituted of one people sharing a 'common political destiny'.[42] All the citizens from every European nation should thus consider any individual living in another European state as being 'one of us'.[43]

This temptation is widespread among the supporters of a European constitutional patriotism. The French philosopher Jean-Marc Ferry has convincingly shown that constitutional patriotism differs both from a 'legal' patriotism in that it rests upon a relationship with one's history and from a 'historical' patriotism for it rests on a *critical* relationship to one's history).[44] Yet, Ferry does not abandon the prospect of a 'European state' or that of a 'European demos' beyond national borders.[45] For Ferry, the European construct should bridge the gap between the 'moral' and the 'legal' communities. To be sure, Jean-Marc Ferry does not think that the European legal and moral communities should be completely congruent.[46] Although he borrows Michael Walzer's terms, he does not contemplate a fully fledged European state supported by a warm sense of belonging. But he nevertheless thinks of pan-European distributive policies and reforms of the European public sphere with a view to provide European citizenship with warmer and thicker moral foundations. In the end, his philosophical ambition remains like Habermas to go beyond Rawls's 'overlapping consensus' by making norms and values coincide. What used to be a 'liberal–republican' point of view is not far from shading into a new form of Euro-patriotism.

'WE VERSUS WE': THE EUROPEAN UNION FROM CONSTITUTIONAL PATRIOTISM TO CONSTITUTIONAL SELF-DISCIPLINE

Seen through an American lens, the European Union thus seem to be faced with the following dilemma: either it remains a 'hollow shell', or it transforms itself into a fully-fledged federal republic with its own distinctive patriotic *ethos*. The Constitutional Treaty signed by the heads of state and government in October 2004 echoes this 'patriotic' ambition. Although the temptation to root the EU in religious values was rejected by a majority of the members of the European constitutional convention, they quite enthusiastically chose to stress the EU's values in a solemn preamble and a long Charter of Rights. In so doing, the drafters of the European 'Constitution' were moved by a desire to dwell on what distinguishes the EU from 'the

[42] Derrida and Habermas, n 39 above, at 45.
[43] *Ibid.*
[44] J-M Ferry, *La question de l'Etat européen*, Paris: Gallimard, 2000), 168.
[45] *Ibid.*, 38.
[46] *Ibid.*, 39.

other Union', and scholars will now endeavour to demonstrate the coherence and distinctiveness of this moral patrimony, and to present it as the first step towards a 'thick constitutional patriotism'.[47] Against this view, we argue that this temptation should be resisted. Those who pretend to promote a distinctive EU should bear in mind that replicating the 'we versus them' pattern of thought which made constitutional patriotism possible in the US would paradoxically destroy what is so unique in the EU's constitutional grammar.

The first and most simple critique that could be raised against 'constitutional patriotism' is simply that Europe doesn't need it. If the EU were based on constitutional hierarchy, it would be necessary to guarantee the 'primacy' of the citizens' loyalty to the Union. This is the classic idea of 'constitutional patriotism', inspired by the Greek and Roman tradition. Yet, the European Union differs from other 'compound republics' in that it does not rest on the supreme authority of a single *demos,* and does not reduce national feelings to mere sentimental rituals.[48] Since its creation, the European construct has established itself as a new kind of polity defined by the persistent plurality of its peoples.[49] Indeed, what is so unique about the European process is not that it promotes universal democratic values. Rather, Europe's singularity lies in that it does not seek to rely on one *demos* but on multiple *demoi* working together without becoming one. Joseph Weiler has powerfully shown that this European peculiarity has two consequences. First, the European constitutional discipline does not enjoy (nor need to enjoy) the same kind of authority as may be found in the US—and for that matter in all federal states—where federalism is rooted in a single and sovereign will . Second, the primacy of European law does not go on a par with the primacy of legislative authority. European federalism is 'constructed with a top-to-bottom hierarchy of norms, but with a bottom-to-top hierarchy of authority and real power'.[50]

This doesn't amount to saying that European integration is a purely horizontal process. European states and their citizens accept constraints defined in the Union's basic rules to make their coexistence possible, and these constraints are, in several respects, more demanding than those of US federalism.[51] They accept the primacy of European law—including the

[47] M Kumm, 'Thick Constitutional Patriotism and the Treaty Establishing a Constitution for Europe', paper presented at the Cidel Conference, Constitutionalism and Democracy in the European Union, London, 11–13 November 2004.

[48] R Bellamy and D Castiglione, 'Between Cosmopolis and Community: Three Models of Rights and Democracy within the European Union' in D Archibugi, D Held and M Kölher (eds) *Re-Imagining Political Community* (Cambridge: Polity, 1998).

[49] K Nicolaïdis, 'We the Peoples of Europe' (2004) 83(6) *Foreign Affairs* 97–110

[50] J Weiler, 'Federalism without Constitutionalism: Europe's Sonderweg' in K Nicolaïdis and R Howse (eds) *The Federal Vision, Legitimacy and Levels of Governance in the United States and the European Union* (Oxford: Oxford University Press, 2001), 57.

[51] D Halberstam, 'Of Power and Responsibility: The Political Morality of Federal Systems' (2004) 90(3) *Virginia Law Review* 101–98.

charter—over their own law. They accept to be outvoted in some matters, and to be brought to Court when they breach their obligations. The EU is far more than a confederation of sovereign states. Since *Van Gend and Loos* (1963) the direct effect and the supremacy of Community law is grounded in a direct relation between European norms and the peoples. But these peoples are also organised as states which remain at the core of the Union. In the EU's peculiar constitutionalism, the Member States abide by constitutional discipline, not because they are subordinate to a higher sovereignty and authority attaching to norms validated by the federal people, but by their own will.[52] Their discipline is 'an autonomous voluntary act, endlessly renewed on each occasion, of subordination, in the discrete arenas governed by Europe to a norm which is the aggregate expression of other wills, other political identities, other political communities'.[53]

Such a constitutional discipline is inherently different from 'patriotism', even of the 'constitutional' variety. Patriotism evokes 'loyalty', which is an affective representation: 'It is not a considered choice but what we feel for our kin and club. It is simply an expression of our whole personality'.[54] More often than not, loyalty is the kind of discipline required by groups of which one does not choose to belong—a family, nation, an ethnic or religious group, and so on. It may sometimes be the result of a deliberate adhesion—such as in the case of party membership—but even then it entails 'a commitment that is affective in character and generated by a great deal more of our personality than calculation or moral reasoning'.[55] Such a feeling might be needed in a state, which involves the redistribution of wealth, accepting the rule of the majority, and ultimately being prepared to die for one's country. It is not required in the EU because the EU is not a state. Here, all we need is 'obligation', a relationship which is 'evoked by rules whose validity we assess and recognise for a variety of explicit reasons, whether they be prudential or ethical or both'.[56] We accept rules on rational grounds because they serve our interests; because we realise that they protect us against potential abuses, or because they correspond to our idea of political justice. What this requires is not a sense of loyalty to a people over our attachment to the smaller groups it contains; not a simple subordination to the broader legal order, as in Cicero's republican patriotism. What the EU demands is an attitude of self-restraint and a capacity to restrain one's own national passions when they conflict with the others'. We believe this is a more accurate description of why states and citizens actually accept EU discipline: they abide by norms, not because they reflect

[52] M Maduro, 'Contrapunctual Law : European Constitutional Pluralism in Action' in N Walker (ed) *Sovereignty in Transition* (Oxford: Hart, 2003).
[53] Weiler, n 50 above, at 68.
[54] Shklar, 'Waltzer' in Hoffman (ed), n 5 above, at 380.
[55] Shklar, 'Obligation' in Hoffman (ed), n 5 above, at 41; Fletcher, n 27 above.
[56] Shklar, 'Waltzer' in Hoffman (ed), n 5 above, at 381.

'values' or 'shared understandings', but out of calculation or of consent to the rules. In any case, for rational reasons.

This leads us to a second critique of constitutional patriotism. By stressing the 'values' which allegedly underlie our commitments, constitutional patriotism could deprive the EU of its most original asset: its 'rational' nature. Because they are rational, our European obligations force us to constantly reflect on our national loyalty. In Weiler's terms:

> European integration may be seen, then, as an attempt to control the excesses of the modern nation-state in Europe ... . The European Community was to be an antidote to the negative features of the state and statal intercourse.[57]

The European Union would break with its own principles if it were to become a 'normal' polity, based on a single 'demos' and a widespread emotional attachment to the 'values' encapsulated in the 'federal' constitution, for the European process was precisely deemed a 'political practice of refusing and resisting particular identifications'.[58] Instead of 'patriotism', nurtured by an opposition to another (a principled opposition like a family quarrel today, but what tomorrow?), the EU needs a 'constitutional discipline' founded on rational calculations and a readiness to assess critically one's own national loyalty. Europe's finality has been to ensure that no patriotism is immune from a sceptical check. It forces us to re-examine, in permanence, the reasons of our obligation. And prevent it from deriving towards loyalty.

Still, one should not reduce the dynamics of integration to a one-way opposition between a national '*Eros*' and a supranational 'Civilization'.[59] It would be a historical misreading to consider the nation as a mere emotional community. Social scientists and historians have convincingly shown that, more often than not, nations were born as artificial communities promoting universal norms against communal and religious ties. To be sure, in their struggle against those traditional links, nations had to 'invent traditions' and to use the language of ethnicity, history and mythology. This amounts to say that the nation encompasses the two dimensions of '*Eros*' and 'Civilization'. Consequently, the European integration process should not be seen as a top-down movement in which a rational Europe tames an 'erotic' nation. Sometimes, national loyalty will conflict with European obligations. Far from being a problem, this is precisely what makes the EU valuable.[60] By criticising the EU in the name of values associated with our

[57] J Weiler, *The Constitution of Europe* (Cambridge: Cambridge University Press, 1999), 341.

[58] P Markell 'Making Affect Safe for Democracy', (2000) 28 *Political Theory* 38–64 at 57.

[59] J Weiler, 'To Be a European Citizen: *Eros* and Civilization' (1997) 4(4) *Journal of European Public Policy* 495–519.

[60] P Magnette, *L'Europe, l'Etat et la démocratie: Le souverain apprivoisé* (Brussels: Complexe, 2000); and his 'European Citizenship: Between Cosmopolitanism and Nationalism' in K Nicolaïdis and S Weatherhill (eds) *Whose Europe? National Models and the Constitution of the European Union* (Oxford: Oxford University Press/European Studies, 2003).

national links, we prevent it from its own abuses. In his only comment on the European Union, John Rawls evoked such a risk, that of a 'civil society awash in a meaningless consumerism of some kind'. Rawls stressed the value of nationalities, and he did so by contrasting the EU to the American model.

> One question the Europeans should ask themselves, if I may hazard a suggestion, is how far reaching they want their Union to be. It seems to me that much would be lost if the European Union became a federal union like the United States. Here there is a common language of political discourse and a ready willingness to move from one state to another. Isn't there a conflict between a large free and open market comprising all of Europe and the individual nation-states, each with its separate political and social institutions, historical memories, and forms and traditions of social policy. Surely these are of great value to the citizens of these countries and give meaning to their life.[61]

Rawls did not elaborate this critique but it points to an interesting intuition. Against those who denounce the EU's weakness, he stressed the necessity to preserve national identities. More than that, he seemed to consider that preserving Europe's cultural diversity would be the best antidote against the drive towards a 'market society'. In this quasi-Rousseauist critique, he described national feelings as a resource against the impoverishment of our personal development. National loyalties remain valuable in the EU to the extent that they prevent the anomie generated by abstract norms. This is were the originality of the Union lies: in this constant process of dialogue between national values and European norms, which has managed so far to prevent both the excesses of loyalty and the anomie of asbtract normativity.

CONCLUSION

This chapter has argued that those who think about the EU's constitutional identity should not be upset by the 'American experience': seeing it as a model that could be imitated conceals the EU's uniqueness; using it as a counter-model, an 'other' which could help Europe take conscience of its own identity, paradoxically amounts to replicating the American path and undermines the EU's foundations. Instead of looking towards an hypothetical 'moral community' based on conscious 'values', Europeans should rather discriminate between the 'thick' values embedded in their national identities and the 'thin' European norms, and see the virtues of a constant and peaceful opposition between these two forms of relationships. This distinction

[61] J Rawls and P Van Parijs, 'Three letters on The Law of the Peoples and the European Union', (2003) *Revue de philosophie économique* 7–20 at 9.

between 'values' and 'norms', between 'moral' and 'legal' obligations[62] or between 'loyalty' and 'obligation'[63] is a key element of liberal constitutionalism. It does not amount to saying that 'values' pertain to a pre-modern world that should be gradually bypassed, and that human beings liberated from traditionalist contexts will feel happy to abide by abstract, cold and rational norms. It simply means that in a pluralist world, agreed norms are a better way to deal with conflicts of loyalty than so-called 'shared values'. In this spirit, the 'abstractness' and the 'value-free' character of the European construct, often seen as its main weaknesses, might be Europe's most original assets since this abstraction helps peoples with different values find compromises compatible with their agreed norms. Turning our 'rational' adhesion to the EU into a 'thicker' attachment based on deep 'moral' values could raise conflicts with our other moral links. It could generate 'conflicts of loyalty', leaving no choice but to assert the predominance of the EU over national links, or to dissolve the EU. Adhering to a cold, thin, abstract community such as the EU protects our personal autonomy against the sometimes extravagant claims for loyalty inherent in 'moral communities'. *Pace* Ackerman, the EU will not give rise to 'pride and hope', but it is precisely for this reason that it will prevent the replication of those 'fears and humiliations' which justified its creation.

[62] JS Mill, *On Liberty* (Cambridge: Cambridge University Press, 1986).
[63] Shklar, n 5 above; Fletcher, above n 27.

14

Governance and American Political Development

MARK TUSHNET

INSTITUTIONAL INNOVATIONS OCCUR almost constantly in the United States, and each is presented by its proponents as a new and better way of doing whatever the proponents think is worth doing. An interesting question, which I explore in this Chapter, is this: What are the political circumstances under which some innovations become significant in shaping large-scale policy?[1] In my view, we can identify those circumstances by examining the large-scale structures of national governance—the functional constitution. Those structures in turn have been shaped by several constitutional features: The United States has a presidential system in which, over time, the President has come to play the leading role in initiating policy on the national level; it has a separation-of-powers system in which presidential initiatives must obtain approval by—and are reshaped by—Congress; and its elections are first-past-the-post elections by districts. These features conduce to the development of a nationally focused two-party system, and the interests of the two major national parties play the dominant role in my account of the circumstances under which institutional innovations will become stabilised.[2]

The United States has experienced a series of what I call constitutional orders or regimes—combinations of ideological presuppositions and institutional arrangements that are compatible with and reinforce those presuppositions.[3] From the 1940s through the 1970s there was something identifiable as a New Deal–Great Society constitutional order. Its ideological presuppositions included: (1) a rather strong commitment to ascriptive

[1] Here 'large-scale' could refer to policies adopted on the national level or policies adopted by a large number of local jurisdictions.

[2] I note that my attention to the functional rather than the textual Constitution is at least partially justified by the fact that the textual Constitution of the United States is old and general (in the respects relevant to my discussion). As a result, essentially any institutional innovation is, or can with a lawyer's ingenuity be made to be, consistent with the textual Constitution. (This assertion would of course be challenged by originalists of a certain sort. In the event that institutional innovations stabilise in ways compatible with the *other* commitments of such originalists, I believe that they would not have much influence.)

[3] Mark Tushnet, *The New Constitutional Order* (2003).

equality, that is, the proposition that a person's generic characteristics were irrelevant to his or her place in society; (2) a modest commitment to substantive equality, that is, the proposition that everyone should receive roughly similar shares of material wealth unless there were good reasons to depart from equality; and (3) a commitment, of varying strength over time, to the view that economic markets when regulated in only traditional ways generated more social distress than was acceptable, accompanied by the view that new forms of regulation developed and guided by technical professionals could alleviate that distress. Its institutional embodiments included a strong commitment to governing through decisions made by national-level institutions, presidential initiative in law-making at that level, and the incorporation of interest groups and professionals into the processes of making and especially administering policy.

The New Deal–Great Society constitutional order is no longer with us. What has replaced it remains unclear. Some believe that the United States is undergoing an extremely long transition from the old order to a new, substantially more conservative one. I have argued, in contrast, that the United States has had a new constitutional order for perhaps a decade. Its institutional arrangements include divided government at the national level; its ideological commitments include a scaling-back of the ambitions of the prior order without, however, repudiating that order's fundamental commitments to national power, ascriptive equality and economic regulation. Importantly, the set of institutional arrangements currently in place in the United States continues to incorporate interest groups in policy making and administration.

In this chapter I draw on the literature on American political development to speculate about where the current constitutional order might go. That literature emphasises the role of presidents in transforming constitutional orders. Transformative presidents set two processes in train. They offer cogent articulations of new ideological presuppositions, which they and, again importantly, their successors can elaborate and embody in specific policies. And, transformative presidents begin to develop new institutional arrangements that will mature to displace the ones against which such presidents must contend. The literature on American political development also emphasises the accumulated weight of institutional forms. It argues that the institutional forms of one regime are layered on to those of its predecessors, and that the accumulated weight of those forms becomes increasingly difficult to displace.[4] So, to use an example that will play a large role in what follows, the interest groups and professional organisations that played such a large role in the New Deal–Great Society constitutional order retain a great deal of political power, which will pose a more

[4] I believe that this layering is what Karen Orren and Stephen Skowronek capture in their awkward term *intercurrence*, although they also use that term in a broader, and in my judgment less analytically helpful, sense. For their discussion, see Karen Orren and Stephen Skowronek, *The Search for American Political Development* (2004), 108–18.

substantial obstacle to a new transformation than did the institutional arrangements displaced by the New Deal order.

I begin by sketching the manner in which the New Deal–Great Society constitutional order decayed—again, leaving us either with a new constitutional order or awaiting one. I then examine the possibilities for a president-led transformation of the existing arrangements and ideological commitments. Unsurprisingly, those possibilities are greater for Republican presidents, and I outline how we can see some recent Republican policies as incipient strategies of transformation. I then turn to the Democrats, for whom the possibilities seem much more limited.[5]

Franklin Roosevelt put in place the essential components of the New Deal–Great Society constitutional order. Overcoming the Supreme Court's constitutional objections to a system in which economic policy would be developed and implemented at the national level, Roosevelt centralised policy-making capacity in the presidency. The Great Depression gave force to long-standing views held by progressives that economic markets needed more interventionist regulation if they were to operate smoothly. Roosevelt put technical professionals in charge of developing and implementing new regulatory policies to stabilise the economy. Overcoming political objections from Southern and other conservative Democrats, Roosevelt made ascriptive equality the heart of substantive policy, supporting the claims of African Americans to enhanced political participation in the South. Roosevelt also built substantive equality into the policy agenda, through his creation of a national pension system and his support of labour organising. Both these aspects of the policy agenda were, of course, consistent with a political strategy aimed at entrenching the Democratic Party in positions of national power. The political benefits of supporting a modest programme of substantive equality were obvious; labour unions could provide important political support for Roosevelt; and the beneficiaries of old-age pensions would be cemented into the New Deal coalition by the Social Security system. Mobilising those subordinated by ascriptive inequality was a useful way to overcome the political power of conservatives who opposed the *other* aspects of Roosevelt's preferred policies.[6] Finally, economic regulation under the guidance of technical professionals built those professionals into the operation of the national government, giving them a stake in making the national government the locus where policy was made.

Institutionally, Roosevelt's programmes were to be administered by national bureaucracies. Those bureaucracies were staffed from two sources.

[5] I doubt that anything analytically important turns on focusing on the role of presidents in transforming constitutional orders. What matters, I believe, is this: Possibilities for transformation always exist, as do small-scale 'models' of institutional arrangements that might become more widespread, but it takes political leadership to convert those small-scale models into larger forms that constitute a new constitutional order. As it happens, US presidents provided that leadership in the twentieth century (with Representative Newt Gingrich offering a modest exception).

[6] For a recent analysis, see Kevin J McMahon, *Reconsidering Roosevelt on Race: How the Presidency Paved the Road to* Brown (2004).

Roosevelt looked to the interest groups that he was incorporating into the Democratic political coalition to provide the staff for the agencies that dealt with substantive policies of most concern to each such interest group. In doing so, he began to construct the so-called 'iron triangle' of domestic policy-making, with the interest groups at one apex, the federal bureaucracy at another, and (in the usual formulation) Congress as the third. In addition, Roosevelt endorsed the view, articulated in prior decades by the progressives, that trained and specialised professionals—lawyers, economists, social workers and the like—were particularly well-suited for implementing substantive policy because their training made them sensitive to the range of considerations that had to be taken into account if well-designed policies were to be executed well.

Lyndon Johnson's Great Society programmes deepened the New Deal's commitments to equality and an interest-group-driven political system. Notably, the War on Poverty was designed so as to make possible an alliance between newly mobilised poor people and social-welfare bureaucrats, to be used by national political leaders to weaken the political power of local politicians.[7] The New Deal–Great Society coalition began to decay in the 1960s. The War in Vietnam contributed to discrediting claims that national-level decision makers were particularly talented at making policy,[8] as did the corruption associated with Richard Nixon. In addition, the fiscal conditions for executing the New Deal–Great Society commitments to substantive equality disappeared, and yet the interest groups supporting those commitments continued to press for implementing them. The consequences were national economic policies that were neither economically nor politically sustainable.[9]

The conditions for replacing the New Deal–Great Society constitutional order were there. Conservative Republicans tried to take advantage of them, and achieved some degree of success. Their difficulties, though, tracked the two components of the existing constitutional order, its substantive commitments and its institutional arrangements. Barry Goldwater and, following him, Ronald Reagan did articulate a vision of government that contrasted sharply with the New Deal–Great Society vision. They were proponents of government policies that, they asserted, would enlarge the domain within which people could order their activities free of government supervision. Such policies, they argued, would not impair, but might even enhance, ascriptive and substantive equality, as individuals choosing freely

[7] It failed to do so, of course. Written before the language of American political development became widely used (and from a perspective unsympathetic to the political strategy the programme embodied), Moynihan's analysis provides strong support for the arguments made by scholars now using that language. Daniel Patrick Moynihan, *Maximum Feasible Misunderstanding: Community Action in the War on Poverty* (1969).

[8] David Halberstam captured the point in the ironic title of his examination of national policy making during the Vietnam War. David Halberstam, *The Best and the Brightest* (1972).

[9] An early diagnosis of the looming difficulties was James O'Connor, *The Fiscal Crisis of the State* (1973).

would generate a larger economic pie that could be divided according to each person's individual willingness to work and contribute to society. And, they argued, the policies they supported scaled back the New Deal's regulatory innovations because the economic problems to which the New Deal and Great Society addressed themselves were smaller than their opponents believed and because, in any event, the New Deal–Great Society's regulatory interventions were badly designed to deal with what problems there were.

The ideological component of the conservative challenge to the New Deal-Great Society constitutional order had its own difficulties, though. The conservatives' claims that their policies would achieve equality were unpersuasive, partly because the length of time the prior constitutional order had been in place meant that many people could not believe that anything other than New Deal–Great Society policies could actually promote equality, and partly because many individual conservatives had long personal histories of rejecting in principle the claims of equality. Claims that better regulations could be designed were in tension with claims that the economy did not require New Deal-style regulation, leading to scepticism about the possibility that conservative Republicans were the right people to come up with better regulations.

Perhaps most important, though, there was an inconsistency at the heart of the conservatives' ideology considered as a programme of political transformation. Substantively, the conservatives called for reducing the role of government, and in particular for reducing the role of the national government, in everyday life. Yet, this substantive programme was to be achieved by deploying the power of the national government. *Presidents* were to remain the central figures in the political order envisioned by the conservatives—as they would have to, if the conservative political order was to have any staying power.

The conservatives' institutional difficulties proved even more daunting. They faced national bureaucracies that had been entrenched for a decade and more. The staffs of those bureaucracies were adept at using the tools of government to defeat efforts to transform the bureaucracies' missions. They could use processes—studies, hearings, openness to outside comments, and the like—that were seemingly neutral as to substance as a means of impeding policy change. The entrenched bureaucracies made policy change so difficult that it became credible to claim that conservative policies had been tried and had failed.

There was an obvious strategic response, but it was one that would reproduce rather than replace the institutional arrangements of the New Deal–Great Society constitutional order. The response was to accept the role that interest groups would play in developing national policy, but to replace one set of interest groups with another. Instead of staffing the bureaucracy with people drawn from the interest groups that made up the Democratic Party coalition, staff it with people drawn from business- and Republican-oriented interest groups. Two recent examples of the strategy are the so-called 'K Street Project', which involved threats by Republican members of Congress to penalise lobbyists who did not contribute to the Republican party (and thereby accepted the role of lobbyists in policy making),[10] and Vice President Cheney's Energy Task Force, to which industry-based lobbyists had differential access relative to consumer- and environmental-oriented lobbyists.[11]

What we have now in the United States is a constitutional order in which the institutional arrangements of the prior constitutional order have been eroded only slightly and in which the ideological positions of the New Deal–Great Society order have not been fully repudiated or replaced by consistently conservative ones, but have instead been tempered or, as I sometimes put it, chastened. Notably, though, at least on the right the ideological programme is reasonably clear. Several generations of conservative thinkers and politicians have put forth a vision of government that, with sufficient political support, would change national policy dramatically. Ascriptive equality would remain important, as the conservative rejection of affirmative action indicates, but substantive equality would become irrelevant as a policy matter.[12] Economic activity would be subject to fewer non-traditional forms of regulation, and the regulations that remained in place would attempt to capitalise on economic incentives rather than use the New Deal's command-and-control form. The challenge to conservatives lies in connecting their ideological vision to a set of institutional arrangements that would provide stable support for politicians who sought to implement that vision.

I find it convenient to distinguish between institutional strategies that involve undermining the opposition and those that involve strengthening one's own support. There are of course a large number of discrete strategies—including gerrymandering and purging the voting rolls—that can be used to weaken the opposition. Yet, these are unlikely to be stable institutional arrangements, because their successes, and the length of time they will remain successful, depend on a large number of contingencies, such as continuing control over the processes of districting (in a nation with a mobile population).

More stable, but more problematic, are substantive programmes that have the effect of weakening the ability of non-Republicans to vote.

[10] For a description of the K Street Project, see Nicholas Confessore, 'Welcome to the Machine: How the GOP Disciplined K Street and Made Bush Supreme,' *Washington Monthly* (July/August 2003).

[11] The argument developed here would be better supported by examples from the late 1980s than by contemporary examples. My primary defence is the limits of time, but a secondary one is that if I am right in thinking that the new constitutional order has been in place since the early 1990s, contemporary examples are almost as good as ones drawn from the earlier period.

[12] Here the key move would be to defend tax programmes aimed at increasing the differential in wealth between the higher and the lower income brackets as desirable in principle, and not on the ground that aiding the rich indirectly aids the poor. One can see hints of this move in the use of the phrase 'class warfare' to attack those who point out the effects of such policies on substantive equality, but I do not think that the position has yet received a full ideological articulation.

Restricting public assistance programmes to the point where recipients have to spend so much time complying with the programme's requirements that they cannot realistically be expected to vote is one possibility. My sense, though, is that the level to which assistance would have to be reduced to have these effects is so low that the programmes would run up against continuing attachment to norms requiring a commitment to a modest version of substantive equality.

More interesting are strategies aimed directly at the institutional arrangements of the New Deal–Great Society order, and in particular at the interest groups and professionals in the 'iron triangle'. The most prominent among these have been efforts to 'de-fund the left', by restricting or eliminating federal programmes that provide financial support, directly or indirectly, to the New Deal–Great Society interest groups and professionals. More subtle strategies exist. Converting the Great Society's discretionary social welfare programmes into programmes in which the only task of bureaucrats is to assemble information and check it against rigid rules has the effect of de-professionalising the administration of such programmes.[13] Gradually, such programmes become staffed by non-professional administrators, and the investment professionals have in such programmes is reduced. Recent reforms in public education have a similar effect. They induce teachers to 'teach to the test' rather than exercise independent judgment in designing programmes appropriate to their particular students. Teachers become 'workers' rather than professionals. Republican efforts at 'tort reform' can be understood in these terms as attempts to weaken the financial position of plaintiff-side tort lawyers, who have become an important source of campaign financing on the Democratic side.[14]

This second set of strategies is obviously quite attractive from the point of view of conservatives seeking to transform the US constitutional order. These strategies have an important drawback, though. They are more or less direct challenges to the interest groups and professionals, who can be expected to fight hard against them, using all the resources that bureaucrats typically have—delay, subversion by overly rigid interpretation of rules,

[13] See William H Simon, 'Legality, Bureaucracy, and Class in the Welfare System' (1986) 92 *Yale Law Journal* 1198.

[14] Why plaintiff-side tort lawyers became financial supporters of the Democratic Party remains underexplored. One possibility is this: Plaintiff-side tort lawyers are organised in the American Trial Lawyers' Association, which 'began in 1946 as an organisation of attorneys concerned about the lack of effective representation of injured laborers in the workers' compensation system' (Thomas F Burke, *Lawyers, Lawsuits, and Legal Rights: The Battle over Litigation in American Society* (2002), 47. These lawyers were already on labour's side. In addition, the legal structure of the US workers' compensation system induced them seek remedies against manufacturers for making defective equipment (as a way of getting around the fact that workers' compensation remedies were the exclusive means of getting redress from the workers' employers but did not preclude remedies against third parties). The expertise developed in these lawsuits then allowed the plaintiffs-side trial lawyers to become generalists in suits against large businesses for all types of defects in their products, not simply those that caused injury to workers. I am confident that the full story is much more complex than this sketch suggests.

leaks to sympathisers in the press, academy and Congress, and the like. Scholars of American political development are especially sceptical about the likelihood that such direct challenges can today be powerful enough to overcome the advantages entrenched interest groups and professionals have.

Instead of taking on the interest groups and professionals directly, conservatives might attempt to go around them. The idea is to develop institutions that mobilise political support from citizens 'on the ground', without the intervention of the New Deal–Great Society interest groups and professional organisations. One example is provided by the Bush administration's faith-based initiatives, which—if implemented so as to advance the transformative project—would provide support from the national government to religious institutions and their members, by-passing both the traditional interest groups of the New Deal–Great Society order and the professionals who traditionally have administered the service programmes encompassed in the faith-based initiatives.[15] Innovations in health care policy aim to make individuals more direct participants in the process of choosing modes of treatment.[16] Privatisation of the government supported pension system would have a two-fold effect: It would provide brokers with substantial fees for administering the private pension programmes individuals developed, and it would displace the national pension bureaucracy in favour of individual choice and responsibility. Because these programmes pose a threat to the New Deal–Great Society interest groups, they too have been resisted strenuously.[17]

A final obstacle to the consolidation of a new conservative constitutional order is, ironically, posed by the successes conservatives have already

[15] The churches that would administer the programmes are themselves institutions, of course, but they would be connected directly to the national government instead of having that connection mediated through some central organisation that itself dealt directly with the national government.

[16] Supreme Court decisions giving substantial constitutional protection to commercial advertising under the First Amendment's free speech clause encouraged regulatory agencies to reduce the degree of attention they paid to advertising of prescription medications directly to the public, with the result that patients now are in a position to ask their physicians to prescribe a particular medication. (This was predicted by then-Justice William Rehnquist in a dissent from the Court's first foray into the area of commercial advertising. *Virginia Board of Pharmacy v Virginia Citizens Consumer Council*, 425 US 748, 788 (1976) (Rehnquist, J., dissenting):

> Quite consistently with Virginia law requiring prescription drugs to be available only through a physician, 'our' pharmacist might run any of the following representative advertisements in a local newspaper:
>
> > Pain getting you down? Insist that your physician prescribe Demerol. You pay a little more than for aspirin, but you get a lot more relief.
> >
> > Can't shake the flu? Get a prescription for Tetracycline from your doctor today.
> >
> > Don't spend another sleepless night. Ask your doctor to prescribe Seconal without delay.

[17] I devote only this note to a more conventional constitutional law analysis. One of the weapons of the New Deal–Great Society's interest groups and professionals is the constitutional law developed to support the New Deal–Great Society constitutional order. For a discussion of the way in which the Supreme Court collaborated in constructing and supporting that order, see Mark Tushnet, 'The Supreme Court and the National Political Order: Collaboration and

achieved. In Stephen Skowronek's terms, conservatives have already had their transformative leaders—Ronald Reagan and Newt Gingrich.[18] Now they can have only successors to those leaders. And, as Skowronek emphasises, successor presidents face peculiar difficulties in articulating programmes that can inspire real transformation. Their difficulty is that they must (if they are to become successful in themselves, as politicians desire) simultaneously continue the transformation their predecessors initiated and place their distinctive mark on the transformation. That is never easy. It remains an open question whether conservatives now have the leadership that could accomplish this task, and sustain the transformation in the longer run.

The problems for Democrats are even larger, primarily because the party has not substantially reduced its dependence on the New Deal–Great Society interest groups and professionals for important political support. Consider, for example, the modifications of the contemporary party's commitments to ascriptive and substantive equality. Driven primarily by the political need to satisfy demands from the party's African American constituency, as represented by the leadership of nationally oriented interest groups, the party has become committed to affirmative action programmes that are in some tension with ascriptive equality. Yet, when characterised properly as programmes dealing with equality of outcome, such programmes are ways of implementing substantive equality. The modification of the party's commitments to equality so as to blend ascriptive and substantive themes is reflected as well in support for accommodation mandates in non-discrimination laws more generally.[19]

The interest-group dependence of the party, though, has meant that this modification has not yet been extended beyond traditional (African American) and newer (disabilities rights, religious organisations) interest groups to become a more general programme of securing substantive equality, particularly for the relatively poor. That same dependence impeded President Clinton's attempt to reformulate the modification of ascriptive and substantive equality in terms of promoting opportunity. Clinton emphasised investment in human capital through education and health care, as

Confrontation' in Ronald Kahn and Kenneth Kersch (eds) *The Supreme Court and American Political Development* (2005). The Supreme Court developed strongly separationist doctrines of church–state relations, under which direct monetary grants to religious institutions, even to support non-religious programmes, were constitutionally questionable. More recently the Supreme Court has modified that doctrine, allowing service-recipients to use *their* monetary grants for services provided by religious institutions. *Zelman v Simmons-Harris*, 536 US 639 (2002). But—indicating the way in which constitutional doctrine from an earlier era can itself impede the development of a new constitutional order, the Supreme Court has not (yet) held that general programmes of service provision *must* include religious institutions among those entitled to administer the benefits. *Locke v Davey*, 124 S Ct 1307 (2004).

[18] The terminology and analysis are drawn from Stephen Skowronek, *The Politics Presidents Make: Leadership from John Adams to George Bush* (1993).

[19] For a discussion of the equivalence of accommodation mandates and affirmative action, see, e.g., Christine Jolls, 'Antidiscrimination and Accommodation' (2001) 115 *Harvard Law Review* 642.

ways of offering people opportunities that, when seized, would promote equality. In doing so, he appropriated some of the themes articulated by the Reagan–Gingrich ideology.[20] Those themes, and Clinton's version, were in tension with the commitments of the Democratic Party's interest-group and professional constituencies, which were directly opposed to the modified versions of ascriptive and substantive equality, and as a result never gained a deep foothold within the party.

The Democratic Party's regulatory agenda has also been modified, in a way that simultaneously presents opportunities for developing new institutional arrangements and poses political difficulties within the party. I am most familiar with developments in regulation of health and safety in the workplace, but those developments are, I understand, mirrored in other substantive domains. The Clinton administration's project of 'reinventing government' had two components. The first, and probably the more prominent in public presentations, involved simple improvements in managerial efficiency. This component was entirely compatible with the existing structure of the national New Deal–Great Society bureaucracy.

The other component was more innovative. Exemplified by the administration's (thwarted) effort to expand nationally its Maine 200 programme for workplace safety and health, the new regulatory agenda called for regulation on the shop-floor, with participation by *local* regulatory professionals, both professionals employed by the government and those employed by the regulated entity. Participants in these programmes were encouraged to develop more effective health and safety programmes that would be responsive to shop-floor conditions and draw on local knowledge while remaining aware of developments elsewhere that might be emulated (though not commanded).[21]

The general structure of these and similar programmes is roughly the one commended by proponents of democratic experimentalism. They promise political gains to the Democratic Party because they incorporate professional expertise—at the local level—rather than repudiating it, as Republican programmes do. To that extent the programmes do not weaken the structural supports for the Democratic Party. Yet, the programmes do pose a different threat, not to professionals as such, but to the professional organisations operating at the national level in the manner of traditional interest groups. These programmes resemble the Republican ones discussed earlier in by-passing national-level organisations to elicit support directly from the local level. To capture the political valence of the programmes, we might say, for example, that in education the programmes seek to empower teachers (and parents), not teachers' unions. Yet, in doing so they pose some

[20] As the literature on American political development suggests a president from the 'opposition' party would.

[21] For a general and theoretically informed discussion of these innovations, see Orly Lobel, 'The Renew Deal: The Fall of Regulation and the Rise of Governance in Contemporary Legal Thought' (2004) 89 *Minnesota Law Review* 342.

threats to teachers' unions, or at least to the current leadership of those unions.

Party leaders as well as interest-group leaders have struggled, not entirely successfully, to figure out what stance to take toward these new modes of regulation.[22] Consider the 'problem' posed by the existing leadership of teachers' unions. As Louise Trubek has suggested,[23] the new institutions of governance elicit support in several stages.[24] First, they undermine the existing interest-group structure, then reconstitute it in a different form by re-professionalising teachers in their schoolrooms, redefining but not eliminating the craft elements that make teachers professionals. The political difficulty occurs because the reconstitution cannot take place until the existing interest-group structure has been undermined, but the occupants of positions within that structure will obstruct the transformative efforts.

Presumably, success can come when a party leader devises a way of defending the policies that generates enough support on the ground to either transform the positions taken by interest-group leaders or to render them largely irrelevant.

I turn finally to prevalent approaches to constitutional law and theory in the United States.[25] If the practical political problems for liberals are more serious than those for conservatives, the difficulties for conservative theorising are more serious than those for liberals. Reacting to the approach to constitutional law taken by the Warren and Burger Courts in their collaboration with the New Deal–Great Society constitutional order, conservatives pitched their hopes on a jurisprudence of original intent, now—after some transformations—a jurisprudence that makes the public understandings of the Constitution's terms, when those terms were adopted, controlling. For all practical purposes, they have achieved consensus among themselves on only one result from that jurisprudence—a defence of a constitutionally strong presidency independent of substantial constitutional control.[26] And,

[22] As William Simon's brief discussion in his chapter for this book suggests, opportunities for criticism and legal challenge arise because these programmes are set within a larger regulatory framework that remains committed to *some* version of command-and-control, prescriptive regulation. Standards drawn from the statutes creating that type of regulation provide the basis for legal and policy challenges to the newer forms of regulation. (One useful quotation refers to one of the newer programmes of environmental regulation: 'If it isn't illegal, it isn't XL.' Cited in Tushnet, n 3 above, at 171.)

[23] In comments on an earlier version of this chapter.

[24] The methods by which the New Deal–Great Society constitutional order was constructed suggest that there may be a number of mechanisms at work here. Sometimes the 'undermine, then reconstitute' approach is a strategy consciously adopted by political leaders. Sometimes the undermining is a side effect of actions taken for other reasons, which then provides the opportunity for constructing new modes of political support.

[25] I touch on here only the main lines of constitutional theorising in the United States. As always, there are other, often more interesting theorisations rattling around. I focus on the main lines because, of any, they are the most likely to have some political purchase in the short run.

[26] The position has achieved such a high degree of agreement within the conservative community that the Department of Justice's Office of Legal Counsel thought it unnecessary even to cite a major precedent suggesting otherwise in the recently released 'torture memo'.

as I have suggested, that result fits uncomfortably with programmatic conservativism. Beyond that, there is disagreement, fostered in part by the incompatibilities on the level of theory among the conservative movement's social conservatives, its economic conservatives and its libertarians.

Even more, the jurisprudence of original understanding almost by definition stands as an impediment to the constitutional justification of new forms of social order, because it requires that what the government does be justified with reference to understandings widely held in the eighteenth and nineteenth century, not the twenty-first. The use of federal funds to support faith-based initiatives, for example, is at least as vulnerable to originalist challenge as are the command-and-control regulations of the New Deal and Great Society. The best conservative theorisation of which I am aware presents a substantive account of constitutional law in which so-called intermediate institutions play the central role, rather than either individual choice or the institutions of government.[27] But, even that account is flawed by the author's commitment to an originalism that in the end cannot support the substantive account.

Liberal constitutional theorising is characterised by the disarray natural to a theory that has lost its relation to the constitutional order's actual practices and has not yet found other practices to attach to. Symptomatic is Cass Sunstein's restless exploration of possibilities for a new anchor for liberalism. First that anchor was to be what Sunstein called 'liberal republicanism'.[28] More recently he has found a new anchor in a form of non-judicial constitutionalism that would revitalise Franklin Roosevelt's 'Second Bill of Rights', with some modest gestures in the direction of identifying the appropriate methods of institutionalising the new rights (primarily, by limiting the degree to which those rights would be enforceable by courts).[29] Over the past several years, though, some degree of agreement has been reached that liberal constitutional theory should at least be attentive to, and perhaps should elevate into a primary role, popular constitutionalism, understood as the expression of constitutional values in non-judicial venues.[30] This has been coupled with an increasing appreciation of the place that social welfare rights should hold in a liberal constitutional theory.[31] These areas of agreement provide a decent basis for new constitutional theorising about new forms of governance. In addition, liberal constitutional theorists nurtured in the New Deal–Great Society tradition have not thought themselves

[27] John O McGinnis, 'Reviving Tocqueville's America: The Rehnquist Court's Jurisprudence of Social Discovery' (2002) 90 *California Law Review* 485.

[28] Cass R Sunstein, 'Beyond the Republican Revival' (1988) 97 *Yale Law Journal* 1539.

[29] Cass R Sunstein, *The Second Bill of Rights: FDR's Unfinished Revolution and Why We Need It More Than Ever* (2004). Bruce Ackerman's more flamboyant spewing out of one programmamatic suggestion after another for liberals to pursue is another symptom of disarray.

[30] See, eg, Larry Kramer, *The People Themselves* (2004), and, of course, Mark Tushnet, *Taking The Constitution Away From The Courts* (1999).

[31] See, eg, Robin West, *Progressive Constitutionalism: Reconstructing the Fourteenth Amendment* (1994).

tied to the Constitution's text.[32] This enables them to theorise more comfortably than conservatives about small-c constitutionalism in the United States.

Yet, liberal theorisation is impeded somewhat by, once again, the continuing effects of the institutional arrangements of the New Deal–Great Society constitutional order.

Specifically, liberals simply cannot *both* (1) be sceptical about the importance of the courts in a new constitutional order and still insist, as the interest-group constituencies of the older order require (2) that the heart of those constituencies' policy agendas be protected by the courts against erosion.[33] Again to speak more generally: Liberal constitutional theorising about innovative modes of governance must preserve the traditional modes of justification for, and of enforcement of, what liberal theorists must treat as fundamental or core rights—in my terms, the rights crucially important to central supporters of the Democratic Party. At the same time, it must accept the use of innovative justifications for and methods of enforcing new rights of constitutional dimension, what Sunstein calls 'constitutive commitments'—relatively deep commitments of principle that have some staying power and that affect a broad range of policies And, finally, it must come up with an acceptable theoretical account of why some rights are allocated to traditional modes and others to innovative ones. The latter condition is particularly tricky, because at least some core rights have characteristics similar to those of the new ones. So far, the past weighs too heavily on liberal constitutional theorists for them to have developed any constitutional theory that satisfies these constraints.[34]

The result has been a rhetoric about popular constitutionalism and the courts that suggests a half-hearted commitment to the former: It often seems as if the advocates of popular constitutionalism have given up on the courts simply because they have lost control of them, and—as their defence of judicial enforcement of the core agendas indicates—would happily use the courts as aggressively as they could were they to regain control. Popular

[32] The clearest examples are suggestions by Bruce Ackerman and Akhil Reed Amar for the recognition of processes of constitutional amendment that do not conform to the prescriptions of Article V of the US Constitution, that is, for the recognition of constitutional amendments by means other than those provided in the text. Reva Siegel and Robert Post have developed similar though narrower ideas.

[33] The role in discussions of popular constitutionalism of *Brown v Board of Education* and *Roe v Wade*, as well as liberal scepticism about direct democracy (through referenda) and the possibility of a new constitutional convention, are symptomatic of these difficulties. Defenders of the idea of popular constitutionalism have responses to these forms of liberal scepticism, but, as I can testify, the responses have gained essentially no support within the community of liberal constitutional thinkers.

[34] A variant of this difficulty is that much liberal constitutional theorising has been committed to some version of process-based justifications for strong judicial enforcement of certain constitutional rights, and that determining *which* rights should be subject to *what* processes is extraordinarily hard when, as is typically the case when institutional innovations seem imperative, there is disagreement not merely about means to reach an agreed-upon goal, but about what goal is to be sought in the first place.

constitutionalism, that is, seems like a merely strategic retreat rather than a principled commitment around which constitutional theorising is formed. It may be inevitable, and even if not inevitable it may be desirable, to take as the starting place for theorising the strategic position one happens to be in. Yet, I have suggested, stabilising institutional innovations requires the development of some principled (non-strategic) ideology that explains and justifies those innovations. As yet, liberals have done little to convert their strategic situation into a theorised ideology.

The conditions I have described suggest that substantial changes in the present organisation of the national government are not in ready prospect. A conservative transformation might occur, whereas a liberal one seems quite unlikely. Nothing in political life is guaranteed, of course, and the unexpected might occur—new events reshaping politics, new political leaders coming to the fore or ones already on the scene transforming themselves and then transforming politics. For now, though, I think the soundest judgment is that the new constitutional order is the one we have.

Epilogue: Accountability Without Sovereignty

CHARLES F SABEL AND WILLIAM H SIMON

THERE IS SUBSTANTIAL agreement among contributors to this volume that the body of rights and rules that goes generally by the name of law is changing. Municipal law is becoming more responsive to changes in the supranational setting. Think, for example, of the influence of international human rights law and environmental conventions, or the effect of EU law on Member States of the Union. It is also becoming more sensitive to the particularities of local contexts within nation states. At the same time this body of rules and rights is reaching into new realms and striving to take account of the effects of intervention in one realm on the others. Think of the regulation of social responses to disability or of water quality. There is further agreement that the effort to make rights and rules more responsive while increasing their reach and integration increasingly takes the form of frameworks subject to revision in the light of the experience of implementing initial conceptions.

Doubts emerge, however, as to whether law can be made an instrument of these changes and still be law in the sense of holding officials accountable for their acts and assuring that citizens are otherwise secure in the enjoyment of their rights. In their introduction to this volume Gráinne de Búrca and Joanne Scott formulate these doubts as a chain of successively less forbidding theses regarding the (in)compatibility of the ensemble of innovations just invoked, or 'new governance', with traditional law.

According to the 'gap thesis', the most daunting of all, there may be a fundamental incompatibility between law and new governance. According to some versions of the 'hybridity thesis', new governance can be a (complementary) part of law, but only by relying on and leaving unaltered elements, substantive as well as procedural, of tradition. According to the transformation thesis, new governance can combine with traditional law so as to transform the latter. But even in this last case, there is a concern that the transformational law may need to rely on the elements of a traditional, separation of powers constitution.

In their separate contributions to this volume de Búrca and Scott/Holder have furnished rich case studies of traditional law/new governance hybrids in, respectively, and rights against discrimination ecological regulation, with special attention to the institutional innovations that, in linking revision of the legal framework to the experience of implementation in civil society, create what is arguably a hybrid form. Many other chapters are in this same spirit, reporting carefully on messy facts, and drawing conclusions from this close observation that avoid at one extreme the claim of an unbridgeable gap or fundamental contradiction between traditional law and new governance, and at the other, the claim that new governance is not just a part of law, but its bright future.

In this brief epilogue, we try to explain why we are drawn to the latter, transformation thesis. Our reluctance to see traditional legal institutions as either a basic foundation that must be protected from erosion by new governance or as a constituent of a stable partnership with it does not arise from confidence in the superiority and ultimate triumph of new governance, and still less on a belief that its innovations are never used for bad ends. Rather, it springs from two other sources.

First, both the gap and the hybridity theses treat traditional legality as more coherent and more potent than it is. Modern jurisprudence casts an enormous shadow of doubt over the stronger claims of traditional legality, and history gives no reason to think that traditional legal institutions could perform the tasks of insuring accountability and protecting rights in a world of rapid technological and organisational change, and cross-border transactions, migration and externalities.

New governance may or may not be an answer to the dilemmas of this situation, but distinctions between working traditions and fanciful innovations are not. Indeed the suggestion at the core of much new governance discussion that societies can and should innovate at the margin without profoundly perturbing the arrangements that enable the innovations ignores the enduring insight of nineteenth-century social theory that great innovations only arise in conditions that undermine their antecedents. The hope of innovation that only augments but otherwise does not alter our existing capacities is certainly a more harmless fable of social engineering than the idea of a deliberate and all encompassing revolution, but it is no less a fable, and no less informed than its revolutionary cousin by the idea of a knowing social apex or centre.

The second source of our inclination toward the transformation view is empirical. The accounts of new governance in this volume present just the kind of evidence we have in mind: The more detailed they are, the more they suggest, not the co-existence of old and new, but their mutual transformation—the creation of institutions whose very function or role has no precise analogue in prior legal regimes, and whose operation therefore forces us to reconsider familiar terms such as 'accountability, 'penalty' and 'compliance.'

GAPS: TONIC AND TOXIC

The 'gap' concern comes in two forms: tonic and toxic. In the tonic form the worry is that new governance innovations are in tension with current law, perhaps in a mutually disruptive way, because the law lags the innovative practice. It is easy to find suggestive evidence for this concern in the awkward evasiveness with which the EU Constitutional draft treated new governance, as discussed by Claire Kilpatrick, and in US court decisions that obstruct new governance initiatives in, for example, occupational health and safety, as discussed by Orly Lobel.

But it is hard to know just how serious a worry this is. Social development in general and jurisgenerative social development in particular are seldom synchronised with the development of law. There are a few justly celebrated instances where the law is far in advance of any consolidated and deliberate social practice. The American Constitution comes to mind. There are cases where the courts side vigorously with what Whig history liked to call the forces of progress. Recall the nineteenth-century US cases in which common law judges took the side of improving land users in their disputes with neighbours who claimed protection under traditional common law property rights against any disruption in the flow of their stream water or the view from their windows.[1]

But on balance the intuition (standing in here for the summary evidence we might want but do not have) is that law and courts lag development, often egregiously so. The most notorious cases have to do, fittingly enough, with judicial foot dragging in the recognition of the traditional administrative state, as for example Supreme Court resistance to the New Deal—the paradigmatic new governance institution of its day. And even when courts have accommodated such large changes as the advent of a new administrative regime, they have frequently lagged, or deliberately resisted ongoing adjustments to changing circumstance within that new regime. For US administrative lawyers a persistent instance of this is the opposition of the Supreme Court to innovations in rule-making procedures prompted by new requirements for information gathering and assessment, but not authorised by the Administrative Procedure Act.[2]

A benefit of this judicial 'obstruction' is presumably to weed out or retard the diffusion of innovations that are in fact best uprooted or contained. But even assuming that the costs of persistent legal tardiness in the recognition of worthy social innovations exceed the benefits, no one, to our knowledge, has argued that the judicially contrived delays have fundamentally changed the course of development in the past; and there is no strong evidence for the view that belated legal recognition of new governance institutions would have more than transitory effect.

In the toxic version of the gap concern, however, the tension between law and new governance becomes a contradiction, and the choice is either/or: either new governance, with its capacity to contextualise and update rules, or the rule of law by means of stable and constraining rules. The deep

[1] See Morton J Horwitz, *The Transformation of American Law: 1780–1860* (Cambridge, MA: Harvard University Press, 1977) pp 31–62.

[2] Richard B Stewart, 'Vermont Yankee and the Evolution of Administrative Procedure' (1978).91 *Harvard Law Review* 1805

worry here is that the explicit provisionality of new governance framework laws obligates those who 'follow' the legal rules to re-write them in the act of applying them; that this revision is at the discretion of those who do the revising; and that this inevitable exercise of discretion is incompatible with the kinds of accountability on which citizens of a democracy rightly insist in the elaboration of administrative rules and constitutional rights. We entrench rights in Constitutions to make them difficult to revise by legislatures, administrators or judges. We declare administrative agencies to be the agents of the sovereign, democratic principal, embodied in the legislature, to make manifest, and subject to judicial review, the administrators' obligation to act within the limits established and for the purposes set by the democratic principal.

The ideal of accountability is compelling, but the model of accountability that the toxic gap thesis invokes is not realistic. In essence, the critics have in mind an idea of law as hierarchical and the associated idea of principal–agent accountability—fidelity of law-applying agents down in the legal hierarchy to law-making sovereigns at its apex. The sovereign is a democratically elected government; its enactments are legitimate because of its representative status. The law-applying judgments of the government's unelected agents are legitimate only to the extent they can be traced to the enactments of the legislative principal. Accountability is thus a matter of pedigree. Ideally, pedigree is tested by an independent judiciary in proceedings that can be initiated by individual citizens. Accountability in this view is upward- and backward-looking; the court looks upward toward the sovereign and backward toward some prior authorisation.

From this point of view, new governance seems radically unsettling because of its flagrant disrespect for the distinction between enactment (or law making) and enforcement (or law application) on which principal–agent accountability depends. In new governance, agents are expected to revise their mandates in the course of implementing them. Sovereigns set frameworks that describe vague goals and invite elaboration. They do not purport to confine discretion within narrow channels. Because many of the traditional connotations of the 'rule of law' are linked to principal–agent views of accountability, the renunciation of the latter seems threatening.

Yet long-recognised problems with the principal–agent version of the rule of law, amply illustrated in these essays, indicate that it is implausible.

First, for the sovereign to perform the role ascribed to it in principal–agent accountability, it must know what it wants, and it must know this at a level of detail that meaningfully circumscribes its agents' discretion. New governance institutions arise from the recognition that rule makers do not have sufficient knowledge to do this. This is not a novel situation, but it has been intensified by rapid technological and institutional change, and by the need to coordinate activities among increasingly diverse constituencies. Rule makers know that today's solutions may not be optimal by the time they have embodied them in specific decrees. And they know that effective solutions must accommodate the interests of an expanding range of constituencies that they do not have detailed knowledge of. It often appears that solutions to problems can only be identified as they are pursued; that actors have to learn what problem they are solving through the very process of problem solving. It is this condition of severely bounded knowledge that drives the legislators to abandon the idea of prescribing solutions and instead to establish the kind of frameworks described in this book that induce and facilitate problem solving by diffuse constituencies.

Second, even an omniscient sovereign could not embody its intentions in instructions sufficiently detailed to obviate discretion. Given the limited time it would have to formulate them and the limited time the agents would have to absorb them, she would have to simplify and generalise. Simplification and generalisation, however, involve ambiguity or rigidity or both. Either the agent must be held strictly to the text of the instruction, or she must be urged to seek out its underlying intent. The first strategy restricts discretion only at the cost of introducing arbitrariness (since text, strictly interpreted, will diverge from intent). The second increases ambiguity and opens up a space for competing interpretations of intent. Given these limits on cognition, it is no surprise that the insistent lesson of modern jurisprudence is the inevitability of ambiguity and contestation in law application.

New governance acknowledges these problems more directly than traditional legality. It seeks to respond to them through explicitly provisional and incomplete legislative frameworks that set the terms for diffuse groups of stakeholders to elaborate in particular applications, which will then be reviewed at the centre with an eye toward revision of the frameworks. New governance thus officialises and subjects to public discipline this process of resolution of ambiguity, rather than, as traditional judicial practice tends to do, treating it as an insider's secret.

Third, the argument for principal–agent accountability in the US and the EU rests on the assumption that the relevant sovereigns are democratically representative of the people affected by the agents' law-applying activity. Yet, it is increasingly the case that people are affected by the actions of many sovereigns, while generally only one, or at most a few, are democratically accountable to them. People move around more. They engage in more cross-border transactions and activities. They engage in local activities with cross-border effects. In this situation, they constantly find themselves affected by activities regulated, facilitated, or authorised by states of which they are not citizens. The accountability of agents to democratic sovereigns would not legitimate the effects of the agents' conduct as to these people. Concerns about the extra-territorial effects of state conduct were key to the founding of both the US and the EU, and at least in the EU have remained so. New governance is in part an effort to create accountability with respect to cross-border effects without creating an encompassing sovereign that would tightly constrict Member State autonomy.

Finally, it's worth recalling how limited the range has been in which courts historically have even purported to hold state agents accountable to the mandates of their sovereign principal. Vast spheres of government activity have been exempt from traditional rule-of-law principles. Sovereign immunity has precluded judicial review of both routine activity and major discretionary decisions. Decisions that do not directly infringe traditional private rights have historically been exempt from challenge. No doubt the proper scope of such immunity is debatable, but most people would concede that full-scale judicial review would not work for many such decisions, whether because they cannot be objectively substantiated, judges lack the requisite expertise, review would be too costly or necessary confidentiality would be compromised. Yet, many of the new governance approaches discussed in this book do reach such decisions. Claire Kilpatrick makes this point with respect to the European Employment Strategy, which reaches into areas such as macro-economic policy that traditional legality has not purported to regulate. Thus, the flexibility of new governance modes has made it possible to extend forms of discipline into areas that would otherwise be unregulated.

It is correct, then, that new governance repudiates the rule of law in its principal–agent variation, mostly fundamentally by disrespecting the distinction between enforcement and enactment. On the other hand, it suggests an alternative discipline that could be seen as a reinterpretation of the basic rule-of-law ideal of accountability. The alternative, instead of looking backward to a prior enactment and upward toward a central sovereign, looks forward and sideways: forward to the ongoing efforts at implementation, sideways to the efforts and views of peer institutions.

Peer review is the answer of new governance to the inadequacies of principal–agent accountability. Peer review imposes on implementing 'agents' the obligation to justify the exercise of discretion they have been granted by framework-making 'principals' in the light of pooled comparable experience. In peer review, the actors at all levels learn from and correct each other, thus undermining the hierarchical distinction between principals and agents and creating a form of dynamic accountability—accountability that anticipates the transformation of rules in use. Dynamic accountability becomes the means of controlling discretion when that control cannot be hard wired into the rules of hierarchy.

To see how intuitively compelling the logic of peer review is to thoughtful administrative lawyers confronted with the dilemma of an ex-ante unknowable world, consider the work of Phedon Nicolaides on policy implementation in the EU. His explicit aim is not to transcend the tested and true principal–agent framework, but on the contrary to apply that framework to what appears to be, from the standpoint of traditional notions of accountability, the ramshackle structure of the EU. Even after heroically assuming that the European Parliament and Council of Ministers together amount to something approximating a unified principal, Nicolaides must take two oddities into account. The first is that this unified principal, the EU, has multiple agents: the national administrative authorities who implement EU law in their respective jurisdictions. Agents being what they are in principal–agent theory, each of these national administrations can be expected to interpret the EU's instructions—a directive, say—in a self serving way; and the principle will of course be determined to minimise the 'drift' away from its original intentions produced by these multiple agents. The second is that (in the EU) the principal is realistically presumed to have only a vague or provisional idea of its own goals. Sometimes self-interested drifting by national administrative agencies will therefore be only that; while other times it may reveal possibilities that the principal has overlooked, and prefers more than any of the options entertained ex ante. In other words, the principal can sometimes learn from the agents. Since accountability cannot under these circumstances be established by comparing rule to performance, how can it be achieved? The device is simple:

> Accountability is strengthened not when the actions of the agent are constrained but when the agent is required to explain and justify his actions to those who have the necessary knowledge to understand evaluate those actions. We conclude, therefore, that effective delegation must confer decision-making discretion to the agent, while effective accountability mechanisms must remove arbitrariness from the agent's actions by requiring him to (a) show how he has taken into account the impact of his decisions on others, (b) explain sufficiently his decisions and (c) be liable to judicial challenge and, preferably, to some kind of periodic peer review. The latter is very important because only peers have the same knowledge to evaluate the agent's explanations.[3]

Notice that in the case of both principal–agent accountability and peer review the mechanism for evaluating the exercise of discretion is distinct from the mechanism for rewarding the acceptable use of discretion or sanctioning its abuse. Moreover the results of peer reviews are in principle and practice no harder or easier to enforce than the judgments of agents by principals, a point we touch on below and develop more fully in the next section.

These qualities are strikingly manifested in the EU variant of peer review accountability: Initial framework goals (such as full employment, social inclusion, a unified energy grid) and measures for gauging their achievement are established by joint action of the Member States and EU institutions; lower-level units (such as national ministries or regulatory authorities and the actors with whom they collaborate) are given the freedom to advance these ends as they see fit; but they must report regularly on their performance, especially as measured by the agreed indicators, and participate in a review process with other Member States in which their results are

[3] Phedon Nicolaides, Improving Policy Implementation in an Enlarged European Union: The Case of National Regulatory Authorities (Maastricht: European Institute of Public Administration , 2003) p 46.

compared with those pursuing other means to the same general ends. Framework goals, metrics and procedures themselves are periodically revised by the same combination of actors that initially established them.

Under the name of fora, networked agencies, councils of regulators, open methods of coordination or more generally processes, this peer review, with its reliance on recursive, disentrenching deliberation, has become all but ubiquitous in EU governance: for instance in the regulation of telecommunications, energy, pharmaceutical licensing, environmental protection, occupational health and safety, food safety, maritime safety, rail interoperability and safety, financial services, employment promotion, social inclusion and pension reform. Similar arrangements are incipient in other key areas such as health care and anti-discrimination policy; and the basic architecture of framework making and revision is now routinely used to address new problems such as GMO regulation and the fight against terrorism, and to renovate solutions to familiar ones such as competition policy, state aid and fiscal coordination.

A body of 'EU administrative law' requires that decision making at key steps in these iterative process be transparent, accessible to relevant parties in civil society as well as affected administrations, and deliberate in the sense of providing reasons for decisions.[4] This law notwithstanding, the degree to which peer review is binding on national participants and cumulatively influential in the revision of frameworks varies from domain to domain. But this variation only underscores that peer review is a defining feature of (EU) governance in an ex-ante unknowable world, while the degree to which the norms produced by that innovative governance are 'transposed' to practice is, as legal anthropology and law and society have taught us to expect of norms in general, a matter of context.

The democratic legitimacy of these peer review processes cannot depend on the conformity of their results to prior legislative decision. Rather, democracy will have to be established within the review processes themselves. Legitimacy will depend on their transparency and more ambitiously, on their openness to directly deliberative participation by affected stakeholders. Deliberative because preferences, even ideas of the possible, change in the course of decision making (otherwise we could count on principals to define solutions in advance); directly so because new preferences and possibilities arise through hands-on problem solving by those in urgent need of an answer, not dispassionate reflection of first principles by a magisterial elite secure against life's pressures.

A range of questions remain to be answered. Who, in view of any particular problem, is to be included in the process of directly deliberative problem solving? Who decides on the criteria of inclusion? What is the relation of these particular problem-solving 'publics', as John Dewey called them, to each other? To a public sphere that includes them all? To the self rule of the

[4] See Mario P Chiti, 'Forms of European Administrative Action' (2004) 68 *Law & Contemporary Problems* 37.

polity? To pose these questions is to conclude that new governance, precisely because of its successes in displacing the old, will in the end require us to rethink the very ideas of democracy on which our inveterate ideas of accountability are founded.

These are critical problems, but progress need not await theoretical solutions to them. Just as law and jurisgenerative social development are seldom synchronised, so the theory and practice of democracy are frequently, perhaps normally, disjoint. (Lawyers, especially administrative lawyers, make a profession of this condition; at least they can live with it, resembling in this the unlikely creatures who prosper in the crevices of Antarctic glaciers or the boiling spume of deep-ocean volcanoes that seem utterly inimical to life. The traditional administrative state did not shut down upon discovery that the delegation doctrine was an unworkable fiction, and therefore often ignored by the high courts that promulgated it—see for the US the endless discussion of *Chevron*, for the EU *Meroni*.)

Many of the great crises of the development of democracy—the New Deal first and foremost—result from the clash between sub-national advances in governance and the existing frame of national democracy. The crises are resolved, when they are, by some adjustment of the frame and the advance that permits a synthesis of the two. To go by this crude rule of thumb, the relevant worry for our time is likely to be that the 'local' successes of new governance—made possible partly by the availability of institutions that check discretion without directly renewing democracy—provoke broad crises of legitimacy, not that the absence of a new account of legitimacy checks the spread of new governance. An explosion, not a logjam, is likely to be the signal that discussion of the democratic legitimacy of new governance can no longer be deferred. This is not a reason to be insouciant about the problems of democratic legitimacy waiting beyond the horizon of accountability issues addressed by peer review. But it is a reason to expect that new governance innovations of questionable legitimacy will proceed because they promise results when more legitimate methods no longer do, and perhaps a reason as well to search in the interaction between traditional law and new governance for clues to the solution to large questions of democratic justification that the progress of the later are already provoking. The hybridity thesis, discussed in the next section focuses attention on this interplay; the constitutionalism question, with which we conclude, asks us to draw first conclusions from what we find.

LAW AND NEW GOVERNANCE HYBRIDS: CONSERVATIVE OR TRANSFORMATIVE?

The hybridity thesis takes for granted the compatibility of some variant of law and some variant of new governance and invites us to reflect on the precise conditions of the relation.

The conservative form of the hybridity thesis asserts that old and new are complementary but inert, in that old stays old and new is new. De Búrca and Scott's 'baseline hybridity' belongs in this category. From this perspective, new governance institutions can supplement traditional ones, increasing the reach of law without jeopardising the core protections it affords.

In its radical variants the hybridity thesis implies reciprocal change: old and new react upon each other, creating institutions with no close analogue in either of the original classes. Its appeal is that transformative combination produces novel ways of securing traditional protections while extending those protections in ways traditional norms would have precluded. We class in this perspective de Búrca and Scott's 'developmental' and 'default' hybridity, as well as their 'transformation thesis'.

As a practical matter, to agree that old and new governance form a hybrid at all is to agree that profound changes of a certain general kind are underway—agreement enough certainly to frame a research programme, as the current volume illustrates, and beyond that debate about institutional and political reform. But a virtue of the hybridity and transformation ideas is to press for further conceptual and empirical clarification against the backdrop of the common orientation they afford. In this spirit we use the cases of discrimination directives and the emergence of penalty defaults in US environmental law—both presented in this volume at least as much as instances of conservative as transformative hybridity—to argue that the hybridisation in progress is transformative: changing our concepts of law and right by refashioning the institutions that give expression to both. Discussion of the anti-discrimination directives returns us to the relation between new governance and fidelity to the foundational values of the polity: the counterpart in the domain of fundamental rights to the problem of administrative accountability. Discussion of penalty defaults puts on the table questions about the enforcement of peer review accountability deferred until now and suggests that the notion of enforcement too is being transformed by its suffusion with new governance.

As de Búrca recounts, in 2000 the EU adopted two anti-discrimination framework directives and an 'action programme' to combat discrimination. The Race Discrimination Directive addresses ethnic and racial discrimination in a wide range of social and economic settings; the Directive on Equal Treatment in Employment and Occupation addresses workplace discrimination on a wide range of grounds, including sexual orientation, age, disability, ethnicity and religious belief. The action programme to combat discrimination aims to increase the capacity of national administrations, EU bodies, and networks of experts and NGOs at the national and EU levels to assess and propose reforms of the rapidly evolving law and practice of ending discrimination. These measures are in turn part of a continuing effort to include fundamental rights in an eventual EU Constitution, and to monitor their application, for example through the creation of an EU Fundamental Rights Agency for this purpose.

From the standpoint of conservative hybridity—the portrayal of old and new as complementary but not mutually transformative—the directives and programme fall naturally and attractively into two parts. The first is a categorical prohibition on discrimination, understood as a practice or decision that disadvantages an individual or group relative to others solely on grounds of ethnicity, faith, age, disability or other attribute judged irrelevant to relations among equal citizens. This is the 'traditional' right, similar in kind to human and civil rights; its effectiveness, like theirs (on the traditional understanding) derives largely from unequivocal textual requirements easily intelligible to courts.

The second, novel part of the hybrid is contained in provisions establishing equality of treatment of potentially disadvantaged groups as an open-ended goal. Consider, for instance, the case of persons with disabilities. A rule permitting employers to consider in hiring decisions only those attributes of job applicants directly relevant to their prospective employment prohibits many kinds of discrimination, yet does not protect persons with disabilities which could affect performance. Anticipating this difficulty the Employment Directive obligates employers to provide 'reasonable accommodation' to persons with disabilities, where 'reasonable' depends on the accommodations actually afforded in the practice of various national administrations.

These parts of the directives put us in the province of the framework regulation characteristic of new governance in general and EU governance in particular. Certainly courts acting in isolation from other institutions have a poor record of giving corrigible meaning to requirements of this kind. But peer review of implementation efforts by relevant authorities and civil society actors, and subject to judicial scrutiny, has, at least in some circumstances, proved able to make effective sense of such open-ended goals. This is arguably the premise of the action programme for augmenting the evaluative capacities of key actors: Linked together in forms that are already familiar from the regulatory realm of EU governance, these newly capacitated actors could, as de Búrca suggests, extend the system of peer review from regulation to rights, creating along the way a conservative hybrid of traditional anti-discrimination law and new-governance law of equality.

The limit to this interpretation is that the very distinction between a traditionally justiciable, textually unambiguous prohibition on discrimination and an open-ended requirement of equality (vindicated through new governance) proves in practice untenable, even in what might seem its natural habitat of anti-discrimination rules. The distinction breaks down because the core meaning of the prohibition against discrimination often depends on new-governance mechanisms in just the way the conservative hybridity thesis disallows.

The ambiguities that come to light in addressing discrimination against pregnant women is a familiar illustration. Gender-blind rules or practices that penalise the career disruptions associated with child bearing discriminate against pregnant women even if they nowhere announce or even intend this. So a bright-line rule requiring gender-blind interpretations is obviously useless in these circumstances. Indeed the only general way to address, rather than aggravate, this and many other kinds of discrimination is to convert them into questions of accommodation: to require, for instance, that differences in physiology between the sexes be accommodated so that men and women have equal chances to advance precisely because these differences are openly acknowledged, not ignored. By this route the prohibitions of discrimination come to resemble the requirement of reasonable accommodations needed to secure equality, and to raise with the latter the problem of defining a standard or comparison group—a comparator—with reference to which the reasonableness of any particular accommodation can be judged. Bright-line rules of doctrine give way to investigation of open-ended, rapidly evolving social possibility.

The proposal to establish an EU Fundamental Rights Agency formalises and generalises this synthesis. In response to the populist electoral successes of Jörg Haider in Austria in the late 90s, and the fears of widespread xenophobia that they aroused, the Treaty of Nice granted the EU Council, in Article 7 of the Union Treaty, the authority to sanction Member States for persistently offending the common values on which the Union is founded, including human rights.[5] But just as the determination of a 'reasonable' accommodation depends in part on the accommodations actually afforded, so the non-arbitrary determination of persistent breaches of rights depends on a (continually corrected) baseline of practices in Member States of identifying and sanctioning rights abuses. As two leading protagonists in the construction of the new institutions put it:

> In order to ensure that such a mechanism [of sanctions] is used in a non-selective manner, it should proceed on the basis of a systematic monitoring by independent experts, providing comparable data and objective assessments on the situation of fundamental rights in all the Member States of the Union.[6]

To this end a network of independent experts in fundamental rights was created to 'detect fundamental rights anomalies or situations where there might be breaches or the risk of breaches of these rights falling within Article 7 of the Union Treaty', and to 'help in finding solutions to remedy confirmed anomalies or to prevent potential breaches'.[7] If, as seems likely, this network does become the core of the Fundamental Rights Agency, then peer review of fundamental rights will have been in some important measure officialised in the EU.

From this it does not follow, as proponents of the conservative hybridity thesis might fear, that the protection of new rights to equality comes at the price of the evisceration of the old protection against naked discrimination. To say that rights are open ended, and that their determination is dependent on a (disciplined and accountable) evaluation of social possibilities is

[5] See Philip Alston and Olivier De Schutter, 'Introduction' in Philip Alston and Olivier de Schutter (eds) *Monitoring Fundamental Rights in the EU: The Contribution of the Fundamental Rights Agency* (Oxford: Hart Publishing, 2005) pp 1–21; and Olivier De Schutter, 'Mainstreaming Human Rights in the European Union' in *ibid.*, pp 37–72.

[6] *Ibid*, p 7

[7] *Ibid.*

not to say that they are hostage to shifting social preferences, or at the mercy of just the kinds of utilitarian calculations that the commitment of values to rights is meant to forestall. Certainly the history of institutions such as the EU Fundamental Rights Agency does not suggest that their purpose is to allow civil society to subvert or degrade onerous rights, new or old, if it finds this useful.

On the contrary: as we just saw, the Agency was originally created precisely to police and when necessary to sanction politically motivated rights violations in accord with, if not directly animated by at least some important currents of popular sentiment. Its mandate is to detect and where possible identify means of preventing breaches of right, not to register what citizens aggrieved by the protections accorded others prefer to do with those protections. From this perspective the intent of the Agency, and of other such benchmarking institutions is to establish a kind of non-court-centric judicial review, 'horizontalizing' determination of fundamental values by engaging elements of civil society in their interpretation (via the regular surveys of changing practice), and so extending the range of justiciable claims to protection in ways that courts can not.

Of course, founding intentions do not directly and reliably determine ongoing practices and outcomes. Institutions can fail, betraying the intentions that animated them. The judiciary, for example, has been notoriously derelict in protecting vulnerable citizens against violation of their rights by state authorities in times of national crisis, even in countries such as the US, with well entrenched traditions of judicial review of actions by other branches of government. The consensus, at least in the US, is that such failures are corrigible lapses, not proofs of the fundamental inadequacy of judicial review as a means of vindicating rights. The new-governance forms of rights determination will periodically fail too—inevitably, given the novelty of the task and the institutions addressing it. If we credit the consensus view of the failures of judicial review, then we ought to treat the inevitable breakdowns of non-court-centric or benchmarking judicial review as corrigible institutional problems as well, at least until we have evidence of their persistent incorrigibility.

As a second instance of the transformative character of experimentalist new governance consider the penalty default as elaborated by Brad Karkkainen and the changes it works on our understanding of law as an instrument of inducing compliance with authorised social ends. As first introduced by Ian Ayres and Robert Gertner,[8] the idea draws attention to deficiencies in the standard, contract law understanding of a default rule (the rule courts apply when the agreement lacks a relevant provision) as rule the majority of contracting parties would have agreed on had they bargained over the issue. They pointed out that such rules will be unjust or

[8] Ian Ayres and Robert Gertner, 'Filling in the Gaps in Incomplete Contracts: An Economic Theory of Default Rules' (1989).99 *Yale Law Journal* 87

inefficient in a significant range of cases where there are asymmetries of information. Default rules that would not be chosen by a majority of parties may nevertheless be desirable, if they can be cheaply contracted out of by those who don't want them, because they will induce the disclosure of information that would otherwise be withheld. A default rule that says that sellers are liable only for foreseeable consequences of a breach is better than one that provides liability for all harm incurred by the buyer, even if most sellers would ultimately agree to the unlimited damage rule. The foreseeability rule is better because it gives the buyer an incentive to inform the seller of any unusual risks non-performance presents, and such disclosure in turn encourages the parties to bargain in an informed fashion to their own rule. In formulating a penalty default, the rule maker does not try to approximate the optimum outcome. Rather, it tries to create incentives for the parties to produce a rule that approximates the optimum outcome.

Karkkainen's innovation is to extend the idea of a penalty default from one-shot transactions to ongoing regimes where sequences of rules have to be written in circumstances where information is not only asymmetrically distributed and inaccessible to outsiders, but also so incomplete and rapidly changing as to be highly unreliable for even the party best informed at any moment. These are, you will have noticed, the very circumstances in which principal–agent accountability breaks down because there is no actor with reliable knowledge of what to do. Examples range from the identification and mitigation of environmental harms to the reform of whole school system found to be in violation of constitutional or statutory obligations. Under these conditions a court or administrative agency imposes, in new governance, a penalty on the actors if they do not establish a system for warranting to one another the information they disclose, and then acting on what they currently know.

Thus, the US Endangered Species Act precludes development of certain lands entirely unless relevant stakeholders develop and implement a conservation plan for endangered species. California's Proposition 65 creates vague but potentially large liability in connection with sometimes onerous warning requirements about toxic substances and then creates an exemption for businesses that disclose pertinent information to an agency and comply with minimum tolerance levels announced by the agency. Note that there is nothing intrinsically 'soft' about such regimes. If anything, the new penalty default is more overwhelmingly coercive than conventional legal penalties. New governance defaults are often potentially draconian. Severe criminal penalties can apply for failure to comply with environmental and workplace safety reporting rules; non-performing schools under the US No Child Left Behind Act can be dissolved. Enforcers often hold back from imposing such harsh penalties, but the prospect of leniency comes only at the cost of uncertainty. In contract, penalties for breaches are costs, and parties prefer (efficient) breach to compliance with the agreement when the penalty is less expensive than performance. In new governance penalty defaults, the parties sometimes must choose between performance—creating the requisite information warranting regime—and a future so incalculable as to be chaos.

The new penalty default is not transformative because it can be draconian. Rather the new penalty transforms the character of law by shifting the obligations of compliance, and the coercion directed to enforce those obligations, from rules to frameworks for creating rules. This shift is of course of a piece with, and helps establish the background conditions for, the shift from accountability as rule following to accountability as the justifiable exercise of discretion subject to peer review: The penalty default motivates the actors to provide the information on the basis of which the peer reviewers can determine whether discretionary choices under uncertainty are warranted.

CONSTITUTIONALISM

Supposing then that new governance is law, and transformative law at that, what is the relation between such law and conventional constitutionalism? At its broadest, this question asks for a specification of the relation between new governance and constitutional democracy. It is a very broad question indeed—much too expansive for discussion here. A narrower version, better suited to present purposes, asks only for clarification of the minimum conditions of compatibility between experimentalist law and its enabling constitution—what the latter must and must not provide if it is to accommodate the former. But note that even a response to this limited question is necessarily speculative. As we suggested a moment ago, changes in—constitutional—frameworks lag changes in law, just as changes in law lag changes in social organisation. So while we have tried to build the case for new governance as transformative law on the innovative practice of courts and administrative bodies, with regard to the constitutional dimension of new governance, assuming there can be one, we are anticipating, not reporting developments.

We can begin with features that a constitution must *not* contain if it is to be compatible with experimentalist governance. The crucial preclusion here is a strict specification of the separation of powers, at least as understood in the conventional sense of a delineation of the roles the legislative, executive, and judicial branches of government. This separation of powers has come to map onto the democratic pedigree view of law and the principal–agent model of accountability, with (in the simplest version) the legislature charged with setting goals, the executive and administration charged with realising them and the courts charged with ensuring that the other branches meet their obligations while respecting the rights of the citizens. Since experimentalist law blurs the distinction between conception and execution—between legislative enactment and administrative implementation—a constitution that insists on separating them is inimical to new governance. Any constitution, or constitutional interpretation, that established judicial sovereignty—assigning a court exclusive authority to police this separation of powers by deciding itself how to resolve conflicting claims to authority among the branches of government—would by the same token be inimical to any broad expansion of experimentalist governance.

Yet, this rejection raises fears that the courts will not be able to perform their role in protecting the individual rights. So in addition to saying what an experimentalist Constitution must not do, we must indicate how it might provide a form of constitutional self-restraint and accountability other than by the separation of powers. In the language of the earlier discussion the question is whether there is a constitutional analogue to peer review. In fact we have already encountered a candidate example: the planned Fundamental Rights Agency of the EU and the emergent system of monitoring, interpreting and enforcing rights of which it is a part. Recall that in this system the varying national practices of rights enforcement—each the outcome of particular interactions between the domestic courts and administrations—create the benchmarks or precedents against which the others are judged and the frontier of just enforcement. Member States of the EU are held to constitutional account; but the standards of accountability are set by their peers, on the basis of a comprehensive evaluation of practice, not by a court trying to determine whether each organ of government acted within the bounds legitimately set for it. This method is already being applied to ensure respect for the core—common—values of the EU; and there is nothing in principle to prevent its generalisation to many other domains as well.

In American constitutional discussion the view that the branches of government jointly resolve conflicting interpretations of their authority under the Constitution by creating competing precedents and debating or evaluating their significance is called departmentalism. For leading historians of the US Constitution departmentalism was taken for granted in the early period of the Republic, at least through the first quarter of the nineteenth century. Encounters between and (temporary) co-habitation of first people and colonisers in Canada and elsewhere in the late eighteenth century produced similarly fluid 'dialogues' on the meanings of constitutional forms.[9] Judicial sovereignty is a late development in all these settings, the result of the ossification of the legal profession and popular democracy generally. But for our purposes the historical fact of departmentalism is less significant than the periodic re-discovery of the need for some form of dialogue among the branches—an elementary form of peer review—when some authority (typically the Supreme Court in the US) tries, in the spirit of a separation of powers view of the constitution, to rectify definitively the division of labour between Congress, administrative agencies, and the executive, or between any combination of these and the court itself.[10] The protests are typically

[9] James Tully, *Strange Multiplicity: Constitutionalism in an Age of Diversity* (Cambridge: Cambridge University Press, 1995).

[10] See Larry Kramer, *The People Themselves: Popular Constitutionalism and Judicial Review* (Oxford and New York: Oxford University Press, 2004), and Robert A Burt, *The Constitution in Conflict*. (Cambridge, MA: Belknap Press of Harvard University Press, 1992).

founded on the demonstration of the impossibility of an ex ante determination of an optimal division of responsibility; and the appeals to dialogue are motivated by the consequent need for mutual learning among the branches: just the conditions, again, that render principal–agent accountability unfeasible and peer review effective.

But despite the recurrence of these episodes—itself an indication of a persistent and perhaps increasingly burdensome limit to the constitutionalism of a fixed separation of powers—contemporary versions of departmentalism have been more often invoked to criticise the defects of current practices, such as judicial sovereignty, than to construct alternatives to them. Part of the explanation for this programmatic hesitation is surely the presumed absence of institutional mechanisms for realising the constitutional dialogue and disciplining—holding accountable—the participants. In the absence of such mechanisms departmentalism seems to depend on the disposition of the actors: some joint, civic commitment to the common good or an intercultural sensitivity to the way of being of those, other than ourselves, with whom we are unavoidably living. The difficulty is that Constitutions that can count on such conciliatory dispositions may seem superfluous when the dispositions prevail, and unworkable when they do not. But just as experimentalist law is providing institutions that allow for rule making that is flexible but not unaccountable, and for the vindication of open-ended rights to equality that is not arbitrary, so too it may provide the matrix for creating institutions that permit the branches of government to resolve their different understandings of their roles as peers, not as supplicants before judges acting as the exegetes of an eternal, and unworkable plan. Such an innovation would not yet be a revolution in democracy. But it would bring a transformation of constitutionalism as surely as experimentalist governance is bringing a transformation of law.

Index

Accountability
constitutionalism, and, 410–11
and see **Constitutionalism**
discretion, exercise of, 401
environmental governance, and, 239, 295
and see **Environmental governance**
experimental governance, and, 98
and see **Experimental governance**
explanation, 401
governance mechanisms, and, 202, 205, 208
see also **Governance mechanisms (EU)**
importance, of, 398
institutional intermediation, and, 356
judicial challenge, 401
judicial review, and, 400
justification, 401
nature, of, 398
new governance, and, 330–1, 334, 398–400
and see **New Governance**
occupational safety, and, 278
see also **Occupational safety (USA)**
peer review, and, 400–4, 410
and see **Peer review**
principal-agent version, 398–9, 401
rule of law, and, 400
sovereign immunity, 400
sovereignty, and, 398–9
ADVANCE programmes
see also **Gender equity (USA)**
adoption, of, 339
ADVANCE institutions, 337
bridge builders, 354–5
collaborative agreements, 340–1
coordination, 341
departmental incentives, 344
development, of, 339
grantees, and, 339–40
grant making, 344
guidelines, 339
hybridity, and, 351
and see **Hybridity**
intermediation, 345
internalisation, 349
leverage, 344
organisational processes, 353
problem framing, 350
role, of, 339, 345
University of Michigan, 346–8, 355
Agencies (EU)
accountability, 112
and see **Accountability**
emergence, of, 112–13
powers, of, 112
public enforcement agencies, 135
regulatory agencies, 112
role, of, 112–13
American constitutionalism
see also **Constitutionalism**
accountability, 411
and see **Accountability**
American Revolution
moral decay, and, 367
moral significance, 367
public virtues, 367
self-government, 367
anti-Europeanism, 369
citizenship, 364
departmentalism, 410–1
epistemic democracy, 368
identity, and, 364
nationalisation, 363
patriotism, 364–9
peer review, and, 410–11
and see **Peer review**
public enlightenment, 368
re-interpretation, 368, 370
responsibility, division of, 411
US Constitution
compound republic, 366
dispersed sovereignty, 365–7, 369
European references, 366, 368
framework of rights, 364
judicial support, 370
sacralisation, 370
transformation, o, 411

Anti-discrimination
see also **EU Race Directive**
action programme, 404
categorical prohibition, 405
equal treatment, 405
framework directives, 404–5
gender equity
see **Gender equity (USA)**
mainstreaming, 117–19
policy integration, 117–18
race discrimination
see **Race discrimination**
reasonable accommodation, 405–6

Broad Economic Policy Guidelines (BEPGs)
fiscal policy, and, 68, 83
and see **Fiscal policy**
national diversity, and, 93
operation, of, 83
purpose, of, 83–4
reform, of, 84
reliance, on, 93

Classic Community Method (CCM)
experimental federalism, and, 212
healthcare services, and, 181
see also **Healthcare services (EU)**
limitations, 77
nature, of, 77
operation, of, 77
Clean Air Act
see also **Environmental governance (USA)**
emission limits, 308
enforcement programmes, 308
federal implementation plan (FIP), 308–10
monitoring requirements, 308
state implementation plan (SIP), 308–10
Comitology
development, of, 239–40
effect, of, 204–5
environmental governance, and, 239
and see **Environmental governance**
regulation, of, 240
Common Implementation Strategy (CIS)
accountability, 233, 239
and see **Accountability**
collaborative governance, 227, 237
decision-making, 239
embedded constitutionalism, and, 238–9
endorsement, 232
formalisation, 232–3
guidance documents, 229–30
informal process, 230–1
institutional arrangements, 231, 233, 238
key activities, 229
legal constraint, 238
normative expectations, 238
Open Method of Coordination (OMC), and, 227
and see **Open Method of Coordination (OMC)**
participation, under, 228, 237
procedure, 238
reflexivity, 233
reorganisation, 231–2
review, 231–2, 237
revision, of, 231
working levels
Strategic Coordination Group, 227–8, 233
Water Directors, 227–8, 233, 239
Working Groups, 227–8, 233, 237
working procedures, 238
Constitutional Treaty (CT)
see also **European constitutionalism**
competences, under, 194–5, 202
constitutionalism, and, 143, 145–7
fundamental rights, and, 404
health
healthcare services, and, 193–6, 202
health policy, 195
human health, protecting, 194–5
interpretative issues, 195–6
public health, 194
see also **Healthcare services (EU)**
patriotism, and, 376
ratification, 18, 19
transformative effect, 375
Constitutionalism
see also **American constitutionalism**
accountability, and, 410
and see **Accountability**
administrative implementation, 409
authoritative ordering, 33
common interest, 33
constitutional aims, 17
constitutional authority, 16
constitutional common law, 240

constitutional materialism, 235
constitutional resources, 33
constitutional rules, 240
definition, 15–6
embedded constitutionalism, 238–40, 242
employment governance, and, 142–3, 146–7
and see **Employment governance**
environmental governance, and, 235, 238–40, 242
and see **Environmental governance**
European constitutionalism
see **European constitutionalism**
experimental governance, and, 409–11
formal constitutionalism, 239–40
governance, and, 1, 33
and see **Governance**
intergovernmental constitutionalism
Constitutional Treaty (CT), and, 147
employment governance, and, 147–9
focus, of, 147
legitimacy, and, 149
judicial protection, 241
judicial sovereignty, 409–11
legal framework, 33
legislative enactment, 409
legitimacy, and, 10
majoritarianism, 369
nature, of, 16–7
new governance, and, 33, 409
and see **New governance**
normative aspirations, 17
particularism, and, 16–7
political intrusion, 241
processual constitutionalism
Constitutional Treaty (CT), 146–7
employment governance, 146, 150
environmental governance, and, 235
Open Method of Coordination (OMC), 146–7
significance, of, 151
public policy, and, 10
reflexivity, and, 33–6
self-government, and, 1, 4, 10
self-restraint, 410
self-understanding, and, 17
separation of powers, 409–11
social technology, and, 28, 33, 35
statehood, and, 17–8
state tradition, 34
symbolic value, 16
transformative constitutionalism
Constitutional Treaty (CT), and, 143, 145
meaning, of, 143
social rights, 144–5
state of nation-states, 144
universalism, and, 16–7
Council of Ministers (EU)
institutional balance, and, 204
and see **Institutional balance**
powers, of, 22

Death penalty administration
charging decisions, 62–3
error data, 62–3
political implications, 62
post-conviction relief, 61–2
reform, of, 61–2
review procedures, 62–3
sentencing policy, 62–3
Destabilisation rights
see also **Environmental governance (USA)**
administrative control mechanism, 317
administrative destabilisation right, 296, 315, 317
definition, 314
effect, of, 296
experimentalist collaboration, 315–16
institutions
institutional failure, 315, 317, 321
institutional restructuring, 315
judicial redress, 296
local arrangements, 317, 321
local governance, and, 296
process failure, and, 317
public institutions, and, 315
public law litigation, 296, 315, 321
underperformance, and, 317
Discrimination
see also **Race Discrimination**
anti-discrimination
see **Anti-discrimination**
gender equity
see **Gender equity (USA)**
judicial elaboration, 136
public enforcement agencies, 135
voluntary associations, 135

Economic and Monetary Union (EMU)
effect, of, 129–30
introduction, of, 129
Educational reform
see **School reform**
Employment discrimination (USA)
see also **Gender equity (USA)**
compliance agencies, 325
intervention
public intervention, 325
regulatory intervention, 325
National Science Foundation (NSF), and, 325
and see **National Science Foundation (NSF)**
Employment governance
see also **Employment regulation**
constitutionalism
differing constitutional positions, 143
effect, of, 142–3
extent, of, 148
intergovernmental constitutionalism, 147–8, 19
processual constitutionalism, 146, 150
relationship, between, 143
transformative constitutionalism, 143
and see **Constitutionalism**
demographic influences, 130
discrimination regulation, 132
see also **Race discrimination**
economic influences, 129–30
employment guarantees, 144
employment law, and, 131
European Employment Strategy (EES), 131–2, 140–1
and see **European Employment Strategy (EES)**
European Social Fund (ESF), 131, 133
and see **European Social Fund (ESF)**
gender equality, 132
see also **Gender equity (USA)**
hybridity, and, 130–4
and see **Hybridity**
integrated regime, 131, 134
norms
elaboration, 134, 135
revision, 134, 135
Open Method of Coordination (OMC), 130–4
and see **Open Method of Coordination (OMC)**
peopled governance spaces
bargained agreements, 136–7
bargained compliance, 137
development, of, 134–5
discrimination regulation, 135–6
employment legislation, and, 135
public enforcement agencies, 135
public-private links, 135–8, 140–2
structural funds, and, 137
worker representation, 136–7
practical difficulties, 134
public institutions, and, 135
structural funds
see **Structural funds**
work directives, 131–2
worker's rights, 133
Employment law
see also **Employment regulation**
hard law, 126, 128–9
soft law, 126, 128–9
Employment policy
see also **European Employment Strategy (EES)**
competitive efficiency, 127
coordination, of, 67
cross-national comparisons, 124–5
development, of, 128
employment legislation, and, 82
employment strategy, and, 400
EU Member States, and, 124–5, 128
European Employment Strategy (EES), 82, 124, 129–30
and see **European Employment Strategy (EES)**
governance, of, 124
guidelines, use of, 124
hard law, and, 126–7, 129
hybridity, and, 129–30
and see **Hybridity**
job creation, 127
need, for, 129–30
Open Method of Coordination (OMC), and, 81–2
and see **Open Method of Coordination (OMC)**
part-time work, 128
social inclusion, and, 127–8
social justice, and, 127–8
soft law, and, 126–7, 129

state innovation, 128–9
structural funds, 82
unemployment, 127–8
worker protection, 127–8

Employment regulation
Amsterdam Treaty, under, 123
bargaining
bargained agreements, and, 136–7
bargained compliance, 137
constitutionalism, and, 121
and see **Constitutionalism**
development, of, 122–4
discrimination directives, 135
see also **EU Race Directive**
diversification, of, 128
EC Treaty, under, 122
European Social Fund (ESF), 123–4, 127, 130–1
and see **European Social Fund (ESF)**
hybridity, and, 129–30
and see **Hybridity**
judicial activity, 123
lack, of, 122–3
Maastricht Treaty, under, 123
new governance, and, 121–3
and see **New governance**
parental leave, 136
public-private links, 135–6
state innovation, 128–9
transformation, of, 122
workers
representation, 135–7
worker's rights, 133
working time, 136

ENAR network
establishment, of, 116
role, of, 116

Endangered Species Act (ESA)
see also **Environmental governance (USA)**
forestry, and, 302
habitat conservation plan (HCP), 302–4
land use rules, 303, 408
net environmental benefit, 302
species
protection, 303
survival, 303
urban development, and, 302–3

Environmental assessment
see also **Environmental governance**
Aarhus Convention, effect of, 218
alternative solutions, consideration of, 213, 223
anticipatory control, 214
assessment procedure, 213
behavioural change, 234
best practice, 220–1
consultation, provision for, 220
cross-level experimentation, 223–4
decision-making, and, 213–4
development, of, 234
environmental effects, 217
Environmental Impact Assessment Directive, 214–16, 218, 222
environmental protection, and, 213–4
expansion, of, 223
experimentalist processes, 221–3
experimentalist revision, 234–5
guidance, on, 221
harm
identification, of, 408
mitigation, 408
implementation practice, 221
importance, of, 211–12
information deficits, 218
law, role of, 234–5
local knowledge, 218
meaning, of, 213
nature conservation, 214
new governance, and, 234
and see **New governance**
participation, and, 213, 218–21
regulation
environmental impact assessment (EIA), 214–6, 218, 222
flexibility, 216–17
framework rules, 214
implementation reports, 217, 220–1, 231
information exchange, 215–7
procedural instruments, 214
spill-over effect, 222–3
strategic environmental assessment (SEA), 215, 221–3
regulatory nature, 214
reporting requirements, 224, 230–1, 234
revision process, 234
significance, of, 213
Strategic Environmental Assessment Directive, 215, 221–3
sustainability assessment, 223

Environmental governance
see also **Environmental governance (USA)**
collaborative governance, 212, 237
comitology, and, 239
and see **Comitology**
constitutionalism, 235, 238–40, 242
and see **Constitutionalism**
courts, role of, 241–2
environmental assessment
see **Environmental assessment**
environmental policy, and, 211
experimental federalism, and, 212, 233
hybridity, and, 235
and see **Hybridity**
implementation powers, 236
judicial protection, 241
law, role of, 234–5
legislative procedures, and, 235
multi-level governance, 233
participation, 237
reflexivity, 242
revision process, 234
visibility, and, 236
Environmental governance (USA)
air pollution, 308
air quality standards, 309
citizen suits
collaborative governance schemes, 319
destabilisation, and, 319–20
disentrenchment, and, 319–20
effects, of, 318–19
institutional failure, and, 319
purpose, of, 318
Clean Air Act, 308–10
and see **Clean Air Act**
cooperative federalism, and, 308–9, 312
destabilisation rights
see **Destabilisation rights**
Endangered Species Act (ESA), 302–4
and see **Endangered Species Act (ESA)**
environmental assessment, and, 304
environmental objectives, 293
finding of no significant impact (FONSI)
mitigated, 304–6
significance, of, 305–6
flexible strategies, 293
interventionist approach, 293
local needs, 295
National Environmental Policy Act (NEPA), 298, 304, 306
new governance
accountability, 316, 321
co-ordination, 316, 321
destabilisation rights, 315
local experiments, 315
monitoring, 316
penalty default rules, 310–1
reactions, to, 316
transparency, 316
and see **New governance**
Proposition 65
see **Proposition 65**
reforms
accountability, 295
collaborative governance, 294–5
devolved governance, 294–5
environmental contracting, 293–4
information pooling, 295
integrated management, 295
market-based mechanisms, 293–4
public-private collaboration, 295
regulatory penalty defaults
see **Regulatory penalty defaults**
Resource Conservation and Recovery Act (RCRA)
hazardous waste disposal, 307
land ban, under, 307, 310
phased prohibition, 307
watershed management
see **Watershed management**
EU Charter of Fundamental Rights
employment rights, 144–5
freedom of association, 145
healthcare, and, 197
see also **Healthcare services (EU)**
significance, of, 144
social rights, under, 125–6, 129, 142, 144, 197
solidarity, under, 162
and see **Solidarity**
strike action, 145
EU Constitution
see also **Constitutional Treaty (CT)**
allure, of, 18
competences, 26
consequentiality, 26, 27
constitutionalism
see **European constitutionalism**

governance, and, 18
ideological controversy, 17–8
integration, and, 18
legitimacy, 27
new governance, and, 25
and see **New governance**
nominalism, and, 18–9
and see **Nominalism**
normative authorisation, 27
Open Method of Coordination (OMC)
see **Open Method of Coordination (OMC)**
ratification, 18–9
statehood, and, 17–8
status
constitutional status, 27
legal status, 27
textualism, and, 19
and see **Textualism**
EU law
cooperation, resulting from, 198
direct effect, 20–1, 182, 377
fundamental rights, and, 197
funding, and, 198
interpretative communications, 201
Open Method of Coordination (OMC), and, 197
and see **Open Method of Coordination (OMC)**
policy coordination, and, 198
primacy, of, 376
procedural obligations, 197
role, of, 196–7
soft law, 196–7
supremacy, 377
EU Member States
cooperation, between, 5
employment policy, and, 124–5, 128
and see **Employment policy**
healthcare services, 179, 196, 198, 202–3
and see **Healthcare services (EU)**
EU Race Directive
action programme
access, to, 105
analysis/evaluation, 104–5
awareness-raising, 105
capacity-building, 104–5
development, of, 103–5
importance, of, 104
legislative reference, 105
networking, 105
objectives, 104
prevention, 104, 105
quantitative indicators, 105
trans-national cooperation, 105
adoption, of, 99, 104
analysis/evaluation
data collection, 107–8
data protection, 107
equality bodies, 106, 115
funding, for, 106, 107–8
independent experts, 108
indicators, development of, 107
legal working group, 108–9
non-governmental participation, 109
privacy, 107
provision, for, 104–5
research, 107
awareness-raising
funding, for, 111
provision, for, 105
publicity campaign, 111
capacity-building
funding, for, 109–10
non-governmental organisations (NGOs), and, 110–11
provision, for, 104–5
trans-national partnerships, 109–10
content, of, 100–1
criticism, of, 99–100
development, of, 104
direct/indirect discrimination, 100–1
discriminatory treatment, 100
enforcement of rights, 102, 119
equality bodies, 101, 106, 115
framework nature, 100–2, 119
hybridity, 97, 101–3, 119–20
and see **Hybridity**
implementation, 104
institutional context, 103–4
institutional support
agencies, role of, 112–13
European Fundamental Rights Agency, 112, 114, 116
European Union Monitoring Centre (EUMC), 113–5
extent, of, 111–12
judicial remedies, 101
minimum standards, 101
new governance approach, 101
see also **New governance**
purpose, of, 100
revision, 101
rights-based approach, 102

significance, of, 99, 103
victimisation, 100
European Commission
policy dissemination, 204
role, of, 2, 22, 203–4
European constitutionalism
see also **Constitutional Treaty** (CT)
American reference, 371–2
see also **American constitutionalism**
autonomy, and, 34
citizenship, 372–3
common values, 363, 370
competences
allocation, of, 202
contested competences, 209
shared competences, 203
constitutional concepts
accountability, 202
constitutional discipline, 376–8
constitutional patriotism, 370–5, 377–8
constitutional values, 202, 205, 207, 209
equal access, 202
individual rights, 202
institutional balance, 203–5
problems, associated with, 202
public resources, use of, 202
solidarity, 202
development, of, 16, 363
effect, of, 142–3
federalism, 370, 373
fundamental rights, 373
German experience, 370–1
hierarchy
institutional hierarchy, 20
judicial *kompetenz-kompetenz*, 20
legal-normative hierarchy, 20
legal order, and, 20
significance, of, 20
identity
civic identity, 374
collective identity, 372
European identity, 374
national identity, 371, 379
integration, 376, 378
intergovernmental constitutionalism, 147
legal framework, 33
legal order
direct effect, 20, 21
implied powers, 20
importance, of, 20
judicial involvement, 21
legal hierarchy, 20
rule of law, 21
statehood, 21
supremacy, 20–1
liberal democracy, 370
nationality, 373
national loyalty, 377–9
national tradition, 371–2
new governance, and, 5, 11, 27–9, 33
and see **New governance**
nominalism, 16, 18–9
and see **Nominalism**
obligation, importance of, 377–8, 380
patriotism
constitutional patriotism, 370–5, 377–8
Euro-patriotism, 364, 374–5
legal patriotism, 375
post-nationalism, 374–5
processual constitutionalism, 146–7
reflexivity, and, 33–6
republican tradition, 372
rule of law, 370
self-containment
constitutional authority, 28
legal order, and, 20–1, 28
new governance, and, 27–9
regulatory control, 20
significance, of, 20–1
self-restraint, 377
social market economy, 370
state
statehood, 21
state structures, 28–9
state tradition, 21
textualism, and, 19
and see **Textualism**
transformative constitutionalism, 143, 145
European Court of Justice (ECJ)
jurisdiction, of, 21
European Employment Strategy (EES)
achievement, of, 82
development, of, 140
difficulties, 140
effectiveness, 140
employment governance, and, 131–2, 140–1
and see **Employment governance**

employment policy, and, 82, 124, 129–130
and see **Employment policy**
equal opportunities, 132–3
guidelines, 67–8, 140–1
health & safety, 132–3
hybridity, and, 82
and see **Hybridity**
implementation, 140
legitimacy, 140
Lisbon Strategy
implementation, 141
review, of, 141
Open Method of Coordination (OMC), and, 76, 78
and see **Open Method of Coordination (OMC)**
operation, of, 68, 76, 130
public-private involvement, 140–1
purpose, of, 67
quality indicators, 134
recommendations, use of, 134
significance, of, 76, 124–5, 129, 131
visibility, 140
European Fundamental Rights Agency
creation, of, 404, 406–7, 410
role, of, 112, 114, 116
European law
see also **EU law**
direct effect, 20–1, 182, 377
primacy, of, 376
supremacy, 377
European Parliament
powers, of, 22
European Social Fund (ESF)
employment governance, and, 131, 133
and see **Employment governance**
employment regulation, and, 123–4, 127, 130–1
see also **Employment regulation (EU)**
employment strategy, and, 133
hybridity, and, 82
and see **Hybridity**
objectives, 133
European Structural Fund
see also **Structural funds**
consultation requirements, 139
EQUAL initiative, 138
social partners
access, 139
participation, 139
territorial dimension, 139
European Union (EU)
agencies, within, 112–13
and see **Agencies**
citizenship, 363
civic foundations, 372
Classic Community Method (CCM), use of, 212
and see **Classic Community Method (CCM)**
common values, 363, 370
constitutionalism
see **European constitutionalism**
demographic position, 130
economic interests, 72
economic role, 130
employment guarantees, 144
employment policy, 67
and see **Employment policy**
Euro-patriotism, 364
European law
see **European law**
European social model, 144
fiscal policy, 68
and see **Fiscal policy**
framework regulation, 405
funding
integration, 198
judicial review, 199
legislative activity, 199
policy development, 199
global economic integration, 144
governance mechanisms
see **Governance mechanisms (EU)**
healthcare services, 179, 194
and see **Healthcare services (EU)**
integration, 65–6, 69, 72, 92, 149, 198, 376, 378
intergovernmental nature, 147–8
legislative authority, 376
legitimacy, 78, 142, 147–9
national identity, 371, 379
patriotism
constitutional patriotism, 370–2
Euro-patriotism, 364
plurality, 376
political community, as, 34–5
rational nature, 378
reflexive entity, as, 34–5
regulatory dynamics, 15
responsible self-government, 34–5

self-government, and, 15
self-restraint, 377
self-understanding, 35
shared epistemic frame, 35
social rights, 144–5
social spending, 144
social welfare guarantees, 144
soft law, 76
and see **Soft law**
solidarity, within, 153
and see **Solidarity**
sovereignty, and, 72
European Union Monitoring Centre (EUMC)
data collection, 113–14
development, of, 115
difficulties, affecting, 113–14
establishment, of, 113
human rights, and, 115
reform, of, 114–15
role, of, 113, 115
structure, of, 114
Excessive Deficit Procedure (EDP)
failure, of, 90
fiscal policy, and, 83, 93
and see **Fiscal policy**
rules, governing, 85–6
sanctions, 86–7, 93
Experimental governance
see also **New governance**
accountability, 98
and see **Accountability**
constitutionalism, and, 409–11
and see **Constitutionalism**
flexibility, 98
framework directives, 99
human rights model, distinguished, 97–8
judicial involvement, 98
participation, 98
revision, and, 98
Experimentalist federalism
Classic Community Method (CCM), and, 212
and see **Classic Community Method (CCM)**
environmental governance, and, 212, 233
and see **Environmental governance**
Expert Advisory Fora (EAFs)
role, of, 237

Fiscal policy
Broad Economic Policy Guidelines (BEPGs), 68
budgetary performance, 82–3
budget deficits, 83
constructivist approach, 90
coordination, of, 68, 76, 82–3, 90, 93–4
eurozone, within, 82–3
fixed rules, 68–9
hard law, and, 89–90
and see **Hard law**
hybridity, 87, 93
and see **Hybridity**
multilateral surveillance, 84–5, 93
non-compliance, 90
sanctions, 69, 90
self-interest, 89
soft law
competition, 89
compromise, 88
consistency, 89
cooperation, 89
flexible implementation, 88
incrementalism, 89
information dissemination, 89
information flow, 89
learning, 89
negotiation costs, 88
sovereignty costs, 88
uncertainty, 88
and see **Soft law**

Gap thesis
accountability, and, 5, 398
see also **Accountability**
administrative procedures, 6
law, and, 4–5
nature, of, 4
normative dimension, 4
political constraints, 5–6
traditional law, and, 395–7
Gender equity (USA)
see also **National Science Foundation (NSF)**
academic sciences
cultural issues, 335
ethnic inequality, 336
faculty administration, 336
gender bias, 335–7
gender equity initiatives, 336
institutional change, 337

multilevel intervention, 335, 337
racial inequality, 336
regulatory systems, 336
remediation, 337
small treatment differentials, 335
women's under-participation, 334–5
comparative strategies, 326
new governance, and, 326
and see **New governance**
Governance
see also **New governance**
constitutionalism
see **Constitutionalism**
experimental forms, 2, 97–9
see also **Experimental governance**
governmental authority, 3
human rights model
development, 98
enforcement, 98
experimental governance, and, 97–8
flexible goals, 97
judicial involvement, 98
monitoring, 98
self-regulation, 98
voluntarism, 98
infrastructure, and, 3
institutional failure, 407
judicial review, 407
soft law, and, 3
and see **Soft law**
US experience
see **US governance**
Governance mechanisms (EU)
see also **European Union**
accountability, 202, 205, 208
and see **Accountability**
administration, 200
Constitutional Treaty (CT), 202
and see **Constitutional Treaty (CT)**
cooperation, 198
coordination, 198
deregulatory litigation, 205, 209
destabilisation, and, 208
funding, 198
hard law framework, 207–8
information
collection, of, 200–1
dissemination, of, 200–1
interpretative communications, 201
law, role of, 196–8
legitimate governance, 205
litigation, 207–9
multilevel, 203
non-litigation routes, 200
Open Method of Coordination (OMC), 197
and see **Open Method of Coordination(OMC)**
participation, 206
policy discussions, 208
policy generation, 208
public scrutiny, 205
representation, 205–6

Hard law
critiques, of, 66–7
employment law, and, 126, 128–9
fiscal policy, and, 89–90
and see **Fiscal policy**
framework, 207–8
international relations (IR), 69, 71, 73
and see **International relations (IR)**
soft law
distinguished, 65–6
hybrid constellations, 67–8
interaction, with, 67
and see **Soft law**
Hazard Analysis and Critical Control Point (HAACP)
corrective action, and, 60–1
experimentalist trends, 55
food safety, and, 55, 58, 60
significance, of, 3
Health & safety
see also **Occupational Safety (USA)**
best practice, 56
compliance, 56
experimentalist trends, 55
hazards
corrective measures, 56
dealing, with, 55–6
identification, of, 56
management-based regulation, 55
minimum standards, 56
Healthcare (USA)
children, and, 259–60
Clinton health plans, 246, 248, 259, 262, 264
delivery, of, 245, 248
eligibility, 259, 261
entitlement programmes, 259, 263
ethnic/racial disparities

benchmarking, 258
chronic care management, 258
civil rights litigation, 256, 258, 266
data collection, 258
elimination, of, 255–6
lawyers, changing role, 258
malpractice framework, 257
persistence, of, 255–6
physicians, performance of, 258
quality-based response, 256–8
reduction, in, 257
regulatory governance, 257
regulatory structure, 256
self-regulation, 257
extent, of, 245
families, 259–61
funding
federal funding, 261
fiscal constraints, 261
governance
conventional governance, 261–2
deregulation, 245
failures, in, 246, 248
new governance, 246
old systems, 245–6
regulation, 246
self-regulation, 246
government
monitoring, by, 265
privatisation, 266
responsibilities, 266
role, of, 265–6
Health Insurance Portability and Accountability Act (HIPAA)
effect, 254–5, 267
provisions, 253
hybrid solutions, 268
incremental approach, 259–61
insurance, lack of, 259, 262
malpractice
framework, 257
litigation, 257, 267
market forces, 246
Medicaid, 258, 260
Medicare, 245
new governance
benchmarking, 246, 252
data collection, 246, 252
development, of, 267–8
devolution, 246, 252, 254
effect, of, 246
experimentation, 254–5
flexible rules, 261
government involvement, 261
informal sanctions, 261
judicial review, and, 263
monitoring, 246, 252
network creation, 246, 252, 255
participation, 261–2
procedural requirements, 263
public-private networks, 261, 264
public-private partnerships, 246, 252–3, 255
regional structures, 264–5
representation, 263–4
social problems, and, 246
soft law, 261, 266
stakeholder collaborations, 246–7
subsidiarity, 254
technology, use of, 252, 264
and see **New governance**
participation
access, expansion of, 262
consumer-physician alliances, 262
disadvantaged groups, 262–3
evaluation, 263
gender bias, 262–3
legal regime, for, 265
local participation, 265
monitoring, 263, 265
patient empowerment, 262–3
racial bias, 262–3
representation, 263–4
stakeholder collaborations, 247–52, 263
uninsured persons, 262, 264
physician/patient relationship, 260
privatisation, 246
public-private networks
infrastructure, for, 265
local autonomy, 265
managed care, and, 264
state experimentation, 264
use, of, 261, 264
seamless enrolment, 261
soft law
benchmarks, 266–7
courts, role of, 267
data collection, 267
guidelines, 266
importance, of, 266
legislative requirements, 267
reporting, 267
and see **Soft law**

stakeholder collaborations
see **Stakeholder collaborations**
state-based system, 260
tax credits, 260
technology
benefits, of, 252–3, 261
bio-terrorism, and, 253
commitment, to, 264
cost savings, 253–4
interoperable systems, 254
legislation, encouraging, 253
local health systems, 254, 265
local technology standards, 253
medical records, 253–4
use, of, 252–3, 264
universal coverage, 248, 259–60
viability, 245
Healthcare services (EU)
Byrne Reflection Process (BRP), 186–8, 204
capacity sharing, 203
case studies, 179–80
competences
see **European constitutionalism**
constitutional concepts
see **European constitutionalism**
constitutional law, and, 180
constitutional reform, and, 180, 193–4
Constitutional Treaty (CT), and, 193–4, 202
and see **Constitutional Treaty** (CT)
cross-border services, 190
data protection, 186–7
delivery, of, 179
deregulation, and, 183
direct effect, and, 182
e-health, 186, 190
European social model, and, 180
free movement, and, 187–8
funding, 180, 186, 188–9, 197–9, 208
governance processes, 180, 185, 205–8
see also **Governance mechanisms** (EU)
harmonisation, 180, 186–7, 194, 196, 198
health technology, 189
high level reflection process (HLRP), 185–6, 188, 191, 204, 206–7
information
collection, of, 180, 188, 197, 200
dissemination, 180, 189, 197, 200
information strategy, 190
pharmaceuticals, on, 190
infrastructure, 186, 188
institutional balance
see **Institutional balance**
Kohll litigation, 180–1, 184–5
and see ***Kohll* litigation**
medical research, 199
Member States, and, 179, 182, 196, 198, 202–3
national policies, 198
new governance, and, 181, 186, 196
and see **New governance**
Open Method of Coordination (OMC), 180, 186, 190, 192, 193, 197, 206
and see **Open Method of Coordination** (OMC)
organisation, of, 179
participation
extent, of, 206
policy initiation, 206
representation, 206–7
patients
patient mobility, 182, 185–6
patients' rights, 201
persuasive convergence, 180, 191, 197
policy convergence, 197
prior authorisation, 182
provision, of, 182
reimbursement, 182
research centres, 189
restrictions, on, 182–4
skills development, 186, 188
social market tradition, 183
specialised treatment, 189
structural funding, 186
Human rights
importance, of, 395
Hybridity
anti-discrimination measures, 404–5
and see **Anti-discrimination**
baseline hybridity, 6, 7, 8, 23, 404
conservative form, 403–4, 406
development, of, 119
emergence, of, 93
employment governance, and, 130–34
and see **Employment governance**
employment policy, and, 93
and see **Employment policy**

evidence, of, 119
fiscal policy, and, 93
and see **Fiscal policy**
framework regulation, and, 405
fundamental hybridity, 6–8, 23, 404
hybrid governance, 3
hybrid thesis
baseline hybridity, 6–8, 23, 404
default hybridity, 6, 9, 23, 404
developmental hybridity, 6, 8, 404
law, and, 6
nature, of, 6
soft law, and, 6
traditional law, and, 395–6, 403
interpretative issues, 405
open-ended rights, 406–7
radical variants, 404
reciprocal change, 404
soft law, and, 91, 93
and see **Soft law**
transformation thesis, and, 40

Institute of Nuclear Plant Operation (INPO)
operating standards, 58
performance indicators, 60
safety regimes, 55, 58
Institutional balance
comitology, 204–5
and see **Comitology**
entitlement, to, 205
EU Member States, 204
European Commission, 203–4, 209
European Council, 204
Open Method of Coordination (OMC), 204
and see **Open Method of Coordination (OMC)**
Institutional intermediation
see also **Gender equity (USA)**
accountability, 356
and see **Accountability**
bridge builders
boundary spanning, 356
conceptual orientation, 355
fluency, 356
legitimacy, 356
problem-solving, and, 355–6
role, of, 354–5
systems change, and, 356
functional integration
ADVANCE initiatives, 349
institutional change, 349
institutional internalisation, 349
organisational processes, 349, 353
pivotal strategies, 349
problem framing, 349–51
role hybridity, 349, 351, 353
intermediaries, 345–6
leadership
commitment, and, 357
encouragement, of, 357–8
formal authority, 357
importance, of, 357
mobilisation, 357, 359
regeneration, 357
linkages, 343
pivot points, 343
International law (IL)
behaviour
constraint, 70
transformation, 70, 75
customary international law, 70
rationalist approach, 70–1, 73, 76
soft law, and, 69
and see **Soft law**
International relations (IR)
constructivist approach, 70, 72–3, 76
customary international law, 70
see also **International law (IL)**
domestic politics, 71
institutions
influence, of, 75
role, of, 71, 75
legalisation
delegation, 69, 70
obligation, 69
precision, 69
legally binding obligations, 70–1
social environment, 72, 75
soft law, and, 69, 73
and see **Soft law**
sovereignty, 72

***Kohll* litigation**
see also **Healthcare services (EU)**
Classic Community Method (CCM), 181
and see **Classic Community Method (CCM)**
data protection, 187
deregulation, and, 183
disruptive effects, 182–4
financial arrangements, 208

juridical process, and, 184
reflection processes, 185–8, 191, 204, 206–7
regulatory responses, 187–8
services
provision, of, 182
restrictions, on, 182
specialised treatment, 189
significance, of, 180–1, 184–5
traditional constitutionalism, and, 181
treaty interpretation, 183

Legal system
see also **Toyota Production System (TPS)**
approaches
law and economics, 39–40, 42–3, 52, 64
rights and principles, 38, 40–2, 52, 64
rules and standards, 39
case decisions, 40
compensation, 43
conflict resolution, 39–40
corporate liability, 43
decision-making, 39–41
discretion
limits, on, 39
sentencing, 39–40
dispute resolution, 38, 40
due process, 38
fairness, 40–3
judicial decisions, 40–41
legal reasoning, 40
liability, 42–3
nature, of, 38
negligence, 42
norms
formal norms, 39
informal norms, 39
primary norms, 38–9
secondary norms, 38–9
predictability, 40
punishment, 42–3
reasonableness, 42–3
retrospective inquiry, 42–3
social values, and, 38–9

Municipal law
importance, of, 395
local contexts, 395
scope, of, 395

National Science Foundation (NSF)
ADVANCE programmes, 337, 339, 340–2
and see **ADVANCE programmes**
benchmarking, and, 346
capacity building, 342–3, 358
change, ongoing, 346
collaborative agreements, 341
communication, 341
data gathering, 341, 343
error detection, 346
evaluation, 341
gender equity, and, 338–9, 345
see also **Gender equity (USA)**
grantees, position of, 340–2
institutional intermediaries, 345–6
leveraging, by, 344–5
linkages, 345, 349, 359
monitoring, 346
pivot points, 345–6, 349
problem-solving, 346
problem-solving intermediation, 346, 359
quantitative indicators, 341
reciprocity, 340–1
role, of, 337–40

New governance
accountability, 330–1, 334, 398–400
and see **Accountability**
change, ongoing, 330
collaborative problem-solving, 328, 333
common features, 2
constitutionalism, and, 1, 3–4, 10–12, 15–16, 24, 34–6, 409
and see **Constitutionalism**
definition, 15–16, 21–2
democracy, and, 4
democratic justification, 403
destabilisation, and, 329
disempowered groups, 331
enactment, and, 400
enforcement, and, 400
environmental assessment, and, 234
and see **Environmental assessment**
error-identification
benchmarking, 327
information, use of, 327
problem-solving, 327–9
resource requirement, 327
skills requirement, 327
European experience
analysis, of, 23–4, 30

binary model, 22, 29
boundaries of governance, 32
collective trust, 32
constitutionalism, 24
constitutional ordering, 22
coordination, 32
definition, 21–2
democratic experimentalism, 30–2
democratic government, and, 31
development, of, 23
governance philosophy, 30–1
hybridity, 30
institutional design, 30
institutional powers, 22
integration, 22
justice, and, 32
legal ordering, 22
methodology, 23
nature, of, 22, 30
non-legislative character, 22
normative support, 29
participation, 22
political culture, 32
political organisation, 30
power-sharing, 22
regulatory capacity, 32
regulatory *desiderata*, 30, 32
regulatory forms, 22
supranational context, 32
feasibility, 331
flexibility, 400
framework regulation, 405
gap thesis, 4, 395–7
and see **Gap thesis**
gender equity
see **Gender equity (USA)**
healthcare services, and, 181, 186, 196
see also **Healthcare services (EU)**
hybrid thesis, 3–4, 23–4, 395–6, 403
see also **Hybridity**
innovation, and, 396–7, 403
institutionalism, 328, 332
intervention
judicial, 332
regulatory, 332
judicial obstruction, 397
juridification, of, 27
learning
individual level, 326
institutional learning, 327–9, 332
ongoing learning, 326
organisational level, 326
legal dimension, 3, 4
legal revision, and, 398
legitimacy, 403
local experimentation, 331–3
local organisations, and, 333
local practice, 332
meaning, 2–3
nominalism, and, 24–5
and see **Nominalism**
occupational safety, 274–5, 278, 286–7
see also **Occupational Safety (USA)**
participation, and, 3, 5, 22, 329–31
peer review, 400–2
and see **Peer review**
penalties, strength of, 408
performance
evaluation, 327
metrics, 333
performance standards, 332, 334
problem-solving, 328, 330–1, 333
professionals, role of, 329
public agencies, role of, 332–3
quantitative metrics, 333–4
reflexive constitutionalism, 34–6
see also **Constitutionalism**
regulation, and, 2, 3, 22, 405
and see **Regulation**
regulatory penalty defaults, 407–9
and see **Regulatory penalty defaults**
remediation, 334
representation, and, 330
resistance, to, 329
self-diagnosis, 334
significance, of, 12
social development, and, 397
solidarity, and, 153, 176–7
and see **Solidarity**
symbolic compliance, 332
theories
gap thesis, 4
hybridity thesis, 4
transformation thesis, 4
traditional law
gap thesis, 395–6
hybridity thesis, 395–6, 403
incompatibility, 395–6
traditional legality, 396
transformation thesis, 395–6
transformation thesis
see **Transformation thesis**

transformative law, as, 409
transformative leadership, 329
transformative nature, 407
transparency, and, 3
Nominalism
constitutional authority, and, 16
constitutional discourse
dilution, of, 25
rhetorical device, as, 25
constitutionalism, and, 24–5
and see **Constitutionalism**
EU Constitution, and, 18–19
see also **Constitutional Treaty (CT)**
meaning, of, 16
new governance, and, 24–5, 29
and see **New governance**
social technology, and, 17
Nuclear Regulatory Commission
safety regimes, 55

Occupational Safety & Health Administration (OSHA)
see also **Occupational safety (USA)**
Alliance Program, 277
changes, to, 275–6
compliance
compliance assistance, 276
cooperative compliance, 285
comprehensive safety and health programmes (CSHP), 279
controversy, surrounding, 271
cooperative programmes, 269, 275–9, 284–5, 290
data
collection, 285
transparency, 286
discretionary approach, 280
enforcement, by, 271–4, 278, 280
establishment, of, 269
experimental trends, 55, 275–6, 288
funding, 292
hazardous substances, and, 55, 59
interdisciplinary teams, 59
penalties, imposed by, 271–2
regulatory approach, 272–3
regulatory mandate, 270–2
regulatory standards, 272–4
repeat inspections, 275
resistance, to, 273–4, 279
resources, 271, 278
role, of, 269–70
safety culture, 276–7, 286
strategic partnership, 277, 290
Strategic Partnership Program (SPP), 277
targeting, use of, 278–80, 285
voluntary programmes, 279–80
weakness, of, 272
worker participation, 281–3
Occupational safety (USA)
see also **Occupational Safety & Health Administration (OSHA)**
accident rates, 271, 284
compliance, 287
cooperative strategies, 284
costs, associated with, 271
governance
administrative governance, 269–70
transitional governance, 284–5, 289
government spending, 271
hazards
hazard control, 287
identification of, 284, 287
judicial review, and, 273
legislation
governing legislation, 270
reform, of, 280
National Labour Relations Act (NLRA), 282–3
new governance
accountability, 278
data transparency, 286
development, of, 275, 278, 288
doctrinal divides, 286–7
evaluation, 286
flexibility, 281
integration, 280, 286–7
legal boundaries, 286–7
measuring success, 284–6
monitoring, 286
need, for, 274
political support, 278
transparency, 278
and see **New Governance**
participation
benefits, 284
employee participation, 282–3
employer-employee partnerships, 282–3
safety committees, 282
stakeholder participation, 281–2
penalties, 271–2
regulatory approach, 270, 272–3
risk prevention, 287

Teamwork for Employees and Managers Act (TEAM), 283–4
unionisation, and, 281–2
worker participation, 281–3
workplace environment, 275

Open Method of Coordination (OMC)
advantages, 77–8, 133–4
constitutional status, 26
constructivist perspective, 81
elements, of, 77
employment governance, and, 130–4
and see **Employment governance**
employment policy, and, 68
and see **Employment policy**
European Employment Strategy (EES), and, 76, 78
and see **European Employment Strategy (EES)**
governance, and, 28
and see **Governance**
healthcare services, and, 180, 186, 190, 192–3, 197, 206
see also **Healthcare services (EU)**
hybridity, and, 82, 130–1
and see **Hybridity**
impact
administrative reorganisation, 80
mutual learning, 80–1
participation, 80–1
policy change, 80–1
policy making, 80
transparency, 80–1
law
alternative, to, 1, 82, 131
complementary, to, 131
legislative action, 1, 82
national policy, and, 26
nature, of, 76–7
operation, of, 77–8, 81
policy changes, and, 78
positive effects, 79
problem-solving, and, 78
scope, of, 78
self-authorisation, 28
significance, of, 3, 22, 25
social policy, and, 26, 76, 78
soft law, and, 6
and see **Soft law**
state structures, and 29
structural funds, and, 82
supranational competences, 26
treatment, of, 26
voluntary compliance, 28

Peer review
accountability, and, 400–2, 410
and see **Accountability**
deliberative participation, 402
enforcement, of, 404
fundamental rights, 406
legitimacy, 402
new governance, and, 400–2
and see **New Governance**
review processes, 402
transparency, 402

Penalty defaults
see **Regulatory penalty defaults**

Problem-solving
institutional resistance, 324
local problem-solving, 323
new governance, and, 323–5, 329
and see **New governance**
participatory problem-solving, 324–5
peer comparisons, 324
performance, information on, 323
public agencies, role of, 323
symbolic process participation, 324

Proposition 65
see also **Environmental governance (USA)**
effect, of, 299, 301
environmental exposures, 299
penalty default approach, 301
regulatory standards, 301
risk assessment, 300
warning requirements, 299–301, 408

Public law
death penalty administration
see **Death penalty administration**
experimentalist trends, 55
governance, and, 239
innovation
benchmarking, 60, 63
continuous revision, 57–8, 63
decision-making, 58, 63
dispute resolution, 57, 62
improvement, 57
learning, 57, 62
performance standards, 57–8
problem-solving, 57, 59, 61
prospectivity, 61
punitive intervention, 61
remediation, 61
root cause analysis, 60, 63
management-based regulation, 55
usage, and, 239

Race discrimination
see also **EU Race Directive**
hybridity
development, of, 119
evidence, of, 119
and see **Hybridity**
mainstreaming, 117–19
networks
ENAR network, 116
Independent Experts on Fundamental Rights, 116
RAXEN network, 112–16
new governance approach, 119
see also **New Governance**
non-governmental organisations (NGOs), 117
policy integration, 117–18
rights-based approach, 119
RAXEN network
see also **Race discrimination**
role, of, 112–16
structure, of, 116
Regulation
command and control, 2
framework regulation, 405
legal process, and, 1
regulatory forms, 1
Regulatory penalty defaults
see also **Environmental governance (USA)**
action-forcing, 296, 298, 321
behavioural change, 297
Clean Air Act, 308–10
conventional rules, as, 301–2
default
accidental penalty default, 304, 306
agency action, 307
default procedure, 306
penalty default, 295–6
definition, 297
effect, of, 296–8
Endangered Species Act (ESA), 302
and see **Endangered Species Act (ESA)**
environmental costs, and, 297
environmental impact statement (EIS), 298, 304, 306
environmental regulation, 297, 310
examples, of, 298
information-forcing, 296, 298, 321
land ban, effect of, 307–8
mitigation
adaptive mitigation, 306
mitigation measures, 306–7
new governance, and, 407–9
and see **New governance**
Proposition 65, and, 299–301
and see **Proposition 65**
regulatory rules, as, 296, 321
watershed management, 311–14
and see **Watershed management**

School reform
accountability, 56, 59, 60
experimentalist trends, 55
interdisciplinary teams, 59–60
management-based regulation, 55
performance measures, 57, 59
standard-setting, 56–7
Social Europe
notion, of, 26
single market, and, 26
Social rights (EU)
constitutionalism, and, 125
and see **Constitutionalism**
EU Charter of Fundamental Rights, 125–6, 129, 142
fundamental rights, 125
hard law, and, 126–7
jurisdictional problems, 126
market integration, and, 125–6
political problems, 126
Social Action Programme (1974), 125
soft law, and, 126–7
Worker's Charter (1989), 126
worker's rights, 125–6
Soft law
advantages, 75–6
behavioural change, and, 6
constructivist approach, 73, 75–6, 81, 91–2
contracting costs, 73
diversity, 74, 77–8
effectiveness, 6
employment law, and, 126, 128–9
European integration, and, 65–6, 69
flexibility, 74, 77
function, of, 91
hard law
distinguished, 65–6
hybrid constellations, 67–8
interaction, with, 66
hybridity, and, 6, 91, 93
and see **Hybridity**

incrementalism, 74, 78
integrated approach, 91
international law, and, 69
and see **International law (IL)**
international relations, and, 69, 73
and see **International relations (IR)**
meaning, of, 65, 69
multilateral governance, and, 69
new governance, and, 65
and see **New governance**
objections, to, 66
Open Method of Coordination (OMC)
see **Open Method of Coordination (OMC)**
participation, 74
policy changes, and, 78
problem-solving, and, 78
rationalist approach, 73, 75–6, 91–2
significance, of, 6
simplicity, 74
social rights, and, 126–7
sovereignty costs, 74
speed, 74
synthetic approach, 91–3

Solidarity
agricultural sector, and, 158–9
Cohesion Policy, and, 174–5
cooperation, and, 163
definition, 154
deliberation, importance of, 176–7
duty, as, 157
economic policy, and, 161
employment policy, and, 161
and see **Employment policy**
equal treatment, and, 172
financial obligations, and, 170–2, 176
fisheries sector, and, 160
flexible nature, 156, 173–4
free movement, and, 170, 176
fundamental rights, and, 162
host states, responsibilities of, 170–3, 176
identity, and, 154
judicial response
employment rights, 176
individual use, to, 165
legislative use, to, 163–4
maternity insurance schemes, 166
migrants, funding of, 170–3, 176
pensions schemes, 165–6
recognition, 162–3
residence requirements, 176
residence rights, 170–1
retirement schemes, 167
sickness schemes, 165–6, 169
social welfare systems, 168
state aid decisions, 164
support, 164
undertakings, use by, 165
migrants, funding of, 170–3, 176
nationality, and, 154
new governance, and, 153, 176–7
and see **New governance**
objective, as, 155–6, 160
origins, 153
principle, as, 155–6, 159, 161
production quotas, involving, 158
proportionality, and, 171, 175
residence
length, of, 172
rights, of, 170–1
responsibility, resulting from, 154
social cohesion, and, 160–1
social dialogue, and, 174
social policy, and, 153, 161, 169, 174
social welfare systems, and, 153
state aid, and, 164
steel sector, involving, 157
subsidiarity, and, 169, 174
transport sector, and, 160
treaties, promoting, 15–5, 176
use
anti-crisis policy, 157–9
flexible use, 173–4
hard uses, 156
horizontal use, 173–4
individuals, by, 165
judicial use, 162
legislative use, 156–7, 15, 160, 163–4
pro-active use, 169–70
softer uses, 160–162, 174
undertakings, by, 165
vertical use, 173
value, as, 155–6, 160

Stability and Growth Pact (SGP)
fiscal policy, and, 83
and see **Fiscal policy**
nature, of, 87
rationalist perspective, 89
reform, of, 90
soft law, and, 89
and see **Soft law**

Stakeholder collaborations
see also **Healthcare (USA)**
benchmarking, 251
business groups, 247
consumer groups, 247–8, 250, 252
data collection, 247, 251
development, of, 248
employers, and, 248–50, 252
expertise, sharing of, 247
external mechanisms, affecting, 251
government involvement, 247, 249–52
healthcare institutions, 247
information
dissemination, of, 251
information technology, 248
internal mechanisms, affecting, 251
Leapfrog Group, 250
managed care, 248
need, for, 248
participation, 263
patients, involvement of, 250
physicians, role of, 248–9, 251–2
policy entrepreneurs, 249
professional influence, 252
quality control, 251
Structural funds
EQUAL Development Partnerships (EDPs), 138–9
EQUAL initiative, 138
European Community initiatives, 138
European Structural Fund, 138–9
and see **European Structural Fund**
healthcare services, and, 186
see also **Healthcare services (EU)**
partnership principle, 138–9
public-private links, 137–8, 142
reform, of, 138
Subsidiarity
healthcare provision, and, 254
solidarity, and, 169, 174
and see **Solidarity**

Textualism
drawbacks, 25
effect, of, 19
new governance, and, 25, 29
and see **New governance**
power politics, and, 25–6
significance, of, 19
Toyota jurisprudence
see also **Toyota Production System (TPS)**
distinctive features, 38
Toyota Production System (TPS)
health & safety regulation, 37
jurisprudential implications, 37
legal system contrasts
articulated norms, 47–8
benchmarking, 60, 63
codified practice, 48
comparisons, 37, 45
consensus, 46
continuous revision, 57, 63
decision-making, 48–9, 51–2, 58, 63
destabilisation, 49–52
dispute resolution, 45–6, 54, 57, 62
fairness, 54
formality, 47–8
improvement, 47
individualistic concerns, 53
innovation, 47, 57
instrumental thought, 52–3
judicial decisions, 51
learning, 47, 57, 62
legitimacy, 52
liability analysis, 53
performance, 57–8
prescriptive thought, 52–3
primary norms, 45
problem-solving, 46, 48–9, 57, 59, 61, 64
punitive intervention, 61
reasonableness, 49
retrospective concerns, 53
root cause analysis, 60, 63
secondary norms, 45, 54
uncertainty, 46
see also **Legal system**
legal theory, and, 37–8
manufacturing process
benchmarking, 49
cost minimisation, 46
customer satisfaction, 47
decision-making, 48–9, 52
destabilisation, 49–50, 52
dispute resolution, 54
fairness, 54–5
flexibility, 44
incentives, 54–5
information dispersal, 48–9
job security, 54
kaizen (continuous improvement), 45, 47, 49
kanban system, 45
personnel system, 54

plant design, 51
problem-solving, 45, 48–50, 52–3
product design, 52–3
production problems, 45, 48
quality, 46–7
root cause analysis, 50, 53
speed, 44
superior performance, 49
supervisory judgment, 54
system design, 53
teamwork, 4, 49
traditional processes, distinguished, 44–5
public services, delivery of, 37
stock price maximisation, 46–7

Transformation thesis
hybridity, and, 404
and see **Hybridity**
law, and, 9–10
nature, of, 9
traditional law, and, 395–6

US governance
see also **Governance**
affirmative action programmes, 389
campaign finance, 387
conservative challenges, 384–8
constitutional influences, 381
constitutionalism, and, 392–4
see also **American constitutionalism**
constitutional law, 391–2
constitutional theory, 392–3
economic market regulation, 382–3, 386
equality
ascriptive equality, 381–4, 386, 389
substantive equality, 382–4, 386, 389
faith-based initiatives, 388, 392
health & safety programmes, 390
see also **Occupational safety (USA)**
healthcare policy, 388–9
see also **Healthcare (USA)**
human capital, investment in, 389
ideological presuppositions, 381
innovation, 381
institutional arrangements, 386–7
institutional strategies, 386
interest groups, 385, 387–9
large-scale policy, 381
lobbyists, 386
national bureaucracies, 384–5
national governance, 381
new constitutional order, 382, 386–8, 394
New Deal-Great Society, 381–4
original understanding, 392
pension programmes, 388
political development, 381–4
presidential role, 382, 389
privatisation, 388
public assistance programmes, 387
social welfare programmes, 387
transformation
conservative transformation, 394
difficulties, with, 391
transformative leaders, 389

Water Framework Directive (WFD)
see also **Environmental governance**
application, 224
collaborative governance, and, 212
Common Implementation Strategy (CIS), 226–8
see **Common Implementation Strategy (CIS)**
ecological assessment, 225
ecological status, 224–5
experimentalist governance, 226,–7
governance forum, emergence of, 224
groundwater, 224
implementation, 212, 225–7, 231, 236
information pooling, 224, 234
legislative framework, 224
purpose, 224
reporting requirements, 224, 230, 231, 234
soft law, recourse to, 226
surface water, 224

Watershed management
Clean Water Act (CWA), 311–12
cooperative federalism, 313
integrated watershed management, 311–12
litigation, involving, 312
penalty default, and, 312
Total Maximum Daily Load (TMDL), 311–14
water quality, 312–13